VOLUME II

# HISTORY

## *of the*

# CANADIAN

# *Peoples*

## 1867 TO THE PRESENT

### SECOND EDITION

**ALVIN FINKEL**
*Athabasca University*

**MARGARET CONRAD**
*Acadia University*

Copp Clark Ltd.
Toronto

Publisher: *Ron Doleman*
Managing Editor: *Linda Scott*
Editor: *Barbara Tessman*
Proofreader: *Madhu Ranadive*
Production Coordinator: *Wendy Moran*
Manufacturing Coordinator: *Sharon Latta Paterson*
Design: *Wycliffe Smith Design Inc.*
Printing and binding: *Best Book Manufacturers*

**Canadian Cataloguing in Publication Data**

Finkel, Alvin
History of the Canadian peoples

2nd ed.
Contents: v. I. Beginnings to 1967 / Margaret Conrad, Alvin Finkel. - v.
II. 1867 to the present / Alvin Finkel, Margaret Conrad.
Includes bibliographical references and index.
ISBN 0-7730-5530-4 (v. I)   ISBN 0-7730-5531-2 (v. II)

1. Canada - History.   I. Conrad, Margaret.   II. Title.

FC164.H57 1998     971     C97-931377-5
F1033.H57 1998

ISBN 0-7730-5531-2

Addison-Wesley
College Division
26 Prince Andrew Place
Don Mills, ON  M3C 2T8
Tel. (416) 447-5101
Fax. (416) 447-7755
http://www.aw.com/canada/

**Printed and bound in Canada.**

A B C D E -BB- 01 00 99 98 97

*For our students past and present.*
*We hope that this is the kind of text where*
*they can identify something of their personal past.*

# CONTENTS

Preface                                                                          x

Introduction:   INTERPRETING CANADA'S PAST                                        xi

                What Is History?                                                  xi
                The Context of This Text                                          xii
                History and Geography                                            xiv
                History and Culture                                              xiv
                Gender and History                                               xv
                Working-Class History                                            xv
                History and the Life Cycle                                       xvi
                Constructing a Narrative                                         xvi

      Part 1   Inventing Canada:
               State Formation and Industrialization                             1

Chapter 1      PEOPLE IN SEARCH OF A NATION                                       5

               Canada in 1867: The Context                                       5
               Canada's Peoples                                                  8
               Economy and Society                                              12
               Community and Culture                                            19
               Intellectual Revolutions                                         23
               Political Change                                                 26
               The Road to Confederation, 1864-1867                             28
               Conclusion                                                       32

Chapter 2      NATION BUILDING, 1867-1911                                        35

               Consolidating the Union                                          36
               Nova Scotia's Secessionist Movement                              37
               Annexing the Northwest: The Red River Rebellion                  38
               British Columbia and Prince Edward Island                        42
               Newfoundland's Perspective                                       43
               Pacific Scandal and the Defeat of Macdonald                      44
               The Liberals at the Helm                                         46
               The National Policy                                              47
               The Northwest                                                    48
               The Clash of Cultures                                            51
               Provincial-Dominion Conflict                                     54
               The North Atlantic Triangle                                      56
               Laurier Liberalism                                               58
               Provincial Rights and the Management of Progress                 60
               Imperialism, Nationalism, and Reciprocity                        61
               The 1911 Election and the Conservative Agenda                    64
               Conclusion                                                       65

               The Métis Migrations: *A Historiographical Debate*               65

Chapter 3    THE NEW INDUSTRIAL ORDER, 1867-1921                                    71

             Assessing the National Policy                                          72
             Transportation and Communication                                      73
             Secondary Industry                                                     75
             Deindustrialization in the Maritimes                                   77
             Staples: Old and New                                                   78
             Serving the Industrial Economy                                         85
             Retailing                                                              85
             Mass Production and Modern Management                                  87
             Financial Institutions                                                 89
             Private Initiative and Public Policy                                   90
             Work and the Family                                                    91
             Life in the Workplace                                                  93
             Conclusion                                                             95

             The National Policy and Regional Development: *A Historiographical Debate*  95

Chapter 4    A NATION ON THE MOVE, 1867-1921                                        99

             The Problem of Outmigration                                           100
             Immigration Policy                                                    101
             Settlers and Sojourners                                               104
             "White Canada Forever"                                                107
             Settling In                                                           110
             Native Peoples and the Dominant Culture                               112
             Northern Exposure                                                     116
             Canadian Cities in Transition                                         117
             Conclusion                                                            121

             Urban Poverty During the Laurier Boom: *A Historiographical Debate*   122

Chapter 5    COMMUNITY RESPONSES TO THE AGE OF INDUSTRY, 1867-1921                 127

             The Age of Reform                                                     128
             The Radical Response                                                  139
             The Rural Response                                                    140
             The Woman Movement                                                    143
             The Changing Canadian Family                                          147
             The Demand for Female Suffrage                                        149
             Conclusion                                                            150

             The Suffragists: *A Historiographical Debate*                         151

Chapter 6    CULTURAL CURRENTS IN THE INDUSTRIAL AGE, 1867-1921                    157

             Defining Canada                                                       158
             French-Canadian Nationalism                                           160
             A Changing Protestantism                                              163
             A Combative Catholicism                                               164
             Schooling and Society                                                 166
             Reinventing Nature                                                    171
             The Growth of Organized Sports                                        173
             Cultural Life in the Cities                                           176
             Architecture in the Modern Age                                        178

The Arts     180
Conclusion     188

Late Victorian Protestantism: *A Historiographical Debate*     188

**Part 2**    **The Modern Age:**
**Corporate Economy and Mass Society**     193

**Chapter 7**    THE GREAT WAR DECADE, 1911-1921     197

The Borden Administration, 1911-1914     197
Preparing for War     200
The Wartime Economy     202
Financing the War     204
The War in Europe     205
The War at Home     207
Enemies Within     210
A White Man's War     212
The Halifax Explosion     213
Canada on the World Stage     216
Demobilization and Reconstruction     217
What Brave New World?     218
Conclusion     222

Conscription: *A Historiographical Debate*     222

**Chapter 8**    THE STATE IN TRANSITION, 1921-1939     227

The Mackenzie King Era     228
Regional and Class Protest in the 1920s     229
Political Women     234
First Nations in the Age of Democracy     235
Labour Politics     237
The Bennett Years, 1930-1935     238
Protest From Left and Right     239
Third Parties     242
From Laissez-Faire to Welfare     246
Towards an Independent Canada     250
Conclusion     251

Populism, Right and Left: *A Historiographical Debate*     252

**Chapter 9**    CAPITALISM IN CRISIS, 1919-1939     255

Riding the Economic Roller Coaster     255
The Turbulent Twenties     257
The Dirty Thirties     262
Newfoundland on the Rocks     267
Hanging on by the Fingernails     267
Trade Unions in the Interwar Period     268
Making Ends Meet     270
Conclusion     272

What Caused the Great Depression? *A Historiographical Debate*     272

Chapter 10    MASS CONSUMER SOCIETY AND THE SEARCH FOR IDENTITY, 1919-1939    275

The Communications Revolution    276
Sexuality and Respectability    278
Motherhood in the Modern Age    282
Housing Canadians    283
Women, Work, and the Family    284
Rural Life    285
Religion in a Secular Society    287
Education    289
Culture and Leisure    292
Music and Theatre in the Interwar Years    295
Population    298
Conclusion    301

The Farming Community: *A Historiographical Debate*    301

Chapter 11    CANADA'S WORLD WAR, 1939-1945    305

Canada's War    306
Descent into War    309
The Business of War    315
Controlling the Enemy Within    318
The Welfare State    320
Labour and the State    323
The New World Order    324
Demobilization and Postwar Reconstruction    326
Conclusion    328

Origins of the Welfare State: *A Historiographical Debate*    329

Part 3    **Reinventing Canada,
1945-1997**    **333**

Chapter 12    REDEFINING LIBERALISM: THE CANADIAN STATE, 1945-1975    337

Federal Parties and Leaders    338
Provincial Politics    341
Newfoundland Enters Confederation    342
Politics and Representation    343
Shaping the Welfare State    344
Housing Policy    349
The Provinces and the New Liberalism    349
Quebec and the French-Canadian Nation    352
International Relations and the New Liberalism    356
Conclusion    357

The Development of Quebec Nationalism: *A Historiographical Debate*    358

Chapter 13    THE AMERICAN DREAM:
CANADA AND ITS SOUTHERN NEIGHBOUR, 1945-1975    361

The Cold War    362
Continental Economic Integration    368
Ottawa and Economic Nationalism    369
Americanization of Canadian Culture    374

From Red Baiting to Student Rebellion 376
Conclusion 378

Vietnam: What Role Did Canada Play? *A Historiographical Debate* 379

**Chapter 14 GROWTH AT ALL COSTS: THE ECONOMY, 1945-1975** 383

The Government's Postwar Strategy: The Welfare and Warfare Economy 384
Economic Growth in the Fabulous Fifties 385
The Postindustrial Economy 388
The Costs of Growth 393
Economic Disparity 398
The Trade Union Movement 401
Conclusion 403

Causes of and Solutions for Stagflation: *A Historiographical Debate* 404

**Chapter 15 COMMUNITY AND NATION, 1945-1997** 407

Population 408
Changing Social Mores 410
Education 412
Cities and Suburbs 414
The Immigrant Experience 416
Asian-Canadian Communities 417
Native Peoples Find a Voice 420
The Women's Movement 425
A Culture of Protest Emerges 427
Religion in a Secular Age 431
Conclusion 433

Consumerism and Loss of Community: *A Historiographical Debate* 434

**Chapter 16 CREATING A CANADIAN CULTURE, 1945-1997** 437

Quebec's Cultural Revolution 438
Cultural Development in the "Rest of Canada" 443
Professional Sports 449
Television and the Public Broadcaster 452
Media Concentration and Censorship 454
Conclusion 455

Who Speaks for a 'Culture'? *A Debate* 455

**Chapter 17 CANADA IN THE GLOBAL VILLAGE, 1975-1997** 459

Economic Stagnation and the Political Response 460
Canadian Politics and the Free Trade Agreement 463
The Free Trade Era 465
Quebec Sovereignty 467
The Meech Lake Accord 471
The Charlottetown Accord 474
Quebec After the Defeat of the Charlottetown Accord 476
Post-Prosperity Ontario 478
The Post-Prosperity West 480
Provincial Politics 481
Federal Cutbacks 484

The Trade Union Movement                                          485
Canada in the World                                              486
The Federal Election of 1997                                     487
Does Canada Have a Future?                                       488

If Quebec Leaves: *A Debate*                                     489

Index                                                           493

## List of Maps

Map 1.1    British North America, 1867                            6
Map 2.1    Canada, 1898                                          55
Map 2.2    Canada, 1905                                          59
Map 7.1    Canada, 1914                                          199
Map 7.2    The European Front, 1914-1918                         205
Map 11.1   The European Front, 1944-45—
           Italian Campaign and Northwest Europe Campaign        311
Map 11.2   Principal Routes Flown by Ferry Command, 1940-45      313
Map 12.1   Canada, 1949                                          350

## List of Figures and Tables

Table 1.1     Population of Canada, 1871                          7
Table 1.2     Religious Affiliation in Canada, 1871              23
Table 3.1     Percentage Sectoral Distribution of GNP, 1880-1920 76
Table 4.1     Canada's Population, 1861-1921                     100
Table 4.2     Population of Selected Canadian Cities, 1871-1921  118
Figure 8.1    Rural and Urban Infant Mortality by Province, 1943 247
Table 9.1     Percentage Sectoral Distribution of the Gross
              National Product, 1920-1940                        256
Table 9.2     Percentage Sectoral Distribution of the Gross
              National Product, 1920-1940                        264
Table 9.3     Per Capita Income by Province, 1928-29, 1933       266
Figure 10.1   Birth Rates, 1851-1941                             279
Table 10.1    Urban Percentages of Population for Regions and
              Provinces, 1901-1941                               285
Table 10.2    Canada's Population, 1911-1941                     298
Table 11.1    Marriages, Divorces, and Births in Canada, 1939-1948 327
Table 12.1    Social Expenditure by Country                      347
Table 13.1    Percentage of Foreign Control of Selected Canadian
              Industries, 1939-1973                              368
Table 13.2    Destination of Domestic Exports, 1946-1975         369
Table 13.3    Origins of Canadian Imports, 1946-1975            369
Table 14.1    Canada's Economic Growth, 1945-1976               386
Figure 14.1   Farm Populations in Canada, 1941-1971             393
Figure 14.2   Percent Distribution of Income of Families and
              Unattached Individuals, 1951 and 1971             399
Table 15.1    A Growing Population, 1941-1991                    409
Figure 15.1   Total Fertility Rates, 1946-1990                  410
Table 15.2    Religious Affiliations of Canadians               433
Figure 17.1   Unemployment and Inflation Rates in Canada,
              1970-1994                                         460
Table 17.1    1997 Federal Election Results                     487
Table 17.2    1997 Federal Election Results by Region           487

# PREFACE

Like Volume I, Volume II of the *History of the Canadian Peoples* devotes as much attention to the ordinary people of the past as to those who dominated the political and economic spheres of Canadian society. We have reprinted here the Introduction from Volume I, which explains our general approach to this project.

Volume II begins with a survey of British North America on the eve of Confederation as a review for those who have read Volume I and as an introduction for those who have not. The rest of the book is divided into three chronological sections: one devoted to the period from Confederation to the outbreak of the First World War; the second from the beginning of the First World War to the end of the Second World War; and the third to the period since the Second World War. For each period, there are separate chapters on politics, economics, social organization, and cultural developments. A separate chapter is devoted to each of the world wars, and to the impact of American influence on Canada in the period after the Second World War. Political and economic developments after the Second World War are divided between two periods with 1975, the date often given as marking the closing of the post-war economic boom, as the major turning point. Post-1975 political and economic developments are combined in the final chapters of the book.

The authors wish to thank Veronica Strong-Boag, Michael Behiels, Brian Henderson, and Cornelius Jaenen for their role in the initial conceptualization of this project. We owe a particular debt to Barbara Tessman, former managing editor at Copp Clark Pitman, and editor of both editions of Volume II, whose contribution to the organization, content, and writing of Volume II was above and beyond the call of duty. Douglas Baldwin, Michael Behiels, Jeff Miller, Maurice Tugwell, Brian VanBlarcom, and Brian Young suggested changes to the first edition and saved us from many errors. For the second edition, we owe thanks to Gerald Friesen and Mark McGowan for their comments on the entire manuscript and to Marilyn Barber, Jim Miller, Ernest Forbes, Ruth Brouwer, Kathryn McPherson, and Graham Decarie for comments on the various sections of the book. Danelle D'Alvise did an excellent job of canvassing professors for their evaluations of the first edition and we thank both Danelle and the university teachers who took the time to answer her questions. First Jeff Miller and Barbara Tessman at Copp Clark Pitman and then Ron Doleman and Linda Scott at Addison-Wesley worked closely with us to plan the second edition and to move it through the various necessary phases before the work could be completed. Madhu Ranadive and Richard Holt did the photo and artwork research for this edition and Maral Bablanian performed the same task in the first edition.

As is usually the case in projects such as these, secretarial services were fundamental to the project, and we wish to thank Myrna Nolan and Claire Gemmell of Athabasca University and Brenda Naugler and Carolyn Bowlby of Acadia University for their help with the first edition. We equally thank Judy McCluskey and Jan Cleveland of Mount Saint Vincent University and Lorette Kisinski and Yvette Hetze of Athabasca University for their help with the second edition. Of course, the authors alone bear responsibility for any problems remaining in the text.

NTRODUCTION

# INTRODUCTION

## INTERPRETING CANADA'S PAST

IN 1829, SHAWNADITHIT, THE LAST SURVIVING Beothuk, died of tuberculosis in Newfoundland. Thirty-eight years later, three British North American colonies united to form the Dominion of Canada. The second of these two events has always had a central place in Canadian history textbooks. The first, until recently, has been ignored. For students of history, it is important to understand why the focus of historical analysis changes and what factors influence historians in their approaches to their craft.

## WHAT IS HISTORY?

Simply stated, history is the study of the past. In non-literate societies, people passed oral traditions from one generation to the next, with each generation fashioning the story to meet the needs of the time. When writing was invented, history became fixed in texts. The narrative was often revised, but earlier texts could be used to show how interpretations of the past changed over time. Although ordinary people continued to tell their stories, they were considered less important than "official" written histories that reflected the interests of the most powerful members of society. Some of the official texts, such as the Bible and the Koran, were even

deemed to be divinely inspired and therefore less subject to revision than the narratives of mere mortals.

In the nineteenth century, history became an academic discipline in Europe and North America. Scholars in universities began to collect primary historical documents, compare texts, develop standards of accuracy, write histories, and train students to become professional historians. At first, professional historians focused on political and military events that chronicled the evolution of empires and nation-states. Gradually, they broadened their scope to include economic and social developments that, it was increasingly believed, helped to explain relations of power.

No matter how meticulously researched, most academic histories written before 1970 ignored, or treated unsympathetically, the experiences of ordinary people and issues relating to private life. Sex was almost never mentioned, despite the fact that its regulation preoccupied politicians, spiritual leaders, and nearly everybody else at most times in human history. Family life was taken for granted, and gay and lesbian relationships unacknowledged. When aboriginal and minority peoples were brought into the narrative, it was almost always to outline their deficiencies. Women and the working class, two of the largest groups in virtually every society, remained largely invisible.

Part of the reason that history was so narrowly focused lies in the sources of information available to historians. Until the twentieth century, the literate few, such as monarchs, politicians, and bishops, left behind far more written records than the millions of people whose lives they dominated. Our knowledge of medieval Europe, for example, is largely based on the accounts of church officials. Their belief that religious convictions governed the lives of the masses can be neither confirmed nor denied by direct statements from serfs, who left no written records. Although social historians have found indirect evidence suggesting that clerical leaders exaggerated the piety and subservience of the majority, the fact remains that serfs, slaves, labourers, and peasants have received far less attention from historians than have the elites who ruled them.

Another reason for the narrow focus is that history was written by a small group of privileged white men to be read by others like themselves. Their interests understandably turned to war and political developments in which their peers participated and whose perspective they adopted. In the second half of the twentieth century, the history profession underwent a major transformation. Women, children of the working class, and cultural minorities began entering universities in larger numbers and soon demanded that "their" history also be taken into account. Their questions not only encouraged the exploration of new topics but also influenced the way historians understand change over time. Instead of seeing history as a sequence of events orchestrated by a small and powerful elite, scholars began to interpret it as an arena in which classes, cultural groups, and individual men and women struggled to control the values that shaped their collective lives.

When history is approached as a contested terrain, events must be analyzed from a variety of perspectives. For example, when we discuss the rebellions of 1837 in Upper and Lower Canada, we recognize the importance of understanding not only the actions and attitudes of British officials and the ruling elite within the Canadas, but also those of the ambitious middle classes, and the frustrated farmers and landless poor. The goals of the rebels in Lower Canada varied depending on whether the focus is on an habitante with no bread to feed her children or a high-status seigneur like the rebel leader Louis-Joseph Papineau. Similarly, the conclusions reached about the significance of events such as the rebellions depend upon whose point of view is being considered.

Historians now realize that primary documents cannot "speak for themselves." They must be analyzed critically to understand who produced them, in what circumstances, and for what purpose. Because each historian brings individual values and concerns to the study of the past, it is also important to know something about the people who write secondary documents, such as history texts. The social and political perspective of the historian, as well as the time of writing, are often reflected, consciously or unconsciously, in decisions about what subjects to analyze, what documents to consult, and how to interpret their relative meaning and importance.

## THE CONTEXT OF THIS TEXT

The authors of this book are university-trained historians, schooled in the theories and methods of what was once called "the new social history." Since the new social history is now over three decades old, it can no longer be considered new, but its findings have informed our decisions about what to include in this introductory textbook.

Social historians have made a concerted effort to broaden the scope of historical inquiry. To fill the gaps in written sources, they have taken an interdisciplinary approach, drawing upon other disciplines (including geography, economics, political science, sociology, anthropology, archaeology, and psychology) to answer their questions. Sources such as material evidence from archaeological excavations, data from censuses and immigration lists, and oral traditions have helped historians to develop a more complex sense of the lives of the silent majority in past times. When personal computers became widely available in the 1970s, historians were able to process larger amounts of historical information. The science of demography, which analyzes population trends and draws upon vast quantities of data, has proved particularly useful in helping historians to trace changes in family size, life-cycle choices, and migration patterns.

At the same time that new methodologies extended the scope of history, historians were being influenced by new theoretical perspectives. Scholars who studied minorities, women, and the working class brought insights from multicultural studies, feminism, and Marxism to their analysis. By focusing on social structures such as class, culture, gender, and race, historians raised new questions about old topics and revolutionized the way the past is perceived.

Critics often remark that social history focuses the energy of historians into narrow topics, that it yields interesting but ultimately insignificant findings, and that it destroys the unifying national focus that earlier political studies offered. In response to such charges, we argue that there cannot be and never was a single narrative of Canadian history. The claim that there is a narrative ideal to which all historians must bow is, we believe, as damaging to the historical enterprise as are some postmodernist theories that dismiss history—and the view that the present can be informed by an understanding of the past—as a figment of the modernist imagination.

From the foregoing discussion, it is clear that history is a dynamic and evolving discipline. Debates rage, methods come and go, different conclusions are drawn from the same body of evidence. At various points in this text we discuss historiography—that is, debates about historical interpretation. In a survey text we can only touch upon a few examples of common historical assumptions that recent writings have challenged. It might be useful at this point to highlight some of the themes that give rise to controversy and that are

## WHAT'S IN A NAME?

Contemporary political movements that are changing the face of Canada are also forcing historians to think about the words they use. Thirty years ago, most textbooks referred to people with black skin as "negroes." In the 1960s, this term was replaced by "black," and more recently by "African Canadian," despite the fact that not all Africans are black. Similarly, the words used to describe aboriginal peoples have changed in recent years. "Savages" was quickly dropped from textbooks in the 1960s. Although the misnomer "Indian" has particular applications that seem as yet unavoidable, the preferred term seems to be "First Nations" or "Native peoples." "Amerindian" is a scholarly term used to encompass a wide range of aboriginal cultures.

Women, too, have insisted on being described in more respectful terms. Feminists have objected strongly to the use of the word "girl" when adult women are being discussed, and dismiss "lady" as being condescending or elitist. Because "man" was adequate for the male of the species, "woman," they argued, was the most appropriate term, although some radical feminists prefer a different spelling, such as "wymyn." Only the most hidebound of scholars still insist that the word "man" can be used to describe the entire human species.

Many scholars complained loudly about being asked to abandon words long established in their vocabularies. A few even argued that "political correctness" restricted freedom of speech. We do not hold such views. Since English is a living language and changes over time, we see no reason why it should not continue to reflect the new consciousness of groups in Canadian society. In our view, the words "politically conscious" more accurately describe attempts by groups to name their own experience.

Language, of course, is not only about naming things; it is also about power. Attempts by oppressed groups to find new words to fit their experiences should be seen in the context of their struggles for empowerment. In this text, we attempt to keep up with the changing times while bearing in mind that people in the past used a different terminology. We are also aware that in the future we may revise the words we use, as groups continue to reinvent their identities. Even the word "Canada" has changed its meaning over the past five hundred years, and it is our job as historians to shed light on the way this term came to be applied, for a time at least, to all the people living on the northern half of the North American continent.

explored in our two-volume study.

## HISTORY AND GEOGRAPHY

Historians have long recognized that geography has played an important role in the understanding of Canada's past, if for no other reason than that we have so much of it. Since Canada occupies over 7 percent of the global land mass, it is not surprising that regions figure prominently in the country's historical development, and that an individual's sense of place is defined locally and regionally more often than nationally. This insight has informed a vigorous historical inquiry in recent years on the so-called "peripheral" regions of Canada: the Atlantic Provinces, Western Canada, and the North.

In older history texts, historians, most of them working in central Canadian universities, focused on people and events in Ontario and Quebec. They structured their chapters around dates that reflected significant episodes in the St Lawrence–Great Lakes region, such as the conquest and the rebellions, and interpreted historical developments from the point of view of their central location. In this text we openly acknowledge that the tensions between the St Lawrence–Great Lakes "heartland" and the "hinterland" to the east, west, and north play a part in Canadian historical development. We attempt not only to discuss topics relevant to the "peripheral" regions of the nation, but also to introduce regional perspectives on national developments, along with time frames that reflect the larger Canadian experience.

With the growth of the environmental movement in the 1970s, historians began to explore Canada's changing ecology. Ten thousand years ago, most of the area that makes up present-day Canada was covered by ice. The nation's rugged terrain reflects its ice-age origins and explains why the northern half of the North American continent was less attractive to First Nations and European immigrants than the warmer and more fertile regions to the south. While twentieth-century developments in transportation and communication have largely eliminated geographical barriers

to the movement of peoples and ideas, much of what happens in Canada reflects identities based on earlier regional histories. Indeed, Canada's federal system of government is constructed around a sense of place that existed even before the arrival of Europeans. Volume 1 of this text begins with a discussion of the changing natural environment which, we now acknowledge, plays a significant role at all times in the nation's history.

From the moment that human beings began moving into what is now Canada, they left their mark on the landscape, and not always in a positive way. We can now see new significance in the statements made by New Brunswick historian Peter Fisher in the 1820s to the effect that moose were being indiscriminately slaughtered and lumber companies were stripping the land of trees. In attempting to trace the changes in the natural environment over time, we offer a historical perspective on the environmental challenges that Canadians face today.

## HISTORY AND CULTURE

The questions raised about the relationship of human beings to the planet have also prompted Canadian historians to re-evaluate their interpretations of human interaction. In the past, historians simply assumed that the European conquest of Canada represented a step in the upward progress of "western civilization." They were conditioned to accept notions of European moral superiority over other groups, the right of Europeans to establish dominion over "inferior" peoples, and the value of technological progress.

Such views no longer go unchallenged. Aboriginal leaders reject the Eurocentric view of the contact between Europeans and the indigenous people of the Americas. They suggest that the First Nations embodied more egalitarian and peaceful values than the technologically superior European societies of the time. They also argue that Native peoples had a more positive relationship with the environment.

There is much evidence to support the Native interpretation of the past. By the time of contact, the Europeans, or at least their elites, had embraced social values that stressed domination: domination of women by men, domination of the majority of people by a relatively tiny ruling elite, and domination of the natural world by humankind. In contrast, most Native societies—like many European societies in earlier stages of their development—emphasized harmony among their members and with nature. While European values resulted in the exploitation of natural resources to the point of depletion, the Natives of North America generally avoided the environmental destruction that dogged European "progress."

Many scholars now accept the Native perspective of events relating to the contact period. As we show in this text, there is evidence that, prior to contact, Canada's Native peoples had rich cultures that were subsequently weakened by European influence. In some cases this influence turned egalitarian, self-sufficient tribes into poverty-stricken groups riddled by disease, drunkenness, and abuse of women and children. This insight developed in part because historians now have a greater appreciation of the devastation wrought by European diseases on the Native peoples of the Americas. Although pre-contact populations are difficult to estimate, it would appear that between 1500 and 1650 the Native populations of the Americas were reduced to a mere fragment of their original numbers. In the face of such human devastation it is not difficult to see why the Europeans came to dominate the Canadian landscape. They were not morally or even necessarily technologically superior to the aboriginal peoples; they were only more immune to the diseases they brought with them.

While a positive re-evaluation of pre-contact Native life has emerged in recent years, many scholars warn of the dangers of going too far in this direction. Some aboriginal nations were militaristic, others clearly practised slavery, and the evidence regarding the treatment of women in various tribes is, at best, contradictory. Moreover, it has been argued that the disappearance of various animal species in the pre-contact period and evidence of wasteful hunting practices suggest that small populations, rather than conscious environmentalism, may account for the lesser destruction of the land's resources in the pre-contact period compared to the period of European trade and settlement.

## GENDER AND HISTORY

As with Native history, the emergence of a large literature on women's history has done more than "add women and stir"; it has challenged many of the conclusions reached by historians who examined only the rhetoric and behaviour of male elites. In Canadian history, we now see the winning of responsible government in the mid-nineteenth century as a gendered development in which middle-class men gained political ascendancy. Women were denied the vote for another seventy years and continue to struggle for an equal place in the formal political institutions of the nation.

Historians are quick to point out that women were not merely passive victims of the historical process. Throughout the nineteenth century, for instance, parsons and pundits proclaimed that woman's place was in the home. They also focused upon motherhood as woman's primary function in society. Despite such admonitions, women entered the workforce in increasing numbers and dramatically limited the number of children they produced. So concerned were male legislators about the decline in the birth rate that they passed a law in 1892 denying people access to birth control and making abortion illegal. Nevertheless, the birth rate continued to decline. As is often the case with subordinate groups in society, women in the nineteenth century left few records to indicate why or how they limited births, but statistical evidence clearly demonstrates that they did so. Smaller family sizes, in turn, had an impact on women's life choices that contributed to their increased involvement in the public sphere in the twentieth century.

## WORKING-CLASS HISTORY

The history of the working class has also provided a new perspective on the past. By looking at history "from the bottom up," historians have been able to explain more clearly how power is exercised in

Canadian society. Class, of course, is a difficult concept to analyze in the Canadian context and changes dramatically over time. In the eighteenth and early nineteenth centuries, old aristocratic notions of the class structure, emphasizing land and heredity, dominated colonial life. The Industrial Revolution in the mid-nineteenth century increased the power of the middle class and created a landless working class, which was itself highly stratified.

Despite—or more likely because of—the large number of studies conducted on the working class, there is disagreement on a number of important questions. Historians take different views on the extent to which the values of skilled workers in the early stages of the Industrial Revolution differed from those of their employers, and they debate the degree to which the union movement served the interests of the larger working class. While early unions benefited skilled workers to a considerable degree, they were usually closed to women, non-whites, and unskilled labour. This information helps historians to understand the limited impact of the union movement at certain points in Canadian history and raises interesting questions about the ways in which masculinity and femininity were expressed in working-class homes.

## HISTORY AND THE LIFE CYCLE

In recent years, historians have also become more conscious of the fact that documents capture only a moment of reality. Time, as the old adage goes, does not stand still: values change, people grow older, and new ways of doing things come into practice. It is important, therefore, when studying individuals, to think about where they are in their life cycles. The impact of head taxes or famine migrations on children might well be quite different from that of middle-aged adults, and different still from that of people nearing the end of their lives. Only a few documents, such as personal diaries, remind us that individuals are moving through time and that where they are in their own lifetimes is a critical part of understanding their—often changing—point of view.

The report of the Royal Commission on the Relations between Capital and Labour in 1889 offers some perspective on the importance of life course in understanding human behaviour. Charged with investigating alleged abuses in some of Canada's earliest factories, the commissioners assembled the testimony of hundreds of child and adult workers. This testimony was influenced by a number of factors, including the age and gender of the workers being questioned. Twenty-two-year-old Georgina Loiselle, who was beaten with a cigar mould by her employer, Mr Fortier, reported the incident with little emotion and no sense of outrage. She may well have been relatively sanguine about the event, not only because Fortier claimed to be acting in place of her parents, but also because she saw her situation as transitory. Like many young women of her generation, she undoubtedly hoped to marry and leave the factory forever. Her testimony in the 1880s must be viewed as one part of an ongoing process, a part that makes only limited sense in isolation.

## CONSTRUCTING A NARRATIVE

This two-volume text attempts to integrate the findings from social history with earlier work on social elites to produce a more comprehensive portrait of Canadian society. While social history is emphasized, political history remains central to the narrative. We also show how the two are joined. For instance, in our discussion of the complicated class structure within the fur-trading empire of the Hudson's Bay Company in the mid-nineteenth century, we note that decisions made in London as well as those made by Governor Sir George Simpson in Canada helped to put this structure in place. We also show that the men who created the structures could not always control them. The Hudson's Bay Company's ability to focus its profit-making attention on fur trading alone was weakened by Métis resistance to company rules, by changing fashions in European markets, and by changing relations between women and men on the fur-trade frontier. It is this interaction—leading at times to compromises and at times to conflict—

that is the focus of our history of Canada.

There is, we maintain, nothing inevitable about historical processes. At times in this text the limitations on an individual's behaviour set by age, class, culture, gender, race, or region may appear to suggest that many, perhaps most, of our ancestors were hopeless victims of forces beyond their control. A closer reading should reveal that people sought in various ways to transcend the limits placed on their lives. Social struggles of every sort changed or at least sought to change the course of history. As you read this book, we hope that you will gain a greater appreciation of how earlier generations of people in what is now called Canada responded to their environment and shaped their own history.

# 1

## INVENTING CANADA:
### State Formation
### and Industrialization

# T I M E L I N E

| | |
|---|---|
| **1867** | • Confederation; first federal and provincial elections; anti-confederates win in Nova Scotia |
| **1867-73** | • John A. Macdonald serves as prime minister |
| **1868** | • Canada First movement founded |
| **1869** | • First Northwest Rebellion; Nova Scotia and federal government come to terms; Newfoundland votes decisively against joining the Dominion of Canada; first Canadian Immigration Act passed; beginning of Guibord affair in Montreal; Timothy Eaton opens his first store |
| **1870** | • Province of Manitoba established; first Canadian branch of the YWCA opens in Saint John |
| **1871-77** | • Negotiation of treaties with First Nations of the Northwest |
| **1872** | • Dominion Lands Act; Trade Union Act removes common-law prohibitions against trade unions |
| **1873** | • Prince Edward Island joins Confederation; Royal North West Mounted Police established; Pacific Scandal |
| **1873-8** | • Economic recession; Alexander Mackenzie serves as prime minister |
| **1874** | • Creation of Women's Christian Temperance Union in Canada |
| **1875** | • Caraquet Riot; union of Presbyterian churches; Grace Anne Lockhart becomes first woman in British Empire to receive a university degree |
| **1876** | • Passage of Indian Act; founding of Toronto Women's Literary Club |
| **1877** | • Saint John fire leaves 15 000 homeless |
| **1878** | • Canada Temperance Act |
| **1878-96** | • Conservatives in power federally |
| **1879** | • Increase in tariff marks implementation of National Policy; Provincial Miners' Association founded in Nova Scotia |
| **1880** | • Canadian Pacific Railway contract granted; Britain transfers the Arctic Archipelago to Canada |
| **1881** | • Founding of the Société nationale des Acadiens |
| **1883** | • Founding of Trades and Labour Congress and the Wholesale Grocers Guild; breakthrough of Knights of Labour; union of Methodist churches; Queen's and University of Toronto open facilities to train women |
| **1884** | • Creation of Imperial Federation League; Ontario passes the nation's first Factory Act |
| **1885** | • Second Northwest Rebellion; potlatch banned; pass system introduced for treaty Indians in the Northwest; first head tax imposed on Chinese immigrants; major smallpox epidemic in Quebec; Quebec Factory Act; Canadian Pacific Railway completed |
| **1886** | • Parti national wins Quebec provincial election; "repealers" win Nova Scotia provincial election; establishment of Royal Commission on Relations of Labour and Capital |
| **1887** | • Provincial premiers' conference; British–American Joint High Commission on inshore fisheries |
| **1888** | • Jesuit Estates Act passed in Quebec |
| **1889** | • Federal government concedes that the area from Kenora to Thunder Bay forms part of Ontario |

| 1890 | • Manitoba renounces official bilingualism and removes public support for separate schools |
|---|---|
| 1891 | • Papal encyclical, *Rerum novarum*, published; Goldwin Smith's *Canada and the Canadian Question* published |
| 1891-92 | • John Abbott heads government |
| 1892 | • Federal government bans contraceptives and abortifacients; North-West Territories legislative assembly restricts French-language education; St John's fire leaves 10 000 homeless |
| 1882-94 | • John Thompson is prime minister |
| 1894-96 | • Mackenzie Bowell serves as prime minister |
| 1895 | • Clara Brett Martin becomes Canada's first female law graduate |
| 1896 | • Canada's economy begins a long-term expansion; Klondike gold rush begins; Charles Tupper briefly serves as prime minister |
| 1896-1911 | • Laurier Liberals form government |
| 1897 | • Wheat boom begins; First Women's Institute established |
| 1898 | • National referendum on prohibition |
| 1899-1902 | • South African War |
| 1901 | • First transatlantic wireless signal received by Marconi in Newfoundland |
| 1902 | • Formation of INCO |
| 1903 | • Board of Railway Commissioners established; Laurier government provides loan guarantees and subsidies for two new transcontinental railroads; Quebec legislates compulsory vaccination for smallpox |
| 1904 | • Founding of L'Association Catholique de la Jeunesse Canadienne-francaise |
| 1905 | • Saskatchewan and Alberta achieve provincehood; Industrial Workers of the World established |
| 1907 | • Industrial Disputes Investigation Act passed; recession grips Canadian economy; anti-Asian riots in Vancouver; Doukhobors in Saskatchewan have half their land confiscated; Bell telephone operators strike |
| 1908 | • Founding of Moral and Social Reform Council of Canada; *Anne of Green Gables* published; Indian Act amendments give federal government power to expropriate reserve lands |
| 1909 | • Fishermen's Protective Union founded in Newfoundland; Canadian Council of Agriculture established |
| 1909-10 | • Miners' strike in Springhill |
| 1910 | • *Le Devoir* begins publication; National Hockey Association formed; Steel Company of Canada created by mergers; Laurier government's Naval Service Bill |
| 1911 | • Reciprocity treaty with United States rejected in federal election; École Sociale Populaire founded in Quebec |
| 1911-20 | • Robert Borden is prime minister |
| 1912 | • Ontario's Regulation 17 restricts education in languages other than English; radical Doukhobors relocate from Saskatchewan to British Columbia |
| 1913 | • Group of Seven begin their work together |
| 1913-14 | • Major recession |
| 1914 | • Outbreak of the First World War; Komagata Maru incident |

This section explores the processes by which Canada was transformed from a string of isolated British colonies in 1867 to a nation that was ready to make its mark on the world's stage during the First World War (1914-18.) In this period, immigration, western settlement, the growth of cities, and new value systems signalled the onset of Canada's modern age. Two themes are particularly noteworthy: first, the emergence of the state—federal, provincial, and municipal—as a major force in nation building; and second, the role of industrial capitalism in defining Canada's economic and social realities. Together, the interventionist state and vigorous industrial growth changed the lives of all Canadians and "invented" a nation that was vastly different from the one that had come together so inauspiciously in 1867.

# CHAPTER 1

## PEOPLE IN SEARCH OF A NATION

LET US SEE WHAT THESE CANADIANS DESIRE to do. They are not ... a very harmonious or homogeneous community. Two-fifths of the population are French and three-fifths are English. They are therefore perplexed with an internal antagonism.... The wisdom of Solomon and the energy and strategy of Frederick the Great would seem to be required to preserve and strengthen such a people, if formed ... into "a new nationality."... A more unpromising nucleus of a new nation could hardly be found on the face of the earth.[1]

These words were written in 1866 by Joseph Howe, a leader of the anti-confederate movement in Nova Scotia. Although Howe's criticism focused on the United Province of Canada—divided into Ontario and Quebec at Confederation—much the same point could be made about the new Dominion of Canada, which came into being with the passage of the British North America Act (BNA Act) in 1867. What had been the United Province dominated the federation in population and power, and even bequeathed its name and capital to the infant nation. In Howe's opinion, such a lopsided arrangement could spell nothing but disaster for Nova Scotia and New Brunswick, the two Maritime colonies that had become reluctant

partners in the Confederation project. Subsequent developments proved that Howe was right: cultural and regional tensions were indeed defining features of the Dominion of Canada.

Nevertheless, the fledgling nation survived and even thrived in the half century following its birth. By the 1880s, Canada's territorial jurisdiction had been extended to the Pacific and Arctic Oceans, making it physically the second largest nation on earth. In the twentieth century, Canada emerged as one of the world's industrial giants. Even the most optimistic supporters of Confederation would have been surprised by the success of their venture.

## CANADA IN 1867: THE CONTEXT

On 1 July 1867, by an act of the British Parliament, the Dominion of Canada was born (see map 1.1). The new nation was composed of four provinces— Ontario, Quebec, New Brunswick, and Nova Scotia—and had a population of less than 3.5 million (see table 1.1). Clustered along the Great Lakes–St Lawrence waterway and the northeast coast of North America, these colonies were in closer communication with the two empires— Great Britain and the United States—that dominated their existence than they were with each other. They had scarcely any links with the other British colonies in North America—British Columbia, Prince Edward Island, and Newfoundland and Labrador—or with the vast Northwest Territories, known as Rupert's Land and administered by the British-chartered Hudson's Bay Company since 1670. The Arctic archipelago, also claimed by Britain, was out of bounds for most "southerners," who tended to succumb to the rigours of its cold weather and difficult terrain.

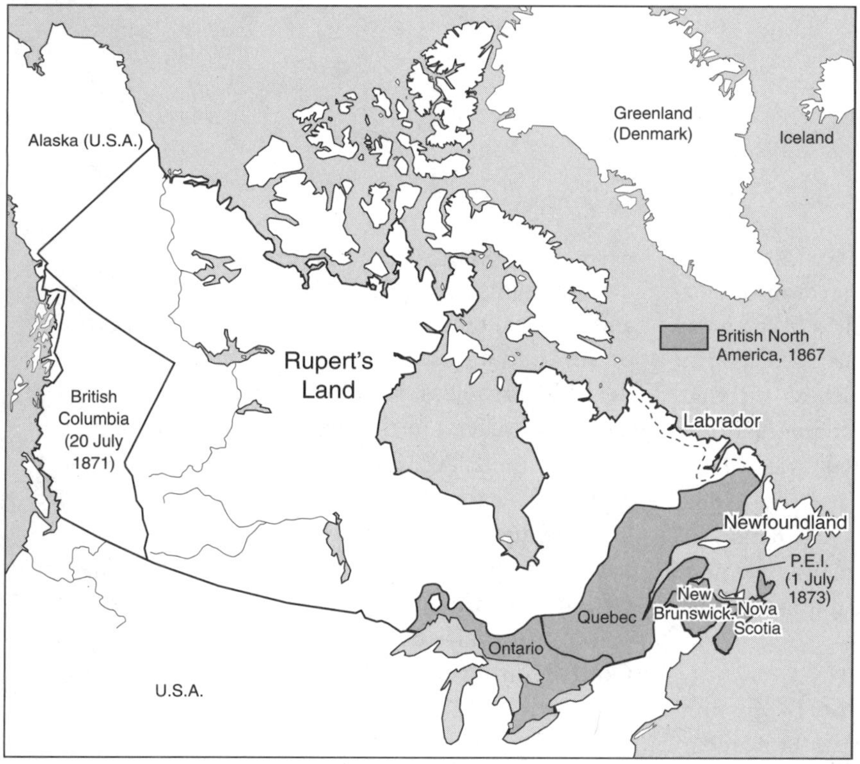

**Map 1.1** *British North America, 1867.*

In the settled areas, railroads were beginning to supplant the stagecoach services that had linked major communities, but there was no direct rail communication, and only a poor excuse for a road, between Quebec and New Brunswick. Portland, Maine, was the eastern terminus and winter port of the Grand Trunk Railroad, the longest rail line in Canada in 1867. When Canadians travelled to the Northwest, they usually did so through the United States, which boasted a transcontinental railroad by

1869. Even telegraph lines, the fastest form of communication, were often routed through the United States rather than directly from one colony to the other.

Yet, citizens of the new nation shared one significant feature with other peoples living in the northern half of the North American continent: they were subjects of Great Britain, the world's most powerful empire in the nineteenth century. Like the Dominion of Canada—which remained a dependency of Great Britain under the BNA Act—all of the British North American colonies possessed, to a greater or lesser degree, the political, legal, and social institutions of the mother country. Queen Victoria, who ascended the British throne in 1837, presided over the British Empire. When she died in 1901, many Canadians looked back fondly to the Victorian Age, which they associated with prosperity and social propriety.

It was this shared heritage, and Britain's eagerness to relinquish direct involvement in the internal administration of its North American colonies, that enabled the Canadian government to move so quickly in expanding its borders following Confederation. By 1873, the Northwest Territories had been transferred to Canada, and Manitoba, British Columbia, and Prince Edward Island had become provinces. New provinces were soon carved out of the southern territories while the boundaries of several provinces were extended northward (see maps 2.1 and 2.2). By 1914, the map of Canada (see map 7.1) looked very much as it does today, with one notable exception: Newfoundland and Labrador remained a separate self-governing colony under the British Crown, and the boundary between Quebec and Labrador was still in dispute.

## MEASURING THE CANADIAN POPULATION

In the nineteenth century, reformers argued that statistical tables revealed patterns that could help governments develop public policy. Section 91(6) of the BNA Act made census enumeration and vital statistics—that is the record of births, marriages, and deaths—a responsibility of the federal government. Because of the costs involved, Ottawa was slow to take up its role as collector of vital statistics, but, beginning in 1871, it conducted census enumerations every ten years. Canada's first census was a major endeavour, taking seven years to complete and costing over half a million dollars.

Covering the four original provinces of Confederation—Ontario, Quebec, New Brunswick, and Nova Scotia—the 1871 census provided a record of population distribution (see table 1.1) and indicators of economic growth. The quality of the data depended to a large extent on the diligence and ability of the enumerator. Notwithstanding its flaws, the manuscript census remains one of the best sources available for historians and genealogists to gain information on the lives of ordinary Canadians at the time of Confederation.

**Table 1.1**

| POPULATION OF CANADA, 1871 | |
| --- | --- |
| Ontario | 1 620 851 |
| Quebec | 1 191 516 |
| New Brunswick | 285 594 |
| Nova Scotia | 387 800 |
| **Total** | **3 485 761** |

*Source: Census of Canada, 1871*

Canada's closest neighbour, and the object of grudging admiration, was the United States. Like Canada, the Thirteen Colonies, which formed the original United States, had begun their existence as dependencies of Great Britain. They had declared their independence in 1776 and sustained their resolve in a fiercely fought war. When the United States of America was officially recognized by the Treaty of Paris in 1783, it was not much larger in population and territory than Canada in 1867. The United States soon expanded its borders westward to the Pacific. By the mid-nineteenth century, Americans were making threatening noises about their "manifest destiny" to dominate the whole North American continent. This goal was temporarily deflected by a bitter Civil War, which raged from 1861 to 1865 between the slave-owning South and industrialized North. Following the war, the Americans resumed their expansionary policies, purchasing Alaska from the Russians in 1867 and casting covetous eyes towards Rupert's Land.

The question of defence was very much on the minds of Canadians in the decade prior to Confederation. For over a century, British North Americans had relied on imperial troops to protect them against external attack and internal disorder. British troops had been instrumental in pushing back an American invasion during the War of 1812 (1812–14) and had effectively, if brutally, put down the rebellions of 1837–38 in Upper and Lower Canada. During the Crimean War (1854–56), in which Britain and France were allied against Russia, most of the ten thousand imperial troops in the colonies were moved to the European front. All able-bodied men in British North America between the ages of fifteen and sixty were theoretically members of the sedentary militia, but it was unorganized, ill-equipped, untrained, and usually unenthusiastic about military service.

The threat of hostility from the United States during and immediately following the American Civil War brought the issue of defence home to all British North Americans. Because the British continued to trade with the South and even supplied it with military vessels, the British colonies bordering on the northern states were vulnerable to retaliatory attacks. Nearly seventeen thousand British troops were stationed in the colonies at the height of the conflict, but this number was no match for the massive northern army which was a million strong by the end of the war. Although the Americans did not turn their military might northward, Canadians continued to keep a watchful eye on their potentially aggressive neighbour.

## CANADA'S PEOPLES

Despite their shared colonial identity, the peoples of Britain's North American colonies in 1867 were a mixed lot, scarcely the building blocks of a nation bound together by ties of a common history and culture. The land's First Nations could be found in every region, but their numbers were declining rapidly. Of the approximately 120 000 Indians in British North America at the time of Confederation, the vast majority lived in British Columbia and Rupert's Land, along with some 10 000 Métis, the progeny of European traders and Native women. Inuit peoples, certainly no more than 10 000 in total, confined themselves to the northern regions of the continent, where, perhaps to their benefit, they had only sporadic contact with European culture.

The vulnerable condition of Native peoples at mid-century was a far cry from the independence they had once known. With the invasion of their cherished farming, fishing, and hunting grounds by European settlers, aboriginal peoples had difficulty making a living. Deprived of their land, they lacked the resources to live well off the fur trade that had once sustained them or to return to traditional lifestyles. In the eastern colonies, about twenty thousand Algonkin and Iroquois peoples lived primarily on reserves that were often encroached upon by rapacious settlers. The Beothuk of Newfoundland, pushed into the interior of the colony by conflict with the fishing communities along the coast, had died out in the 1820s. Meanwhile, the Métis and Blackfoot of the southwestern plains watched with dismay as western settlement in the United States resulted in the virtual extinction of the buffalo and the marginalization of aboriginal peoples. Would the same process destroy them? Coastal Indians in British Columbia already knew the answer to that question. They had prospered from the fur trade in the first half of the nineteenth century but had lost much of their land as settlers poured into the region following the gold rush of 1858.

In 1867, at least thirty thousand people of African descent lived in Canada. The first Africans in the colonies in both the French and British regimes were usually slaves. After the American Revolution, thirty-five hundred free blacks arrived in the Loyalist migration. Wealthy Loyalists also brought their black slaves with them to British-controlled colonies. Slavery was abolished in Upper

*One of the best-known "conductors" on the underground railway was Harriet Tubman, who made an estimated nineteen trips into slave states to rescue over three hundred people. Between 1851 and 1857, Tubman was based in St Catharines, Canada West, where she made a living cleaning and cooking for people in the town.*

Library of Congress

Canada in 1793 and for all practical purposes ceased elsewhere in British North America early in the nineteenth century, but it remained legally sanctioned in the United States. Following the War of 1812, black refugees—slaves who had run away from their American masters to join the British forces—sought refuge in Nova Scotia and New Brunswick. In the 1850s, a secret process known as the "underground railroad" was

*During the American Civil War, the British North American colonies feared an invasion from the United States. African Americans living in Victoria formed the Victoria Pioneer Rifle Corps to help defend the colony.*

British Columbia Archives and Records Service/C-6124

developed to bring escaped slaves into British North America, most of them to Canada West, where a number of African-American communities had been established in the 1830s and 1840s.

Despite the official opposition to slavery, whites in British North America were no less prejudiced than their American neighbours. Black refugees faced discrimination in land grants, voting rights, schooling, and employment. Given the gender imbalance and the difficulty of gaining acceptance in their new environment, some of those who had travelled the underground railroad decided that their prospects were better in the United States after slavery was abolished there in 1863.

In the wake of the gold rush, the West Coast became home to some seven thousand Chinese, the majority of them from the gold fields of California. Most of the Chinese immigrants were men who worked as merchants, prospectors, and servants, but a few women worked with their merchant husbands or made a living as prostitutes. When the gold fields were depleted, fewer than two thousand Chinese remained to form the basis of Canada's

oldest Chinese community. The hostility of the white majority, the lack of work, and the difficulties of finding marriage partners encouraged the majority of Chinese to return either to California or to their homeland.

The legacy of the French regime in North America (1604–1760) was present in the nearly one-third of Canadians whose first language was French. Concentrated in Quebec, the heartland of the old French empire, French Canadians also included the Acadians in the Maritimes and a growing number of francophone settlers in the eastern sections of Ontario. The French-speaking Métis population of Red River and other areas of the Northwest testified to the earlier influence of France in the fur trade. Although it had been over a century since the Acadian deportation (1755) and the conquest of Quebec (1763), the historical memory of the bitter conflict between the British and French for ascendancy in North America was still very much alive and helped to inspire strong francophone nationalism in Quebec and a common identity among Acadians.

British immigrants began settling the eastern

seaboard a century before Great Britain officially gained control of the French colonies in North America by the Treaty of Utrecht (1713) and the Treaty of Paris (1763). By the end of the eighteenth century, the best sites in the Maritimes and Newfoundland had been settled. Between 1815 and 1870, some 1 300 000 British subjects sailed to British North America, the majority destined for Upper Canada, known as Canada West following union with Lower Canada in 1840. While an unknown number of these immigrants eventually drifted to the United States, enough stayed in the colonies to ensure a British majority in every province except Quebec by 1867.

A British heritage did not guarantee a common culture or even a strong allegiance to the British Empire. Welsh, Scots, and Irish immigrants shared a history of hated English imperialism, which had culminated in acts of union with Wales (1535), Scotland (1707), and Ireland (1801), to create "Great" Britain. The Welsh, Scots, and Irish differed from each other in significant ways and were divided by internal conflicts. With their clan structure, Gaelic language, and Roman Catholic faith, Scots Highlanders contrasted dramatically with the more individualistic, English-speaking, Presbyterian Lowland Scots, and no one in 1867 could confuse Irish Protestants, either Presbyterian or Anglican, with the Irish who professed Roman Catholicism. Even those who traced their ancestry to England brought widely divergent cultural experiences. Military officers who retired in the colonies following the French and Napoleonic Wars (1793–1815) had little in common with the descendants of eighteenth-century West Country settlers in Newfoundland or the New England Planter, Loyalist, and "late" Loyalist migrants to the Maritimes and the Canadas.

The Irish made up one-quarter of the Canadian population at the time of Confederation. Those who identified themselves as English and Welsh accounted for about 20 percent, and the Scottish nearly 16 percent. While all the colonies were home to immigrants from Great Britain, they each had a different mix. At 45 and 33 percent, respectively, Prince Edward Island and Nova Scotia had the highest proportion of

people claiming Scottish ancestry, and Scots fur traders were the overwhelming majority of the Europeans in the Northwest Territories. The Irish represented between one-quarter and one-third of the population of Ontario but, unlike the Maritime colonies, where Irish Protestants and Catholics were represented in nearly equal numbers, Ontario attracted a majority of Irish Protestant immigrants. In Newfoundland, Catholics were the dominant element among those who claimed Irish origins.

The victims of the Great Famine, which struck Ireland in 1845, were the most obvious newcomers in 1867. Between 1845 and 1855, nearly 350 000 Irish immigrants poured into British North America in an effort to escape the troubles that gripped their homeland. While not as numer-

*By the 1860s, Irish women, who outnumbered men in the post-famine migration, dominated the ranks of domestic service in every large urban centre in Canada except Quebec City. This sketch, drawn by Juliana Horatia Ewing shortly after her arrival in Fredericton in 1867, was inspired by her experience with an Irish housekeeper who had a fondness for the bottle and had to be fired. Like most English immigrants, Ewing arrived with a prejudice against the Irish, who had also moved to England in large numbers following the Great Famine.*

National Archives of Canada/C126434

ous as the 445 000 Irish who had arrived in British North America in the previous two decades, the famine migrants had fewer resources and therefore encountered greater difficulty in their efforts to make a living. Most of them entered through quarantine stations on Grosse Île (Quebec) or Partridge Island (Saint John), where unmarked graves still bear silent testimony to the suffering of these ill-fated people. Destitute and disease ridden, the famine migrants filled up the remaining, often marginal, lands on the agricultural frontier and formed the backbone of the labouring classes in most colonial cities.

People who traced their origins to the German-speaking states—German unification was achieved only in 1871—were the largest ethnic group in Canada other than British and French in 1867. Although most Germans were not recent immigrants, they retained their cultural identity in areas where their settlements were concentrated such as Lunenburg County in Nova Scotia and Waterloo County in Ontario. In Waterloo County, the town of Berlin had Lutheran, Mennonite, Evangelical, and Roman Catholic churches, as well as German-language newspapers and schools, to serve its overwhelmingly German citizens. The close relationship of the British monarchy to Germany assured the place of Germans in the Canadian mosaic, at least until 1914 when antagonism between Germany and Great Britain erupted in war.

While over 90 percent of Canadians at the time of Confederation traced their origins to France or Britain, most of them had never set foot in Europe. Fully 93 percent of the inhabitants of Quebec and Nova Scotia in 1871 were born in Canada. The percentages were lower in New Brunswick and Ontario—87 percent and 73 percent respectively—but it was clear that Canada was no longer a preferred destination for immigrants. By the mid-nineteenth century, even the Canadian-born, especially from the Maritimes and Quebec, were beginning to move in large numbers to the United States, where frontier lands and industrial employment offered attractive opportunities. The supporters of Confederation hoped to stimulate industrial growth and secure a western frontier so

that Canada could keep its sons and daughters at home.

With over half of its citizens under the age of twenty-one, Canada was a young nation in 1867. Fertility—the number of births per thousand women of child-bearing age (that is, between age fifteen and forty-nine)—was high, especially in francophone families and rural areas of the country. In urban centres, there was evidence of a dramatic decline in family size that demographers call the "fertility transition." People began limiting the size of their families for reasons that are not entirely clear but seem to be linked to a lower death rate and the adoption of new values associated with industrialism. Women born in 1825 bore, on average, 7.8 children, while those born in 1845 bore 6.3. By the end of the century this figure had dropped to under 4.

Ninety-five percent of Canadians living in 1867 were married or would enter into a marriage relationship at some point in their lives. Although rudimentary birth control was practised by some couples, most people controlled the size of their families by delaying marriage. Men, on average, were over twenty-five when they married, while women were twenty-three. Cultural values and ethnic origins had an impact on family formation. On one end of the spectrum, francophones tended to marry in their early twenties; at the opposite extreme, Protestants of Scottish background were nearly thirty years old when they took their wedding vows. On average, Roman Catholics tended to marry younger and have larger families than did people of evangelical persuasion such as Baptists, Methodists, Presbyterians, and Lutherans.

For women who bore children outside of marriage, the penalties were often severe. "Illegitimate" children were easily "adopted" by kin or neighbours in close-knit families and communities, but such support networks were not always available, especially among poor immigrants living in cities. Desperate women often sought illegal abortions, while those who took their pregnancy to term sometimes committed infanticide, a practice that had increased in the two decades before Confederation. Most unmarried mothers gave their babies to church- and state-run orphanages, where overcrowding and poor nutrition resulted in horrific death rates: of the six hundred babies abandoned at the doors of a Montreal foundling hospital in 1863, for example, fewer than sixty survived.

Community proscriptions against premarital sex were part of a rigid sexual code that also included harsh legal penalties against intimate relations between people of the same sex. Homosexuality in the Victorian era was considered a crime punishable by imprisonment and even death. In practice, the latter penalty appears not to have been imposed in the colonial period, but there were cases of men being imprisoned for engaging in homosexual relationships. There may well have been networks of gays and lesbians—terms that did not exist to describe same sex relationships in 1867—but, because the legal system forced homosexuals to keep their intimate lives secret, their history remained unrecorded.

While average life expectancy in early Victorian Canada was forty, this figure is somewhat misleading. One in five children died before their first birthday, primarily as a result of diseases spread by impure water and contaminated milk. In Montreal, the most unhealthy city in the dominion, the infant death rate was closer to one in three. Those who survived childhood and adolescence had a life expectancy of close to sixty years, but this figure only represents an average. At any age, death was likely, and no Canadians could be assured of a long life or robust health. Illness was an ever-present threat to Canadians, and cures were often worse than the disease. Epidemics of cholera, the most recent in 1854, killed thousands in cities, while diseases such as tuberculosis, smallpox, and diphtheria were common in both rural and urban environments. Although some municipal jurisdictions had taken steps to improve sanitation, urban water and sewer systems were rudimentary. The germ theory of disease, only recently advanced, was still not widely accepted. Many doctors clung to the view that patients were best cured by heavy doses of morphine or by applying leeches to extract "bad humours" from the blood—or both.

Canadians were a rural people in 1867, with 80 percent living in communities of fewer than a thousand inhabitants. While some areas of the nation had been farmed for over two hundred years, huge sections, especially in remoter regions, were not far from the frontier stage. Newcomers from Europe frequently remarked on the untidy appearance of the landscape, where fields of charred stumps, left from the land-clearing process, greeted them. Despite the frontier character, pioneers in Eastern Canada had been aware for some time that the "new world" was rapidly becoming more like the "old" European world they had left behind. In most settled regions, wild animals no longer existed in sufficient quantities to make the fur trade profitable, while several species of birds, such as the great auk, had become extinct from over-exploitation. The stands of white pine, much in demand for the shipbuilding industry, were also fast disappearing. In 1867, Canadians relied almost entirely on wood for their fuel, with the result that there was little forested land remaining near major cities. Coal contributed less than 10 percent and oil scarcely any of the energy production.

Boasting a population of over a hundred thousand, Montreal was Canada's largest city, nearly twice the size of its nearest rivals, Quebec City and Toronto. Saint John and Halifax, whose populations approached thirty thousand, were the largest cities in the Maritimes. Whether large or small, cities were highly concentrated. The transportation technology necessary to sustain suburbs, most notably electric street cars, was still three decades away. While most cities were primarily commercial and administrative centres, a few were developing impressive industrial potential and extending their influence well beyond their boundaries through elaborate transportation networks.

## ECONOMY AND SOCIETY

In 1867, the lives of individual Canadians were being transformed by the Industrial Revolution. This term is used to describe the changes in technology and the organization of production that swept the North Atlantic world in the nineteenth century. The first major industrial nation was Great Britain whose "mechanics" and capitalists had pioneered in the application of steam-powered machines to production in key sectors of the economy: agriculture, manufacturing, and transportation. Strongly influenced by the British experience, British North Americans experimented with new transportation and production processes in the first half of the nineteenth century. Steam-propelled machines, trains, and ocean-going vessels changed the way that people performed their most basic activities, and created the context that made Confederation possible.

Manufacturing in Canada, as elsewhere, encouraged the growth of cities. With its large domestic market, low-wage structure, and pivotal location on the St Lawrence trading system, Montreal was Canada's leading industrial centre in 1867. Factories built along the Lachine Canal benefited from nearby hydraulic power and an abundant labour supply, enabling them to establish a dominant position in a variety of consumer and heavy industries. Although quick off the mark in exploiting its industrial potential, Hamilton failed to recover from the recession of the late 1850s and was eclipsed by Toronto in the race for industrial ascendancy in Ontario. Between 1851 and 1871, Toronto was transformed from a city of independent artisans to one where over 70 percent of the labour force worked in shops employing over thirty people. Saint John emerged as the leading manufacturing centre in the Maritimes. By the time of Confederation, its foundry, footwear, and clothing industries each exceeded shipbuilding in the value of their output.

Railroad companies were Canada's largest corporations in 1867. With their personnel departments, complex accounting systems, quality control procedures, specialized division of labour, machine shops, and rolling mills, they were in the forefront of practices associated with the Industrial Revolution. Every community in the new dominion longed for a railroad to bring capital investment, quicken the pace of travel, and put them on the map. Significantly, Maritimers made an intercolonial railroad link one of their few conditions for joining Confederation, and

the promise of a railway, or of assuming the debt of one already in existence, clinched the Confederation negotiations with British Columbia and Prince Edward Island.

Industrialism not only revolutionized production processes, it also changed the way that people related to each other and to their work. In pre-industrial society, artisans had controlled their workplace, making a product from start to finish and determining their own standards and prices. Machines, in contrast, encouraged the division of labour into repetitive tasks and the centralization of production in factories owned by a few wealthy capitalists who could finance such expensive ventures. Under the factory system, labourers lost control of their work and often found it difficult to make a living wage. Meanwhile, successful capitalists with their imposing new factories could produce more, make greater profits, and enjoy a level of material wealth hitherto only imagined.

At first, workers tried to destroy the new machines that threatened their traditional practices, as was the case among shoemakers in Montreal when the sewing machine was introduced in 1852. Gradually, workers began organizing to

*At the time of Confederation, illustrated newspapers often included lithographic scenes of industrial sites such as this one of the Toronto Rolling Mills. The size and complexity of operations associated with railway development elicited much comment and symbolized Canada's entry into the Industrial Age.*

Metropolitan Toronto Reference Library, J. Ross Robertson Collection/T10914

press for better working conditions and a fairer distribution of the profits of mechanized production. Only skilled labourers could risk joining unions, which were considered seditious conspiracies by factory owners. Unskilled workers, who could easily be replaced, were fired if they were caught trying to organize the shop floor. At the time of Confederation, only a tiny minority of workers belonged to unions, but whether unionized or not, wage earners were determined not to become slaves to their capitalist masters. On 10 June 1867, just three weeks before the first Dominion Day, over ten thousand workers in Montreal, parading behind the *patriote* flag of the Lower Canadian rebels of 1837, took to the street in a show of worker solidarity.

Canada's industrial workforce was dominated by men, who were hired exclusively in the milling, woodworking, and metal industries, and who held supervisory positions throughout the industrial structure. Women, both married and single, and children, some as young as eight years old, were employed in clothing, soap-making, and tobacco factories and made up a significant proportion of those hired in printing, footwear, and confectionery industries. Women and children who worked in factories earned half the wage paid to men and also formed the majority of workers employed in the "sweated trades," a term used to describe industrial tasks performed in the home at appallingly low rates. By the 1860s, there was growing concern about the exploitation of women and children in the industrial system, but capitalists resisted reforms that would deprive them of a cheap labour supply.

Professional services were also being transformed by the pressures of the new industrial order. At the beginning of the nineteenth century, doctors, lawyers, and clergymen of the Roman Catholic and Anglican Churches were considered the professional elite of colonial society. Professional men traditionally came from the upper classes, had some schooling in the liberal arts, and served an apprenticeship for a prescribed number of years before setting up a practice. Although there were no specific programs of study required to enter the professions, most colonies had licensing boards to determine who should be allowed to practise their skills in law and medicine, while the church hierarchies served as gatekeepers for those allowed into the pulpit.

By the mid-nineteenth century, the professions were undergoing a major transformation. Roman Catholic and Anglican clergymen lost ground to evangelical preachers, doctors found their territory invaded by quacks, homeopaths, and patent medicine salesmen, and lawyers came under attack for their outmoded legal opinions. At the same time, practitioners of skills much in demand in the industrial age, such as surveyors, accountants, and teachers, were gaining in prestige and began aspiring to professional status.

In an effort to impose control over their rapidly changing work processes, professionals set out to secure legislation giving them the right to establish standards, which usually involved some combination of university training and standardized exams, and to determine who should be admitted to professional practice. The reconstruction of the professions was only in the early stages by the time of Confederation. With the creation of the Canadian Medical Association in 1867, doctors were well on the way to securing exclusive control over their profession. Pharmacists, dentists, lawyers, engineers, and accountants were not far behind. At the same time, through courses offered in their newly minted universities, evangelical churches were moving closer to a professionally defined clergy.

As well as changing the economic structures that organized the way people made a living, the Industrial Revolution also prompted changes in the political institutions governing the British Empire. From the early days of European overseas expansion, the mercantile system had dominated imperial policy. Under this system, colonial economies were strictly controlled in the interests of advancing the wealth and power of the mother country. High customs duties were placed on merchandise imported from outside the empire, while colonial products and shipping capacity were restricted to the closed circle of imperial trade. To maintain such a system, the mother country kept a tight control over colonial governments. The high cost of maintaining troops and administrators in the colonies was accepted as one of the necessary burdens of empire.

A source of constant friction between Britain and its colonies, mercantilism had been one of the reasons that thirteen American colonies had declared independence from Great Britain in 1776. Thereafter, colonial policy became the source of endless debate, fuelled by the theories of British economist Adam Smith, who argued that a free trade system worked more effectively than one hobbled by restraining mercantile legislation. The logical extension of such thinking had major implications for colonial policy. If colonies populated by British settlers were not required for economic reasons, why should Britain put up with the expense and bother of governing them?

The British North American colonies had been slow to reject mercantilism. Their exports— primary products such as furs, fish, timber, and wheat—found ready markets in a rapidly industrializing Great Britain, and benefited from the preferences built into the mercantile system. Yet, as British North Americans would soon discover, colonial interests had never been the major consideration in formulating imperial policy. In 1846, precipitated by the Irish Famine and the need to import food from any source, Great Britain adopted a policy of global free trade and within three years had entirely dismantled the old mercantile system.

For many British North Americans, the introduction of free trade turned their world upside down. A few merchants, especially those tied to the timber and wheat trade, even advocated annexation to the United States as the only solution to their temporarily failing fortunes. Although the crisis passed, it produced three new strategies that would change the economic direction of the British North American colonies. First, Great Britain negotiated a free trade treaty with the United States as a means of relieving some of the economic distress experienced by the colonies. In effect from 1854 to 1866, the Reciprocity Treaty applied only to primary products such as fish, timber, minerals, and agricultural products, but it proved particularly valuable when these commodities were in high

demand during the American Civil War. Second, the link between economic policy and political structures proved as close in practice as it was in theory. Between 1848 and 1855, the British North American colonies with elected assemblies were granted a limited form of colonial self-rule known as responsible government. Armed with their new powers, the colonies embarked on a third strategy to meet the challenges of the age: free trade among themselves and tariff protection against imports from the rest of the world. The United Canadas and New Brunswick led the colonies in developing a protectionist strategy. Following Confederation, protectionism would become the cornerstone of Canada's national policy.

We now know that the Industrial Revolution would transform Canadian society, but it is important not to overestimate the degree of social change that it caused before 1867. At the time of Confederation, over half of the working adult population made a living by farming, fishing, lumbering, and trapping animals (compared to fewer than 5 percent by the end of the twentieth century). The products of industrial processes were changing the way people conducted their primary pursuits, but the social implications were only beginning to be recognized. In 1867, farming families still consumed much of what they produced. For them, and for most Canadians, the family, rather than the factory or office, was still the basic unit of economic and social organization, and their major goal in life was to accumulate enough wealth to help their children achieve land ownership.

The goal of landed independence had been within reach of many British North Americans in the century before Confederation. In 1871, fully 85 percent of farmers in Ontario over the age of fifty owned some land. Those who remained tenants on the estates of others, as was the case of the Irish immigrants who lived on Amherst Island in Lake Ontario, often did so because it was profitable. In Ontario's bustling towns and cities "working on one's own account" as an artisan or small shopkeeper was a widespread phenomenon, not yet eclipsed by factory production and corporate practices.

As Canada's frontier province, Ontario was

probably exceptional in the degree of opportunity available to its citizens. People in other parts of Canada, where settlement had proceeded earlier and often under less democratic circumstances, were facing difficult choices. In Quebec, seigneurialism, a system of landholding that predated the conquest, had been abolished in 1855 but had left a legacy of small and overcrowded farms. Prince Edward Island was still struggling to rid itself of the system of proprietary land ownership that had been imposed on the colony in 1767. Despite a generation of efforts to solve the "land question," some 60 percent of the island's farmers in 1861 were either tenants or squatters. Because of the importance of the timber trade to the New Brunswick economy, much of the land there remained locked up in Crown leases. Nova Scotia's land frontier was entirely gone, and the physical extent of settlement, much of it on marginal agricultural land, was greater in the 1860s than it is today.

By 1867, farmers living on the best agricultural lands had moved well beyond the subsistence stage, producing significant surpluses for markets at home and abroad. Stimulated by mechanization, new seeds and breeds, better methods of transportation, and expanding markets, commercial agriculture grew dramatically in the mid-nineteenth century. Ontario was Canada's breadbasket, producing 84 percent of the nation's wheat, much of it destined for export. Ontario farmers also produced livestock, butter, milk, and wool in exportable quantities. Quebec specialized in livestock, potatoes, and coarse grains, most of which was consumed locally. Surplus grains, potatoes, apples, and other foodstuffs from Maritime farms found markets in Newfoundland and the Caribbean. Such sales increased a family's disposable income without threatening their primary goal of producing for subsistence.

Farming in 1867 was a term that covered an enormous range of activities. In most households men, women, and children worked together with the plant and animal resources to produce a livelihood. Men usually worked in the fields and woodlot, handling the heavier tasks with their oxen and horses, and increasingly with the help of machinery

## WOMEN'S WORK

Material abundance made possible by industrial production was beginning to have an impact on the lives of Canadian women in 1867, but there were still many tasks that had to be performed to ensure a family's well-being through the Canadian seasons. When twenty-seven-year-old Juliana Horatia Ewing, an accomplished writer of children's literature and the wife of a British officer stationed in Fredericton, was asked to provide advice on a woman's domestic responsibilities to friends back in England who were planning to emigrate to Canada in 1868, she wrote the following:

> She must learn to make her own soap & candles if not to spin her own yarn. She must get her neighbours to tell her if she ought to have her house banked for the winter with sawdust to keep the frost from the cellar. She must keep a strong (metal if she can get it) saucer or pot of water on her stove if she feels giddy from the stove heat. She must keep her wood ashes to make soft soap ... & be very, very careful as to where she stores them till the heat has gone out because of fire. Wood ashes & water make ley [sic] to scrub the floors with.

> Hard soap is made with lime & grease—so she must save her bits of fat. In the winter the children had better wear 2 pairs of socks & moccasins instead of boots. She can learn to make them herself I think. What I should especially advise them to take are good seeds for next year. At least in Fredericton vegetable seeds were got out from England and dear. In the short & hot summer vegetation is wonderful. Squash & cucumbers & vegetable marrows will rampage over the ground. Everything is luxuriant. I advise plenty of carrots & beetroots, things that will store in a frost proof cellar for winter consumption as one gets a little tired of the monotony of winter fare. She will have to pack butter & eggs in autumn for winter consumption.... I use to grease my eggs all over with butter & pack them in coarse salt the narrow end downwards. Meat is frozen and keeps any length of time, & is "thawed out" for cooking. It is best to thaw it gradually. Tell her not to frighten herself with thoughts of a barbarian outlandish life. I have gone through all of that & it is a great mistake.[2]

such as the new self-raking reaper. In communities by oceans, lakes, and rivers, men did most of the fishing. Many farmers possessed skills that enabled them to serve their family and neighbours as blacksmiths, carpenters, cobblers, tanners, and wheelwrights. When it came time to erect a house, barn, or other building, men managed the construction process. The male head of the household was also usually responsible for supervising and paying the hired help during peak seasons of planting and harvest.

Women's work included gardening, dairying, poultry raising, food preparation, spinning, weaving, and sewing. Although the first priority was meeting family needs, many women sold or bartered the surplus from their kitchen, garden, dairy, and loom in urban markets. They also served their communities as nurses, midwives, and teachers. In fishing communities, women cleaned and dried the fish that their male relatives caught. Native women fished, trapped, prepared hides, sewed clothes, gathered nuts, berries, and herbs, and served as guides, while Native men often moved farther afield in search of elusive game. Both men and women in Native communities made baskets, brooms, leather goods, and highly prized bead and quill work for sale locally and internationally. Everywhere, women, aided by older children, had the major responsibility for raising children, cooking, and cleaning. More affluent households had servants, who were also mainly female and who were generally supervised by the mistress of the house.

In areas where farming alone could not sustain a family, members combined a number of activities to ensure survival. Fathers and older sons often worked in the fisheries or the woods for part of the year, while adolescent children moved to the city to find work and wages to supplement the family income. When these strategies failed, entire families moved to industrial towns to take work in expanding factories. The family-based work practices of rural farm life often worked effectively in the unregulated urban landscapes of Victorian Canada. If the income of the head of household was insufficient for the family's needs, one or more of the children were sent out to work, and, if the

*At the time of Confederation, the bead and quill-work of aboriginal artists was highly prized, selling well in domestic and foreign markets. The nineteenth-century cradle pictured above is covered with panels of Mi'kmaq porcupine quill-work.*

Panels by Christianne Morris/Des Brisay Museum, Bridgewater, Nova Scotia. Photo by Ron Merrick/ Courtesy of the History Collection of the Nova Scotia Museum, Halifax

space was available, boarders would become part of the household. Working-class families also planted gardens and raised animals in their backyards to provide food.

Many men worked in the variety of forest operations, producing everything from potash, staves, and firewood to railway ties, planks, and ship timber. Rivers and streams throughout the new nation were choked with logs during the spring drive when gangs of men brought their winter's harvest to waiting mills. In the period from 1850 to 1870, the value of wood exports increased from $6.4 million to $20.4 million. The proportion sent to the British market declined from 80 to 50 percent in the same period, while the American market soared. With a flourishing shipbuilding industry in Quebec and the Maritimes, a vigorous construction industry in the rapidly expanding cities, and new factories producing barrels, furniture, doors, and sashes, the local market for timber also increased significantly.

By 1867, the fur trade was experiencing a period of transition. The Hudson's Bay Company dominated the industry, but in 1867 its days as a privileged monopoly were numbered. Although the depletion of fur-bearing animals posed some difficulties for the company, the major problems were

*Carleton House on the North Saskatchewan River was a favourite stopping point for fur traders making the long trek between the Red River and Edmonton.*

Glenbow Archives/NA-1408-8

economic and political. Competition from free traders and the eagerness of visionaries to convert the great Northwest to an agricultural frontier meant that the company would have to expand its range of activities and transform itself from a monopoly to a competitive corporation.

The challenges facing the fisheries were more complex. Cod was still the chief export of the fisheries in Newfoundland and the Gulf of St Lawrence, while a mixed fishery had developed along the coasts of New Brunswick and Nova Scotia. In the 1860s, the mixed fishery was facing a crisis, in part because of the destruction of river spawning grounds by dams and sawdust-spewing mills. The increased competition from Americans, who were granted access to the inshore fisheries by the Reciprocity Treaty, only added to the problem of more people chasing fewer fish. With its base on St Pierre and Miquelon, and rights to fish along the west coast of Newfoundland (commonly called the French shore), France brought still more pressure on the beleaguered Atlantic fisheries.

Because their own sources were depleted, Nova Scotians began encroaching on the fishing areas formerly dominated by people from Newfoundland and Labrador, who, in turn, responded with violence and vandalism. The collapse of the seal fisheries in the 1860s had forced many Newfoundlanders to depend on charity for survival. Not surprisingly, they were not inclined to have much sympathy for Nova Scotians who could combine fishing with farming and thereby sustain a much higher standard of living. The "truck" system, by which many fishing families in the region were held in perpetual debt to the merchants who marketed the fish and provided supplies, made any attempt to reform the structure of the fisheries a social as well as an economic problem.

The riches under the vast Canadian terrain offered exciting prospects for a nation on the verge of an industrial boom. While the gold rush on the West Coast was running down, the smaller rush in Nova Scotia peaked in 1867. The expansion of coal mining in Nova Scotia was one of the success stories of the decade. Between 1858, when the General Mining Association's monopoly over Nova Scotia coal was abolished, and 1865, fourteen new coal mines were opened in Cape Breton alone, and more on the mainland. Nova Scotia was the mineral capital of Canada in 1867, with over three thousand men and boys employed in coal mines and seven hundred more in the gold industry.

No matter where one lived in Canada in 1867, luck and individual determination played a role in deciding who would prosper. A bad season could put a farm, fishing, or hunting family close to destitution. Unless one had a needed skill, finding work in Canadian cities could be difficult. Many urban jobs, such as dock work and construction, waxed and waned with the seasons and the capitalist cycles of boom and bust. Even those who had achieved middle-class affluence could find their security swept away when misfortune, especially the premature death of the principal breadwinner, struck. Few people bought personal insurance in 1867, and unemployment insurance was still only an ideal.

Despite the uncertainty, the prospects for the good life were better in the 1860s than they had been at the beginning of the century. The transition from a commercial to an industrial economy brought glimpses of an improved lifestyle, even for the most menial labourers. Unlike construction projects and dock work, factories offered the possibility—if not always the reality—of year-round employment, sometimes for several family members. Working conditions were likely to be harsh and the wages modest, but for an increasing number of working-class families, these jobs offered a degree of security hitherto unknown. For men with a little capital, some skill, and much ambition, there were opportunities to grow with the new nation and end one's days with a substantial legacy to pass on to one's children.

*By the time this picture was taken in 1867 or 1868, most of the easily accessible gold had been mined in the Cariboo. The ore embedded in hard rock could only be extracted by a hydraulic process with water wheels such as the one pictured here.*

British Columbia Archives and Records Service /1379, A-613

## COMMUNITY AND CULTURE

Canadians in 1867 were moving quickly towards new ways of defining their sense of community. Following the arrival of Europeans, older ways, based on local identities, face-to-face relationships, oral communication, and a holistic sense of community, had gradually been replaced by literate societies where written documents bound people through commercial, religious, and political institutions across greater expanses of time and space. While many immigrants could not read and write and still lived largely in local settings, everyone was aware of written texts, such as the Bible, calendars, and contracts, and understood their importance. The growth of literacy and advances in communications at mid-century precipitated a third stage of cultural development. As railways, newspapers, and state institutions diminished distance and accelerated the pace of change, ordinary people were wrenched from their local contexts of kin and community. Few Canadians understood the transformation of their world in this way, but many people were profoundly disturbed by the changes taking place around them and over which they seemed to have little control.

The family was changing both in form and function, and in its relation to other institutions, but it was still the basic unit of social life. More than simply an economic entity, the family was the context in which children learned gender roles, heard stories of their ancestors, received their earliest lessons on the meaning of life, and were taught their "place" in society. That place was largely determined by socially constructed categories such as class, ethnicity, and religion. While an individual might move from one class to another, change religious affiliation, or lie about ethnic origins, it was rarely done. Even more difficult to escape were one's race, gender, or age identities, which also played a major role in determining individual destiny.

No distinction in Canadian society was more fundamental than that between the sexes. Men and women contributed different skills to the family economy and were treated separately under the law. Upon marriage all personal property belonging to the wife and any wages she earned were under the absolute control of her husband. Husband and wife were declared to be one under British common law, which prevailed outside of Quebec. It was impossible for a wife in common law jurisdictions to sign a contract, sue or be sued in her own name, or take her husband to court if he mistreated her. Nor could a married woman engage in business separate from her husband without his consent. The husband also had complete control over the children of the marriage and had easier access to divorce than did his wife.

The subordination of women was based on the pre-industrial ideal of a male-headed household in which women, children, apprentices, and servants were provided for and protected. Although it is unlikely that this patriarchal ideal was ever entirely reflected in practice, the gulf between the ideal and reality had widened in the nineteenth century. Women were excluded from the boards of banks and railways, professional and skilled occupations, university education, and formal politics. Despite the changes taking place around them, women were told that they must continue to take their status from that of their husbands and inhabit the private sphere of the home. Women who avoided their roles as wives and mothers to stay in the paid labour force or, worse, who espoused the doctrines of "woman's rights," were the objects of criticism and ridicule. So, too, were men who failed to maintain their wives in a domestic setting.

Race was also a source of individual and institutional discrimination. Notwithstanding the great range in ability and wealth among aboriginal, African, and Asian peoples, they were all, virtually without exception, treated shabbily by the white majority of Canadians, and racism, rather than disappearing following the abolition of slavery, was becoming more systemic. New scientific theories about origins of species and the survival of the fittest were quickly adapted to make claims about the superiority of the white "race." Such ideas, in turn, fed prejudices about racial intermarriage that fuelled segregationist tendencies. As a result, peo-

ple of African and Asian background were often found in separate schools and churches, excluded from skilled trades and professions, and segregated in the outskirts of communities dominated by whites.

In 1867, aboriginal peoples could still be seen in the towns and cities of Canada, but they were being pressured to live on reserves, out of the sight of white communities upon which they depended to make a living. Indians living on reserves were denied the vote, allegedly on the grounds that they were wards of the state. They were also often forced to endure religious schooling and paternalistic regulations and, on many occasions, were subjected to physical and sexual abuse from the very people who professed to be helping them. Because of such treatment, many Natives living in Canada questioned the wisdom of adapting to the world taking shape around them.

Canadians at the time of Confederation were making life choices that differed considerably from those made by their parents and grandparents. This helped to create what in the twentieth century would be called a "generation gap," with younger people finding their elders "old fashioned," and elders feeling that they lacked the respect they deserved. The gap was especially wide between illiterate parents and their literate children. With the increase in schooling and the postponement of marriage, adolescence—a term that was coined only at the end of the century—was emerging as a stage of the life cycle. Childhood also received new emphasis. In middle-class homes, the child was increasingly perceived as innocent and angelic rather than as a primitive creature to be socialized to adult behaviour as quickly as possible and sent into the labour force.

Hereditary privileges such as existed in Europe failed to take root in North America, but people in Canada still managed to sort themselves on the basis of class. Tight little cliques of businessmen, professionals, and politicians dominated all aspects of public life. With the exception of Quebec, where the elite were predominantly francophone and Catholic, most members of Canada's ruling class were white, English-speaking, Protestant men. These men, along with their wives, imposed their values on Canadian society to a degree out of all proportion to their numbers and in direct proportion to their wealth—and they were destined to increase in power as the century advanced.

The middle class of farmers and artisans constituted the bone and sinew of the nation, but there were wide variations in the wealth and status in this occupational group. While many families lived close to subsistence on the margins of society, others were poised to expand their operations and join the ranks of the economic elite. Most of the "middling sort" were facing pressures that would result in the erosion of their status. In retrospect, they would see the mid-nineteenth century as a golden age before the factory system, corporate management practices, and commercial agriculture completely undermined their independence.

In both town and country, a class of propertyless labourers survived by doing manual work, often on a seasonal basis. This class was expanding rapidly and was anything but uniform in its composition. For some Canadians, wage labour was only a stage in their life cycle, a chance to earn a little money before returning to the family farm or setting up in a business or profession. Others who joined the working class were destined to stay there for the rest of their lives, their status defined by the skills they could acquire and the occupational choices that came their way.

Wealth, like power, was unevenly distributed. For example, 20 percent of the farmers in Ontario owned 60 percent of the land, while in cities such as Toronto the wealthiest 10 percent of householders held well over half of the assessed estate and personal wealth. Among the middle class it was becoming increasingly fashionable to display one's wealth in fine homes. The Victorian parlour—crammed with furniture, knick-knacks, photographs, and paintings—became a popular site for conspicuous consump-

tion, and a source of much grumbling by the domestic servants whose job it was to dust the objects that cluttered the room.

Formal education, with its emphasis on teaching the skills of reading and writing, offered the key for improving one's prospects in life. By the

*The splendour of the Victorian parlour is clearly evident in this Notman photograph, taken in 1884, of the living room in the Montreal home of George Stephen (1829–1921). Born in Scotland, Stephen emigrated to Montreal where he worked as a draper. By 1860, he was the head of his own drapery shop. A shrewd businessman, he invested his capital in banking and railways and soon rose to the top of two of the companies in which he invested. He was president of the Bank of Montreal (1876–81) and the first president of the Canadian Pacific Railway (1880-88). Created a baronet in 1886, he retired to England two years later.*

Notman Photographic Archives, McCord Museum of Canadian History, Montreal/II-73825

mid-nineteenth century, 60 percent of children claimed at least a few years of schooling. Once seen as the responsibility of parents and left to the voluntary sector, schooling had become a state responsibility in most provinces by the time of Confederation. Under the new education acts, taxes were assessed on all property holders to finance the state-operated schools. This policy was considered such an invasion of privacy that in some communities there were violent protests against the hated school tax.

Despite the goals of school reformers, the common schools, or "free" schools as they were sometimes called, were not equally accessible to all children and were certainly not uniform in their curriculum and administration. In Quebec, Roman Catholics ran their own schools and shared government grants equally with the Protestant schools. The Newfoundland government also provided assistance to a school system that was developed entirely along denominational lines. While school attendance under the new system increased impressively, most children attended erratically and for only a few years. Parents in many families viewed children as contributors to the family economy and took them out of school to work in the fields or to perform household chores. In the 1860s, compulsory school attendance was a goal of education reformers, but it was still too controversial a policy to force on reluctant citizens.

As this discussion of schools suggests, religion played a crucial role in defining individual identity in Canada. The growth in membership, power, and institutional complexity of Christian churches was a trend of major significance in the decades immediately before Confederation. Nearly every individual claimed to be a Christian, and those who did not were under intense pressure to become one. Not only were religious leaders reaching out to the unconverted both at home and abroad, they were also mounting campaigns to build new churches, found universities, and establish social services. The church had a higher profile than the state in most communities and played a central role in the spiritual, economic, social, and political life of the nation.

The energy displayed by the institutional church was in part fuelled by the competition among the various denominations. At the time of Confederation, over 40 percent of Canadians were Roman Catholics (see table 1.2). They were a

*Cull's schoolhouse in West Garafraxa in 1867. Many communities in Victorian Canada boasted new one-room schoolhouses, built to the latest specifications of heat, light, and ventilation and staffed by teachers hired by the government.*

From the collection of the Wellington County Museum and Archives/PH6130

majority in Quebec and Rupert's Land and formed a significant minority nearly everywhere else. Roman Catholics had participated in the political life of most of the colonies before it was possible to do so in Great Britain, where "Catholic Emancipation" was achieved only in 1829. The deep roots of Roman Catholicism in British North America, combined with a reinvigorated papacy in Rome and the arrival of a large number of Irish Catholics in the colonies, virtually guaranteed a growing rivalry with Protestants.

By the 1840s, the Roman Catholic Church was asserting its authority everywhere, but especially in Quebec. Papal enthusiasts resisted the separation of church and state, maintained a tight control over social services and education, and intervened directly in political matters when secular authorities threatened their power. In social terms, the Roman Catholic Church touched the lives of its adherents at every level. The number of priests and nuns grew dramatically at mid-century, and church-sponsored institutions ran the gamut from day nurseries and orphanages to universities such as Laval which included faculties of medicine and law.

| Table 1.2 | |
|---|---|
| **RELIGIOUS AFFILIATION IN CANADA, 1871** | |
| **Denomination** | **Percentage** |
| Anglican | 14.00 |
| Baptist | 6.80 |
| Jewish | 0.03 |
| Lutheran | 1.00 |
| Roman Catholic | 43.00 |
| Congregationalist | 0.60 |
| Methodist | 16.30 |
| Presbyterian | 16.20 |
| Other | 2.07 |

*Source: Census of Canada, 1871*

At the time of Confederation, Ontario was the most Protestant of provinces, with over 80 percent of its population belonging to one of the Protestant denominations. There was little uniformity among Protestants, except in their determined opposition to Roman Catholicism. The Church of England had made valiant efforts to become the "established" church in the colonies, with special access to government assistance and exclusive control over higher education. By the mid-nineteenth century, Anglican leaders had been forced to admit defeat in the face of resistance led by the Baptist, Methodist, and Presbyterian churches. The diversity of religious beliefs in colonial society made separation of church and state, and voluntary support for church organization, the preferred option for the majority of Protestants.

Although Protestants subscribed to the voluntary principle in religious matters, this did not mean that they recoiled from political action. Protestant alliances came together during elections to ensure the defeat of Roman Catholic candidates, while in larger communities, organizations such as the Orange Order were devoted to the exclusion of Roman Catholics from all areas of public life. Initially composed of Irish Protestants, the Orange Order broadened its membership at mid-century by offering assistance and camaraderie to anyone eager to fight papal influences. Violent clashes between Orange and Green (Irish Catholic) groups often accompanied the parades marking important events in the history of Ireland, while a "mixed" marriage between a Protestant and a Roman Catholic might result in a noisy, and even violent, charivari by disapproving neighbours.

Brute strength often outweighed notions of Christian charity in motivating individual behaviour in Victorian Canada, where political conflict, drunken brawls, and family violence were common. Many parents and teachers encouraged discipline in children by beating them, and the law permitted husbands to use physical force to control their wives. Popular pastimes such as cockfighting, bear-baiting, wrestling, and fisticuffs carried violence into recreation. Along the waterfront in Quebec City's Lower Town and on Water Street in Halifax, the incidence of violent crimes and brawls, along with prostitution and drunkenness, was an extreme manifestation of the generalized brutality that many British North Americans experienced. The resort to violence was not confined to the lower classes. While there were laws against fighting duels, upper-class men continued to challenge each other to physical contests to defend their honour against even the most trivial verbal slights.

There was a growing concern among the middle class about the ignorance and violence that characterized Canadian society. Dedicated to individual discipline and self-help, middle-class reformers urged others to follow their lead in establishing "companionate" marriages, displaying good manners, and practising moderation in their public behaviour. Only a minority of people were committed to such a degree of self-discipline in 1867, but time was on their side. As the middle class grew and gained power in the later decades of the nineteenth century, the concern for moderation and control became features of a set of "modern" values that would increasingly govern behaviour in Canada.

## INTELLECTUAL REVOLUTIONS

Canadians in 1867 were heirs to the Enlightenment, a term applied to a dramatic shift in the tenor of European intellectual life in the eighteenth century. Building on developments in science and philosophy that had been gaining momentum since the Renaissance, intellectuals in the eighteenth century called into question the claims of revealed

*Cricket Club in Vancouver.*
*At the time of Confederation, there was little that could be called a Canadian literary or artistic culture, but,*
*Canadians had developed their own unique contribution to leisure and sports activities.*
*Lacrosse and snowshoeing clubs, first organized in Montreal, reflected the popularity of sports*
*introduced by Canada's aboriginal peoples. By the 1860s, these activities were giving way*
*to European leisure pursuits—cricket, racing, yachting, rowing, skating, and curling.*
*Although a form of ice hockey was played in a few places before 1867,*
*it was not the popular sport it would later become.*

religion and a divinely sanctioned social order. Such questioning helped to fan the flames of the American (1776–83) and French (1789–95) Revolutions and became the dominant ethic of those members of the new middle class who championed economic growth, political change, and social reform.

The transformation sweeping Canada at the time of Confederation was reinforced by the Enlightenment view that human beings were essentially good and that worldly progress was a desirable end of human endeavours. This was in sharp contrast to the older Christian belief that humans were born in sin and that release from the pain of human existence came only in a heavenly afterlife. As a result of the progressive perspective, Canadians began to adopt the view that education and moral training would reduce class and cultural differences and bring greater unity to their society.

"Improvement" became the watchword of the nineteenth century. One of the most effective vehicles for improvement in urban centres was the Mechanics Institute. Founded in Scotland to serve the educational needs of skilled labourers, Mechanics Institutes in the colonies catered primarily to the business and professional classes. Literary societies and subscription libraries also offered opportunities for adult education. In the rural areas, people flocked to hear about the latest scientific discoveries and literary achievements from itinerant lecturers or grappled with new ideas around their kitchen tables by the light of candles and kerosene lamps.

Middle-class reformers turned their reforming zeal on the poor, criminal, and insane. Once considered the world's unfortunate souls, less advantaged groups were now believed to be "curable." Reformers urged the establishment of Houses of Industry (where the poor could be taught useful work habits), model prisons (where criminals could be reformed), and asylums (where the mentally ill could get remedial treatment). Like many other developments in the nineteenth century, this reform impulse was documented by imposing buildings that testified to the public nature of the perceived solution to society's problems.

Reformers placed a special emphasis on saving the child, who, it was believed, was highly responsive to socialization. Although public schools were the primary agents of social control, orphanages, industrial schools, and urban hostels were also established to target the nation's youth. The Young Men's Christian Association, founded in Great Britain in the 1840s, had branches in a number of Canadian cities by the time of Confederation, and pressure was mounting to create a similar institution to serve the needs of the single women who were moving to urban centres to find work.

Concerned about the widespread consumption of alcoholic beverages, reformers were enthusiastic promoters of temperance. By 1867, the temperance movement, led by the Sons of Temperance, was seen by many people as the single most effective solution to the complex problems facing a rapidly changing society. Not content to encourage individuals to discipline themselves in such matters as alcohol consumption, many temperance advocates began urging the passage of laws prohibiting the manufacture and sale of liquor.

Nothing symbolized the progressive impulse of the Confederation period better than the promise and practice of science in Canada. Science stimulated industry, advanced civilization, filled hours of leisure time, and even, some believed, brought people closer to an understanding of God's purpose for the universe. By the 1860s, most Canadian universities had scientists on their faculties, and travelling lecturers could almost always guarantee a good audience if they spoke on a scientific subject. Practical inventions were the stock-in-trade of Canadians who, like their southern neighbours, were obsessed with finding better ways of doing things.

Most Canadians accepted the new science as part of the larger movement towards a better society. In 1859, their complacency was shaken when British scientist Charles Darwin published *The Origin of Species*. Darwin's view that all living things evolved from a single primitive form of life and had developed by a process of natural selection and survival of the fittest flew in the face of Christianity's human-centred view of creation and the notion of a God who, if not benevolent, was at least not deliberately cruel. Darwinism was hotly debated in intellectual circles, but it did little to dampen religious enthusiasm or deflect the rage for reform.

In their quest for improvement, Canadians had laid the foundations for seventeen universities by the time of Confederation. While they symbolized the increasing importance of formal education, universities in the nineteenth century bore little relationship to the large educational factories that today grace the Canadian landscape. Most institutions of higher learning were sponsored by churches, and those claiming to be non-denominational, including Dalhousie, the University of New Brunswick, McGill, and the University of Toronto, often had close ties to one of the major churches.

Opened only to men, universities catered primarily to a small elite who could do without the labour of their adult sons. In 1867, only about fifteen hundred students attended Canadian universities. Professors, most of them trained outside of Canada, taught small classes and offered a narrow range of courses. While law and medicine were taught in a few of the larger universities, and theology in the denominational institutions, the liberal arts, dominated by courses in Greek, Latin, and philosophy, was the most popular program of study. Science was taught on most campuses, but pedagogical techniques left much to be desired. "I can remember," S.S. Nelles of Victoria College reminisced of the 1850s and 1860s, "when a Canadian university could venture to issue a calendar with the announcement of a single professor for all the natural sciences, and with a laboratory something similar to an ordinary blacksmith's shop, where the professor was his own assistant and compelled to blow not only his own bellows, but his own trumpet as well." [3]

In 1867, people received their information, other than by word of mouth, largely from newspapers. There were 380 newspapers published in British North America, one for every ten thousand people. Most newspapers appeared once or twice weekly and consisted of four pages cramped with editorials, shipping information, local items, serialized novels, advertisements, and news of the wider world. With the successful laying of the Atlantic cable in 1866, news from Europe suddenly was available in a few minutes rather than a week or two. Newspapers were sustained by political parties or religious denominations and by their subscribers; it was not until the twentieth century that advertisements became the dominant source of newspaper funding. As the purveyors of "knowledge," Canada's newspapers editors—men such as George Brown, Thomas D'Arcy McGee, and Joseph Howe—wielded considerable political power, and their high profile often lead them to a career in politics.

## POLITICAL CHANGE

Political values in Victorian Canada reflected developments in the wider North Atlantic world. In Europe, the old order, in which power was concentrated in the hands of a small hereditary elite bolstered by a state-supported church and a standing army, was crumbling. The growing middle class demanded that power be shared by all men with a stake in society, and they often had the power to make their views prevail. These contrasting ways of organizing power, labelled "conservative" and "liberal," were challenged by a few people who argued that every man—and even women—be given an equal political voice, and that equality of condition, not just equality of opportunity, should be the goal of public policy. Although such doctrines, labelled "radical" or "socialist," were quickly dismissed by the colonial elite, they developed a larger following as the Industrial Revolution gained

ground. The organizational activities of European intellectuals Karl Marx and Friedrich Engels, culminating in the First International in 1864, also encouraged a more systematic approach to socialist efforts to combat the inequities of the industrial order.

The struggle between conservatives and liberals dominated colonial legislatures in British North America for the first half of the nineteenth century. Although there were rebellions in Upper and Lower Canada in 1837–38, the transition to "responsible government," the term used to describe the limited form of liberalism prevailing in the colonies, was a relatively peaceful affair. Political parties became the vehicle for delivering democratic government, and in most colonies they assumed the names of the theoretical positions they espoused: Conservative (Tory) and Liberal (Reform). In Quebec these parties were known by their colours: *bleu* (Conservative) and *rouge* (Liberal). By the time of Confederation, the Conservative Party, inspired less by liberal doctrines than by its ambition to undermine the opposition, sported the name Liberal-Conservative Party, one which it continued to use on official documents until the 1920s.

The Roman Catholic Church in Quebec, under firm instructions from Rome, remained adamantly opposed to liberalism. It subscribed to the belief that the pope was infallible, proscribed controversial books listed on the papal Index, and excommunicated Catholics who became members of the liberal-inspired Institut canadien. At election time, leaders of the Roman Catholic Church threw their considerable weight behind Conservative candidates, who represented the least of the evils on the political spectrum.

Even outside the Roman Catholic hierarchy, there was only qualified support for liberalism in Canada. It might be acceptable to support public schools, provide government funding to railway companies, or dismantle feudal property relations such as existed in Quebec and Prince Edward Island, but few were willing to take the notion of equality before the law too far. Colonial politicians toyed with the idea of adopting universal manhood suffrage but fell back on property and rental quali-

## D'ARCY MCGEE

One of the most eloquent advocates of a British North American nationalism was Thomas D'Arcy McGee. A native of Ireland and a participant in the Irish rebellion of 1848, McGee emigrated to North America and finally settled in Montreal in 1857. As editor of the **New Era**, a newspaper that catered to the growing Irish community in Montreal, McGee quickly gained a high profile and was elected to the legislature of the United Canadas. Rejecting the militant practices of his youth, he supported a new "northern nationality" for the British North American colonies within the larger imperial context. For McGee, a moderate nationalism based on economic progress offered an alternative to the ethnic and sectional conflicts that he felt impeded the progress of British North America, just as they had poisoned the potential of his beloved Ireland. In a speech delivered to the Assembly of the United Canadas on 2 May 1860, McGee captured the enthusiasm that westward expansion and economic development inspired in many British North Americans:

*Honorable Thomas D'Arcy McGee, Montreal, 1863.*
Notman Photographic Archives, McCord Museum of Canadian History, Montreal/I-7382

portion of it more particularly, is incapable of maintaining to the end of the century the ratio of the past progress?... I look to the future of my adopted country with hope, though not without anxiety; I see in the not remote distance one nationality bound, like the shield of Achilles, by the blue rim of Ocean. I see it quartered into many communities, each disposing of its internal affairs, but all bound together by free institutions, free intercourse, and free commerce; I see within the round of that shield the peaks of the Western mountains and the crests of the eastern waves—the winding Assiniboine, the five-fold lakes, the St. Lawrence, the Ottawa, the Saguenay, the St. John, and the Basin of Minas—by all these flowing waters, in all the valleys they fertilize, in all the cities they visit on their courses, I see a generation of industrious, contented moral men, free in name and in fact,—men capable of maintain-

I begin by entreating the House to believe that I have spoken ...with a sole single desire for the increase, prosperity, freedom and honour of this incipient Northern Nation. I call it a Northern Nation—for such it must become, if all of us do our duty to the last. Men do not talk on this continent of changes wrought by centuries, but of the events of years. Men do not vegetate in this age, as they did formerly, in one spot—occupying one position. Thought outruns the steam car, and hope outflies the telegraph. We live more in ten years in this era than the patriarchs did in a thousand.... What marvels have not been wrought in Europe and America from 1840 to 1860?—and who can say the world, or our own

ing, in peace and in war, a Constitution worthy of such a Country.

McGee's views were highly unpopular among militant Irish nationalists, who in the 1850s banded together to form the Irish Republican Brotherhood and Clan-na-Gael, popularly known as the Fenians. With supporters on both sides of the Atlantic, their goal was to lift the yoke of British oppression and secure independence for Ireland by any means possible—including violence. They were opposed to any plan whereby the British North American colonies willingly chose to remain part of the British Empire.

fications as the basis for political citizenship. No public figure suggested that women should be granted suffrage. When elections were called for the Canadian Parliament in 1867, only about 20 percent of the entire population was eligible to vote.

The blending of a liberal economic regime with a conservative social order was particularly evident in the way colonial politicians approached legal reform. In an effort to embrace the opportunities of the industrial age, new laws relating to contract, debt, and bankruptcy were adopted in most colonies prior to Confederation. The acceptance of liberal principles in family law took much longer to achieve. Legal reform was particularly complicated in Quebec where, since 1763, French and British legal systems had been applied in a confusing mix. In 1857, the government appointed a commission of three legal experts to bring order out of the chaos. The result was a new Civil Code (1866) and a Code of Civil Procedures (1867), which introduced liberal thinking with respect to commercial relations but maintained a more conservative approach to laws relating to family, marriage, inheritance, and the legal position of women.

The Confederation movement itself was inspired by a new idea—nationalism—that was modified to accommodate particular Canadian circumstances. In part a reaction against the cold rationalism of the Enlightenment, nationalism in Europe inspired movements among peoples who could point to a common cultural, often linguistic or religious, identity. Nationalism was unleashed during the American and French Revolutions and quickly took hold in Latin America and Europe. In the mid-nineteenth century, British North Americans watched with growing interest the movements to unify the German and Italian states, and efforts by Irish patriots to liberate Ireland from the hated union with Great Britain.

Many British North Americans saw nationalism as something that could spur the colonies to greater achievements, but nationalist sentiment posed problems in a society where culture divided rather than united its people. French Canadians, whose common language, religion, and history provided the basis for a separate national identity,

were particularly leery of romantic talk about a larger British North American cultural unity. Safer ground for the new nationalism was the economic potential of the northern half of the continent, which stirred the hearts and imagination of both the romantic idealist and the practical businessman. In the late 1850s, with the discovery of gold in British Columbia and scientific studies proclaiming the agricultural potential of the Prairies, the possibility of a transcontinental nation rivalling the United States suddenly seemed more than a pipe dream.

## THE ROAD TO CONFEDERATION, 1864–1867

Over the years, a number of statesmen had suggested a union of the British North American colonies, but nothing had come of such musings. In the 1860s, Confederation was achieved relatively easily and without the violence and bloodshed typical of many national movements elsewhere. How did this achievement come about?

As with most successful undertakings, the context was critical to the final outcome. The revolution in imperial policy signalled by the adoption of free trade and the granting of responsible government was an important prerequisite. So, too, was the rapid advance in communication and transportation made possible by telegraph and the railroad. The Civil War in the United States and its troubled aftermath added an air of urgency to constitutional discussions. Despite fierce provincial loyalties and long-held cultural identities, the fact that most people in 1867 had been born in British North America helped to make them more receptive to notions of a homegrown nationalism. Leadership, it could be argued, was also essential to the outcome of the Confederation movement. Both centre stage and behind the scenes during the negotiations was a purposeful group of businessmen and politicians, mostly based in the United Canadas, who were determined to make their vision a reality. With a generation of experience behind them in colonial administration and capitalist development, they drew up the Confederation agreement, manoeuvred it through colonial and imperial legislatures, and played a central role in defining the policies that governed the new nation through its early years of development.

The event that set the ball rolling early in 1864 was the collapse of yet another administration in the United Province of Canada. Engineered by Great Britain before the colonies had been granted responsible government, the union of Upper and Lower Canada in 1840 had been designed to solve the problems of ethnic antagonism, economic stagnation, and political conflict in the two colonies. It failed to produce the desired results. Instead, sectional politics became the order of the day in the United Canadas, with a predominantly Roman Catholic francophone population in Canada East aligned against a largely Protestant anglophone population in Canada West.

Under the conditions laid down by the Act of Union, Canada East (formerly Lower Canada) and Canada West (formerly Upper Canada) had equal representation in the assembly. This situation became increasingly unacceptable to the rapidly growing population of Canada West. Policies favoured by one side were invariably imposed on the other, creating hard feelings on both sides. While Canada West tended to support public schools, an ambitious economic program, expansion of the militia, and a more democratic distribution of seats in the assembly, Canada East resisted such policies. By the late 1850s, the opposing parties in the assembly were so equally balanced that it became difficult to form a government. The resignation of another coalition government in the Canadas in March 1864 was only the last in a long string of administrative failures that frustrated politicians and made capitalists uneasy about the investment potential of the colony.

By this time, too, the government of the United Canadas was deeply in debt, much of it generated by the loan guarantees and massive subsidies given to the Grand Trunk Railway. Although the Grand Trunk linked the colony from Sarnia to Quebec City, it carried less traffic than was predicted, was badly administered, and threatened to take the government with it if it filed for bankruptcy. Investors in the Grand Trunk saw Confederation

as the best way to recoup their failing fortunes. If the colonies united and expanded westward, the Grand Trunk could become a transcontinental railway carrying foodstuffs from a new agricultural frontier as well as products from the Orient to markets in Great Britain. With this vision before them, some of the Grand Trunk's British investors bought controlling interest in the Hudson's Bay Company in 1863, planning to link the Northwest to the eastern colonies once Confederation was achieved.

There was widespread support for such an ambitious venture in the United Province. As the major financial, industrial, and transportation centre of British North America—and the headquarters of the Grand Trunk—Montreal stood to benefit from westward expansion and any project that improved the prospects of its troubled railway company. Toronto businessmen were also on side, convinced that their city could beat Montreal in the race to capture the new markets that would develop in the West. With most of the farm land already taken up in the Canadas, the idea of opening a new agricultural frontier on the Prairies also appealed to families anxious about their children's future.

In theory, the Province of Canada could have acquired the Northwest Territories and reached an agreement with the Maritime colonies regarding intercolonial railway lines and trade without resorting to formal political arrangements. But the fractious politics of the United Canadas and the heavy debts of its government made it difficult to take any action in this direction. British investors, led by the large Baring Brothers Bank, would only agree to finance new railway ventures in British North America if the colonies were united. From the bank's point of view, it would be easier to deal with one government in the region than several, and projects would be more likely to succeed if intercolonial squabbling—which had scuttled earlier negotiations for a railway to the Maritimes—could be averted. Colonial politicians quickly realized that if they refused to meet the terms of the international business community, they might never be able to realize their dreams of economic development.

George Brown, leader of the Reform Party in

Canada West, was an ardent exponent of western expansion and promoted his frontier vision to readers of his Toronto-based newspaper, the *Globe*. Eager to advance the fortunes of his city and colony, Brown took the initiative in calling for a legislative committee with representatives from all parties to find a solution to the constitutional impasse. The committee met in May and early June of 1864. Although Brown preferred a smaller federation encompassing only Canada East and Canada West, he was prepared to accept the majority view that a larger federation should be attempted. When the government collapsed on 14 June—the very day the committee brought down its report—Brown become part of the so-called Great Coalition, which included his long-time rivals John A. Macdonald and George-Étienne Cartier. Its sole purpose was to settle the constitutional difficulties in the United Canadas. The first step in that direction was to approach the Maritime colonies with a proposal for the union of British North America.

The political crisis in the Upper Provinces coincided with discussions in the Lower Provinces on the topic of Maritime union. Primarily of interest to Nova Scotians and New Brunswickers who were riding high on their success in shipbuilding and international trade, Maritime union had become a fall-back position when the Canadians abruptly withdrew from discussions relating to an intercolonial railway in 1862. Maritime union offered the prospects of creating a larger stage for local politicians and, with any luck, the weight necessary to get British investors to look favourably on their region. The ice-free ports of Halifax and Saint John stood to benefit from any railway project the union could mount, and the region's rich reserves of coal would fuel the engines that ran the trains and factories.

When the Canadians sent letters asking to be invited to a proposed Maritime union conference, they initiated a chain of events that led to three conferences: one in Charlottetown in September 1864, a second one a month later in Quebec City, and a final one in London in the fall and winter of 1866–67. Prince Edward Island and Newfoundland opted out of negotiations after the Quebec Conference, but the advocates of Confederation in the other self-governing colonies persevered, and, at the end of March 1867, the British North America Act passed in the British Parliament.

The Canadians who signed the act all had different expectations about what the new federation would accomplish and therein lay the seeds of discord. While Ontario businessmen and farmers saw it as a chance to expand their markets and take a lead in developing the western plains, leaders of church and state in Quebec saw it as an opportunity to create a province with a francophone and Roman Catholic majority. Even the sceptical Maritimers sometimes allowed themselves to imagine a future in which their ice-free ports bulged with the imports and exports of a great transcontinental nation. The British North America Act reflected these diverse interests and the power relationships that prevailed in the colonies in the 1860s.

The Confederation agreement was largely the handiwork of the politicians from the United Canadas. For them, the most important goal was to preserve the liberal principle of majority rule while at the same time satisfying the demands of the francophone minority. This was achieved through the creation of a federal system by which the powers of the state were divided between national and provincial administrations. Canada West and Canada East would each have provincial status, thus ending once and for all the indignities imposed by the Act of Union. To protect the Protestant minority in Canada East, the separate school system in place there was specifically guaranteed. Representation by population, with seats being weighted slightly in favour of rural ridings, would prevail in the House of Commons. Sectional equality was the proposed basis for appointments to the Senate: Ontario and Quebec were each allotted twenty-four seats, the same number that the Canadians were prepared to let the Maritimers divide among themselves.

The Canadians presented this blueprint for union at the Charlottetown Conference and hammered out the details in resolutions adopted at the October meetings in Quebec City. So determined were they to adhere as closely as possible to their principles that they even refused Prince Edward

Island's request for an extra seat in the House of Commons. According to the formula developed for representation by population, the island received only five seats, an awkward number to divide among its three constituencies. The delegates were also unwilling to find a solution to the island's land question. With little inducement, the islanders withdrew from the negotiations to enter Confederation. Newfoundlanders were equally unimpressed by the proposals presented by the Canadians, whose interests in railways and westward expansion were far removed from the issues that dominated the Newfoundland economy.

There were dissenting voices in Nova Scotia and New Brunswick as well. Anti-confederates in the Maritimes noted, with some justification, that Confederation was a scheme of Canadian politicians and business interests who regarded the proposed new nation as an extension of the boundaries of the United Canadas. By virtue of the concentration of over three-quarters of the colonial population within its territory, it would dominate the new federation. Moreover, anti-confederates argued, the financial proposals in the Quebec Resolutions gave the provinces inadequate income to pay for the responsibilities assigned to them, such as schools, roads, and social services. All customs duties, the main source of government funds in the 1860s, were to be absorbed into the federal coffers, while the provinces would be forced to manage on a per capita grant. The small population base in the Maritimes meant that their provincial administrations would have little money to work with. Although Maritimers desperately wanted to be connected to the other colonies by an Intercolonial Railway, they saw little benefit coming their way from a line to the Pacific, or indeed from an agricultural frontier on the distant Prairies. The Acadians and many Irish Catholics in the region were suspicious, on principle, of any union that reflected British models in Ireland, Scotland, and Wales.

In Quebec, there were strong anti-confederate arguments too, most of them voiced by *rouge* leader A.-A. Dorion. He maintained that the federal government, with control over trade, foreign affairs, interprovincial railways, justice, and defence, as well as the right to take on extraordinary powers in times of emergency, would dictate to the provinces. Under such an arrangement Quebec would have little control over its destiny. Eventually its culture would be eroded and its people assimilated into an anglophone Protestant state. The *rouges* pressed for an election or a referendum on Confederation but to no avail. Despite tensions among its leaders, the Great Coalition held together. The *bleu* majority from Canada East joined Reformers and Conservatives from Canada West to give the Confederation proposals a comfortable majority in the legislature of the United Canadas in the winter of 1865.

The opposition to Confederation in the Maritimes was not so easily brushed aside. Early in 1865, in a hotly contested election, Samuel Leonard Tilley's pro-Confederation forces were defeated by an anti-Confederation coalition headed by A.J. Smith. Resistance to Confederation in Nova Scotia developed so quickly under Joseph Howe's leadership that Conservative premier Dr Charles Tupper decided against introducing the Quebec Resolutions in the legislature for fear that they would be rejected. Since Prince Edward Island and Newfoundland also showed little interest in Confederation, it looked as if Atlantic Canada was out of the picture entirely.

The pro-Confederation forces soon showed their hand. By 1865, the Colonial Office was fully behind Confederation as a vehicle for reducing imperial commitments in North America, and it had instructed its representatives in the colonies to use their influence to see that the scheme succeeded. The actions of Lieutenant-Governor Arthur Gordon in New Brunswick provide perhaps the best example of how imperial pressure could be exercised even in a colony that had responsible government. On a dubious technicality, he forced the resignation of his recently elected government and called another election. Gordon made it clear to everyone who would listen that Britain expected New Brunswick to support union with the Canadas. At the polls, Tilley's pro-Confederation party, which promised to negotiate substantial alterations to the Quebec Resolutions to make them more acceptable to the Maritimes, won a resounding victory.

Gordon's influence was not the only factor determining the outcome of the 1866 election. With the Reciprocity Treaty due to come to an end in 1866, timber interests in New Brunswick were thinking more seriously about alternative economic strategies. The Roman Catholic hierarchy, originally opposed to Confederation, was also coming around to a more positive view. For those who were still wavering, money supplied by the Canadians and their Grand Trunk allies helped to legitimize the Confederation forces. Further drama was added to the contest when, in the days leading up to the election, an American wing of the Fenian Brotherhood launched raids on New Brunswick and Canada West from their bases in the United States. Although easily deflected, the attacks gave emphasis to the pro-confederate position that defence could be better handled by a strong federal government for all of the colonies.

The end of reciprocity, which threatened markets for coal, timber, potatoes, and fish, also put Nova Scotia in a vulnerable position. In 1866, the prospects were so bleak that a few Nova Scotians even argued that annexation to the United States was the only sensible course of action. Tupper saw his main chance and took it. Unable to convince his own party to support the hated Quebec Resolutions, he managed to get the Nova Scotia Assembly to authorize further negotiations on union. Thus, neither the Nova Scotia voters nor their elected representatives gave their approval to the proposals that ultimately became the basis of the British North America Act.

At the London meetings, the Canadians were adamant that the Quebec Resolutions remain the basis of negotiations. Assurances were provided that the Intercolonial Railway would be built and that subsidies to provincial governments would be improved but no substantial changes were made to the federal structure to meet the concerns of the Maritimers. The pressure from the Roman Catholic hierarchy for protection of separate schools outside Quebec was handled by including guarantees to separate schools legally in existence at the time the act went into effect and by the possibility of appeal to the federal government for remedial legislation should the laws be violated.

Federal and provincial powers were defined in the British North America Act of 1867. Section 91 of the BNA Act enumerated a wide range of federal powers, running the gamut from trade and commerce to patents and copyright, that were, in the words of the act, deemed to be in the interest of the "Peace, Order and Good Government" of Canada as a whole. The list of responsibilities delegated to the provinces in section 92 of the act seemed much more modest when it was drawn up in 1867. In later years, with the expansion of matters of a "local or private Nature," such as municipal institutions, social services, and education, the provinces faced the challenge of finding money to pay for the responsibilities that fell to them under the BNA Act.

The finishing touches to the agreement included giving the new union a title, name, and rank. It was decided to refer to the union as a confederation rather than a federation on the grounds that the latter term implied a loose political arrangement that many of the architects of Confederation sought to avoid. A number of names were considered for the new nation, but an agreement was quickly reached that it should be called Canada. Although suggestions were made that Canada should be ranked as a kingdom or viceroyalty, it was finally decided that it should be a dominion, a term apparently drawn from a biblical reference in Psalm 72: "He shall have dominion also from sea to sea, and from the river unto the ends of the earth." The colonial secretary, the Earl of Derby, was not impressed: "I do not know that there is any objection to the term "Dominion," he wrote to the British Prime Minister Benjamin Disraeli, "though it strikes me as rather absurd."

## CONCLUSION

Absurd or not, the deed was done, and people would have to live with it, at least for a while. There was, of course, nothing inevitable about Confederation. The most that can be said is that the essential elements for success were in place, the timing was good, and those who supported Confederation had the necessary skills and resources to see it through to completion. Nor was there any guarantee that the wobbly structure put in place primarily to promote railways and to accommodate certain cultural sensibilities, would survive any length of time. Federations are notoriously unstable political arrangements and often last only a few years. To be sure, people like George Brown, John A. Macdonald, and D'Arcy McGee spoke passionately about creating a "new nationality," but few Canadians, if asked, would have been able to say what the new nation stood for, and in

the Maritimes there was genuine grief over the loss of colonial autonomy. Fortunately, the die-hard anti-confederates were a restrained lot and seemed to have no serious plans to dissolve the union by force. If their diaries and letters are any indication, most citizens of the new nation paid little attention to the political manoeuvring taking place around them. They diligently went about their daily routines, and just hoped that their politicians had not landed them in another fine mess.

## NOTES

[1] Quoted in James L. Sturgis, "The Opposition to Confederation in Nova Scotia, 1864–1868" in *The Causes of Canadian Confederation*, ed. Ged Martin (Fredericton: Acadiensis Press, 1990), 125

[2] Donna McDonald, *Illustrated News: Juliana Horatia Ewing's Canadian Pictures, 1867–1869* (Toronto: Dundurn Press, 1985), 44–45

[3] Cited in A.B. McKillop, *Matters of the Mind: The University in Ontario, 1791–1951* (Toronto: University of Toronto Press, 1994), 111

## SELECTED READING

This chapter summarizes material in the later chapters of *History of the Canadian Peoples*, volume 1. Following is an abbreviated list of books dealing with the history of individual colonies and Confederation.

A useful starting point for any discussion of Canada in the mid-nineteenth century is the *Historical Atlas of Canada*, vol. 2, *The Land Transformed, 1800–1891* (Toronto: University of Toronto Press, 1993). *The Horizon* series, *The Dictionary of Canadian Biography*, and *Canada's Visual History Series* offer valuable perspectives on aspects of Canadian social and cultural history.

Regional studies include Jean Barman, *The West Beyond the West: A History of British Columbia* (Toronto: University of Toronto Press, 1996); Gerald Friesen, *The Canadian Prairies: A History* (Toronto: University of Toronto Press, 1987); J.M.S. Careless, *The Union of the Canadas: The Growth of Canadian Institutions, 1841–1857* (Toronto: McClelland and Stewart, 1967); John A. Dickinson and Brian Young, *A Short History of Quebec*, 2nd ed. (Toronto: Copp Clark Pitman, 1993); Paul-André Linteau, René Durocher, and Jean-Claude Robert, *Quebec: A History, 1867–1929* (Toronto: Lorimer, 1983); W.S. MacNutt, *The Atlantic Provinces: The Emergence of Colonial Society, 1712–1857* (Toronto: McClelland and Stewart, 1965); and Phillip A. Buckner and John G. Reid, eds., *The Atlantic Region to Confederation* (Toronto and Fredericton: University of Toronto Press and Acadiensis Press, 1994).

The Confederation movement is surveyed in W.L. Morton, *The Critical Years: The Union of British North America 1857–1873* (Toronto: McClelland and Stewart, 1964); P.B. Waite, *The Life and Times of Confederation 1864–1867* (Toronto: University of Toronto Press, 1962); and Donald Creighton, *The Road to Confederation: The Emergence of Canada 1863–1867* (Toronto: Macmillan, 1964). Several important essays on confederation itself appear in Ramsay Cook, ed., *Confederation* (Toronto: University of Toronto Press, 1967), and Ged Martin, ed., *The Causes of Canadian Confederation* (Fredericton: Acadiensis Press, 1990). Quebec attitudes to Confederation are discussed in A.I. Silver, *The French-Canadian Idea of Confederation, 1864–1900*, 2nd ed. (Toronto: University of Toronto Press, 1997).

# 2

# NATION BUILDING,
# 1867-1911

Oɴ 1 Jᴜʟʏ 1867, Cᴀɴᴀᴅɪᴀɴs ᴄᴇʟᴇʙʀᴀᴛᴇᴅ Confederation Day. George Brown's *Globe* described festivities in the city of Toronto:

> On the roofs of houses and elsewhere, in all directions, flag-poles were being hoisted into the air to do their part in the celebration of Confederation Day. A programme of celebration arranged by the Government included a grand review of Her Majesty's Troops, regulars and volunteers, on the Bathurst Street Commons at ten a.m. At three o'clock there was a grand Balloon Ascension from Queen's Park. In the evening there were concerts given by the Bands of the Tenth Royal Regiment and the Grand Trunk Brigade in the form of a grand promenade at Queen's Park accompanied by the most magnificent display of fireworks ever exhibited in Canada.

> Another grand celebration took place on the evening of the same day at the Horticultural Gardens....The gardens were brilliantly lighted, and a large tent set up for refreshments of strawberries, ice cream, etc. The concert was at eight p.m. and dancing commenced at ten-thirty. Tickets were twenty-five cents, children's tickets ten cents. The bands of the Thirteenth Hussars and the Seventeenth Regiment played, among

other selections, pieces by Donizetti, Kappe, Burchart, Rossini, and Benedict.

The *Globe* also recorded that as part of the Confederation Day celebrations, "an immense ox" was roasted and the meat "distributed among the poor of the city."

Not all communities in the new Dominion celebrated Confederation in such grand style. In Nova Scotia and New Brunswick, anti-confederate feeling ran so high that several editors printed black banners on the front pages of their newspapers, and many people hoisted black flags to announce their deeply held hostility towards the union. Francophones in Quebec were also restrained in their enthusiasm, preferring to wait and see what Confederation would mean for their newly proclaimed province.

It had taken nearly three years to bring Nova Scotia, New Brunswick, and the United Province of Canada into Confederation, but the work of creating a nation had only just begun. In addition to convincing the original signatories to the British North America Act to stay in the federation, political leaders were also determined to round out the boundaries and develop a national policy that would appeal to the hearts and minds of the diverse

*At age twenty-nine, John A. Macdonald was elected to the legislature of the United Canadas and quickly became a leading figure in the Conservative Party. He helped to engineer an alliance with the French Canadian bloc and in 1856 emerged as joint premier of the United Canadas. A quick-witted and practical politician, Macdonald was also a shrewd businessman and lawyer, but he was overly fond of alcohol. During his first term in office as prime minister of Canada, his drinking frequently caused embarrassment for his government and may well have contributed to the mismanagement of the railway negotiations that resulted in the Pacific Scandal.*

National Archives of Canada/PA12848

peoples in an immense territory. They had their work cut out for them.

## CONSOLIDATING THE UNION

The task of choosing the nation's first prime minister was assigned to the governor general, Lord Monck. He selected John A. Macdonald, an opponent of Confederation before 1864, but thereafter its most energetic promoter. If anyone could bring the scattered elements of the new nation together, it would be John A., whose ability to charm his opponents and sustain the faithful with well-placed patronage was legendary. Macdonald had hoped to put an end to party politics by maintaining the coalition of Reform and Tory politicians that had championed Confederation, but this was not to be. Suspicious of Macdonald's motives, George Brown had resigned from the Great Coalition in 1865 over what he felt to be the mishandling of negotiations to renew the reciprocity treaty with the United States. Macdonald was able to convince the remaining Reform members of the coalition to support his leadership, and he also maintained his pre-Confederation partnership with the *bleus* led by George-Étienne Cartier. In the Maritimes, Samuel Leonard Tilley, the Liberal premier of New Brunswick, and Charles Tupper, Conservative premier of Nova Scotia, also agreed to bring their pro-Confederation forces, such as they were, into Macdonald's Liberal-Conservative party.

The regional, religious, and cultural issues that plagued the colonies before Confederation did not go away. When Macdonald created his first cabinet, he was forced to accommodate various interests—Protestant and Catholic, French and English, province and nation. The delicate balancing act meant that two men who were central to the success of Confederation, Charles Tupper and D'Arcy McGee, were dropped from the cabinet so that an Irish Catholic from Nova Scotia, Edward Kenny, could ensure the required cultural and regional balance. Despite such challenges, the new ministry won a handy victory at the polls in the first election, carrying 108 of the 180 seats.

A closer look at the 1867 election results indicated that Macdonald had no cause to be complacent. Although it did not translate into seats, almost half of the popular vote went to candidates running in opposition to the Liberal-Conservatives. Macdonald's coalition benefited from the fact that the opposition was divided among George Brown's Reformers, Dorion's *rouges*, and the Maritime anti-confederates, but, in time, this opposition would form a coalition that would become the basis of the Liberal Party.

## VOTING IN THE NEW DOMINION

In 1867, elections were carried out much differently than they are today. Voters openly announced the candidate of their choice, often to jeers and menacing gestures from the crowd around the polls, and under the watchful eyes of relatives, employers, and party workers. Violence between supporters of opposing sides was not uncommon. For example, no member was elected for the riding of Kamouraska in 1867 because a family feud between the Chapais and the Letelliers led to riots that made polling impossible.

The lack of a national franchise policy also caused difficulties. From 1867 to 1884, provincial election lists were used to determine who could vote. The 1867 contest was particularly confusing because all the provinces were electing new assemblies, and in Ontario and Quebec candidates were allowed to sit in both the federal and provincial legislatures. Except in Nova Scotia, where voting occurred simultaneously in all constituencies on 18 September, elections were conducted at different times across the Dominion. Thus, voting took place from late July to September in the 180 constituencies

electing members to the first Canadian House of Commons. As government leader, Macdonald could ensure that elections were held in the easy ridings first so that momentum could be used to sway votes in the constituencies where government support was uncertain.

The number of people eligible to cast a ballot was relatively small. All provinces at the time of Confederation limited the vote to men over twenty-one years of age who owned or rented property of a certain value. Status Indians, regarded as wards of the state, had no vote, and property qualifications kept most unskilled workers and farm labourers off electoral lists. As a result of gender, property, and age restrictions, only 15 percent of the Quebec population, for example, could vote in the provincial or federal elections in the early years of Confederation, and only about 20 percent had this right by the end of the century. Today, by contrast, under universal suffrage for people over eighteen years of age, almost 70 percent of the population has the right to vote, with most of the disenfranchised being either children or immigrants who have not yet fulfilled the requirements for citizenship.

## NOVA SCOTIA'S SECESSIONIST MOVEMENT

The election results also highlighted another serious problem. Although the Liberal-Conservatives won huge majorities in Ontario and Quebec, pro-Confederation candidates won barely half the seats in New Brunswick, while Tupper was the only government candidate in Nova Scotia to scrape through. Tupper's Conservative government was also defeated in the elections to the provincial assembly where all but two seats went to anti-Confederation candidates. With such a clear indication of discontent in his native province, Joseph Howe felt that he had a mandate to transform his anti-Confederation campaign into a demand for repeal of the union. A repeal league quickly took shape, and Howe was dispatched to London to get permission to take Nova Scotia out of Confederation.

The threat of secession posed a serious challenge to Macdonald's government and to the new nation. Yet, what was to be done? On the face of

things, Maritimers had every reason to feel aggrieved. The Liberal-Conservative Party proved little more than the old Conservative–*bleu* alliance of the United Canadas writ large; the federal cabinet was dominated by politicians from Ontario and Quebec who held nine of the thirteen ministerial positions; and the nation's capital, Ottawa, was run by civil servants who had formerly served the United Canadas. Further, when the Canadian Parliament opened on 8 November 1867, it endorsed policies that reinforced Nova Scotian alienation from the federation, including a rise in the tariff rate from 10 to 15 percent, which pleased the Montreal industrialists but angered Maritime shippers dependent on international trade.

In Britain, Howe's request for repeal of the union fell on deaf ears. Neither the Conservatives nor the Liberals in the British Parliament were interested in restoring autonomy to the provinces. Accepting defeat, Howe began negotiating with the Canadians for better terms for Nova Scotia within Confederation. Howe's willingness to compromise was due in part to growing militancy among his anti-confederate supporters. Neither a populist nor a republican, Howe was repulsed by talk of popular revolt or annexation to the United States, which the die-hard anti-confederates saw as their only alternatives to the hated union. It was wiser, Howe reasoned, to make the best of a bad bargain than to risk the possibility of severing ties with the mother country, and even of bloody conflict.

At meetings held in Portland, Maine, over the winter of 1868–69, Howe and Finance Minister John Rose hammered out "better terms" for Nova Scotia. The federal government agreed to pay an additional $1 million of pre-Confederation Nova Scotia debt and to increase the province's annual grant by $82 698 per year for ten years to help it meet the ongoing costs of government. In a rare gesture of conciliation, Howe and Hugh MacDonald, another anti-Confederate from Nova Scotia, were given seats in the cabinet. The strategy was only partly successful. Despite his high profile, Howe had difficulty winning his own seat in Hants County and proved unable to deliver all of the anti-confederates from Nova Scotia into Macdonald's hands.

In conjunction with Tilley and Tupper, who was finally awarded a seat in the cabinet in 1870, Howe urged his colleagues to move quickly on the construction of the Intercolonial Railway and to press for a new reciprocity treaty with the United States. All regions of Canada lamented the end of free trade with the United States in 1866, but Maritimers were particularly eager to restore American markets for their timber, fish, coal, and agricultural products. Because of negotiations in 1866 in which Britain gave Americans access to the inshore fisheries without offering anything in return, Maritimers were convinced that their interests were being sacrificed on the altar of larger Canadian and imperial goals.

In 1871, Macdonald represented Canada in a British delegation that met with their American counterparts in Washington to resolve the issues dividing the two countries. Macdonald hoped to exchange American access to the Canadian inshore fisheries for a new reciprocity treaty but was unable to do so because of opposition from the protectionist Republican Congress. While there would be no

reciprocity treaty, the Treaty of Washington offered some relief to Canadian fishers. Their catch was granted free entry into American markets, and financial compensation, to be decided by arbitration, would be forthcoming in return for American access to Canada's inshore waters. There were cries of sell-out in Nova Scotia, but only two Nova Scotian members of Parliament voted against the treaty. By the time of the 1872 election, two-thirds of the Nova Scotian MPs supported Macdonald. Anti-confederates remained strong in the provincial legislature, but much of the energy had gone out of their fight. The threat of secession, it seemed, had passed—at least for the time being.

## ANNEXING THE NORTHWEST: THE RED RIVER REBELLION

The first parliamentary session of the Dominion of Canada moved swiftly to negotiate the transfer of the Northwest to the new country. By 1869, an agreement had been reached with the Hudson's Bay Company, which held legal title over the region, to sell its claim to the land for £300 000 (about $1.5 million) and a grant to the company of one-twentieth of the land most suitable for farming. This agreement represented a financial coup for the financiers who had bought control of the company in 1863. They received a cash return on their initial investment of about £1.5 million, retained their fur-trading operations, and stood to gain immensely from the sale of land once the area was settled. Eventually, the land sales netted the company $120 million.

The Métis and aboriginal peoples were treated less generously than the European "owners" of the land. Eager to open the Northwest to immigrants, the federal government sent land surveyors to the Red River colony in August 1869 to prepare for an influx of settlers, which was expected when the official transfer of title occurred in December. Consulted by neither the company nor the Canadians, the Métis were afraid that they would lose possession of the land they farmed. Their fears seemed confirmed when the surveyors began mea-

*Louis Riel (second row, centre) with his provisional government.*

suring the land in square lots, ignoring the narrow river-lot system used by the Métis to mark off land.

The behaviour of the Canadians already living in the Red River area reinforced Métis anxieties. Largely land speculators who hoped to make their fortunes when Canada acquired the Northwest, these men were openly racist towards the non-white majority in the region. Unlike the fur traders, who were often paternalistic but rarely contemptuous towards aboriginal peoples and Métis, the "Canadian Party," as they came to be called, regarded Natives as uncivilized people whose presence in the region was a deterrent to European settlement. The Canadian Party was a minority in a population that the 1871 census recorded as just under 12 000 (5757 French-speaking Métis, 4083 English-speaking Métis—the offspring of English traders and aboriginal women—1500 whites, and 558 Indians) but only the "Canadians" had the ear of Ottawa.

On 11 October 1869, a group of unarmed Métis stopped a road-building party from its work, angry that the contract had been given to John Snow, an openly racist Canadian land speculator. Five days later, a Métis National Committee was formed. The committee's goal was to block the Canadian takeover of Red River until firm guarantees for Métis land rights had been granted. As secretary of this committee, the Métis chose Louis Riel. The twenty-five-year-old Riel had spent nearly ten years in Catholic educational institutions in Quebec. Literate and articulate, he was seen as someone who could negotiate with the Canadians on their own terms but who, as a Métis, could be counted on not to sell out his people.

Meanwhile, William McDougall, the minister of public works in Macdonald's cabinet, was appointed the first lieutenant-governor of what became known as the Northwest Territories, and he immediately set out to take possession of Canada's new colony. When McDougall attempted to enter Hudson's Bay territory on 2 November, he was prevented from doing so by a group of armed Métis. Early in December, the Métis established a provisional government under John Bruce and Louis Riel to coordinate resistance to Canadian imperialism.

The heart of the resistance lay with French-speaking Métis. Although most Canadians and aboriginal people in the area opposed the provisional government's actions, many people were caught in the middle. The English-speaking Métis were particularly torn and shifted allegiance depending upon the circumstances. Yet, when Macdonald tried to undermine the resistance by encouraging divisions between the French-speaking Métis and their English-speaking counterparts, and by using the influence of the Catholic Church over the leaders of the provisional government, his efforts failed.

The Canadian Party in Red River attempted to overthrow the provisional government soon after it was established, but they were no match for the well-organized Métis. Sixty-five Canadian conspirators were captured and imprisoned in Fort Garry. Yet another attempt to seize control of the colony was foiled in February 1870. One of the prisoners captured in the second incident was Thomas Scott, an Orangeman from Ontario who had been employed as a road builder before the rebellion started. Showing contempt for his Métis guards, he called on his fellow prisoners to escape so they could continue their resistance to the provisional government. Pressured by angry Métis guards bent on vengeance, as well as by the challenge to his government's legitimacy, Riel agreed to have Scott executed in March 1870.

The situation was further complicated by the presence of American agents in Red River. Afraid that the United States would take advantage of the political crisis to seize control of the region, Macdonald reluctantly agreed to negotiate with representatives of the provisional government. They were led by Abbé N.J. Ritchot who had the confidence not only of Riel but also of the Bishop of Saint Boniface, A.A. Taché. Church officials opposed the rebellion but supported the Métis land claims and demands for protection of the French

language and Roman Catholic religion.

By May 1870, negotiations between the Canadian and provisional Red River governments concluded with an agreement that, on the surface, met Métis demands. The Red River colony and its environs would become the province of Manitoba, a tiny jurisdiction that initially encompassed only the area around Red River. Like the other provinces, it would have an elected legislative assembly and an appointed upper chamber. Both English and French were officially recognized in legislative and court proceedings; denominational schools, Protestant and Catholic, would be maintained. Unlike other provinces, Manitoba would, until such time as the federal government decided otherwise, have its land and other resources controlled by Ottawa. For the Métis, the major victory was the guarantee in the Manitoba Act that they would receive title for lands they currently farmed as well as 1.4 million acres of farmland for the use of their children.

This victory soon proved hollow. With a settlement in hand, Macdonald convinced Britain that a military expedition should be sent to Red River to assert Canadian control against American designs and any further difficulties from the Métis. Led by Colonel Garnet Wolseley, the army included in its ranks Ontario Orangemen who saw Riel and his followers as the agents of Roman Catholic domination in the West. They imposed a virtual reign of terror on the Métis. Riel fled to the United States, and other members of the provisional government went into hiding. In the wake of the army, white settlers poured into the province and received title for land, while the Métis were kept waiting for their land grants. With the buffalo in Manitoba disappearing, no land settlement in sight, and continued hostility from their white neighbours, many Métis moved west to territory that is now part of Saskatchewan, where they could still hunt buffalo and where they could establish communities under their own control.

## THE INDIAN TREATIES

The Macdonald government was determined not to repeat the Métis experience with aboriginal peoples in the newly acquired territories. Between 1871 and 1877, seven treaties were concluded with aboriginal peoples living east of the Rockies, whose estimated population was thirty-four thousand. Adams Archibald, the first lieutenant-governor of Manitoba, was the negotiator of Treaty One, which covered the Indians of Lower Fort Garry. In his speech to those assembled for the occasion, he made clear the intentions of the federal government: "Your Great Mother [Queen Victoria] wishes the good of all races under her sway. She wishes her red children to be happy and contented. She wishes them to live in comfort. She would like them to adopt the habits of the whites, to till land and raise food, and store it up against a time of want."[1] The Natives agreed to the treaties because they feared the changes that were taking place and wanted some guarantees for their future well-being which was being threatened by the disappearance of the buffalo as well as by the influx of settlers.

Treaty One, like the six subsequent treaties, established reserves where aboriginal peoples would have their farms, and promised implements, seed, and training to launch them in agricultural careers. It also promised that traditional hunting and fishing rights would be recognized. Despite treaty promises, the aboriginal peoples were soon frustrated by the failure of the Canadian government to provide farm aid. Indian commissioner Weymss Simpson interpreted the Lower Fort Garry treaty to imply that implements and seed would be provided only when aboriginal peoples had settled on reserves and built homes to demonstrate their readiness for an agricultural life. The distraught Lower Fort Garry Natives replied eloquently but with little impact: "We cannot tear down trees and build huts with our teeth, we cannot break the prairie with our hands, nor reap the harvest when we have grown it with our knives."[2]

The political status of Prairie aboriginal peoples was actually determined before the treaties were negotiated. Under the British North America Act, aboriginal people throughout Canada were placed under the jurisdiction of the federal government. Aboriginal peoples living on reserves in the eastern colonies were registered by the federal government, as were the "treaty Indians" in the new areas acquired by Canada. In 1876, the federal government consolidated its policies with respect to aboriginal peoples in the Indian Act. The act was revised periodically over the following century, but its basic premise—that aboriginal peoples were still incapable of integrating into "civilized" society and therefore needed supervision in their economic, political, and social activities—remained unaltered.

The act replaced traditional political structures with band chiefs and councils chosen according to the legislation, and subjected all reserve activities to the supervision of regional and national bureaucracies dominated by whites. In defining Indian status, the act made gender distinctions: the wives, widows, and children of registered men were declared to be status Indians even if they had no Indian heritage; an aboriginal woman who married a white man lost her status as an Indian, as did her children. Status Indians were also eventually denied the right to perform traditional religious practices or to drink alcohol, restrictions that were incorporated during periodic revisions of the act. In theory, reserves were designed to isolate aboriginal peoples so that they could learn European ways at their own pace and be introduced to white society when they were ready; in practice, it brought them together in closed political and social arrangements that made future integration highly unlikely.

As the provisions of the Indian treaties and Indian Act suggest, the government's priority in the Northwest was for European, not aboriginal, settlement. In 1872, the Dominion Lands Act granted free homesteads of 160 acres to farmers who cleared 10 acres and built a home within three years of registering their intention to settle. In 1873, the North-West Mounted Police was established to maintain law and order in the Northwest. Though planning for the force was already in the works, its speedy approval by Parliament was assured after the massacre of twenty-two Assiniboine in the Cypress Hills by American wolf hunters bent on avenging the alleged theft of horses. This atrocity emphasized the threat from the Americans who eyed the lands claimed by Canada. Threats from the United States also stiffened Macdonald's resolve to negotiate the entry of

British Columbia and Prince Edward Island into Confederation.

## BRITISH COLUMBIA AND PRINCE EDWARD ISLAND

The gold rush in British Columbia was over by the mid-1860s, resulting in a large outflow of prospectors, miners, and merchants. Before the slump, the two west coast colonies—Vancouver Island and British Columbia—had spent liberally to build courts, roads, and other public works. After the gold rush, both colonies were nearly bankrupt. The Colonial Office engineered their union in 1866, but, with combined debts of $1.3 million, the new colony of British Columbia was not in a position to initiate public projects. The jealousy between mainlanders and islanders further complicated the colony's politics. For two years New Westminster and Victoria fought over which city would be the capital before the latter prevailed. The lack of full responsible government also drew fire from the growing number of immigrants.

By the 1870s, new economic activities were taking root on the West Coast. Coal mines were operating in Nanaimo, sawmills had been established along Alberni Canal and Burrard Inlet, a British naval base was located in Esquimalt, and small agricultural settlements were scattered through the colony. Victoria continued its role as the centre of banking, commerce, and shipbuilding for the colony. British capital dominated these economic initiatives, but during and after the gold rush, close economic ties developed with the American territories south of the border.

While a few business people in Victoria called for admission of British Columbia into the United States, such a proposal was denounced by the dominant British interests in the colony. The Canadian option was championed by Amor de Cosmos, a colourful Victoria-based newspaper editor whose adopted name—he was plain William Smith from Nova Scotia—reflected his flamboyant style. In March 1867, de Cosmos countered annexationist proposals with a resolution in the legislative council that British Columbia be included as a province of Canada. Britain rejected the proposal at the time

on the grounds that it was premature to incorporate the Pacific Coast into the new federation before the Northwest had been acquired by Canada.

Once the fate of the Northwest had been sealed, the Colonial Office was quick to let the colonists know that Britain favoured British Columbia's entry into Confederation. Lieutenant-Governor Andrew Musgrave, following the pattern set by Britain's chief representatives in other colonies, actively promoted the union. After an inconclusive debate in the legislative council on the merits of union with Canada, it was agreed that a delegation would meet with representatives of the Dominion government. The council's terms for British Columbia's entry into Confederation included the immediate building of a wagon road connecting New Westminster to Fort Garry, with a railroad along that route to follow in due course; the assumption by Canada of British Columbia's existing debt; and a grant to the province of $100 000 per annum to enable it to undertake necessary public works.

During the negotiations held in June 1870, the Canadian delegation was led by George-Étienne Cartier. He proved more than willing to accept the conditions demanded by the British Columbians and even agreed to start building the railway within two years and complete it within ten years of British Columbia joining Confederation. These generous terms raised more than one eyebrow in Ottawa. How could a railway be built across such difficult terrain in such a short time? What would the other provinces say about the $100 000 per annum grant that was much more on a per capita basis than they had been offered? Since aboriginal peoples were excluded from the population count because they were governed separately under the Indian Act, British Columbia would have needed a non-aboriginal population of 120 000 to justify its grant request. Instead, it had only about 10 500: 8576 Europeans, 1548 Chinese, and 462 African-origin residents. Despite these concerns, the Macdonald government stood by the agreement. British Columbia would give Canada a Pacific boundary and fulfil the Confederation promise of a dominion from sea to sea. It could not be lost to the Americans.

Elections in November 1870 gave every seat in the British Columbia legislature to supporters of Confederation on the terms worked out in the June negotiations. On 18 January 1871, the legislative council unanimously agreed to bring the colony into Confederation, and in June British Columbia became the sixth province of Canada. Few people in British Columbia—and certainly not the aboriginal people who made up 80 percent of the population and had no say in the matter—felt any real attachment to Canada. The economic stimulus of the proposed railway and Canadian government grants made Confederation appear to be a lucrative economic arrangement that should not be rejected.

Similar economic reasons led Prince Edward Island into Confederation in 1873. In the 1860s, the promise of an intercolonial railway connecting the Maritimes to potential markets in Central Canada seemed irrelevant to residents of the island colony. The 1867 election was fought not over Confederation but on the persistent land question, the role of the Conservative government in repressing the Tenant League—organized to intimidate landlords—and denominational schools, an issue of intense interest to the Roman Catholics who made up 45 percent of the island's population.

Supported by a majority of the Roman Catholic voters, the Liberals defeated the Conservatives in the 1867 election. Once in office, the Liberals proved as unwilling as their Conservative predecessors to establish a system of publicly funded denominational schools. Consequently, they lost much of their support and, in turn, suffered defeat in the 1870 election. The Conservatives under James Pope, a leading island businessman and one-time supporter of Confederation, formed the new government in alliance with the Roman Catholic independents who had broken away from the Liberals.

When the Conservatives took office, the economy of the island colony was stable, if not thriving. Its 94 021 people found export markets for the products of their farms and fisheries and, like other Maritimers, boasted a healthy shipbuilding industry. In the wake of several decades of steady growth, the island's elite had established three banks and several newspapers. Only one thing was missing: railroads. An apostle of progress, Pope set out to fill the gap with a line that wound a serpentine route through many of the island's communities. Islanders soon found, as had others before them, that railway building was hard on the public purse. Faced with huge public debt, Pope argued to Prince Edward Islanders that only by joining Canada and letting that country assume the island's debt could they avoid the paralysis that repayment would entail.

Once more the Americans were on the scene. General Benjamin Butler of Massachusetts had come to the island in 1869 to offer a special trade deal, which appeared to be a first step towards luring it into the American union. Although the American offers came to nothing, the Canadian government decided not to take any chances. Macdonald agreed not only to assume the railway debt and establish year-round communications between the island and the mainland, but also to use federal moneys to buy out the remaining absentee landlords so that tenants could become freeholders. With its interests thus addressed, Prince Edward Island agreed to become the seventh province of Canada in 1873.

## Newfoundland's Perspective

There was little prospect that Newfoundland, the remaining Atlantic colony, would follow in Prince Edward Island's footsteps. Dependent largely on the fisheries, the island's 150 000 people looked out to sea and international trade for their livelihood. The economy was experiencing some difficulties in the 1860s, but Confederation promised more problems than it solved. British North America bought only 5 percent of Newfoundland's exports and provided 16 percent of its imports. With markets in southern Europe, the West Indies, and Brazil, and 70 percent of its imports supplied by Britain and the United States, Confederation threatened Newfoundland's long-standing trading patterns with tariffs against foreign trade and policies designed to create an integrated national economy.

Not surprisingly, the merchants of St John's and Conception Bay, who dominated the local economy, were firmly set against union with Canada. In 1865, the St John's Chamber of Commerce concluded that Confederation "can open no new or more extensive market for the product of our fisheries, nor does it hold out the prospect of developing new resources within the Colony or extending those we now possess."[3] Most of the island's Roman Catholic population, and particularly the church leaders in the colony, many of whom were Irish immigrants, wanted no part of a union backed by Great Britain. With so little support for it, Confederation was not even an issue in the 1865 election.

Unlike the other Atlantic colonies, Newfoundland faced neither an overwhelming debt nor intense British pressure to enter a union with Canada. The issue of defence, which preoccupied leaders in the mainland colonies, conjured up only fears that the colony's young men would be conscripted to fight Canadian wars. Nevertheless, Confederation remained on the political agenda. Conservative Premier Frederick Carter, a principled man who had done much to mute sectarian politics in his province, supported the idea of union. In the months preceding the 1869 election, he persuaded the assembly to pass draft terms for union, and an agreement was negotiated with the Canadian government for the colony's entry into Confederation.

Newfoundland voters were still not convinced that their destiny lay with Canada. Led by merchant Charles Fox Bennett, the anti-Confederation forces won over two-thirds of the seats in the Newfoundland legislature. Even Protestant areas of the colony, which usually voted Conservative, deserted the party that flirted with "the Canadian wolf." Several generations would pass before Newfoundlanders debated the issue of Confederation again. In the 1880s, railway mania swept Newfoundland with the usual accompanying public debt. Although Canada again put out feelers, local politicians, smarting from their earlier defeat, refused to touch the Confederation issue.

## PACIFIC SCANDAL AND THE DEFEAT OF MACDONALD

Despite Macdonald's success in rounding out Canada's borders, his government barely survived the 1872 election. Even Cartier lost his seat in Montreal East and only re-entered Parliament through a by-election in Manitoba. Without the nine seats contributed by the new provinces of Manitoba and British Columbia, Macdonald would have had difficulty continuing to govern. When the final tally was in, the Conservatives could claim a small majority in the House of Commons, but their position was precarious because so many members refused to align themselves either with the government or the opposition.

Macdonald's biggest threat came from Ontario where Alexander Mackenzie's Reformers —or Liberals as they were increasingly called— revived criticisms of the Tories as corrupt spendthrifts and papist sympathizers. In the wake of the Red River uprising, sectarian issues intensified, and the Ontario Liberals were not above reminding Protestants that Macdonald had failed to bring the Métis murderers of Thomas Scott to justice. Such views clashed dramatically with those of opposition members from Quebec, who denounced Cartier for having done nothing to settle Métis land claims or to win amnesty for Louis Riel.

Other issues also surfaced during the campaign. Macdonald had failed to convince the United States to sign a new reciprocity agreement, a major item on the wish list of most primary producers. Nor, apparently, had his government been able to resolve the question of who was to build the Pacific railway. Moreover, as a means of appealing to the skilled workers, many of whom had sufficient property holdings to allow them to vote, Macdonald had legally recognized unions. George Brown, the *éminence grise* of the Ontario Liberals, was particularly outraged by this move, which scuttled the union-breaking tactics practised in his *Globe* newspaper offices, and he redoubled his efforts to have his long-time political enemy defeated.

The difficulty of gaining enough support to

remain in power led Macdonald to indulge in activities that ultimately led to his downfall. In May 1871, the government introduced legislation to provide for the construction of a Pacific railway. The bill offered $30 million in cash and twenty million acres of land as an incentive to any company that would sign a contract to build the line. Opposition members, led by Alexander Mackenzie's Ontario contingent, balked at such extravagance and confidently predicted that the awarding of a railway charter would be marked by political corruption. They were right.

Two companies sought the lucrative railway-building contract. One was headed by Ontario Senator David MacPherson and included the leading lights of the Toronto business community. The other, headed by Hugh Allan, president of the Allan Steamship Lines, represented Montreal business interests and had backing from the Northern Pacific Railway in the United States. Attempts by the Macdonald administration to effect a merger of these two Canadian groups, and keep the Americans out, stalled the awarding of a contract but bore no fruit.

Cartier had a major interest in seeing his city prevail in the contest with Toronto, but even he initially regarded Allan's demands as extreme. Yet, Cartier was politically vulnerable, and Allan made clear his determination either to force Cartier's full support or to engineer his political defeat. As the 1872 federal election loomed, a beleaguered Cartier, suffering from the Bright's disease that would cause his death the following year, capitulated to Allan's demands. In return for Cartier's support, Allan gave at least $162 000, and perhaps as much as $360 000, to the Conservative election effort.

Most elections in the mid-nineteenth century were marked by fraud, intimidation, and violence, but the 1872 election was eventually revealed to be one of the most corrupt. In February 1873, the Macdonald government named Sir Hugh Allan as president of the Canadian Pacific Railway Company. Two months later, Lucius Huntington, a Liberal MP, charged that Allan had bought his presidency with $360 000 in donations to the Conservative Party. Macdonald reluctantly

**CONFEDERATION !**
THE MUCH-FATHERED YOUNGSTER.

*This spoof on Confederation is one of many drawn by Canada's first great cartoonist, J.W. Bengough, who between 1873 and 1892 produced the satirical weekly newspaper* **Grip***, named for the raven in Charles Dickens's* **Barnaby Rudge***. Born in Toronto in 1851, Bengough worked for the* **Globe** *before launching his own publication. The Pacific Scandal of 1873 gave him ample material for satire and launched him on a successful career, as a newspaper editor, cartoonist, and public lecturer.*

J.W. Bengough/National Archives of Canada/C78676

appointed a select committee to examine the charges. It soon became apparent that the Liberals had a mole in the Conservative organization: incriminating letters and telegrams proved Cartier's corruption and left little doubt of Macdonald's as well. Even more damaging was the fact that Allan was being financed by American investors, who were poised to assume control of Canada's major railway company. They might even be planning to undermine the project so that Canadian traffic would be forced to use the Northern Pacific, which was dominated by Allan's American backers. Sensing that the government was doomed, many independents joined the Liberal opposition. On 5 November 1873, Macdonald informed Governor General Lord Dufferin that he no longer enjoyed a parliamentary majority and therefore, following the principle of responsible government, was resigning as prime minister.

## THE LIBERALS AT THE HELM

Dufferin invited Alexander Mackenzie, member for Lanark, Ontario, to form a government. A Highland Scot, a stonemason, and a Baptist, Mackenzie had quit school at the age of thirteen to contribute to the family economy. He was a teetotaller and had a tremendous capacity for hard work, but, like many self-made men, Mackenzie had little sympathy for anyone who was unable to succeed. He had taken the position of prime minister more out of duty than ambition after Edward Blake, a former premier of Ontario, and A.-A. Dorion had turned it down. Mackenzie cobbled together a Liberal coalition consisting of Ontario Reformers, Quebec *rouges*, moderate Liberals, and Maritimers of all political stripes disillusioned by Macdonald's government.

Hoping to use the Pacific Scandal to win a majority in support of his government, Mackenzie called an election for the winter of 1874. Macdonald, who remained Conservative leader, campaigned on a nationalist platform that emphasized the need for the Pacific railway to hold the Northwest and fulfil pledges to British Columbia. In keeping with the more cautious program favoured by his followers, Mackenzie promised a new Pacific railway contract that did not involve large public expenditures for the benefit of private entrepreneurs. Emphasizing provincial rights and the need for economy, he presented a vision of the new dominion markedly at odds with the "new nationality" that the Conservatives preached. Mackenzie won a majority of seats in every province except British Columbia whose 2063 voters returned Conservatives in all of their six ridings.

Despite their strong mandate, the Liberals survived only one term in office. Canada was gripped in a worldwide recession in the 1870s, which made it difficult to pursue an ambitious national policy. When the United States rejected the new government's efforts to negotiate a reciprocity treaty, the Liberals had no economic strategy other than retrenchment. It did not inspire enthusiasm. British Columbia threatened secession if the federal government failed to build a railway within the time frame promised by their Confederation agreement, and Canadians continued to move to the United States to find work.

The Liberal interlude nevertheless left its mark on the new nation. In addition to introducing electoral reforms that included simultaneous voting, the secret ballot, and trial of disputed elections by the courts, the Liberals negotiated with Britain to enlarge the powers of the dominion. Such aggrandizement was the special goal of Edward Blake, who agreed to serve in a number of portfolios under Mackenzie's leadership. A brilliant but thin-skinned individual, Blake had associated himself briefly with the Canada First movement, dominated by a group of young Canadian nationalists based in Ontario. The Canada Firsters envisioned a vigorous Anglo-Saxon and Protestant nation allied with Great Britain. In a speech delivered in Aurora, Ontario, in October 1874, Blake captured the essence of the Canada First position and his own sense of superiority in his approach to national policy:

> The future of Canada, I believe, depends very largely upon the cultivation of a national spirit. We are engaged in a very difficult task—the task of welding together seven Provinces which have been accustomed to regard themselves as isolated from each other, which are full of petty jealousies, their Provincial questions, their local interests. How are we to accomplish our work? How are we to effect a real union between these Provinces? Can we do it by giving a sop now to one, now to another, after the manner of the late Government?... Do you hope to create or preserve harmony and good feeling upon such a false and sordid and mercenary basis as that? No so! That day I hope is gone for ever, and we must find some other and truer ground for Union than that by which the late Government sought to buy love and purchase peace.[4]

Blake resisted the attempts of Canada Firsters to recruit him as leader of their short-lived party, the Canadian National Association, founded in the wake of the Pacific Scandal. Nevertheless, he was sympathetic to their emphasis on Canada achieving greater autonomy within the British Empire. As Mackenzie's minister of justice, Blake extended the nation's powers to create admiralty courts, exercise authority over shipping on the Great Lakes, and pardon criminals. He also established the Supreme Court of Canada in 1875 but failed in his attempts to make it the final court of appeal, which remained the Judicial Committee of the Privy Council of Great Britain until 1949.

It was widely conceded that the voters preferred Sir John A. drunk to Mackenzie sober, and the federal election of 1878 confirmed that verdict. Despite the Pacific Scandal and a weak performance in the House while the Liberals were in office, Macdonald's Conservatives won 142 of the 206 seats in the House and carried majorities in every province except New Brunswick. During the campaign, Macdonald advocated a development program that is often described as the National Policy. The centrepiece of the program was a policy of high tariffs to stimulate a strong manufacturing sector in the Canadian economy. In addition, Macdonald underlined the importance of a rapid completion of the Pacific railway and the encouragement of population growth through immigration. Inspired by the slow economic climate of the 1870s, these policies would form the framework of national development under both Conservative and Liberal administrations until the First World War.

## THE NATIONAL POLICY

Following the election, the Macdonald government acted quickly to implement its National Policy. In 1879, Finance Minister Tilley raised the tariff from 15 percent to levels ranging from 17.5 to 35 percent. Manufacturers were delighted with a policy that they had long been promoting to support their industries against foreign competition. Counting the members of the Canadian Manufacturers Association among his principal supporters,

Macdonald increased tariffs throughout the 1880s, reportedly relying on casual billiard room discussions with entrepreneurs to determine the appropriate level of protection.

Meanwhile, the government moved on a second aspect of the National Policy in 1880 when it entered into negotiations for a new Canadian Pacific Railway company. Headed by George Stephen, president of the Bank of Montreal, and his cousin Donald Smith, a major stakeholder in the Hudson's Bay Company, the company included Norman Kittson and James J. Hill, two men who in the 1870s had developed a successful partnership with Stephen and Smith in the St Paul, Minnesota, and Manitoba Railway Company. The CPR was from the outset a multinational enterprise. In the early years of the company's existence, only about one-sixth of the CPR stock was held in Canada; the rest was purchased by investors in New York, Paris, and London.

The Macdonald government offered the CPR syndicate generous support for its efforts: a cash grant of $25 million in aid of construction; a land grant of twenty-five million acres (half of the land within thirty-two kilometres of the CPR's main line would be set aside until the company decided which parcels of land it wished to claim); an additional land grant for railway stations and road beds; the eleven hundred kilometres of completed track built in the Mackenzie years, valued at over $37 million; a guarantee of a twenty-year monopoly on western rail traffic; exemption of the company from the tariff on all materials required in railway construction; and a twenty-year exemption for all CPR properties from federal and provincial taxation and from taxation by municipalities not yet incorporated. More grants were required before the line was completed in 1885, and in 1888 the government guaranteed a $15 million bond issue in compensation for dropping the monopoly clause in the original contract.

In the third area of the National Policy—immigration—the Macdonald government had less obvious success. Over 900 000 immigrants arrived in Canada in the 1880s, but this was balanced against over a million people who left Canada in the same time period. The exodus of people from the Maritimes and Quebec to the United States was a cause of some alarm in both regions. In Ontario, people were more likely to take up the challenge of western settlement, but the numbers were not large. The population of the Prairies was only about 400 000 by 1901, not the millions that optimists had predicted earlier in the century.

During Macdonald's second term in office the boundaries of Canada were further extended. In 1880, by an imperial order-in-council, the Arctic archipelago was added to Canadian jurisdiction as the District of Franklin. This move was precipitated by a request from the Americans in 1874 for mineral rights on Baffin Island. There was no thought of developing or settling the region on the part of British or Canadian authorities. As one member of the Colonial Office remarked at the time, the main reason for turning the islands over to Canada was "to prevent the United States from claiming them, not from their likelihood of their being any value to Canada."[5]

## THE NORTHWEST

In the two decades following Confederation, no region of the nation experienced greater changes than the old Northwest. Its society came to resemble that of Eastern Canada in many—though not all—ways. Outside of Manitoba, whose boundaries were extended in 1881, the Northwest Territories remained under the jurisdiction of the federal government. The Northwest Territories Act of 1875 determined that the area would be governed by an appointed council until such time as the population warranted the inclusion of elected officials. Since no provision was made for responsible government, power was concentrated in the hands of the lieutenant-governor and his Ottawa advisers. The act guaranteed denominational schools, and, by an amendment in 1877, French and English were made the official languages of the courts and council. The capital of the vast region was Battleford until 1882 when, with the arrival of the railway, it was moved to Regina.

The heavy hand of Ottawa was soon called into question. In 1879, the council, by then called the legislative assembly, resigned en masse, charging that the lieutenant-governor, Edgar Dewdney, often ignored its advice. The federal government

*In both Canada and the United States, railway companies employed Chinese labourers to do some of the most dangerous and backbreaking work. They were responsible for the jobs of tunnelling and handling explosives, which helps to account for the death of 600 Chinese workers during the CPR construction process. In the words of the 1884 Royal Commission on Chinese Immigration, they were "living machines" working for the benefit of the capitalists who employed them and the fragile nation that was bound together by iron rails.*

Notman Photographic Archives, McCord Museum of Canadian History, Montreal/2117

responded two years later by granting the assembly most powers held by provinces except the right to borrow money. By the mid-1890s, pressure was mounting for the creation of one or two provinces within the territories.

As historian Gerald Friesen has pointed out, Native peoples of the western interior experienced a revolution in the last half of the nineteenth century.[6] The disappearance of the buffalo, the building of the railway, the influx of white settlers, and the arrival of the federal government in the form of police, law courts, and legislatures were each occurrences of profound significance. The fact that they all happened in the short period between 1875 and 1885 meant that special care was needed to prevent disaster for both Native and newcomer. Unfortunately, administrators in the Northwest Territories and their political masters in Ottawa proved ill-equipped to handle the volatile situation developing in their rapidly changing western empire.

With the disappearance of the buffalo and other game, the plains Indians reluctantly accepted treaties that they believed guaranteed them government help to become farmers. The transition proved difficult. Before the promised government assistance arrived, Dewdney reduced rations as a cost-cutting measure. This policy was implemented in the early 1880s just as the buffalo were disappearing from the Canadian prairies—the last Canadian hunt occurred in 1879. The crisis facing the aboriginal peoples was real. Between 1880 and 1885, an estimated three thousand Natives in the Northwest died from starvation.

In desperation, some Natives stole cattle from the settlers in the region. This inevitably got the culprits into trouble with the North-West Mounted Police (NWMP), which was charged with the responsibility of upholding laws against theft. As the situation worsened, aboriginal peoples began to organize against the whites in the region, who symbolized the threat to the old way of life on the plains. Cree chiefs such as Big Bear and Poundmaker played key roles in aboriginal resistance. From the outset of negotiations with Ottawa, Big Bear had regarded the treaty provi-

sions as insulting. He had refused to sign Treaty Six until starvation among his band forced his hand in 1882. Like his white counterparts in Ottawa, Big Bear dreamed of creating a larger political organization, but his confederation was one in which the plains tribes would unite to force the Canadian government to renegotiate the treaties and provide aboriginal peoples with ironclad assurances of the right to hunt and live in their traditional territories.[6]

In 1884, about two thousand Cree from several reserves gathered outside Battleford in an attempt to coordinate their resistance. Several councils held that year demonstrated a growing cohesion of the Cree in resisting government mistreatment. When the government response was slow in coming, young militants in the band began calling for armed struggle. Unrest among the Natives coincided with growing discontent among the Métis, many of them migrants from Manitoba, living along the South Saskatchewan River. While the Métis had come to terms with the fact that hunting would have to give way to a largely agricultural existence, they wanted the same assistance as was offered other settlers in the West. Encouraged by the clergy, the Métis began to petition Ottawa for land, agricultural aid, schools, and a locally run police force. Their biggest concern was that they be able to maintain community control over new institutions and thereby preserve their distinct way of life.

When Ottawa ignored their petitions, the Métis decided in 1884 to invite Louis Riel to return to Canada from his home in the United States to lead his people. During his years in exile, Riel had suffered from mental problems and increasingly became obsessed with what he viewed as his mission to establish a new North American Catholicism with Bishop Bourget of Montreal as the pope of the New World. He eventually became an American citizen, joined the Republican Party, and was teaching school in Montana when he received the call from his people in the Northwest. Despite his emotional instability, Riel still had the skills required to make Ottawa listen. Initially he attempted to pursue the peaceful route of pressuring the Macdonald government for concessions. In this approach he had the support of many white settlers in the region who were growing impatient with their own treatment by Ottawa and Lieutenant-Governor Dewdney.

Ottawa ignored Riel's petitions, with predictable results. On 18 March 1885, Riel proclaimed a provisional government and demanded that Ottawa grant the moderate demands outlined in a Bill of Rights. Riel still hoped for a peaceful settlement to the stand-off, but many Métis, including Riel's military adviser, Gabriel Dumont, felt that militant action was called for. Dumont advocated seizing government buildings, attacking NWMP detachments, and blowing up the railway tracks used by the federal government to send troops westwards. Skirmishes between Métis and NWMP at Batoche and Duck Lake, in which the police fared badly, resulted in the government's decision to send a militia force under Major-General Frederick Middleton to the scene. Within two weeks of the Duck Lake incident, the first detachment of militia arrived on CPR trains.

When word of the Métis rebellion reached Cree ears, the young militants attacked the base at Frog Lake, killing a hated Indian agent and eight others. In another incident, two farming instructors regarded as hostile to Natives were murdered in the Battleford district. These developments alarmed white settlers, who feared nothing so much as an "Indian War." Forced to choose sides, they would volunteer to help the army sent by Ottawa to put down the uprising.

Riel withdrew his supporters to Batoche where they held out against the army for six weeks before surrendering. Tried for treason, Riel was found guilty by an all-white jury in a Regina courtroom and was hanged in November 1885. Riel's defence of his actions during his trial was a mixture of a madman's confused ramblings and a clear-sighted analysis of the plight of aboriginal peoples. Since his death, Riel has become a symbol of his people, and assessments of his behaviour have often varied greatly. It is more generally conceded now than it was a century ago that, whatever the merits of this complicated man, the cause for which he fought in 1885 was a noble one.

## THE "BILL OF RIGHTS," 1885

Métis demands suggest that Riel's program was neither separatist nor racist, as Canadian opponents of Riel charged at the time. While the concerns of the Métis were uppermost in Riel's mind, the Bill of Rights included calls for better treatment of all peoples in the Northwest Territories. Following is a condensed version of the demands:

1. That the half-breeds of the Northwest Territories be given grants similar to those accorded to the half-breeds of Manitoba by the Act of 1870.

2. That patents be issued to all half-breeds and white settlers who have fairly earned the right of possession to their farms; that the timber regulations be made more liberal; and that the settler be treated as having rights in the country.

3. That the provinces of Alberta and Saskatchewan be forthwith organized with legislatures of their own, so that the people may be no longer subject to the despotism of Lieutenant-Governor Dewdney; and, in the proposed new provincial legislatures, that the Métis shall have a fair and reasonable share of representation.

4. That the offices of trust throughout these provinces be given to residents of the country, as far as practicable, and that we denounce the appointment of disreputable outsiders and repudiate their authority.

5. That this region be administered for the benefit of the actual settler, and not for the advantage of the alien speculator; and that all lawful customs and usages which obtain among the Métis be respected.

6. That better provision be made for the Indians, the parliamentary grant to be increased, and lands set apart as an endowment for the establishment of hospitals and schools for the use of whites, half-breeds, and Indians, at such places as the provincial legislatures may determine.

7. That the Land Department of the Dominion Government be administered as far as practicable from Winnipeg, so that settlers may not be compelled, as heretofore to go to Ottawa for the settlement of questions in dispute between them and land commissioners. [7]

felony-treason. While the hanging of Louis Riel was an issue of public debate for many years, the hanging of eight aboriginal leaders and the long jail sentences for many of their followers created little interest except among Native peoples. Military might and the legal system had broken organized resistance to white colonialism, but aboriginal peoples continued to perform individual acts of defiance. They secretly practised religious ceremonies that were banned under the Indian Act, and they protected each other against attempts by the NWMP to arrest them when accused, often falsely, of failing to meet the standards of the white man's laws.

## THE CLASH OF CULTURES

Natives were not the only people questioning Macdonald's interpretation of Confederation. For francophones, Ottawa's handling of guarantees for French-language rights and denominational schools was a major cause of concern. Both policies were resisted by provincial legislatures outside Quebec. Dominated by representatives of the English Protestant majority, the federal government also remained unmoved by pleas for legislation that would protect francophone and Roman Catholic minorities throughout the country.

At the time of Confederation, Cartier led a Conservative bloc in Quebec that included both moderates and ultra-conservatives, known as ultramontanists. The latter were determined to organize society according to the principles of the Roman Catholic Church, which would have control over the most important institutions in society. In the 1871 provincial election in Quebec, the ultramontane wing of the Conservative Party launched the Catholic Program, requiring that all candidates make Catholic doctrine the basis of their political action and comply with directives issued by Roman Catholic bishops. The *programmistes*, as they were called, won only one seat, but they were a force to be reckoned with in the Conservative Party both in

*Following his capture in July 1885, Big Bear was incarcerated for three years in Stoney Mountain penitentiary, north of Winnipeg. Like other prisoners, he had his hair cropped and was forced to do menial jobs. He was reported to have converted to Roman Catholicism while in prison. Released in 1887, he seemed broken in spirit and died within a year.*

National Archives of Canada/C1873

The aboriginal people paid dearly for their acts of frustration. Of eighty-one arrested during the turmoil, forty-four were convicted. Of these, eight were hanged, three were sentenced to life imprisonment, and many others were incarcerated for shorter periods. Even Big Bear and Poundmaker, who had tried to prevent violence, were sentenced to three-year prison terms on charges of

Quebec City and in Ottawa.

The first contest over denominational schools outside of Quebec occurred in New Brunswick. The New Brunswick Common Schools Act of 1871 authorized municipalities in the province to tax all ratepayers to support the public school system whose institutions henceforth would be the only ones to benefit from government funding. The omission from the act of Roman Catholic schools, which had hitherto received public funding, though by convention rather than by law, was intentional. When Premier George King went to the polls to defend the new legislation, he campaigned under the slogan, "Vote for the Queen against the Pope." He won a resounding victory.

In response to what they perceived as an unfair law, Roman Catholics in New Brunswick, who constituted one-third of the population, appealed to the courts. The legislation was declared valid, so they turned to the federal government. Education was normally a provincial matter, but the BNA Act authorized the federal government to intervene when education laws in place at the time of Confederation were violated. Since grants to Roman Catholic schools in the province had been the practice but not the law, the government let the New Brunswick legislation stand.

Roman Catholics in New Brunswick responded by refusing to pay their assessments, and they were prosecuted for non-payment. When the assessment legislation was ruled unconstitutional on a technicality, the government moved to close the loopholes in the act. Again, Roman Catholics in New Brunswick appealed to Ottawa. To Macdonald's embarrassment, the motion to disallow the New Brunswick assessment act was carried with votes from the French Canadians in his party. Macdonald passed the responsibility to the imperial government, which advised the governor general to sign the act to confirm the principle of provincial responsibility in education.

While most Roman Catholics in New Brunswick vigorously opposed the school legislation, resistance was especially fierce among the province's Acadian population. They made up about half of the adherents to Roman Catholicism in the province and did not always see eye to eye with their English-speaking co-religionists, most of whom were Irish. Since only one Acadian child in six received any schooling, and few attended school for more than five or six years, most Acadians were unwilling to pay taxes to support any school, much less a school from which Catholic education was excluded. The poverty that existed in many Acadian communities made the school tax particularly onerous.

Matters came to a head in the village of Caraquet. In January 1875, a group of angry Acadians broke up the meeting of Protestants who were trying to set aside parish elections on the grounds that most voters had been ineligible to cast ballots because they had not paid their school taxes. The Acadians had numbers on their side in Caraquet, where only seventy-nine Protestants resided in a population of over three thousand.

*The Caraquet Riot of 1875 resulted in two deaths and encouraged leaders in church and government to compromise on the issue of school policy in New Brunswick.*

When constables and volunteers tried to arrest the Acadians who broke up the meeting, a mêlée ensued in which one volunteer and one Acadian were shot. The trial of nine Acadians for murder became a cause célèbre and forced the government to back down from its rigid position. In addition to dismissal of the charges against the accused Acadians, the government agreed to allow Roman Catholics to be taught by members of religious orders in areas where their numbers warranted.

While the issue of denominational schools had been resolved in New Brunswick, language remained a problem for all Acadians, whose numbers in the three Maritime provinces were approaching a hundred thousand by the 1870s. Teachers in areas with mainly Acadian populations taught in French, but provincial normal schools taught only in English, and there were few resources available for French-speaking teachers. In an effort to improve the conditions in their Acadian schools, the New Brunswick Department of Education prepared a few elementary readers in French, but most textbooks made available to Acadian students were in English.

By the 1880s, religious and cultural concerns had become as important as economic issues in determining party loyalties and shaping national policies. This was amply revealed in the aftermath of Riel's hanging in 1885. Because the Métis involved in the rebellion were primarily French-speaking Roman Catholics, neither Orangemen nor Quebec nationalists took account of the regional and aboriginal concerns behind the uprising. Instead, Orangemen regarded Riel as a French-speaking Roman Catholic determined to deprive the British Empire of the Northwest, while Quebec nationalists saw him as a hero whose undoing proved that French-Canadian rights would not be respected outside Quebec.

Macdonald's decision to let Riel hang was undoubtedly a calculated one designed to reassure anglophones that he was not a pawn of Roman Catholics; but it was also a decision made with the tacit support of the Roman Catholic hierarchy, who found Riel's religious beliefs increasingly unacceptable. Such evidence was conveniently forgotten by the extremists on both sides. After Riel's execution, an outpouring of grief and rage, including a demonstration in Montreal attended by over fifty thousand people, testified the extent of Québécois alienation. Building on francophone discontent, Honoré Mercier led the Parti national, which included Quebec's Liberals along with Conservative dissidents, to a provincial election victory in 1886. Mercier's success demonstrated the erosion of the political alliance between the Conservatives and the Roman Catholic Church that had exercised power both federally and in Quebec in the post-Confederation era. By using the word *national* in the party name, Liberals also reminded the francophone majority in Quebec that they were a nation even if it was submerged in the larger nation-state of Canada.

French Canadians in Ontario, who numbered over a hundred thousand by the 1880s, became hostages to the cultural bigotry spreading across the country. Unlike New Brunswick, Ontario's denominational schools were protected by the British North America Act, but French linguistic rights had no similar guarantees. Before 1885, provincial officials tolerated education in both French and German. In the wake of Quebec campaigns against Riel's execution, the Ontario government limited the hours of instruction in languages other than English and required teachers to be tested to ensure proficiency in the English language. Since local school boards were left to enforce this regulation, most initially chose to ignore it.

The Jesuit Estates Act of 1888 galvanized the anti-Roman Catholic forces of Ontario into more concerted action. When the Jesuits returned to Quebec in the 1840s, they demanded compensation for the properties confiscated by Great Britain following the conquest in 1763. The Quebec government, at a loss as to how to arbitrate among the contending Roman Catholic claimants, invited Pope Leo XIII to help to determine monetary compensation. Although the final settlement included funds for Protestant universities in Quebec, Protestant extremists in Ontario decried Vatican involvement in Canadian affairs. An Ontario-based group calling itself the Equal Rights Association launched a campaign to rid the province and the nation of papal influences of any kind. Riding the wave of anti-Catholic sentiment, D'Alton McCarthy, one of the Conservative Party's most able lieutenants, urged the abolition of public funding for separate schools and called for the assimilation of French Canadians.

In an effort to curry favour with its overwhelmingly English and Protestant electorate, the Liberal government of Ontario removed all French textbooks from the authorized list of books in 1889. Meanwhile, local school boards threw roadblocks in the way of instruction in the French language. In Caledonia Township, for example, where francophones made up one-third of the population, anglophone Catholics refused to establish any French-language schools to supplement the nine English-language schools in operation by 1871.

While anglophone and francophone Catholics fought for control within the Ontario separate schools system, their counterparts in Manitoba were forced to cooperate to defend the right to have publicly supported separate schools at all. The Manitoba Act of 1870 and the Northwest Territories Act of 1875 provided for official bilingualism on the Prairies, but demography worked against such a policy. Although francophones were half the population of Manitoba in 1870, they represented only 11 000 of the 152 000 residents in 1891. Across the West, including British Columbia, only 4.6 percent of the population reported French as their mother tongue in 1901. The anti-French, anti-Catholic rhetoric of English Protestant settlers in the West and the ingrained image of the western lands as bleak and infertile, discouraged extensive Québécois migration to Canada's frontier.

In 1890, Thomas Greenway's Liberal government passed legislation to eliminate official bilingualism and the separate schools system guaranteed by the Manitoba Act. Following Manitoba's lead, the Northwest Territories in 1892 legislated an end to education in French after the third grade and removed French as an official language in legislative proceedings. The Roman Catholics of Manitoba (as well as the Anglicans who also ran their own schools) decided to challenge the validity of the schools legislation in the courts.

The Manitoba schools legislation became a national issue for those fighting the battle between Roman Catholic and Protestant ways of organizing education. When the Judicial Committee of the Privy Council in Britain ruled that Manitoba had acted legally, but that the federal government had the constitutional right to pass remedial legislation to restore public funding for denominational schools, the Conservatives were caught in a quandary. Should they offer assistance to the aggrieved minorities of Manitoba or insist that education remain a matter for provincial jurisdiction?

Macdonald enjoyed exercising federal authority over the provinces, but he died in 1891, leaving the decision to his successors. In 1896 the federal Conservatives included remedial legislation as part of their election platform. Since they lost the election, it was left to the new prime minister, Wilfrid Laurier, to negotiate a compromise acceptable to Liberals, who supported the principle of provincial rights. The Manitoba legislation was allowed to stand, but religious instruction and instruction in a language other than English (the French langauge was not specifically mentioned) were permitted in areas where the number of pupils warranted such practices.

## PROVINCIAL–DOMINION CONFLICT

As the foregoing discussion suggests, the defence of provincial interests emerged as a major feature of the Canadian federal system. Macdonald had hoped to create a strong federal state, with the provinces as subordinate political entities. Instead, he was faced with ambitious principalities that claimed powers equal and even superior to those of the federal government in areas under their jurisdiction. Macdonald made extensive use of the power of disallowance, which enabled the federal government to set aside provincial legislation, but the provinces challenged his actions in the courts. Much to Macdonald's dismay, the Judicial Committee of the Privy Council in Great Britain, which was the final court of appeal in cases relating to the interpretation of the British North America Act, often sustained the less centralized view of

Confederation favoured by the provinces.

The tension between Ottawa and the provinces was in part a natural result of the give and take of party politics. When Liberal parties were in office provincially it was easy for them to take the Conservative government in Ottawa to task. This was certainly true in the case of Ontario, where the Liberal Party held office from 1871 to 1905. But Ontario's battles with Ottawa involved more than partisan politics. At stake was the issue of who would dominate the new federation: the national government or the government of the province with nearly half the nation's population.

Oliver Mowat, premier of Ontario from 1872 to 1896, emerged as the undisputed champion of provincial rights in the generation following Confederation. A lawyer and former articling student in Macdonald's law firm, Mowat was an implacable foe of Macdonald's centralizing vision of Confederation. Mowat insisted that Confederation was an agreement among provinces and that the provinces retained the jurisdiction they held prior to Confederation except for specific responsibilities that they granted to the federal government. From this "provincial compact" point of view, there was no new "political nationality" formed in 1867. Such a reading of the constitution meant that the federal power to legislate for the "peace, order, and good government" of the nation should never intrude upon provincial jurisdiction in matters of a "local or private" nature.

Mowat believed that the federal government's frequent disallowances of provincial legislation amounted to unconstitutional interference in Ontario's sovereign areas of authority. He also resented Macdonald's favouritism towards provinces that supported Conservative administrations. When Macdonald attempted to have Ontario's boundaries restricted by placing territories north and west of Lake Superior within the province of Manitoba, Mowat challenged the decision in the courts and argued the case before the

Privy Council in London. Only after several judicial decisions upholding Ontario's claim did Macdonald agree in 1889 to concede the boundary that Ontario demanded.

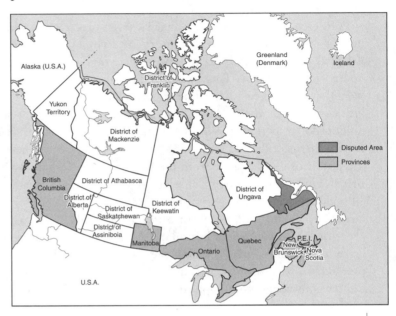

**Map 2.1** *Canada, 1898.*

## THE PREMIERS' CONFERENCE, 1887

The Ontario boundary dispute was in full swing when Quebec premier Honoré Mercier suggested to the other premiers that they meet to discuss matters of common interest. Not surprisingly, Mowat was enthusiastic about the idea. In the Maritimes, provincial governments were also open to constitutional change. They were having difficulty managing on their federal subsidies and were alarmed by the impact of federal economic policies on their regional economies. In May 1886, Liberal premier W.S. Fielding introduced a resolution in the Nova Scotia legislature calling for repeal of the British North America Act and establishment of a Maritime union. The Liberal premier of New Brunswick, A.G. Blair, was not prepared to go that far but he, like Fielding, was interested in cooperating with other premiers in a revision of the terms of Confederation. In Manitoba, economic growth encouraged plans for railways to the United States, but these were banned by the CPR's monopoly clause. John Norquay, Canada's first premier of Métis descent, was sued by the CPR and harassed by the federal government for his defiant approach to such matters. Although a Conservative, he, too, agreed to attend a conference of premiers.

In October 1887, five of Canada's seven premiers—the Conservative premiers of Prince Edward Island and British Columbia stayed home—met in Quebec City to demand changes in federal–provincial relations. The twenty-two resolutions passed by the premiers included calls for a million-dollar increase in subsidies to the provinces (which then stood at $3.2 million); the handing of the power of disallowance from the federal to the British government; provincial selection of half of all senators; provincial consent before local works could be placed under dominion control; and recognition of Ontario's boundary. Macdonald ignored the conference, accusing the four Liberal premiers of partisan mischief, but federal-provincial tensions would not disappear.

## THE NORTH ATLANTIC TRIANGLE

Canada had no Department of External Affairs until 1909. The self-governing dominions and crown colonies within the British Empire accepted British primacy in the international arena and had little desire to establish foreign policy at odds with British interests. Nonetheless, Canada's leaders expected to be consulted by the British government on diplomatic initiatives that affected the new nation's interests. In the discussions leading to the Treaty of Washington in 1871, and on several occasions thereafter, Britain included Canadian representatives on their negotiating teams. The issues at stake invariably involved Canadian-American economic relations.

Many of the problems between Canada and the United States revolved around fish. Fishing disputes grew out of the Anglo-American convention of 1818 that had excluded Americans from British North American inshore fisheries—defined as a three-mile limit from shore—and from access to the harbours, bays, and creeks of British North America except for shelter, repairs, and supplies of

wood and water. During the periods in which the Reciprocity Treaty (1854–66) and Washington Treaty (1871–83) prevailed, the Americans had free access to the inshore fisheries, but thereafter American access again became a point of contention. When the terms of the Treaty of Washington came to an end, Americans showed little interest in coming to the bargaining table, with the result that Canada began enforcing measures to protect its fisheries. In 1886, nearly seven hundred vessels were boarded, and some of them were seized for violations; the number doubled the following year. The Americans threatened to retaliate by cutting off all commercial relations with Canada if satisfactory redress for the seizures was not forthcoming.

In 1887, a British–American Joint High Commission was established to deal with the problem. Canada was invited by Britain to name a representative to the British delegation. Although Canada's delegate, Sir Charles Tupper, was eager to secure Canadian access to the American market for fish and, if possible, a larger reciprocity agreement, he ran into a brick wall of American resistance. Again there would be no reciprocity treaty. Even the limited arrangement negotiated by the British delegation, which gave Canadians free access to the American market for fresh fish, was rejected by the American Senate. Americans paid a licence fee for access to Canadian ports, and Canadian fishermen were left high and dry.

Canada fared better with regard to its sealing industry in the North Pacific. After buying Alaska from the Russians in 1867, the Americans claimed exclusive rights to the Bering Sea. The United States leased sealing rights off the Pribilof Islands in the Bering Sea to the North American Commercial Company, which was enraged when British Columbia interests also began sealing in the region. The Americans charged that indiscriminate sealing was destroying the seal herd and seized Canadian vessels. Britain, which had not recognized Russian claims in the area, countered that the North American Commercial Company was the major perpetrator of the slaughter. In the face of a stand-off, the two sides agreed to an arbitration panel, which met in Paris in 1893, and decided largely in Britain's favour. The slaughter of the seals could continue, with all sides participating until a moratorium on sealing in the Bering Sea was imposed in 1911.

## CANADA IN QUESTION

Notwithstanding the protectionist sentiment in the United States, the Liberals, under their new leader Edward Blake, still clung to their free trade agenda. It did little to enhance their popularity with voters in the 1882 election, which Macdonald, trumpeting the virtues of the National Policy, won handily in every province except Ontario. In Quebec, Blake's principled Protestantism was rewarded with only seven of the province's seventy-five seats.

Blake and Macdonald battled it out on the same issues in 1887 and again Macdonald won a majority, but this time the Quebec voters split almost evenly between Liberals and Conservatives. Macdonald hoped that he could go on beating Blake every four or five years, but it was not to be. With francophones now willing to vote for Liberals like Honoré Mercier, it was only a matter of time before the Liberal Party turned to Quebec to find a leader. Their choice was Wilfrid Laurier, who assumed leadership of the federal Liberal Party in June 1887. Within a decade, he had reshaped it into an election-winning machine, but he had to deal with the free trade issue first.

The idea of closer trade relations with the United States was popular with many Liberal Party supporters. Among party radicals, there was even support for commercial union, a policy that would harmonize the tariff structures of the two North American nations as well as open the border to trade in natural and manufactured products. Those who championed the National Policy pointed out that such a union would compromise Canada's ability to determine its own economic policy, but primary producers considered such concerns to be irrelevant. In 1887, the Conservatives tried to spike the Liberal guns by securing a limited trade agreement with the United States, but the Americans were moving in a more protectionist direction for reasons that had little to do with Canadian inter-

ests. When the United States introduced the McKinley Tariff in 1890, the latest in a series of tariff hikes, Macdonald's hopes for a reciprocity treaty were completely dashed.

Opposition to reciprocity usually rested on economic arguments, but emotional issues also entered the debate. Among many Canadians, there was a lingering fear that overly close commercial ties with the United States would weaken economic and cultural relations with Great Britain. Even Canadians who were not of British origin recognized that the British connection and the institutions it represented were one of the main pillars of the Canadian identity. They argued that any policy threatening Canada's ties to the world's greatest empire should be avoided since British power and prestige gave Canada a higher international profile than its population and wealth warranted.

Imperial sentiment was on the rise in the late nineteenth century. During the 1880s, many Canadian communities were celebrating the centenary of their Loyalist origins, while in Great Britain there was support for strengthening the bonds of empire. Imperial enthusiasts established the Imperial Federation League in 1884 and called for a conference to take place in 1887 on the occasion of Queen Victoria's Golden Jubilee. Thereafter imperial conferences were held periodically in London. Canadians, representing the senior dominion in the empire, usually played a leading role in their deliberations. Although imperialists disagreed among themselves about what form closer imperial ties should take, most discussion centred around a common imperial tariff, colonial representation in an imperial parliament, and cooperation in imperial defence.

During the 1891 election, a scandal erupted that seemed to confirm the fact that there was a conspiracy between members of the Liberal Party and American business interests to sever Canada's ties with Great Britain. The Conservative Party secured a copy of a private pamphlet written by Edward Farrer, editor of the *Globe*, which suggested ways of pressuring Canada into union with its southern neighbour. The Conservatives used this seemingly clear evidence of treason to help them win the election, but they could not stop people from voting with their feet and moving to the United States.

During the 1891 election, the very future of the nation seemed to be at stake. Should Canadians seek closer ties with the United States or, failing that, with Great Britain? Perhaps they should dissolve their unwieldy federation and go it alone as separate dominions within the British Empire, as Newfoundland had done. Or was there something to be said for staying the course? A few visionaries saw Canada's future as that of an independent nation such as those emerging in Europe and Latin America, but they were a definite minority in the late nineteenth century.

In this, his last election, Macdonald offered no new remedies for his divided country. The Conservative slogan in the campaign—"The Old Man, The Old Flag and the Old Policy"—said it all. With Macdonald at the helm, the British flag as their inspiration, and the tariff as their crowning achievement, the Conservatives squeaked through. The Liberals boldly declared their support for "unrestricted reciprocity." Such a position, which retreated from the idea of commercial union, appealed to the radical wing of the party, but made many Liberals—and many Canadians—extremely nervous. It failed, however, to deter francophones in Quebec, who, for the first time since the Pacific Scandal, elected Liberals in a majority of their constituencies.

As Macdonald lay on his deathbed in June 1891, he must have wondered what manner of political entity he had helped to shape. Canadians were still at odds with each other, and there were few signposts offering a clear direction for the future. Even the party he had worked so hard to build was in disarray. Following his death, it broke into squabbling factions and had four leaders— John Abbott, John Thompson, Mackenzie Bowell, and Charles Tupper—in five years.

## LAURIER LIBERALISM

Canadians voted for the Liberals in 1896 for a variety of reasons. Laurier's success in improving the party's organization was one of them. Another was the party's retreat in 1893 from its rigid free-trade philosophy, which was increasingly alienating voters in Ontario, where the tariff was credited with much of the province's recent economic growth. Laurier's talent for political management and his sensitivity to provincial aspirations no doubt helped as well. These qualities were evident in the formation of his first cabinet. In it he included powerful local chieftains—W.S. Fielding of Nova Scotia, Oliver Mowat of Ontario, and A.G. Blair of New Brunswick—and rising newcomers like Clifford Sifton of Manitoba, who in 1897 became minister of the interior, responsible for development of the West.

Laurier's government survived three more elections and marked a high point in Canadian national development: industries flourished, immigrants flocked to the West, and two more transcontinental railways were built. Indeed, national policy seemed to change little as the reins of government passed from the Conservatives to the Liberals. Canada, however, changed dramatically during Laurier's term in office.

Trained as a lawyer, Laurier joined the Parti rouge as a young man and edited a newspaper, *Le Défricheur*, in the Eastern Townships of Quebec. He was among those who opposed Confederation, but, after serving a term in the Quebec legislature (1871–74), he decided to run federally in 1874. For a short time, he was minister of inland revenue in the Mackenzie cabinet. A stout defender of political liberalism and Canadian unity, he was Edward Blake's choice as party leader and was chosen over the objections of several prominent Liberals. His opposition to the *programmistes* earned him few friends among ultramontanists in Quebec, but such views made him acceptable to the majority of English Protestants, who admired his courage in standing up to conservative forces in his province. Like Macdonald, Laurier had the personality for politics. He developed into a skilful and practical politician who sought compromise among the discordant groups in Canada battling for ascendancy.

Laurier's willingness to compromise was reflected in the tariff policy developed early in his adminstration. In 1897 his finance minister, W.S. Fielding, introduced the so-called British preference that applied lower tariffs to any country admitting Canadian products on a preferential basis. Since Great Britain had a policy of global free trade, it was automatically granted tariff preference. This policy pleased those with imperialist leanings and did little to hurt Canadian manufacturers whose main competition came from the United States.

It was fortunate for the Liberals that they came to office just as international economic conditions were on the upswing and when most of the farmland on the American frontier had been taken up. Under the supervision of Clifford Sifton, immigration was vigorously pursued, and the results were spectacular. Over two million people came to Canada between 1896 and 1911, many of them settling in the four western provinces. In 1905, the Laurier government created two new provinces—Alberta and Saskatchewan—out of the Northwest Territories. Laurier invited Liberals to form the government in both new provinces, giving his party a substantial patronage advantage over the rival Conservatives. He also created a continuing source of federal–provincial friction in deciding, as Macdonald had in the case of Manitoba, to keep public lands and natural resources under federal control.

Encouraged by what seemed to be unending growth, Laurier decided to assist the eastern-based Grand Trunk and the western-based Canadian Northern railway companies to complete transcontinental lines. The vast sums of taxpayers' money invested in the projects meant that they, like the CPR, encouraged extravagance and political cor-

ruption. Unlike the CPR, the two new railways failed to make a profit and continued to be a drain on the federal budget long after Laurier had departed the scene.

Coinciding with Laurier's success at the polls

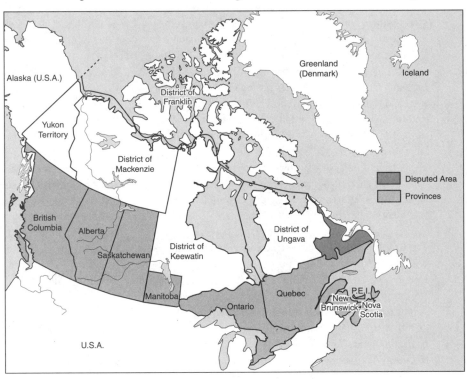

**Map 2.2** *Canada, 1905.*

was the discovery of gold in the Klondike in 1896. Within two years, the lure of instant wealth brought forty thousand people to the Yukon and transformed Dawson from a tiny fur-trading post into Western Canada's second largest city. Within another two years, a railway connected the Yukon with Skagway on the Pacific coast, and the Yukon Territories had been carved out of the Northwest Territories as a separate area of jurisdiction under the federal government. Like other territorial governments, the Yukon was originally governed by a commissioner and appointed officials, backed by the NWMP. Elected officials were gradually added to the council. By the early twentieth century, individual prospectors were giving way to international corporations, and Canada's wild and woolly northern frontier settled down to a more mundane existence.

## RAILROADING CANADA

Donald Mackenzie, from Kirkland Lake, Ontario, began his career as a subcontractor for the CPR and then made his fortune by investing in street railways and other utilities in Canada's burgeoning cities. In 1895 he teamed up with Donald Mann, another CPR subcontractor, to build a railway to Hudson Bay. This project failed to materialize, but the two men began buying short rail lines in Manitoba and soon had the basis for a second transcontinental railway. With bond guarantees and land grants from the Manitoba government, they marketed $14 million of securities for their Canadian Northern Railway in London and New York. Neither promoter put up any of his own money: one-third of the capital was guaranteed by governments at various levels, while Mackenzie's Toronto associate, George Cox, added the financial muscle of the Bank of Commerce.

The Grand Trunk Railway, whose conservative London-based directors saw their future survival dependent on tapping the booming West, tried to buy the Canadian Northern, but negotiations for a merger of the two companies failed. Under their new American general manager, Charles M. Hayes, the Grand Trunk embarked on a project to build its own new railway, incorporated as the National Transcontinental. Both companies would demand and get land grants, subsidies, and loan guarantees from the Laurier government. When Quebec and the Maritimes laid on pressure, the federal government even agreed to build the Grand Trunk's Eastern Division from Moncton to Winnipeg and lease it to the company. Not to be outdone, Mackenzie and Mann knit together eastern lines to establish their claim to an Atlantic terminus.

Extravagance, greed, and patronage dogged the two ventures. When a royal commission was struck by the Borden government in 1911 to look into the skyrocketing costs of the Eastern Division, it was discovered that the project cost $70 million (out of $160 million) more than it should have. Nevertheless, the two companies pressed forward with construction, floating new security issues in London and demanding more subsidies and loan guarantees from Ottawa. Hayes was planning even grander schemes when he died in the sinking of the **Titanic** in 1912. Mackenzie and Mann continued to expand their railroad empire, but their days were numbered. European investors were beginning to have second thoughts about investing in Canadian railways, and the outbreak of the First World War closed European financial markets completely. Faced with bankruptcy, Mackenzie and Mann were forced to let their railway empire be amalgamated with other government-owned railways into the Canadian National Railway system, which was created in a series of mergers between 1917 and 1923.

## PROVINCIAL RIGHTS AND THE MANAGEMENT OF PROGRESS

While prosperity helped to cover up the cracks in Confederation, it did not stop the growing regional disparity that increasingly defined the country. Nor did it stop the provinces from demanding that Ottawa pursue their interests, whether or not they conflicted with national policies.

Throughout the West, a political storm was brewing over the high tariffs that favoured eastern manufacturers and that forced farmers to pay higher prices for their agricultural machinery and supplies. People in the Prairie provinces also resented the fact that Ottawa retained control over their natural resources. After 1905, Manitoba became insistent that its northern boundary be pushed to the 60th parallel to give it a territorial base equal to the new western provinces. Westerners also wanted a railway to a Hudson Bay port to provide an alternative route to export markets. In British Columbia, the white majority were alarmed by the growing number of Asians arriving on their shores and insisted that Ottawa restrict Asian immigration.

In the Maritimes, regional resentment flourished as all three provinces fell behind the rest of the nation in economic growth. The expansion of industries related to coal and steel in the first decade of the twentieth century masked some of the deep structural problems facing the region's economy, but no one could deny that the Maritimes generally were losing power within Confederation. In 1867, the region had held over

*The Yukon gold rush drew many people into the Canadian North, but few became permanent residents.*
*One person who stayed was Martha Munger, who married George Black and in 1935 became the second woman*
*to hold a seat in the Canadian House of Commons.*

M.L. Black Collectionl/Yukon Archives

20 percent of the seats in the House of Commons; by 1914, its representation had dropped to 13 percent. Declining representation made it difficult for the Maritime region to shape national policies to meet its needs or to exert influence in federal–provincial conferences.

Like Macdonald, Laurier built his success on support in Canada's two largest provinces. Yet, Laurier could not count on Ontario to keep him in office. The province's seats split evenly between Conservatives and Liberals in 1896, but thereafter the Conservatives won a majority of Ontario's seats in federal elections. In 1905, James Whitney's Conservatives put an end to the thirty-four-year reign of the Liberals in Ontario's provincial government. Holding more than a third of the seats in the House of Commons, Ontario wielded considerable influence in the corridors of power and caused Laurier as many problems as the other provinces put together. The strength of the province's industrial interests threatened the delicate balance between regional and national interests, while growing imperial sentiment within Ontario's overwhelmingly anglophone population continued to clash with nationalist sentiment in Quebec.

Laurier won large majorities in Quebec throughout his political career, but the nationalist movement remained an on-going threat to his francophone support. Henri Bourassa, the grandson of Louis-Joseph Papineau—the *patriote* leader in the Rebellion of 1837–38—emerged as the new leader of the nationalist cause. Although he was widely respected in his native province, Bourassa's vision of a bilingual and bicultural Canada put him at odds with some nationalists who felt that Quebec should pursue a destiny independent from the rest of Canada. Bourassa concentrated on influencing public opinion and existing parties rather than forming a new organization to promote his policies. Founded in 1910, his newspaper, *Le Devoir*, emerged as a major force in developing public opinion in Quebec.

## IMPERIALISM, NATIONALISM, AND RECIPROCITY

The growing rivalry between Germany and Great Britain for imperial and industrial ascendency

*A one-time protégé of Laurier (right), Bourassa (above) resigned from his seat in the House of Commons over Liberal policy on the South African War. He returned to Parliament as an independent in 1900 and soon emerged as the intellectual and moral leader of French-Canadian nationalism.*

National Archives of Canada/A-119 and C27360

in the conflict, which had nothing to do with Canada's interests. French Canadians, rather than seeing imperialism as another form of Canadian nationalism, identified with the Boers, who were fleeing the clutches of an aggressive world empire.

True to form, Laurier offered a compromise: Ottawa would equip and raise volunteers, but once in South Africa they would be paid by the British. On the grounds that the effort would cost Canada little financially, he refused to debate the issue in the Commons. More than seven thousand Canadians eventually saw service in the so-called Boer War. Laurier's compromise pleased neither side: it lost him the support of Henri Bourassa, who resigned from the House of Commons in 1899 to protest the Liberal Party's policy on the war; at the same time, it did little to improve his image among the jingoistic imperialists.

Laurier's refusal to give more assistance to the British war effort encouraged a number of private initiatives. Donald Smith, raised to the British peerage as Lord Strathcona, funded an entire contingent. In Montreal, Margaret Polson Murray launched a patriotic organization of women, the Imperial Order Daughters of the Empire (IODE), to support empire unity and assist in the war effort. Its motto, "One flag, one throne, one country," appealed to many women who identified Canada's interests with those of Great Britain, and branches of the IODE sprang up across the country. The enormous interest that the war sparked on the home front also inspired the establishment of a Patriotic Fund, a Canadian branch of the Soldiers' Wives League, and a Canadian Memorial Association. This latter organization was dedicated to marking the graves of the 244 Canadian fatalities and to erecting monuments to the men who fought

inevitably created problems in Canada. When Britain declared war against Dutch settlers—called Boers—in South Africa in 1899, many anglophone Canadians felt it was their war too. Laurier faced enormous pressures to send a Canadian contingent to South Africa, not only from imperialist-minded English Canadians, but also from the commander of the Canadian militia and the British Colonial Secretary. In sharp contrast, Bourassa and other French-Canadian nationalists in Laurier's party were determined that Canada not be involved in South Africa.

The South African War increased tensions between English and French Canadians, especially in Montreal, where both anglophone imperialists and francophone nationalists lived in close proximity. On 5 March 1900, a group of McGill University students, celebrating the liberation of the South African town of Ladysmith from the Boers, attacked the offices of two French-language newspapers and then paraded to the Montreal campus of Laval University (now the University of Montreal) where they tried to provoke the French students into retaliatory action. The following day, the Laval students held a peaceful demonstration to protest the behaviour of the McGill students, which, in turn, provoked a crowd of English-speaking students and townspeople, armed with sticks, clubs, and frozen potatoes, to march on Laval University. The mob was dispersed by police with water hoses, but the militia had to be called out to preserve public order in the ethnically divided city.

For those fighting in South Africa, the glamour of warfare quickly wore off. The Boers inflicted humiliating defeats on British forces in the first few weeks of the war, and when the empire finally threw enough troops into the field to win formal engagements, the Boers refused to surrender. Instead, they resorted to guerrilla warfare, which prolonged the war for two years. Most of the Canadian casualties were a result of the diseases that ravaged the military camps rather than of the shooting skills of the Boers.

Following the war, Laurier was determined to find a middle ground between subordination to imperial authorities and total independence, but the task proved difficult. Canada still needed British support in negotiating with the Americans, who, like the British, seemed to be entering another expansionary phase. In 1898, the Americans had trounced the Spanish in a nasty little war over

*In 1899, Minnie Affleck was one of four Canadian nurses who went with the First Contingent to South Africa. In 1901, the Canadian Army Nursing Service was established as part of the Army Medical Corps, making nurses the first women to officially serve in the Canadian army.*

National Archives of Canada/C51799

Cuba and then went on to take Puerto Rico, Guam, and the Philippines from the humiliated Spaniards. Would they use the same tactics with Canada?

The disputed boundary between Alaska and the Yukon seemed to be the testing ground. With the discovery of gold in the Klondike, the width of the Alaska Panhandle suddenly became important for determining who owned the ports through which people and goods entered the fabled gold fields. Canada's dependence on Britain in foreign affairs was reflected in the makeup of an international judicial tribunal to decide the issue in 1903. The two Canadian delegates on the three-man British negotiating team found an uncertain ally in the British appointee, Lord Alverstone. In their negotiations with three American commissioners, all loyal appointees of President Theodore Roosevelt, Alverstone sided with the United States, demonstrating, at least in the minds of many Canadians, that Anglo-American friendship was more important to Britain than were good relations with its senior dominion. The boundary decision sparked anti-British outbursts and strengthened an autonomous nationalism among many Canadians.

As a result of the meddling of British officers in Canada's affairs during the South African War, and the bad feelings lingering from the Alaska boundary decision, the Laurier government insisted in 1904 that the officer commanding the Canadian militia be appointed by Canada rather than by Britain. Canada theoretically also assumed greater responsibility for its own defence when Britain, in 1906, withdrew its troops from Halifax and Esquimalt, the last two British bases in Canada. Given the escalating Anglo-German naval rivalry,

*During the 1911 election campaign, companies opposed to free trade bought advertising space in their local newspapers to promote their anti-free trade position. This cartoon was drawn by Donald McRitchie, who had previously published much of his work in the* **Eye Opener**, *a Calgary-based journal.*

The Gazette (Montreal), 22 and 23 September 1911

and Canada's reliance on Britain for naval protection, what should Canadians do? Was the dominion to make a direct financial contribution to the British Admiralty or should it establish its own navy?

Laurier's genius for compromise again surfaced. His Naval Service Bill, introduced in 1910, proposed a Canadian navy that, in times of war, could be placed under imperial control. There would be no direct contribution to the British Admiralty. United in their disdain for Laurier's "tinpot navy," the Conservatives were nevertheless deeply divided between an English-Canadian majority demanding a direct contribution, and a small band of French Canadians who opposed both a contribution to Britain and a separate Canadian navy.

Laurier was in political difficulty as the 1911 election neared, but a timely economic initiative by the Americans seemed to provide an issue to unite the country and defeat the prime minister's enemies. Under President William Howard Taft, the Americans proposed a comprehensive trade agreement that allowed the free entry of a wide range of natural products and set lower rates on a number of manufactured goods, including agricultural implements so dear to the hearts of Canadian farmers. Here, it seemed, was the solution to agrarian grievances and a means of satisfying those who had long worked for closer trade relations between Canada and the United States.

## THE 1911 ELECTION AND THE CONSERVATIVE AGENDA

At first glance, the phlegmatic Robert Laird Borden, federal Conservative leader since 1901, was not the man to challenge the charismatic Laurier. Yet this respectable Halifax lawyer had managed to rebuild a party shattered by the divisions of the 1890s. His Halifax Platform of 1907 included endorsement of progressive policies such as free rural mail delivery, civil service reform, and federal aid to technical education. By 1911, the Conservatives were also backed by effective local organizations. Conservative spirits were raised further still by the defection of two key interest groups from the Liberal fold. Enraged by the prospect of reciprocity, eighteen prominent Toronto business-men and financiers, along with long-time Liberal allies such as the Canadian Manufacturers Association, deserted the party they had formerly supported so generously. Together with dissident Liberal MPs like Clifford Sifton, they denounced reciprocity as a threat to Canadian survival, a step towards absorption by the United States, and a threat to the dominion's manufacturing interests. Laurier's Quebec stronghold also crumbled as Bourassa's nationalists, damning the naval policy as a sell-out to English Canada, found common cause with Quebec francophone Conservatives.

The federal election of 1911 was preceded by months of heated debate and pamphleteering. Reciprocity and the naval policy, the two issues that more than any other posed the question of Canada's future, combined with the usual appeal of patronage, local issues, and individual candidates to defeat the Liberals. Although the popular vote was close, the distribution of seats was decisive. The Liberals won only 13 of Ontario's 86 constituencies and altogether won only 87 ridings; the Conservatives took 134 seats, including 27 in Quebec, where the alliance with nationalists boost-ed Conservative fortunes. Neither Laurier's liberalism nor his efforts to steer a middle course between differing visions of Canada proved sufficient to the problems of the day.

## CONCLUSION

Despite the difficulties, Canada survived the challenges to its existence in the years immediately following Confederation and, by the twentieth century, seemed to be doing very well in the race for economic success. Not everyone took courage from this achievement. Aboriginal peoples would see the early decades of Confederation as ones of defeat and marginalization, while the outlying regions of West and East still wondered about their place in a Canadian firmament dominated by Ontario and Quebec. Even in Central Canada, religious and cultural differences focusing on school and language policy made some people feel that imperial federation, annexation, or provincial independence were happier alternatives to being yoked in a federation where every national policy was ringed with compromise and bitterness. Moreover, the rapid economic growth that Canada's leaders had sought and at last seemed to have achieved, brought with it a host of new problems to bedevil the nation. It is to this growth and its consequences for Canadians that we now turn.

## THE MÉTIS MIGRATIONS

### A Historiographical Debate

In the decade and a half following the 1869 Métis rebellion, about 40 percent of the Red River mixed-bloods moved further west, either joining existing Métis communities in the Northwest or founding new ones. The migrants, many of whom had figured among the rebels of 1869, played key roles in the 1885 rebellion as well. Why did they move and why did they join in a second rebellion against Canadian authority?

For most historians before the 1970s, there was a simple answer. The Métis were "savages" or "half-savages" and were uninterested in becoming part of the new agriculture-based European society that Ontario immigrants were establishing in Red River. They wanted to hunt, not farm, and moved to areas where agricultural settlement had yet to be established. Disillusioned when their nomadic lifestyles came once again under attack from agricultural settlers, they engaged in a futile rebellion in 1885. From this perspective, the "pull" of a promised "primitive" life further west explained the Métis migration.

In the 1980s, several historians suggested that "push" factors were more important than the lure of a pre-agricultural existence. Douglas Sprague, using archival evidence of government thinking in the 1870s and 1880s, accused governments of having dispossessed the Métis and provoked them into leaving Red River. He outlined a variety of stratagems that governments used deliberately to deprive the Métis of lands promised to them in 1870. Stalling was the major tactic. From 1870 to 1873, the Macdonald Conservatives ignored their promise to grant lands to the Métis, while the subsequent Mackenzie Liberal administration placed innumerable judicial roadblocks in the way of Métis who attempted to get title to land. The mistreatment of the Métis, to which both the federal and Manitoba governments turned a blind eye, caused many Métis to give up in frustration and move further west, abandoning or selling land claims in Manitoba. As settlement and the railway again began to stretch into their new territories, at the same time that the buffalo disappeared, the Métis demanded guarantees of land from the Canadian government. The government made a pretence of dealing with these demands, but its previous duplicity in Manitoba and continuing inaction in the Northwest Territories provoked a violent Métis reaction.[8]

The dispossession thesis has been disputed by several scholars of the Métis, particularly political scientist Thomas Flanagan and historian Gerhard Ens. Flanagan has provided evidence to bolster the older view that the Métis did not want to farm. This, rather than government delays, official hostility, or mistreatment by European settlers, persuaded them to move west. He also argues that delays both in the Manitoba and Northwest land settlements resulted from disagreements and misunderstandings between the Métis and the federal government and not from deliberate stalling by the latter.[9]

Ens, while suggesting that the hostility of racist Ontario settlers in Manitoba did exert some influence on Métis decisions to migrate, argues that this was not their major concern. Instead, he suggests that the desire to participate in the flourishing trade of buffalo robes with American merchants informed the Métis decision to migrate. Ens uses censuses of the population of the older, established communities in Red River at different periods to demonstrate that the move west had begun before the rebellion, as buffalo hunters came to terms with declining numbers of buffalo in the Red River region. He infers that many Métis, though once "peasants" content to eke out a living from small-scale farming and from hunting, had become consumers on the European model. Buffalo robes could be traded for consumer goods.[10]

Sprague has countered Ens's data, suggesting that many of the alleged migrants of the pre-1870 period only migrated to newer communities within the Red River colony. The overall population of the colony increased rapidly until 1870, only beginning a steep decline after 1875 when it had become clear that the governments of Canada and Manitoba intended to dispossess the Métis.[11]

Diane Payment takes issue with Ens's suggestion that the migrants to the territories were in search of buffalo robes and in retreat from a subsistence agriculture/hunting economy. Her careful study of the evolution of the large Métis community of Batoche emphasizes that the Métis sought a settled, not a nomadic, life. They built stores, schools, and churches, and started farms. Though they also hunted buffalo, the robe trade was not the central feature of their lives. Payment concludes that the "push" factors, both the racism of the Manitoba settlers and the broken promises of governments regarding land, caused the Métis to migrate, since they established new communities much like those they left behind rather than becoming nomadic free spirits.[12]

Payment has also raised some questions about the tendency of most historians of the Métis to leave gender out of the equation in their studies of Métis migrations, rebellions, and life in general. Ens and Flanagan largely ignore Métis women and often appear to speak of the "Métis family" as if its only real decision makers were men. Payment observes the important role of women in establishing the institutions of Batoche. Métis women were generally more devout than their menfolk and more committed to establishing a sedentary lifestyle for themselves and their children. Payment argues that women's networks played an important role in migration from Red River to Batoche. She notes: "Over half of the approximately 500 inhabitants of Batoche in 1883 were women. The general resettlement pattern was by extended families; grandparents, parents, brothers, sisters, cousins, and cross-cousins but closer analysis reveals a particularly strong female kinship tie."[13]

The debate about the Métis migration patterns is far from purely academic. It has become entangled in Métis land claims. The Manitoba Métis Federation hired Professor Sprague to make its case that the federal government has failed to fulfil its 1870 promises, while the federal Department of Justice contracted with both Flanagan and Ens to help prepare its case against the Métis claims.

## NOTES

[1] Alexander Morris, *The Treaties of Canada with the Indians of Manitoba and the North-West Territories* (Toronto: Belfords Clarke, 1880; reprinted Coles, 1971), 28

[2] Quoted in Manitoba Indian Brotherhood, *Treaty Days: Centennial Commemorations Historical Pageant* (Winnipeg: Manitoba Indian Brotherhood, 1971), 24

[3] Cited in James Hiller, "Confederation Defeated: The Newfoundland Election of 1869" in *Newfoundland in the Nineteenth and Twentieth Centuries: Essays in Interpretation*, ed. James Hiller and Peter Neary (Toronto: University of Toronto Press, 1980), 74

[4] Cited in P.B. Waite, *Canada, 1874–1896: Arduous Destiny* (Toronto: McClelland and Stewart, 1971), 35

[5] Cited in Shelagh D. Grant, *Sovereignty or Security: Government Policy in the Canadian North, 1936–1950* (Vancouver: UBC Press, 1988), 5

[6] Gerald Friesen, *The Canadian Prairies: A History* (Toronto: University of Toronto Press, 1984), 129

[7] Bill of Rights, 13 April 1885, Provincial Archives of Alberta

[8] D.N. Sprague, *Canada and the Métis, 1869-1885* (Waterloo: Wilfrid Laurier University Press, 1988)

[9] Thomas Flanagan, *Riel and the Rebellion: 1885 Reconsidered* (Saskatoon: Western Producer Prairie Books, 1983)

[10] Gerhard J. Ens, *Homeland to Hinterland: The Changing Worlds of the Red River Métis in the Nineteenth Century* (Toronto: University of Toronto Press, 1996)

[11] D.N. Sprague, "Dispossession vs. Accommodation in Plaintiff vs. Defendant Accounts of Métis Dispersal from Manitoba, 1870-1881," *Prairie Forum* 16, 2 (Fall 1991): 137-56

[12] Diane Payment, *"The Free People—Otipemisiwak" Batoche, Saskatchewan, 1870-1930* (Ottawa: National Historic Parks and Sites, 1990)

[13] Diane Payment, "'La Vie en Rose?' Métis Women at Batoche, 1870-1920," in *Women of the First Nation: Power, Wisdom and Strength*, ed. Patricia Chuchryk et al. (Winnipeg: University of Manitoba Press, 1995), 20

## SELECTED READING

There is an extensive literature on Canada in the years immediately following Confederation. The standard surveys include W.L. Morton, *The Critical Years: The Union of British North America, 1857–1873* (Toronto: McClelland and Stewart, 1964); P.B. Waite, *Canada, 1874–1896: Arduous Destiny* (Toronto: McClelland and Stewart, 1971); and R.C. Brown and Ramsay Cook, *Canada, 1896–1921: A Nation Transformed* (Toronto: McClelland and Stewart, 1974). The provincial perspective is covered in Kenneth G. Pryke, *Nova Scotia and Confederation, 1864–1874* (Toronto: University of Toronto Press, 1979); Alfred G. Bailey, "The Basis and Persistence of Opposition to Confederation in New Brunswick," *Canadian Historical Review* 23, 4 (Dec. 1942): 374–97; Ian Ross Robertson, "Political Realignment in Pre-Confederation Prince Edward Island," *Acadiensis* 15, 1 (Autumn 1985): 35–58; F.W.P. Bolger, *Prince Edward Island Confederation, 1863- 1973* (Charlottetown: St Dunston's University Press, 1964); David Weale and Harry Baglole, *The Island and Confederation: The End of an Era* (Charlottetown: Ragweed, 1973); James Hiller, "Confederation Defeated: The Newfoundland Election of 1869" in *Newfoundland in the Nineteenth and Twentieth Centuries: Essays in Interpretation*, ed. James Hiller and Peter Neary, (Toronto: University of Toronto Press, 1980), 67–94; Arthur I. Silver, *The French-Canadian Idea of Confederation, 1864–1900* (Toronto: University of Toronto Press, 1982); Christopher Armstrong, *The Politics of Federalism: Ontario's Relations with the Federal Government, 1867–1942* (Toronto: University of Toronto Press, 1981); and H.V. Nelles, *The Politics of Development* (Toronto: Macmillan, 1974).

In addition to the works listed in chapter 1, regional and provincial surveys that cover this period include Margaret Ormsby, *British Columbia: A History* (Toronto: Macmillan, 1971); Morris Zaslow, *The Opening of the Canadian North, 1870–1914* (Toronto: McClelland and Stewart, 1971); W.L. Morton, *Manitoba: A History* (Toronto: University of Toronto Press, 1957); Lewis H. Thomas, *The Struggle for Responsible Government in the North-West Territories, 1870–97* (Toronto: University of Toronto Press, 1978); Joseph Schull, *Ontario Since 1867* (Toronto: McClelland and Stewart, 1978); Susan Mann Trofimenkoff, *The Dream of Nation: A Social and Intellectual History of Quebec* (Toronto: Gage, 1983); E.R. Forbes and D.A. Muise, eds. *The Atlantic Provinces in Confederation* (Toronto and Fredericton: University of Toronto Press and Acadiensis Press, 1993); J. Murray Beck, *Politics of Nova Scotia*, 2 vols. (Tantallon, NS: Four East Publications, 1985–88); S.J.R. Noel, *Politics of Newfoundland* (Toronto: University of Toronto Press, 1971); Ken S. Coates; and William R. Morrison, *Land of the Midnight Sun: A History of the Yukon* (Edmonton: Hurtig, 1988).

There is a vast literature on the two Northwest rebellions including Gerhard J. Ens, *Homeland to Hinterland: The Changing Worlds of the Red River Métis in the Nineteeth Century* (Toronto: University of Toronto Press, 1996); D.N. Sprague, *Canada and the Métis, 1869–1885* (Waterloo: Wilfrid Laurier University Press, 1988); Joseph Kinsey Howard, *Strange Empire: A Narrative of the Northwest* (New York: William Morrow, 1952); Fritz Pannekoek, *A Snug Little Flock: The Social Origins of the Red River Resistance, 1869-70* (Winnipeg: Watson & Dywer, 1991) and two books by George Stanley: *The Birth of Western Canada: A History of the Riel Rebellions* (Toronto: University of Toronto Press, 1970) and *Louis Riel* (Toronto: McGraw-Hill Ryerson, 1963). The causes and events of the 1885 rebellion are detailed in the two Stanley works as well as Bob Beal and Rod MacLeod, *Prairie Fire: The Northwest Rebellion of 1885* (Edmonton: Hurtig, 1984). A qualified defence of Canadian government actions is found in Thomas Flanagan, *Riel and the Rebellion: 1885 Reconsidered* (Saskatoon: Western Producer Prairie Books, 1983). The military aspects of the rebellion are outlined in Desmond Morton, *The Last War Drum* (Toronto: Hakkert, 1972). Biographies of the major Métis protagonists of the 1885 rebellion include Stanley's *Louis Riel* and George Woodcock, *Gabriel Dumont: The Métis Chief and His Lost World* (Edmonton: Hurtig, 1975). Life for Native peoples in the West following the defeat of the rebellions is the subject of several essays in F.L. Barron and James B. Waldram, eds., *1885 and After: Native Society in Transition* (Regina: Canadian Plains Research Center, 1986). An important community study focusing on the Métis is Diane Payment, *Batoche, 1870–1910* (St Boniface: Les Éditions du Blé, 1983). The gendered discourse of the rebellion's opponents is discussed in Sarah A. Carter, "The Exploitation and Narration of the Captivity of Theresa Delaney and Theresa Gowanlock, 1885," in Catherine Cavanaugh and Jeremy Mouat, *Making Western Canada: Essays on European Colonization and Settlement* (Toronto: Garamond, 1996): 31-61.

On aboriginal issues, see Olive P. Dickason, *Canada's First Nations* (Toronto: McClelland and Stewart, 1992); Arthur J. Ray, *I Have Lived Here Since the World Began: An Illustrated History of Canada's Native People* (Toronto: Lester and Key Porter, 1996); Frank Tough, *"As Their Resources Fail": Native People and the Economic History of Northern Manitoba, 1870-1930* (Vancouver: University of British Columbia Press, 1996); J.R. Miller, *Skyscrapers Hide the Heavens: A History of Indian–White Relations in Canada* (Toronto: University of Toronto Press, 1989); Katherine Pettipas, *Severing the Ties that Bind: Government Repression of Indigenous Religious Ceremonies on the Prairies* (Winnipeg: University of Manitoba Press, 1994); Brian Titley, *A Narrow Vision: Duncan Campbell Scott and the Administration of Indian Affairs in Canada* (Vancouver: UBC Press, 1986); Sarah Carter, *Lost Harvests: Prairie Indian Reserve Farmers and Government Policy*

(Montreal: McGill-Queen's University Press, 1990); R.E. Cail, *Land, Man and Law: The Disposal of Crown Lands in British Columbia, 1871–1913* (Vancouver: UBC Press, 1974); Tina Loo, *Making Law, Order, and Authority in British Columbia, 1812–1871* (Toronto: University of Toronto Press, 1994). The North-West Mounted Police are discussed in R.C. McLeod, *The North-West Mounted Police and Law Enforcement, 1873-1905* (Toronto: University of Toronto Press, 1976); and Keith Walden, *Visions of Order: The Canadian Mounties in Symbol and Myth* (Toronto: Butterworths, 1982).

On the formation of political parties in Canada, see R. Kenneth Carty and W. Peter Ward, eds., *National Politics and Community in Canada* (Vancouver: UBC Press, 1986) and Gordon T. Stewart, *The Origins of Canadian Politics: A Comparative Approach* (Vancouver: University of British Columbia Press, 1986). Ideological debates are traced in Denis Monière, *Ideologies in Quebec: The Historical Development* (Toronto: University of Toronto Press, 1981); Douglas V. Verney, *Three Civilizations, Two Cultures, One State: Canada's Political Traditions* (Durham, NC: Duke University Press, 1986); and Carl Berger, *The Sense of Power: Studies in the Ideas of Canadian Imperialism* (Toronto: University of Toronto Press, 1970). On Canada's external relations see R.C. Brown, *Canada's National Policy, 1883–1900: A Study of American–Canadian Relations* (Princeton: Princeton University Press, 1964); Edelgard E. Mahant and Graeme S. Mount, *An Introduction to Canadian–American Relations* (Toronto: Methuen, 1984); J.L. Granstein and Norman Hillmer, *For Better or For Worse: Canada and the Unitied States to the 1990s* (Toronto: Copp, Clark, Pitman, 1991); and C.P. Stacey, *Canada and the Age of Conflict: A History of Canadian External Relations, Vol. I, 1867-1921* (Toronto: MacMillan, 1971). The South African War is extensively covered in Carman Miller, *Painting the Map Red: Canada and the South African War, 1899-1902* (Montreal: McGill-Queen's University Press, 1993).

General background on French–English and Protestant–Catholic conflict is provided in Ramsay Cook, *Provincial Autonomy, Minority Rights and the Compact Theory, 1867–1921* (Ottawa: Queen's Printer, 1969); Ramsay Cook, R. Craig Brown, and Carl Berger, eds., *Minorities, Schools and Politics* (Toronto: University of Toronto Press, 1969); H.B. Neatby, *Laurier and a Liberal Quebec: A Study in Political Management* (Toronto: McClelland and Stewart, 1973); Robert Choquette, *Language and Religion: A History of English–French Conflict in Ontario* (Ottawa: University of Ottawa Press, 1975); Richard Wilbur, *The Rise of French New Brunswick* (Halifax: Formac, 1989); Jean Daigle, ed., *Acadia of the Maritimes: Thematic Studies* (Moncton: Chaire d'études acadiennes, Université de Moncton, 1995); Sheila A. Andrew, *The Development of Elites in Acadian New Brunswick, 1861-1881* (Montreal and Kingston: McGill-Queen's University Press, 1996); Jacques Paul Couturier et Phyllis E. LeBlanc, dir., *Économie et société en Acadie, 1850-1950* (Moncton: Éditions d'Acadie, 1996); Robert Painchaud, "French-Canadian Historiography and Franco-Catholic Settlement in Western Canada, 1870–1915," *Canadian Historical Review* 59, 4 (Dec. 1978): 447–66; Paul Crunican, *Priests and Politicians: Manitoba Schools and the Election of 1896* (Toronto: University of Toronto Press, 1974); Kenneth Munro, "Official Bilingualism in Alberta," *Prairie Forum* 12, 1 (Spring 1987): 37–48; and Chad Gaffield, *Language, Schooling and Cultural Conflict: The Origins of the French-Language Controversy in Ontario* (Montreal: McGill-Queen's University Press, 1987).

Biographies of major national political figures include Donald Creighton, *Sir John A. Macdonald: The Old Chieftain* (Toronto: Macmillan, 1955); Dale C. Thompson, *Alexander Mackenzie: Clear Grit* (Toronto: Macmillan, 1960); Brian Young, *George-Étienne Cartier: Montreal Bourgeois* (Montreal: McGill-Queen's University Press, 1981); J. Murray Beck, *Joseph Howe*, vol. 2, *The Briton Becomes Canadian, 1848–1873* (Montreal: McGill-Queen's University Press, 1982); P.B. Waite, *The Man from Halifax: Sir John Thompson, Prime Minister* (Toronto: University of Toronto Press, 1985); and Joseph Schull, *Laurier: The First Canadian* (Toronto: Macmillan, 1965); Blair Neatby, *Laurier and a Liberal Quebec: A Study in Political Management* (Toronto: McClelland and Stewart, 1973); Real Bélanger, *Wilfrid Laurier: quand la politique devient passion* (Québec: Presses de l'Université Laval, 1986). See also Michael Bliss, *Right Honourable Men: The Descent of Canadian Politics from Macdonald to Mulroney* (Toronto, HarperCollins, 1995) and Marcel Hamelin, ed., *The Political Ideas of the Prime Ministers of Canada* (Ottawa: Éditions de l'Université d'Ottawa, 1969).

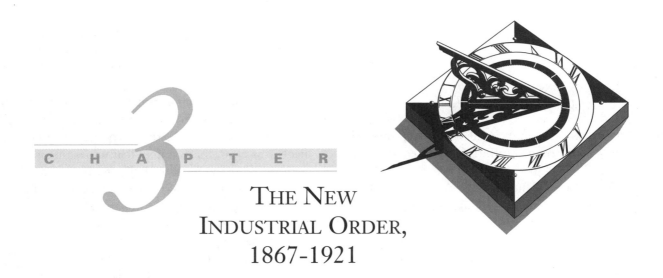

# THE NEW INDUSTRIAL ORDER, 1867-1921

E DWIGE ALLARD, A MONTREAL CARPENTER'S wife living in St Jacques ward, kept a one-acre garden that provided much of the food for her household of nine: herself, her husband, their six children, and Edwige's father-in-law. In 1871, she produced ten bushels of beans, ten bushels of potatoes, and four bushels of other root crops.[1] Families in some Montreal neighbourhoods also kept cows, pigs, and chickens in their backyards. By the twentieth century, it had become difficult for women in Canada's rapidly growing cities to contribute to the family economy through their farming activity: only the wealthy could afford a home with enough land for a garden, while municipal by-laws made it illegal to keep animals in urban spaces. Where once a woman could contribute to the family economy by raising animals, making butter, or selling eggs and vegetables, now her options were limited to sharing her home with boarders, taking in laundry or sewing, doing piecework at home, or going out to work for wages herself.

During the half-century following Confederation, the lives of all classes and cultures in Canada changed dramatically. The 1921 census showed that nearly half the population of Canada lived in towns and cities, up from 20 percent in 1871. With their mechanized equipment,

Canadian farms were more productive than ever before, but fewer people were living on farms. Meanwhile, urban-based industries were employing people in unprecedented numbers. The forces influencing the contours of human labour had also changed greatly in the fifty years following Confederation. Business cycles began to have more impact than the seasons in determining the rhythms of work, and the words "unemployment" and "labour union" were becoming familiar terms in the Canadian vocabulary.

While not everyone had an easy ride on the rocky road to industrialization, the overall economic trends were in the direction of impressive growth. The total output of goods and services, known as the gross national product (GNP), multiplied five times between 1867 and 1921, and the population rose from 3.5 to nearly 8.5 million. By 1915, three rail lines stretched across the continent and linked cities, towns, and villages, many of which had not even existed in 1867. Wherever it went, the railway quickened the pace of economic life and laid the foundations for a national economy dominated by the banks and businesses in Montreal and Toronto. Little wonder that Canada's obvious potential prompted Prime Minister Wilfrid Laurier to claim in 1904, "As the nineteenth century was that of the United States, so I think the twentieth century shall be filled by Canada."

## ASSESSING THE NATIONAL POLICY

As we have seen in the previous chapter, three policies—a protective tariff, transcontinental railways, and sponsorship of immigration—emerged as the cornerstones of the Conservative Party's national development strategy. By linking the provinces, the railways enabled tariff-protected goods to find national markets. Immigration provided both the railway and manufacturing companies with business. Together, these policies were designed to bring Canada into an age of sustained industrial growth. In retrospect the National Policy looks impressively integrated, but it actually developed in a piecemeal fashion and was challenged by regional, occupational, and even individual agendas.

The importance of the National Policy in promoting industrial growth and economic expansion has long been debated. Detractors of the policy, then and now, charge that the tariff benefited producers at the expense of consumers, and encouraged investors to establish firms destined for failure. By protecting domestic manufacturers from foreign competition, they argue, the National Policy encouraged the development of industries that could never compete in international markets. Regional critics maintain that the policy favoured central Canadian economic growth to the detriment of the Maritimes and the developing West.

In contrast, supporters of the National Policy have argued that protection is necessary to allow infant industries to succeed against competition from established companies in other countries. Canada's model, after all, was the United States, where the importance of tariffs in promoting industrial development is generally conceded. Moreover, supporters point to statistics showing that, in the decade following the implementation of the National Policy tariff, capital investment increased 114 percent, total wages paid by manufacturers rose by 68 percent, and the number of manufacturing establishments grew by 52 percent over the previous decade. They also argue that,

because of the National Policy, Canada was in a better position to take advantage of improved economic conditions when they returned in the late 1890s.

While the role of tariffs in Canadian economic development will probably always be the subject of controversy, there are several points of agreement. It is clear, for example, that under the protective cloak of the National Policy tariff, Canadian entrepreneurs moved to fill needs hitherto met by American imports. Toronto, in particular, became the centre of specialized industries that served a national market. The piano manufacturing industry is a good case in point. In 1876, some 90 percent of the pianos that graced fashionable Canadian parlours were imported; by 1891 nearly all pianos were made by Heintzman, R.S. Williams, or Mason and Risch of Toronto.

The agricultural implements industry also expanded under the tariff. Already well established in Ontario at the time of Confederation, the industry grew significantly after 1867 as farmers invested in machines for mowing, raking, reaping, and binding their harvest. Using American patents as well as developing their own lines, the Ontario firms of Massey Manufacturing of Toronto and A. Harris and Son of Brantford emerged as leaders in the industry. The implementation of a 35 percent tariff on imported agricultural machinery in 1883 gave them a tremendous boost in the Canadian market. To press their advantage, they used aggressive sales techniques, including displays at county fairs, field contests, "delivery day" parades, catalogues, newspaper advertising, and easy credit terms. When in 1891 the two companies merged as Massey-Harris, capitalized at $5 million, they formed Canada's largest corporation, controlling over half the Canadian sales of agricultural machinery.

There is also clear evidence that the National Policy laid the foundations for a branch-plant economy in Canada. Despite the success of such companies as Massey-Harris, many of the new companies, including Singer Sewing Machine, Gillette, Swift's, Coca-Cola, and Westinghouse, were American-owned. Their managers built manufacturing facilities in Canada to sell in a market that was protected from direct imports by high tariffs. In this period, the government welcomed foreign companies that sought to scale the tariff wall, and it remained unconcerned about the nationality of company owners or the address to which profits were delivered.

Canada's manufacturing sector was large by 1914, but it was weak relative to that of other major manufacturing nations. In part, this was due to the nation's continued dependence on external sources, primarily Great Britain and the United States, for capital and technology. A dependence on foreign technology led Canadian corporations to spend less of their profits on research, with the result that their manufactured products had trouble competing in global markets, and unprocessed primary products continued to make up the bulk of Canadian exports.

Because of Canada's dependence on foreign capital and technology, the National Policy did little to shield Canada from international economic trends. Rising tariffs in the United States, fluctuating capital markets in Great Britain, and recessions in either country were immediately felt in Canada, and there was little Canadians could do economically or politically to alter that reality. Long swing cycles in economic performance, relating to the opening of new economic frontiers and Great Britain's dominant role in the international financial market, were particularly important prior to 1914. Economic growth remained sluggish from 1867 to 1896, then soared upward until 1912; two years later, the First World War sent it soaring again. Shorter business cycles resulting in slowdowns in 1873–79, 1893–96, and again in 1903–7 were also felt in Canada. Historian Paul Craven argues that the brutal recession of the 1870s was only the worst of a prolonged period of economic hardship experienced by Canadian working people in the last third of the nineteenth century.[2] Economic fortunes were influenced as well by seasonal rhythms. In port cities such as Montreal, the seasonal cycle of work and wages was particularly onerous. The winter freeze-up heralded higher unemployment rates and lower incomes for the city's working families, who frequently had trouble keeping body and soul together until employment prospects picked up again in the spring.

It is impossible to determine whether another approach to economic development would have been more successful. No matter what they did, Canadians lived on the border of the United States, an emerging industrial giant whose economy would dominate the world in the twentieth century. When the Canadian economy was experiencing healthy growth, the American economy was often performing even better, encouraging people to move across the border to find work. In global terms, Canada's economic performance in the fifty years following Confederation was spectacular, but compared to the United States, where economic activity occurred on such a grand scale, the results seemed less impressive.

## TRANSPORTATION AND COMMUNICATION

Railways played a major role in Canada's Industrial Revolution. By 1915, Canadians boasted over fifty-five thousand kilometres of track capable of shuffling goods and people from the Atlantic to the Pacific and even into the Yukon. Most Canadian railways were built by private corporations, generously supported by federal, provincial, and municipal governments. Governments were prepared to subsidize railway development and bail railway companies out of their financial difficulties because it was felt that an integrated transportation network was crucial to the growth of a national economy.

By reducing transportation costs, railways expanded the geographic range in which products could be marketed. There was little likelihood of a bushel of wheat selling at a profit in the London market before the completion of the Canadian Pacific Railway because the cost of transporting grain by cumbersome boat and overland trails made the product uncompetitive in international markets. With the introduction of lower freight rates on eastbound grain under the Crow's Nest Pass Agreement of 1897, and cutthroat competition resulting from the railway-building orgy of the early twentieth century, Prairie wheat farmers emerged as highly competitive players on international grain exchanges. Similarly, manufacturers in Montreal and Toronto would have had great difficulty capturing markets in the Maritimes and the West without the network of railways that fanned sales teams and products across the northern half of the continent. Economists might debate the cost advantages of investment in railways as opposed to some other opportunity, but Canadians knew that their community was doomed if it did not have a railway.

*Intercolonial Railway works.*
*Moncton's development as a manufacturing and distributing centre in the late nineteenth century had much to do with the fact that it became the eastern headquarters of the Intercolonial Railway.*

Moncton Museum Collection

Railways not only expanded in length, they also improved in efficiency and service. Standard gauge steel rails, better bridges over rivers and gorges, more powerful locomotives, and specialized cars—box, pullman, and refrigerator—brought railways into the golden age of freight and passenger service. By 1900, a train trip between Halifax and Vancouver took only six days, a far cry from the months required to travel the distance by ship around South America or overland by river and road. The increased efficiency of rail communication was reflected in the postal service. Daily mail service was inaugurated across the nation in 1886, and rural postal delivery was introduced in 1908.

Ocean travel was also improving in safety and capacity. Reliable steamship service carried Prairie wheat, Ontario bacon, and Nova Scotia apples to British markets on time and usually in good condition. Under the auspices of the federal government, which had responsibility for navigational aids, Canada's coasts and inland waterways sprouted lighthouses, channel markers, and wharves. When the ill-fated *Titanic* was sunk by an iceberg in 1912, it shocked Canadians, who had become less accustomed to marine disasters than their grandparents had been. Increased capacity and lower rates also encouraged the traffic in immigrants.

While the steam engine provided the original power for an industrializing Canada, electricity and gasoline made their debut prior to the First World War. Electrically powered transportation was too expensive to compete with the steam-powered train on a national level, but the proliferation of electric streetcars in Canadian cities in the 1890s transformed the urban landscape. With more efficient transportation, burgeoning industrial cities sprawled into suburbs where people fled to escape the congestion of the urban core.

The major threat to the supremacy of steam-powered transportation was the internal combustion engine, used in both automobiles and aircraft. After the first manufacturing plant—a Ford branch plant—opened in Windsor, Ontario, in 1904, the auto industry thrived in Canada. Automobiles were used mostly for pleasure, but the commercial potential of motor vehicle transport was beginning to be established, and provincial Departments of Highways began improving the roads to facilitate the latest revolution in transportation. By contrast, aircraft transportation did not come into its own until after the Second World War, notwithstanding the early aeronautical experiments by J.A.D. McCurdy and F.W. Baldwin under Alexander Graham Bell's Aerial Experiment Association in

*The longest steel cantilever bridge in the world, the Quebec City bridge, opened in 1919, was designed to carry trains across the St Lawrence. It collapsed twice during construction, killing, in total, eighty-four workers, thirty-seven of them Mohawk high steel workers from Kahnawake.*

Archives de la Ville de Québec

Cape Breton. Curtiss Aeroplanes of Toronto, an American subsidiary, produced aircraft for military purposes during the First World War, but Canadians remained on the periphery of the aircraft industry.

Developments in transportation were matched by equally revolutionary advances in communication. Before he experimented in aviation, Alexander Graham Bell had become a household name with his highly publicized telephone call between Brantford and Paris, Ontario, in 1876. Initially perceived as a novelty, the telephone quickly became a popular necessity for business and personal communication. Yet another communication first occurred in 1901 when a wireless signal was sent across the Atlantic. Guglielmo Marconi picked up the first signal by hoisting antennae on kites flown on Signal Hill in St John's. In 1902, Marconi's Wireless Telegraph Company of Canada began to operate a transatlantic radio link from Glace Bay, Nova Scotia, the same year that an underwater cable linked Canada with Australia. Meanwhile, Canadian-born Reginald Fessenden was experimenting with wireless telegraph and voice transmissions, conducting ground-breaking work that would lead to the development of radio. Fessenden's first broadcast of the human voice by radio took place from his laboratory in Massachusetts on Christmas Eve 1906.

This conquest of time and space through developments in transportation and communication made traditional ways of telling time awkward. In 1867, clocks were set by astronomical calculations in each major locality. This meant, for example, that 12:00 noon was fifteen minutes earlier in Halifax than in Moncton. The railway and telegraph demanded a more standardized approach, especially in a country as big as Canada. Appropriately, it was a Canadian, Sandford Fleming, who advocated a global system of telling time based on hourly variations from a standard mean. Fleming was instrumental in convincing those attending the International Prime Meridian Conference in 1884 in Washington to adopt such a system, which is still in use today.

## SECONDARY INDUSTRY

In the fifty years following Confederation, secondary industry went from strength to strength. The first phase of Canada's Industrial Revolution, which occurred roughly between 1850 and 1900, was characterized by a rapid expansion of consumer goods industries, such as textiles, clothing, footwear, and cigars. The second phase, beginning around 1900, was fuelled by a surge in capital goods industries, such as machinery and equipment, and new technologies that spurred development in mining, pulp and paper, electrical and chemical industries. By 1921, nearly 30 percent of Canada's GNP was derived from manufacturing and construction (see table 3.1), a proportion that has remained virtually constant to the end of the twentieth century.

The emergence of a vigorous iron and steel industry at the turn of the century signalled

## MEASURING THE CANADIAN ECONOMY

Economists divide the economy into three sectors: primary or staple industries such as hunting, fishing, forestry, farming, and mining; secondary or manufacturing industries that add value through the processing of primary resources; and tertiary or service industries that facilitate the use and development of primary and secondary resources. The tertiary sector includes financial services, trade, transportation, utilities, and public administration as well as services ranging from street cleaning to teaching. Rents, investment income, indirect taxes, and income paid to non-residents are often grouped separately. Together, the output of goods and services is called the gross national product (GNP). Since the goods and services produced outside of the market economy, such as housework and voluntary labour, are not included in calculations of GNP, the national output is considerably greater than the official figures indicate. In 1986, Statistics Canada adopted gross domestic product (GDP) to measure the nation's economic performance. The GDP is calculated in the same way as the GNP except that it excludes payments on foreign investment.

**Table 3.1**

### PERCENTAGE SECTORAL DISTRIBUTION OF THE GNP, 1880–1920

| Year | Primary | Secondary | Tertiary | Other |
|------|---------|-----------|----------|-------|
| 1880 | 43.5 | 22.7 | 22.4 | 11.4 |
| 1890 | 36.6 | 28.1 | 26.7 | 8.6 |
| 1900 | 36.5 | 25.0 | 29.4 | 9.1 |
| 1910 | 30.2 | 27.8 | 33.6 | 8.4 |
| 1920 | 26.6 | 29.7 | 35.3 | 8.4 |

*Source: William L. Marr and Donald Paterson,* Canada: An Economic History *(Toronto: Gage, 1980), 22*

Canada's arrival as an industrial nation. In 1900, the Nova Scotia Steel Company of New Glasgow, which had been producing steel since 1882, acquired coal mines in Cape Breton, built a new steel plant in Sydney, and reorganized as Nova Scotia Coal and Steel, capitalized at $7 million. Hard on the heels of this triumph came the Dominion Iron and Steel Company, the brainchild of Boston industrialist H.M. Whitney and a syndicate of Boston, New York, and Montreal businessmen. The capital of $15 million was raised largely in Montreal, and American interests soon withdrew in favour of Canadian shareholders. By 1902, the company employed four thousand men at its blast and steel furnace works in Sydney, which had temporarily become the centre of Canada's Industrial Revolution.

Ontario also spawned two steel complexes. After several false starts, the Hamilton Steel and Iron Company began pouring open-hearth steel in 1900 and established its dominance in the field following its reorganization as Stelco in 1910. Meanwhile, American visionary Francis Hector Clergue capped his industrial empire at Sault Ste Marie with a massive steel and iron works. In 1902, Clergue's Algoma Steel Company produced the first steel rails in the dominion, but the following year Clergue ran out of money, and Algoma Steel became the sickly cousin of the "big four" steel companies of Canada. Algoma was only a minor setback in the otherwise rapid growth of Canada's iron and steel industry. Between 1877 and 1900, Canadian iron production increased over sixfold and multiplied tenfold again by 1913, at which time Canadian plants poured over one million tons of iron, much of it converted to the steel required to run the wheels of modern industry.

Canada's heavy industry expanded impressively during the first two decades of the twentieth century. In addition to the rails and rolling stock required for the railways, Canadian factories turned out binders and seed drills, bicycles and carriages, furniture and appliances to satisfy the Canadian market. Canadians also enthusiastically embraced the automobile age. By 1920, no less than thirty-nine Canadian and eight American companies were established to build cars in Ontario alone, and the Canadian automobile industry employed over eight thousand people. Ford, General Motors, and Chrysler, the "big three" American companies that would eventually dominate the North American automobile industry, were well established in Canada, finding it a useful base from which to supply the British Empire.

As manufacturing became more complex, intermediate goods required in the production process became a larger segment of secondary

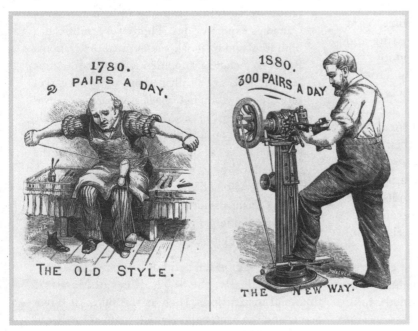

*What a difference a century makes in the shoe industry.*

Print by John Henry Walker. Ink. Notman Photographic Archives, McCord Museum on Canadian History, Montreal /M930.50.5,142 and M930.50.262

industry. Acids, alkalis, and heavy chemicals were essential ingredients in pulp and paper, iron and steel, oil refining, the electrical industry, and even in agriculture. Because chemical production often required vast quantities of electricity, plants were located near power sources. The Canada Carbide Company, for instance, became a subsidiary of Shawinigan Water and Power which controlled the vast Shawinigan dam in Quebec. In the 1890s, Thomas "Carbide" Willson, a Canadian inventor, discovered a process for producing calcium carbide at a fraction of the cost of earlier methods, and the compound was soon widely used in the manufacture of products as diverse as fertilizer, bleaching powder, and ammunition, the latter an item in high demand during the First World War. Among the most successful intermediate goods industries were those producing the bolts, nails, nuts, screws, and similar products that quite literally held the products of industry together.

Stimulated by economic growth, construction materials such as lumber, bricks, glass, stone, and cement figured prominently in the secondary sector. The demand for factories, public buildings, homes, and tenements sustained a construction industry that accounted for over 5 percent of the GNP by 1921. Although the construction industry itself was highly decentralized in this period, patterns of consolidation and centralization were at work in the manufacture of construction materials. A good case in point is Portland cement. Rock cement had a long history of use in construction, but Portland cement, or concrete, was only invented in the early decades of the nineteenth century. Canadians began producing concrete on a commercial basis early in the 1890s, and output increased at a rapid rate. In an effort to control the industry, nine firms—five in Ontario, three in Quebec, and one in Alberta—were consolidated into the Canada Cement Company in 1909 by the flamboyant entrepreneur Max Aitken.

## DEINDUSTRIALIZATION IN THE MARITIMES

There was a clear geographical structure to the Canadian economy as it emerged under the National Policy. Neither the Maritimes nor the western provinces managed to emulate the manufacturing success of the central Canadian provinces, whose head start in the Industrial Revolution was evident even before Confederation. By 1901, Ontario accounted for fully half of the gross value of Canadian manufacturing and Quebec for nearly one-third. Once set, this pattern remained remarkably constant, although for a brief period during and after the First World War Quebec's manufacturing sector dropped well below 30 percent of the national output, as Ontario surged ahead under the twin impact of war and western development.

The Maritime provinces, in the long run, benefited less from national economic policies than did the rest of the country. In the short run, prospects looked good. The Intercolonial Railway, completed in 1876, brought welcome investment and inspired efforts to produce for a national market. While Halifax was slow to industrialize, Saint John, the region's major timber-exporting and shipbuilding centre, initially thrived on the National Policy tariff, emerging as the nation's main supplier of nails and brass products in the 1880s. Other urban centres along the Intercolonial—Moncton, Amherst, Truro, New Glasgow, and Sydney—also developed their industrial potential. By 1885, the Maritimes, with less than 20 percent of the nation's population, had eight of Canada's twenty-three cotton mills, three of its five sugar refineries, two of its seven ropeworks, and had pioneered the nation's steel-making efforts.

The impressive industrial base that emerged in the Maritimes following the implementation of the National Policy tariff quickly eroded as the recession of the 1890s led to factory closures and industrial consolidations by Montreal financiers. First the cotton industry and then sugar, rope, and glass became victims of the consolidation movement. By 1895, the control of all secondary industries except for confectioneries and iron and steel had fallen into the hands of outside interests. Some industries continued to operate under distant management; others were closed down in efforts to "rationalize" production. By the first decade of the twentieth century, the trends were clear. Between 1880 and 1910, manufacturing in the Maritime region grew at an annual rate of 1.8 percent, compared to 3.1 for the nation as a whole. Overall, in the same period, the Maritime economy grew by only 2.2 percent, no greater than that of the holdout colony Newfoundland, and substantially less than the national growth rate of 3.8 percent.

The wooden shipbuilding industry, the focus of much pre-Confederation investment in the Maritimes, reached a peak in the 1870s and then declined precipitously. In the 1880s, the shipbuilders had to decide whether to invest in iron steamers or put their profits in other sectors. In all three Maritime provinces, the decision was to move away from shipbuilding. Historians Eric W. Sager and Lewis R. Fischer note:

> It is not self-evident that [Maritime] economic and political interests were best served by the collective failure to sustain a shipping industry to serve Canada's export trades. There were politicians, both local and national, who wanted the National Policy to include a shipping industry and Atlantic seaports as part of a truly national economic structure. But the vision of Canada as a maritime power soon faded, even in the Maritimes. It is impossible to know how far a shipping industry might have contributed to prosperity in the Maritimes in the twentieth century. We are spared the knowledge by the decisions of the late nineteenth century, when Canadians pursued a landward development strategy and left the people of the Maritimes to dream of past glories and foregone opportunities. [3]

As the region fell behind the rest of the country economically, the head offices of Maritime financial institutions, such as the Bank of Nova Scotia and the Merchants Bank (renamed the Royal Bank in 1901) moved to Central Canada. Even Nova Scotia's much prized steel industry, which benefited from the geographic proximity of major coal and iron deposits, had fallen into the hands of outside interests by the first decade of the century. Although the general economic growth associated with the Laurier boom and the First World War helped to hide the structural problems that characterized the region's industrial base, economic underdevelopment would long remain the defining feature of the Maritime economy.

## STAPLES: OLD AND NEW

Primary industries reeled under the impact of new technological and bureaucratic processes. By 1921, Canada was one of the world's great resource frontiers from which furs, fish, timber, wheat, and minerals poured forth to markets around the world. Moreover, Canada's most successful secondary products in the export market, such as bacon and sawn lumber, often remained closely tied to Canada's abundant natural resources.

Commercialization of farming occurred first in Ontario, where agriculture flourished, stimulated by local demand and the almost insatiable British market for staple foods. With rail and steamship service offering more reliable transportation, cold storage facilities, and lower freight rates, huge quantities of Ontario's bacon, cheese, butter, and eggs found their way to British larders by the end of the nineteenth century. Ontario farmers also branched into industrial crops such as sugar beets, grapes, and tobacco and grew most of the fruit and vegetables that were canned in Canada prior to 1920.

One of the most successful entrepreneurs in the overseas trade was William Davies. An immigrant from Britain in 1854, Davies established a plant for curing and smoking meat in Toronto in 1861. The popularity of his bacon in Britain led to the opening of a larger plant in 1874. For a short time in the 1880s, Davies was forced to buy hogs in the Chicago market. Ontario farmers soon increased their production to supply the needs of the industry. By the end of the century, William Davies Company in Toronto slaughtered nearly 450 000 Canadian-grown hogs, employed three hundred workers, and boasted export sales of over $3.5 millions.

The cheese industry experienced an even more dramatic expansion. Once the Dairymen's Association solved their problems with quality control, Canadian cheese, like Canadian bacon, found a British market. Export sales skyrocketed from 8.3 million pounds in 1871 to 189.8 million in 1899. Cheese production remained a decentralized activity throughout all the eastern provinces, but its greatest success was in Ontario. Although Canadian producers made their reputation with cheddar, they also invented processed cheese, upon which A.F. McLaren of Ingersoll built a thriving business. Following the First World War, he was bought out by another Canadian-born cheese maker, J.L. Kraft, who, in 1905, had moved to Chicago where he became the world's most successful cheese maker.

Cattle raising in Quebec's Eastern Townships proved a highly profitable venture, and Quebec farmers exported butter and cheese to Great Britain. However, Ontario's farms were more productive than those of Quebec, where families were larger, mechanization slower, and farm surpluses less abundant. Continued colonization in the St Maurice–Lac St Jean area, the St Maurice Valley, and the back country south of the St Lawrence increased the land base in Quebec by almost 40 percent in the second half of the nineteenth century, but much of the land was marginal and could only support a family through the sale of its wood products. Even with this agricultural expansion, Quebec had only two-thirds as much land under cultivation as did Ontario in 1900.

The Maritimes, like Quebec, had a large number of marginal farms but, in fertile areas such as the St John River Valley, the Annapolis Valley, and Prince Edward Island, farmers took up commercial farming to take advantage of expanding urban markets at home and abroad. Potatoes were a successful crop throughout the region. In the Annapolis Valley of Nova Scotia, apple production increased nearly tenfold between 1881 and 1911, and doubled again by 1921 as orchards planted during the prewar euphoria came to maturity. With an average annual output of over five million bushels in the 1920s, Nova Scotia grew nearly half of Canada's apple crop and sold most of it on the British market.

The Prairie wheat boom is the most spectacular agricultural success story of this period. Between 1901 and 1913, Prairie wheat production expanded from 56 million to 224 million bushels, grain exports increased by 600 percent, and wheat soared from 14 to 42 percent of total Canadian exports. A variety of factors came together to make the wheat boom possible: faster maturing strains of wheat, the chill steel plough (which could handle the prairie sod), gas-driven tractors, rising world prices, lower transportation costs, a steady supply of immigrant labour, and encouragement from public and private agencies. Together, these factors transformed the Prairies from a fur trade frontier to the breadbasket of the world, its wheat production second in volume only to that of the United States.

The dramatic expansion of the Prairie wheat economy was once believed to have been the engine of Canada's economic growth from 1896 to 1913. While a debate among economic historians on the relative importance of this staple's impact on economic growth still rages, estimates of wheat's significance are now generally more modest than they once were. Technological change in manufacturing as well as improved markets for hydro-electricity and pulp and paper together were far more important factors in Canadian economic growth than the expanding wheat economy. Exaggerated expectations of profit from the wheat economy led to an overexpansion of railway facilities in Western Canada and to an orgy of land speculation throughout the Prairies before the First World War. By the time that more realistic estimates of the potential of wheat had been accepted, many individuals had gone bankrupt, and municipal finances were shaky throughout the wheat belt.

Although significant, wheat was by no means the only product of western agriculture. Dairy farming was important in Manitoba as was mixed farming in the Park Belt of the Prairies and in British Columbia. Between 1885 and 1905, cattle ranching flourished in the Alberta foothills. Canada's "wild West" was developed by "gentlemen farmers" such as Senator Matthew Cochrane, a pioneer cattle breeder and successful shoe manufacturer from the Eastern Townships. With an embargo on American imports, generous terms for leasing land, and the completion of the CPR—all provided by the obliging Macdonald government in the 1880s—ranching fever gripped Alberta. The first cattlemen's association was founded in 1882, and Calgary, the capital of ranching country, was incorporated as a town in 1883. With stockyards, slaughterhouses, tanneries, and packing plants all catering to the domestic and overseas beef trade, Calgary was controlled by the elite cattlemen who communed together at the exclusive Ranchmen's Club. Cattle ranching also flourished in the Okanagan Valley in the wake of the gold rush.

Despite their initial success, ranchers in both Alberta and British Columbia were soon fighting a rearguard action against farmers who, armed with dryland farming techniques, insisted on breaking up the cattle range. Battles between rancher and farmer were bitterly fought. In 1919, one crusty rancher directed the executors of his will to use the money from the sale of his estate for "the extermination of that class of Vermin, commonly known as farmers."[4] By that time, the days when the rancher reigned supreme had already gone, but livestock remained an important industry in the western provinces.

Scientific and technological innovation had an enormous impact on agricultural production. It has been estimated that the development of the fast-maturing Marquis wheat by Dominion Cerealist Charles E. Saunders added over $100 million to farm income between 1911 and 1918. While horse and human power continued to be the chief sources of energy on Canadian farms, engine power was introduced as early as 1877 when the first steam threshing machine was used in Woodbridge, Ontario. Steam threshers could process more in a day than the average farmer produced in a year and soon transformed the harvesting process. Gasoline engines and tractors became practical in the second decade of the twentieth century, but few farmers actually owned one until the 1920s.

As farming evolved from a way of life to an industry, a number of patterns emerged. Commercial farms were on average larger, more highly mechanized, and consequently more valuable than subsistence farms, which increasingly were abandoned. In marginal areas where farming had been only one of a variety of occupations including fishing and lumbering, commercial farming proved impossible. Not all commercial farms were successful even in prime agricultural areas. Usually small and lacking financial resources, most commercial farms operated close to the margin, resulting in many failures both in the long-settled East and the booming West. Bad weather, bad markets, and just plain bad luck could make it impossible to carry on, especially if the farm were highly mortgaged to pay for new improvements. One of the major problems facing farmers was that large volumes and low prices prevailed as the productivity of the agricultural sector multiplied under the influence of new farming techniques. The decline in the relative importance of farming in this period reflects the fact that fewer farms were required to meet the Canadian and international demand for food.

The fishing industry, like agriculture, adjusted unevenly to the new economic order. In the second half of the nineteenth century, inshore fishers came under increasing competition from deep-sea fleets, while canning and cold storage emerged as new ways of preserving fish, supplementing salting, drying, and pickling. New investment poured into canning factories designed to process lobster, herring, and sardines, and into cold storage facilities to handle fresh fish. While technology and transportation dictated that the fresh fish industry would become centralized in a few communities such as Yarmouth, Halifax, and Mulgrave, the canned and salt fishery remained dispersed and uncoordinated. Because virtually every fishing port had a canning factory, the product varied widely in quality, and workers were relegated to seasonal employment. Quality control also plagued the saltfish industry, which was beginning to face stiff competition in its traditional Latin American and southern European markets.

The ocean fisheries differed from most primary industries in that they were a "free resource," one that Canadians could not own, at least beyond the three-mile limit recognized by international law. In the industrial age, proximity alone would not give Canadians an advantage over their competitors. Norway, France, and other European countries used state-of-the-art vessels, government bounties, efficient marketing operations, and a superior product to increasingly dominate the North Atlantic fisheries. Undercapitalized, internally fragmented, and undermined by the "truck system," the east coast fishery failed to develop the abundant resource found at its very doorstep.

On the West Coast, the salmon fishery developed quickly in the final decades of the nineteenth century, and by 1900 salmon had become the most profitable fishery in Canada, surpassing cod in the value of sales. Steveston, where a large number of canneries were built, became known as the sockeye capital of the world, exporting its canned salmon largely to a British market. A complex division of labour based on race and gender became a feature of the British Columbia fishing industry. White managers, millwrights, and engineers supervised Chinese men and Japanese and Native women in the canneries while Native, white, and, later, Japanese men caught the fish.

*The influx of immigrants and the rapid spread of salmon canneries in British Columbia at the turn of the century resulted in a series of laws that restricted salmon fishing licences in the interests of the canning industry and the recreational fishery. Invariably, the laws had a negative impact on the Natives who were less likely than immigrants to own canning companies. This picture shows a federal fisheries officer removing an "illegal" Kwakwaka'wakh salmon trap on the Marble River, Quatsino Sound, Vancouver Island, in 1912.*

Vancouver Public Library/13904

In 1902, much of the industry was centralized under the British Columbia Packers Association. A company backed by eastern Canadian and American capital, it was incorporated in New Jersey, a state whose liberal incorporation laws made it a popular base for companies avoiding anti-trust legislation. The new company consolidated and mechanized the packing process, increasing its profits by reducing the costs of both labour and fish supply. The Smith butchering machine, whose popular name, the "Iron Chink," reflected the racist attitudes towards Asian cannery workers, processed sixty to seventy-five fish a minute and encouraged the mechanizing of filleting, salting, and weighing. When the sanitary can and the double seamer were introduced in 1912, the automated assembly line became a reality.

Aboriginal peoples suffered most from the commercialization of the salmon fishery. For centuries the economies and cultures of Natives on the Pacific Coast had been based on the salmon fisheries. Indeed, the commercial fishery in the early years depended on Native skills as fishers, processors, boat builders, and net makers. By the end of the nineteenth century, federal and provincial governments began passing legislation to control the fishery. Historian Dianne Newell has traced the process by which fishery regulations were used to deny Natives access to their traditional fishing sites and methods. She concludes: "As the industry spread and mechanized in the twentieth century, changes in labour supply, in markets for fish, in technology, and in government regulation rendered Indians less central to fishing, and eventually to fish processing."[5] By adapting to new technologies, new regulations, and white hostility, Indian families and villages managed to maintain a toehold in the industry until the second half of the twentieth century, but they were no longer central to the fishery they once had dominated.

British Columbia was also Canada's new timber frontier. By the 1880s, most of the white pine forests of Eastern Canada had been laid to waste. The demand for lumber for construction in rapidly growing North American cities was met by the majestic Douglas fir and cedar of the West Coast. Between 1871 and 1880, some 350 million board feet of timber were cut in British Columbia; in the second decade of the twentieth century, the figure had risen to a staggering 13.5 billion, and lumbering had emerged as one of British Columbia's most lucrative industries.

The forests of Eastern Canada continued to produce lumber, fine woods for furniture, pit props for mines, railway ties, shakes, shingles, and laths. They also came into their own in the production of pulp and paper. Although the first groundwood paper mill was established in Valleyfield, Quebec, in 1869, it was not until the end of the nineteenth century that the pulp and paper industry took off. The growing demand for newsprint in the United States and the expiration of important patents on newsprint production attracted capital investment, while legislation restricting the export of unprocessed logs encouraged a Canadian base for the industry. With the cost of newsprint soaring in the United States, the American government removed its tariff on pulp and newsprint from Canada in 1913. By 1920, Canada was rapidly emerging as the world's leader in newsprint production, over 80 percent of which was destined for the United States.

Canada's mining industry came virtually from nowhere in the nineteenth century to international prominence by 1921. As late as 1890, nearly 40 percent of Canada's mineral output consisted of non-metallic substances such as gypsum, grindstones, clay, and cement, but the twin impact of technological innovations and rising demand generated by new manufacturing processes brought rapid changes as the twentieth century dawned. The new era of mining activity got off to a dramatic start when gold was discovered in the Klondike in 1896, but it had relatively less impact on the Canadian economy and business community than other mining ventures. Since the Industrial Revolution was built on resources of coal, iron, and other base metals, the discovery and exploitation of these resources drew most of the investment, if not the popular attention.

Coal mining in the Maritimes, Alberta, and British Columbia expanded in the late nineteenth century to supply Canadian trains, factories, and homes. By the beginning of the twentieth century, huge quantities of coal and iron were processed in Canada's steel plants. Even so, the demand outstripped domestic supply.

Surveys conducted for the CPR and the Canadian Geological Survey revealed the potential wealth locked in the Canadian Shield and the western mountain ranges. When the chemical and mechanical processes for separating complex ores were developed at the turn of the century, the nickel-copper deposits around Sudbury and zinc-lead-silver deposits in British Columbia became profitable fields for exploitation. Capital poured into Canada from all over the world to bring the vast storehouse of mineral wealth into production.

The discovery of copper-gold deposits at the base of Red Mountain in 1887 created an instant boom town at Rossland, British Columbia, which a decade later boasted eight thousand people. By that time, an American promoter, F.A. Heinze, had built a smelter at Trail, which was connected to Rossland by a narrow-gauge railway. Following its decision to build a line through the Crow's Nest Pass, the CPR bought Heinze's interests and incorporated them in the Consolidated Mining and Smelting Company of Canada (Cominco) in 1906. As a CPR subsidiary, Cominco had access to extensive capital resources, which were used to develop hydro-electrical power in the region and to solve the metallurgical problem of separating ores. By 1910, British Columbia's mineral output was second in value only to Ontario's, much of it extracted from the fabulous Kootenay region.

Rich mineral resources were concentrated in "New Ontario," the area between Sudbury and Hudson Bay, which was granted in huge sections to Ontario by the federal government or the courts between 1874 and 1912. Following the discovery of copper sulphides in the Sudbury Basin in 1883, there was a rush to stake claims in the area. As in the Yukon and British Columbia, prospectors and speculators were soon replaced by large corporations. In 1886, American promoter Samuel J. Ritchie established the Canadian Copper Company to develop Sudbury's deposits for refining by the Orford Copper Company in New Jersey. Two years later, a smelter was constructed at Copper Cliff to concentrate the nickel-copper matte prior to shipping. Initially considered a nuisance, nickel was soon found to have valuable steel-hardening qualities. In 1902, Canadian Copper and Orford merged to form the International Nickel Company, or Inco, of New Jersey. The increasing demand for nickel-steel armour plate in a rapidly militarizing Europe led Mond Nickel of Wales to establish a base in Sudbury, which soon became the world's major supplier of nickel. At the same time, discoveries of gold, silver, and cobalt along the route of the Timiskaming and Northern Ontario Railway put the names of Cobalt, Timmins, Kirkland Lake, and Porcupine on the map. The value of minerals produced in Ontario increased fourfold between 1900 and 1910 and nearly doubled again in the next decade, making Ontario Canada's leading province in the mining industry.

Quebec's rich mining frontier was slow to develop, but the extraordinary range of mineral resources inspired a variety of initiatives. At the end of the nineteenth century, foreign companies began working the asbestos deposits in the Eastern Townships. Although Quebec quickly became the world's leading producer of this rare mineral, most of the processing was done outside of Canada, and the fierce competition between mining companies resulted in overproduction, gluts, and slowdowns that made the industry highly unstable. The copper and gold deposits of the Abitibi region of Quebec were known prior to the First World War but not seriously exploited until the 1920s.

One of the major attractions of Ontario and Quebec as mining and processing centres was the availability of cheap electrical power. Ontario's initiative in developing Niagara Falls gave the province a massive source of hydro-electric power. In Quebec, American capital developed the mighty Shawinigan Falls on the St Maurice River, which was second only to Niagara Falls in its generating capacity. Shawinigan soon attracted an aluminum smelter, pulp mill, and chemical factories. By 1903, hydro lines carried Shawinigan power to Montreal. Unlike Ontario, Quebec left the hydro industry to private enterprise, giving entrepreneurs free rein to charge lower rates to commercial customers if they chose to do so. Whether publicly or privately owned, the abundant supply of hydro-electric

*The introduction of manufactured goods eroded the advantage that aboriginal peoples had in most of their labour-intensive crafts. Snowshoes, however, remained a vital trade commodity for aboriginal peoples in the North, who found a ready buyer in the Hudson's Bay Company.*

National Archives of Canada/C38174

power served as a magnet to industry. With nearly 80 percent of Canada's generating capacity in 1918, Ontario and Quebec were in the vanguard of the second industrial revolution based on mining, chemicals, and pulp and paper, which relied on abundant energy resources.

Canadian furs fetched premium prices on European markets after 1867, and Canadians, in particular Canada's aboriginal peoples, continued to hunt and trap furs. As in other primary industries, new technology and modern business practices had a transforming effect on the way the fur industry was conducted. The Hudson's Bay Company, faced with competition, introduced bureaucratic management structures, used railways and steamships where possible, and pushed into new fur trade frontiers. Under the direction of C.C. Chipman, who was appointed director in 1891, the trade was retrenched and reorganized, much to the disgust of the old commissioned officers, who increasingly found their bureaucratic jobs

bewildering and distasteful. During the First World War, the international market for Canadian furs shifted from London to New York. Montreal, Winnipeg, and Edmonton became centres of the rapidly changing fur industry. The value of Canadian pelts in 1920 was over $20 million, a figure that would not be surpassed for many years.

By the first decade of the twentieth century, fur farming had begun to emerge as an alternative to hunting and trapping. Based primarily in Prince Edward Island, the raising of fox, mink, and other fur-bearing animals in captivity was made more practical by the introduction of woven wire enclosures in the late 1890s. Thereafter, the industry developed quickly, stimulated by improved breeding methods, the growing demand of the fashion industry, and the declining population of the world's wild fur-bearing animals. By 1910, Prince Edward Island

*Natives in New Brunswick played an important role as guides and canoe builders for vacationers who came to the province for recreational hunting and fishing.*

Provincal Archives of New Brunswick, Taylor Collection/P5-381

breeders fetched as much as $15 000 a pair for their silver fox on the London market, and people were mortgaging their farms to invest in the industry.

## SERVING THE INDUSTRIAL ECONOMY

While the primary and secondary sectors provided much of the drama surrounding Canada's rise to industrial maturity, the service sector emerged as the major contributor to Canada's GNP by the end of the First World War. The Industrial Revolution in Canada and elsewhere was carried forward by a growing army of clerks, cleaners, cab drivers, cooks, and secretaries as well as managers, bankers, lawyers, engineers, and civil servants. In 1921, as many people worked in service industries as in the primary sector, performing jobs, such as electrical repair, automobile sales, and switchboard operation, that could scarcely have been imagined in 1867.

Clerical work was one of the fastest growing occupations in an industrializing Canada. While the general labour force grew by 10.4 percent between 1891 and 1901, the clerical sector rose 73.3 percent. The growth continued in the first decade of the twentieth century and reached an astounding 109.3 percent between 1911 and 1921. By the latter date, clerical workers represented nearly 7 percent of the labour force. Another change had also taken place in this thirty-year period. In 1891, women comprised only 14.3 percent of those working in clerical positions; by 1921, 41.8 percent of clerical workers were women, and the trend towards feminization of clerical work continued throughout the twentieth cen-

tury. Women were reputed to be better at the painstaking detail required by the modern office, but they were hired because they were paid less than their male counterparts. Since most women remained in the labour force only until they married, employers could get away with paying them less than men and making few provisions for their long-term economic well-being. Women office workers thus helped to increase the profitability of

*The woman in this 1904 portrait of the Vancouver main branch of the Royal Bank is probably Jennie Moore, one of the first women employed by the bank. Until the First World War, men worked as tellers while women were assigned less visible roles as clerks and stenographers.*

**Royal Bank Archives**

the modern corporate enterprise and soon became indispensable to its operations.

## RETAILING

Marketing the products of field and factory was the central function of industrial capitalism. As transportation improved and nationwide markets emerged, retail operations grew and changed. The availability of a vast array of manufactured products

## ENTERPRISING WOMEN

While men dominated the business world, a few women became economic actors in their own right. The passage of Married Women's Property Acts in most provincial jurisdictions in the late nineteenth century enabled women to hold property and conduct business free from the supervisory control of their husbands. As historian Peter Baskerville has shown, British Columbian women were quick to take up their new rights in the marketplace. In 1891, one out of five non-institutional property holders was a woman, up from one in twenty-five in 1863. Women also established their own businesses. Although women tended to operate on the margins of the business world and in areas firmly within the traditional sphere of women's activities, such as sewing, cooking, and teaching, their efforts point to the growing trend of women of all ages and classes to take advantage of the opportunities opening in the market economy.

Fourteen-year-old Eva Clarke of Victoria, for example, petitioned the Supreme Court on her own behalf upon the death of her mother and the imminent bankruptcy of her father:

I have been learning to play the piano for about eighteen months altogether. My present teacher is W. Sharpe of Victoria. It is my intention to qualify myself for a teacher of music of which I am very fond. It is necessary for me to have a piano in order that I may practice. I practice on the piano daily about two hours but it will not be possible for me to continue this practice unless I have a piano in the house where I live.[6]

It is not known whether Eva kept her piano, but the court ordered that all income from her mother's legacy be used to support the education of Eva and her brother and that it be administered by the court rather than by her father. As Baskerville observes: "Eva's reaction to the death of her mother, in 1888, provides a poignant illustration of individual perspectives within families, and, as well, suggests the possibility that many young women in late nineteenth century Victoria openly sought independent career goals." The growing tendency of making a living outside the context of marriage and motherhood meant that the role of women in the Industrial Age was increasingly under negotiation.

transformed many people from producers to consumers and ushered in a material age that challenged the values of a society built upon scarcity and spiritual salvation.

The changes in retailing activity can be seen in the meteoric rise of the T. Eaton Company. In 1869, Timothy Eaton opened a dry-goods and clothing store on Yonge Street in Toronto. What distinguished Eaton from his many competitors was his method of selling, which included fixed prices, cash only, and money-back guarantees. The approach was so popular that Eaton moved to larger premises, equipped with an elevator, in 1883. Weekly "bargain days" and the latest technological innovations, such as elevators, electric lights, and escalators (the latter installed in 1907), drew curious crowds and increased sales. In 1884, Eaton reached across the country to grab business from local retailers when he issued his first mail-order catalogue. Telephone sales were instituted the next year. By 1903, the Eaton mail-order business was so large that it moved to separate premises. The

expansion in sales allowed Eaton's to manufacture its own merchandise, thus by-passing wholesalers and suppliers. In 1893, it established its first overseas operation in London. Soon Eaton's wholesale operations circled the globe, with offices in such places as New York, Paris, and Yokohama. Eaton's also opened a branch in Winnipeg in 1905, the first in a chain-store business that would expand dramatically in the 1920s. Robert Simpson, also of Toronto, paralleled the Eaton experience. No corner of Canada reached by the postal service was left unchanged by the rise of the great department stores and their catalogues.

The appearance of department stores and nationwide chains on the scale of Eaton's or Simpson's posed a challenge to the local retail trade. The Wholesale Grocers Guild, established in 1883, tried unsuccessfully to prevent direct sales from manufacturers, and retailers launched campaigns to urge customers to buy locally. In areas like the Maritimes and the Prairies, retailers painted lurid pictures of grasping central Canadian mail-order stores sucking the lifeblood from the regional economy, but consumers bought the best product at the lowest price. Local retailers survived by providing specialties or services, such as long-term credit, unavailable from the big chains. Charles Woodward on the West Coast was the most conspicuous example of someone who defied the power of the central Canadian retailers by establishing his own chain of department stores. In the final analysis, local retailing expanded despite the activities of men like Timothy Eaton as more people and products were drawn into the market economy.

## MASS PRODUCTION AND MODERN MANAGEMENT

Market expansion led to reorganization of the structure of industry, encouraging small-scale, owner-operated businesses to evolve into bureaucratic, multipurpose, and multinational corporations. Even the census categories were changed in 1901 to reflect new concepts of business activity. In calculating manufacturing establishments, only those operations employing more than five people were enumerated. Three decades earlier, the average number of people employed in an establishment had been under five.

The progress of Massey-Harris following its creation in 1891 is a good example of the evolution of corporate enterprise. The largest company in Canada, it quickly gobbled up the Canadian competition and increased sales in the United States and Europe. Between 1890 and 1911, Massey-Harris accounted for 15 percent of the manufactures exported from Canada. Production was concentrated in Toronto, Brantford, and Woodstock, while management was "rationalized" into departments specializing in such areas as sales, advertising, and accounting. In its mechanized factories, Massey-Harris produced a high volume of standardized products with interchangeable parts. Parts and service became an important selling point for the company, as it would later become for automobile manufacturers. Before the end of the century, Massey-Harris had established a major facility for

research and development, explored the use of moving pictures for advertising, and diversified into bicycle production. Meanwhile, the Massey name graced the great concert hall in Toronto, and the family fortune sustained such public charities as Toronto's Fred Victor Mission. Although International Harvester located in Canada in 1903, Massey-Harris survived the competition from the American branch plant and established its own branch plant in New York State in 1910.

The Massey-Harris story was repeated, usually with less success, in a variety of Canadian industries. As family firms and partnerships grew in size and complexity, they often turned into corporate enterprises. The limited liability corporation separated individual wealth from corporate wealth and made corporations independent legal entities. No longer tied to the fate of a single person or a few individuals, the corporation took on a life of its own. At the same time, ownership was divorced from management functions, which were increasingly carried out by salaried employees. No individual, no matter how energetic or gifted, could keep on top of the details of such rapidly expanding businesses. Nor was such control desirable. Chief executive officers needed their time to mobilize capital and plot long-range corporate strategy.

Control over day-to-day operations of large corporations was achieved through structural reorganization. At the turn of the century, management techniques became the focus of attention for business people trying to maximize the profits of their enterprises. Scientific management, a term coined by American Frederick W. Taylor, advocated that managers take responsibility for coordinating work processes and that employees be deprived of any initiative or authority in deciding how to do their work. On the shop floor this meant that the labour process was broken down into simple repetitive tasks and that employee output was closely monitored by supervisors. At the management level, rigid hierarchies with clear lines of authority were developed and new accounting procedures implemented to control production and labour costs. When Henry Ford perfected the assembly line for his Model T in 1914, artisans who once performed the most skilled of manufacturing operations—the assembly of complex machinery—were forced to submit to the dictates of management and the machine.

Service industries quickly adopted the structures of secondary industries. *The Monetary Times* of 1 October 1920 offered the following observation: "The construction of the modern office grows constantly more like the construction of the factory. Work has been standardized, long rows of desks of uniform design and equipment now occupy the offices of our large commercial and financial institutions. With the increased division of labour each operation becomes more simple. The field in which each member of the staff operates is narrower." Like the mechanized factory and the limited liability corporation, the modern office was a hallmark of the industrial age. As industries became larger, efficient administration determined entrepreneurial success or failure. Managers and clerks staffed the new offices of corporate capitalism, taking orders, checking inventories, corresponding with suppliers, and generally ensuring that the company operated smoothly and at a profit. New notions of management efficiency were applied in the office much as they were in the factory. By 1921, the general bookkeeper and office worker had been replaced by accountants, stenographers, secretaries, filing clerks, and telephone operators, while typewriters, telephones, and Hollerith punch-card machines were an integral part of the bureaucratic process. Those who worked in offices might wear white collars, but the structure of their work increasingly resembled that of blue-collar factory workers.

The bureaucratic structures in place, corporations could survive their founders. Indeed, control often passed out of the hands of founding families altogether if there were no talented sons or nephews to inherit the business (daughters and nieces being systematically excluded from corporate boardrooms). The only limit to the continued success of corporate enterprise was failure to compete in the marketplace. Driven by the Darwinian logic that held that only the fittest survived, successful corporate managers were forced to keep ahead of the competition.

Canadian entrepreneurs were decidedly unen-

thusiastic about unrestrained competition. While giving lip-service to the god of free enterprise, they secretly agreed to fix prices and agitated publicly for policies that would guarantee them a "living profit." Nationwide associations, such as the Dominion Wholesale Grocers Guild, Retail Merchants Association, Canadian Manufacturers Association, and Canadian Bankers Association, tried to regulate the activities of their members, but restrictions on "unfair" trading practices often failed to bring order to the marketplace because it took only one entrepreneur to break an agreement. For most businesses, growing bigger meant becoming more efficient, reaping the benefits of economies of scale, and gaining an edge over competitors. The consequences of "bigger is better" thinking soon became obvious. If a company could become big enough, it might be possible to sweep all competition aside and establish a monopoly over the marketplace.

Monopoly was a bad word in industrializing Canada. It had unsavoury connotations reaching back to the mercantile era when monopolies had been granted to the King's favourites; it also flew in the face of the liberal doctrine of free enterprise. When American business people began using trusts and holding companies to dominate the market, their government passed anti-combines laws designed to prevent such monopolistic practices. Canada did likewise as early as 1889, though the combines tradition that emerged in Canada followed British precedents, which held that combination in itself was not illegal unless it was demonstrably against the public interest. A spate of mergers in the 1880s was followed by an even bigger merger movement in the early twentieth century. Between 1909 and 1912, some 275 Canadian firms were consolidated into 52 enterprises, capitalized at nearly half a billion dollars.

The merger movement brought to the fore some of Canada's major corporate giants. Vertically integrated, companies were capable of handling all the functions of the industry, including supplying their own raw materials and shipping their products in company-owned boxcars. Their vast assets enabled them to mobilize capital on a scale hitherto unimaginable. Although such companies were technically not monopolies, their size gave them tremendous power in the reorganized marketplace. They could outbid and outlast their smaller competitors and make it difficult for new competitors to break into the industry. The fact that many of the companies established at the turn of the twentieth century are still household names in Canada—Imperial Oil, Bell Canada, General Electric, Stelco, and the Canada Cement Company—is visible testimony to their triumph over the "invisible forces" of the marketplace.

## FINANCIAL INSTITUTIONS

The longevity and stability of corporations has been a key feature of industrial capitalism. So, too, has been the emergence of an array of financial intermediaries whose chief purpose is to mobilize capital for investment. As the Canadian economy soared to new heights, conventional sources of capital—banks, governments, and wealthy individuals—proved inadequate to the task of financing large-scale ventures. New institutions and mechanisms, many of which developed around the financing of railways, emerged to fill the vacuum. By 1920, the Canadian financial community included two stock exchanges and a complex web of insurance, mortgage, and trust companies, bond brokers, and securities dealers, all designed to move money to where it could reap the greatest return.

Much of the financial frenzy of the first decade of the twentieth century was encouraged by legislation that permitted companies to issue both preferred and common stock. Bonds and preferred stock had first claims on company dividends. Common shares were virtually worthless when issued but had the potential to return dividends if the profits of the company materialized. Stock issues were often much abused, with huge paper values piled high on shaky assets. Referred to as "watered" stock when based on speculation rather than assets, common shares were a gamble both for the buyer and the promoter. But the latter usually had inside information about the corporate issue and made money from commissions even if the stocks themselves proved worthless.

Despite the potential for abuse, common stocks were a surprisingly effective vehicle for mobilizing domestic and foreign capital for investment. Stock exchanges, although they had existed in Montreal and Toronto from the middle of the nineteenth century, suddenly came to life, while securities companies joined bankers and insurance agents as important players in the financial field. When mergers were in the offing, such firms as Royal Securities, Dominion Securities, or Wood Gundy were often pulling the strings and arranging for the transfer—on paper of course—of the vast sums of money required to finance the transaction.

Canada's most flamboyant financier was Max Aitken. The son of a Presbyterian minister, Aitken grew up in northern New Brunswick and turned to selling bonds and insurance when he failed the entrance examination to Dalhousie Law School. As the protégé of Halifax businessman John Stairs, Aitken became president of Stairs's new holding company, Royal Securities, in 1903. After speculating in utilities in the Caribbean and Latin America, Aitken moved to Montreal, used Montreal Trust to take over Royal Securities, and was a key figure in the merger movement of 1909–12. His crowning achievement was putting together the Steel Company of Canada in 1910, a conglomerate that included the Montreal Rolling Mills, Hamilton Steel and Iron, Canada Screw, and Canada Bolt and Nut. Having made his fortune, Aitken moved to London where he had marketed much of his speculative stock, became a member of Parliament, bought himself a title—Lord Beaverbrook—and continued to keep an eye on his Canadian interests. Among Beaverbrook's merger-making associates was a future Canadian prime minister, R.B. Bennett, whose millions were earned in part by collaborating with Aitken to merge grain elevators and hydro-electric stations on the Prairies.

Although Canadian banks were usually reluctant to speculate on the grand scale typical of securities houses, they nevertheless responded to the changes in the business climate. The BNA Act gave the federal government sole jurisdiction over banking institutions. In 1871, Ottawa passed an act requiring banks to have assets of at least $500 000, resulting in the eventual dissolution of small banks such as the Farmers Bank of Rustico in Prince Edward Island. In banking, as in other businesses, consolidation was the order of the day. The number of banks operating under dominion charter declined from forty-four to eighteen between 1880 and 1920, while the number of branches rose from under 300 to 4676. Although some twenty banks had failed in this period, many more had been absorbed by the giants in the field. Successful private bankers, such as Alloway and Champion in Winnipeg, sold out to the chartered banks, in this case the Bank of Commerce in 1919, when the partners became too old to continue the operation.

No longer simply vehicles for facilitating exchange, banks encouraged savings accounts by paying interest on deposited money, transferred funds from their many branches to profitable investment frontiers, and developed modern management structures. The major banks often figured prominently in mergers and takeovers and formed close relationships with trust and securities companies. By 1920, the Canadian banking community had developed a reputation for stability much like the solid buildings that dominated the main streets of most Canadian towns. And, like large corporations, they were built to last. Four of the five major banks of the second half of the twentieth century— Nova Scotia, Commerce, Montreal, and Royal— had established their position in the financial firmament by 1920. They also moved their head offices to Toronto or Montreal, the centres of Canadian business activity.

Much of the capital required to finance Canada's industrial economy was raised domestically, channelled from personal and business savings either directly or through financial intermediaries to potential profit-making ventures. When it came to large projects such as railways or corporate mergers, Canadians tapped foreign capital markets, usually British or American, but in some cases French and German. The pattern was set in the mercantile era when British capitalists developed the fur, fish, and timber frontiers; it continued with the use of British capital to build canals and railways. At the turn of the century, foreign investment, more than half as large as domestic savings, was a significant factor in fuelling the spectacular growth in Canada's age of industry. Foreign investment in the Canadian economy rose to nearly $5 billion by 1920. For many Canadians, this was a source of pride rather than concern, visible proof that the National Policy had worked. Moreover, domestic investment far outstripped foreign investment in this period. As late as 1926, less than 20 percent of Canadian industry was controlled by foreigners.

## PRIVATE INITIATIVE AND PUBLIC POLICY

In Canada, as in the United States and Britain, private capitalists were the preferred agents for undertaking risky economic ventures. Governments at all levels encouraged and assisted private enterprise but only became directly involved as a last resort. Largely unfettered by government regulation before the First World War, capitalists also reaped most of the profit of their risk-taking activities. Successful entrepreneurs paid no income tax whatsoever prior to 1917 and were subject to few estate or corporation taxes. A general view prevailed that the "captains of industry" were the authors of their own success and deserved to enjoy the wealth that their ability and hard work had earned them. By 1921, Canada had a charmed circle of multimillionaire businessmen who capped their careers with palatial homes, knighthoods, and unprecedented power. The people who laboured in the mines, factories, and offices of industrial Canada received far less compensation for their long hours of work, while governments at all levels accumulated huge debts through grants and guarantees to private corporations.

In the first decade of the twentieth century, entrepreneurs came under increasing criticism, and governments were encouraged to take action to protect the public against private greed. Regulatory commissions became a popular means of establishing some control over the activities of private corporations. In 1903, a Board of Railway Commissioners was set up to serve as a buffer between the disgruntled public and the railways. Federally chartered telephone companies came under the commission's jurisdiction in 1906.

Public money continued to provide much of the infrastructure, or basic services, upon which private fortunes were built. Apart from involvement in railways, Ottawa sponsored the Geological Survey, established a system of experimental farms, and subsidized cold storage facilities to enhance economic development. In 1916, at the height of the First World War, the federal government created the Honorary Advisory Council for Science and Industrial Research (later renamed the National Research Council) to take initiative in scientific research, increasingly the key to economic development.

Provincial governments enjoyed important economic powers, especially if Ottawa did not control their natural resources. Most provinces passed legislation to encourage settlement and disposed of timber and mineral rights by sale or lease. In 1897–1900, Ontario imposed an excise tax on the export of unprocessed logs to encourage manufacturing in the province. As a result of this legislation, sawmills and pulp and paper plants were established in Ontario, leading other timber-producing provinces such as Quebec and New Brunswick to adopt similar legislative measures. The Ontario government also took the dramatic step in 1906 of establishing a provincially controlled Hydro-Electric Power Commission to regulate private power companies, to distribute power, and ultimately to generate its own power. Promoted as a policy to bring "power to the people," Ontario Hydro was supported by entrepreneurs throughout southwestern sections of the province who wanted access to a cheap and reliable source of power for industrial purposes.

Like Ontario, the Prairie provinces experimented with government-owned utilities, but most provincial administrations preferred to avoid the political pitfalls of direct government ownership. Municipal governments could not afford the luxury of remaining so aloof. As cities grew and services became more complex, direct involvement seemed increasingly necessary. Private companies providing water, sewerage, street lighting, communication, and transportation services in urban settings were often granted monopoly powers, and, in the opinion of consumers, many abused their privileged position. After the 1890s, many municipal governments either assumed direct control over utilities or created regulatory commissions to keep an eye on private corporations. The result of the spate of utility development in a burgeoning industrial economy was a typically Canadian system of mixed public and private services, reflecting the circumstances in individual localities.

## WORK AND THE FAMILY

The shift to an industrial economy had an enormous impact on the Canadian family. While self-sufficiency was rare even in pre-industrial British North America, a majority of family units produced a substantial proportion of the goods they consumed, relying only peripherally on the sale of their products and their labour in the marketplace. By the twentieth century, the market played a major role in the lives of virtually every Canadian. Urban dwellers, in particular, lacked the resources to produce most of their own food, clothing, or shelter, but even in the countryside, the true subsistence farm family was becoming rare and was, in most cases, desperately poor.

Families responded to the new market economy in a gendered way. In many farming families, women began in the mid-nineteenth century to increase their production for off-farm sales, becoming major producers in dairying, poultry raising, market gardening, and fruit growing. As these areas of farming expanded and wheat farming declined east of Ontario, men took over what had previously been considered women's work. Dairying was entirely transformed in the second half of the nineteenth century. Increasingly the pasturing, feeding, calving, and milking, once regarded as women's work, were appropriated by men. For many women, this shift in farm responsibilities was welcomed as a reduction of the heavy physical labour that characterized their daily lives.

Most families depended upon the labour of all their members, including their children. Although a romantic view of childhood innocence was maintained by middle-class families who had the money to keep servants to perform household chores, the working classes could rarely afford to be sentimental about their children. Children in farm and factory households fetched water from wells, ran errands, and helped with the cooking, cleaning, gardening, baby sitting, and care of the aged and infirm. In rural areas, children were frequently kept home from school during planting and harvesting seasons. When the household economy was faced with a crisis such as the death or illness of a parent, the older children were called upon to take on adult roles.

Children, rather than wives, were the secondary wage earners in early industrializing Canada. Working-class children often entered the paid labour force at age eleven or twelve—and even younger—and lived with their parents for perhaps another fifteen years before marrying. In 1871, the

passed in Ontario and Quebec in the mid-1880s, and later replicated in other provinces, prohibited employment of boys under twelve and girls under fourteen in factories, but these laws were poorly enforced and frequently circumvented by families close to destitution.

Most working-class families were poor at some stage in their evolution. Generally, at the time of marriage, savings and two incomes allowed a couple to enjoy an acceptable, if modest, standard of living, but poverty was especially pronounced for large families consisting of children too young to work or to be left unsupervised while the mother entered the labour force. In such cases, the wife's marginal earnings from piecework, laundry, or boarders often meant the difference between a family's subsistence and destitution.

Families headed by women—those who had never married, were widowed, or whose husbands had deserted them—as well as families where the husband was too ill to work were in a particularly precarious position. Although legislation was passed in 1869 that made it a criminal offence for a man to refuse to provide his wife with food, clothes, and lodging, few women were successful in pursuing their claims. Nor could a woman expect the state or private charity to offer anything more than temporary assistance, if that. Families and individuals in early industrializing Canada were largely left to sink or swim. In this respect there was little change from the pre-industrial era when

*Farm children at work on the Prairies, circa 1900.*

Glenbow Archives/NA2157-1

census reported that 25 percent of boys and 10 percent of girls between the ages of eleven and fifteen had occupations outside the home. Factory Acts

luck and good health played a greater role than planning in determining income levels.

## LIFE IN THE WORKPLACE

Life in the industrial workplace was hard. In many occupations, ten- and twelve-hour days were common. Conditions were sometimes better in small businesses where people worked in kin or community settings, but in such cases there was often even less recourse from a cruel or capricious boss. Women and children in the workforce were particularly vulnerable. For example, young cigar makers in Montreal who were unable to keep up with unrealistic demands, or who were unwilling to defer to the whims of management, often had their wages docked and were subjected to physical discipline and confinement. Punishments were imposed to exact conformity, break a child's independence, and ensure regular work habits. In families where the child's income was critical to survival, it was not uncommon for parents to support employers in their efforts to "train" young workers.

Given their value to the family economy, many children no doubt preferred workplaces to schools. In Cumberland County, Nova Scotia, where children made up 16 percent of the coal-mining work force in the 1880s, young boys were proud to be doing "a man's job." Coal miners, working with relatively uncomplicated technology, produced an indispensable product, and their ability to shut down a mine gave them power within the workplace and the community. Yet a coal mine was a dangerous place to work. In 1891, the first of many mining disasters in Springhill, Nova Scotia, resulted in the deaths of 125 men and boys.

In keeping with the gendered notions of work that prevailed in industrializing Canada, skill, while arguably an objective concept, was also socially constructed. Certain jobs were treated as requiring special abilities or training while others were not. For example, printing, though it required little talent or training, was a well-paid "skilled" occupation that excluded women, while dressmaking, which required considerable skill, was a poorly paid "unskilled" line of work in which women were

*Garment workers in Quebec City.*
Archives nationales du Québec à Québec/P535/N-79-12-43

employed. Although women were the food manufacturers at home, in a candy-making factory such as Ganong Brothers in St Stephen, New Brunswick, only men were confectioners. Women were hired at low wages to decorate and box the prepared candies.

As the structures of industrialization were gradually put in place, it became the ideal that married men earned incomes in the marketplace while their wives stayed home to do the housework and rear the children or, in middle-class families, to supervise servants who did this work. Professionals and unionized craftsmen could often earn a wage sufficient to maintain a family, but the vast majority of wage earners could not. Nevertheless, the belief that the male head of household should, and could, earn enough to feed, clothe, and shelter a family was used to justify underpaying women workers. The future prime minister, William Lyon Mackenzie King, writing in 1897 on the sweatshops of the clothing-manufacturing sector in Toronto, quoted an owner who noted: "I don't treat the men bad, but I even up by taking advantage of the women. I have a girl who can do as much work, and as good work as a man; she gets $5 a week. The man who is standing next to her gets $11. The girls, however, average $3.50 a week, and some are as low as two dollars."[7]

On the railroads and in the highly mechanized manufacturing sectors, employers in the late nineteenth century capitulated to male worker demands that women and children not be hired as cheap labour. Such demands were often ignored in unskilled labour-intensive industries where competition to provide goods at the lowest possible cost occurred mainly on the backs of workers. The cigar makers of London, Ontario, for example, learned in the 1880s how easily a well-paid skilled occupation could be turned into a poorly paid "unskilled" job. While unionized cigar makers tried to maintain quality, restrict new entrants to the trade, and hold the line on wages, their employers were eager to reduce labour costs. When unionized workers refused to accept a cut in wages, their employers replaced most of them with women and children. By the mid-1880s, only 13 of the 150 cigar makers in town were adult males.

Company owners also kept Canadian labour in line by supporting an open door policy for immigrant labourers who agreed to work as strike breakers or under conditions that Canadians found unacceptable. In response to demands from workers, the Laurier government passed an Alien Labour Act (1897) designed to make it unlawful for "any person, company, partnership, or corporation, in any manner to pre-pay the transportation of, or in any other way to assist or solicit the importation of immigration of any alien or foreigner into Canada under contract or agreement ... to perform labour or service of any kind in Canada." Despite

its sweeping scope, the Alien Labour Act failed to prevent companies from importing contract labour and strikebreakers when they were determined to do so. The act was rarely enforced and applied only to the importation of labour from the United States.

Modern management techniques and hiring practices reduced the autonomy of many workers; so did the company-town phenomenon. Mining and textile-mill towns were frequently owned lock, stock, and barrel by companies. Homes, stores, schools, doctors, and even churches were firmly under corporate control. Cape Breton, Alberta, and British Columbia coal, Quebec asbestos, and Ontario gold, silver, and nickel were mined by workers who lived in company towns. While some factory owners took a paternal attitude towards their workers, most resorted to authoritarian control to keep their workers in line. During their 1909–10 strike, members of Cape Breton's United Mine Workers were summarily evicted from their homes and locked out of company stores. Company officials even ordered sympathetic ministers to stop sheltering the homeless in their churches.

Disease and injury were often the fate of industrial workers. Although the 1889 Royal Commission on the Relations of Labour and Capital had reported dangerous working conditions and recommended reform, little action was taken. Workers stricken by injury or disease were in the difficult position of having to prove employer negligence in order to sue for compensation. In the second decade of the twentieth century, Ontario, Nova Scotia, British Columbia, Alberta, and New Brunswick passed Workman's Compensation Acts, which conceded a limited right to industrial compensation. Still, many employees found no protection from the high levels of zinc, mercury, asbestos, dry-cleaning fluids, dyes, and other chemicals that went unregulated. Coal miners and textile workers "retired" exhausted and prematurely aged, their lungs so damaged by coal dust and fabric fibres that they coughed themselves to death. Anonymous graves along rail tracks or near remote mines bear testimony to the existence of immigrant labourers who worked under draconian conditions in industrializing Canada.

## CONCLUSION

By the turn of the century, few people could ignore the inequality that characterized the age of industry. In every Canadian town and city, hideous slums stood in sharp contrast to the elegant homes of the wealthy. William Mackenzie and Donald Mann, the swashbuckling financiers of the Canadian Northern, escaped from the collapse of their railway with a profit of $10 million while the public was left to pick up the tab. In 1914, the American investigative journalist Gustavus Myers claimed that fewer than fifty men controlled $4 billion, or one-third of Canada's wealth. Certainly no one could have made such a claim in 1867. The total estate of Nova Scotia's Enos Collins, reputed to have been one of the wealthiest men in British North America when he died in 1871, was little more than $6 million.

The conflict between labour and capital was a troubling feature of the industrial age, but it was by no means the only problem facing the new nation. As we shall see in the next chapter, immigration and urbanization were changing Canada's social fabric in ways totally unanticipated by the Fathers of Confederation.

---

## THE NATIONAL POLICY AND REGIONAL DEVELOPMENT

### A Historiographical Debate

It is a commonplace in Western and Atlantic Canada that the National Policy of the late nineteenth century was biased in favour of Central Canada. Some historians of these regions confirm popular perceptions and suggest that central Canadian industrialization occurred at the expense of the outlying regions as a result of deliberate public policy. There are also scholars, past and present, who argue that the National Policy had negligible impact on the economic fate of these two regions. Who is right?

S.A. Saunders argued in the 1930s that the economic problems of the Maritimes stemmed from decline in demand or price for the key staple exports. When British demand for timber and ships fell off in the 1880s, the region's economy began a decline from which it could not recover. The region's carrying trade meanwhile suffered a fatal blow from the competition of steam and steel ships.[8] This explanation, of course, does not address the issue of why the region's entrepreneurs did not adjust to changing economic times. According to T.W. Acheson, the failure of the Maritimes to generate a major metropolitan centre in the age of the National Policy contributed to the region's drift to outside control and industrial stagnation. "With its powerful mercantile interests," Acheson argues, "Halifax could have most easily adapted to this role, but its merchants preferred, like their Boston counterparts, to invest their large fortunes in banks and American railroad stocks than to venture them on building a new order."[9]

Economist Ken Norrie and historian Doug Owram, the authors of an economic history of Canada, are sceptical about the possibility of extensive industrialization of the Maritime region in the late nineteenth century. They are even more sceptical of attempts to pin the blame on the National Policy: "To find the argument credible, one would need to believe that fairly small changes in transportation rates or in Dominion subsidies could have had enormous effects on industrial prospects. Simply putting the issue in that manner suggests the probable answer."[10]

Norrie and Owram are equally sceptical

of claims that the National Policy discriminated against Western Canada. T.D. Regehr, for example, states, "there has been deliberate and admitted freight-rate discrimination against the West."[11] Only constant battles by westerners resulted, over time, in partial amelioration of these rates, argues Regehr. In contrast, Norrie and Owram claim flatly, "rail freight rates in the development phase of the wheat economy were at least as low as they would have been under the next most likely alternative to the national policy."[12] Norrie rejects the view that federal tariff and freight rate policies hindered western industrialization:

> In some instances, Prairie industrialization being perhaps the best example, the problem lies in being small and isolated rather than with discriminatory treatment. The present economic structure of the region is adequately explained by standard location theory concepts. It is incorrect to suggest that the federal government or other institutions have industrialized the East at the expense of the West. It must be recognized rather that any significant decentralization of industry in Canada can only be achieved by committing real resources to that end and that this means a subsidy for persons residing in the recipient regions at the expense of other Canadians.[13]

Norrie's argument perhaps makes too little allowance for the role the state has played in the marketplace, demonstrating, in its purchasing policies, for example, a strong central Canadian bias. But he correctly points out a fallacy in the claims of many who focus on alleged discrimination against the regions: the assumption that the free market, left to its own workings, would have produced a more equitable distribution of industry in Canada. The tendency of capital left on its own to concentrate in a few areas with transportation and population advantages is a universal phenomenon of the capitalist system. In some countries, the state has intervened to force industries to locate in less favoured areas, but there is little evidence that in late-nineteenth-century Canada there were significant sections of popular opinion in any region who favoured more draconian intervention in the marketplace than that envisaged by John A. Macdonald and his business community supporters.

## NOTES

[1] Bettina Bradbury, "Pigs, Cows, and Boarders: Non-Wage Forms of Survival Among Montreal's Families, 1861-91," *Labour/Le Travail* 14 (Fall 1984): 46

[2] Paul Craven, *Labouring Lives: Work and Workers in Nineteenth-Century Ontario* (Toronto: University of Toronto Press, 1995), 10

[3] Eric W. Sager and Lewis R. Fischer, "Atlantic Canada and the Age of Sail Revisited," *Canadian Historical Review* 63, 2 (June 1982): 150

[4] David H. Breen, "On the Range," *Horizon Canada* (Quebec: Centre for the Study of Teaching Canada, 1987), 1234

[5] Dianne Newell, *The Tangled Webs of History: Indians and the Law in Canada's Pacific Coast Fisheries* (Toronto: University of Toronto Press, 1993), 206

[6] Peter Baskerville, "She Has Already Hinted at 'Board': Enterprising Urban Women in British Columbia," *Histoire sociale/Social History* 26, 52 (Nov. 1993): 225

[7] Quoted in Ruth Frager, "Class and Ethnic Barriers to Feminist Perspectives in Toronto's Jewish Labour Movement, 1919–1939," *Studies in Political Economy* 30 (Autumn 1989): 148

[8] S.A. Saunders, *Economic History of the Maritime Provinces* (Ottawa: Royal Commission on Dominion–Provincial Relations, 1940)

[9] T.W. Acheson, "The National Policy and the Industrialization of the Maritimes, 1880–1910," *Acadiensis* 1, 2 (Spring 1972): 27–28

[10] Kenneth Norrie and Douglas Owram, *A History of the Canadian Economy* (Toronto: Harcourt Brace Jovanovich, 1991), 402

[11] T.D. Regehr, "Western Canada and the Burden of National Transportation Policies" in *Canada and the Burden of Unity*, ed. D.J. Bercuson (Toronto: Macmillan, 1977), 115

[12] Norrie and Owram, *History of the Canadian Economy*, 327

[13] Kenneth H. Norrie, "Some Comments on Prairie Economic Alienation," *Canadian Public Policy* 2, 2 (Spring 1976): 222

## SELECTED READING

Major economic histories include Kenneth Norrie and Douglas Owram, *A History of the Canadian Economy* (Toronto: Harcourt Brace Jovanovich, 1991); W.T. Easterbrook and Hugh G.J. Aitken, *Canadian Economic History* (1956; reprint Toronto: University of Toronto Press, 1988); and William L. Marr and Donald G. Paterson, *Canada: An Economic History* (Toronto: Gage, 1980). Business developments are discussed in Graham D. Taylor and Peter A. Baskerville, *A Concise History of Business in Canada* (Toronto: Oxford University Press, 1994); Michael Bliss, *Northern Enterprise: Five Centuries of Canadian Business* (Toronto: McClelland and Stewart, 1987) and *A Living Profit: Studies in the Social History of Canadian Business, 1883–1911* (Toronto: McClelland and Stewart, 1974); and Tom Naylor, *The History of Canadian Business, 1867–1914*, 2 vols. (Toronto: Lorimer, 1975). State–business relations are illuminated in H.V. Nelles and Christopher Armstrong, *Monopoly's Moment: The Organization and Regulation of Canadian Utilities, 1830–1930* (Toronto: University of Toronto Press, 1988). Biographies of early Canadian tycoons include Michael Bliss, *A Canadian Millionaire: The Life and Business Times of Sir Joseph Flavelle, Bart., 1858–1939* (Toronto: Macmillan, 1978); Gregory P. Marchildon, *Profits and Politics: Beaverbrook and the Gilded Age of Canadian Finance* (Toronto: University of Toronto Press, 1996); and Joy L. Stantik, *Timothy Eaton and the Rise of the Department Store* (Toronto: University of Toronto Press, 1990). A good history of one of the "big five" banks is found in Duncan McDowall, *Quick to the Frontier: Canada's Royal Bank* (Toronto: McClelland and Stewart, 1993).

Geographically focused studies include Morris Zaslow, *The Opening of the Canadian North, 1870–1914* (Toronto: McClelland and Stewart, 1971); Chester Martin, *Dominion Lands Policy* (Toronto: Carleton Library, 1973); V.C. Fowke, *The National Policy and the Wheat Economy* (Toronto: University of Toronto Press, 1957); John Herd Thompson, *The Harvests of War: The Prairie West, 1914–1918* (Toronto: McClelland and Stewart, 1978); Ian M. Drummond, *Progress Without Planning: The Economic History of Ontario from Confederation to the Second World War* (Toronto: University of Toronto Press, 1987); H.V. Nelles, *The Politics of Development: Forests, Mines and Hydro-electric Power in Ontario, 1849–1941* (Toronto: Macmillan, 1974); Jean Hamelin and Yves Roby, *Histoire économique du Québec, 1851–1896* (Montreal: Fides, 1971); J.I. Little, *Crofters and Habitants: Settler Society, Economy and Culture in a Quebec Township, 1848–1881* (Montreal: McGill-Queen's University Press, 1991); Normand Séguin, *La Conquête du sol au 19e siècle* (Montreal: Boréal Express, 1977); J.H. Dales, *Hydroelectricity and Economic Development: Quebec, 1898–1940* (Cambridge: Harvard University Press, 1957); William F. Ryan, *The Clergy and Economic Growth in Quebec, 1896–1914* (Quebec: Les Presses de l'Université Laval, 1966); Robert Armstrong, *Structure and Change: An Economic History of Quebec* (Toronto: Gage, 1984); Ronald Rudin, *Banking en français: The French Banks of Quebec, 1835–1935* (Toronto: University of Toronto Press, 1985); S.A. Saunders, *Economic History of the Maritime Provinces* (Ottawa: Royal Commission on Dominion–Provincial Relations, 1940); David G. Alexander, *Atlantic Canada and Confederation: Essays in Canadian Political Economy* (Toronto: University of Toronto Press, 1983); and Eric W. Sager with Gerald E. Panting, *Maritime Capital: The Shipping Industry in Atlantic Canada, 1820-1914* (Montreal: McGill-Queen's University Press, 1990).

Ontario's relative success over other regions is explored in John Isbister, "Agriculture, Balanced Growth and Social Change in Central Canada since 1850: An Interpretation," in *Perspectives on Canadian Economic History*, ed. Douglas McCalla (Toronto: Copp Clark Pitman, 1987): 58–80; Douglas McCalla, *Planting the Province: The Economic History of Upper Canada, 1784–1870* (Toronto: University of Toronto Press, 1993); and N.R.M. Seifried, *The Regional*

*Structure of the Canadian Economy* (Toronto: Nelson, 1984). See René Hardy, *La Sidérurgie dans le monde rural* (Québec: Les Presses de l'Université Laval, 1995) for a discussion of the decline of Quebec's iron industry at the turn of the twentieth century.

On the post-Confederation fur trade, see Arthur J. Ray, *The Canadian Fur Trade in the Industrial Age* (Toronto: University of Toronto Press, 1990). On changes in a major fishery, see Rosemary E. Ommer, *From Outpost to Outport: A Structural Analysis of the Jersey–Gaspé Fishery* (Montreal: McGill-Queen's University Press, 1991). The continuing importance of "truck" is examined in Rosemary E. Ommer, ed., *Merchant Credit and Labour Struggles in Historical Perspective* (Fredericton: Acadiensis Press, 1990).

On the aboriginal economy in the Industrial Age, see Bruce W. Hodgins and Jamie Benidickson, *The Temagami Experience* (Toronto: University of Toronto Press, 1989); Sarah Carter, *Lost Harvests: Prairie Indian Reserve Farmers and Government Policy* (Montreal: McGill-Queen's University Press, 1990); Kerry Abel, *Drum Song: Glimpses of Dene History* (Montreal: McGill-Queen's University Press, 1993) and Dianne Newell, *The Tangled Webs of History: Indians and the Law in Canada's Pacific Coast Fisheries* (Toronto: University of Toronto Press, 1994).

On the evolution of the tariff, see Ben Forster, *A Conjunction of Interests: Business, Politics, and Tariffs, 1825–1879* (Toronto: University of Toronto Press, 1986) and J.H. Dales, *The Protective Tariff in Canada's Development* (Toronto: University of Toronto Press, 1966). Railway development is assessed in W. Kaye Lamb, *History of the Canadian Pacific Railway* (New York: Macmillan, 1977); G.R. Stevens, *History of the Canadian National Railways* (New York: Macmillan, 1973); T.D. Regehr, *The Canadian Northern Railway: Pioneer Road of the Northern Prairies, 1895–1918* (Toronto: Macmillan, 1976); John Eagle, *The Canadian Pacfic Railway and the Development of Western Canada* (Montreal and Kingston: McGill-Queen's University Press, 1989); and Ken Cruikshank, *Close Ties: Railways, Governmemt, and the Board of Railway Commissioners, 1851-1933* (Montreal and Kingston: McGill-Queen's University Press, 1991). Vernon Fowke's *National Policy and the Wheat Economy* (Toronto: University of Toronto Press, 1957) makes the Prairie case against the National Policy. An opposing view is presented in Kenneth H. Norrie, *The National Policy and the Prairie Region* (New Haven, CT: Yale University Press, 1971). Maritime assessments of national economic policies should begin with the much-reprinted essay by T.W. Acheson, "The National Policy and the Industrialization of the Maritimes, 1880–1910," *Acadiensis* 1 (Spring 1972): 3–28. On the foreign ownership debate, see Glenn Williams, *Not for Export: Toward a Political Economy of Canada's Arrested Industrialization* (Toronto: McClelland and Stewart, 1983); and Gordon Laxer, *Open for Business: The Roots of Foreign Ownership in Canada* (Toronto: Oxford University Press, 1989).

Working-class life, described more fully in chapter 5, is analyzed in Terry Copp, *The Anatomy of Poverty: The Condition of the Working Class in Montreal, 1897–1929* (Toronto: McClelland and Stewart, 1974); Michael Piva, *The Conditions of the Working Class in Toronto, 1900–1921* (Ottawa: University of Ottawa Press, 1979); Judith Fingard, *The Dark Side of Life in Victorian Halifax* (Halifax: Pottersfield Press, 1989); Paul Craven ed., *Labouring Lives: Work and Workers in Nineteenth-Century Ontario* (Toronto: University of Toronto Press, 1995); and Bryan D. Palmer, *Working Class Experience: Rethinking the History of Canadian Labour, 1800–1991* (Toronto: McClelland and Stewart, 1992).

# 4
# A NATION ON THE MOVE, 1867-1921

IN 1877, MANZO NAGANO, A NINETEEN-YEAR-old Japanese sailor, jumped ship at New Westminster, British Columbia. Probably the only Japanese in Canada for about fifteen years, Nagano earned his living longshoring and fishing for salmon. He returned to Japan for a time, travelled to the United States, and finally settled in Victoria in 1892, where he established a shop selling Japanese products. Later he branched into the salmon-exporting business. He brought a woman from Japan to be his wife, and they opened a hotel. Nagano's industry and achievement were characteristic of many early Japanese immigrants to Canada, but his visibility made him a target of economic jealousy and the racial fears of his Victoria neighbours.[1]

Nagano was one of nearly five million immigrants who arrived in Canada between 1871 and 1921 (see table 4.1). As his story suggests, newcomers had mixed experiences. Optimism and opportunity were often blunted by uncertainty and disappointment. Some people prospered; others did not. The same could be said for most Canadians, over four million of whom left Canada in the same period. Whatever their hopes and fears, Canadians, old and new, were on the move in the half century following Confederation. They struggled, sometimes individually, increasingly together, to come to terms with a country whose families, communities, and institutions were changing, often dramatically.

*Galicians at immigration sheds in Quebec City.*

National Archives of Canada/C4745

**Table 4.1**

CANADA'S POPULATION (IN THOUSANDS), 1861–1921

| Year | Natural Increase | Immigration | Emigration | Net Migration | Population |
|------|------------------|-------------|------------|---------------|-----------|
| 1861 | | | | | 3230 |
| 1861–71 | 650 | 186 | 376 | -191 | 3689 |
| 1871-81 | 720 | 353 | 438 | - 85 | 4325 |
| 1881-91 | 714 | 903 | 1 108 | -205 | 4833 |
| 1891-01 | 719 | 326 | 507 | -181 | 5371 |
| 1901-11 | 1120 | 1782 | 1 066 | 751 | 7207 |
| 1911-21 | 1349 | 1592 | 1 360 | 233 | 8788 |

*Source: David C. Corbett,* Canada's Immigration Policy: A Critique *(Toronto: University of Toronto Press, 1957), 121*

## THE PROBLEM OF OUTMIGRATION

In the early years of Confederation, the slow rate of population growth was as great a concern as railways and tariffs for Canadian leaders. Despite the passage of the Dominion Lands Act in 1872, most immigrants to North America in the late nineteenth century preferred to settle in the United States. So, too, it seemed, did many Canadians. Frontier lands and industrial jobs, as well as a better climate, attracted Canadians like a magnet, and there seemed to be nothing that the nation's leaders could do to stop the exodus.

In Atlantic Canada, close family ties and geographic proximity had long made New England a place to find work. Once the trend was set, other family members followed, producing what demographers describe as a chain migration. Nearly half a million people left the Maritimes between 1880 and 1921, a number representing over one-third of the total population remaining in the region. Maritime carpenters thrown out of work by the collapse of the shipbuilding industry helped to build the suburbs of American cities, former farm boys delivered milk in horse-drawn vans, fishing families found the protected American markets easier to supply from Gloucester and Salem in Massachusetts than they did from Barrington and Yarmouth in Nova Scotia. Women worked as domestics, factory hands, clerks, secretaries, teachers, and nurses. Early in the twentieth century, one commentator estimated that as many as 70 percent of the nurses in Massachusetts were "Provincials," the term used to describe Canadians living in the United States.

Newfoundland experienced similar trends. While most Newfoundlanders moved to Massachusetts or New York, a significant number also found work in the industrializing areas of the Maritimes, particularly Halifax and Cape Breton. The development of the iron reserves on Bell Island to supply Nova Scotia's steel industry led naturally to the migration of labour across the Cabot Strait to Cape Breton. From there, the Newfoundlanders often joined the Nova Scotians moving to better opportunities in the United States.

In the same period, large families and limited agricultural opportunities encouraged over seven hundred thousand Quebeckers to leave Canada, many of them destined for mill towns in New England. With factories employing men, women, and children, whole families joined the exodus and thereby became the founders of a Franco-American community that still retains its distinctiveness. Quebec's Roman Catholic Church tried to keep its flock at home by developing colonization societies to settle frontier areas of the province, but such efforts had little success.

The experience of Norbert Dubois is a good example of the options facing Quebec's farmers in the late nineteenth century. Born in St Cuthbert, Bethier County, in 1855, Norbert was the younger son of a farming family. Since there was little likelihood of receiving enough land from the family holdings to make a success of farming, he moved to Rhode Island in 1878, soon after having married a woman from his local parish. Their first child was born in the United States. In 1881, the family moved back to St Cuthbert, where they took up farming, eventually purchasing a small plot of land. Early in the 1900s, the family returned to Rhode Island. When his father died, Norbert sold his share of the family property to one of his brothers for $950, apparently preferring to remain in the United States, where he died in 1932.

The Canadian West had little attraction for

*It was lumber mills such as this one on the Rimouski River that enabled some families in the colonization regions of Quebec to survive the difficulties of farming in marginal agricultural regions.*

National Archives of Canada/PA22075

Quebec's rural migrants. Efforts by Bishop Taché and his successors in St Boniface to repatriate francophones from New England bore some fruit in the 1870s, but the numbers trickled off despite attempts to maintain interest through a federally sponsored newspaper, *Le Colonisateur*, distributed throughout Quebec and New England in the 1880s. In 1901, there were only twenty-three thousand French-speaking settlers on the Prairies, many of them from France, Belgium, and Switzerland rather than Quebec. Francophones were scattered throughout the West in communities such as St Albert, Grande Clairière, Montmartre, St Brieux, and Gravelbourg. Together they had an important influence on the culture and politics of the region, but they found their culture increasingly submerged in a flood of immigrants who spoke any language but French.

At the same time, the numbers of francophones living in Ontario and the Maritimes increased significantly in the half century following Confederation. Quebeckers crossed the border into eastern and northern Ontario to take advantage of employment opportunities in farming, resource

development, and the federal bureaucracy. The number of Franco-Ontarians jumped from 102 743 in 1881 to 158 671 in 1901 and 202 442 in 1911, an increase that brought their numbers to nearly 10 percent of the provincial population.

Although some Acadians were attracted to jobs in New England, they were less likely than their anglophone neighbours to leave the Maritimes. They were also more likely than anglophones to have large families. As a result, those claiming a French heritage in New Brunswick rose from less than 16 percent of the population in 1871 to over 31 percent in 1921. By the latter date, Acadians increased to 10.8 percent of the population in Nova Scotia and 13.5 percent in Prince Edward Island.

Rural Ontario lost population to the developing western territories as well as to the agricultural, forest, and urban frontiers of the United States in the last three decades of the nineteenth century. However, unlike the Maritimes and Quebec, where outmigration exceeded immigration until the 1930s, Ontario was able to stem the outward flow in the first decade of the twentieth century. Ontario's rapidly developing industrial economy and resource frontier employed not only the surplus population from the rural areas of the nation but also a rising tide of immigrants who flooded into Canada in the early years of the twentieth century.

## IMMIGRATION POLICY

Under the British North America Act, immigration was a responsibility shared by federal and provincial jurisdictions. Ottawa took an early lead with the passage, in 1869, of an act defining immigration and citizenship procedures. The act established immigration offices in Great Britain and continental Europe, quarantine stations in Halifax, Saint John, and Quebec, and immigration branches in various Canadian cities. On paper, Canada's immigration policy was an open one; only criminals were denied admission. In practice, people who were deemed destitute, physically unfit, or mentally disabled were required to post a bond, and were often turned away.

In the first three decades following Confederation, Canada's ethnic balance changed very little. The 1901 census reported that 88 percent of Canadians were of British or French descent, just 4 percent fewer than in 1871. But that picture was changing. Unlike many Canadians, Minister of the Interior Clifford Sifton was prepared to welcome Eastern Europeans, assessing them as good prospects to survive the rigours of pioneering on the Canadian Prairies. "I think a stalwart peasant in a sheep-skin coat, born on the soil, whose forefathers have been farmers for ten generations, with a stout wife and a half-dozen children is good quality," Sifton declared.[2] Business people were similarly enthusiastic about such recruits, seeing them as ideal candidates for the hard, low-wage labour needed in factories, resource industries, and homes.

Under Sifton's direction, the Department of the Interior, in cooperation with transportation companies and other private recruitment agencies, advertised extensively in Europe and the United States for immigrants to settle the Prairies and work in Canada's expanding industries. These efforts proved effective in part because they coincided with a number of global trends that combined to make immigration an attractive option for many people. In Europe, ethnic and religious tensions, outright persecution, industrial upheaval, and the collapse of peasant farming systems "pushed" many potential emigrants to seek a new life in Canada. An upswing in the international economy, vigorous recruitment campaigns, improved transportation by steam and rail, technological breakthroughs in farming, and the relatively high wages in Canada "pulled" people to what was increasingly perceived as a land of opportunity.

Sifton's ministerial successor, Frank Oliver, pursued a much more restrictive immigration policy: "It is not merely a question of filling the country with people," he opined. "It is a question of the ultimate efforts put forward for the building up of a Canadian nationality. This can never be accomplished if the preponderance of the people should be of such a class and character as will deteriorate rather than elevate the condition of our people and our country at large."[3] In 1906, the Immigration Act was revised to incorporate such views. The prohibited categories were expanded to include the "feeble minded," those "afflicted with a loathsome disease," professional beggars, prostitutes and those living off of their avails, persons convicted of crimes of "moral turpitude," and anyone "likely to become a public charge," or who "may become dangerous to the public health." Later amendments barred women or girls coming to Canada for "any immoral purpose" as well as those persons suffering from alcoholism, mental or physical defects, or a condition of "constitutional psychopathic inferiority." Because these terms were so vague, immigration officials had considerable latitude to make arbitrary judgements about the suitability of applicants.

These laws failed to stem the flow of people into the country before the First World War. From a low of 16 835 arrivals in 1896 to a high of 400 000 in 1913, immigrants came from Britain, Europe, the United States, and Asia, many of them settling in the four western provinces. Between 1896 and 1914, nearly a million immigrant farmers were found for Canada's agricultural economy. Other immigrants found work, usually on a temporary basis, as farm labourers. In 1891, sixty-three hundred seasonal workers were employed in the wheat harvest; by 1921 the number had increased to sixty-three thousand. Many of the people employed on western farms came from the eastern provinces on "harvest trains," placed in service specifically to cater to the labour needs of the wheat economy.

Immigrant workers were also common in the mining, lumbering, and railway camps scattered throughout industrializing Canada. With the assistance of the federal government and private agencies, company officials recruited Slavs,

Scandinavians, and Italians for these jobs, but when their numbers proved insufficient, companies pressed the government to admit Chinese, Japanese, and East Indian labourers. Historian Donald Avery estimates that between 1907 and 1914, when all three of Canada's transcontinental railway systems were engaged in construction projects, fifty thousand to seventy thousand workers were required annually by the railway companies alone.[4] Still other immigrants were attracted to the jobs opening up in Canada's industrial cities. Statistics show that the percentage of unskilled labourers entering Canada rose from 31 percent of total immigration in 1907 to 43 percent in 1914, while the percentage of agriculturalists declined from 38 percent to 28 percent in the same period.

Between 1901 and 1921, over three million immigrants arrived in Canada. The majority of them—perhaps as many as two-thirds—came from the United States and Great Britain, but enough came from other nations of the world to alter the ethnic composition of Canada. By 1920, over 20 percent of Canadians traced their origins to countries other than Great Britain and France. The three Prairie provinces, with 54 percent of the foreign-born, were entirely transformed by the newcomers. There, Canadian, British, and American settlers lived side by side with eastern and western Europeans, each of whom contributed about 20 percent to the population. On the Pacific Coast, the cultural mix varied again. Sixty percent of the 40 000 Chinese and virtually all of the 16 000 Japanese enumerated by the 1921 census were located in British Columbia, which otherwise was 60 percent British. Only the Maritime region, with its agricultural frontier taken up and its industrial base languishing, failed to attract a significant number of immigrants outside of its coal-mining and steel-making communities.

Because of the high birth rate among francophones, their percentage of the population of Canada dropped only marginally, from 31.1 percent in 1871 to 28.2 percent in 1921. The percentage of non-francophones and non-anglophones (called allophones) in Quebec rose from 1.6 percent in 1871 to 4.9 percent in 1921. While this increase did not represent a major demographic shift, its effect was particularly noticeable in Montreal, where 80 percent of the allophones—and 60 percent of the anglophones—chose to live.

By the second decade of the twentieth century, the population patterns of the "new" Canada were beginning to take shape. Over half of the Dominion's population continued to live in Quebec and Ontario, but the proportion of Canadians living in these two provinces dropped from nearly 75 percent in 1891 to 60 percent in 1921. Maritimers accounted for only 11.4 percent, down from 18.2 percent thirty years earlier. Indeed, Prince Edward Island's population in 1921 was smaller than it had been in any decade since the 1860s. By contrast, the West registered explosive growth. Prairie populations rose from 7.8 percent to 22.3 percent of the Canadian total in the first two decades of the twentieth century, while British Columbia in 1921 accounted for 6 percent of the nation's people.

Canadians harboured deep fears about immigration. For many English-speaking Canadians, the tide of foreigners threatened the dominance of British culture. Francophones were even more cautious. Since most immigrants came from English-speaking countries—and those who did not quickly assimilated to the Anglo-Canadian culture—French Canadians saw themselves disappearing in a sea of English-speaking North Americans. Between 1900 and 1940, virtually all nationalist organizations in Quebec went on record as opposing Canada's "open door" immigration policy. Quebec's leading nationalist advocate, Henri Bourassa, urged a federal policy of bilingualism to reassure francophones, but most English Canadians were determined to keep Canada British. To that end, they insisted that new arrivals should be moulded to the values and institutions of the British majority, in what Howard Palmer has termed "Anglo-conformity."[5] As a result of such views, there was little likelihood of Canada becoming a "mosaic" of different but equal peoples, or the "melting pot" favoured in the United States. Rather, the nation become a battleground for many cultures trying to establish their place in a rigid social pecking order.

## SETTLERS AND SOJOURNERS

The federal government's early difficulties in attracting large numbers of farmers to the West created an interest in sponsoring block settlements for ethnic minorities. In the 1870s, about seventy-four hundred German-speaking Mennonites left their homes in western Russia to settle in Manitoba; two decades later, their descendants spread into the area that would become the province of Saskatchewan. The Mennonites proved excellent farmers, introducing crop rotation and planting trees as wind breaks. Because they were pacifists, farmed communally, and stuck to themselves, they were initially viewed with suspicion by their neighbours. Despite their exclusiveness, the Mennonites created prosperous farming communities and soon established good relations with the people living around them.

Also in the 1870s, two thousand Icelanders settled in Gimli ("Paradise"), Manitoba, driven from their homeland by economic depression and volcanic eruptions. Just after the colony was founded, a devastating outbreak of smallpox resulted in an armed quarantine of the settlement and the death of a hundred people, mainly young children. This tragedy was followed by floods in 1879 and 1880. Religious tensions between adherents of the Church of Iceland and the more conservative Lutherans also racked the community and caused a number of the settlers to move to the United States. Such difficulties notwithstanding, the colony thrived. Within a generation, its members had begun to adapt to English-Canadian norms, while retaining pride in their distinct culture, which was reflected in their own schools, churches, and Icelandic-language newspaper.

In the 1880s, the first wave of Jewish immigrants, fleeing persecution in the Russian Empire, established farming settlements in what would become Saskatchewan. It was a new experience for a people who had been barred by law from farming in their homeland. By the end of the century, Jews subjected to discriminatory policies in Poland, Austria-Hungary, and Germany, also turned to Canada as a place of refuge, but they found that

Canada was not without its own discriminatory practices. General hostility towards non-Christians forced Jewish immigrants to stick together, despite their diverse cultural backgrounds. At the same time, discrimination in employment and quotas restricting Jewish entrants to legal and medical schools focused them into a narrow range of occupations. In Winnipeg, Jews took up jobs as unskilled labourers, pedlars, and small shopkeepers and congregated in the city's north end. Wherever they settled, socialist political beliefs distinguished many Jewish settlers from their usually more conservative neighbours.

The Prairies were home to about twenty-five thousand Jews by 1921. Even more could be found in Quebec and Ontario, which each counted almost fifty thousand Jews in their population in 1921. Because Montreal and Toronto had Jewish communities and offered urban employment, many Jews chose to make these cities their home, and Montreal's Jewish community quadrupled between 1901 and 1911. The Jewish presence in Quebec put tremendous pressure on the Protestant English-language schools, which the Jews attended because they could not get provincial grants to create their own schools. By a 1903 ruling, Jews were considered Protestants for the purposes of school taxes, but they received few benefits from this ruling. By the 1920s, nearly 40 percent of the Protestant School Board's students were Jewish, but there were no Jewish high school teachers. Protestant prayers and religious instruction were imposed upon Jewish children, who were also denied the right to stay at home on Jewish holidays.

Not all group settlers came from Europe. The Mormons, adherents of the Church of Jesus Christ of the Latter-Day Saints, began moving to Canada from their base in Utah in the 1880s. The first eight families, under the leadership of Charles Ora Card, arrived in the Northwest Territories in 1887. Using dryland farming techniques developed in Utah, the Mormons brought into agricultural production areas of the Prairies that had hitherto supported only open-range ranching. The aim of permanent settlement was reflected in one of Card's advertisements: "Come along with your capital and build our flouring mills, sugar refiner-

*The Cardston Temple of the Church of Jesus Christ of the Latter-Day Saints.*
Glenbow Archives/ND27-12

ies, electric railways and electric lights, and aid to establish other industries and grow up with an enterprising and healthy country. Don't forget to secure a good farm adjacent to one of the grandest irrigation systems of modern times."[6]

The Mormon population in Alberta rose to seven thousand by 1912. In the following year, building began on a temple located in Cardston, Alberta. Completed ten years later, it was distinctive not only for its size and style of architecture but also because it was the first Mormon temple to be built outside of the United States. Like other religiously defined cultural groups, the Mormons often felt the prejudice of neighbours who condemned their religious beliefs, most notably their advocacy of polygamy. The Mormons gave up this practice soon after their arrival in Canada, but Canadians were slow to forget that this had once been a distinguishing feature of Mormon culture.

One of the first groups to respond to Sifton's stepped-up recruitment program in the 1890s was a block of Doukhobors in Russia who were being persecuted by the tsar for their ethnic traits and religious practices. Under an agreement negotiated in 1898 with the help of Russian intellectual Leo Tolstoy and University of Toronto professor James Mavor, some seventy-four hundred Doukhobors settled on 400 000 acres of land near Yorkton, Saskatchewan. Mainly followers of visionary leader Peter Veregin, who required his flock to live comunally, they soon became divided over the degree of loyalty the group should maintain to their leader's beliefs. The most fervent followers, called the Sons of Freedom, began in 1902 to destroy their property and conduct nude demonstrations as visible evidence of their faith. For shocked Canadians, such behaviour was only visible evidence that the whole group should be brought into conformity with Anglo-Canadian norms. In 1906, the government began forcing Doukhobors to follow the strict letter of the homestead law with respect to their communal landholdings. About a third of the group agreed to abandon their communalism, and remained in Saskatchewan under their leader Peter Makaroff. In 1912, the rest joined Veregin in the creation of a new utopia in the interior of British Columbia.

During the First World War, the Hutterites, a German-speaking pacifist group with communal practices, negotiated entry into Canada. Most of

*With their strongly held beliefs about the appropriate spheres for men and women, middle-class Canadians objected to the hard physical labour performed by women in Doukhobor families and the extreme patriarchal control that Doukhobor men held over women and children.*

National Archives of Canada/C8891

them had spent one or two generations in South Dakota before moving northward. Settling in Manitoba and Alberta, they established communities that resisted all efforts at assimilation. Their distinctive communal arrangements included a children's nursery, women's spinning hall, and common dining room. When a community reached a population of between one hundred and two hundred people, another one was established, which remained as self-sufficient, remote, and autonomous as its predecessor.

Canada also became the homeland for thousands of people from the Hapsburg provinces of Galicia and Bukovyna. Known today as Ukrainians, they were the largest and the most visible of all

European peasant cultures to come to Canada. As many as 150 000 Ukrainians had arrived by 1914 and another 70 000 came in the interwar years. The exact numbers are difficult to determine since the newcomers were designated in a variety of ways in immigration records and came from countries whose boundaries were notoriously fluid. Often poor, illiterate, and oppressed in their homeland, they were the prototype of Sifton's peasant in a sheepskin coat. Prior to 1910, the vast majority of Ukrainian migrants were men, the most destitute of whom began their Canadian experience clustered in tenements in the north end of Winnipeg and worked as railway navvies and farm labourers. As soon as they could do so, they moved to their own farms, many of them in the vicinity of Dauphin, Manitoba, Yorkton, Saskatchewan, or the Edna-Star district northeast of Edmonton. The Ukrainians quickly earned a reputation for hard work and determination, though their cultural practices brought widespread criticism from their Canadian-born neighbours.

The onion-shaped dome of their church architecture was the most visible symbol of a Ukrainian presence in the dominion. The thatched-roof homes built by first-generation Ukrainians were also unlike any others found in the West, and they elicited much comment. Because of their numbers and varied political experiences, the Ukrainians were never a uniform cultural group. They held political views ranging from socialist to conservative and subscribed to a wide range of religious beliefs, although a majority of those who came before the First World War were Catholics of the Byzantine Rite. Some of them assimilated to

Anglo-Canadian norms quickly; others less so. Nevertheless as a group, the Ukrainians left an indelible mark on Canada. In their insistence on maintaining their cultural distinctiveness, they became a "third" force in Canadian social development. Historian Gerald Friesen argues that, "As much as any other single ethnic group, the Ukrainians were responsible for the official adoption of today's bilingual-multicultural definition of Canadian society." [7]

The majority of newcomers came to stay, but another category of immigrant, called sojourners, planned to return to their homelands with some money in their pockets. Most Chinese and Japanese immigrants fell into this category. So, too, did a number of eastern Europeans, such as the people from the mountain villages where the borders of Greece, Bulgaria, Serbia, and Albania meet. Now known as Macedonians, they began migrating to Canada to find work in the first decade of the twentieth century. Overwhelmingly single or young married men, many of them found jobs in Toronto's factories, abattoirs, and construction sites. While in Toronto, they lived in boarding houses located in ethnic enclaves such as Cabbagetown. During the recession of 1907, some three hundred Macedonian sojourners were deported to prevent them from becoming objects of Canadian charity, but their numbers continued to grow. Mutual support soon found expression in the creation in 1910 of a "national" Eastern Orthodox parish centred in SS Cyril and Methody Church in Toronto. When Balkan Wars in 1912-13 divided their homeland, many Macedonian sojourners decided to become permanent settlers, a decision confirmed by the difficulties of returning to Europe during the First World War.

Italians came both as settlers and sojourners, their numbers swelling in the first two decades of the twentieth century when over 120 000 Italians arrived in Canada. Like the Macedonians, most of the early Italian immigrants were young single men. They were often recruited by Italian labour agents (*padroni*) based in Montreal and Toronto who sponsored contract labour for railway and mining companies. The majority of the Italians who chose to stay in Canada lived in Montreal and

Toronto; others settled in communities across the nation. The low proportion of women among them—10 834 out of a population of 45 411 in 1911—suggests one of the reasons why ten years later only 66 769 people of Italian origin were reported living in Canada. Some men returned to their homeland once their work contracts expired; others moved to the United States where the vast majority of Italian immigrants to North America chose to settle.

## "WHITE CANADA FOREVER"

While eastern and southern Europeans were subjected to discrimination, non-white immigrants bore the brunt of Canadian hostility. The Chinese, who performed the most dangerous jobs in the construction of the CPR, were almost universally despised. In defending his policy of importing Chinese workers, John A. Macdonald revealed his contempt when he told a Toronto political meeting: "Well they do come and so do rats. I am pledged to build the great Pacific Railroad in five years, and if I cannot obtain white labour, I must employ other." [8] Following the completion of the railway, many of the labourers stayed in Canada because their families back in China depended upon the money they sent home. Angry whites complained that they were unfair competition for jobs, and began to lobby for their deportation.

Responding to pressure from the province of British Columbia where most of the Chinese had settled, the federal government imposed a $50 head tax on Chinese immigrants in 1885. The tax was raised to $100 in 1901 and an astounding $500 in 1904, equivalent to a year's wages. The result was a gender imbalance in the Chinese-Canadian population. In the period before the First World War, most of the small number of Chinese women in the country were the wives of merchants who could afford to pay the tax or prostitutes who were already in Canada when the tax was instituted. Shunned by the broader society, the Chinese lived in segregated Chinatowns where support was available for the homeless, ill, and aged.

Like the Chinese, most Japanese immigrants

to Canada (known as Issei) viewed themselves as sojourners who would return home after making some money. Many did so, but by 1910 a number

*Chinatowns such as this one in Victoria are among the legacies of racial segregation in Canada.*

National Archives of Canada/C23415

of Japanese men in Canada had established themselves in farming, fishing, and trade in the Vancouver and Steveston areas of British Columbia. Soon they began to bring in Japanese women and establish families. Known as "picture brides" because husbands had only their pictures when they "proposed," the women were married by proxy in Japan, after negotiations between the couple's families. The economic success of the Japanese drew the ire of their racist neighbours who made no secret of the fact that they wanted to keep British Columbia "white forever."

Whether immigrant or Canadian-born, Chinese and Japanese were denied the franchise in the western provinces, barred from access to the professions, subjected to discriminatory housing covenants, and segregated in public places. They were also threatened with physical violence. In 1907, whites marched through Japanese and Chinese sections of Vancouver, breaking windows and shouting racist slogans. While an isolated example, the incident indicated the depth of the hostility faced by Asian immigrants. The federal government responded to these racist sentiments

by negotiating an agreement with Japan that restricted the number of Japanese allowed to enter the country to four hundred annually. Anti-Asian feeling was not limited to the West Coast. In Calgary, where the Chinese formed less than 1 percent of the population, a smallpox outbreak in 1892 was blamed on the Chinese community because four of its members were included among those quarantined. When the four were released, a mob of three hundred tried to find them, destroying several Chinese-owned laundries in the process.

While it was difficult for Canadians to impose restrictions on immigrants from India, which, like Canada, was a colony of the British Empire, it did not stop them from trying. The federal government passed an order-in-council in 1908 requiring East Indians to come to Canada by continuous passage from India. Since there was no direct steamship line between the two countries, the regulation virtually precluded immigration. In 1913, thirty-eight Sikhs contested the restriction and were admitted. This experience encouraged others to charter the *Komagata Maru*, a Japanese-owned freighter to bring 376 Punjabis, mostly Sikhs, to Canada in 1914. Detained on board for two months in Vancouver harbour while their case was heard before the courts, the would-be immigrants were eventually ordered to leave. To give point to the court order, the Royal Canadian Navy cruiser *Rainbow* was sent to the scene. Due to such policies, only 1016 East Indians were enumerated in Canada in 1921, down from 2342 (2315 men and 27 women) ten years earlier.

By the late nineteenth century, most whites had become adherents of racist beliefs that held blacks to be mentally and morally inferior. Even Wilfrid Laurier was heard to proclaim in 1910 that: "We see in the United States what grave problems may arise from the presence of a race unable to become full members of the same social family as ourselves."[9] Thus the arrival between 1910 and 1912 of some thirteen hundred African-American homesteaders from Oklahoma, where statehood brought deteriorating conditions for blacks, caused a major uproar. Because they were healthy American citizens and held property, immigration regulations could not be used to keep them out. Public petitions from all three Prairie provinces urged Ottawa to ban further admission of black immigrants and the federal government prepared an order-in-council to prohibit black immigration for a year but it was never proclaimed. Fears that relations with the United States would be damaged, and that black voters in Ontario and the Maritimes would be alienated, apparently caused politicians to exercise restraint. Instead, agents were sent into the United States to discourage black immigrants, and border officials were rewarded for the rigorous application of immigration regulations against blacks trying to enter the country— policies that, sadly, had the effect that was intended.

The majority of immigrants in this period were caucasian and came from Great Britain and the United States. Because most of them spoke English and came as individuals, they attracted less attention from nativistic Canadians. This was especially the case with the English-speaking Canadians living in the United States who took advantage of the incentives offered in the Canadian West to return to the land of their birth. Not only were they better able to adapt to institutions that were familiar to them, they were also likely to have extended family members in Canada upon whom they could draw for assistance.

*William Peyton Hubbard (third from right) laying the last stone for Toronto's new city hall, 1898. Canada's treatment of blacks was not always characterized by prejudice and exclusion. Once the chauffeur for George Brown, Hubbard became a successful businessman and in 1894 was elected alderman in Toronto. He was re-elected thirteen times and often served as acting mayor.*

City of Toronto Archives/SC 268-216

## THE HOME CHILDREN

Between the 1860s and the 1920s, over eighty thousand poor and orphaned children from Great Britain were sent to Canada. Most of them were indentured to farm families as cheap labour. Known as "Home Children" because they came from homes or orphanages, they seldom received the love and care reserved for "blood" relations. Maggie Hall, a child immigrant, described a typical work day to her friend in 1890:

> I have to get my morning's work done by 12 o'clock every day to take the children for a walk then I have to get the table laid for lunch when I come in then after dinner I help to wash up then I have to give the little boy his lessons then for the rest of the afternoon I sew till it is time to get afternoon tea and shut up and light the gas then by that time it is time for our tea after which I clear away get the table ready for Miss Smith's dinner then put the little boy to bed & after Miss Smith's dinner I help wash up which does not take very long then I do what I like for the rest of the evening till halfpast nine when we have Prayers then I take Miss Smith's hot water & hot bottle, the basket of silver & glass of milk to her bedroom shut up & go to bed which by the time I have done all it is just about ten. [10]

The demand for servants by Canada's growing middle class inspired immigration officials to recruit female domestics in Great Britain and elsewhere. Between 1904 and 1914, some ninety thousand British women came to Canada to work in domestic service: 60 percent came from England, 29 percent from Scotland, and 10 percent from Ireland. This breakdown meant that the Irish servant, so typical of the 1870s, had almost vanished by the early twentieth century. British sources made up about three-quarters of the immigrants who came to work as domestic servants in this period. Others came from Scandinavia and Central and Eastern Europe. Domestic servants were believed to be especially desirable immigrants because they made the most likely marriage partners for the male farmers and labourers who were the majority of newcomers in the migration process. Not surprisingly, the open door for domestics and wives did not include African, West Indian, or Asian women.

Despite their talk about keeping the country British, Anglo-Canadians were not always welcoming of immigrants from their imperial homeland. Many Canadians found the superior attitude adopted by some British immigrants particularly hard to swallow. An even greater cause for concern, especially for employers, was the socialist perspective held by those who had been associated with labour politics in Great Britain. Because many of the British immigrants came from urban backgrounds, they often made disgruntled homesteaders. Dubbed "green Englishmen" by their neighbours, they drifted to Prairie towns to find work, where they were sometimes met with signs indicating that "No Englishmen need apply."

While many British immigrants came as single men looking for work in Canadian towns and cities, in at least one instance it was British women who were actively sought as factory operatives. John Penman, the owner of Penman's woollen factories in Paris, Ontario, recruited seven hundred skilled hosiery workers from the east midlands of England between 1907 and 1928. Many of them were single women who were accustomed to lifelong wage earning. In her investigation of these women, Joy Parr found that they maintained this tradition in Paris, relying on female networks, public services, and family practices to sustain their continued labour force participation. She also found that "patterns in the whole municipality changed to accommodate the schedules of the mills and the habits of the mill workers."[11] The commercial provision of laundry services, the hours for Saturday shopping, and early school-leaving laws all reflected the fact that Paris was a "woman's town."

## SETTLING IN

The journey to Canada in this period was dramatically different from that facing earlier immigrants. Atlantic crossings, while not always pleasant, usually lasted less than two weeks and rarely resulted in marine disaster. Train travel, even in roughly fitted colonist cars, was palatial compared to the discomfort of crossing the country before the advent of the railway. All the same, survival in Canada proved a good deal harder than settlers and sojourners had been led to expect by the optimistic pamphlets, films, and lectures supplied by the recruitment agencies. Once at their destination, immigrants were left to fend for themselves, without public assistance. On the Prairies, the new arrivals faced the back-breaking work, poor living conditions, and homesickness that pioneers in other regions had experienced. Historians estimate that as many as 40 percent of those who filed for homesteads eventually sold or abandoned their claim.

The Canadian homestead policy of 160 acres for a $10 fee and minor settlement duties seemed a bonanza to many people, but families settling on the land needed more than hope and industry to succeed. The minimum investment required in ploughs, oxen, cattle, poultry, wagons, and basic household utensils, as well as seed and sufficient supplies to tide families over until the first harvest, was reckoned to cost even thrifty families close to $1000. Few came with such a sum: it had to be earned in Canada. The solution for many immigrants was to work as labourers and domestics on more prosperous farms or to take jobs with the railways or in mines before taking up farming. While husbands and older sons and daughters looked elsewhere for the cash stake to guarantee the family's future, married women regularly maintained homesteads, living for long, lonely winter months in what were often little more than shacks—or in the somewhat less uncomfortable "soddies" constructed out of the prairie land itself—caring for young children and tending livestock.

One of the sons of Maria Aho, a founding settler of a Finnish community established in southwest Saskatchewan in 1888, recalled how difficult the early years were for his family:

> My mother was so homesick, she never allowed us to dismantle her trunk insisting that she would not stay in this bush with no roads, nothing, just a small two-room hut with branches as a roof. The roof leaked. But every second year she had a new baby until there were twelve of us. She worked all the time, I never saw her sleep and still she kept insisting we act civilized. I was not allowed out to the nearest town till I could read and write. She taught us all that and she told us about Finland, her hometown Lapua. We dug a well by hand, but it kept drying up. Still we had a sauna every week and we were all scrubbed. Then we read the Bible and sang from the hymn book.... Mother never saw Finland again, she died at seventy-six, and I have never seen that country, but still if people ask me I tell them that I am a Finn. [12]

Belonging to the dominant Anglo-Canadian culture did not always make matters better. For example, Roy and Verna Benson who settled in Munson, Alberta, were less than enthusiastic about their experience. Roy wrote in January 1911:

> I suppose you are wondering what kind of country we have struck well there are a lot of people right here that are doing the same thing wondering. This past year has made a lot of them sit up and notice. Some have left the country, some couldn't.... I had a 10 a[cres] broke a year ago (cost me $50) last July. Last spring I let a fellow put in on shares and put $20 into a fence—this fall I told him he could have it all but the fence.

In May of the same year, Verna offered her perspective:

> I surely don't care anything about putting in another winter like last winter. I went to one of the neighbours New Years day and I wasn't away from home again until the last of April. There was two months last winter I never saw a woman and in fact the only persons I did see during that time was Roy and our bachelor neighbor. Then the men all wonder why the women don't like it here and the women all wonder what there is about the country that the men like so well. [13]

Verna's bachelor neighbour probably also suffered from loneliness. In her study of male labour in Prairie agriculture, Cecilia Danysk cites the case of Ebe Koeppen from Germany, who recorded in his diary that he had reached a "very sad point." [14] For Koeppen, life without a wife was "slow spiritual death." He admitted that he did not write home about such things because "the staggering dreariness of such existence is too difficult to make understandable." A popular prairie song, "The Alberta Homesteader," made light of this familiar lament of single men:

> My clothes are all ragged, my language is rough,
> My bread is case-hardened and solid and tough
> My dishes are scattered all over the room
> My floor gets afraid of the sight of a broom.

Despite the hard times, uncertain reception, and lack of women, newcomers found encouragement and support in both rural and urban settings. Mutual aid societies, church organizations, cooperatives, and just plain neighbourliness rescued many families and individuals from destitution. Ethnic solidarities proved invaluable. Minority communities such as Vancouver's "Little Tokyo" and Saskatchewan's Jewish agricultural colonies near Wapella, Hirsch, Cupar, Lipton, and Sonnenfeld gave inhabitants opportunities to share cherished customs and to work out collective ways of dealing with life's many hardships. In the Ukrainian settlements of east-central Alberta, over ninety community halls had been built by 1913 to host meetings, lectures, plays, concerts, dances, and choir practices. For navvies and sojourners, the fellowship found in the boarding houses, stores, cafés, and restaurants run by their compatriots sometimes helped to compensate for Canadian inhospitality.

This is not to say that ethnic solidarity was an entirely positive experience. Among immigrant Italians, for example, the middlemen who arranged contract labour for Canadian companies often extorted substantial commissions from their desperate clients. On the West Coast, Chinese prostitutes were sometimes virtual slaves of merchants who sold their sexual services to both Chinese and white customers. The police records of Canadian cities show a high incidence of crime, especially assault and theft, within immigrant communities. While this evidence perhaps reflects the fact that immigrants were more likely to be singled out by the forces of law and order, it also testifies to the tensions that, not surprisingly, surfaced among unhappy immigrants thrown together in less than ideal circumstances.

## NATIVE PEOPLES AND THE DOMINANT CULTURE

As immigrants invaded the western areas of the continent, aboriginal peoples there, as elsewhere in the dominion, found themselves on the defensive. Disease, malnutrition, and low morale continued to take a large toll on aboriginal populations. In the eastern regions of Canada, aboriginal peoples had developed immunities to European diseases, but in the West and North they were more vulnerable. The Cree of the Northwest, for example, suffered major losses as a variety of epidemics plagued them in the 1870s; northern Native peoples, whose contact with Europeans was still relatively recent, suffered repeated fatal epidemics, which stopped only in the 1930s. Because of poor diets and overcrowding on reserves, tuberculosis was a particular scourge. The combination of immigration and high death rates quickly reduced both the absolute and relative numbers of aboriginal people in Western Canada. For instance, in 1911 Native peoples constituted a mere 3 percent of the population of Alberta. Fifty years earlier, they had been the overwhelming majority in the territory. By the beginning of the twentieth century, with their total numbers dipping below two hundred thousand, the very

survival of Canada's First Nations seemed seriously in doubt.

Because white settlers tended to view Native peoples as a nuisance in the path of "progress," the major goal of federal Indian policy became the removal of aboriginal peoples from their lands without provoking a violent reaction. In 1908, Frank Oliver, who served as minister of Indian affairs as well as minister of the interior from 1905 to 1911, introduced a measure that would allow aboriginal people to be removed from reserves near towns with more than eight thousand residents. Oliver won a further amendment to the Indian Act in 1911 that allowed portions of reserves to be expropriated by municipalities or companies for roads, railways, or other public purposes. Under this legislation, almost half of the Blackfoot reserve was sold for slightly over a million dollars. When Natives refused to cooperate, the government applied pressure. The Blood of southern Alberta, for example, were forced to sell off their lands in 1916 and 1917 after the Department of Indian Affairs, to the consternation of the local Indian agent, withheld funds needed for farming operations until they consented to the sale. Despite their refusal to bow to government pressure, Indians in British Columbia achieved few successes. The McKenna-McBride Commission, created in 1912 to resolve federal–provincial differences regarding Indian land claims in the province, ignored Indian claims and exchanged over fourteen thousand hectares of reserve land for larger but significantly less valuable holdings.

Like many Canadians facing the challenges of industrialization, Native peoples sought jobs in the industrial economy developing around them. Reports from Indian agents before the First World War indicate, for example, extensive employment of Ojibwa and Swampy Cree near Lake Manitoba in fishing, lumbering, and gypsum mining. With the rise of tourism, many Natives secured jobs as guides for recreational hunters and fishers. The Iroquois of Kahnawake, near Montreal, took construction jobs in that city as well as in Ontario and the United States. Cree women and girls did laundry and cleaning for wages while men worked on railway construction. In the Maritimes, a few

Mi'kmaq worked in the coal mines, on the railroads, and in ironworks. On the West Coast, women and men from Native communities worked in the lumbermills, mines, canneries, and commercial fishery. Unfortunately, the position of aboriginal peoples in the industrial economy was often marginal, and became even more so as economic growth became defined in terms of the immigrant population.

Those lucky enough to hold on to good lands in the face of predatory settlers often prospered. As early as the 1880s, the Cowichan and Fraser River Valley Indians raised livestock, cereals, and market produce. In Saskatchewan, Natives practised mixed farming, with the Assiniboine Reserve reporting in 1893, for example, the harvesting of good crops of wheat, barley, oats, potatoes, turnips, carrots, and onions. They also raised cattle and sheep. On many reserves, Natives made a reasonable living as carpenters, blacksmiths, cobblers, printers, and craftspeople; others owned trading schooners, hotels, inns, cafés, and small logging and sawmill operations.

The Woodlands Indians in Central Canada lacked viable agricultural lands and increasingly found the fur trade frontier receding. While some moved north with the fur trade, others engaged in commercial fishing to make up for lost income. The Temagami Indians in northeastern Ontario, who had not been included in pre-Confederation treaty negotiations, found themselves fighting a rearguard action against the advance of the lumbering, farming, mining, and recreational frontiers. Chief Aleck Paul told anthropologist Frank Speck in 1913:

> When the white people came they commenced killing all the game. They left nothing on purpose to breed and keep us the supply, because the white man don't care about the animals. They are after the money. After the white man kills all the game in one place he can take the train and go three hundred miles or more to another and do the same there. But the Indian cannot do that. He must stay on his own section all the time and support his family on what it produces. [15]

Remedies for injustice did not come easily. As litigants in a European-based judicial system, Indian people faced major social, cultural, and economic obstacles. They gradually responded by using the tactics of their adversaries: cooperation among themselves, organized protest, and demands that white men's laws relating to property rights and personal freedom be applied equally to Native peoples. The Grand Indian Council of Ontario and Quebec, founded in 1870 by Iroquois and Ojibwa, protested Ottawa's legislation designed to expropriate their land near towns and cities. In British Columbia, land claims were the subject of a Squamish delegation to King Edward VII in London in 1906 and of a petition from the Nisga to the Judicial Committee of the Privy Council in 1913. Pan-Indian revival movements such as the Council of Tribes were still more outspoken, stating bluntly that whites had demoralized and defrauded Native peoples, who should now fight back. The pressure from the Department of Indian Affairs, the indifference and outright hostility of most Canadians, and the military might of the majority doomed such protests, at least for the time being.

As a last resort, Natives practised widespread defiance of measures taken to restrict their freedom. A pass system was introduced on reserves in the Northwest Territories after the rebellion of 1885, under which residents required written permission from an Indian agent before leaving a reserve even for short periods. This regulation proved largely unenforceable. Attempts to ban the sun dances of the Prairie Indians in the 1890s simply drove them underground: the dances were an essential component of communion with the spirit world and, like all dances among Native peoples, were an expression of group solidarity.

In British Columbia, Indians similarly defied the 1885 government ban on potlatches, the elaborate gift-giving ceremonies widely practised in west coast cultures. The government regarded the time spent potlatching as a diversion from productive work and a deterrent to the development of capitalist values. For the Natives, it was a means both of redistributing wealth and conferring honours within the tribe. Similar cultural imperialism inspired government efforts to end the practice of wife exchange among the Kwakiutl of Vancouver Island. Kwakiutl women tended to ignore government attempts to restore them to their first husbands because in their culture a woman who had been married to several men reaped more honours and was entitled to perform certain sacred dances at ceremonies.

Not all Indians in British Columbia coped with the onrush of European settlement by asserting their traditional values. A significant number responded to the spiritual messages preached by Protestant and Roman Catholic missionaries. For example, in 1862 William Duncan of the Anglican Church Missionary Society established the community of Metlakatla, near the mouth of the Skeena River. Like most missionaries, Duncan

aimed to remould Indian society in the image of Victorian Britain. Appalled by the drunkenness, disease, and prostitution that the presence of white miners in the Skeena area let loose on the Tsimshian, he made liquor and prostitution illegal in Metlakatla. He personally set the school curriculum and designed homes for the residents, who numbered nine hundred in 1876. Indian rituals were also forbidden in this authoritarian community, which collapsed when six hundred of its residents moved to Alaska after disputes between Duncan and church authorities.

Education policies were characterized by similar contradictions and difficulties. The federal government delegated responsibility for Native education to the major churches, which had sent

*Native dancing off reserves had already been banned under the Indian Act when this picture was taken in South Edmonton in 1898.*
Glenbow Archives/NA614-1

missionaries to reserves to convert the Indians to their brand of Christianity. While the churches professed support for assimilation of aboriginal peoples into white society, their school curricula suggested that Indians were only welcome in the lower ranks of the social hierarchy. Little time was devoted to academic subjects; instead, much of the day was divided between religious instruction and training in manual labour for boys and household work for girls. Indian parents complained that boarding schools separated children from their families and forbade pupils the use of their birth languages. They also argued that youngsters were overworked, poorly fed, and subject to corporal punishment, which Native societies did not inflict on children. Although about two-thirds of the Native children enrolled in schools at the end of the century attended a day school on their reserve, the government policy favoured schools well away from reserves. A cabinet minister expressed the government's philosophy in 1883: "If these schools are to succeed, we must not have them too near the bands; in order to educate the children properly we must separate them from their families. Some people may say that this is hard, but if we want to civilize them, we must do that." [16]

*Native industrial school students and their father, Saskatchewan, circa 1900.*

National Archives of Canada/C37113

---

## THE LAND ISSUE

Natives often expressed disbelief at the heavy-handedness by which they were dispossessed of their lands and resources. This letter to the Victoria **Daily Colonist**, published on 15 May 1880, expressed views common among Native leaders.

I am an Indian chief and a Christian. "Do unto others as you wish others should do unto you" is Christian doctrine. Is the white man a Christian? This is a part of his creed—"take all you want if it belongs to an Indian"? He has taken all our land and all the salmon and we have nothing. He believes an Indian has a right to live if he can on nothing at all....

The Indians are now reduced to this condition— THEY MUST ROB OR STARVE. Which will they do? I need not answer. An Indian is a man; and he has eyes. If you stab him he will bleed; if you poison him he will die. If you wrong him shall he not seek revenge? If an Indian wrongs a white man what is his humility? Revenge. If want compels us to execute the villainy they teach they may discover when it is

TOO LATE that an Indian can imitate the lightning and strike in a thousand places at the same time. We are not beggars. In the middle of the magnificent country that was once our own we only ask for land enough to enable us to live like white men by working in the fields. If the Indians get no land this spring you MAY BE SURE the white man will have a very bad harvest this year, and the Indians will eat beef next winter. Fine talk won't feed an Indian. "Her Majesty's Indian subjects," whose rights are limited to living on nothing at all if they can, are prepared to face the worst—anything but death by starvation. In a court of justice we could prove that we are the only persons who have any right or title to this land. If the Queen has no power to aid us; if all the power belongs to the parliament, then I say again may the Lord have mercy on the Indians—AND ON THE WHITE-MEN.

WILLIAM,
Chief of the Williams Lake Indians [17]

## THE LOST MÉTIS NATION

The Métis, whose sense of purpose was badly fractured in the years following the Northwest Rebellion of 1885, fared little better than the Indians. Although they continued to demand lands as their aboriginal right, the Métis met a brick wall of government indifference. Meanwhile, the pressures of white settlement forced them to inhabit areas with little agricultural potential. They hunted, fished, and trapped in unsettled territories and moved on when white settlers arrived. Instead of the unified nation that the rebels of '85 hoped to create, the Métis were dispersed across the Prairies in communities such as Green Lake, Saskatchewan, and Lac Ste Anne and Lac La Biche, Alberta. The Métis in Batoche finally won a land settlement in 1899–1900, receiving individual land grants rather than a reserve. Since farming required capital that the Métis lacked, many sold their lands.

In 1896, the Roman Catholic Church, spurred by the missionary Albert Lacombe, established a reserve, St Paul des Métis, one hundred kilometres northeast of Edmonton. Promises of livestock and equipment failed to materialize, and it soon became clear that neither the church nor the federal government planned to invest much money in the enterprise. By 1908, most of the Métis farmers had moved away. For decades, the Métis remained a forgotten people, invisible even in the census until 1981 when, for the first time, "Métis" was recognized as an ethnic group.

## NORTHERN EXPOSURE

Canada's concept of the North was gradually changing in the years following Confederation. The provinces of Quebec, Ontario, Manitoba, Saskatchewan, and Alberta achieved their present configuration early in the twentieth century, and the general view developed that the "true North" was above the sixtieth parallel. In the late nineteenth century, the North still belonged to the aboriginal peoples. Before the Yukon gold rush, over half of the white population living in northern climates could be found in Labrador.

As the fur stocks in the south dwindled, aboriginal peoples in the North were increasingly drawn into the fur trade. This was particularly the case among the Dene who inhabited the Mackenzie River Valley. In the second half of the nineteenth century, free traders (many of them Métis), missionaries, and scientists (most of them associated with the Geological Survey and the Dominion Lands Branch of the Department of the Interior), increasingly encroached on the North. The Dene also became the target for salvation by two missionary organizations, the Oblate Missionaries of Mary Immaculate and the Anglican Church Missionary Society. Like other aboriginal peoples who became Christians, the Dene responded to the spiritual message of Christianity while shaping their religious practices to their own traditions and needs. They were particularly bemused by the competition between the Protestants and the Catholics, which was in contrast to the message of brotherly love that the missionaries preached.

The potential wealth of the north, especially the oil-laden Athabasca tar sands and the iron-bearing rocks of Ungava, was gradually recognized by the federal government. In 1895 and 1897, orders-in-council affirmed the British cession of the Arctic to Canada, laid claim to all territory between 141° west longitude and a vague line running west of Greenland, and created three new northern administrative districts—Mackenzie, Yukon, and Franklin. As early as 1891, the federal government declared its determination to negotiate treaties with the Dene but was slow to do so until the discovery of gold in the Klondike galvanized them into action. Treaties 8, 10, and 11 were signed with various Dene bands beginning in 1898.

Because Canada's claim to its Arctic sector was called into question by other nations, the federal government sponsored forays into the north by Captain Joseph Bernier between 1906 and 1911. Canada's pretensions notwithstanding, American explorer Robert Peary claimed the North Pole for the United States in 1909, but the Americans failed to follow up the claim. In 1913, Vilhjalmur Stefansson led an expedition under Canadian auspices to study the marine biology, oceanography, and Inuit people of the North. Soon after setting out, the primary government vessel, the *Karluk*, was crushed in the ice, and most of its crew, who set out on foot over the ice, were never heard of again. A few managed to reach Wrangel Island, 110 miles off the coast of Siberia. Rumours that they had claimed the island for Canada set in motion a protracted sovereignty debate with the Soviet Union in the 1920s. For his part, Stefansson claimed to have explored a hundred thousand square miles of Arctic territory, travelling twenty thousand miles by sled and dog team while living off land and marine resources during his five-year

*Fond du Lac, on the east end of Lake Athabasca, became the site of a Hudson's Bay post in 1853 and soon thereafter the Oblate mission, named Our Lady of Seven Sorrows, was established. Despite the ravages from European diseases and suspicions that priests were the sources of their difficulties, the Dene gradually began to incorporate aspects of Roman Catholicism into their world view.*

J.B. Tyrell/Thomas Fisher Rare Book Library, University of Toronto

adventure. He remained convinced that the North was the last frontier and spent the years following his return from the Arctic trying to convince someone to help him pursue his northern dream.

Although the Inuit of the eastern Arctic remained largely outside European influences until the 1930s, the peoples of the central and western Arctic were not so fortunate. The uncontrolled

slaughter of whales and walrus from the 1860s to the 1880s left starvation in its wake among a people already weakened by European diseases. As a result, the original Inuvialuit people disappeared from the region and were replaced by Alaskan Inuit.

## CANADIAN CITIES IN TRANSITION

Emigration, immigration, and the growth of population in the western and northern frontiers was paralleled by an unprecedented movement of people from rural to urban areas of the country. In the boom years from 1901 to 1911, the populations of Montreal and Toronto increased by 49 and 58 percent, respectively. Even this growth paled in comparison with that of Winnipeg, Calgary, Edmonton, and Vancouver (see table 4.2). Cities in Western Canada grew out of nowhere to dominate their rural hinterlands. A sleepy village in 1871, Winnipeg would have remained a backwater except for the determination of local merchants to have the Pacific railway put its main line through town and construct its western yards and shops there as well. The CPR Syndicate had planned to build through Selkirk, northeast of Winnipeg, but the railway directors could always be persuaded to change their minds. By building a bridge across the Red River and securing two rail loops that could link a Pacific railway with the United States, Winnipeg had something other locations lacked. It offered the CPR free passage on the bridge, a $200 000 bonus, free land for its station, and a permanent exemption from municipal taxes on railway property.

With the railway in place and Prairie agriculture under way, Winnipeg grew quickly and emerged as the third largest city in Canada by 1911. Other Prairie cities, including Edmonton,

**Table 4.2**

### POPULATION OF SELECTED CANADIAN CITIES, 1871–1921
(RANKED IN ORDER OF SIZE FOR 1921)

| City | 1871 | 1891 | 1901 | 1921 |
|------|------|------|------|------|
| Montreal | 115 000 | 219 616 | 328 172 | 618 506 |
| Toronto | 59 000 | 181 215 | 209 892 | 521 893 |
| Winnipeg | 241 | 25 639 | 42 340 | 179 087 |
| Vancouver | | 13 709 | 29 432 | 163 220 |
| Hamilton | 26 880 | 48 959 | 52 634 | 114 151 |
| Ottawa | 24 141 | 44 154 | 59 928 | 107 843 |
| Quebec | 59 699 | 63 090 | 68 840 | 95 193 |
| Calgary | | 3 867 | 4 392 | 63 305 |
| London | 18 000 | 31 977 | 37 976 | 60 959 |
| Edmonton | | 700 | 4 176 | 58 846 |
| Halifax | 29 582 | 38 437 | 40 832 | 58 375 |
| Saint John | 28 805 | 39 179 | 40 711 | 47 166 |

*Source: Alan Artibise,* Winnipeg: A Social History of Urban Growth *(Montreal: McGill-Queen's University Press, 1975), 132; George A. Nader,* Cities of Canada *vol. 2,* Profiles of Fifteen Metropolitan Centres *(Toronto: MacMillan, 1976)*

Like Winnipeg, Vancouver owed its growth to the CPR. To become the terminus of that company's transcontinental line, Vancouver provided subsidies and tax holidays to the company. Competing with Victoria, whose commission merchants continued for another twenty years to control trade with Britain and California, Vancouver's merchants sought to dominate the British Columbia economy. They convinced city council to provide a $300 000 subsidy to local promoters of a railway to the Upper Fraser Valley, spent $150 000 on a bridge across False Creek to connect the city with roads to the Fraser Valley, and gave subsidies to the initiators of a sugar refinery and a graving dock.

Calgary, and Regina, had begun to expand by the end of the century, but the railyards and Winnipeg's position as the main distribution point for the region gave it an advantage in attracting new industry. It became the home of the grain exchange whose speculators bid on the wheat crop, and developed a substantial manufacturing sector, including clothing, furniture, and food processing firms as well as metal shops dependent on the railway.

Wherever they were located, cities harboured the worst features of uncontrolled growth in this period. Noise, overcrowding, poor sewerage systems, and inadequate roads combined to make life unpleasant for most city dwellers. When immigrants flooded into the country at the turn of the century, their presence was seen as a further problem. The *Missionary Outlook* observed in 1910: "Every large city on this continent has its fourfold problem of the slum, the saloons, the foreign colony and the districts of vice. The foreign colony may not properly be called a slum, but it represents a community that is about to become an important factor in our social life and will become a menace in our civilization unless it learns to assimilate the moral and religious ideals and the standards of citizenship."[18]

Montreal, Canada's largest city, manifested all the worst features of uncontrolled growth. By the

*Jasper Avenue in Edmonton, 1890 and 1910 (top).*

Provincial Archives of Alberta, E.Brown Collection/B4755 and National Archives of Canada/C7911

*A one-room dwelling in Winnipeg, circa 1915.*

Provincial Archives of Manitoba/N2438

end of the nineteenth century, most of its working class citizens lived in rundown tenements; its infant mortality rate was among the highest in the Western world; and the hierarchy of ethnic privilege was rigidly maintained. Toronto was only marginally better off. Although falling land prices made home ownership possible for an increasing number of Toronto's working families, slum conditions prevailed in the back-lane cottages of St John's Ward and in areas close to railyards, factories, and packinghouses. Indeed, the gap between rich and poor was evident in the segregated neighbourhoods of all major Canadian cities and in the stark contrast between the spectacular homes and office buildings of the wealthy and the substandard housing and dust-ridden factories of workers.

The best contemporary survey of living conditions in a Canadian city was carried out in 1896 by Herbert Ames, a businessman and social reformer, in Montreal. Ames focused on two areas of the city, areas he labelled "the city below the hill" and "the city above the hill." The former consisted of the part of west-end Montreal bounded by Westmount, the city limits, and the St Lawrence River, the latter the high terraces and plateaus along the base of Mount Royal. The city below the

hill was home to about 38 000 people divided almost equally among French, English, and Irish Canadians; the city above the hill was peopled largely by those of English and Scottish background.

Above the hill, Ames noted, there were "tall and handsome houses, stately churches and well-built schools," while below the hill "the tenement house replaces the single residence, and the factory with its smoking chimney is in evidence on every side." Beautiful parks and abundant greenery added to the charms of the homes in the upper city; below, "one paltry plot of ground, scarce an acre in extent, dignified by the title of Richmond Square, is the only spot where green grass can be seen free of charge." Above the hill, all the homes had modern plumbing and looked out on wide, well-paved, clean streets; below the hill, half the houses lacked running water and made use of pit-in-the-ground privies.

Below the hill, population density was more than double the city average, but Ames concluded that it was not overcrowded except in an area called the "Swamp." According to Ames, the poorest of the poor were the residents whose homes faced a rear court and were not visible from the street. These homes were poorly built, and their residents suffered disproportionately from disease, crime, drunkenness, poverty, and early death. Summing up the conditions below the hill, Ames noted that for every ten families in the area, "One family might secure an entire house to itself, but nine families must needs share theirs with another."[19]

Later studies have confirmed the view that there were two cities in Montreal, with the rich and poor living completely different lives. As late as the 1920s, children of Montreal's wealthier families had a much higher life expectancy than those who were born into poor families. The continuing high infant mortality rate in poor districts of Montreal can be traced in large part to contaminated milk and water. While affluent families could afford to purchase milk that was certified pure, 90 percent of the milk shipped to Montreal in freight cars was unfit for human consumption. The elite were also more likely to be able to afford better food and to live in areas served by adequate water, sewerage mains, and municipal parks. Moreover, when bad weather or epidemics rendered urban life especially unsafe or uncomfortable, they could escape to hideaways outside the city, like those in Ontario's Kawarthas or along Quebec's North Shore.

Because the rich could avoid most of the problems created by poverty, urban improvements were often a long time coming. It was not until 1926 that the province of Quebec made the pasteurization of milk mandatory, and only the threat posed to wealthy residents by disease helped to encourage some early public health efforts such as compulsory vaccination for smallpox in 1903 and a water filtration plant in 1914.

Most of the laws governing Canada's municipal development were patterned on Ontario's pre-Confederation model. By opting for municipal incorporation, cities, towns, and villages were given special rights to raise money and make laws governing activities within their jurisdiction. (Rural areas were divided into units called townships, districts, counties, or parishes, depending on the province, and these became the basis of local elected government.) When Canadians decided to reform the new industrial order, they turned to their municipal government as the most accessible political structure to help them achieve their goals.

The requirement that a person had to own property to acquire the municipal franchise ensured that local governments attended mainly to the needs of ratepayers. Urban reformers argued that measures to reduce disease and the spread of fires benefited everyone, since neither germs nor flames spared the rich. Over time, their arguments carried the day, but reluctance to pay higher property taxes slowed the process. In Charlottetown, where waterworks, sewerage, and improved sanitation appeared in the last two decades of the century, the *Patriot*, a local newspaper, complained in 1874:

The rich citizen can have his residence in the suburbs where the air and water are both pure, or if he chooses to live in the city he can afford to buy spring water, and he has always a doctor at hand to attend to any of his family who shows any symptoms of being unwell. [The poor man] must bring up his family in the neighbourhood of reeking cesspools and filthy pig-sties. He can not well afford to buy pure water at a very expensive rate; and he has to think twice before he calls in a doctor.[20]

Despite the general recognition by the 1870s of the role of polluted water in carrying disease, many city governments were slow to install better water systems outside the wealthy neighbourhoods. Vancouver in the 1880s was an ugly, smelly city without sewers or any hint of planned development. By the late 1890s, the city had acquired a waterworks and extended water mains to most areas. With the mountains supplying pure water, Vancouver's water-related disease problems were minor compared to most cities. In Winnipeg, just 10 percent of the population had sewers and waterworks in 1890: only in central Winnipeg, where the commercial elite lived and conducted their business, was the water supply adequate. In the working-class north end, water was delivered to homes, but the sewerage system emptied into the river with the result that deadly Red River fever (typhoid) was a continuing problem in the area. The combination of wooden buildings and a poor water supply could translate into uncontrolled fires that destroyed many homes. Winnipeg was not unique in this regard. A major fire left fifteen thousand people homeless in Saint John in 1877, and fifteen years later the homes of ten thousand people were destroyed by fire in St John's.

Nor was the nation's capital immune to problems facing urban dwellers. While the city named a health officer in 1874 to demand that householders dispose of garbage, Ottawa had no dump. Smallpox spread through the tenements of Lower Town in 1875. It has been estimated that one-quarter of the population of Ottawa were working poor, people able to find work during part of the year, but unemployed and often destitute during the winter.

*In the 1890s, Halifax, like most Canadian cities, switched from horse-drawn to electric streetcars.*
Public Archives of Nova Scotia/N-0405

There were also people who could not find work at all: men maimed in mill, construction, and bush accidents; pregnant serving girls; the handicapped and those ill with diseases such as tuberculosis. Both the working poor and the unemployables required aid from private charities to survive when relatives or friends were unable or unavailable to help.

Halifax, with its military base, was unique among Canadian cities. When the British withdrew their troops from Canada in 1871, they retained their garrison in Halifax, which served as Britain's naval and military base for the North Atlantic. The Church of England bishop declared in 1889 that "the military were a curse to this city and were the cause of a great deal of demoralization among the poor."[21] Since cities without military bases also had demoralized poor in their midst, it is doubtful that the good bishop was correct in laying the entire blame on the military. It was nevertheless the case that grog shops, brothels, and disreputable board-ing houses thrived on Barrack Street just below the Citadel and helped to sustain the lifestyle of the

repeat offenders committed to Rockhead Prison, a substantial octagonal building located in the north end of the city. After Barrack Street was closed to the military and its name changed to South Brunswick in the early 1870s, "soldiertown" drifted to adjacent areas and continued to be a major cause for concern among urban reformers.

## CONCLUSION

By the turn of the century, industrialization and immigration were changing the face of Canada. Rising urban populations quickly overran what amenities, natural and otherwise, the city had to offer. Middle-class residents soon became uncom-fortable with the glaring contrast between their standard of living and that experienced by the poor. While much of this concern was a result of their fears that the poor might one day rise up and dis-possess them of their conspicuous wealth, it was, as we will see in the next chapter, also a manifestation of a new spirit of reform that swept the nation in the industrial age.

# URBAN POVERTY DURING THE LAURIER BOOM

## *A Historiographical Debate*

While most historians agree that the period coinciding with Laurier's term of office (1896–1911) was one of economic growth, there are various opinions about its impact on the people who flocked to the booming Canadian cities to take up industrial and service jobs. Until the 1970s, most historians, following the interpretations of those who lived during the period, claimed that all Canadians benefited, although perhaps at differing rates, from the unparalleled prosperity created by immigration, western settlement, and industrial development. Social historians who studied the working-class experience in industrial cities in this period, came to different conclusions. Did the living standards of the working poor improve during the Laurier Boom, or did only some people reap the advantages of this period of economic growth?

One of the most positive descriptions of this period of Canadian history was penned by Liberal partisan O.D. Skelton in the multi-volume study *Canada and Its Provinces* (1913).[22] Because Skelton and many of his contemporaries were gripped by the drama of western settlement and resource development, they were less likely to take into account the conditions in the industrial cities, where the majority of immigrants and a large number of rural-born Canadians eventually settled. Social gospellers such as J.S. Woodsworth, who worked among the urban poor in Winnipeg's north end, were more aware of the growing inequalities that characterized the age of industry. "In country districts people are to a large extent on a level," he asserted in 1909, "but in the cities we have the rich and the poor, the classes and the masses, with all that these distinctions involve."[23]

In the 1970s, social historians returned to Woodsworth's theme of social inequality. Terry Copp examined the standard of living of Montreal's working class at the turn of the century and concluded that "as far as real income is concerned the average wage earner in Montreal was less well off during the period of economic expansion [of the Laurier era] than during the 'depression' of the nineteenth century."[24] Michael Piva reached similar conclusions in his study of conditions of the working class in Toronto.[25] In the Maritimes, deindustrialization made the Laurier Boom something of a bust. In his study of female industrial workers in Amherst, Sydney, and Yarmouth, Nova Scotia, at the turn of the century, D.A. Muise reveals that the earnings of both women and men were suppressed in the first two decades of the twentieth century.[26] This contributed to the continuing trend of outmigration that further weakened the region's economic potential.

New research also showed that, within the working class, age, culture, and gender dictated who suffered most from the growing gap between rich and poor. Howard Palmer documented the discrimination that immigrants without capital or skills faced in both the rural and urban job markets. For many immigrants, Palmer argued, stereotypes emphasizing peasant origins "played a role in determining job opportunities for new immigrants and functioned to disparage those who would climb out of their place."[27] Discrimination not only forced immigrants to take backbreaking jobs as navvies, bunkhouse men, and farm labourers in rural areas of the nation; it also helped to create ghettos with names like "Little Italy" and "Little Africa" within the working-class districts of Canada's industrial cities. While detailed studies have yet to be undertaken, there is little indication that any of these "cultural communities" ranked very high in terms of wealth.

Working-class women also benefited little from the Laurier Boom. As Joan Sangster points out in her article on the 1907 Bell telephone strike in Toronto, women were not only systematically paid less than men for their labour, they were also less likely to be unionized and therefore generally unsuccessful in their efforts to resist wage reductions and oppressive working conditions.[28] In her study of the "girl problem" in Toronto, Carolyn Strange notes that "Toronto's service and light manufacturing industries were built on the back of working girls," whose low wages were justified on the basis of "their age,

their marital status and their sex."[29] By encouraging young women to act in a "respectable" way and to seek security in family life, social reformers in the early decades of the twentieth century made it virtually impossible for women to find equality in the public sphere of work and wages.

In the 1990s, when the gap between rich and poor is steadily widening even as the Canadian economy is growing, it is perhaps easier to understand that statistics indicating overall economic growth do not always translate into better living conditions for everyone. Some people prosper more than others in periods of rapid economic change, and there is often an underclass who bears the brunt of economic "progress."

## NOTES

[1] Patricia Roy, J.L. Granatstein, Masako Iino, and Hiroko Takamura, *Mutual Hostages: Canadians and Japanese during the Second World War* (Toronto: University of Toronto Press, 1990), 3

[2] Cited in J.W. Dafoe, *Clifford Sifton in Relation to His Times* (Toronto: Macmillan, 1931), 142

[3] Quoted in Reg Whittaker, *Canadian Immigration Policy Since Confederation* (Ottawa: Canadian Historical Association, 1991), 8

[4] Donald H. Avery, *Reluctant Host: Canada's Response to Immigrant Workers, 1896–1994* (Toronto: McClelland and Stewart, 1995), 30

[5] Howard Palmer, "Reluctant Hosts: Anglo-Canadian Views of Multiculturalism in the Twentieth Century" in *Immigration in Canada: Historical Perspectives*, ed. Gerald Tulchinsky (Toronto: Copp Clark Longman, 1994)

[6] Cited in Jacqueline Hucker, "Temple of the Church of Jesus Christ of the Latter-Day Saints" (Agenda Paper No. 32, Historic Sites and Monuments Board, 6–7 Nov. 1992), 163

[7] Gerald Friesen, *The Canadian Prairies: A History* (Toronto: University of Toronto Press, 1984), 265

[8] *Daily Globe*, 7 June 1882

[9] Cited in James W. St. G. Walker, *Racial Discrimination in Canada: The Black Experience* (Ottawa: Canadian Historical Association, 1985), 4

[10] John Bullen, "Hidden Workers: Child Labour and the Family Economy in Late Nineteenth-Century Urban Ontario," *Labour/Le Travail* 18 (Fall 1986): 181

[11] Joy Parr, *The Gender of Breadwinners: Women, Men, and Change in Two Industrial Towns, 1880–1950* (Toronto: University of Toronto Press, 1990), 94–95

[12] Varpu Lindström-Best, *Defiant Sisters: A Social History of Finnish Immigrant Women in Canada* (Toronto: Multicultural History Society of Ontario, 1988), 27

[13] Cited in John W. Bennett and Seena B. Kohl, *Settling the Canadian-American West, 1890–1915: Pioneer Adaptation and Community Building* (Lincoln: University of Nebraska Press, 1995), 68

[14] Cecilia Danysk, *Hired Hands: Labour and the Development of Prairie Agriculture, 1880–1930* (Toronto: McClelland and Stewart, 1995), 71–72

[15] Cited in Bruce W. Hodgins and Jamie Benidickson, eds., *The Temagami Experience: Recreation, Resources, and the Aboriginal Experience in the Northern Ontario Wilderness* (Toronto: University of Toronto Press, 1989), 142

[16] J.R. Miller, *Skyscrapers Hide the Heavens: A History of Indian–White Relations in Canada* (Toronto: University of Toronto Press, 1989), 298

[17] Quoted in Penny Petrone, ed., *First People, First Voices* (Toronto: University of Toronto Press, 1983), 68–69

[18] Cited in Robert Harney, "Ethnicity and Neighbourhoods" in *Cities and Urbanization: Canadian Historical Perspectives*, ed. Gilbert A. Stelter (Toronto: Copp Clark Pitman, 1990), 228

[19] Herbert Brown Ames, *The City Below the Hill* (Toronto: University of Toronto Press, 1972), 103, 105, 48

[20] Quoted in Douglas Baldwin, "'But Not A Drop to Drink': The Struggle for Pure Water" in *Gaslights, Epidemics and Vagabond Cows: Charlottetown in the Victorian Era*, ed. Douglas Baldwin and Thomas Spira (Charlottetown: Ragweed Press, 1988), 110

[21] Cited in Judith Fingard, *The Dark Side of Life in Victorian Halifax* (Porters Lake, NS: Pottersfield Press, 1989), 16

[22] O.D. Skelton, "General Economic History, 1867–1912" in *Canada and Its Provinces*, vol. 9, ed. Adam Smith and Arthur G. Doughty (Toronto: Glasgow, Brook, 1913)

[23] Quoted in Paul W. Bennett and Cornelius Jaenen, *Emerging Identities: Selected Problems and Interpretations in Canadian History* (Scarborough: Prentice-Hall, 1986), 355

[24] Terry Copp, "The Conditions of the Working Class in Montreal, 1867–1920," *Historical Papers* (1972): 172. This conclusion is further developed in his monograph *The Anatomy of Poverty: The Condition of the Working Class in Montreal, 1897–1929* (Toronto: McClelland and Stewart, 1974)

[25] Michael J. Piva, *The Condition of the Working Class in Toronto, 1900–1920* (Ottawa: University of Ottawa Press, 1979)

[26] D.A. Muise, "The Industrial Context of Inequality: Female Participation in Nova Scotia's Paid Labour Force, 1871–1921," *Acadiensis* 20, 2 (Spring 1991): 30

[27] Howard Palmer, "Reluctant Hosts: Anglo-Canadian Views of Multiculturalism in the Twentieth Century," in *Multiculturalism as State Policy* (Ottawa: Canadian Consultative Council on Multiculturalism and Supply and Services Canada, 1976), 96

[28] Joan Sangster, "The 1907 Bell Telephone Strike: Organizing Women Workers," *Labour/Le Travailleur* 3 (1978): 109–30

[29] Carolyn Strange, *Toronto's Girl Problem: The Perils and Pleasures of the City, 1880–1930* (Toronto: University of Toronto Press, 1995), 39, 41

## Selected Reading

On immigration and immigrants, the major surveys are Jean Burnet with Howard Palmer, *"Coming Canadians": An Introduction to the History of Canada's Peoples* (Toronto: McClelland and Stewart, 1988), and Gerald Tulchinsky, ed., *Immigration in Canada: Historical Perspectives* (Toronto: Copp Clark Longman, 1994). Among other key works are Donald Avery, *Reluctant Host: Canada's Response to Immigrant Workers, 1896–1994* (Toronto: McClelland and Stewart, 1995); Howard Palmer, *Patterns of Prejudice* (Toronto: McClelland and Stewart, 1982); and Barbara Roberts, *Whence*

*They Came: Deportation from Canada 1900–1935* (Ottawa: University of Ottawa Press, 1988). Much valuable information on immigration and settlement in this period is condensed in the pamphlets of the Canadian Historical Association's Canada's Ethnic Groups series, several of which are cited in this chapter. See also D.J. Hall, *Clifford Sifton*, 2 vols. (Vancouver, University of British Columbia Press, 1985).

Publications dealing with specific groups and regions include Orest Martynowych, *The Ukrainian Bloc Settlement in East Central Alberta, 1890–1930: A History* (Edmonton: Alberta Culture, 1985); Lubomir Luciuk and Stella Hryniuk, eds., *Canada's Ukrainians: Negotiating an Identity* (Toronto: University of Toronto Press, 1991); George Woodcock and Ivan Avakumovic, *The Doukhobors* (Ottawa: Carleton Library, 1977); Lillian Petroff, *Sojourners and Settlers: The Macedonian Community in Toronto to 1940* (Toronto: University of Toronto Press, 1995); Bruno Ramirez, *The Italians of Montreal: From Sojourning to Settlement, 1900–1921* (Montreal: Éditions du Courant, 1980); John Zucchi, *Toronto Italians* (Montreal: McGill-Queen's University Press, 1988); Irving Abella, *A Coat of Many Colours: Two Centuries of Jewish Life in Canada* (Toronto: Lester and Orpen Dennys, 1990); Gerald Tulchinsky, *Taking Root: The Origins of the Canadian Jewish Community* (Toronto: Lester Publishing, 1992); Hans Lehmann, *The German Canadians 1750–1937: Immigration, Settlement and Culture* (St John's: Bassler Gerhard, 1986); Frank H. Epp, *Mennonites in Canada, 1786–1920: The History of a Separate People* (Toronto: Macmillan, 1974); Bruno Ramirez, *On the Move: French-Canadian and Italian Migrants in the North Atlantic Economy, 1860–1914* (Toronto: McClelland and Stewart, 1990); Hugh Johnson, *The Voyage of the Komagata Maru: The Sikh Challenge to Canada's Colour Bar* (Delhi: Oxford University Press, 1979); Patricia E. Roy, *A White Man's Province: British Columbia Politicians and Chinese and Japanese Immigrants 1858–1914* (Vancouver: UBC Press, 1989); W. Peter Ward, *White Canada Forever: Popular Attitudes and Public Policy Toward Orientals in British Columbia*, 2nd ed. (Montreal: McGill-Queen's University Press, 1990); and J. Brian Dawson with Patricia Dawson, *Moon Cakes in Gold Mountain: From China to the Canadian Plains* (Calgary: Detselig, 1991). On child immigrants, see Joy Parr, *Labouring Children: British Immigrant Apprentices to Canada, 1896–1924* (Montreal: McGill-Queen's University Press, 1980).

On outmigration, see Patricia A. Thornton, "The Problem of Outmigration from Atlantic Canada, 1871–1921: A New Look," *Acadiensis* 15, 1 (Autumn 1985): 3–34, and Bruno Ramirez, *On the Move*. A good case study of social mobility in an Ontario town is David G. Burley, *A Particular Condition in Life: Self-Employment and Social Mobility in Mid-Victorian Brantford, Ontario* (Montreal and Kingston: McGill-Queen's University Press, 1994). On western settlement, see John W. Bennett and Seena B. Kohl, *Settling the Canadian–American West, 1890–1915: Pioneer Adaptation and Community Building* (Lincoln: University of Nebraska Press, 1995); David Jones and Ian Macpherson, eds., *Building Beyond the Homestead* (Calgary: University of Calgary Press, 1988); David Jones, *Empire of Dust: Settling and Abandoning the Prairie Dry Belt* (Edmonton: University of Alberta Press, 1987); Paul Voisey, *Vulcan: The Making of a Prairie Community* (Toronto: University of Toronto Press, 1988); Elizabeth B. Mitchell, *In Western Canada Before the War: Impressions of Early Twentieth Century Prairie Communities* (Saskatoon: Western Producer Prairie Books, 1981); David Breen, *The Canadian Prairie West and the Ranching Frontier* (Toronto: University of Toronto Press, 1983); Susan Jackel, ed., *A Flannel Shirt and Liberty: British Gentlewomen in the Canadian West* (Vancouver: University of British Columbia Press, 1982); Frances Swyripa, *Wedded to the Cause: Ukrainian-Canadian Women and Ethnic Identity, 1891–1991* (Toronto: University of Toronto Press, 1993); Carol Fairbanks and Sara Brooks Sundberg, *Farm Women on the Prairie Frontier: A Sourcebook for Canada and the United States* (Metuchen, NJ: Scarecrow Press, 1983); Linda Rasmussen et al., *A Harvest Yet to Reap: A History of Prairie Women* (Toronto: Women's Press, 1976); Nellie McClung, *Clearing in the West* (New York, 1936); Eliane Silverman, *The Last Best West: Women on the Alberta Frontier, 1880–1930* (Montreal: Eden Press, 1984); and Georgina Binnie-Clark, *Wheat and Women* (Toronto: University of Toronto Press, 1979).

On Native peoples, see, in addition to works cited earlier: Gerhard J. Ens, *Homeland to Hinterland: The Changing Worlds of the Red River Métis in the Nineteenth Century* (Toronto: University of Toronto Press, 1996); J.R. Miller, *Shingwauk's Vision: A History of Native Residential Schools* (Toronto: University of Toronto Press, 1996); Douglas Cole and Ira Chaikin, *An Iron Hand upon the People: The Law Against the Potlatch on the Northwest Coast* (Vancouver: Douglas and McIntyre, 1990); Rolf Knight, *Indians at Work: An Informal History of Native Indian Labour in British Columbia, 1858–1930* (Vancouver: New Star Books, 1978); Paul Tennant, *Aboriginal Peoples and Politics: The Indian Land Question in British Columbia, 1849–1989* (Vancouver: UBC Press, 1990); Katherine Pettipas, *Severing the Ties that Bind: Government Repression of Indigenous Religious Ceremonies on the Prairies* (Winnipeg: University of Manitoba Press, 1994); David C. Mandelbaum, *The Plains Cree: An Ethnographic, Historical and Comparative Study* (Regina: Canadian Plains Research Center, 1978); Peter Schmalz, *The Ojibwa of Southern Ontario* (Toronto: University of Toronto Press, 1990); Ellice B. Gonzalez, *Changing Economic Roles for Micmac Men and Women: An Ethnohistorical Analysis* (Ottawa: National Museum, 1981); Ruth Holmes Whitehead, *The Old Man Told Us: Excerpts from Micmac History, 1500–1950* (Halifax: Nimbus, 1991); Keith J. Crowe, *A History of the Original Peoples of Northern Canada* (Montreal: McGill-Queen's University Press, 1991); and Ken S. Coates, *Best Left as Indians: Native–White Relations in the Yukon Territory,*

*1840–1973* (Montreal: McGill-Queen's University Press, 1991). Missionary work among Native peoples is discussed in John Webster Grant, *Moon of Wintertime: Missionaries and the Indians of Canada in Encounter since 1534* (Toronto: University of Toronto Press, 1984); Martha McCarthy, *From the Great River: Oblate Missions to the Dene, 1847–1921* (Edmonton: University of Alberta Press, 1995); and Robert Choquette, *The Oblate Assault on Canada's Northwest* (Ottawa: University of Ottawa Press, 1995).

On city life, see G. Stelter and A.F.J. Artibise, eds., *The Canadian City: Essays in Urban History* (Toronto: Copp Clark Pitman, 1984); A.F.J. Artibise, ed., *Town and City: Aspects of Western Canadian Urban Development* (Regina: University of Regina, 1981); and J.M.S. Careless, *The Rise of Cities: Canada Before 1914* (Ottawa: Canadian Historical Association, 1978). A series of illustrated urban histories published by James Lorimer is useful for studying the growth of the late-nineteenth-century city. Included are *Winnipeg* by Alan Artibise (1977); *Calgary* by Max Foran (1978); *Vancouver* by Patricia Roy (1980); *Toronto to 1918* by J.M.S. Careless (1984); *Hamilton* by John C. Weaver (1984), and *Ottawa* by John H. Taylor (1986). Also see Doug Baldwin and Thomas Spira, eds., *Gaslights, Epidemics and Vagabond Cows: Charlottetown in the Victorian Era* (Charlottetown: Ragweed, 1988); John English and Kenneth McLaughlin, *Kitchener: An Illustrated History* (Waterloo: Wilfrid Laurier University Press, 1983); Judith Fingard, *The Dark Side of Life in Victorian Halifax* (Porters Lake, NS: Pottersfield Press, 1989); Paul André Linteau, *Maisonneuve: Comment des promoteurs fabriquent une ville* (Montreal: Boréal Express, 1981). An examination of legal and police systems can be found in John C. Weaver, *Crimes, Constables and the Courts: Order and Transgression in a Canadian City, 1816–1970* (Montreal: McGill-Queen's University Press, 1995). A critical study of law-making is Carolyn Strange and Tina Loo, *Making Good: Law and Moral Regulation in Canada, 1867-1939* (Toronto: University of Toronto Press, 1997), while policing generally is treated in Greg Marquis, *Policing Canada's Century* (Toronto: University of Toronto Press, 1993).

# CHAPTER 5

## COMMMUNITY RESPONSES TO THE AGE OF INDUSTRY, 1867-1921

IN 1912, FOURTEEN-YEAR-OLD SENEFTA KIZIMA arrived in Canada with her parents. Immigrants from the Ukraine, the family had initially intended to homestead, but decided instead to settle in Calgary where Senefta found work as a domestic.

> In 1915 at the time of the First World War, I got a job washing dishes in a restaurant. One time some drunk soldiers broke into the restaurant and demanded that the owner fire "Austrians" because they were "enemies." The owner, afraid the drunk soldiers would break windows, had to fire us. Because of his "Austrianness," my father also lost his job.

> Someone began rounding up workers for a coal mine in the area near Canmore. Father had once worked in a mine. He hired on at Georgetown.... [H]e sustained a serious injury in the mine—his leg was crushed and he was an invalid for the rest of his life. At that time there was no compensation; once you were injured you had no reason to live....

> We returned to Calgary to our house which had stood empty for a year. I got a job in a restaurant as a waitress. I was paid $7 a week. One time two people came into the restaurant and asked me how many hours I worked and how much I earned.

> They were organizing restaurant workers into a union. This was 1916 or 1917. Having organized the workers, they called a strike in restaurants and hotels in Calgary.

> At the time of the strike I understood many things, experienced injustice, and saw great dishonesty among people. The results of this struggle were higher wages for restaurant workers. Therefore, to the Ukrainian progressive movement I came, because of the union, because of the strike battle.[1]

The labour union that attracted Kizima was only one of many organizations that drew the support of Canadians in the early decades of the twentieth century. In response to the dislocation caused by immigration, industrial development, urban growth, and rural depopulation, people came together to demand reform of a social order that seemed to favour a lucky few over the mass of the nation's citizens.[2] Reform became the watchword of the industrial age, and few individuals or institutions escaped the rage to make improvements on a system that clearly was less than ideal.

People in organized pressure groups commissioned studies, collected signatures for petitions, buttonholed mayors and councillors, marched in the streets, and even clashed with militias in an effort to make their demands known. Elected politicians ignored community-based groups at their peril. With new notions of citizenship and political entitlement gaining widespread acceptance, politicians were forced to accommodate the wishes of their aggrieved constituents or face the prospect that the system that served them so well would be entirely swept away in the whirlwind that followed in the wake of industrial growth.

## THE AGE OF REFORM

The reform impulse in industrializing Canada took many forms. In the early years of Confederation, conservative reformers blamed the poor themselves for their plight, observing that the poor were often transient, drank too much, and failed to attend church. Ignoring the economic causes that produced the transients (commonly labelled "tramps"), conservative reformers emphasized the need to make the tramping life unpalatable. Able-bodied men were often required to work for charity, usually at breaking stones or sawing wood. If the poor would just "shape up," the conservative argued, they would soon be on the road to healthier and happier lives.

By the end of the nineteenth century, reformers were more likely to see larger forces as a cause of destitution and to look to the state to create laws that would ameliorate the worst abuses of the industrial order. They saw themselves as more progressive than conservative reformers, who focused on individual discipline to solve social problems. Whether conservative or progressive, reformers shared one characteristic: they claimed that they had knowledge—religious, scientific, or political—that would bring about a better world for themselves and others.

## THE TEMPERANCE MOVEMENT

Alcohol was a favoured target of conservative reformers, who saw it as the cause of many of Canada's social problems. Over the course of the nineteenth century, the movement to encourage temperance in the consumption of alcohol had given way to a demand that the state impose laws to prohibit its manufacture, sale, and consumption. This transition from the personal to the political prompted a mass movement for reform. By the end of the nineteenth century, the Protestant churches, led by the Baptists, Methodists, and Presbyterians, and voluntary organizations, such as the Sons of Temperance and the Woman's Christian Temperance Union (WCTU), had forged a formidable alliance. In their zeal to achieve prohibition, they conducted a vigorous education campaign, solicited signatures for enormous petitions, and lobbied politicians at all levels of government.

Pressed by the mounting support for action, the federal government passed the Canada Temperance Act in 1878. Known as the Scott Act, it allowed municipalities to hold a plebiscite to determine whether liquor could be sold within

*Beer parlour, Boisetown, New Brunswick, 1912.*

National Archives of New Brunswick/ P145-61

their boundaries. Many areas of Canada voted "dry," and the consumption of alcohol actually declined, but it never totally stopped. A royal commission investigation reported in 1895 that liquor flowed almost as freely in supposedly dry municipalities as in "wet" ones. In Moncton, for example, after prohibition forces carried the day in an 1879 plebiscite, bootleggers quickly stepped into the breech left by the closing of licensed liquor outlets. Prohibitionists in the community pointed fingers at the Roman Catholic Acadians, but they were not alone in availing themselves of the services of bootleggers or in refusing to obey the provisions of the Scott Act. The municipality resisted paying the costs of enforcing prohibition, and the police soon tired of vain attempts to prosecute the bootleggers in court. In Moncton, as in most other "dry" municipalities in Canada, people continued to consume alcohol, only under different retail conditions.

Drinking was a real problem in early industrializing Canada, where liquor flowed freely and was consumed in great quantities. As a result, temperance in the consumption of alcohol was supported by Roman Catholics as well as Protestants, and by people in all classes and regions of the country. What separated the wets from the drys was not the problem itself but the means of addressing it. For many people, the demand for state intervention went too far. This was the position taken in Quebec, where the Roman Catholic Church scorned state intervention on the issue and where people were less likely than other Canadians to exercise the local option to ban alcohol. Thus, in demanding a national policy on a contentious issue, anglophone Protestant prohibitionists came dangerously close to imposing their values on a reluctant and increasingly beleaguered cultural minority.

Prime Minister Laurier tried to avoid immediate action by agreeing to a national referendum on the issue. Held in 1898, it yielded a predictable result: a majority for the drys in every province outside Quebec. The relatively small overall majority and a low voter turnout allowed Laurier to sidestep the issue that bitterly divided the country. For the time being, prohibition advocates had to be content with the existing system of local option. However, their forces were not yet spent. Prohibitionists turned to their provincial governments for action on the liquor trade. They also demanded a wholesale reform of the political system, including giving women, who were believed to be more supportive of the temperance cause, the right to vote.

## LEGISLATING MORALITY

Most conservative reformers focused on the moral issues associated with the problems they were trying to address. Nowhere was this approach more diligently pursued than in Toronto, which earned the appellation "Toronto the Good" for its earnest efforts to legislate morality. In 1886, Toronto's reforming mayor, William Howland, established a Morality Department in the city police force. Anyone involved in prostitution, the illicit sale of liquor, gambling, or the mistreatment of children and animals was hauled into court by the new morality squad. Under the charge of vagrancy, young women innocently walking on the streets at night could be interrogated by the morality police.

Women and children were the special concern of moral reformers, who had difficulty accepting the freedom from parental and patriarchal control that city life encouraged in these vulnerable members of society. As Carolyn Strange points out in her study of the "girl problem" in Toronto, that city took the lead in the social purity movement, creating a flurry of institutions designed specifically to focus on the plight of women and female children. A Children's Aid Society, two industrial schools for girls, a children's court, and a women's court were all established in the period between 1880 and 1910. In addition, women in Toronto had access to the expanded services of the YWCA, Big Sisters, the WCTU, and a variety of "safe" settlement houses.[2] Despite this energetic response, young women in Toronto continued to ply their trade as prostitutes, practise infanticide, and sink into destitution. Journalist C.S. Clark, in an 1898 exposé entitled *Toronto the Good*, shocked the citizens of Toronto with his lurid account of the vice that flourished under the noses of Morality Department officers.

## THE PROGRESSIVE IMPULSE

By the turn of the century, it was becoming clear to many thinking people that reforming the individual would not produce a reformed society. Something more was needed. As with so many of the reform activities adopted in Canada in this period, the United States led the way in developing a "progressive" approach to the problems of the industrial age. Unlike evangelical reformers and social purity advocates who saw social problems as both individual and inevitable, progressives argued that problems were social and open to solution.

Progressivism drew together an impressive coalition of forces including professionals, journalists, church leaders, union organizers, and women's rights activists. Through their voluntary agencies and carefully documented studies, they shed a bright light on the darkest corners of Canadian society and promoted the view that through hard work, judicious laws, scientific management, and reformed political structures, everyone could enjoy the benefits of the industrial system. The force of their logic was irresistible. By the second decade of the twentieth century, most Canadians, consciously or not, imbibed the spirit of progressivism that had swept the North American continent.

At the forefront of the progressive movement was an army of health professionals led by medical doctors and nurses. They argued that public health should be a priority of reform, and provided municipal officials and school boards with scientific evidence of the need for vaccinations, medical inspection, and better nutrition. Throughout the country energies were marshalled to build new hospitals, establish clinics for young mothers and their babies, and teach school children that "Cleanliness

is next to Godliness." Campaigns against smoking and spitting—both connected for those who pursued the popular pastime of chewing tobacco—encouraged habits that would lead to healthier Canadians.

Churches were central to progressive reform efforts in many communities. By the turn of the

*Toronto Department of Health well-baby clinics instructed new mothers on how to care for their infants.*

City of Toronto Archives/DPW 32-234

century, the Methodists, Presbyterians, and Baptists, in particular, had adopted what is termed the "social gospel" approach to their work. While still concerned with spiritual salvation and social purity, they expanded their charitable activities to address the appalling conditions created by the industrial system. The Protestant churches cooperated with union leaders, through the Lord's Day Alliance, to pressure the federal government to legislate Sunday observance. Passed in 1907, the Lord's Day Act banned paid employment, shopping, and commercial leisure activities on Sunday, a policy the churches argued not only conformed to Canada's Christian beliefs but also gave working people a day of rest.

Both the Methodist and Presbyterian Churches established social reform agencies that came together in 1907 as the Moral and Social Reform Council of Canada. In 1913, the council changed its name to the Social Service Council of

Canada and hosted a congress in Ottawa the following year. The program testified to the broad range of interests that motivated the social gospellers: a weekly day of rest, the Canadian Indian, the church and industrial life, the labour problem, child welfare, the problem of the city, the problem of the country, social service as life work, commercialized vice and the white slave traffic, immigration, political purity, temperance, prison reform, and humanizing religion. Wartime tensions would drive a wedge between the reformers

---

### THE GRENFELL MISSION

In Newfoundland, the social gospel movement was represented in a dramatic way by the mission of Wilfred Grenfell. Born in England in 1865, Grenfell was a student at London Medical School when he was converted to active Christianity by American evangelist Dwight L. Moody. He subsequently joined the Royal National Mission to Deep Sea Fishermen. In 1892, he visited the coasts of Newfoundland and Labrador where he saw a great opportunity to combine medical and missionary work among people who rarely saw a doctor or a minister. The following year, he opened a hospital in Battle Creek, and by the end of the century had established his mission headquarters at St Anthony's on the northern tip of Newfoundland. Backed by supporters in the United States, Canada, and Great Britain, Grenfell expanded his activities to include nursing stations, schools, cooperatives, and an orphanage. His well-publicized efforts to bring services to isolated areas—including a close brush with death on an ice floe in 1908—made him a popular hero and enabled him to earn more money for his mission through the lecture circuit. Following his marriage to a Chicago heiress in 1909, Grenfell spent less time in missionary work, which was carried on by dedicated men and women inspired by Grenfell's pioneering efforts.

---

and the radicals in the social gospel movement, but in 1914 great plans were afoot for a mass effort to establish "God's kingdom on earth."

The churches also established missions, labour churches, and settlement houses in the inner city to minister to the spiritual and physical needs of the working class. In Halifax, the Methodist Church's Jost Mission reached out to working-class mothers, while the Fred Victor Mission in Toronto ministered to the needs of destitute people. Between 1907 and 1913, Methodist minister J.S. Woodsworth served as superintendent of Winnipeg's All People's Mission, which catered to the city's culturally diverse immigrant population. His surveys of social conditions in Winnipeg, *Strangers Within Our Gates* (1909) and *My Neighbor* (1911), offered sensitive analyses of the situation facing his clients, but they also revealed a condescending attitude towards immigrants and the poor that typified many of those who championed the progressive movement.

Class and racial biases were reflected in the pseudo-scientific theories of eugenics, which gained wide currency among progressives. Drawing on scientific findings relating to reproduction in the plant and animal world, eugenicists argued that society could be improved by preventing people with undesirable mental and physical traits from reproducing. Those who embraced eugenics believed that inherited traits rather than social conditions predisposed people to poverty and crime. Because of such views, reform leaders such as the Reverend S.D. Chown, Moderator of the Methodist Church, could make statements such as the following without fear of being challenged:

> The immigration question is the most vital one in Canada today, as it has to do with the purity of our national life-blood. It is foolish to dribble away the vitality of our own country in a vain endeavour to assimilate the world's non-adjustable, profligate, and indolent social parasites.... It is most vital to our nation's life that we should ever remember that quality is of greater value than quantity and that character lies at the basis of national stability and progress.[3]

The concern for racial purity and social control led the progressives to focus on reform of sexual practices. Although 1892 legislation prohibiting birth control made it difficult for progressives to champion eugenics, they were determined to educate people to sexual hygiene and self-control. The Methodist Church, for example, distributed sex manuals targeted at various age levels for women and men. While criticized today as moralistic and wrong-headed, they incorporated the thinking of the time in the field of "sexology" and moved some distance from the puritanical approach to sex characteristic of the Victorian age.

The support for controlling sexuality sprang from a number of motives. With the rise of prostitution and the increasing incidence of venereal disease, many Canadians felt that some form of social control over sexuality was necessary. Women in particular were eager to eliminate the double standard of sexual behaviour by extending to men the strict codes that governed female sexuality. For most reformers, a lifelong monogamous marriage—what the WCTU described as "the pure white life for two"—was the bedrock of the nation. With correct family formation, reformers argued, a wide range of social evils would be eliminated, including divorce, wife battery, child abuse, sexually transmitted disease, and prostitution.

The desire for social control and scientific analysis led to same-sex relationships being labelled "homosexual" and deemed unnatural. While social purity advocates insisted that homosexuals be put in jail, the medical profession began describing same-sex attraction as a form of insanity requiring confinement in a lunatic asylum rather than a prison. Practising homosexuals could face either fate in a society that still subscribed to the view that sex should be confined only to married couples. In Victoria, two men convicted of sodomy in 1891 were each sentenced to fifteen years in prison, a sentence later commuted to seven years. Sentences of a year or two were more common. Sometimes the offenders were simply asked to leave town. In Regina, for example, Frank Hoskins, a leading merchant, was arrested in 1895 and charged with "gross indecency of an unnatural character" after being found engaging in sexual activity with two other men. As a result of a local petition that asked for leniency because of his good character prior to this incident, he was spared a prison sentence on the condition that he leave the Northwest Territories.

Progressives also took up the cause of environmental reform, arguing that Canada lagged behind other industrialized nations in attending to the problems of pollution and resource depletion. The example of the United States inspired the federal government to set aside Banff Hot Springs Reserve and Rocky Mountain Park for public use in 1885. Following the North American Conservation Conference called by President Theodore Roosevelt in 1909, the federal government established a Canadian Commission of Conservation (CCC). Under the energetic direction of Clifford Sifton, the CCC investigated everything from fur farming and migratory birds to urban planning and power development. Frustration with jurisdictional disputes and federal inaction caused Sifton to resign in 1918, and the commission was abolished three years later. Nevertheless, a number of issues it raised would continue to preoccupy environmental reformers, and its achievements were considerable. It produced over two hundred studies of environmental issues, encouraged the creation of parks and game reserves, inspired the passage of laws to protect migratory birds and wild animals, and forged a link between conservation and urban planning that left a legacy in a number of Canadian cities.

The "city beautiful" movement, with its notions of rational planning, handsome buildings, and public spaces, appealed to many progressives. Originating in Europe and the United States, the movement soon had Canadian converts, including Herbert Ames who, as we have seen, had catalogued Montreal's problems in his book *The City Below the Hill*. Urban reformers established their own voluntary associations, such as Montreal's City Improvement League, and enlisted the support of the Union of Canadian Municipalities. Urban planning experts argued that changing cities would also change the people who lived in them.

Determined to eliminate urban slums, progressives advanced programs for subsidized housing that would replace overcrowded tenements. Ames recommended that the city of Montreal enter into arrangements with developers to build working-class homes at cost, with a 5 percent profit factored in the calculations. While the scheme caught on neither with developers nor the city, progressives continued to press their case for improved urban housing. The garden city, or new-town, movement in Great Britain, with its most celebrated example in Letchworth Garden City north of London, offered them a model for action. While the city beautiful movement emphasized urban aesthetics, the garden city planners stressed health and housing. Parks, playgrounds, sewers, public baths, water filtration systems, and planned housing developments, it was argued, would offer urban dwellers better health and, by extension, make them better citizens. In 1914, the Canadian Commission of Conservation hired British town planner and former Letchworth city manager Thomas Adams to advise them on their proposals for urban reform. Although Canadians failed to produce a garden city of their own, they adopted the movement's ideas in a number of suburban developments, including the Toronto Housing Company's plans for Riverdale and Spruce Court.

Progressive reformers were suspicious of private utilities in water, power, telephones, and transport, arguing for government control of such essential services. As we have seen in chapter 3, municipal and provincial governments in the first decade of the twentieth century often responded to pressure from urban reformers to take over the utilities from private developers. Montreal's private utilities weathered the tide of consumer grievance, while Edmonton's streetcars, electricity, and telephones all became publicly owned. In Toronto, Bell survived as a private monopoly, but the Toronto Transit Commission assumed control of the street railways.

As progressives encountered resistance from municipal governments, they became critical of political processes. The ratepayers, critics argued, had become passive pawns in the hands of corrupt developers who could influence voting in the poorer wards. To counter the power of "special interests," cities were urged to establish boards of control, elected on a city-wide franchise. Because middle-class voters had a much higher turnout at the polls than working-class voters, they were more likely to influence the results in a city-wide election, thereby putting an end to ward politics. Boards of control were adopted in Winnipeg (1906), Ottawa (1907), Montreal (1909), Hamilton (1910), and London (1914) prior to the First World War. A more extreme attempt to wrest

power from the masses was the trend of delegating authority to "expert" city managers and appointed commissioners, policies adopted in Edmonton in 1904, Saint John in 1908, and a few years later in Regina, Saskatoon, and Prince Albert.

The faith in expert urban management came naturally to middle-class progressives who were eager to establish peace, order, and good government on their own terms, but the progressive agenda gained limited support from the poorer districts of many cities. The francophone working class in Montreal, resentful of the self-serving policies of the anglophone elite who took little interest in the well-being of those who lived in the city below the hill, gave a resounding victory to populist mayoral candidate Médéric Martin in 1914. It was just one manifestation of the potential power of the working class.

## THE UNION MOVEMENT

Opposition to features of the industrial order led working people to form unions for the purposes of making collective demands on employers and providing mutual aid in times of hardship. Gradually, unions also began to lobby governments for legislative changes that would improve the lives of working people. While organizations of manufacturers remained more powerful than those formed by workers, unions took root in industrializing Canada and managed to win a few battles in their war to shape the system to their advantage.

Early labour organizations were craft unions. These were alliances of men and (very rarely) women attempting to maintain control over working conditions and wages in the face of employer attempts to introduce new administrative methods and new technologies that would transform their craft. Workers doing repetitive and less complex tasks were more easily replaced than craftspeople and proved largely unable to create lasting unions. Even the crafts had difficulty maintaining their organizations during recessions in which the oversupply of willing hands gave employers the advantage. Moulders in Toronto, working in stove, machinery, and agricultural implements industries, were able to dictate apprenticeship regulations, wage rates, and the pace of work in their factories. By contrast, Toronto coopers witnessed the destruction of their craft in the 1870s, and the city's shoemakers lost a long battle with their employers by 1890. Mechanization, employer hostility, and recession made it difficult for coopers and shoemakers to restrict entry into their profession as moulders continued to do.

At the time of Confederation, unionized labour was still too weak to exert much political pressure. It was not until the Trade Union Act of 1872, passed by the Macdonald government, that common-law prohibitions against unions as combinations in restraint of trade were removed. The act legalized only unions that agreed to be liable for the individual acts of their members—including, for example, damages inflicted on company property during strikes—so few unions chose to register under its provisions. No laws forced employers to bargain collectively with their employees or prevented employers from dismissing their employees without cause. Many employers simply refused to hire union labour and fired any employee who was suspected of advocating unions.

Despite the obstacles, workers organized resistance. In 1871, Toronto printers struck all of the city's newspapers in an attempt to force the nine-hour day on the whole publishing industry. The publishers, led by Reform Party notable George Brown, successfully prosecuted the strikers for seditious conspiracy, while ten thousand people paraded in support of the accused and their strike demands. Throughout 1872, the movement for the nine-hour day reverberated throughout industrial Canada, only to be quelled by the crushing recession of 1873. While the movement failed to achieve its objective, it produced a degree of solidarity among craftsmen and labourers that re-emerged once the recession lifted. In a curious twist of fate, George Brown was fatally shot in March 1880 by George Bennett, a disgruntled and deranged employee who had been fired for intemperance.

In the 1880s and 1890s, the strike became firmly established as labour's chief method of attempting to win improvements for workers. While there had been only 56 strikes in British North America from 1815 to 1849, and 204 in the 1870s, there were 425 recorded strikes in the 1880s and 600 in the 1890s. A key player in the strike wave was the Noble and Holy Order of the Knights of Labor. The Knights originated in 1869 among Philadelphia garment cutters concerned about the loss of worker control in their industry. The group's emphasis on secret rituals, reminiscent of pre-industrial culture, appealed to workers, and the organization spread across the United States and into Canada in the 1880s.

Unlike craft unions, the Knights were open to all workers regardless of skill, and the organization encouraged workers to support each other's struggles. In the preamble to their constitution, the Knights argued that workers must fight the "alarming developments and aggressiveness of great capitalists and corporations" to secure "full enjoyment of the wealth [workers] create, sufficient leisure in which to develop their intellectual, moral, and social faculties, all the benefits of recreation and pleasure of association, in a word, to enable them to share in the gains and honours of advancing civilization."[4] But they were unclear how best to work to these ends. Their American leaders focused on creating cooperatives as alternative workplaces, but capital for such ventures was always difficult to find.

The Knights' major breakthrough in Canada occurred in 1883 when they organized workers for a strike "against the monopolistic telegraph companies, symbol for much that was despised in the new industrial capitalist society."[5] Over the next several years, they organized workers across Canada in a variety of industrial sectors and broke union taboos against including women and blacks—though not Orientals—in their ranks. In the late 1880s, about sixteen thousand Canadian workers were members of the Knights, with Toronto, Hamilton, and Montreal enjoying particularly large memberships. Locals in Toronto ranged from shoemakers, barbers, and plumbers to carpenters, journalists, and a group of women tailors.

While their efforts to organize workers according to industry rather than along craft lines attracted many workers, the Knights were regarded by leaders of the craft unions as a dangerous rival.

The class consciousness of the Knights contrasted with the group consciousness of the craft unions, whose leaders claimed that the exclusive right of craftspeople to practise certain trades would be whittled away if all-inclusive workers' unions succeeded. During the recession of the late 1880s, the craft unions began to force workers to choose between the Knights and separate craft unions. Throughout the 1890s, the Knights retained many locals, especially in Quebec, but their isolation increased as the Trades and Labour Congress (TLC), created in 1883, emerged as the major political voice of Canadian labour. Dominated by craft-based unions, the TLC fought against industrial unions almost as hard as it did against employer intransigence. It also adopted the policy of its counterpart in the United States—the American Federation of Labor—of calling for higher wages and improved working conditions rather than for radical changes to the capitalist system. The national organization and its municipal counterparts, such as the Montreal Trades and Labour Council, lobbied governments for such reforms as shorter work days, safer workplaces, and an end to child labour. Their efforts led to greater government regulation of the workplace, though workers constantly complained that governments were lax in enforcing such regulations.

In 1902, at a meeting in Berlin, Ontario, the TLC formally affiliated with the American Federation of Labor. It then proceeded to expel industrial unions such as the Knights of Labor from its ranks and to consolidate its position as the dominant labour organization in the country. The TLC exiles established a rival organization, the National Trades and Labour Congress, in 1907. Although its numbers were small, it offered a nationalist alternative for the dominion's working men and women. Even within its own ranks, the TLC continued to harbour a radical contingent that pressed for industrial unionism and for direct political action.

During Canada's rise to industrial maturity, labour organizations were fragmented along regional and cultural lines. In Nova Scotia, the Provincial Workmen's Association (PWA) emerged as the most powerful voice of the province's working class. The PWA began in 1879 as the Provincial Miners' Association but changed its name and broadened its focus in 1880. It shared with the Knights a decentralized organization and a solidarity among members based on participation in various rituals. Unlike the Knights, the PWA included only workers in recognized crafts. The association was dominated by Nova Scotia's large mining population, and its lobbying efforts led to mine safety legislation and other laws of benefit to miners. Although the organization became increasingly conservative after the turn of the century, the nineteenth-century PWA was relatively militant. It shut down all the province's mines on two occasions, and its fiercely independent locals waged over seventy strikes before 1900. When strike activity increased during the first decade of the twentieth century, Maritime coal miners turned to the more radical American-based United Mine Workers (UMW) of America to help them in their struggles. In Springhill, workers conducted a bitter twenty-two-month strike in a failed attempt to have the UMW recognized as their legitimate bargaining agent.

Miner militancy on the East Coast was matched on the other side of the country. In British Columbia, coal miners had spontaneously struck several times before a Mutual Protective Society was established in 1877 among workers at Dunsmuir, Diggle and Company. The society protested wage cuts and short-weighing of coal on company scales (the workers were paid by the ton) and closed down the Wellington mine on Vancouver Island. Robert Dunsmuir, the province's leading capitalist, was able to convince the government to use the militia to force the miners back to work, but a long history of miner organization and militancy in British Columbia had begun. By 1905–6, the UMW had gained a foothold in the coal fields of southwestern British Columbia and Alberta, but not before the miners were forced to strike to have the union of their choice.

In Quebec, francophone workers were encouraged to look for assistance from the Roman Catholic Church rather than from secular unions, which the church condemned as foreign dominated and materialistic. Church-sponsored unions were initially conservative in their approach to labour rights, but priests assigned to the unions soon became sensitive to the plight of working people. In 1921, Catholic unions came together as the Confédération des travailleurs catholiques du Canada with an outlook similar to that of the TLC.

While many unionized workers held their own in the workplace, the position of common labourers remained precarious. Generally, navvies—the men who worked in construction gangs that built the railways and other public works—were victims of the subcontracting system: subcontractors prospered by placing the lowest bid and then wringing profits by paying low wages and feeding and housing the workers in the cheapest way imaginable. Living in grim bunkhouses and eating stale bread, a navvy had experiences of the work world far removed from those of the proud craftsman.

Such workers were ripe for the message of Industrial Workers of the World (IWW), an American-based organization, founded in 1905, that rejected both the parliamentary process and traditional unionism. The Wobblies, as they were

called, focused on the strike as the most effective political weapon and called on their members to walk off the job collectively when a fellow worker was unjustly treated by an employer. The IWW leadership hoped that worker solidarity and general strikes would eventually force employers to hand over their properties to their workers. Although these policies failed to capture the imagination of a majority of Canadian workers, the IWW had a wide following in the first two decades of the twentieth century among railway construction workers in the West and in northern Ontario.

Women were largely excluded from labour organizations but this did not stop them from protesting labour practices in trades that they dominated. In 1900, female spoolers in Valleyfield's cotton industry walked off the job when apprentices were hired to perform their work. The women had limited bargaining power because textile work was no longer a highly skilled trade, and experienced workers could easily be replaced. But women in more skilled occupations fared no better than their sisters in the textile industry. In 1907, over four hundred Bell telephone operators, commonly known as "hello girls," went on a much-publicized strike to protest a reduction in hourly rates for their highly skilled and physically taxing work. Operators were subject to electrical shocks from their equipment and to the stress of constant demands from a growing number of callers. After less than a week, the strikers agreed to submit their grievances to a federal arbitration commission. The commissioners chastised Bell for its labour practices but avoided the wage issue with the statement that it was better left "to the market." Like many people in this period, the commissioners were more concerned about the impact of dangerous working conditions on the maternal potential

*Bunkhouse men experienced some of the worst working and living conditions in industrializing Canada.*

National Archives of Canada/PA115432

of the women, most of whom were between the ages of seventeen and twenty-two, than about the ability of the women to make a living wage.

People of colour were generally excluded from unions, most of which had specific racial qualification for membership. As we have seen, white workers objected to the hiring of Orientals, and violence sometimes erupted when employers tried to introduce foreigners of any type into the workplace. Most racial minorities worked in manual jobs, many of them seasonal and part-time, which made it difficult for them to form their own unions. One exception was the occupation of railway porters. Because blacks were associated with servant status, they became the preferred employees for sleeping car and station porters. Porters and their families made up the nucleus of black communities in railway cities such as Halifax, Montreal, Toronto, Winnipeg, Calgary, and Vancouver. Although their hours were long and the pay low, working on the trains was almost a rite of passage for many African-Canadian men. In 1918, porters of the Canadian Northern Railway, then in the process of becoming part of the CNR system, organized Canada's first black union, the Order of Sleeping Car Porters. The Canadian Brotherhood of Railway Employees initially refused to accept the union but relented in 1919 to become the first craft union to abolish racial restrictions on membership.

Unions made their presence felt during Canada's rise to industrial maturity, but they had little success in restructuring capitalist development in the interests of labour or in expanding their membership. Only 5.6 percent of the labour force in Ontario and 8.4 in Quebec was organized by 1911. While some of the difficulties can be attributed to the conservative agenda promoted by the international unionism of the TLC, this was only partly the cause. Union leaders were often overtly racist and sexist, thereby alienating a significant proportion of their potential membership. Further, the strike as a vehicle for exerting the power of workers often provoked repression. With military power in the hands of the state, and that state generally eager to respond to the corporate agenda, workers had little hope of wresting either concessions or fundamental changes.

*As this photo of the 1914 Street Railway Strike in Saint John suggests, peaceful demonstrations sometimes led to violence when police tried to disperse demonstrators.*
Provincial Archives of New Brunswick/P338-200

## LABOUR AND THE STATE

The increased visibility of organized labour and the threat it constituted to the established order prompted a variety of responses. In the 1880s, governments at all levels conducted a series of investigations to determine the causes of worker discontent. The Macdonald government appointed the Royal Commission on the Relations of Labour and Capital in 1886. Its majority and minority reports and five volumes of evidence submitted in 1889 provide a wealth of information on the shocking conditions in Canadian factories, but the commissioners' recommendations yielded few reforms, other than the declaration in 1894 of a holiday—Labour Day—for Canada's working people.

## ONE HUNDRED AND TWO MUFFLED VOICES[6]

The Royal Commissioners studying the relations between labour and capital heard the testimony of nearly 1800 witnesses. Only 102 of those who testified were women. Although women made up over 20 percent of the paid labour force in 1891, nobody on the commission was very interested in hearing from them. As historian Susan Mann Trofimenkoff has revealed, it took a great deal of courage for working people generally and women in particular to speak before a formal body such as a royal commission. Saying something that offended employers might threaten a worker's job. Nearly half of the women testified anonymously; only thirty of the close to seventeen hundred male witnesses did so.

The most dramatic testimony relating to women's work came from a woman identified as Georgina Loiselle. Beaten by her employer for her "impertinent" refusal to make a hundred extra cigars, she was still employed at the factory five years later when she gave her testimony. Her employer justified his behaviour to the commissioners on the grounds that "her mother had prayed me ... to correct her in the best way I could." With three of Georgina's brothers also employed by the company, the factory's owner had assumed the role of disciplinarian to the fatherless Loiselle children. Georgina was eighteen at the time of the beating, and no one, including Georgina herself, seemed particularly surprised by her employer's brutality.

When the commissioners submitted their report, they indicated much greater concern over the moral consequences of women working in unchaperoned settings and using common washrooms with men than they did about the poor salaries and working conditions that were uniformly the lot of women in waged labour in Victorian Canada.

---

Many employers, harking back to the paternalism that they felt characterized pre-industrial relations, tried to earn the loyalty of their skilled and experienced employees by sponsoring company picnics, excursions to nearby tourist sites, and even company bands. When such inducements failed to work, employers used force, calling upon governments to send in police, militia, and troops to put down strikes and to coerce labour into compliance. In 1899, militia cleared the London streets of people protesting in support of the Amalgamated Association of Street Railway Employees against the Cleveland-based corporation that ran the streetcars. A year later, the fishers on the Fraser River, striking for better prices for their fish from canning factory owners, were met by militia and provincial police. Coal mining towns in the Maritimes and the West were particularly susceptible to official intervention on behalf of the mine owners.

For all its short-term success in forcing labour to toe the company line, military or police intervention in disputes between capital and labour proved counterproductive. It was usually expensive, often provoked sympathy for workers, and always increased class conflict. As a result, governments at all levels tried to find a "middle way" that would reduce the worst excesses

*The Massey Company Band was one of the many efforts undertaken in the 1880s to encourage worker loyalty.*
Ontario Agricultural Museum, Massey Ferguson Archives

of the capitalist system while leaving its structure largely intact. In 1900, the federal Liberals established a Department of Labour and hired a university-trained labour relations expert, William Lyon Mackenzie King, to be its first deputy minister. King championed conciliation and compromise and believed in enhancing the role of government as the umpire between labour and capital.

In 1907, King helped to engineer the Industrial Disputes Investigation Act (Lemieux Act), which prohibited strikes and lockouts in public utilities and mines until the dispute had been investigated by a tripartite board of arbitration representing labour, capital, and government. By establishing a compulsory cooling-off period, the act deprived organized labour of its strongest weapon, the surprise strike, without any compensatory protection against retaliation by the employer, such as hiring strikebreakers. The TLC asked the Conservatives to repeal the act when they were elected to power in 1911, but Robert Borden let the legislation stand.

The state's bias in favour of business interests, evidenced by military intervention and legislation like the Lemieux Act, made many labour leaders question traditional party loyalties. In Britain, workers were throwing their support behind the Independent Labour Party, and socialist parties in Europe also found their base of support among working people. While socialists preached the total abolition of capitalism, labourites focused on improving the lot of workers within the capitalist system. In addition to supporting public ownership of railways, banks, and utilities, Labour Party leaders urged state enforcement of safe working conditions and the introduction of social insurance programs such as unemployment and health insurance and old age pensions.

In the first decade of the twentieth century, labour parties began to appear on the Canadian scene. In 1900, A.W. Puttee, a founder of the Winnipeg Labour Party, and Ralph Smith, TLC president, were elected to Parliament. Rejecting the more radical Socialist Party of Canada, the TLC endorsed the creation of provincial labour parties. It was, for instance, instrumental in the founding of the Montreal-based Parti ouvrier in

1904. Opposed by the Roman Catholic Church, such a party had little hope of gaining a victory at the polls, though Alphonse Verville, the head of the plumbers' union, was elected to Ottawa in a 1906 by-election in the working-class district of Maisonneuve.

## THE RADICAL RESPONSE

By 1914, a growing number of Canadians were pursuing more radical visions than those championed by the progressives and labourites, whose main goal was to impose rational order on capitalism. Those advocating socialism were in the forefront of an international movement to abolish a system that they believed put property ahead of people and pitted labour against capital in an uneven struggle refereed by a state clearly biased in favour of the rich. Socialists disagreed on the best means of achieving a society where each would receive according to his or her needs, but the goal nevertheless had wide appeal in early industrializing Canada.

The socialist movement that took root in Canada was a strange amalgam of Marxism, Christian socialism, and reformism. On one end of the spectrum, radicals such as the Industrial Workers of the World preached syndicalism, the view that labourers should join forces to overthrow the yoke of capitalism. These hardliners argued that a cataclysmic conflict between labour and capital was the only way the new order would be given birth. In this period, most Canadian socialists took a more gradualist approach, focusing on the state as the most likely vehicle for managing revolutionary change.

One of the earliest spokesmen for the gradualist approach was T. Phillips Thompson. Born into a Quaker family in Newcastle-on-Tyne in 1843, Thompson arrived in Canada at the age of fourteen. After studying law, he became a journalist and intellectual based in Toronto. Unlike most Anglo-Canadians, he sympathized with the francophone and Métis minorities and advocated the abolition of the monarchy. A free thinker, he was influenced by the work of American critic Henry George, whose book *Progress and Poverty*, published in 1879, caused a stir throughout Canada. George's message, that industrialism had unleashed an insupportable burden of poverty and distress, was not new, but his solution was: a tax on the property of the rich. Dubbed the "single tax," it had the virtue of simplicity.

Thompson met George on several occasions and incorporated his ideas into a book entitled *The Politics of Labour*, published in 1887. "In the place of the monopolistic rule, which in the true sense now governs the people by prescribing whether they shall work or not, and how they shall receive," Thompson reasoned, "let us have a representative, popular recognized government, conducted on business principles, doing the same thing not for the profit of a few but in the interests of all."[7] While taxing profits and expanding the role of the state may not sound very radical to people today, such ideas were roundly condemned in the nineteenth century.

Socialists rarely won seats in municipal, provincial, and federal governments prior to 1914, but their ideas were influential not only in the labour movement but also among a growing number of intellectuals. Again Thompson's career is instructive. In the 1880s and 1890s, he joined a plethora of organizations established to advance the new millennium: the Single Tax Association, the Nationalist Club, the Anti-Poverty Society, the Toronto Conference on Social Problems, the Toronto Suffrage Association, the Theosophical Society, the Canadian Populist Party, and the Patrons of Industry. Not all of the people in these associations were socialists, but most of them were free thinkers who were deeply influenced by socialist ideas.

At the turn of the century, socialist political parties began to take root in Canada. They ranged from the Christian Socialist League, whose leading spokesman, G. Weston Wrigley, maintained that Christ was the first socialist, to the Socialist Labour Party, whose leaders rejected out of hand the reformism of "middle-class socialism." With the arrival of thousands of immigrants with a tradition of socialist politics, efforts to achieve unity in the cause of socialism were further complicated. No

sooner had local socialist groups on the West Coast come together to produce the Socialist Party of Canada than they were weakened by the defection of members who founded the more moderate Social Democratic Party (SDP) in 1907. With its language locals, the SDP appealed to Finnish, Ukrainian, and Russian communities on the Prairies, who felt excluded from the established political parties. The SDP also proved more open to women's issues, including the problems of unpaid domestic labour and prohibition, than the Socialist Party of Canada, whose leaders considered such issues as detracting from "scientific" socialist goals.

## THE RURAL RESPONSE

While cities served as a focus for reform, people living in the rural communities were far from passively resigned to the changes taking place around them. The prohibition movement, for example, was widely supported in rural areas of Eastern Canada from the middle of the nineteenth century. When the Prairies filled up with settlers, the region added weight to the rural voice that had been losing ground in the decades following Confederation. Western farmers began to question the power of eastern-based institutions such as railways, banks, and governments. In the eastern provinces, rural people were also disturbed by the growing power of urban-based institutions, but their concerns focused on the depopulation of rural areas, which had few of the amenities available to their city-bound neighbours.

The transformation of rural life and the flight of large numbers of people to the city also troubled many urban dwellers. In Montreal, Henri Bourassa wrote frequently and eloquently about the danger to society of abandoning the values associated with rural life. So, too, did Andrew Macphail, a Montreal-based medical doctor who edited *University Magazine* between 1907 and 1920. Macphail looked back nostalgically upon his childhood in rural Prince Edward Island and lamented the rapid disappearance of what he saw as a superior way of life. In 1912, the Board of Moral and

*Milk wagon at St Roche.*
National Archives of Canada/PA11677

Social Reform and Evangelism of the Presbyterian Church established a Summer School on the Country Church Problem and asked John MacDougall, a pastor from Spencerville, Ontario, to lecture on the topic. His lectures were incorporated in *Rural Life in Canada: Its Trend and Tasks*, a publication that documented the crisis apparently facing rural Canada. For all of these men, rural living was as crucial to the moral and spiritual well-being of the nation as it was to physical survival and food production.

The flight of women from the farm was a particular concern of reformers. When markets became the focus of production, the balance of power in the family enterprise shifted in favour of men. Profits from farming, if there were any, were more likely to be invested in farm machinery than in appliances to relieve domestic drudgery. The situation in the West—Canada's much-vaunted land of opportunity—was particularly telling. Discouraged by discriminatory homestead laws, unequal inheritance patterns, and the unending domestic toil that confronted them, women resisted taking up the farming life. Desperate bachelor farmers advertised for women to join them on the farm and many women accepted their proposals but few of them counselled their daughters to marry a farmer. Throughout the nation, young women between the ages of fifteen and thirty left the farm in droves to find jobs in the city. Industrial wages were lower for women than men, but at least in the cities women had access to an income that was often denied them on the farm.

Rural discontent blossomed into a full-blown movement that demanded major changes in Canada's political structures. In Central Canada and the Maritimes, the Grange Movement of the 1870s paralleled efforts by labour and capital to use collective action to achieve their goals. Granges spread from the United States into Canada, and by 1874 a Dominion Grange was formed. Although the Grange movement focused on educational activities and avoided direct political action, it was soon paralleled by another American import, the Patrons of Industry, whose brief political success in the early 1890s led to the election of candidates to the Ontario and Manitoba legislatures as well as to the House of Commons. The Patrons of Industry dissolved as quickly as it began but was succeeded by the Ontario Farmers' Association, which in 1902 emerged as a critic of high transportation costs and the protective tariff. By 1907, it had joined with the Grange to form the United Farmers of Ontario. Led by E.C. Drury and J.J. Morrison, it was determined to make Ottawa listen to the concerns of the farming community.

Meanwhile, on the Prairies, agrarian discontent led to the creation of the Territorial Grain Growers' Association in 1901, which became the basis for provincial associations following the creation of the provinces of Saskatchewan and Alberta in 1905. The Manitoba Grain Growers'

Association was founded in 1902. In 1908, the *Grain Growers' Guide*, a newspaper based in Winnipeg, was established as a mouthpiece for agrarian discontent. Francis Marion Beynon's column in the *Guide* gave women plenty to think about. Recognition of women's contribution to farm life led to the creation of women's auxiliaries to the prairie farm organizations and to support for female suffrage. In Eastern Canada, the Women's Institutes played a similar role but were never as politically focused as the western farm women's organizations.

Western farmers had a rich political legacy upon which to draw. In the United States, farmers had been "raising hell" for years, and many of their programs for action, including separate political parties and mass educational efforts called chautauquas, crossed the border with American homesteaders. When they bumped into democratic socialist ideas brought by British and European immigrants, they created a potent brew.

Rural areas of Newfoundland were also ripe for the message of social reform. Under the dynamic leadership of William Coaker, the Fishermen's Protective Union (FPU), founded in 1909, swept through the outports gaining support from the workers in the fishing and forest industries. It soon earned the hostility of the merchants of St John's and the Roman Catholic Church, which forbade its adherents from becoming members of the "godless" organization. The FPU motto was "To each his own." Does the fisherman receive "his own," Coaker asked, when

> he boards a coastal steamer ... and has to sleep like a dog, eat like a pig and be treated like a serf?... At the seal fishery where he has to live like a brute, work like a dog and be paid like a nigger? Do they receive their own when they pay taxes to keep up five splendid colleges at St. John's ... while thousands of fishermen's children are growing up illiterate? Do they receive their own when forced to supply the funds to maintain a hospital at St John's while fishermen, their wives and daughters, are dying daily in the outports for want of hospitals? [8]

The FPU demanded state intervention to ensure fair return to the people who caught and processed the fish, improvements in education and health care in the outports, and the implementation of an old age pension program. In alliance with the Liberal Party, the FPU won eight seats in the Newfoundland legislature in 1913 and applied pressure on the government of the day, led by Sir Edward Morris, to legislate reforms.

One of the most significant challenges to capitalist industrial development came from the cooperative movement, which was particularly strong in rural Canada. Originating in Britain in the 1840s, cooperatives were organized on the principle of cooperation rather than competition and were owned by their members rather than by anonymous investors. Between 1860 and 1900, farmers in the Maritimes, Quebec, and Ontario developed over twelve hundred cooperative creameries and cheese factories. They also organized insurance companies to provide protection against crop failure and fires. Alphonse Desjardins in Quebec used cooperative principles to establish a chain of credit unions, the caisses populaires. In the West, grain farmers, led by E.A. Partridge, organized the Grain Growers' Grain Company in 1906 to market directly to buyers in Europe. The creation in 1909 of the Cooperative Union of Canada brought like-minded cooperators together for education and lobbying activities.

In the same year, Ontario farmers and western grain growers established the Canadian Council of Agriculture. Tariff policy emerged as the organization's major grievance. Roundly condemned as a charge on society's producers for the benefits of manufacturers, tariffs were seen by the farmers as an instrument of oppression by a class of businessmen who were sucking the nation dry through their greed and corruption.

In June 1910, Prime Minister Laurier set out on a three-month tour of the west where he was besieged by petitions from well-organized farmers. Later in the year, nearly a thousand farmers from all across the country descended on Parliament Hill to demand reforms, including lower tariffs, better rail and grain elevator service, and legislation supporting cooperative enterprises. When the Laurier government negotiated a free trade treaty with the United States in the winter of 1911, it did so not as a throwback to the earlier goals of the Liberal Party but because a clear majority of rural Canadians demanded an end to high tariffs. The fact that the Liberals lost the election late that year only confirmed the belief held by farmers that industrial interests controlled the levers of power in the nation.

## THE WOMAN MOVEMENT

As the foregoing discussion suggests, women were becoming increasingly involved in Canada's reform movements. This involvement was fuelled by the enormous changes in women's lives and by new ideas about the role of women in society. With the introduction of manufactured clothes, foodstuffs, and household products, and the tendency to send children to public schools, much of what was considered women's work moved outside the home. At the same time, middle-class women were told that their place was in the home. To reinforce that injunction, women were denied access to higher education, the professions, boardrooms, and political office. The careful delineation of separate spheres was thus established: men dominated the public sphere with all its opportunities, while women were relegated to the private sphere of motherhood, domesticity, morality, and good works.

The contradictions embodied in the doctrine of separate spheres were particularly obvious in working-class families. When the family economy failed, as it so often did, women could not simply remain "angels in the house." Yet, when they ventured into the public sphere, women were faced with discrimination and exploitation. For working-class women, the notion of living a life of middle-class domesticity no doubt looked attractive, but no matter which class women fell into, they took their status from their husbands and fathers and were confined to a narrow range of options.

The doctrine of separate spheres led middle-class women to organize separately from men in a variety of voluntary organizations. Although such groups began tentatively with the creation of Women's Missionary Aid Societies in various

Protestant churches in the early 1870s, they eventually became more self-serving. Even church-based organizations proved radical in their own way. The Women's Missionary Aid Societies, for example, sponsored single women for overseas service in countries such as India, Burma, and China. While consistent with women's longstanding role in charitable activities, missionary work provided a source of employment for women, often in areas such as medicine and administration largely denied to them at home.

On the home front, the conservatism of the Protestant churches prepared the way for the Salvation Army, a British evangelical organization that attracted large numbers of working-class women when it arrived in Canada in the 1880s. Preaching a doctrine of spiritual equality, the Army evolved into a community service agency, in which women played a prominent role preaching on street corners, "rescuing" prostitutes, and providing food, shelter, and spiritual guidance to some of the destitute in Canadian society. "Hallelujah lasses" often earned the criticism of tight-laced Victorians for their public role, but the Salvation Army, more than the older churches, gave young, single women a home, a job, security, and a purpose in life. [9]

While still rooted in religious service, two of the earliest women's organizations, the Young Woman's Christian Association (YWCA) and the Woman's Christian Temperance Union (WCTU), took middle-class women another step down the road to public service. Founded in Great Britain as a counterpart to the YMCA, the Canadian YWCA was first established in Saint John in 1870. By the 1880s, the "Y" had become a familiar organization in most Canadian cities. It provided both lodging and job training, largely in domestic service, for girls arriving in the "dangerous" urban environment. In the late 1880s, the YWCA also began moving onto university campuses, where most student organizations were closed to women.

As we have already seen, the WCTU focused women's energies in the cause of prohibition. The first Canadian local of this American organization was founded by Letitia Youmans in Picton, Ontario, in 1874. Spreading quickly throughout the nation, the WCTU formed a Dominion Union

*A group of women in front of a YWCA boarding house at 689 Ontario Street, Toronto.*
National Archives of Canada/PA126710

in 1883, and by the 1890s claimed over ten thousand members. Although the WCTU came together around the issue of alcohol, it soon adopted a variety of reform causes.

The women of the WCTU were a formidable force in Canadian society. Not only did the WCTU train women in the arts of public speaking and political lobbying, it also gave them experience in dealing with opposition. *The Ottawa Daily Citizen* published this account of a WCTU action on 5 February 1890:

> A Band of evangelistic workers announced a few days ago by handbills distributed throughout Hull, that meetings would be held every Tuesday evening in that city in a hall on the corner of Duke and Queen Streets.... It seems that preparations were made by a gang of roughs, headed by an unlicensed saloon keeper, to give the new-comers a warm reception; in fact, the intention was more or less

openly expressed to "clean them out." The band of evangelists was composed of Miss Bertha Wright, accompanied by a considerable number of young ladies.... On opening the doors of the Hall a crowd of about TWO HUNDRED MEN well primed with liquor rushed in and filled the place. For a time, their interruptions were confined to noises, etc., but on being remonstrated with they made an attack on the speaker and singers. For a time everything was in confusion, and there was reason to fear the worst, missiles being thrown and blows freely given, but not returned. The young women then joined hands and formed a circle around the speakers, and the roughs refrained from striking them but confined their efforts to separating the little band.... Finally the police managed to clear the hall and took the Ottawa people to the station, fighting off the crowd with their batons all the way. At this time some of the young women were badly hurt by the missiles that were thrown. [10]

Despite the "warm reception," Bertha Wright and her "little band" from the Ottawa Young Woman's Christian Temperance Union were back in Hull the following week, this time to take on an angry mob of four hundred "roughs."

*Established in 1887 by the Ottawa Young Woman's Christian Temperance Union, the Home for Friendless Women supported itself by operating a laundry. WCTU "Y"s were a popular branch of the temperance organization in the 1880s and 1890s and were distinguished from their more conservative parent organization by their evangelical zeal.*

National Archives of Canada/PA27434

While many of the voluntary organizations that appealed to women originated in Great Britain and the United States, Canada made its own contribution to the voluntary cause in the form of the Women's Institutes. The first Women's Institute was established in Stoney Creek, Ontario, in 1897 by Adelaide Hoodless. As a mother who watched her youngest child die as a result of drinking impure milk, Hoodless wanted to improve women's domestic skills through education on matters relating to nutrition and sanitation. Her major causes included domestic science courses in the schools, pure milk legislation, and public health reforms. These causes were taken up with zeal by the Women's Institutes after the Ontario govern-ment began subsidizing their efforts in 1900. By the 1920s, the Women's Institutes had spread throughout Canada and had taken root in rural areas of Great Britain and around the world.

For francophone women in Quebec, the possibilities for community service were narrower than for women elsewhere in Canada. Religious orders in the province took most of the responsibility for health, welfare, and education, and it is in the female religious orders that can be found the counterpart to anglophone Protestant voluntarism. Between 1837 and 1899, thirty-four new female religious communities were established in Quebec. By 1901, 6.1 percent of the province's single women over twenty were nuns. Religious orders gave Roman Catholic women one of the few avenues by which they could have a direct impact on developments taking place around them. In Montreal, for example, the Grey Nuns organized day-care centres for working-class families in the early 1870s. Many nuns became accomplished administrators. For example, Marie-Elizabeth Casgrain, known as Sister Sainte-Justine, was chief trustee of the Congregation of Notre Dame in Montreal, which expanded from 440 women in 1870 to 1226 in 1901. During her busy career, Casgrain established and administered the Congregation's budget, bought and sold property, and travelled to Europe to hire an architect for a new mother house.

By the turn of the century, lay women in Quebec began to resist the conservative injunctions of their clerical leaders, as illustrated by one remarkable family.

Marie Lacoste-Gérin-Lajoie, used the Fédération nationale Saint-Jean-Baptiste, the organization she helped found, as a vehicle to push for access to higher education for women and for improvements

*The Hospital of the Sisters of Charity in Rimouski, 1890.*

R.E. Mercier, Archives nationales du Québec à Québec/P600-6/438-1

in their legal status, and to provide organizational support to women workers. Her sister, Justine Lacoste-de Gaspé-Beaubien, was the founder of the Hôpital Sainte-Justine for children, and remained its president from 1907 until 1964. Marie's sister-in-law, Antoinette Gérin-Lajoie, was one of the co-founders of the École ménagère provincial, the first Quebec domestic science school formed by lay women. Marie's daughter, Marie Gérin-Lajoie, supplemented her religious commitment to Catholic social action by taking courses in social work at Columbia University and observing the British settlement house movement. She ushered in a new age of social service work for both lay women and nuns in her province, and eventually founded a religious order dedicated to training and supporting lay women in their social work.[11]

The growth in Canadian women's activism in the nineteenth century was capped by the formation of a national federation of women's clubs in 1893. Known as the National Council of Women

of Canada (NCWC), it was the brainchild of Lady Aberdeen, the wife of the governor general. She had been elected president of the International Council of Women at the Chicago World's Fair in 1893 and established the NCWC when she returned to Canada. An enthusiastic supporter of reform causes, Lady Aberdeen was a founder of the Aberdeen Association (1890), which distributed reading material to isolated settlers, and of the Victorian Order of Nurses (1897), an organization to provide nursing services in areas where trained medical help was not available.

The NCWC began cautiously but soon encompassed a wide range of causes, including temperance, child welfare, and professional advancement for women. Through their local councils, they mobilized the volunteer energies of women across the country. While the NCWC tried not to alienate male legislators whose votes were needed, they refused to back away from controversial issues once their membership had reached a consensus. In 1910, at their annual meeting in Halifax, the NCWC endorsed women's suffrage, the final step in recognizing women as having public power in their own right. The council avoided most partisan squabbles by refusing to become aligned politically, and it even adopted silent prayer so as not to offend Roman Catholics, Jews, and other non-Protestant women. This stance caused the WCTU and the YWCA to refuse affiliation until 1914 and 1921, respectively, but it showed a sensitivity to cultural diversity that was often lacking in national organizations.

Women's efforts to gain access to a university education began to bear fruit in the 1870s with the opening of Mount Allison to women. When she graduated from the Mount in 1875, Grace Annie Lockhart became the first woman in the British Empire to receive a university degree. By the 1880s, most other universities had followed Mount Allison's lead, although the numbers of women who registered for classes remained low until the twentieth century. Even when their numbers increased, women tended to be channelled into arts programs, steered away from science courses, and excluded completely from the professional schools offering degrees in law, medicine, engineering, and theology.

Men jealously guarded their monopoly on the professions. In 1895, Toronto's Clara Brett Martin became Canada's first woman law graduate, but she faced great resistance from the Law Society of Upper Canada, not only in her efforts to seek education in the legal field but also in attempts to practise. In medicine, Emily Howard Stowe and Jennie Trout were forced to train as physicians in the United States because no Canadian medical school would admit women. Upon their return to Canada, they successfully pressured Queen's University and the University of Toronto to open facilities to train women doctors in 1883, although these universities created separate female medical colleges. Women's College Hospital in Toronto, incorporated in 1913, became the base for many women doctors in the city who found other hospital surgeries closed to them.

While few women became doctors, the number of female nurses was growing rapidly by the end of the nineteenth century. Nurses were expected to be selfless servants of patients and to remain subordinate to doctors, much like the idealized mother in the home. Similarly, many women took up teaching as a profession in this period, but they remained subordinate to male principals and trustees and, like nurses, were paid low salaries compared to those of the men in their profession.

## THE CHANGING CANADIAN FAMILY

The agitation for wider opportunities for women notwithstanding, the major responsibility for most Canadian women remained the home. But the situation was changing there as well, confirmed by a long-term trend towards smaller families. Although Parliament had outlawed contraceptives and abortifacients in 1892, women continued to share birth control information: abstinence, coitus interruptus, self-induced abortion, and the margin of safety provided by breastfeeding helped Canadian women and men space births. Canadians wanted reliable birth control not so much to indulge in the sexual excess that moralists feared but to improve family life, to preserve women's health, and to provide better opportunities for children.

Smaller families were becoming fashionable because ideas about children were changing. In industrializing Canada, middle-class families became increasingly preoccupied with the manner in which children were reared. A rising standard of living and falling birth rate allowed parents, especially mothers, to devote more resources to their offspring. While youngsters had long been, and many remained, important economic assets to their families, they became more than ever the focus of emotional and psychological expenditure by women whose domestic responsibilities were believed to centre on a perfected modern motherhood. For middle-class children, shifting views about mothering and childhood meant better health, more sympathy, and greater opportunity for individual self-expression.

This was not the case for children from families whose marginal incomes precluded the adoption of modern ideas of childhood that centred on dependence, protection, and delayed responsibilities. Moreover, the young runaways, prostitutes, and labourers who haunt court records, royal commissions, and newspaper columns testify to the fact that poor children were widely exploited and rarely effectively protected. Remedies for the problems of poor and neglected children, although often well-intentioned, frequently penalized this vulnerable group. The Juvenile Delinquents Act of 1908 is a case in point. Under the act, separate juvenile courts were created in an effort to combine crime control with child welfare. When children's courts were created, children lost many of their rights of due process and faced levels of indeterminate sentencing that adults largely escaped. Children were often placed on probation or sentenced to separate institutions, such as the Truro Girls' Home, Toronto's Mercer Reformatory, or Vancouver's Boys' Industrial School, where they were subjected to minimal training in agricultural, technical, or domestic skills. While better than a sentence of hard labour, such training rarely offered troubled children a future of dignified independence, let alone economic comfort.

The law and the courts remained curiously out of step with the needs of women and children in the industrial age. Although Married Women's Property Acts and child custody legislation were passed in the 1880s and 1890s and softened some of the worst excesses of patriarchal authority, the courts remained biased in favour of husbands and fathers. Nowhere was this more obvious than in the issue of wife battery. Most cases of domestic violence never reached the courts, and when they did judges tended to protect the man's right to "discipline" his wife. This injustice was the particular concern of the WCTU, which focused on the fate of women beaten by their drunken husbands. However, the WCTU was not alone in its abhorrence of domestic violence. In Hamilton, police magistrate George Jelf went on record as despising husbands who "hang around hotels, with their wives and little children perhaps starving. They ought to get whipped every day."[12] In some jurisdictions, including Jelf's, whipping remained an option for punishing men who beat their wives long after it was abolished for other offences.

In the new western provinces and territories, women's right to the dower—a one-third interest in her husband's property upon widowhood—was abolished in 1886 and not restored until the second decade of the twentieth century. The fact that men living in western jurisdictions could legally sell or mortgage property without spousal consent was a grievance that rested heavily on pioneering women.

Although men held the reigns of power in industrializing Canada, they did not escape attempts to make them more attentive to the needs of the family. Reformers in this period supported clearly delineated gender roles, but they began to be concerned that men spent too little time at home. In attempts to get men out of private clubs, bars, brothels, and gambling dens, they recommended gardening and exercise as appropriate male leisure activities. The American sex educator Sylvanus Stall, whose works were sold by the Methodist Church in Canada, advised, "In women, the love of home is usually more dominant than in men. By cultivating this in yourself you [men] will produce a harmony of thought and purpose which will contribute greatly to the comfort and well-being of both. Adorn your home with your own hands. Beautify the lawn, the shrubbery; and all external surroundings."[13] This early injunction to what came to be called "companionate marriages" would become a more widely accepted view in the interwar years.

Divorces in early modernizing Canada were expensive and rarely granted. Between Confederation and the 1960s, divorce reform advocates in Canada were few, and the results of their efforts meagre. Historian James Snell notes:

> The absence of significant divorce reform is suggestive of the centrality of the ideal of the conjugal family and of the supportive role of the law. Family solidarity was so central to the belief system of the leaders of Canadian society that significant change in the divorce law could not easily be tolerated. The idea of the child-producing family and of the lifelong, sexually exclusive marriage was fundamental to social reproduction, economic organization, gender relations and sexual morality.[14]

Divorced people, much like women who conceived a child out of wedlock, faced social disapproval.

## THE DEMAND FOR FEMALE SUFFRAGE

By the 1890s, an increasing number of reformers supported what was known at the time as "woman suffrage." People came to the cause in a variety of ways: from lengthy struggles to open universities, professions, and businesses on an equal basis to women; from groups condemning married women's subordination under the law; and from reform movements that felt their goals might be advanced by the support of women. Two feminist perspectives were evident in the suffragists' arguments: equal rights and maternal, or social, feminism. Equal rights advocates hoped to sweep away the unfair laws and attitudes that encouraged discrimination against women. Maternal feminists wanted special laws to support women in their roles as wives and mothers. In both lines of thinking, women's suffrage became a key element in the struggle for reform.

While the equal rights perspective tended to dominate in the years immediately following Confederation, by the turn of the century the rhetoric of maternal feminism prevailed. Expanding on the view that woman's place was in the home, maternal feminists argued that women's special qualities hitherto practised in the private sphere were increasingly needed in the public sphere to reform the abuses of the industrial system. Maternal feminists exploited the widespread nineteenth-century belief that women were instinctively better than men—or at least more sensitive and nurturing—to justify their demands for greater power in both the private and public sphere. Like other middle-class reformers, suffragists were likely to express unflattering views of the working class and immigrants, and frequently pointed to the injustice of allowing illiterate peasant men to vote while Canadian-born women remained disenfranchised. Whatever the justification offered by suffrage advocates, the demand for female suffrage remained fundamentally radical, seeking a direct connection between women and the state rather than allowing male family members to act as mediators.

The hardships of the suffrage campaign wore out several generations of women and deterred the less courageous from expressing their opinions publicly. Misogyny and anti-feminism were widely expressed both verbally and in print by people determined to keep women in their place. In Quebec, Henri Bourassa lashed out against feminism as a dangerous import from a godless Anglo-Saxon culture that would destroy Roman Catholic Quebec. English-Canadian intellectuals such as Stephen Leacock were equally appalled by the notion of equality for women, and resorted to the comfortable view that because women were superior to men they should be shielded from the realities of the public sphere. Canada's union leaders were no better than their middle-class employers who argued that women should be segregated in the workforce and receive lower wages. When immigrants brought with them longstanding feudal views about the subordination of women, further weight was added to the patriarchal perspective. Even Protestant church leaders, whose congregations were increasingly dominated by women, ranted from the pulpit about the horrors of defying the divinely sanctioned subordination of women.

Not surprisingly, given their education and sense of purpose, many of the first generation of professional women became active in the suffrage movement. Dr Emily Howard Stowe, for example, took the lead in establishing Canada's first women's suffrage organization in 1876, whose purpose was cleverly concealed under the name the Toronto Literary Society. By 1883, the group felt confident enough to change its name to the Toronto Women's Suffrage Association and at the same time to launch the Canadian Women's Suffrage Association. Pressure from women's organizations led to gradual municipal enfranchisement of unmarried and widowed women who met the property qualification. Ontario granted this right in 1884, New Brunswick in 1886, Nova Scotia in 1887, and Prince Edward Island in 1888, but many municipalities still refused women the right to hold public office.

The right of women to vote in provincial and national elections was steadfastly resisted. In Nova Scotia, the lobbying of women's groups produced a

*British suffragist Emmeline Pankhurst (first row, fifth from left) stands beside Nellie McClung (left of Pankhurst) during Pankhurst's tour of North America, 1917.*

Provincial Archives of British Columbia/39849

narrow majority in favour of women's suffrage in the legislative assembly in 1893, but manoeuvring by the anti-suffragist attorney-general, J.W. Longley, forestalled passage of the relevant bill. When it was debated in the session of 1894, it lost by one vote. By the end of the century, the tide seemed to have turned firmly against women's suffrage, in part because so many reforms, including prohibition, were predicted to succeed if women ever got a chance to clean up the political system.

Western Canada produced the one individual most identified with the suffrage cause: Nellie L. McClung. Born in Grey County, Ontario, she migrated to Manitoba as a young girl, married a druggist, raised five children, and had a successful career as a fiction writer. Her sense of humour and clever repartee enabled her to survive the many taunts that came her way. In 1914, she packed Winnipeg's Walker Theatre for a performance of "How the Vote was Won." To thundering applause, she played the role of premier of a

Woman's Parliament, and punctured the pretensions of Conservative premier Sir Rodmond Roblin with her speech to an imaginary group of franchise-seeking males: "We wish to compliment this delegation on their splendid gentlemanly appearance. If, without exercising the vote, such splendid specimens of manhood can be produced, such a system of affairs should not be interfered with.... If men start to vote, they will vote too much. Politics unsettles men, and unsettled men means unsettled bills— broken furniture, broken vows, divorce."[15] Such events put the anti-suffrage forces on the defensive and paved the way for opposition parties to embrace a cause whose time had come.

## Conclusion

The arrival of millions of immigrants and the growth of the economy transformed Canada in the half century following Confederation. While Canadians found the changes troubling, they came together in voluntary organizations to address the worst abuses of the industrial order and even envisioned a society where everyone would share in the material wealth made possible by the new technological processes. But being Canadian at the turn of the twentieth century meant more than hard work and reform; it also meant being part of an emerging national culture, the contours of which, like most other aspects of Canadian life in this period, were widely contested and hotly debated. It is to this debate that we turn in the next chapter.

# THE SUFFRAGISTS

## *A Historiographical Debate*

Efforts to reform industrial society proliferated at the turn of the twentieth century. Middle-class reformers, imbued with the progressive spirit of the age, were convinced that political action and social reform could eliminate many of the "social evils" that they saw around them. For many historians, these reformers have become the heroes of Canadian history, and people such as feminist Nellie McClung have been praised for their clarity of vision. Other historians have taken a more critical approach to reformers, who are viewed less as people of vision than as a privileged group who tried to impose their narrow middle-class values on all Canadians. The clash of opinion is clearly drawn around the women's movement, which culminated in the granting of suffrage to women during and immediately following the First World War.

In 1950, Catherine Cleverdon published her pioneering study of the women's suffrage movement. "Political equality is a prize not to be lightly held," she maintained. "Though it came to Canadian women without the harshness and bitterness of the struggle in Great Britain, it was won by the hard work and heartaches of small groups of women throughout the dominion who had the courage and vision to seek it." [16] Cleverdon's perspective was shaped by her strong commitment to the democratic process and her identification with the suffrage leaders, many of whom she interviewed while conducting her research.

When interest in women's history resurfaced in the 1970s and 1980s, scholars were less inclined to see Canada's suffragists as people with only "courage and vision." Carol Lee Bacchi, following the direction taken by feminist scholars internationally, concluded in her study of some two hundred suffrage leaders that: "Most Canadian suffragists were social reformers and members of a social elite. They asked that women be allowed to vote in order to impress certain values upon society, Protestant morality, sobriety and family order." [17] In many suffrage circles, it was revealed, racist and class-bound solutions—including eugenics, exclusive immigration laws, and restrictive voting practices—were openly advocated. Even more damning, especially from the point of view of left-wing scholars, was the fact many middle-class suffrage leaders had the time to devote to "good causes" because they exploited an underclass of household servants. Since a narrow maternal feminist vision—many suffrage leaders saw women's primary role and rationale for public action being rooted in their status as mothers—seemed to motivate most Canadian suffragists, they were ultimately seen as unworthy predecessors to the more purposeful feminists of the modern women's movement. To quote Bacchi, "the female suffragist did not fail to effect a social revolution for women; the majority never had a revolution in mind." [18]

The rejection of the early suffrage leaders as "foremothers" to modern feminism has elicited a vigorous response. In a critique of Bacchi's book, historian Ernest R. Forbes used the experience of women in Halifax, who were described by both Cleverdon and Bacchi as being invariably "conservative" in their approach to female suffrage, to expose the parochialism and present-mindedness of such a position. Halifax suffrage leaders took on a whole range of feminist reforms, Forbes argued, and used any available argument to promote their clearly radical goals. "Reading only the leader's statements in the newspapers one might conclude that the scheme was motivated chiefly by class interests and social control. Having read the minutes [of the Local Council of Women] I do not believe it. Neither, apparently, did the men who rejected their proposals."[19] In her study of women involved in left-wing organizations such as the Social Democratic Party of Canada before 1914, Janice Newton found that many socialist women also espoused maternal feminist goals, often in defiance of their male colleagues. Newton maintains that there was nothing inherently conservative about maternal feminism in this period because many women on the left wanted "nothing less than the socialist transformation of women's maternal and domestic roles."[20]

Contemporary political concern about what constitutes modern feminism clearly motivates such a debate and may obscure more important questions that should be asked about the suffrage movement. Australian scholar Judith Allen, for instance, has called upon scholars to adopt a comparative and international approach to suffrage. By looking at such issues as temperance and sexual consent laws, as well as suffrage, Allen shows that feminist causes were rooted in time and place. For example, developments following the granting of the vote to women in New Zealand and parts of Australia in the 1890s were different from those that followed the success of suffrage in Great Britain, Canada, and the United States where suffrage was granted a generation later. Allen concludes that momentous demographic changes—including the decline in family size, the narrowing in the age gap between spouses, the vast increase in the rate of divorce, the dramatic fall in mortality rates, the change in women's labour force participation rate, and changing values—signalled altered negotiations between men and women.[21] By seeing suffrage and other reform activities in the context of the larger changes taking place within society and the values shaping responses to those changes, individual reform leaders can be better understood. The question then becomes not whether suffrage leaders were heroes or villains, or whether their policies were right or wrong, but why they responded to their world the way that they did.

## NOTES

1 Helen Potrebenko, *No Streets of Gold: A Socialist History of Ukrainians in Alberta* (Vancouver: New Star, 1977), 131–32

2 Carolyn Strange, *Toronto's Girl Problem: The Perils and Pleasures of the City, 1880–1930* (Toronto: University of Toronto Press, 1995), 91

3 Cited in Mariana Valverde, *The Age of Light, Soap, and Water: Moral Reform in English Canada, 1885–1925* (Toronto: McClelland and Stewart, 1991), 106

4 "Preamble to the Knights of Labor Constitution" cited in Martin Robin, *Radical Politics and Canadian Labour* (Kingston: Industrial Relations Centre, Queen's University, 1971), 19–20

5 Gregory S. Kealey, *Toronto Workers Respond to Industrial Capitalism, 1867–1892* (Toronto: University of Toronto Press, 1980), 177

6 Susan Mann Trofimenkoff, "One Hundred and Two Muffled Voices: Canada's Industrial Women in the 1880s," *Atlantis* 3,1 (Fall 1977): 67–82

7 T. Phillips Thompson, *The Politics of Labour* (Toronto: University of Toronto Press, 1975), 221–22

8 Cited in James K. Hiller, "Newfoundland Confronts Canada, 1867 to 1949" in *The Atlantic Provinces in Confederation*, ed. E.R. Forbes and D.A. Muise (Toronto: University of Toronto Press, 1993), 363

9  Lynne Marks, "Working Class Femininity and the Salvation Army: 'Hallelujah Lasses' in English Canada, 1882–1892" in *Rethinking Canada: The Promise of Women's History*, 2nd ed., ed. Veronica Strong-Boag and Anita Clair Fellman, (Toronto: Copp Clark Pitman, 1991)

10  Cited in Sharon Anne Cook, *"Through Sunshine and Shadow": The Woman's Christian Temperance Union, Evangelicalism and Reform in Ontario, 1874–1930* (Montreal: McGill-Queen's University Press, 1995), 3

11  Gail Cuthbert Brandt, "Postmodern Patchwork: Some Recent Trends in the Writing of Women's History in Canada," *Canadian Historical Review* 72, 4 (1991): 453-454

12  Cited in John C. Weaver, *Crimes, Constables, and Courts: Order and Transgression in a Canadian City, 1816-1970* (Montreal: McGill-Queen's University Press, 1995), 78

13  Cited in Valverde, *Age of Light, Soap, and Water*, 31

14  James G. Snell, *In the Shadow of the Law: Divorce in Canada, 1900–1939* (Toronto: University of Toronto Press, 1971), 262

15  Catherine L. Cleverdon, *The Woman Suffrage Movement in Canada*, 2nd ed. (1950; reprint Toronto: University of Toronto Press, 1974), 59

16  Cleverdon, *Woman Suffrage Movement*, 267

17  Carol Lee Bacchi, *Liberation Deferred? The Ideas of the English Canadian Suffragists, 1877–1918* (Toronto: University of Toronto Press, 1983), 3

18  Ibid., 148

19  Ernest Forbes, "The Ideas of Carol Bacchi and the Suffragists of Halifax," *Atlantis* 10, 2 (Spring 1985): 122

20  Janice Newton, *The Feminist Challenge to the Canadian Left, 1900–1918* (Montreal: McGill-Queen's University Press, 1995), 13

21  Judith Allen, "Contextualizing Late Nineteenth-Century Feminism: Problems and Comparisons," *Journal of the Canadian Historical Association*, new series, 1 (1990): 17–39

## SELECTED READING

Social reform in this period is discussed in Mariana Valverde, *The Age of Light, Soap and Water: Moral Reform in English Canada, 1885–1925* (Toronto: McClelland and Stewart, 1991); Ramsay Cook, *The Regenerators: Social Criticism in Late Victorian English Canada* (Toronto: University of Toronto Press, 1985); Joseph Levitt, *Henri Bourassa and the Golden Calf: The Social Program of the Nationalists in Quebec, 1900–1914* (Ottawa: University of Ottawa Press, 1969); Richard Allen, *The Social Passion: Religion and Social Reform in Canada, 1914–1928* (Toronto: University of Toronto Press, 1990); Paul Rutherford, ed., *Saving the Canadian City: The First Phase, 1880–1920* (Toronto: University of Toronto Press, 1974); and Ronald Rompkey, *Grenfell of Labrador: A Biography* (Toronto: University of Toronto Press, 1991).

Surveys of the working class experience and labour movement include Craig Heron, *The Canadian Labour Movement: A Brief History* (Toronto: James Lorimer, 1996); Bryan D. Palmer, *The Working Class Experience: Rethinking the History of Canadian Labour, 1800-1991* (Toronto: McClelland and Stewart, 1992); Desmond Morton, *Working People: An Illustrated History of the Canadian Labour Movement* (Toronto: Summerhill, 1990); Jean Hamelin, ed., *Les Travailleurs Québécois, 1851-1896* (Montreal: Presses de l'Université du Québec, 1973) and Jacques Rouillard, *Histoire du Syndicalisme au Québec* (Montreal: Boréal Express, 1989); Susan Mann Trofimenkoff, "One Hundred and Two Muffled Voices: Canada's Industrial Women in the 1880s," *Atlantis*, 3,1 (Fall 1977): 67-82.

Labour organization is discussed in Gregory S. Kealey and Bryan D. Palmer, *"Dreaming of What Might Be": The Knights of Labour in Ontario* (New York: Cambridge University Press, 1982); A. Ross McCormack, *Reformers, Rebels and Revolutionaries* (Toronto: University of Toronto Press, 1977); Martin Robin, *Radical Politics and Canadian Labour* (Kingston: Industrial Relations Centre, Queen's University, 1971); Donald Avery, *Dangerous Foreigners: European Immigrant Workers and Labour Radicalism in Canada* (Toronto: McClelland and Stewart, 1979); and Ian McKay "'By Wisdom Wile or War': The Provincial Workmen's Association and the Struggle for Working-Class Independence in Nova Scotia," *Labour/Le Travail* (Fall 1986): 13-62. First-hand accounts of working conditions and attitudes are found in Greg Kealey, ed., *Canada Investigates Industrialism: The Royal Commission on the Relations of Labor and Capital, 1889* (Toronto: University of Toronto Press, 1973); Michael Cross, ed., *The Working Man in the Nineteenth Century* (Toronto: Oxford University Press, 1974); T. Phillips Thompson, *The Politics of Labour* (1887; Toronto: University of Toronto Press, 1975); and Edmund Bradwin, *The Bunkhouse Man* (Toronto: University of Toronto Press, 1972).

The impact of industrial capitalism on women and children's work is explored in Marjorie Cohen, *Women's Work, Markets and Economic Development in Nineteenth Century Ontario* (Toronto: University of Toronto Press, 1988); Joy Parr, *Labouring Children: British Immigrant Apprentices to Canada, 1869–1924* (Montreal: McGill-Queen's University Press, 1980), and *The Gender of Breadwinners: Women, Men and Change in Two Industrial Towns, 1880–1950* (Toronto: University of Toronto Press, 1990); Bettina Bradbury, *Working Families: Age, Gender, and Daily Survival in Industrializing Montreal* (Toronto: McClelland Stewart, 1993); John Bullen, "Hidden Workers: Child Labour and the Family Economy in Late Nineteenth-Century Urban Ontario," *Labour/Le Travail* (Fall 1986): 163–88; Janice Acton, Penny Goldsmith, and Bonnie Shepard, eds., *Women at Work: Ontario, 1850–1930* (Toronto: Women's Press, 1974); Franca Iacovetta and Mariana Valverde, eds., *Gender Conflicts: New Essays in Women's History* (Toronto: University of Toronto Press, 1992); Paula Bourne, ed., *Women's Paid and Unpaid Work: Historical and Contemporary Perspectives* (Toronto: New Hogtown, 1986); Graham Lowe, *Women in the Administrative Revolution: The Feminization of Clerical Work* (Toronto: University of Toronto Press, 1987); Elaine Bernard, *The Long Distance Feeling: A History of the Telecommunications Union* (Vancouver: New Star, 1982); and Kathryn McPherson, *Bedside Matters: The Transformation of Canadian Nursing, 1900-1990* (Toronto: Oxford University Press, 1996).

Developments in specific industries and regions are the subject of many books and articles, including: Bryan D. Palmer, *A Culture in Conflict: Skilled Workers and Industrial Capitalism in Hamilton, Ontario* (Montreal and Kingston: McGill-Queen's University Press, 1979); Gregory S. Kealey, *Toronto Workers Respond to Industrialism, 1867-1892* (Toronto: University of Toronto Press, 1980); Craig Heron, *Working in Steel: The Early Years in Canada, 1883-1935* (Toronto: McClelland and Stewart, 1980); Robert A. J. McDonald, "Working-Class Vancouver, 1886-1914: Urbanism and Class in British Columbia," *B.C. Studies* (Spring/Summer 1986): 33-69; Ian McKay, *The Craft Transformed: An Essay on the Carpenters in Halifax, 1885-1985* (Halifax: Holdfast Press, 1985); Eric Sager, *Seafaring Labour: The Merchant Marine of Atlantic Canada, 1820-1914* (Montreal and Kingston: McGill-Queen's University Press, 1989); Ian Radforth, *Bushworkers and Bosses: Logging in Northern Ontario, 1900-1980* (Toronto: University of Toronto Press, 1987); Jeremy Mouat, *Roaring Days: Rossland's Mines in the History of British Columbia* (Vancouver: University of British Columbia Press, 1995); and Ian McKay, "The Realm of Uncertainty: The Experience of Work in the Cumberland Coal Mines, 1873-1927" *Acadiensis* 16, 1 (Autumn 1986): 3-57.

Rural responses are discussed in Vernon C. Fowke, *The National Policy and the Wheat Economy* (Toronto: University of Toronto Press, 1957); David Laycock, *Populism and Democratic Thought in the Canadian Prairies, 1910-1945* (Toronto: University of Toronto Press, 1990); Ian Macpherson, *Each for All: A History of the Cooperative Movement in English Canada, 1900-1945* (Ottawa: Carleton University Press, 1979); Ronald Rudin, *In Whose Interest? Quebec's Caisses Populaires, 1900-1945* (Montreal and Kingston: McGill-Queen's University Press, 1990); Paul Sharp, *The Agrarian Revolt in Western Canada: A Survey Showing the American Parallels* (New York: Octagon Press, 1971); Jeffery Taylor, *Fashioning Farmers: Ideology, Agricultural Knowledge and the Manitoba Farm Movement, 1890-1925* (Regina: Canadian Plains Research Centre, 1994); Ian McDonald, *"To Each His Own": William Coaker and the Fisherman's Protective Union in Newfoundland Politics, 1908-1945* (St John's: ISER, Memorial University, 1987); Terry Crowley, "Rural Labour," in Paul Craven, ed., *Labouring Lives: Work and Workers in Nineteenth-Century Ontario* (Toronto: University of Toronto Press, 1995): 13-104. See also John MacDougall, *Rural Life in Canada: Its Trend and Tasks* (1913; Toronto: University of Toronto Press, 1973); and Andrew Macphail, *The Master's Wife* (1939; Toronto: University of Toronto Press, 1977).

Social histories dealing with changing notions of families and of sexuality include Carolyn Strange, *Toronto's Girl Problem: The Perils and Pleasures of the City, 1880–1930* (Toronto: University of Toronto Press, 1995); Angus McLaren and Arlene Tigar McLaren, *The Bedroom and the State: The Changing Practices and Politics of Contraception and Abortion in Canada, 1880–1980* (Toronto: McClelland and Stewart, 1986); Angus McLaren, *Our Own Master Race: Eugenics in Canada, 1885–1945* (Toronto: McClelland and Stewart, 1990); Gary Kinsman, *The Regulation of Desire: Sexuality in Canada* (Montreal: Black Rose Books, 1987); Sharon Dale Stone, *Lesbians in Canada* (Toronto: Between the Lines, 1990); Neil Sutherland, *Children in English-Canadian Society: Framing the Twentieth-Century Consensus* (Toronto: University of Toronto Press, 1976); Patricia Rooke and Rudy Schnell, *Discarding the Asylum: From Child Rescue to the Welfare State in English Canada, 1800–1950* (Lanham, MO: University Press of America, 1983); James G. Snell, *In the Shadow of the Law: Divorce in Canada, 1900–1939* (Toronto: University of Toronto Press, 1991) and *The Citizen's Wage: The State and the Elderly in Canada, 1900-1951* (Toronto: University of Toronto Press, 1996); and Paul Axelrod, *The Promise of Schooling: Education in Canada, 1800-1914* (Toronto: University of Toronto Press, 1997). Motherhood is the focus of Katherine Arnup, *Education for Motherhood: Advice for Mothers in Twentieth-Century Canada* (Toronto: University of Toronto Press, 1994), and Cynthia R. Comacchio, *"Nations Are Built of Babies": Saving Ontario's Mothers and Children, 1900–1940* (Montreal: McGill-Queen's University Press, 1994).

On women and the church, see Marta Danylewycz, *Taking the Veil: An Alternative to Marriage, Motherhood and Spinsterhood in Quebec, 1840–1920* (Toronto: McClelland and Stewart, 1987); Ruth Compton Brouwer, *New Women for God: Canadian Presbyterian Women and India Missions, 1876–1914* (Toronto: University of Toronto Press, 1990); Rosemary R. Gagan, *A Sensitive Independence: Canadian Methodist Women Missionaries in Canada and the Orient* (Montreal: McGill-Queen's University Press, 1992); and Lynne Marks, *Revivals and Roller Rinks: Religion, Leisure, and Identity in Late-Nineteenth-Century Small-Town Ontario* (Toronto: University of Toronto Press, 1996). Regional studies of women include Denise Lemieux and Lucie Mercier, *Les femmes au tournant du siècle, 1880–1940: Ages de la vie, maternité et quotidien* (Quebec: Institut québécois de recherche sur la culture, 1989); Barbara K. Latham and Roberta J. Pazdro, eds., *Not Just Pin Money: Selected Essays in the History of Women's Work in British Columbia* (Victoria: Camosun College, 1984); Franca Iacovetta and Mariana Valverde, eds., *Gender Conflicts: New Essays in Women's History* (Toronto: University of Toronto Press, 1992); Linda Kealey, ed., *Pursuing Equality: Historical Perspectives on Women in Newfoundland and Labrador* (St John's: ISER, 1993); Carmelita McGrath, Barbara Neis, and Marilyn Porter eds., *Their Lives and Times: Women in Newfoundland and Labrador, A Collage* (St John's: Killick Press, 1995); Margaret Conrad, Toni Laidlaw, and Donna Smyth, *No Place Like Home: Diaries and Letters of Nova Scotia Women, 1771–1939* (Halifax: Formac, 1988); Janet Guildford and Suzanne Morton, eds., S*eparate Spheres: Women's Worlds in the Nineteenth-Century Maritimes* (Fredericton: Acadiensis Press, 1994); and Karen Dubinsky, *Improper Advances: Rape and Heterosexual Conflict in Ontario, 1880–1929* (Chicago: University of Chicago Press, 1993). Victorian medical notions about women are dissected in Wendy M. Mitchinson, *The Nature of Their Bodies: Women and Their Doctors in Victorian Canada* (Toronto: University of Toronto Press, 1991). Women and the law are the subject of Constance Backhouse, *Petticoats and Prejudice: Women and Law in Nineteenth-Century Canada* (Toronto: Women's Press, 1991).

On reform and suffrage movements, see Janice Newton, *The Feminist Challenge to the Canadian Left, 1900–1918* (Montreal: McGill-Queen's University Press, 1995); Linda Kealey, ed., *A Not Unreasonable Claim: Women and Reform in Canada* (Toronto: Women's Press, 1979); Veronica Strong-Boag, *The Parliament of Women: The National Council of Women of Canada, 1893–1929* (Ottawa: National Museum of Civilization, 1976); Naomi Griffiths, *The Splendid Vision: Centennial History of the National Council of Women, 1893–1993* (Ottawa: Carleton University Press, 1993); and Carol Lee Bacchi, *Liberation Deferred? The Ideas of the English-Canadian Suffragists, 1877–1918* (Toronto: University of Toronto Press, 1983). See also Catherine L. Cleverdon, *The Woman Suffrage Movement in Canada* (1950; Toronto: University of Toronto Press, 1972); Nellie McClung, *In Times Like These* (1913; Toronto: University of Toronto Press, 1972).

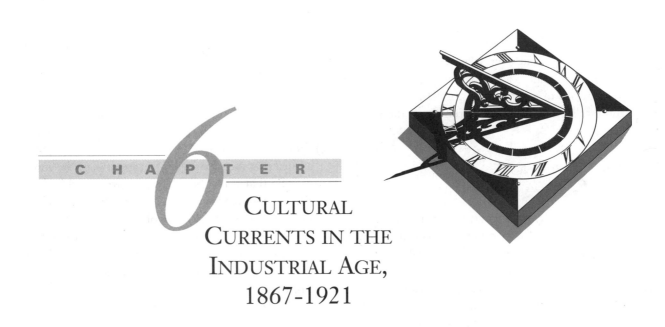

# 6

# CULTURAL CURRENTS IN THE INDUSTRIAL AGE, 1867-1921

IN NOVEMBER 1885, TORONTO LAWYER W.A. Frost wrote to the editor of the *Varsity*, the University of Toronto's student newspaper, to protest the formation of a baseball club at the college. He warned Toronto's students of the unfortunate class of people associated with the game, including a saloon-keeper "who is notorious for his love of baseball and his generosity in bailing out of prison disreputable characters who are unfortunate enough to be placed under the restraints of the law." Frost claimed not to be opposed to baseball as a sport—intrinsically it "may be as good as either cricket or football," he conceded—but worried about the people associated with the game, who, he claimed, were "of the very lowest and most repugnant character." According to Frost, baseball "has been degraded by Yankee professionalism until the name of baseball cannot fail to suggest a tobacco-chewing, loud-voiced, twang-nosed bar-tender, with a large diamond pin and elaborately oiled hair."[1]

Canadians in the half century following Confederation had difficulty defining what made them Canadian. Like Frost, many distinguished themselves from their brash southern neighbours; but, unlike Frost, most seemed unconcerned about the encroachment of American culture. They read American books and magazines, watched and played American baseball, and drifted back and forth across the Canada–United States border without worrying very much about issues of citizenship.

Inevitably, a number of Canadians looked to Great Britain to balance the attraction of the United States. As members of the world's greatest empire, Canadians could at least claim superiority to the Americans by association if not entirely on their own terms. Only a handful of people publicly expressed concern about the fact that Canadians were subjects of the British Empire. When all was said and done, dual citizenship paid dividends, and few Canadians were prepared to put national autonomy ahead of their pocketbooks. French Canadians were the most likely to distance themselves from both the British and the American empires. In Quebec and the Maritimes, francophone leaders forged national visions based on a heady mix of language, religion, history, and grievance. Immigrants from other cultural backgrounds tended to stick to themselves and let the old stock fight it out for ascendancy.

Concern about national identity preoccupied elites much more than it did ordinary Canadians who were just trying to get by. Yet, in making decisions about their lives—where to live and work, what to believe about the nature of the universe, how long to stay in school, which leisure activities to pursue, even whether to establish a varsity baseball team—all Canadians helped to lay the foundations of a nation that in 1914 was culturally and intellectually much different from the one that began in 1867.

## DEFINING CANADA

After 1867, local and regional loyalties remained more important for most people than their identity as Canadians. Only a few intellectuals were troubled by the lack of a "new nationality" trumpeted by supporters of Confederation, such as D'Arcy McGee. Disturbed by the economic focus of much of the Confederation debate, these intellectuals sought to formulate a vision of the country that appealed to the heart and soul.

When the assassination of McGee in 1868 robbed the nation of its most articulate proponent of national idealism, five men in Ottawa decided to take action. The five were Ottawa civil servant and author Henry J. Morgan, Nova Scotia Coal Owners' Association lobbyist Robert Grant Haliburton, poet Charles Mair, militia officer and lawyer George Taylor Denison III, and lawyer W.A. Foster. They became the nucleus of the Canada First movement, which claimed as its mission the promotion of "national sentiment" worthy of a great transcontinental nation.

Reflecting the strained relations between Canada and the United States following the American Civil War, Canada Firsters were initially anti-American. The cancelling of the Reciprocity Treaty, the Fenian invasions, and the Alaska purchase all seemed to confirm the aggressive tendencies of Canada's southern neighbour. After the Washington Treaty was negotiated in 1871, Canada Firsters became concerned about Britain's tendency to sacrifice Canada's interests to the cause of better British–American relations. This concern led them to focus on Canada's North American identity and its independence of both Britain and the United States.

Canada Firsters presented Canada as a country peopled by robust Nordic races disciplined by their efforts to survive in a harsh environment. In the *Canadian Monthly and National Review* and the *Nation*, two journals spawned by the expanding circle of Canada Firsters in the 1870s, they expounded the notion of a new nationality based on a combination of race and geography. They took their cue from R.G. Haliburton, who in 1869 argued that the identifying feature of Canada "must ever be that it is a Northern country inhabited by the descendants of the Northern races." For Haliburton, the superiority of the "Northern races" was self-evident. "If climate has not had the effect of moulding races," he queried, "how is it that southern nations have almost invariably been inferior to and subjugated by the men of the north?"[2]

The place of French Canadians in the new nation was problematic. Although Haliburton and other Canada Firsters were willing in theory to include the "Norman French" among the Nordic elite, they failed in practice to demonstrate even this limited tolerance. Their bigoted attitudes towards French Canadians—and complete contempt for aboriginal peoples—were fully exposed in their efforts to suppress the Red River Rebellion. In Toronto, Denison threatened civil insurrection if Macdonald pardoned Riel and abandoned the West to the Métis. Mair, who had moved to the Red River colony in 1869, was particularly outspoken. An active member of the colony's Canadian Party, Mair declared that Canada was being held back by the inferiority of the Indian and the medievalism of the French, the latter being further tainted by their marriages to aboriginal women. "In general," Mair asserted, "the Frenchman married the Indian and sank to the level of her tastes and inclinations," while "the Englishman married the Indian and raised her to the level of his own." He also concluded that French Canadians were the principal "bar to progress, and to the extension of a great Anglo-Saxon Dominion across the continent."[3]

When industrialized nations led by Great Britain began seizing control of the resources of Africa and Asia in the 1880s, definitions of the new nationality became even more ethnocentric. Bitterness at Britain's alleged abandonment of Canada gave way to a feeling of solidarity with the mother country. Many supporters of closer links between Canada and Great Britain ignored the exploitative character of imperialism, claiming that it was, at least potentially, a means of spreading the message of Christianity throughout the world. While many of the leading imperialists were social reformers, their social critique tended to emphasize the lack of Christian values rather than the faults of capitalism. The imperial goal, it was hoped, would rekindle spiritual purpose and bind Canadians together in a mission to help Great Britain to elevate the world.

The Reverend G.M. Grant typified this brand of imperialism. Born in Albion Mines, Nova Scotia, he became principal of Queen's University, a Presbyterian institution, in 1877 and remained in that post for two decades. Grant pressed for unity among Protestant churches and played a key role in the union of four previously independent Presbyterian denominations into the Presbyterian Church in Canada in 1875. When the factious Methodists united in 1883, he foresaw possibilities for greater unity between Presbyterians and Methodists. Christian, imperial, and Canadian unity were all part of the same organic whole for people like Grant, who believed that by helping to bring the spiritual and cultural benefits of western civilization to "heathen" peoples around the world, Canadians were contributing to global progress.

One expression of the growth of imperialist sentiment was the establishment of Empire Day as a national holiday. First celebrated in Ontario, Nova Scotia, and the Protestant schools of Quebec on 23 May 1898—the day before Queen Victoria's birthday—it was designed to provide an opportunity to use the public schools for the promotion of patriotic sentiments. In his directive to all school inspectors, George Ross, the minister of education in Ontario, nicely blended national and imperial sentiments:

> Part of the forenoon might be occupied with a familiar talk by the teacher on the British Empire, its extent and resources; the relations of Canada to the Empire; the unity of the Empire and its advantages; the privileges which, as British subjects, we enjoy; the extent of Canada and its resources;

readings by Canadian and British authors by the teacher; interesting historical incidents in connection with our own country. The aim of the teacher in all of his references to Canada and the empire should be to make Canadian patriotism intelligent, comprehensive and strong. The afternoon, commencing at 2:30 p.m., might be occupied with patriotic recitations, songs and readings by the pupils, and speeches by the trustees, clergymen and others as may be available. The trustees and public generally should be invited to be present at the exercises. During the day the British Flag or the Canadian Ensign should be hoisted over the school building.[4]

Support for imperialism among English Canadians was by no means unanimous. As the high degree of interest in closer economic links with the United States suggests, many English Canadians were comfortable with the view that Canada was a North American nation, free from the weight of tradition that plagued Europe. Goldwin Smith, a British-born academic who had settled in Toronto in 1871, argued that annexation to the United States was the best option for Canada. In his book *Canada and the Canadian Question* (1891), Smith maintained that annexation would consolidate the peoples of North America into one progressive nation, enhance the global power of English-speaking peoples, and resolve, in one bold stroke, the nationalist issue in Quebec.

Goldwin Smith was not alone in seeing Canada's destiny firmly bound with that of the United States. Especially in the Maritimes and the West, there was strong support for commercial union with the United States among primary producers, though few went so far as calling for political annexation. Canadians who had moved to the United States to find work were also more receptive to closer relations between the two North American nations. In the Canadian Clubs that sprang up in cities such as Boston, New York, and San Francisco, businessmen argued for closer Canada–United States relations, especially in matters of trade. Annexationism was always a latent force, ready to be called into service when economic circumstances looked bleak.

Before 1914, few voices in English Canada called for Canada to cut its ties with Great Britain and forge an independent national identity. John S. Ewart, who served as legal counsel for the French-speaking minority of Manitoba, wrote a series of essays arguing for Canada to become constitutionally independent, but there was little popular support for achieving such a goal. It was only during the First World War that the idea of establishing an independent nation-state gained widespread support. Canada's participation in the war and the support for the self-determination of nations voiced during the conflict spurred Canadians into re-evaluating their lingering colonial relationship with Great Britain.

## FRENCH-CANADIAN NATIONALISM

Few francophones in Canada found much in the national identity debate that appealed to them, though their leading spokesman, Henri Bourassa, shared Goldwin Smith's anti-imperialism. When Laurier gave way to pressure from imperialists in Canada and Great Britain to participate in the South African War in 1899, Bourassa embarked down an intellectual road that made him one of Canada's most original and controversial critics of Canadian public policy. In 1901, he introduced a bill into the House of Commons making the Canadian Parliament the only authority that could declare war on behalf of Canada. Although the resolution was voted down, it put the nation's colonial relationship to Britain on the agenda of public debate.

Bourassa also took the position that Canada should be an Anglo-French nation, with two cultures having equal rights throughout the country. During the debate surrounding the creation of the provinces of Alberta and Saskatchewan in 1905, he argued that Roman Catholics should have control of their own schools in the new provinces, warning that the equality of culture was an absolute condition of French Canadians continuing to accept Confederation. Bourassa gradually retreated from his notion of a bilingual, bicultural Canada because English Canada was so unreceptive to the idea.

Instead, he began to emphasize the Roman Catholic nature of French-Canadian society and the need to protect Quebec's special identity, which, he felt, was being threatened by secularism and materialism. Much troubled by the emergence of big corporations, Bourassa championed the rights of small business and farming families against the greed of corporate capitalism.

Bourassa increasingly became a spokesman for the nationalist forces that had been gaining momentum in Quebec since the Northwest Rebellion. Following the defeat of Honoré Mercier's Parti national government in 1891, nationalist sentiment continued to thrive in a variety of voluntary organizations. The most important of these was La Ligue nationaliste canadienne, established in 1903. Bourassa was a leading figure in the Ligue, which stood for Canadian autonomy within the British Empire, provincial rights, linguistic dualism, separate Roman Catholic schools, and the economic development of Canada by and for Canadians. Although the Ligue had only a few active members, its doctrines were widely disseminated through its newspaper, *Le Nationaliste*, and the speeches and writings of Bourassa and his coterie of young followers.

The enthusiasm of young people for nationalist ideas was captured in L'Association catholique de la jeunesse canadienne-française (ACJC), founded in 1904. Growing out of the determination of male college students to protect French-Canadian and Catholic interests, it was encouraged by church officials and journalists who believed that French Canada was in the midst of a religious and national crisis. The ACJC constitution embodied the idealistic goals of the organization:

1. The members of the Catholic Association of French-Canadian Youth believe that the French-Canadian race has a special mission to fulfil on this continent and that it must, for this end, guard its distinct character from that of other races.

2. They believe that the progress of the French-Canadian race is in a special fashion attached to the Catholic faith, which is one of the essential and specific elements.[5]

The ACJC's motto was "notre maître le passé" (our master the past). The concept was further developed by one of the organization's most prominent members, Lionel Groulx, a priest who taught at the Valleyfield Seminary. In his numerous publications, beginning with *Croisade d'adolescents*, Groulx proclaimed a mission for French Canadians, who, he argued, had been especially chosen by God to advance the cause of Roman Catholicism in North America. When he was appointed to teach history at Laval's Montreal campus in 1915, he had a platform from which to promote his providential view of French-Canadian history, an understanding of which he and other nationalistes felt was essential to the struggle for cultural survival.

## THE ACADIAN RENAISSANCE

French-speaking Canadians outside of Quebec were also influenced by nationalist ideas. Opposition to Confederation served as a catalyst for an Acadian renaissance that built upon the sense of identity generated by the publication of Longfellow's poem "Evangeline" (1847) and Edme Rameau de Saint-Père's historical treatment of the Acadian experience in *La France aux colonies* (1859). In 1867, Israel-D. Landry, a native of Quebec, established the first French-language Acadian newspaper, *Le Moniteur Acadien*, based in Moncton. At the same time, the Collège Saint-Joseph, founded in nearby

---

## THE WRITING OF HISTORY

In the nineteenth century, history emerged as a vehicle for "inventing" Canadian identity. English-Canadian historians portrayed Canada as a collection of peaceful Crown-loving colonies and moderate advocates of responsible government. In such texts as John Charles Dent's **The Last Forty Years: Canada Since the Union of 1841** (1881) and **The Story of the Rebellion** (1885), both oligarchies and radical reformers were given short shrift, while those who supported liberalism were portrayed positively. These historians subscribed to what is known as a Whig view of history—the notion that history is the story of events that reveal the progress of human development.

Nowhere was this view of history more explicitly revealed than in the popular ten-volume **History of Canada**, published by civil engineer William Kingsford between 1887 and 1898. Kingsford was touted as English Canada's counterpart to the famous French-Canadian nationalist historian François-Xavier Garneau whose multi-volume **Histoire du Canada**, published in the 1840s, extolled the history and culture of his people. Although both historians shared a progressive view of history, they differed in their interpretation of events. Garneau regretted the conquest, while Kingsford and most English-Canadian historical writers regarded the conquest as a blessing in disguise for the French Canadians and a necessary step in the march towards civilization.

In the 1890s, the history of Canada become a subject for teaching and research by university professors. The naming of George Wrong to the chair of history at the University of Toronto and the introduction at Queen's University of Adam Shortt's lectures on the economic and social history of Canada, both in 1894, marked the beginning of academic history, which tended to focus less on the heroes and dramatic events of the popular histories. Between 1913 and 1917, Adam Shortt teamed up with Arthur Doughty to produce the multi-volume series **Canada and Its Provinces**. While these authors shared the progressive view of history, they abandoned the romanticism of earlier writers for a detailed analysis of the nation's social and economic development.

In French Canada, the liberal, anticlerical perspective typified by Garneau gave way to histories that emphasized the role of the clergy in developing French-Canadian society. Abbé Jean-Baptiste-Antoine Ferland's histories in the 1860s, for example, painted a portrait of New France as a missionary colony whose history was guided by providence and its earthly representatives in the form of self-sacrificing bishops, nuns, and priests. Even Garneau modified his earlier views in light of the clerical assault. While a few anticlerical historians such as Benjamin Sulte championed secular forces, they tended to glorify rural life and paid little attention to the economic history of French Canada.

Memramcook in 1864, began educating an Acadian professional elite who would take the lead in defining Acadian goals and values. Confrontations over separate schools and language rights in the Maritime provinces reflected the growing sense of political awareness among Acadians.

In 1880, the Société Saint-Jean-Baptiste of Quebec invited all French-speaking communities in North America to a congress in Quebec. Acadians followed up this event with their own congress at Collège Saint-Joseph in July 1881. Over five thousand people attended. In this and a subsequent congress in 1884 at Miscouche, Prince Edward Island, the Acadians chose a national holiday (the Feast of the Assumption), a national flag (the French tricolour with the gold star), and a national hymn ("Ave Maris Stella"). Acadians were proud of their French heritage, but they were determined to develop cultural symbols distinct from those already established in Quebec. In 1903, the Société l'Assomption was founded as a charitable organization by Acadians living in Waltham, Massachusetts. Ten years later, its head office was moved to Moncton, and in subsequent years the Société evolved into a life insurance company.

*Built in 1896 in memory of Father Camille Lefebvre, who founded the Collège Saint-Joseph, the Monument Lefebvre in Memramcook, New Brunswick, became a symbol of the Acadian renaissance.*

La Société du Monument Lefebvre

The emergence of a group identity and an expanding population base soon showed political results. Responding to Acadian pressure, Macdonald appointed Pascal Poirier, a native of Shediac, as the first Acadian senator in 1885. In the New Brunswick provincial elections of 1870, Acadians won four seats and continued to expand their legislative representation in direct proportion to their growing numbers. Acadian representation in the Nova Scotia and Prince Edward Island legislatures was less certain but nevertheless a force to be reckoned with. Until the end of the nineteenth century, Acadians, like the francophones in Quebec, tended to support the Conservative Party. So significant was the Acadian vote in a number of Maritime ridings that Sir Wilfrid Laurier made a point of attending the Acadian congress at Arichat in 1900.

Acadians also followed their Quebec counterparts in focusing on Roman Catholicism as the vehicle for their national aspirations. No Acadian had ever been made a bishop and, indeed, most francophone priests in the region at the time of Confederation had been trained in Quebec. Acadian leaders began to protest their subordination in an institution that played such a prominent role in their daily lives. In 1912, an Acadian, Monseigneur Édouard LeBlanc, was appointed to the episcopal see of Saint John, and two years later the first Acadian parish was established in Moncton. The founding of Collège Sainte-Anne at Pointe-de-l'Église in 1890 and Caraquet's Collège de Sacré-Coeur, which was moved to Bathurst in 1916, ensured that a growing number of educated Acadian men would be available to fill the positions in religious and secular institutions. Acadian women were educated separately from men in their church-sponsored institutions and only achieved access to higher education in the 1940s. As in Quebec, careers in teaching, nursing, and administration in the church attracted a significant number of Acadian women in the second half of the nineteenth century. For example, Anselme and Charlotte Comeau from the municipality of Clare in Nova Scotia raised seven girls who pursued a religious vocation.

## A CHANGING PROTESTANTISM

The changing economic and intellectual climate of the late nineteenth century had a profound impact on Canadian churches. Following the publication of Charles Darwin's works on evolution, the literal truth of church teachings was called sharply into question. If humans were simply the products of millions of years of evolution, where did that leave the Old Testament account of creation? The falling off of church attendance in cities also challenged church leaders. If city life was not conducive to spiritual concerns, how was the church to make itself relevant in an increasingly urbanized society?

Many church leaders responded to the Darwinian challenge by rejecting the theory of evolution as speculative nonsense. In taking this position, they had support from some members of the scientific community, including geologist Sir William Dawson, principal of McGill University and the most influential scientist of his generation. Dawson used scientific evidence to challenge the claims of evolutionists and attempted to reconcile the Bible's account of a six-day creation by suggesting that the term "day" in Genesis be understood as a longer period than a literal day. Many scientists and theologians moved further along this intellectual road by arguing that Biblical stories were figuratively rather than literally true. Protestant "higher critics" borrowed critical methods from contemporary German and British scholars, treated the Bible like any other literary work, and interpreted its truths in mythical rather than literal terms. By the end of the nineteenth century, a widening gulf was developing between church leaders who accepted higher criticism and those who did not.

The social problems accompanying industrialization sparked another major dispute within Canadian churches. While many religious leaders continued to ascribe poverty to personal failings, others began to criticize the new economic order. In the 1880s, the *Canadian Baptist*, under the editorship of Ebenezer William Dadson, called for such legislative measures as prohibition, a guaranteed right to unionize, and legal reforms with respect to the treatment of women, children, and Native peoples. Dadson declared the law of supply and demand "unchristian," a position warmly received by many rank-and-file Baptists.

Presbyterian, Methodist, and Anglican leaders were also increasingly disposed to focus on social problems. Young candidates for the ministry in the Methodist Church, such as J.S. Woodsworth and Albert Edward Smith, were influenced by higher criticism in their classes at Wesley College in Winnipeg and became avid social gospellers in the course of working in the slum-ridden north end of the city. Agnes Machar, a popular author and the daughter of a Presbyterian clergyman, argued that the churches must embrace reform so that working people were not driven towards atheistic communism. A keen critic of the oppression of women in the workplace, Machar was in little doubt about the source of the problem: "The answer lies in the hard necessities of poverty which compels them to take the work on the terms offered, and makes them so much afraid of dismissal that they will seldom ever complain of oppression."[6]

As we saw in chapter 5, most Protestant churches were eventually drawn into the social gospel movement. By focusing on the physical and material condition of people on earth, social gospellers moved away from the evangelical preoccupation with individual spiritual development and life after death. This direction troubled many church members, who became concerned about the abandonment of what they believed to be the fundamental issues of Christianity. As the split between conservatives and social gospellers widened, Protestant churches faced losing the support of leaders on one side or other in the debate.

The ordinary church member was not directly involved in disputes over either the Bible or social philosophy. Although working-class attendance at church was worrisomely low to religious leaders, the middle classes in towns and cities and most people living in rural areas joined a church and regularly attended Sunday services. The establishment of missions, settlement houses, and labour churches helped Protestant denominations to maintain church membership in working-class areas of cities. Nor is there much doubt that the church had a major influence within society as a whole. Otherwise it is unlikely that legislators would have acceded to demands for Sunday closings, or that so many people would have joined missionary societies and prohibition organizations.

Yet, there was less religious enthusiasm in Canadian society than there had been in the early nineteenth century. In mainstream churches, revivalism, which emphasized intense personal experience, was increasingly downplayed. Methodist camp meetings that included several days of open-air preaching to people housed in rudimentary tents gave way to "camps" featuring summer cottages, boat services, and other amenities for the middle class who did not wish their religious observance to interfere with their creature comforts. The *Christian Guardian*, the official organ of the Methodist Church, advertised its Thousand Islands Park camp meetings in the 1870s in a way that would have been incomprehensible to people one hundred years earlier. "There is no more healthy and pleasant summer resort than Thousand Islands Park, on the St. Lawrence. The scenery is picturesque and beautiful. The water is cool and clear. The air is pure and bracing. Good order and interesting services are maintained. Fishing, boating and bathing are available to any extent. The first of the series of services of the season was begun last Friday, under the direction of the Rev. Dr. Hibbard, and is now in full blast."[7]

By seeking middle-class respectability, many churches lost members to religious movements that emphasized old-time religious values. Phoebe Palmer, an American revivalist, had a strong following in Canada, as did home-grown evangelists such as Ralph C. Horner. Expelled from the Methodist ministry for his views, Horner created a splinter church that attracted members in eastern Ontario. The Salvation Army was the most successful and enduring of the new evangelical churches, especially among the urban working

class. A variety of millenarian groups, who believed in the imminent return of Christ, came and went during this period, attracting followers who were disillusioned with the apparent secularization of the established churches. These groups, in turn, often disillusioned their followers when the predicted Second Coming failed to occur.

In the late nineteenth century, scepticism about the teachings of mainstream churches was evident in the spread of spiritualism and theosophy. The range of spiritualist practices varied widely, but all spiritualists shared the belief that the human soul remained alive after the death of the physical body and could be communicated with by the living. Some spiritualists also believed in reincarnation. Theosophists proposed that there was a universal soul to which all individual souls were ultimately identical. Opposed to all forms of discrimination, theosophists proclaimed that individuals of both genders and every race must find their identity in the universal soul. Social reform was integral to theosophical beliefs, which no doubt helped to attract adherents such as Dr Emily Stowe and Phillips Thompson. Unitarianism, which proclaimed the essential unity of all religious beliefs and, like theosophy, embraced social reform and human equality, also won some adherents. Most shocking to the churches were the free-thought societies founded by intellectuals who equated Christianity with superstition and that promoted atheism and agnosticism.

## A COMBATIVE CATHOLICISM

The Roman Catholic Church was not without its sceptics and social reformers, especially in English Canada, where Roman Catholics came from diverse cultural backgrounds. Nevertheless, the clerical hierarchy throughout Canada tried valiantly to keep the dissidents firmly in line with papal pronouncements. The church banned books that it considered irreligious and forbade the faithful from joining secular organizations, such as the Knights of Labor, that it felt distracted people from their religious duties. While clerical rules usually failed to stop Catholics from reading banned literature or joining trade unions, they often pitted the rank and file of church members against their clerical leaders.

*John Joseph Lynch, archbishop of the Roman Catholic Church in Toronto, who tried to stop his parishioners from attending free-thought meetings, is portrayed here as slaying the serpent of free thought with the sword of faith.*

By J.W. Bengough. *Grip*, 22 May 1880

Nowhere was clerical control more successful than in Quebec, where Roman Catholicism claimed the allegiance of 85 percent of the population. A celebrated case of the church's confrontation with its critics occurred in 1869 when it refused to allow the burial of an activist of the Institut canadien in a Roman Catholic cemetery. Founded in Montreal in 1844 to foster French-Canadian culture, the Institut sponsored public forums on controversial issues, championed freedom of conscience, and established a library that included publications placed on the church's Index of forbidden books. Not surprisingly, the Institut earned the opposition of clerical leaders in Quebec, who had it condemned by Rome and its yearbook placed on the Index in 1868. Many members resigned from the Institut because of the church's position, but Joseph Guibord explicitly refused to renounce his membership. When he died in 1869, Bishop Bourget of Montreal denied him burial in consecrated ground. Guibord's widow took the case to court and in 1874, after a series of appeals, the Judicial Committee of the Privy Council ordered that Bourget's ruling be overturned. Because feelings ran so high over the issue, Guibord's body, which had rested in a Protestant cemetery for five years, had to be accompanied by an armed military escort when it was transferred to its final resting place. Even then, Bishop Bourget had the last word: he immediately deconsecrated the ground where Guibord's body lay. Although the Institut declined and eventually closed its doors in 1885, its ideas could not be entirely suppressed.

The church's political influence in Quebec, while significant, was never all-embracing. Although many clerics subscribed to the ultramontanist view that all political policy should be based on church teachings, they were unable to force compliance. Even the Conservative Party, which dominated Quebec politics until 1886, was split between those who accepted ultramontane injunctions and those who believed that politicians must govern without interference from the church. The election of the Parti national as the provincial government, in defiance of continued church support for the Conservatives, demonstrated that many Roman Catholics refused to recognize the right of bishops to dictate their political decisions. Nevertheless, the Parti national could not afford to be too anti-clerical, nor did it challenge church control over education or social services.

The teachings of the Roman Catholic Church were evident in the everyday lives of French Canadians. Despite the fears of church leaders that their control was waning in urban centres, working-class neighbourhoods in Montreal spawned comparatively fewer common-law marriages, illegitimate births, and divorces than among people of other cultural backgrounds. Church attendance also remained high. One wonders, however, how many people followed the proscriptions of Montreal's archbishop Edouard-Charles Fabre (1876–96) against picnics, amusement parks, gambling, Sunday concerts, and the presence of girls at public gatherings.

By the end of the nineteenth century, the Roman Catholic Church in Quebec was increasingly out of step with liberalizing trends in Rome. In 1887, Pope Leo XIII lifted an ineffectual ban on the Knights of Labor, and in his encyclical of 1891, *Rerum Novarum*, he condemned an uncontrolled market economy. While he supported private ownership of industry, the pope urged "a capitalism guided by government, that is to say a competitive market system hemmed in by laws, tariffs and taxes." This position contrasted sharply with that of the Roman Catholic hierarchy in Quebec, which distrusted the state and attempted to influence politics less to promote positive government action than to discourage state rivalry in education, health, and social services.

The pope's injunction that "some opportune remedy must be found quickly for the misery and wretchedness pressing so unjustly on the majority of the working class" eventually spurred a Catholic social action movement. In Quebec, this was centred in the Montreal-based École sociale populaire, established in 1911, which trained Catholic activists to work in the community. The growth of Catholic activism was also reflected in the expansion of the Catholic press, including such clerically controlled newspapers as *Le Droit* in Ottawa, *L'Action catholique* in Quebec City, and *Le Bien public* in Trois-Rivières. In addition, the church supported a Catholic trade union movement, a deliberate attempt to eclipse the secular and increasingly socialist organizations taking root among the working class, but also a check on the exploitation of its flock by profit-seeking capitalists.

Although its influence remained the greatest in Quebec, the Roman Catholic Church expanded throughout Canada, building churches, hospitals, orphanages, and schools to serve its increasingly diverse clients. In the case of Polish immigrants, traditional Catholicism was closely allied to Polish nationalism, a connection that in 1901 turned the congregation of the Winnipeg Holy Ghost parish against the German-speaking Oblate Fathers. At the same time that it was suppressing Native languages in its residential schools, the Catholic Church played an essential role in maintaining minority eastern European languages through its networks of parochial schools. By 1916, for instance, there were eleven Polish and Ukrainian Catholic schools in Manitoba.

## SCHOOLING AND SOCIETY

Perhaps no institution had a greater impact on Canadians than schools. During the second half of the nineteenth century, an increasing number of parents sought at least limited socio-economic mobility for their children by investing in their education. School attendance varied according to region and culture. By 1891, it was estimated that only 6 percent of Ontario residents and 13 percent of Maritime Canadians were totally illiterate. In Quebec, where compulsory schooling was enacted only in 1943, 26 percent of the population was deemed unable either to read or write; in Newfoundland, the figure was 32 percent.

In all provinces outside Quebec, the education system was under a state-directed Department of Education, which set minimum standards for schools. Quebec, in contrast, had two systems, one Catholic and one Protestant, each eligible for provincial subsidies. Two denominational committees made educational policy for the province. The Catholic committee consisted of all Catholic bishops in the province and an equal number of government-appointed lay Catholics, a system guaranteeing that the influence of the church would remain paramount in the Catholic school board. Francophones from working-class and farm backgrounds in Quebec continued to receive far less education than their anglophone counterparts both inside and outside the province. As late as 1926, only one Catholic child in twenty in Montreal stayed in school beyond the primary grades.

The Roman Catholic Church opposed compulsory education, tuition-free schooling, and free textbooks. While the trade union movement in Quebec battled for free, compulsory schooling, the church had the support of the textile, tobacco, and shoe industries, which employed many older children. Poor working-class and farm families also tended to regard the labour and wages of their children as necessary for family survival. Indeed, it has been suggested that rural Quebec migration to New England's textile factories decreased after 1900 because enforcement of laws against child labour in New England made it difficult for poor families to make a living.

Elsewhere in Canada, education was experiencing a rapid transformation. Faith in the value of education, fear of social breakdown, and some agreement that a modern labour market required new skills, contributed to the growth of schools and changes in curriculum. Beginning in Ontario in 1871, the introduction of high schools offered parents who could afford it a chance to further educate their children. By 1905, with the exception of Quebec, all provinces had legislated free schooling and compulsory attendance for youngsters under the age of twelve. Between 1891 and 1922, elementary and secondary enrolments in Canada more than doubled from 942 500 to 1 939 700. The number of teachers grew still faster, from 21 149 in 1890 to 54 691 in 1920. Teachers' qualifications improved steadily, and women increased their numerical predominance to over 82 percent of the profession in 1921. Demand for facilities was such that, by the second decade of the twentieth century, the T. Eaton Company advertised basic school-building kits in its catalogue.

Under pressure from parents, teachers, and administrators, schools became more humane and child centred, as well as more practical and relevant. Kindergartens, with their goal to improve the family life of the poor and to nurture creativity and

independence in the young child, expanded slowly from their Ontario urban base. In all grades, more stress was placed on reasoning with the child and less on the value of corporal punishment. Pressure was also increasing for the establishment of minimum standards of health and safety in the schools. Montreal's schools set the pace in 1906 with the dominion's first regular and systematic medical inspection of pupils. As an integral part of the health-reform effort, formal instruction in physical education was introduced in many schools. For boys this often meant cadet training, an option that regularly pitted peace advocates against more militaristically inclined nationalists.

Other reformers advocated making the curriculum more applicable to the world of work. Under the leadership of Canada's first dairy commissioner, James W. Robertson, philanthropist Sir William Macdonald, and social activist Adelaide Hoodless, manual training and household science were introduced in many schools. Boys were encouraged to think in terms of practical pursuits, in particular a future in agriculture and industry. Girls' training in up-to-date menus and housekeeping was to compensate for the shortcomings of education within the family, to reaffirm female responsibility in the home, and to win recognition for the importance of traditional domestic tasks. The notion of specialized education for girls had a particular appeal in Quebec where *écoles ménagères* were established to give girls a non-academic education designed to make them good housekeepers and bearers of traditional Catholic family values.

Although a national consensus emerged among English-Canadian educational reformers as to what changes were needed within schools, the reality of schooling often varied dramatically. Funding, staffing, equipment, and accommodation differed markedly between town and city, private and public boards, girls' and boys' schools, and among different grades, but a number of common features can be noted. Classes, especially for younger children, normally held over forty pupils, and rural schools regularly grouped children in many grades together in one room. Attendance, although a good deal better than it had been, continued to be a problem as youngsters came more or less regularly depending on their age, sex, and family circumstances. The scattered settlement characteristic of northern areas, with their isolated families of farmers, small mill operators, railway workers, and Native trappers, hunters, and fishers, was never addressed adequately by the public school system. Equally problematic was the situation encountered by the disabled. By 1914, school medical inspection meant that children with mental or physical handicaps were more likely to be identified. For those with minor dental, eye, and ear problems, remedies were possible. Children with serious disabilities found relatively few options. They were likely to be kept at home or to enter the labour force earlier than their contemporaries.

Schools served as a vehicle for assimilating new Canadians, especially on the Prairies. As the region filled up with people from diverse cultures, educational systems based on the cultural conditions of Eastern Canada became entirely unstuck. The 1897 compromise in Manitoba over French and Catholic schools, for example, had permitted a limited number of Catholic teachers, Catholic instruction at the end of the day, and bilingual teaching in English and any other language spoken by at least ten pupils in the school. What was not anticipated in 1897 was the flood of new Canadians who would take advantage of the right to bilingual schooling. Immigrant parents proved intensely interested in both preserving their culture and securing the best schooling possible for their children. In urban areas, they frequently established their own evening schools and sent their children during the day to learn English and Canadian ways in the pub-

lic system. Of the newcomers, Ukrainian Canadians were among the most determined to establish a bilingual school system, but not one that taught English and French.

The English majority in the western provinces refused to accommodate linguistic plu-

*By the end of the nineteenth century, multi-room schools such as the Lunenburg Academy, built in 1895, were emerging in towns and cities as monuments to the faith in education as a panacea for society's ills.*

Lunenburg Academy Foundation

ralism in their schools. In the face of strong opposition from French-Canadian, Polish, Mennonite, and Ukrainian communities, the Manitoba government withdrew funding from all bilingual schools in 1916. Despite the compromise of 1905, Saskatchewan in 1918 abolished instruction in languages other than English beyond the first grade. The Roman Catholic clergy in Alberta had made separate schools, not language, its cause in 1905. The result was that, officially anyway, there were no bilingual schools to outlaw. Nor were there any in British Columbia.

In Ontario, Anglo-Canadians also resisted efforts of the growing francophone minority to secure education in its own language. The ultra-Protestant Orange Lodges and English-speaking Catholics worked together to push Ontario's Department of Education to enact Regulation 17 in 1912. Under this law, only schools with English-speaking teachers, where English instruction was begun upon admission, and where French was not used beyond the second year, could be eligible for government funding. Hostilities escalated to the point where, in 1916, thousands of francophone teachers and students paraded through Ottawa singing, in French:

> Little children, guard our language
> Never obey the oppressor!
> It is a sacred heritage from our ancestors
> Our young hearts must remain French
> O God of Jeanne d'Arc, protector of France,
> Save Canada, conserve forever
> In all our children's hearts the faith and courage
> In spite of everything to remain
> French-Canadian.[8]

Legal appeals were launched, but the courts supported the Ontario government. By the end of the First World War, bitterness was such that Quebec nationalists compared Ontario to wartime Germany in its treatment of minorities. Heightened sensitivity to the survival of language and culture disrupted federal politics as both Laurier and Borden found their parties divided along language lines on the schools question. Ultimately, French Canada could not prevail when English-Canadian nationalism was fully aroused.

In the Maritimes, the school battles of the second half of the nineteenth century gave way to compromise. The New Brunswick government established a French Department in its teacher-training program in 1885, and after 1907 made French-language textbooks available to students. In 1902, Nova Scotia appointed a commission to study Acadian education. Its recommendations resulted in the use of French textbooks and the hiring of bilingual teachers in Acadian areas. On Prince Edward Island, an inspector responsible for Acadian schools was appointed in 1892. Acadians in many parts of the Maritimes were still often subjected to English textbooks and teachers, but they nevertheless retained some concessions to language and culture that were increasingly denied to francophones in Ontario and the West.

## UNIVERSITIES IN THE INDUSTRIAL AGE

While universities served a much smaller clientele than schools, they were important barometers to change in post-Confederation Canada. Most of Canada's seventeen degree-granting institutions in 1867 managed on meagre endowments, tuition fees, and small government grants. Despite pressure from provincial governments in Nova Scotia and Ontario for consolidation, denominational colleges survived, and more were founded, including the Anglican-inspired University of Western Ontario in 1878, and McMaster University in 1887, the latter a special project of Baptist businessman William McMaster and his wife Susan Moulton.

In the western provinces, governments asserted control over universities from the beginning. Manitoba combined Saint Boniface (Catholic), St John's (Anglican), Manitoba College (Presbyterian), and Wesley College (Methodist) under the umbrella of the University of Manitoba in 1877. In each of the other three western provinces, a single provincial university was established: the Universities of Alberta (1906), Saskatchewan (1907), and British Columbia (1908). Modelling themselves after state colleges in the United States, they combined teaching and research functions in the service of their provinces.

In Quebec, higher education remained divided between the two major language groups. McGill and Bishop's, both established before Confederation, catered to anglophone elites, while Laval University, under the control of the Roman Catholic Church, maintained a campus in Quebec City and after 1876 had a branch campus in Montreal. Following the First World War, the University of Montreal gained independence from Laval and emerged as a modern multi-university, including under its auspices the École polytechnique, the École des hautes études commerciales, the Oka Agricultural Institute, and a school of veterinary medicine.

In 1882, under the patronage of the governor general, the Marquis of Lorne, the Royal Society of Canada was established to bring recognition to Canadian scholars who had made major contributions in the arts and sciences. Women were denied access to this exclusive organization until the 1930s, although they were beginning to gain access to universities as students and faculty in this period. By 1921, women made up about 15 percent of the professoriate but they could be found primarily in the bottom ranks.

Despite their reputation for conservatism, universities were changing. Students of the 1880s returning for class reunions in 1914 would scarcely have recognized their campuses: the number of subjects had expanded to include natural and social sciences; women as well as men attended classes; students were less preoccupied with piety than with social issues and participated in a wide range of extracurricular activities; and ornate buildings, housing laboratories, lecture theatres, and lounges had proliferated on expanding, landscaped campuses.

By 1914, students attending Canadian universities were not only taking trendy new courses and getting caught up in sports and social action, but they were also engaging in a youth culture that scandalized their elders. Unchaperoned interaction between male and female students was a particular cause of gossip and concern. Sometimes worse was suspected, as was the case in 1913 when the Toronto *News* broke the story that the University of Toronto campus had been the site of a "tango party" involving five men and some "Chorus girls."[9] It was not only in large urban institutions that young people were demanding more freedom from supervisory control. When seventeen-year-

old Esther Clark from Fredericton arrived at Acadia University in Wolfville, Nova Scotia, in 1912, she objected to being regulated by rules that she had never had to endure at home. "Dr. Cutten added a crazy rule that we have to have permission from home to stay overnight," she informed her brother in December 1914. "Please ask Mother to send in her next letter a statement that she is perfectly willing for me to visit any friends.... I think and hope I've got sense enough not to go visiting anywhere Mother wouldn't approve of." When a visiting lecturer in 1915 presumed to tell the students how to choose a mate and prepare themselves for marriage, Esther Clark was not impressed. She informed her mother: "He told a lot of slushy yarns & gave some advice about choosing the right kind

*Women who attended universities in the second decade of the twentieth century often had high career expectations. Esther Clark (left) earned a PhD in economics at Harvard while her Acadia roommate Lillian Chase became a medical doctor.*

Acadia University/Esther Clark Wright Archives

of husband or wife, about women knowing how to cook & men bringing home flowers & candy to their wives. But it really was hardly worth going to."[10]

The growth of professional schools in universities in this period reflected an increasing demand for career-related education. In their efforts to restrict entry into their fields, professionals pressured the state to grant them self-regulation.

Increasingly, a specific university degree became a condition for receiving a licence to practise a profession. Physicians, lawyers, and engineers succeeded in winning self-regulation in most jurisdictions by the end of the century and required university training as a condition of licensing. As well, in most provinces, specialized technical and agricultural colleges were established to bring academic rigour to practical pursuits. Like other professionals, university professors also expanded their training and increasingly turned to research as the basis for their academic credentials. The PhD, a German innovation, was emerging as the most coveted degree in arts and sciences, though few Canadian universities yet offered it.

Critics warned against the creation of narrow professional monopolies that used education as a means of eliminating rivals. In the health field, for example, homeopaths, midwives, and other proponents of natural medicine complained that "professionalization" was a crude effort to bestow legitimacy on a single approach to medicine—the "scientific" approach stressing chemical-based medicines and surgical solutions espoused by the medical societies. Despite such views, the trend towards professionalization and the scientific approach to the study of human and natural phenomena carried the day both in and outside institutions of higher education.

## REINVENTING NATURE

Industrialization and urbanization led Canadians to approach the natural environment in a different way. While aboriginal people had long treated nature with reverence, early European settlers were more likely to see the rugged Canadian landscape as a cause for panic, an obstacle in their path to progress, or a storehouse of wealth to be exploited. A few colonials commented ruefully on the rapid disappearance of forests, birds, and wild animals, but there was little effort to stop the trend to greater exploitation of Canada's clearly abundant resources.

Influenced by romantic notions of the untamed wilderness emanating from Great Britain and the United States, Canadians in the second half of the nineteenth century began to see the natural environment as a benevolent and healing mother who offered respite from the competition and anxiety of "modern times." Journalist J.W. Dafoe writing in the first issue of *Rod and Gun*, the official journal of the Canadian Forestry Association, noted that, "in these days the country has been discovered anew. No fact of contemporary life is more significant or more hopeful than this return to nature, for breathing space, for those whose daily walk is the tumultuous city streets."[11] Inevitably, such views were most popular among city dwellers, who increasingly encountered "nature" only in small doses.

The back-to-nature movement had an enormous impact on the way all Canadians experienced their country. Organizations such as the Alpine Club and Field-Naturalists' Club initiated many adults into nature's mysteries, while social reformers set up foundations to provide slum children with summer vacations in rural areas. With urban life increasingly redefining what it meant to be a

---

### URBAN PARKS

Even before the city beautiful and garden city movements began having a major impact on urban design, Canadian cities had begun to sprout parks and open spaces within their boundaries. In 1874, Montreal invited Frederick Law Olmstead, who designed New York City's Central Park in the 1860s, to develop Mount Royal according to his design principles. One of Olmstead's pupils, Frederick Todd, established a practice in Montreal and designed projects from Newfoundland to British Columbia. Like his mentor, Todd believed that nature had to be carefully integrated into the park environment and blended into a unified urban plan. Such views inspired the City of Halifax to take over the Public Gardens from the local horticultural society in 1875 and the City of Vancouver to create Stanley Park in 1889, named for the governor general. Manitoba created a public parks board in 1893. By the turn of the century, most cities were creating parks, large and small, as "breathing spaces" for people wearied by the hustle and bustle of urban life.

man, boys became the particular focus of reformers who saw nature as the vehicle for inculcating survival skills and manly virtues. Ernest Thompson Seton, who achieved fame as a naturalist and animal-story writer, inspired a club movement dedicated to teaching boys the skills of tracking, camping, canoeing, and woodcraft. Hundreds of Woodcraft Clubs sprang up all over North America in the first decade of the twentieth century before they were superseded in Canada by the Boy Scout movement. Founded in Britain in 1908 by South African War veteran Robert Baden-Powell, the Boy Scout movement was based on the view that the frontier experience toughened up boys so that they would make better men—and better soldiers. As Robert H. Macdonald argues:

> Young boys may have been in need of direction at the turn of the century ... or they may not; what is important is that in contemporary eyes they appeared to be in danger, and their condition suggested a national crisis.... The Scout movement was a success because it answered so many hopes and anxieties: it was both "progressive'" and reactionary, responding, on the one hand to a number of liberal ideas in education and social theory and, on the other, to a wide range of conservative, imperialist, and militarist opinion. It was a novel solution to the worries of the age, and though it incorporated many different idealisms and gave its recruits a wide variety of experience, its initial stimulus, to use the founder's own emphasis, was the need to BE PREPARED, and that, in essence, meant making *real* men. [12]

Baden-Powell launched the Girl Guides as a counterpart to Boy Scouts in 1909 and by January 1910 Canada had its first Guide group in St Catharines, Ontario. Even more popular among girls was the Canadian Girls in Training (CGIT), an organization established by the YWCA in cooperation with the major Protestant denominations in 1915. Dedicated to training young women between the ages of twelve and seventeen in Christian leadership, the outdoor experience was prominent in CGIT activities. Because of the perceived role of the natural environment in teaching essential values to both boys and girls, schools were also

enlisted in the cause. Through the efforts of naturalist societies, farm organizations, and the Central Experimental Farm in Ottawa, nature study classes were introduced in the public schools of British Columbia (1900), Nova Scotia (1901), Ontario (1904), and Alberta (1908).

Nature enthusiasts also became converts to conservation. Under the combined assault of environmentalists, governments in most provinces passed Game Acts, and people were encouraged to hunt with cameras rather than guns. In 1904, Jack Miner established his first bird sanctuary in Kingsville, Ontario, thereby launching a lifelong career devoted to the preservation of birds. The federal government followed up its initiative in Banff by creating more federally designated national parks, including Yoho (1886) and Jasper (1907), while the Ontario government established the first provincial park reserve, Algonquin, in 1893. Although Canadians continued to gobble up resources at an alarming rate, there was a growing sense that some control over their exploitation was necessary.

Even religion could not escape the call of nature. The notion that spiritual and natural phenomena were in conflict had been a feature of Christian thought since the Middle Ages, but Darwinism called this view into question. Humans, in the post-Darwinian world, seemed not so much enemies of nature but its offspring. Among theologians and creative writers, it became fashionable to refer to nature as a medium whereby people could communicate with God. Poets such as Bliss Carman, Archibald Lampman, and Charles G.D. Roberts wrote eloquently about the kinship between people and nature. In many towns and cities, branches of the Society for the Prevention of Cruelty to Animals gave practical focus to the growing sympathy for the "lower orders."

The idea of nature as a refuge from the city led those who could afford it to buy or rent summer cottages in attractive rural areas outside the city. With railways providing access to hitherto remote areas, people flocked to the Lake of the Woods, Georgian Bay, and the Muskoka regions of Ontario and the Lower Lakes region and Murray Bay in Quebec. In the Maritimes, the options for seaside bliss were endless, but St Andrew's-by-the-Sea, New Brunswick, Cavendish Beach, Prince Edward Island, and the Bras d'Or Lakes in Cape Breton became favourite haunts of the rich and famous from all over North America. For many well-heeled tourists hunting and fishing with an Indian guide was the ultimate wilderness experience, taking them back to simpler times when survival in the great outdoors, rather than in some stifling office tower, was what life was all about.

*With the rise of wilderness tourism, guiding became an important economic activity for Native peoples in many parts of Canada. Guides in the more popular tourist regions could make as much as three dollars a day for their efforts. The Fridays, a Cree family who ran a tourist lodge in Temagami, were popular guides. (Here, Bill Friday is shown, in 1905, with his companions after a successful day's fishing.) While tourists travelling with their guides had glimpses into Native life that few Canadians experienced, they tended to romanticize the Native "instinct" for wilderness skills, thus reinforcing the belief in racial differences that informed most encounters between whites and aboriginals in this period.*

Archives of Ontario/Acc 9348, S 14651

## THE GROWTH OF ORGANIZED SPORTS

As with tourism, sporting activities were shaped by the opportunities and values of the industrial age. Competitive games, the codification of rules regulating play, and commercialization paralleled trends in the marketplace and sparked debates about the purpose of games.

In September 1867, at a convention in Kingston, Ontario, the National Lacrosse Association was formed, the first of many national associations that would eventually impose form and order on sporting pursuits. The expansion of railway and road networks enabled teams to develop regular schedules of intercommunity, interregional, and even international play. By the 1890s, specialized sports pages had become common to most newspapers, an indication that such activities were becoming commercially viable. Electrically lit indoor facilities, such as ice rinks, tracks, and gymnasia, made conditions more predictable for those sports that could be played indoors. In rural areas, recreational activities remained intermittent and less highly structured, but there, too, the impact of new technology and commercial sponsorship was increasingly felt.

The middle class clung tenaciously to the amateur ideal, with its prohibition of payment to participants and its gentlemanly codes of behaviour and training. As the comment by W.A. Frost quoted at the beginning of this chapter suggests, professional sports with its paid players, rough competition, and increasing association with gambling and organized crime was unpopular in many circles. Amateurism became the defining feature of the Olympic Games when they were reinstated in 1896 and also prevailed in athletic programs established in schools, universities, and most social clubs before the First World War.

The Montreal Athletic Association (1881) was the first organization to serve as an umbrella for amateur sports enthusiasts and it became the driving force behind the Amateur Athletics Association of Canada, founded in 1884. In 1893, the governor general, Lord Stanley, donated a cup to the amateur hockey champions of Canada, and his successor, Earl Grey, provided a trophy for the Canadian football champions on the condition that the "cup must remain always under purely amateur conditions." Despite the declarations of their organizers, amateur games increasingly mirrored professional sports in their emphasis on winning as opposed to simply having fun, and in the concern for revenue. Canadians liked winners—men such as Ned Hanlan, who from 1877 to 1884, defended fifteen rowing championships, including the world championship in 1880—and they did not begrudge them deriving commercial benefit from their talent.

Canada ultimately followed the United States down the slippery slope towards the professionalization of sports. By the mid-1890s, a marked expansion in the number of ice rinks and teams effectively transformed ice hockey into a commercial success. The Montreal Wanderers, after winning the last amateur Stanley Cup in 1908, immediately turned professional, and professional hockey soon eclipsed its amateur rivals. Nevertheless, its success ultimately drew on strong amateur play in clubs and universities and on an impressive array of industrial teams from towns like New Glasgow, Glace Bay, Cobalt, and Haileybury.

Baseball emerged as the most popular spectator sport by the end of the nineteenth century, attracting a huge working-class audience throughout English and French Canada. Although scandals over gambling and game fixing erupted from time to time, they failed to dampen the enthusiasm of the fans for very long. Baseball was not only a spectator sport; large numbers of ordinary men, and even a few women, played it as well. In Saint John, conductors' teams played the motormen, spinners played dyers, longshoremen of the North Wharf played longshoremen of the South Wharf, and Roman Catholics played Protestants. Softball emerged as a Canadian adaptation of indoor baseball and, with the help of churches, schools, and city playgrounds, spread quickly.

Popular games varied regionally and along ethnic lines. Cricket, soccer, and English rugby, associated with Britain, were played in Victoria and Vancouver but were of limited interest elsewhere. Curling was popular on the Prairies, and lacrosse, ice hockey, and Canadian football—a curious amalgam of British and American rules—took root in the English-speaking areas of Central Canada. In the Maritimes and southwestern Ontario, enthusiasm for baseball was fuelled by the close relations between those regions and the United States, where baseball was quickly emerging as the nation's most popular sport. With enthusiasts from coast to coast, ice hockey came the closest to becoming Canada's national sport, but until the end of the nineteenth century it had close competition from lacrosse, Canada's only truly indigenous game.

By the turn of the century, Canadians were increasingly participating in international sports events. Canada sent a team to the Olympics in 1900 but its only victory came to George Orton, who won the fifteen hundred metre steeplechase as a member of the American team. Given the migration of so many Canadians to the United States in this period, and the lure of professional salaries, it is not surprising that many Canadians earned their sporting reputations in events sponsored south of the border. Nat Butler, a native of Halifax, began his career in bicycle racing in Boston and broke all records at the Winter Velodrome in Paris in 1905. Nova Scotia-born Burns Pierce teamed up with Archie McEachern from Toronto to win long-distance bicycle races in the United States. Although basketball was developed by a Canadian —James Naismith from Almonte, Ontario—it was pioneered at the YMCA International Training School in Springfield, Massachusetts, where Naismith was a student and later a teacher.

Sports were often closed to racial minorities because whites would not allow them to join their teams and clubs. In the Maritimes, blacks began forming their own baseball teams in the 1880s and by the 1890s were hosting an annual regional championship. The Seasides sporting club in the black community of Africville on the outskirts of Halifax fielded baseball teams in the summer and hockey teams in the winter, while black churches sponsored sports activities in smaller Nova Scotia communities. On the West Coast, a team of Japanese baseball players, known as the Asahi, thrived between 1914 and 1941. Tom Longboat, a rare exception to the increasing exclusion of Native peoples from competitive athletics, came first in the 1907 Boston Marathon. Like whites, individuals from racial minorities were often lured to the United States by professional sporting opportunities. Gabriel Dumont, for example, toured in the United States as a crack marksman in Buffalo Bill's Wild West show in the 1880s, and two black boxers from Nova Scotia, George Dixon and Sam Langford, won acclaim at home as well as in the United States for their successes in the ring.

*The Royals Baseball Club of Saint John, New Brunswick, Intermediate Champions, 1921.*

Public Archives of New Brunswick/P338-2

Working-class Canadians had difficulty finding the time and money that organized sports activities demanded. In some areas, laws prohibited sporting events on Sunday, often the only day a worker was likely to have free time. Mounting regulation of the urban landscape, such as the prohibition of baseball in city parks, added to the constraints upon working-class leisure pursuits. As one critic pointed out in the 1890s, "To the young, the strong, and the rich, the choice is wide and varied; to the poor, the busy and the woman who is [no] longer young, the problem of athletics on ever so modest a scale is a difficult one."[13] While sport reflected the social inequality that was so much a feature of Canadian life in general, opportunities to play and watch sports expanded in the years before the First World War. Somewhat shorter work weeks, at least for skilled male labourers, and the rising influence of school-based sports gave more adults and children the opportunity to experience the enthusiasm of athletic contest.

Sporting activities were also beginning to open up for women. In the 1880s, bicycling joined tennis, curling, and skating as amusements for middle-class women and as a cause for worry among those who identified an increase in women's physical freedom and scandalously scant sporting attire with moral laxity and, worse still, feminist sympathies. Medical misinformation suggesting that physically active women would produce unhealthy babies gave ammunition to those who warned that a sportswoman was in danger of losing her femininity. By the turn of the century, the participation of women in school and university sports, such as basketball, field hockey, and ice hockey, helped to break down proscriptions against female participation in competitive play. Women were allowed to compete in the Olympics for the first time in 1900.

Some sports teams folded during the war, but athletic activity of various kinds continued to flourish. With their support for boxing championships and baseball leagues, army camps provided an important recreational outlet for many soldiers. Golf championships were cancelled during the war, but the game continued its recreational success. When male athletes abandoned swimming facilities, women enjoyed unprecedented opportunities for competition. The war ushered in other changes as well. Cricket, English rugby, and lacrosse failed to thrive, casualties, it seems, of the appeal of other sports and the absence of the high school feeder programs.

By 1920, the prevalence of school athletics and the multitude of programs run by groups such

*One of Canada's outstanding sports stories was supplied by a female basketball team, the Edmonton Grads, students and alumnae of that city's Commercial High School. Beginning in 1915 and continuing for twenty-five years, the Grads put together an unrivalled record of wins over domestic and international opponents.*

Provincal Archives of Alberta/A-11,428

as the YWCA, YMCA, the CGIT, and the Boy Scouts had given sports an unprecedented place in the lives of most Canadians. The discovery by sports promoters that good money could be made presenting professional baseball, football, and

hockey on a regular basis meant that Canadian sport was well on its way to becoming a major North American industry. And, for all the predominance of the anglophone middle class in many areas of sporting life, a shared interest in sporting activity may well have helped to begin to knit together diverse classes and groups of Canadians.

## CULTURAL LIFE IN THE CITIES

In the booming atmosphere of turn-of-the-century cities, Canadians expresses tremendous cultural vitality. Immigrants brought with them a taste for new foods and amusements that even the harsh judgements of native-born residents could not entirely suppress. If the comments of their detractors are any indication, two-day wedding celebrations, church bazaars, and ethnic processions were exuberant events that helped to break the monotony of daily and weekly routines. The immigrant influence was also apparent in city markets— Atwater Market in Montreal, St Lawrence Market in Toronto, and the City Hall Farmers' Market in Winnipeg, for example—which offered a range of sights, sounds, and smells that enriched urban life.

Class as well as culture determined how Canadians enjoyed themselves. For those people who lived in the wealthy enclaves of cities, there were opportunities for fine dining, theatre, opera, yachting, cricket, and camaraderie in exclusive clubs and philanthropic organizations. Working people had access to amusement parks, carnivals, burlesque theatres, lotteries, bazaars, dance halls, and taverns, but risked the disapproval of the church, particularly if such establishments operated on Sundays. City people had more entertainments available to them than did people in rural areas, where small populations and the ever-present eye of church officials often limited the scope of leisure activities.

Canadians were enthusiastic spectators at a host of foreign and domestic touring theatre companies that crossed the country on the expanding railway networks. In 1897, Corliss Powers Walker, an impresario with a string of small theatres in North Dakota, settled in Winnipeg, which he used as a base for controlling bookings and theatre management throughout the West. His flagship theatre seated two thousand people and hosted productions, some of them direct from Broadway, six nights a week, fifty-two weeks a year. The seven touring companies of the Marks Brothers entertained in small towns across the dominion. In the 1890s, the first home-grown professional French-language companies were founded, following on the phenomenal success of Parisian companies that toured Quebec. The British Canadian Theatrical Organization Society (1912) attempted to balance extensive American influence by organizing tours of British theatrical troupes. Although the Trans-Canada Theatre Society (1915) was Canadian owned, it stayed in business by organizing tours of foreign companies. British and Americans gradually acquired controlling interests in Canadian theatres, effectively monopolizing the booking of entertainment by 1914.

The difficulties faced by Canadian talent did not escape notice. In 1907, Governor General Earl Grey created the Earl Grey Music and Dramatic Competition for the dramatic arts, but this venture collapsed in 1911 and had only a minimum influence. There was significant progress in amateur little theatre, notably with the creation in 1905 of the Toronto Arts and Letters Players and in 1913 of the Ottawa Drama League. With the opening of the Hart House Theatre at the University of Toronto in 1919, financed by the Massey family, many distinguished Canadian actors, directors, and playwrights had a forum for their talents.

*In the late nineteenth century, an important event in most black communities across Canada was Emancipation Day, the annual celebration of the freeing of slaves in the British Empire on 1 August 1834. The parade depicted here took place in 1894 in Amherstburg.*

Archives of Ontario/Acc 2537, S 12008

Canadian audiences were also introduced to the international world of dance, though not without earning the disapproval of church leaders. Acclaimed dancers Lois Fuller and Anna Pavlova as well as Nijinsky and the Diaghilev Ballet Russe all made Canadian appearances. Many dance performances were aimed at more well-to-do audiences, but the crowds they drew included Canadians from many walks of life. Spectators also found much to entertain them in dance halls, burlesque theatres, and taverns, where hypnotists, magicians, circuses, and vaudeville drew audiences into a rich world of political satire, popular music, risqué dancing, and bawdy comedy.

These years also saw the appearance of a popular entertainment that would soon outdraw all others: the "movie." In 1896, twelve hundred citizens of Ottawa paid ten cents each to watch Belsaz the magician and—the forerunner of a technology that would put many such performers out of business—a production of Thomas Edison's "Vitascope." Because of the obvious potential of the medium to attract viewers, the Department of the Interior experimented with film in their efforts to promote western settlement. The dominion's first public movie event included *The Kiss*, a short film of less than a minute, showing, among other things, African-American boys eating watermelons, a bathing scene in Atlantic City, and a serpentine dance by Lo Lo Fuller. The controversy, excitement, and moral outrage provoked in these few seconds quickly became characteristic of the medium, and guaranteed that it would find a warm welcome in vaudeville theatres. Shows were seen from one end of the dominion to the other, even in pioneer settlements. The theatre in turn-of-the-century Cochrane, Ontario, for example, was thronged every day not only by locals, but also by gangs of workmen passing to and from railway construction camps.

By 1914, sporadic screenings were beginning to give way to regular shows offered in movie theatres. Vancouver's Schulberg's Electric (1902) and Crystal (1904), Winnipeg's Unique and Dreamland (1903), St John's York (1906), and Montreal's Nationale and Palais Royal (1904) charged each enthusiastic customer a nickel: hence the name nickelodeon. Although pictures were silent, early innovations in accompanying sound came to Canada in 1914, just in time to see service in patriotic wartime newsreels. By then, movies had become a major form of entertainment. With more comfortable theatres, better story lines, and higher prices, films were also making significant inroads among the middle class, who had at first scorned the medium's reputed vulgarity.

## ARCHITECTURE IN THE MODERN AGE

Cities, by 1921, looked nothing like they had a half century earlier. With their banks and department stores, universities and hospitals, museums and libraries, palatial homes and apartment buildings, urban landscapes catalogued the exuberant optimism of the industrial age. For newcomer and long-time resident alike, many buildings must have seemed almost the equivalent of medieval cathedrals, highly visible symbols of success and power. Railway hotels such as Quebec City's Château Frontenac and Victoria's Empress, and private residences such as Toronto's Casa Loma or Edmonton's Beaulieu spoke volumes about the social aspirations of the Canadian business community. Like the fashionable clothes worn by the wealthy, "style" in architecture was essential to the display of conspicuous consumption.

In the 1870s, Victorian versions of medieval or Renaissance buildings were popular. The ornamental mansard roof on Toronto's Opera House was modelled on buildings in Napoleon III's France, while Gothic features reminiscent of the Middle Ages could be found in structures ranging from the Parliament Buildings in Ottawa to the modest homes of the working class. Second Empire and neo-Gothic styles in Canadian architecture were succeeded by a monumental Beaux-Arts style with Roman columns, cornices, and vaults, of which Toronto's Union Station (1915–20), the Saskatchewan Legislature (1908–12), and Montreal's Sun Life Building (begun 1914) are some of the best examples.

Construction advances, notably fireproofed steel framing and reinforced concrete, and the

*Union Station, Toronto, Ontario and Union mine, Cumberland, British Columbia (inset).*
*While cities were becoming architectural monuments to the Industrial Age,*
*company towns on the resource frontier bore a remarkable similarity to one another*
*in their undistinguished architecture and lack of amenities.*

introduction of elevators, changed the type of buildings that could be designed. Under the influence of the Chicago school of architects, early skyscrapers such as the Calgary Grain Exchange (1909) and Edmonton's Tegler Building (1911) began to alter the urban landscape in ways that made Canadian cities increasingly indistinguishable from their British and American counterparts. Since so many important buildings were designed by American and British firms, the similarity is not surprising. McGill University established the first Canadian department of architecture only in 1896, and it was not until 1907 that provincial architectural associations created a national organization.

Buildings in small-town and rural Canada reflected, though more modestly, the international trends in architecture. From the Maritimes to the Yukon, Greek columns, Gothic elements, and mansard roofs reflected the influence of over two thousand years of European architectural history. William Critchlow Harris, for example, produced designs for over ninety high Victorian Gothic buildings in the Maritimes, many of them elegant churches, from his base in Charlottetown. Using architectural texts from Europe and the United States, Canadians easily adapted international designs to their needs, in the process often creating their own unique architectural traditions.

Between Confederation and the First World War, the federal government erected over three hundred public buildings to house national services such as post offices, customs offices, and prisons. All federal buildings were constructed under the direction of the Department of Public Works, whose chief architect from 1881 to 1897 was Thomas Fuller. A native of Bath, England, Fuller was involved as a young man in the design of Canada's Parliament buildings and was determined to create an imposing government presence across the country.

In rural areas of the nation, Canadians displayed architectural distinctiveness in the crafting of barns and storage facilities designed to handle the expanding output of commercialized farming. All across Canada, farmers erected barns to house their expanding herds of cattle, the source of a year-round supply of milk in the rapidly growing cities. The same changes in construction techniques that transformed the urban landscape also made grain elevators a classic form on the Prairie

*Lines of grain elevators, such as this one at Cabri, Saskatchewan, became a familiar sight on the Prairie skyline in the early decades of the twentieth century.*

Saskatchewan Archives/R-B306

landscape. Grain storage facilities in Calgary, Port Arthur, Toronto, and Montreal are said to have been inspirations to world-renowned European architects Walter Gropius and Le Corbusier.

## THE ARTS

In the half-century following Confederation, Canadians lamented their lack of a distinctive artistic and literary culture. The dominion's youth, colonial inheritance, and proximity to the United States were advanced as reasons why Canadian writers, painters, and sculptors rarely achieved international recognition. At the end of the nineteenth century, novelist and essayist Sara Jeannette Duncan commented:

> In our character as colonists we find the root of all our sins of omission in letters.... Our enforced political humility is the distinguishing characteristic of every phase of our national life. We are ignored, and we ignore ourselves. A nation's development is like a plant's, unattractive under ground. So long as Canada remains in political obscurity, content to thrive only at the roots, so long will the leaves and blossoms of art and literature be scanty and stunted products of our national energy .... A national literature cannot be looked for as an outcome of anything less than a complete national existence.[14]

The dead weight of religious conservatism also helped to keep Canada behind developments in the arts in Europe and the United States. In Quebec, most of the home-grown authors stuck to conservative narratives. Quebec was presented in this literature as a devout Catholic nation with a mission to spread the Catholic word throughout the world. In the years immediately following Confederation, glorification of the Papal Zouaves, who fought in 1870 to defend the Vatican against attempts to annex the Holy See to the new Italian state, was especially popular. This was due in large measure to the fact that a contingent of Quebec volunteers had joined the Zouaves in one of the few military ventures approved by the church in Quebec.

With its idealization of country life, the peasant novel, a popular European genre, also took firm root in Quebec. Its most enduring example is Louis Hémon's *Maria Chapdelaine* (1913), which dealt with the difficult choice for many French Canadians of moving either to New England to find work or to communities on Quebec's agricultural frontier. In a few cases, authors transcended the formula writing that characterized this approach to yield a unique literary achievement; for example, Honoré Beaugrand's *Jeanne la Fileuse*, a romanticized presentation of the life of Quebec expatriates in New England, and Laure Conan's *Angeline de Montbrun* (1884), which probed aspects of Quebec's spirituality. Despite the church's injunctions, there was a large audience for great French authors such as Balzac and Stendhal as well as the province's popular writers of mysteries and melodramas.

A realist challenge to the romantic tradition was found in Albert Laberge's *La Scouine* (1918), but this voice remained rare in more ways than one—the novel's first edition was a private printing of only sixty copies. A few writers resisted clerical dictates. Influenced by French modernists like Baudelaire and Rimbaud, bohemian Montreal poets such as Émile Nelligan and members of the École littéraire de Montréal espoused a highly individualistic literature preoccupied with the meaning of life, death, and love. Such writers risked clerical censure and faced minuscule markets for their work.

As a major sponsor of painting, sculpture, and architecture in its great cathedrals, the Roman Catholic church's support could make or break artists. It also resulted in some of the most impressive religious art produced anywhere in the world. Nor was the church's influence confined to direct commissions. Public art reflected the clerically inspired history of Quebec which made mystical figures out of rather ordinary men such as fur trader Dollard des Ormeaux. A combination of church and private commissions supported fine contributions in the art nouveau tradition by painters such as Ozias Leduc and sculptors such as Alfred Laliberté. In Montreal, Louis-Philippe Hébert's monuments to Jacques Cartier and Maisonneuve stand out as some of the best sculpture produced in Canada. Outside of the commissions sponsored by the church, Quebec painters of the late Victorian period focused on landscapes and romanticized

portraits of people's lives. Aaron Allan Edson's landscapes were among the best-known of this genre. Before the First World War, Quebeckers in search of more liberated artistic expression moved to Paris, as was the case with impressionists Maurice Cullen, James Wilson Morrice, and, briefly, Clarence Gagnon.

*Pauline Johnson was the daughter of the chief of the Six Nations and an English woman. Her poems, which celebrated both Canada and her Native heritage, were enormously popular in her day.*

National Archives of Canada/PA111473

The cultural capitals for English-Canadian artists were also outside of Canada. From British Columbia, a young Emily Carr travelled to San Francisco, London, and Paris between 1891 and 1911 to soak up the liberating artistic influences that were lacking at home. Authors also found that the centres of English-language publishing were located in London, and, increasingly, New York and Boston, where there was only a limited market for Canadian themes. Indeed, one of the reasons that Canadians remained within the romantic literary tradition after other countries had abandoned it was that the popular demand for stories about New France, Acadia, aboriginal peoples, and rural life remained strong in foreign markets. Dramatic readings by Pauline Johnson, Canada's "Mohawk Princess," on stages in and outside Canada drew on her Native heritage to conjure up a distinctive northern nationality that was far removed from the experience of most of her listeners. Similarly, the animal stories of Ernest Thompson Seton and Sir Charles G.D. Roberts appealed to audiences in the United States and Great Britain who identified Canada as a northern wilderness.

In the late nineteenth century, English-Canadian literary production was, on the whole, as conservative and prone to romanticizing the past as was its French-Canadian counterpart. Loyalist themes, common in works from the 1820s onward, remained popular and were reinforced by centennial celebrations of Loyalist settlement. Both the initial Loyalist flight from the mad republic to the south and the defence of the Canadas in 1812 were mythologized in Egerton Ryerson's *The Loyalists of America and Their Times* (1880). In 1876, Sarah Curzon, a Toronto suffrage and temperance advocate, produced a play called *Laura Secord, the Heroine of 1812*, which used popular Loyalist mythologies to promote a positive view of women's abilities. Canada Firster Charles Mair won praise for his poems on Loyalist themes. Ironically, Mair, who harboured racist attitudes towards Riel and his Métis followers, presented the Native leader, Tecumseh, who had supported the British in 1812, as a hero in an 1886 drama.

The yearning for simpler days and greater harmony with nature was a frequent theme in the works of the generation of poets who came of age in the post-Confederation period. In poems and serialized novels, Ontario's Isabella Valancy Crawford, who was her family's sole support after the death of her father in 1875, concentrated on bucolic imagery that sold well in New York and Toronto. Charles G.D. Roberts and Bliss Carman celebrated the sea and landscape of their Maritime boyhoods. Duncan Campbell Scott and Archibald Lampman, two Ottawa civil servants, shared with other so-called Confederation poets a tendency to Christian moral-

izing and a focus on natural landscapes unblighted by human greed. In his second book of verse, *Labor and the Angel* (1898), Scott sharply defended society's underdogs, and Lampman, who dabbled in socialist politics, wrote several poems that contrasted the unspoiled beauty of nature with man-made hells. His "The City of the End of Things" was a futuristic vision of an urban nightmare where inhumanity reigned supreme.

By the end of the nineteenth century, cultural production began to increase in range and output, fuelled in part by the growing tendency of newspapers to run serialized novels. Set either in rural areas or in high society within the cities, the narratives were preoccupied with larger-than-life Canadian heroes and beautiful, virginal heroines. Women, who were increasingly able to make a living as writers or journalists, particularly excelled in this genre, and a few managed to distinguish themselves by their themes and writing ability. In her novel, *Roland Graeme Knight*, Agnes Machar fused her reformist, feminist, religious, and patriotic concerns in her highly romantic portrayal of a Knight of Labor and the woman who loved him. Margaret Marshall Saunders, the daughter of a Nova Scotia Baptist minister, published *Beautiful Joe*, the story of an abused dog, in 1894. After winning first prize in an American Humane Society competition, *Beautiful Joe* became a best-seller, reputedly the first work by a Canadian author to sell a million copies.

Regional idylls focusing on the virtues of rural life provided the most popular form of escapism. The new West appeared in fiction such as Nellie McClung's bestseller, *Sowing Seeds in Danny* (1908) and M. Ellis's *Tales of the Klondike* (1898). Ralph Connor chronicled life in Glengarry, Ontario, to demonstrate the relevance of its Scottish Presbyterian morality to the new lands of the West. Norman Duncan looked for inspiration to Newfoundland's fishing villages and W.H. Drummond to old Quebec. Such writers combined a pervasive sense of regional identity with an equally strong dose of Protestant moralism. With few exceptions, such as H.B. Blanchard's *After the Cataclysm* (1899) and Mabel Burkholder's *The Course of Impatience Carningham* (1911), Canadians were slow to address the underside of modern society. Popular writers, like Robert Service, in rollicking verses such as "The Shooting of Dan McGrew" and "The Cremation of Sam McGee," celebrated the energy and enthusiasm of the northern frontier, not its harsher realities.

One of Canada's best-known writers was Lucy Maud Montgomery, whose first published novel, *Anne of Green Gables*, became an instant success when it appeared in 1908. What made Montgomery's work more enduring than that of most of her contemporaries was the fact that she tapped into the aspirations of young women in the industrial age, reflecting their dreams of transcending their rural environments to attend university, pursue a career, and marry a medical doctor. Few women could have it all in this period, but L.M. Montgomery proved that a woman who had superior wit and writing skills could survive an unhappy marriage to a manic-depressive Presbyterian minister and maintain financial solvency by being a successful author.

A new realistic tradition was reflected in the work of Sara Jeannette Duncan, a disciple of the American novelist Henry James and the first woman to be hired as a full-time journalist at the Toronto *Globe*. Her novel *The Imperialist* (1904) dissected small-town Ontario life and explored the need to balance British sentiment with the reality of North American living. Only one major popular writer, Stephen Leacock, in heavily ironic volumes like *Sunshine Sketches of a Little Town* (1912) and *Arcadian Adventures of the Idle Rich* (1914), questioned the values and virtues of North American liberal capitalism. In his *Literary Lapses* (1910), he used a humorous interview to condemn North American business ethics:

So one evening I asked one of the millionaires how old Bloggs had made all his money. "How he made it?" he answered with a sneer. "Why, he made it by taking it out of widows and orphans."

Widows and orphans! I thought, what an excellent idea. But who would have suspected that they had it?

"And how," I asked pretty cautiously, "did he go at it to get it out of them?"

"Why," the man answered, "he just ground them under his heels, and that was how."

For all Leacock's willingness to target the exploitative tendencies of the age, his solutions turned backwards to a Tory conservatism that was highly

*In 1911, thirty-six-year-old Lucy Maud Montgomery married the Reverend Ewan Macdonald and moved from Prince Edward Island to Ontario, where she wrote seven sequels to the highly successful* **Anne of Green Gables** *as well as several other novels and hundreds of short stories and poems.*

authoritarian and, from the perspective of the late twentieth century, racist, sexist, and nativist.

Leading periodicals of the day were somewhat more inclined to express liberal sentiments but were narrow in their focus. The nationalism of *Saturday Night* (established 1887), *Busy Man's Magazine* (1896–1911), which became *Maclean's Magazine*, and *Canadian Magazine* (1893–1939) spoke largely to anglophone Ontario, failing to include Quebec, the Maritimes, or the West, except as reflections of Ontario interests. The First World War tended to accentuate such narrow sentiments, which were given full rein in novels such as Ralph Connor's *The Major* (1917) and Robert Stead's *The Cow Puncher* (1918) to an evangelical Protestant and tribalistic British nationalism. Only the rare writer, such as Francis Beynon in *Aleta Dey* (1919), dared to question the chauvinism and militarism of the Great War, and she retreated to the United States to avoid the repressive atmosphere at home.

Like sports, the interest in literature, music, and art extended beyond professional artists and organizations to embrace a wide range of amateur activities. Maria Tippett has observed that almost everyone was organized in song throughout the country on Sundays. In Toronto, choir master A.S. Voigt enlarged his Jarvis Street Baptist Church choir to 250 voices and formed the Toronto Mendelssohn Choir in 1894, soon to be known throughout North America for its a *cappella* singing. From Bella Bella and Metlakatla to Glace Bay and St John's, brass bands performed at funerals, wedding, and village feasts. Alexander Louks in Delhi, Ontario, is reputed to have organized a community band in the late nineteenth century by dint of teaching all its members how to play their instruments.

Throughout this period, people met in each other's homes at regular intervals to make music, read poetry, and perform plays. Some of these groups gradually became more formal in their efforts to promote cultural activities. In Saint John, the Eclectic Reading Club, established in 1884, had a long waiting list of people wanting to join. The Cavendish Literary Society, founded in 1886 for "the mutual improvement of its members," gave a

young Lucy Maud Montgomery a place to test her ideas, while the Vagabond Club of Vancouver, established in 1914, offered men "an outlet for whatever small talents we possessed in a city in which buying and selling of real-estate was the pre-occupation of the majority of inhabitants."[15] In Toronto, the Arts and Letters Club, founded in 1908, brought artists together to feed off each other's creativity. The Women's Art Association, established in 1890, spawned branches throughout the dominion to bring women together for mutual help and improvement.

Despite the rage for culture, high and low, the number of Canadians with the education, time, and money to indulge in organized cultural activities remained relatively small. More people were influenced by newspapers, the most ubiquitous medium of the age. By the 1890s, an increasing proportion of the population was sufficiently literate to read journalistic prose, and most could afford the money and time to obtain and read an eight-page penny newspaper, increasingly made more enticing through the use of cartoons and photographs. Improved printing processes and cheaper paper made it possible to provide relatively recent news on a daily basis. Advertising by retailers, particularly the large department store owners such as Timothy Eaton, made publishing lucrative and allowed publishers to keep newspaper prices low. Most papers were unabashedly partisan and reported the news in a way that made no pretence to political objectivity, a feature that seemed only to enhance sales. While the nation claimed only 47 daily newspapers in 1873, that number had doubled by 1892 and reached an all-time peak of 138 in 1913. After that date, numbers dwindled in the face of pressure to curb competition and concentrate ownership.

Some papers were sombre enterprises such as the information-crammed *Globe* in Toronto, its rival, the *Mail*, and the ultramontane *Nouveau monde* in Montreal. Increasingly, publishers saw the potential of newspapers for popular entertainment in a society where larger doses of schooling meant more potential readers. The *Montreal Star*, founded in 1869, pioneered "yellow journalism" in Canada, focusing on gossip and events close to home rather than on serious politics and events in Europe. The *Telegram* brought the same formula to Toronto in 1876. *La Presse* of Montreal, which closed the century as Quebec's leading newspaper, also copied this approach, though it included more extensive and internationally oriented news coverage than its English-Canadian counterparts.

While the views expressed in daily newspapers were not greatly different from those of their owners, weekly newspapers offered more varied fare. The *Eye Opener*, based in various locations on the Prairies under its erratic and peripatetic editor Bob Edwards, included saucy cartoons as a way of lampooning social and political attitudes of the day. In socialist circles, weekly newspapers offered an alternative perspective to the capitalist views served up by the dailies. *Cotton's Weekly*, edited by William Cotton on behalf of the Social Democratic Party of Canada, became the largest-selling alternative newspaper in Canada in the years leading up to the First World War, with subscribers from Cape Breton to Vancouver Island.

Although many homes boasted published works by Canadian authors and regularly subscribed to Canadian as well as British and American magazines and newspapers, oral tradition also flourished. Canada drew on a rich folk culture stemming from the diverse backgrounds of its people. In some ways, the whole course of Canadian history was replayed through the medium of folk songs and stories and in this manner spread through lumber camps, fishing fleets, city bars, school playgrounds, and domestic parlours. Then and now, they provide a glimpse of worlds of work, poverty, and conflict that were not so readily available in the published literature of the time. A song from southeastern Newfoundland sums up the costs of marriage for the poor:

> Oh mother dear, I wants a sack
> With beads and buttons down the back...
> Me boot is broke, me frock is tore,
> But Georgie Snooks I do adore...
> Oh, fish is low and flour is high,
> So Georgie Snooks he can't have I.

Other popular songs described the hardships of life for working people and championed the right of legitimate protest. In the historical ballad "Let Us Recall, Brethren, Our Struggle," Doukhobors told the story of their persecution and courageous resistance in tsarist Russia and steeled themselves to withstand assaults from Canadian critics. While they could hardly avoid what the Roman Catholic Church endorsed, French Canadians through their songs and folklore owed something to old traditions that were critical of religious authority. Other elites were also subject to abuse as the criticism of merchants in a folk song suggests:

> Marchand, marchand, combien ton blé?
> Trois francs l'avoin', six francs le blé.
> C'est bien trop cher d'un' bonn' moitié.

Folk art included practical handicrafts like quilts and woven fabric, some of which reached a high order of design and complexity, elaborate images on barns and taverns, and carefully crafted collages of shells and paper. In aboriginal communities, craft production continued to attract attention. This work was rarely recognized by the new artistic elite who distinguished sharply between conventional forms of "high" art and those dismissed as handicrafts, which, not coincidentally, were often the special preserve of women.

Academic art tended to follow the international trends, though often at some distance. In 1868, a Society of Canadian Artists was established to promote formal Canadian artwork in a variety of exhibits. The Royal Academy of Arts and the National Gallery of Canada were created in 1880 at the urging of the governor general, the Marquis of Lorne. Before the end of the century, a number of art schools had been established in urban centres. Overwhelmingly, professional artists were men who, like William Brymner, Robert Harris, and George Reid, trained either in the academic style of the Paris Salon school or later, like Edmund Morris and Curtis Williamson, found inspiration in the atmospheric Hague school. An exception to the habit of European training was Homer Watson, who, like the French-Canadian Ozias Leduc, was self-taught and visited Europe only later in life. Painters regularly took up identifiably Canadian subjects, particularly landscapes of settled areas of the country. In 1907, the creation of the Canadian

*Top:*
**Kwakiutl Mask,** *c. 1900.*
wood, cedar bark, and paint;
29.0 × 20.3 × 86.0 cm;
McMichael Canadian Art Collection,
Purchase 1977;
1977 .2.3

*Left:*
*Clarence Gagnon, 1881-1942,*
**Twilight, Baie St Paul,**
*c. 1920.*
oil on canvas; 49.9 × 65.0 cm;
McMichael Canadian Art Collection,
Gift of Mr. Syd Hoare; 1975.61

*Left:*
*J.E.H. MacDonald, 1873-1932,*
**Beaver Dam and Birches,**
*1919.*
oil on panel; 21.5 × 26.4 cm;
McMichael Canadian Art Collection,
Gift of the Founders, Robert and Signe McMichael;
1966.16.49

*Below:*
*James Wilson Morrice,*
*1865-1924,* **Ice Bridge over**
**the St Charles River,** *1908.*
Montreal Museum of Fine Arts

Art Club (CAC) encouraged showings by early Canadian impressionists. These painters, who focused their attention on light, colour, and mood in their work, were roundly criticized by traditionalists who felt that art, like photographs, should strive to represent objects as they were, not as imagined.

By the time of its last exhibition in 1915, the CAC was being overtaken by men such as Lawren Harris and J.E.H. MacDonald, who were searching for new ways of presenting Canadian subjects. In 1912 they found their inspiration in an exhibition of contemporary Scandinavian landscapes. A year later, along with Tom Thomson, Frank Carmichael, Frank Johnston, Arthur Lismer, Fred Varley, and A.Y. Jackson, they began applying these insights in sketching Algonquin Park. The war and the death of Thomson in 1917 postponed the public arrival of the painters who came to be known as the Group of Seven, but they were part of a significant prewar effort to find artistic expression for what was deemed uniquely Canadian. On the West Coast, Emily Carr was beginning to develop her own powerful, post-impressionist style to convey the majesty of Native life and the coastal landscape. Lacking the sympathetic community available to her eastern male contemporaries, she was forced to support herself by running a boarding house. Both Carr and the Algonquin Group, like the great majority of earlier Canadian painters, tended to avoid the city and its problems. Their world, like that of many writers, most often symbolized an effort to come to terms with the natural rather than the human world of early twentieth-century Canada.

## CONCLUSION

When Canada went to war in 1914, there was still little consensus on what it meant to be a Canadian. There was no distinctive Canadian flag, and while the beaver and the maple leaf seemed to sum up what was distinctive about Canada, they were not adopted as official symbols of the country. Calixa Lavallée, a composer born in Quebec, penned the words to "O Canada" in 1880, but the anthem was not heard in English Canada until the turn of the century. Outside of Quebec, "The Maple Leaf Forever," with its triumphant imperialist lyrics, was much more popular.

Growing cultural diversity and rapid economic development in the first decade of the twentieth century only compounded the natural tendency to emphasize differences. In communities throughout the country, people sorted themselves out in organizations reflecting their class, ethnic, gender, occupational, religious, and regional affiliations and only rarely came together in expressions of solidarity. As participants in the new industrial order, however, Canadians shared more than they realized, including an expanding literacy, a rich popular culture, and a small but growing number of nationwide organizations. Whether these cultural trends were sufficient to hold the nation together under the impact of a world war would remain to be seen.

## LATE VICTORIAN PROTESTANTISM

### *A Historiographical Debate*

Historians debate the causes and consequences of the trend among evangelical churches to achieve respectability and address social problems in the post-Confederation period. Should it be viewed as a sign of capitulation to an increasingly secular society or as a successful attempt to create a Protestant culture in a rapidly changing context?

One approach emphasizes the reaction to external realities: a new urban environment provoked the fear that evangelical religions, with their roots in rural revivals, might become irrelevant. According to this reasoning, the church was forced to adapt to secular realities for the sake of its own survival. Historian Ramsay Cook takes this perspective but argues that the shift in emphasis from saving souls to reforming society had consequences rather different from what was intended. He argues that "the most remarkable consequence ... of the intellectual transformation that took place in English Canada between Confederation and the Great War" was that Protestantism became "a mere sociological instead of a religious doctrine." Once religion became a matter of good works rather than spiritual regeneration, it became easier for people to abandon the church while still remaining good citizens by supporting humanitarian social policies. As many nineteenth-century intellectuals predicted, "the path blazed by nineteenth-century religious liberals led not to the kingdom of God on earth but to the secular city."[16]

Historian William Westfall takes another perspective, arguing that internal church organization must be taken into consideration. In the early years of development, he argues, churches had few members and were preoccupied with converting sinners to Christ. Once the church became a large institution with a mass membership of committed Christians, revivalism became less important than ministering to the faithful. The membership itself remained closely attached to the traditions that had attracted them to evangelicalism and had a real impact on the extent to which the church leadership could change the direction of the church. For Westfall, growing church concerns about social problems reflected not a capitulation to secularism but a challenge to it. Setting aside differences that once kept various denominations at odds with one another, church leaders and their followers worked together to assert a Protestant moral agenda, in the process creating a "Protestant culture:"

> Now arose the prospect that materialism would undermine the religious character of society as a whole and that large numbers of people might not enjoy the benefits of any religion. In the light of that possibility the former religious conflicts became much less important; secularism became the common and omnipresent enemy.

> In this way the new culture provided Christians with a new way of interpreting the world. Inspired by a powerful religious feeling, they caught a glimpse of a glorious future: they then sacrificed their own wealth and ambitions to take up the cause of Christ, and turn their talents to the moral reform of society.[17]

Westfall sees the willingness of evangelical Christians to embark on foreign missions, press for legislation to enforce prohibition and sabbath observance, and volunteer their time and money to help the poor in the inner city as one of the most significant religious movements of this or any other age. The fact that the social gospel impulse eventually waned, he argues, is not sufficient evidence to suggest that it was initially a capitulation to secular forces.

## NOTES

1  Colin D. Howell, *Northern Sandlots: A Social History of Maritime Baseball* (Toronto: University of Toronto Press, 1995), 55

2  Cited in Carl Berger, "The True North Strong and Free" in *Nationalism in Canada*, ed. Peter Russell (Toronto: McGraw-Hill, 1965), 6

3  Cited in David P. Gagan, "The Relevance of Canada First," *Journal of Canadian Studies*, 5 (1970): 38

4  Cited in Robert Craig Brown and Ramsay Cook, *Canada, 1896–1921: A Nation Transformed* (Toronto: McClelland and Stewart, 1974), 31

5  Ibid., 140

6   Cited in Ramsay Cook, *The Regenerators: Social Criticism in Late Victorian English Canada* (Toronto: University of Toronto Press, 1985), 4

7   Neil Semple, "The Quest for the Kingdom: Aspects of Protestant Revivalism in Nineteenth-Century Ontario" in *Old Ontario: Essays in Honour of J.M.S. Careless*, ed. David Keane and Colin Read, (Toronto: Dundurn Press, 1990), 112

8   Brown and Cook, *Canada, 1896–1921*, 258

9   A.B. McKillop, *Matters of Mind: The University in Ontario, 1791–1951* (Toronto: University of Toronto Press, 1994), 251–52

10   Barry Moody, "Esther Clark Goes to College," *Atlantis* 20, 1 (Fall/Winter 1995): 41, 47

11   Cited in George Altmeyer, "Three Ideas of Nature, 1893–1914," *Journal of Canadian Studies*, 11, 3 (Aug. 1976): 23

12   Robert H. MacDonald, *Sons of the Empire: The Frontier and the Boy Scout Movement, 1890–1918* (Toronto: University of Toronto Press, 1993), 26

13   Elizabeth Mitchell, "The Rise of Athleticism Among Girls and Women," *National Council of Women Yearbook* (1896), 106

14   Cited in Gerald Lynch and David Rampton, eds., *The Canadian Essay*, (Toronto: Copp Clark Pitman, 1991), 12

15   Cited in Maria Tippett, *Making Culture: English-Canadian Institutions and the Arts before the Massey Commission* (Toronto: University of Toronto Press, 1990), 6

16   Cook, *The Regenerators*, 229

17   William Westfall, *Two Worlds: The Protestant Culture of Nineteenth-Century Ontario* (Montreal: McGill-Queen's University Press, 1989), 80

## SELECTED READING

On the intellectual history of late Victorian Canada, see Carl Berger, *The Sense of Power: Studies in the Ideas of Canadian Imperialism 1867–1914* (Toronto: University of Toronto Press, 1970), and *Honour and the Search for Influence: A History of the Royal Society of Canada, 1882–1994* (Toronto: University of Toronto Press, 1996); A.B. McKillop, *A Disciplined Intelligence: Critical Inquiry and Canadian Thought in the Victorian Era* (Montreal: McGill-Queen's University Press, 1979); Ramsay Cook, *The Regenerators: Social Criticism in Late Victorian English Canada* (Toronto: University of Toronto Press, 1985); Denis Monière, *Ideologies in Quebec: The Historical Development* (Toronto: University of Toronto Press, 1981); Susan Sheets-Pyenson, *John William Dawson: Faith, Hope, and Science* (Montreal and Kingston: McGill-Queen's University Press, 1996); and Allen Mills, *Fool for Christ: The Political Thought of J.S. Woodsworth* (Toronto: University of Toronto Press, 1991) See also Suzanne Zeller, *Inventing Canada: Early Victorian Science and the Idea of a Transcontinental Nation* (Toronto: University of Toronto Press, 1987); Allan Smith, *Canada–An American Nation? Essays on Continentalism, Identity and the Canadian Frame of Mind* (Montreal and Kington: McGill-Queen's University Press, 1994)

On the writing of history in the late nineteenth century, see M. Brook Taylor, *Promoters, Patriots and Partisans: Historiography in Nineteenth-Century English Canada* (Toronto: University of Toronto Press, 1990); Carl Berger, *The Writing of Canadian History* (Toronto: University of Toronto Press, 1976); and Serge Gagnon, *Quebec and Its Historians, 1840–1920* (Montreal: Harvest House, 1982).

Clerical nationalism is explored in Susan Mann Trofimenkoff, *L'Action Française: French-Canadian Nationalism in the Twenties* (Toronto: University of Toronto Press, 1975); Joseph Levitt, *Henri Bourassa and the Golden Calf: The Social Program of the Nationalists of Quebec, 1900–1914* (Ottawa: University of Ottawa Press, 1969); and Jean Hamelin and Nicole Gagnon, *Histoire du Catholicisme québécois, Part 3, Le XXe siècle* (Montreal: Boréal Express, 1984). The Acadian renaissance is discussed in Cecile Gallant, *Women and the Acadian Renaissance* (Moncton: Les Éditions d'Acadie, 1992), and Jean Daigle, ed., *Acadia of the Maritimes: Thematic Studies* (Moncton: Chaire d'études acadiennes, Université de Moncton, 1995).

Religion and culture is specifically explored in William Westfall, *Two Worlds: The Protestant Culture of Nineteenth-Century Ontario* (Montreal: McGill-Queen's University Press, 1989); John Webster Grant, *A Profusion of Spires: Religion in Nineteenth-Century Ontario* (Toronto: University of Toronto Press, 1988); Neil Semple, *The Lord's Dominion: The History of Canadian Methodism* (Montreal and Kingston: McGill-Queen's University Press, 1996); John S. Moir, *Enduring Witness: A History of the Presbyterian Church in Canada* (Toronto: Presbyterian Church of Canada, 1987); Harry A. Renfree, *Heritage and Horizon: The Baptist Story in Canada* (Mississauga, ON: Canadian Baptist Federation, 1988); Michael Gauvreau, *The Evangelical Century: College and Creed in English Canada from the Great Revival to the Great Depression* (Montreal: McGill-Queen's University Press, 1991) and George Rawlyk, ed., *The Canadian Protestant Experience* (Montreal: McGill-Queen's University Press, 1990). See also Terence Murphy, ed., *A Concise History of Christianity in Canada* (Toronto: Oxford University Press, 1996). On culture, see Keith Walden, *Becoming Modern in Toronto: The Industrial Exhibition and the Shaping of Late Victorian Culture* (Toronto: University of Toronto Press, 1997).

Schools are discussed in Susan Houston and Alison Prentice, *Schooling and Scholars in Nineteenth-Century Ontario* (Toronto: University of Toronto Press, 1988); Donald Wilson, ed., *An Imperfect Past: Education and Society in Canadian History* (Vancouver: UBC Press, 1984); Nancy Sheehan, David C. Jones, and Robert M. Stamp, eds., *Shaping the Schools of the Canadian West* (Calgary: Detselig, 1979); and Roger Magnuson, *A Brief History of Quebec Education* (Montreal: Harvest House, 1980). The best treatment of universities is Brian McKillop, *Matters of Mind: The University in Ontario, 1791-1951* (Toronto: University of Toronto Press, 1994).

Nature, the environment, and conservation are the focus of Chad Gaffield and Pam Gaffield, eds., *Consuming Canada: Readings in Environmental History* (Toronto: Copp Clark, 1995); Patricia Jasen, *Wild Things: Nature, Culture, and Tourism in Ontario, 1790–1914* (Toronto: University of Toronto Press, 1995); Janet Foster, *Working for Wildlife: The Beginning of Preservation in Canada* (Toronto: University of Toronto Press, 1978); J.G. Nelson, ed., *Canadian Parks in Historical Perspective* (Montreal: Harvest House, 1970); James C. Taylor, *Negotiating the Past: The Making of Canada's National Historic Parks and Sites* (Montreal: McGill-Queen's University Press, 1990); Michel Girard, *L'Écologisme retrouvé: Essor et déclin de la Commission de la Conservation du Canada* (Ottawa: Les Presses de l'Université d'Ottawa, 1994); Carl Berger, *Science, God, and Nature in Victorian Canada* (Toronto: University of Toronto Press, 1983); and Robert H. MacDonald, *Sons of the Empire: The Frontier and the Boy Scout Movement, 1890–1918* (Toronto: University of Toronto Press, 1993).

On sports and recreation, see Alan Metcalfe, *Canada Learns to Play: The Emergence of Organized Sport, 1807–1914* (Toronto: McClelland and Stewart, 1987); Colin Howell; *Northern Sandlots: A Social History of Maritime Baseball* (Toronto: University of Toronto Press, 1995); and Bruce Kidd; *Contested Identities: The Struggle for Canadian Sport* (Toronto: University of Toronto Press, 1996). Architecture in this period is comprehensively surveyed in the second volume of Harold Kalman's *A History of Canadian Architecture* (Toronto: Oxford University Press, 1994) and Janet Wright, *Crown Assets: The Architecture of the Department of Public Works, 1867-1967* (Toronto: University of Toronto Press, 1997).

Literary history is discussed in Carl F. Klinck, ed., *Literary History of Canada* (Toronto: University of Toronto Press, 1976), and Dennis Duffy, *Gardens, Covenants, Exiles: Loyalism in the Literature of Upper Canada/Ontario* (Toronto: University of Toronto Press, 1982). Paul Rutherford assesses the explosion in newspaper publication and newspaper readership in *A Victorian Authority: The Daily Press in Late Nineteenth-Century Canada* (Toronto: University of Toronto Press, 1982). See also Minko Sotiron, *From Politics to Profit: The Commercialization of Canadian Daily Newspapers, 1890-1920* (Montreal and Kingston: McGill-Queen's University Press, 1996). On artistic developments, see Carman Cumming, *Sketches from a Young Country: The Images of Grip Magazine* (Toronto: University of Toronto Press, 1997); Maria Tippett, *Making Culture: English-Canadian Institutions and the Arts Before the Massey Commission* (Toronto: University of Toronto Press, 1990); J. Russell Harper, *Painting in Canada: A History*, 2nd ed. (Toronto: University of Toronto Press, 1977); Dennis Reid, *"Our Own Country Canada": Being the Account of the National Aspirations of the Principal Landscape Artists in Montreal and Toronto, 1860–1890* (Ottawa: National Gallery, 1980); Guy Robert, *La peinture au Québec depuis ses origines* (Ste-Adèle, PQ: Iconia, 1978); and Laurent Mailhot and Pierre Nepveu, *La poésie québécoise des origines à nos jours* (Montreal: L'Hexagone, 1986). For an introduction to Canadian theatre history, see Don Rubin ed., *Canadian Theatre History: Selected Readings* (Toronto: Copp Clark Ltd., 1996). Folklore is explored in Edith Fowke and Richard Johnston, *Folk Songs of Canada* (Waterloo, ON: Waterloo Music, 1954), and in several volumes by Edith Fowke: *Sally Go Round the Sun* (Toronto: McClelland and Stewart, 1969), *Folklore of Canada* (Toronto: McClelland and Stewart, 1976), and *Ring Around the Moon* (Toronto: McClelland and Stewart, 1977). For a study of one of Canada's foremost photographers, see Roger Hall, Gordon Dobbs, and Stanley Triggs, *The World of William Notman: The Nineteenth Century Through a Master Lens* (Toronto: McClelland and Stewart, 1993).

# PART 2

# THE MODERN AGE: CORPORATE ECONOMY AND MASS SOCIETY

# T I M E   L I N E

| | |
|---|---|
| **1914-18** | • First World War |
| **1915** | • Battle of Ypres; Saskatchewan leads the English-speaking provinces in banning alcohol |
| **1916** | • Battle of the Somme; labour shortages force temporary abandonment of sexual division of labour; Manitoba, Alberta, and Saskatchewan grant female suffrage; Manitoba government eliminates bilingual schools; National Research Council created |
| **1917** | • Battle of Vimy Ridge; a branch of the Royal Flying Corps established in Canada; Halifax explosion; Ontario and British Columbia women win the vote; conscription (Military Service Act) divides the nation |
| **1917-23** | • Nationalization of interprovincial railways other than the CPR and incorporation, along with publicly owned railways, to form Canadian National Railways |
| **1918** | • Saskatchewan makes English the only language of instruction beyond the first grade; League of Indians of Canada established; Nova Scotia concedes women's suffrage; women win right to vote federally |
| **1919** | • Farmer–Labour government comes to power in Ontario; New Brunswick women win the vote; Winnipeg General Strike and other general strikes mark a year of labour radicalism |
| **1920-21** | • Arthur Meighen heads federal government |
| **1920-24** | • Recession grips Canada |
| **1921-25** | • Progressive Party wins second largest block of seats in House of Commons; United Farmers of Alberta form provincial government |
| **1921-25** | • William Lyon Mackenzie King serves as prime minister |
| **1922** | • United Farmers of Manitoba form provincial government |
| **1925** | • Formation of United Church of Canada; coal miners' strike in Cape Breton; Maritime Rights election in Nova Scotia |
| **1926** | • Arthur Meighen returns briefly to power; Appointment of Duncan Commission |
| **1926-30** | • Mackenzie King's Liberals form government in Ottawa |
| **1927** | • Federal government introduces program for means-tested old age pensions |
| **1928** | • St Francis Xavier Extension Department begins co-operative programs; Alberta passes Sexual Sterilization Act |
| **1929** | • Crash of New York stock market |
| **1930-35** | • R.B. Bennett serves as prime minister |
| **1930-39** | • Great Depression |
| **1931** | • *Quadragesimo Anno*; Statute of Westminster |
| **1932** | • Imperial Economic Conference in Ottawa; establishment of federal relief camps; creation of CCF; Canadian Radio Broadcasting Corporation Act |

| | |
|---|---|
| **1934** | • British-appointed commission of government replaces parliamentary government in Newfoundland; Bank of Canada Act; birth of the Dionne quintuplets |
| **1935** | • Bennett's New Deal; creation of the Canadian Wheat Board; On-to-Ottawa Trek; election of Social Credit in Alberta; Canada–United States trade agreement |
| **1935-48** | • Third King administration |
| **1936** | • Election of Union nationale government in Quebec |
| **1939** | • Establishment of National Film Board |
| **1939-45** | • Second World War |
| **1940** | • Fall of France; Quebec women get the vote; unemployment insurance established as national program; Permanent Joint Board on Defence established |
| **1941** | • Battle for Hong Kong |
| **1942** | • Dieppe landing; national plebiscite on conscription; evacuation of Japanese from coastal areas of British Columbia; Kirkland Lake gold miners' strike |
| **1943** | • Invasion of Sicily; compulsory school attendance legislated in Quebec |
| **1944** | • Liberation of France; establishment of facilities at Chalk River to create plutonium; PC 1003 recognizes right to collective bargaining; Parliament passes legislation to implement family allowances |
| **1945** | • End of war; major Ford strike; United Nations established |

Between 1914 and 1945, Canadians experienced two world wars, a major depression, and the onslaught of mass consumer society. The impact of these developments left people reeling. While some voters turned to new political parties to address their concerns, a majority of Canadians put their faith in traditional parties to meet the challenge of the extraordinary conditions that faced the nation. Warfare demanded saving and sacrifice on the part of most Canadians but, in peacetime, radio, movies, newspapers, and glossy magazines emphasized consumerism and worldly pleasures. Still claiming to be Christians, most Canadians embraced a value system based on material accumulation and individual achievement. Parsons and pundits railed against the attitudes and behaviour that dominated the new era, but they increasingly expressed a minority opinion. The modern age had come to stay.

# 7

# THE GREAT WAR DECADE, 1911–1921

I AM TERRIFIED. I HUG THE EARTH, DIGGING MY fingers into every crevice, every hole.

A blinding flash and an explosive howl a few feet in front of the trench. My bowels liquify. Acrid smoke bites the throat, parches the mouth. I am beyond mere fright. I am frozen with an insane fear that keeps me cowering in the bottom of the trench. I lie flat on my belly waiting....[1]

Charles Yale Harrison, an American soldier in the Canadian Expeditionary Force (CEF), was far from alone in his reaction to a German shelling. Many soldiers—including two future prime ministers, John Diefenbaker and Lester Pearson—found even the thought of the senseless slaughter in Europe too much to bear. As a result of physical or mental illnesses, they were found "unfit for service" and were sent home to Canada. Others refused to volunteer to go overseas and risked being called up when conscription was imposed by the federal government in 1917. Still others volunteered with enthusiasm and, in retrospect at least, remembered the war years as a time when "men were men" and the horrors of modern warfare bonded soldiers together in ways that could not be understood by those outside the military. Whatever the response to the "war to end all wars," which raged in Europe

between August 1914 and November 1918, it touched the lives of most Canadians. It also marked a major turning point in the political history of the nation and served as a catalyst for many of the trends gaining momentum in the industrial age.

## THE BORDEN ADMINISTRATION, 1911–1914

Prime Minister Robert Borden was vacationing in the Muskokas in the week leading up to Britain's declaration of war against Germany on 4 August 1914. Alerted to the impending crisis on 28 July, he hurried back to Ottawa. Three years in office had given him a brutal education in the difficulties of governing a country as big and complex as Canada. Having come to power in 1911 with the support of Quebec nationalists and the anti–free trade business community, he had his hands full just keeping the Conservative coalition together. To make matters worse, the economy began to sink into a recession in 1912. People across the country were thrown out of work, and the unemployed began drifting to cities where they stretched municipal and charitable resources to the limit. Perhaps most frustrating for Borden was his inability to get some of his most innovative policies passed by

Parliament. Although the Conservatives had a majority in the House of Commons, the Liberal-dominated Senate rejected or severely amended much of the government's legislation.

*The Tories on tour in the West in 1911.*
*The lead car is pictured above.*
*Borden is seated behind the driver.*

Like his predecessors, Borden was determined to pursue policies that would foster economic growth, but unlike Macdonald and Laurier, he was a progressive in his approach to policy. Borden emphasized morality, duty, and efficiency in government and struggled, in a way typical of progressives, to eliminate some of the worst abuses of the old patronage-ridden system. In 1907, at a meeting in Halifax, the Conservatives unveiled a new platform designed to emphasize their progressive program. The Halifax platform failed to win many votes in 1908, but it remained the foundation for many of the policies promoted by the Conservatives in the 1911 campaign. Borden crisscrossed the country, promising to introduce the merit system into the civil service, establish a permanent Tariff Commission to set a "scientific tariff," create a Board of Grain Commissioners to regulate the grain trade, implement free rural mail delivery, and provide subsidies to the provinces to improve roads and agricultural education. Prepared to accept increased state intervention in a number of areas, Borden was even quietly considering tak-

ing full control over the Liberal-sponsored Grand Trunk Pacific and Canadian Northern railways if they continued to sap the federal treasury. He was also planning to scrap Laurier's "tin-pot navy." In its place, he proposed to make an "emergency" $35 million contribution to Great Britain's efforts to keep the imperial navy—upon which Canada really depended—strong and efficient. This would buy time, Borden argued, for Canadians to reflect more deeply on their defence policy.

Borden's cabinet included people who had not caught up with the style of progressive politics, but he had a strong ally in his Minister of Finance, Thomas White. The vice-president of National Trust, White represented the Toronto Liberals who had defected from Laurier in 1911 and was a powerful figure in the Canadian financial community. Henri Bourassa also supported Borden in 1911 and might have added a progressive voice to the cabinet, but he refused to consider such a role. As the leader of the Quebec contingent of the cabinet, F.D. Monk was uncomfortable in the predominantly anglophone milieu of Ottawa and, like Bourassa, held views on imperial policy that were diametrically opposed to those promoted by Borden and many of his imperialist-minded colleagues. Quebec nationalists had formed an alliance with the Conservatives in 1911 because they opposed Laurier, but a common enemy was not enough to keep them together once the party came to power. A little over a year after taking office as minister of public works, Monk resigned over the naval question. Like other Quebec nationalists, he was opposed to any policy that smacked of excessive subservience to the British.

Monk's defection from the cabinet did not make it easier to resolve the naval issue. When the Naval Aid Bill was introduced into the House of Commons, it encountered such fierce opposition from the Liberals that the government invoked closure (or limitation) on debate. This was the first time that such a procedure had been used in Canada, and Laurier pointed to it as justification for instructing the Liberals in the Senate to defeat the bill. In making this decision, Laurier undoubtedly took into consideration the views of the nationalists in his native province, but he was probably also taking revenge for Borden's scrapping of his naval program.

Bills creating the Tariff Commission and providing subsidies to provincial highways also fell victim to the Senate's powers to veto and amend bills. In justifying their obstructionism, Liberal senators argued that the Borden administration was usurping powers that were not authorized by the BNA Act. Even the Grain Act of 1912, which created a Board of Grain Commissioners and gave the federal government the power to own and operate terminal grain elevators, had to be carefully administered in order not to invoke the wrath of the Liberal senators.

Not all programs foundered on the rock of Senate intransigence. In the West, Borden's popularity soared when he agreed to support the construction of a railroad to Hudson Bay to provide another outlet for growing grain exports. Farmers were doubtless also pleasantly surprised when many of the provisions of the aborted free trade agreement of 1911 were made available in the Underwood Tariff adopted by the United States in 1913. In 1912, Borden made good on his promise to Canada's most powerful provinces—Quebec, Ontario, and Manitoba—that he would grant them huge sections of federally administered territories on their northern borders. (No effort was made to consult the largely aboriginal populations who lived there.) The Maritimes and western provinces, as well as bankers and brokers, were relieved when the federal government saved the nation's two faltering railway companies from impending bankruptcy in 1914.

On the matter of civil service reform, the government was forced to move more slowly than it had planned. A commission, headed by Sir George Murray, a British public servant with impeccable credentials, had been established in September 1912 to investigate the federal civil service. In his report, Murray recommended a complete overhaul of a system that had become top heavy, patronage ridden, and inefficient. Borden's government took steps to introduce reforms, but the existing system was so inadequate that it was unable—and probably not all that eager—to preside over its own transformation.

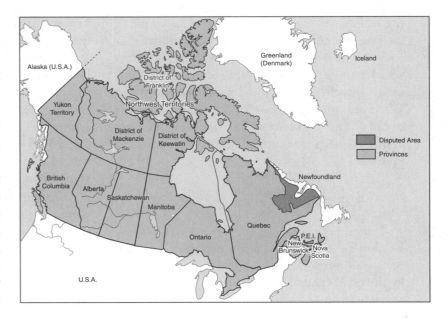

**Map 7.1** *Canada, 1914.*

Perhaps nothing was so disturbing in the long run as the economic recession that descended in 1912. While business and government leaders understood that a credit crunch and overexpansion had created the crisis, most people experienced it as bankruptcy, unemployment, and having inadequate income to purchase the necessities of life. In Ontario, a commission established to study unemployment reported in 1913 that:

Rents are unpaid, families are living on not half rations, and in many homes not knowing where the next meal is coming from. Many heads of families are feeling the pressure mentally; two men, one with a wife and seven small children, the other with a wife and two small children, have been unable to stand up against the depression. One became mentally unbalanced and died of starvation in the hospital, and the other took his own life, both leaving their families destitute.[2]

The federal government responded in 1913 by appointing a commission on the cost of living and by urging the railways to maintain high levels of employment. In the larger cities, municipal governments established employment bureaus. These efforts proved inadequate. Many people were facing real misery and, with immigrants still pouring into the country, there was every possibility that social unrest would be more than local police forces could manage. In May 1914, two thousand immigrants marched through the streets of downtown Winnipeg, waving shovels and shouting "Work or bread." This incident was a harbinger of what could come if economic conditions failed to improve.

## PREPARING FOR WAR

Borden's concerns over the economy and the Senate's obstructionism were quickly superseded by the crisis created by the war. In June 1914, the assassination of Austrian Archduke Franz Ferdinand and his wife in Sarajevo by a Serb nationalist seemed like a remote tragedy. What led to war was not so much the murder of a future head of state as the system of military alliances among European nations, which produced a domino effect when efforts were made to redress the outrage. Austria-Hungary, looking for revenge after the assassination, declared war on Serbia, and turned to its German ally for support. A latecomer to the scramble for overseas colonies, Germany was jealous of the power of France and Great Britain, and for more than a decade its kaiser had been trying to match them in military might and international influence. This was his chance to show the world that Germany was a force to be reckoned with. Germany's eagerness to flex its military muscle led

Russia, an ally of Serbia, to mobilize its army; and France, an ally of Russia, shortly did the same. As Germany prepared to invade neutral Belgium, en route to an attack on France, Great Britain also felt compelled to intervene. The British declaration of war on Germany also meant that Austria-Hungary was aligned against Great Britain. Italy and Rumania eventually joined the effort to stop the German alliance, as did the United States in April 1917. The Ottoman Empire entered the war on the side of Germany in 1915.

As a member of the British Empire, Canada was automatically at war when Great Britain was at war. Canadians nevertheless had a choice about how to participate in the fighting in Europe, or, indeed, whether to participate at all. In August 1914, most people, including Wilfrid Laurier and Henri Bourassa, saw Germany as the aggressor and thought it prudent to support Great Britain. Neither the Canadian state nor the individual citizen was prepared for what this decision meant. The Great War turned out to be a tragedy of unprecedented proportions, eclipsed only by the Second World War in the death and destruction it caused.

Struggling to deal with the demands of war, Conservatives and Liberals in the House of Commons united to pass the War Measures Act early in August 1914. This act gave the federal government authority to do everything deemed "necessary for the security, defence, peace, order and welfare of Canada"—an authority that, in the emergency conditions, allowed it to ignore traditional provincial claims to jurisdiction. Under the provisions of the act, Ottawa imposed tough censorship laws, intervened in the marketplace, and stripped many people of their democratic rights.

Canada entered the war with a standing army of just 3110 men, a navy consisting of two ageing vessels, and not even a hint of an airforce. Since the end of the nineteenth century, most of Canada's defence expenditures had been channelled to the militia, whose budget had risen from $1.6 million in 1898 to $11 million in 1914. Militia strength stood at over seventy-four thousand in the summer of 1914, and it was among these summer-camp soldiers that Canada would draw many of its first eager recruits. Instead of staying in their militia units, infantries were organized on an ad hoc basis as individuals volunteered their services. Volunteers were grouped in numbered battalions, of about a thousand men. Battalions, in turn, were organized into divisions for what became known as the Canadian Expeditionary Force (CEF).

Upon the declaration of war, Borden's Minister of Militia, Sam Hughes, went into action as only a man of his energy and tactlessness could do. Ignoring his department's plans for mobilization in the event of war, Hughes telegraphed his 226 unit commanders, appealing for volunteers for a division of twenty-five thousand men. He was swamped with replies, many of them from recent British immigrants. When the volunteers arrived at the army's new military base at Valcartier a few miles outside of Quebec City, they found construction and confusion all around, with Hughes surveying the scene from a small castle he had built for the purpose. More by good luck than good management, thirty-one thousand men, eight thousand horses, and sundry equipment, much of it useless, were loaded onto transports and dispatched to Europe on 3 October. Among those travelling with the First Division were 101 nurses under the direction of Matron Margaret MacDonald, all full-fledged members of the CEF.

Because there was no sufficiently experienced senior Canadian officer, a British officer, Major-General E.A.H. Alderson, took command. Under Alderson's leadership, soldiers were organized into the 1st Canadian Infantry Division and were drilled into fighting form in England during the winter. The division moved to France in February 1915. At Ypres, Belgium, in mid-April, they had their first real test when they experienced a chlorine gas attack. The Canadians refused to break lines when others around them, who had taken the brunt of the attack, fell back. It soon became clear that the war would be a long one and that Britain needed all the help it could get from the empire. By the summer of 1916, four divisions had been called up and sent overseas. Britain's Lord Kitchener, who was in charge of the War Office, had shocked his cabinet colleagues in the early days of the war by calling for a million soldiers. In the end, Great Britain needed five times that number. Over six hundred thousand of them would be Canadians.

*It was the battle of Ypres that inspired Lieutenant-Colonel John McCrae, a Canadian doctor, to write the poem "In Flanders Fields," a moving call to keep faith with the soldiers who had given up their lives.*

Colonel John McCrae Birthplace society and Guelph Museums

While men and matériel continued to move across the Atlantic, inexperience, corruption, and confusion dogged the mobilization efforts under Hughes. Many of the problems, such as inadequate facilities and bottlenecks in military supplies, would have occurred no matter who was in charge, but Hughes had the unfortunate knack of making even the smallest problem a major crisis. Patronage and corruption riddled the Militia Department's massive purchasing program, and confusion reigned in the command structure of the Canadian forces. Hughes was a stout defender of the Canadian-made Ross rifles, even though the gun had a tendency to jam in the heat of battle. Only gradually were the rifles replaced by the more reliable British-made Lee-Enfields. Even the supply of chaplains for the soldiers, who came from a wide range of religious backgrounds, ended up a hopeless muddle under Sir Sam. Although he was knighted in 1915, Hughes was finally dismissed from his portfolio in 1916. By that time, his administrative incompetence had brought an avalanche of criticism against the government's mishandling of the war effort.

Even before Hughes's dismissal, Borden had seen to it that the work of the Militia Department had been completely reorganized. A variety of committees, including the Imperial Munitions Board, War Purchasing Board, National Service Board, and Ministry of Overseas Military Sources, had been established to bring efficiency into the war effort. Since the government lacked professional civil servants capable of managing an economy suddenly on a war footing, Ottawa was critically dependent on the expertise and good will of business people like Joseph Flavelle, general manager of the William Davies Packing Company, who became chair of the Imperial Munitions Board (IMB). Flavelle spurred private firms to new levels of productivity, enticed American companies to locate in Canada, and, when all else failed, created government-run factories to produce everything from acetone to aeroplanes. By 1917, the IMB was the biggest business in Canada with 600 factories, 150 000 workers, and a turnover of $2 million a day.

## THE WARTIME ECONOMY

Canada's productive capacity received a tremendous boost during the First World War. Although it did not change the direction of the Canadian economy in any major way, the war sped Canadians a little faster down the road to industrial maturity. Markets expanded, at least temporarily, and the value of Canadian exports doubled in the first three years of the war and doubled again by 1919. In 1913, only 7 percent of Canadian manufactures

were sold overseas, a figure that rose to 40 percent during the final two years of the war. Factories ran full tilt producing for the war effort, and grain acreage soared.

Canada's wartime economy, like that of peacetime, depended on private initiative, but the government found it necessary to intervene in the economy in a variety of ways. In addition to setting up the IMB and related committees to ensure that the army was properly equipped, the government brought a wide range of supplies and services under its control. The Board of Grain Supervisors became the sole agent for Canadian wheat sales; the Fuel Controller decided the price and use of coal, wood, and gas; and the Food Board determined policy relating to the cost and distribution of food. The activities of the supervisory boards were many and various. In an effort to increase agricultural efficiency, the Food Board purchased a hundred tractors from the Henry Ford Motor Company to distribute at cost to farmers. The same board urged Canadians to eat more fish so that beef and bacon could be released for overseas armies. Children were encouraged to grow "victory gardens" as their contribution to the war effort.

Inevitably there were complaints about government policy. The Food Board's "anti-loafing law," threatening punishment for any man or boy not gainfully employed, was understandably not very popular, and no one enjoyed the discomfort that resulted from the "fuelless days" mandated by the Fuel Controller. The IMB's pattern of granting contracts sparked accusations from Western Canada that Flavelle and his associates favoured central Canadian firms over those from the less industrialized regions of the nation. When companies producing war supplies recorded huge profits, Canadians became increasingly sceptical about the patriotic claims of corporations. People like Flavelle prospered while servicemen's families, without any resources to sustain them, were often forced to rely on charity.

By 1916, the Canadian economy was fully geared for war. Hostilities rejuvenated the Canadian shipbuilding industry, but in the industrial heartland rather than the Maritime ports. During the war, the British-owned Vickers

Company employed over fifteen thousand people in its shipyards near Montreal, while Davie Shipbuilding of Lauzon, Quebec, produced anti-submarine vessels and steel barges. Between 1914 and 1918, Canada's steel mills doubled their capacity to meet British demands for shells, supplying as much as a third of British artillery needs. Supplemented by the domestic labours of women and children who knit socks, preserved jam, and rolled bandages for the men at the front, farm and factory production increased to meet the demand for food, clothing, and footwear.

Notwithstanding the enhanced role of government and industry, voluntary activities remained essential to the war effort. The twelve hundred branches of the Red Cross in Canada served as a virtual auxiliary of the Army Medical Corps. In many communities, the IODE and the Women's Institute collected money, knit socks, and packed parcels for the men overseas. A range of other organizations—the Great War Veterans' Association, the Next-of-Kin Association, the YM- and YWCA, Consumers' Leagues, Women's Patriotic Leagues, Vacant Lot Garden Clubs, and the Women's Volunteer Army Division—all "did their bit."

Much of the work of caring for the families of soldiers and of the men who returned wounded to Canada was managed by volunteer groups. In the early days of the war, the federal government established a Canadian Patriotic Fund, an organization staffed largely by volunteers whose role was to help the families of soldiers overseas, a growing number of which were dependent on charity. At the beginning of the war, a husband was obliged to secure his wife's permission before offering his services to the military, but this requirement was soon dropped. An enlisted man was required to sign over a portion of his pay to his wife or dependent mother, but this did not always happen. The volunteers

in the Patriotic Fund helped dependants to apply for financial assistance—as much as $50 a month by the end of the war—and also arranged services for a veteran who returned sick, wounded, insane, or addicted to alcohol.

The twin demand for workers and soldiers resulted in a labour shortage by 1916. To address

*Volunteers knitting socks.*
City of Toronto Archives/SC244-873

the problem, women were recruited into jobs in transportation and metal trades that were previously held only by men. In an effort to overcome the prejudices of employers against women, the IMB published a photographic report praising the skills of women workers and offering assurances that there were "many operations in the Machine Shop which can safely be assigned to women." Over thirty thousand women were hired in munitions factories during the war and many more in positions temporarily opened to women because of the conditions created by the war. Women's salaries never matched those of the men they replaced and they were fired from their "untraditional" jobs at the end of the hostilities, but women got a sense of what they could do in the public sphere when they had a chance.

As the economy moved into high gear, Canadians confronted inflation and a soaring cost of living. Wages, controlled by wartime regulation, failed to follow the upward spiral of prices and many people got caught in the financial squeeze. In the last two years of the war, Canada's productive capacity was threatened by rising levels of strike activity and political unrest by an increasingly aggrieved workforce. Canada's War Labour Policy, which was proclaimed in 1918, prohibited strikes and lockouts, while affirming the right to organize and to receive fair wages and equal pay for equal work. Despite such efforts to control the situation, labour shortages blunted the efforts by governments and employers to prevent strikes and protests. There was no desperate reserve army of labour willing to take the jobs of striking workers, and, in the period before another recession struck in 1920, workers recognized their potential power in bringing employers to heel. Union membership increased dramatically, and support for labour parties grew.

In Newfoundland, as in Canada, wartime labour shortages led to a spread of industrial unionism followed by its collapse in the postwar recession. The Newfoundland Industrial Workers' Association organized railway shops, longshoremen, street railway workers, and factory workers. Its Ladies' Branch in St John's orchestrated a series of militant strikes in manufacturing operations in 1918 and 1919. In the outports, fishing families got better prices for their fish but felt that the war effort was very much a St John's affair. When Fisherman's Protective Union leader William Coaker supported the government's efforts to form a coalition and impose military conscription, outport families felt betrayed.

## FINANCING THE WAR

"We are justified in placing upon posterity the greater portion of the financial burden of this war, waged as it is in the interests of human freedom, and their benefit in equal if not in greater degree than our own," Finance Minister Thomas White announced in 1916. With these words the federal government, under the sweeping provisions of the War Measures Act, took a variety of economic initiatives that would have been unthinkable prior to the outbreak of hostilities. It suspended the gold standard, expanded the money supply, and engaged in deficit financing. When British financial markets closed, the federal government for the first time floated loans in the New York bond market. Canadians also extended credit to the mother country for the purchase of the necessities of war.

In an effort to raise money domestically, the government sold Victory Bonds, War Savings Certificates, and, for children, War Savings Stamps. The Canadian economy proved capable of generating nearly $2 billion in loans, and at no time during the war did government expenditures exceed 10 percent of the GNP. In 1917, the federal government began the process of nationalizing half the country's railway capacity by taking control of the Grand Trunk Pacific and Canadian Northern and amalgamating them with other government-controlled railways, such as the Intercolonial, to create the Canadian National Railway system. The government also used the wartime emergency to build a more effective civil service. In 1918, Ottawa placed some forty thousand government workers under a Civil Service Commission whose job it was to ensure that people were hired on the basis of merit rather than patronage.

In response to farmer and labour demands that wealth as well as manpower be conscripted, Ottawa implemented a war profits tax in 1916. It was pegged at 25 percent on all profits greater than 7 percent of capital for corporations and 10 percent of capital for other businesses with a capitalization of $50 000 or more. In 1917, the federal government for the first time imposed personal income taxes. The tax was a mere 2 percent on annual incomes up to $6000, a substantial sum at the time; single persons earning under $1500 and married men with family incomes under $3000 were exempted. Tax rates rose progressively to reach a maximum of 25 percent on income over $100 000. Difficult to collect, the new taxes played a negligible role in paying for the war effort. Eighty-four percent of wartime revenues were raised through customs and excise duties while less than 1 percent came from the personal income taxes. However, the "temporary" income and corporate taxes imposed during the war outlived the crisis that sparked them and by 1939 were generating nearly one-third of the federal government's revenues.

## THE WAR IN EUROPE

Canadian men enlisted in the armed forces for a variety of reasons. Patriotism motivated many young men, but others went overseas in search of adventure. As Larry Nelson, a Toronto enlistee in 1914, recalled, "most of us were young and saw it as a wonderful opportunity to throw off the shackles of working in an office or a factory or on a farm or what-have-you."[3] Still others, victims of the recession, enlisted to secure a steady job. Over 65 percent of the first wave of volunteers were recent British immigrants, and one-half of all

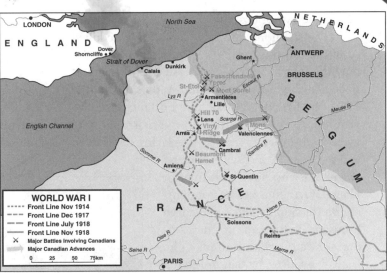

**Map 7.2** *The European Front, 1914–1918.*

enlistees in Canadian forces in the First World War were British born. All were unprepared for a

## THE REALITIES OF WAR

On the front, men lived in trenches that stretched from Switzerland to the English Channel. Their dugouts were pits of thick mud infested with fleas, lice, rats, and germs. Although soldiers devoured their rations of corned beef, biscuits, bread, and tea, it was not a healthy diet and left them constantly hungry and susceptible to diseases. If the enemy missed his mark, dysentery, pneumonia, and "trench fever" might be just as deadly. Chemical warfare was an entirely new and horrifying experience. To survive their first attack of chlorine gas at Ypres, men had urinated in their handkerchiefs and held them to their noses. Rats nibbled the corpses of fallen comrades while those who were still alive dug new trenches and maintained existing ones, moved

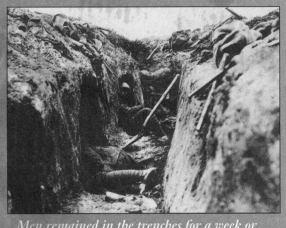

*Men remained in the trenches for a week or more at a time in all kinds of weather before they were relieved briefly to go to makeshift rest camps.*

National Archives of Canada/PA1326

supplies, and tried not to think of their hunger and fear.

Fear was justified. Of the more than 600 000 Canadians who enlisted or were conscripted, about 60 000 died, and at least as many were so severely wounded, physically or mentally, that they were unable to resume a normal life. The mentally wounded, or "shell shocked" as they came to be known, returned to a society that was ill-prepared for such casualties. While a soldier whose wounds put him in a wheelchair received a government pension and the sympathy of other Canadians, there was little comfort for the emotionally disabled who remained unfit to resume their work and family life and who stared vacantly into space or sought comfort in the bottle.

protracted war of unspeakable horror.

The six thousand Canadians who were killed or injured in the April 1915 battle at Ypres were only the first in a long list of casualties that horrified even the most hard-bitten soldier. On 1 July 1916, the first day of the Allied offensive on the Somme, twenty-one thousand British soldiers were slaughtered, among them three hundred and ten men of the Newfoundland Regiment who died at Beaumont Hamel. Over four months of fighting on the Somme left six hundred thousand British and French soldiers dead or wounded. The Canadian Corps, by that time a full four divisions strong, had been brought in to sustain the latter part of the failing offensive and suffered over twenty-four thousand casualties. But the worst was not over. With the Russian front crumbling, the Dardanelles taken by the Turks, and the Germans holding the line in Europe, there was every reason to believe that the Allies might lose the war. There were mutinies in the French army, and some Canadians were being shot for desertion as a warning to anyone else contemplating such a move.

In April 1917, the Canadian Corps took Vimy Ridge after a fiercely fought battle with over ten thousand Canadian casualties. They did not know it at the time, but it was a turning point for Canadians in the war. Until 1917, the soldiers of the CEF fought as "imperials" under Britain's Army Act, and even the commanders of the Canadian Corps were British. All of this was about to change. Although they fought superbly under British command, Canadian soldiers regularly complained about what seemed to them to be second-class treatment by the British military administration in everything from the quarters they were allocated to their place in line as cannon fodder. Borden went overseas in 1916 and became convinced that something had to be done to give Canadians more control over their own war effort.

In the fall of 1916, Borden established a Ministry of Overseas Military Forces under the control of Sir George Perley, the Canadian High Commissioner in London. The order creating the new ministry redefined the CEF as an overseas contingent of the Canadian militia. Gradually many, though not all, of the British officers were

*Commander Currie directs a practice attack near the Canadian front in June 1917.*

Imperial War Museum, London, England

replaced by Canadians until on 9 June 1917, Arthur Currie, the Canadian commander of the First Canadian Infantry Division, was made commander of the entire Canadian Corps.

Under the methodical Currie, Canadians continued to see some of the worst fighting of the war, but they fought with their own maple leaf insignia on their badges. They also developed their own unique reputation for bravery and determination. In October 1917, the Canadians were summoned to Passchendaele, in Belgium, where the British Fifth Army had already lost sixty-eight thousand men. In October and November, the Canadian Corps broke through the German lines, but the price was high: over fifteen thousand men.

While the vast majority of Canadian military personnel were in the land forces, significant num-

*Jack Turner and Lee Allan from Prince Edward Island taking a break from battle in 1917. Lee reads the* **Island Patriot** *while Jack holds* **Jack Canuck**, *a comic strip showing the heroics of soldier life.*

Prince Edward Island Public Archives and Records Office/2767/107

bers also served at sea and in the air. At the outbreak of war, it seemed that the remnant of the Canadian naval service organized by Laurier and ignored by Borden was doing well operating the old cruisers *Niobe* and *Rainbow* with considerable help from the British. The British, for their part, had advised Canada not to attempt to do more at sea but rather to concentrate on the CEF. The unexpected success of German submarines (known as U-boats) in sinking the merchant ships that carried North American war supplies to Britian and Europe brought a new dimension to naval warfare. As a result, nearly ten thousand Canadians served in the navy. Most of them operated Canadian-built anti-submarine craft on the East Coast, but over a thousand served with the British fleet in European waters.

In the summer and fall of 1918, three German U-boats hunted off Nova Scotia and Newfoundland. The Canadian anti-submarine vessels, which escorted merchant ship convoys, helped keep losses of major vessels to only two. It was more difficult to protect the widely scattered fishing fleets, and over thirty schooners and trawlers were destroyed in Canadian and Newfoundland waters. Meanwhile, Borden quietly reversed his earlier political stance that the development of a Canadian navy should have a low priority.

Canada authorized a tiny air unit early in the war, but airmen were encouraged to participate in British units, where they made a major contribution. Over twenty thousand Canadians served in the Royal Flying Corps (FCR), the Royal Naval Air Service, or, after 1 April 1918, the Royal Air Force. One of the most famous of Canada's fighting pilots was Lieutenant-Colonel W.A. "Billy" Bishop, who shot down seventy-two enemy planes and, unlike over fifteen hundred other Canadians who pioneered in the use of the "aeroplane" in wartime, lived to tell about it. The achievements of Canadian airmen such as Bishop, combined with the expertise Canadians gained in the British flying services and the tremendous growth of aircraft technology, helped to ensure national aviation development after the war, including the establishment of the Royal Canadian Air Force as a third armed service.

## THE WAR AT HOME

The slaughter on the European front spread panic in the British War Office and led to the demand for more troops. Borden had pushed the approved strength of the CEF up to two hundred and fifty thousand in the fall of 1915 and then pushed it up again, to five hundred thousand, in his New Year's message for 1916. But where would the soldiers come from? Already voluntary enlistments were lagging and, given the rate of casualties, it was difficult keeping units on the front up to strength.

In the early months of the war, it had looked as if voluntary enlistment would sustain the Canadian war effort. Private units such as the Princess Patricia's Light Infantry, a battalion formed by wealthy Montrealer Hamilton Gault and manned by British reservists living in Canada, offered their services as soon as war was declared. In August 1915, Sam Hughes announced that anyone could apply to form a battalion. Historian Desmond Morton notes that, as a result, recruiting leagues blossomed:

In Edmonton, three battalions competed for men in February 1916; in Winnipeg, there were six; in Toronto, ten. Orangemen, "Sportsmen," "Pals," claimed battalions. Many promised Highland dress; others were reserved for the Irish. One unit promised mothers that its men would never touch liquor. Two battalions were reserved for Americans; another took "bantams," men too short for the CEF minimum height of five foot two. Enthusiastic colonels and good-natured doctors ignored youth, old age, and obvious disability to fill ranks. Only later would such men demand pensions and compensation.[4]

Such recruiting added nearly one hundred and twenty-four thousand men to the CEF's infantry battalions and overall, one in six Canadian men between the ages of fifteen and fifty-four, or nearly two hundred and thirty-three thousand volunteered for the infantry by 1917. Canadians had also joined other branches of the CEF, such as the artillery, engineer, medical, and army service corps, or had responded to appeals to join British forestry and railway units, the Royal Navy, and the Royal Flying Corps, bringing the numbers almost up to the half million demanded by Borden.

While most men of military age never volunteered, preferring to stay at home, raise their families, and participate in the opportunities made available by the war, the proportion of recruits varied dramatically by region and culture. Only thirteen thousand were French-speaking, and men in Ontario and the West were more likely to sign up than those from the Maritimes and Quebec. The attachment of recent immigrants to their European homelands to some extent explains the lower recruitment rates in the longer-settled eastern provinces, but there were other reasons as well.

French Canadians were initially sympathetic to the Allied cause, but this feeling waned as the war progressed. During the first year of the war, French Canadians were dispersed among various units, creating language difficulties. The first and the last entirely French unit, the Royal 22nd Battalion, was established in October 1914. Anger at Ontario's 1912 legislation restricting French-language instruction in public schools, and at the military's reluctance to create French-speaking regiments, reinforced feelings of estrangement from a cause that was identified with Britain and English Canada. As wartime tensions mounted, provincial governments outside Quebec intensified their efforts to suppress French-language education in their jurisdictions, and English Canadians began accusing French Canadians of shirking their duty. These responses were not calculated to make French Canadians any more favourably disposed to fighting overseas.

Borden tried to maintain volunteer strength by stepping up recruitment efforts, conducting a National Registration of all able-bodied men, and creating a Canadian Defence Force that would relieve soldiers stationed in Canada for European service. None of these measures worked. Few volunteers were forthcoming from the national registration program and recruitment efforts were largely ignored. In May 1917, a month after the United States had entered the war, Borden announced his intention to impose conscription, or compulsory military service, on a war-weary nation. Opposition to his Military Service Act, which drafted single men between the ages of twenty and thirty-five, was high, especially in Quebec and among farmers and labourers. Although Borden had postponed calling an election in wartime, he now changed his mind. An election would clear the air about the issue of conscription and give the government a mandate to carry on.

Before dissolving Parliament on 6 October, Borden approached Laurier to join him in a coalition to support an all-out war effort. The seventy-eight-year-old Liberal chief rejected the proposal, concluding, "If I were now to take a different attitude, I would simply hand over the province [Quebec] to the Nationalists, and the consequences may be very serious." In making this decision, Laurier lost the support of many of the party faithful in Ontario and the West. A rump of Liberals joined with the Conservatives to create a Union government that campaigned on a platform of conscription, prohibition, and abolition of party patronage. To ensure a victory for his unstable coalition, Borden also saw to it that the right people got the vote. A Military Voters' Act extended the franchise to every man and woman in the CEF, while the Wartime Elections Act extended the franchise to mothers, wives, and sisters of soldiers—dead or alive—and took it away from citizens of enemy origin naturalized after 1902. The only compensation for those who were disenfranchised was the fact that they would be exempt from conscription.

While some women got the vote for the first time, not all suffrage leaders were pleased about the conditions under which it had been granted. As Dr Margaret Gordon, president of the Canadian Suffrage Association, observed, "It would have been more direct and at the same time more honest if the bill simply stated that all who did not pledge themselves to vote Conservative would be disfranchised." Even these draconian measures failed to convince Unionists that they would carry the day. Running scared during the election campaign, they promised sons of farmers that they would not be conscripted, a promise that was later broken.

The results of the election held on 17 December surprised few people: the Union government won 153 seats, while the Liberals won 82. Sixty-two of Quebec's 65 seats went to Laurier, but the Liberals carried only 10 of 28 seats in the Maritimes, 8 of 82 in Ontario, and 2 of 57 in the West. While the distribution of seats made the Union victory look impressive, the popular vote told another story. Civilian voters in the Maritimes gave a slight majority of their votes to anti-conscription candidates; even in Ontario, anti-conscriptionists, though winning only 10 percent of the seats, won almost 40 percent of the civilian vote.

If anti-conscriptionists constituted a substantial part of the electorate in English Canada, they were the overwhelming majority in Quebec, where anti-conscription, and thus anti-government, feeling continued to run high after the election. In 1918, the Quebec legislature even debated a secessionist resolution. When conscription tribunals began hearing applications for military exemptions, violence erupted in the province. The worst incident occurred in late March 1918 in Quebec City, where furious crowds attacked the military service registry and trashed English businesses. When the police refused to intervene, Ottawa sent in troops from Toronto who, when provoked, opened fire, killing four people and injuring many more.

Whether conscription served its military purpose has been much debated, not only at the time, but also by subsequent generations of historians. Defaults and desertions were common, and tribunals were often sympathetic to local boys. Of the more than four hundred thousand men who registered under the legislation, less than one hundred thousand were successfully drafted and only twenty-four thousand went to France. Because of the difficulty of raising conscripts, the Fifth Division in Britain was dis-

*Canadian nurses at a hospital in France vote in the 1917 election.*

National Archives of Canada/PA2279

solved and its soldiers distributed among the thinning ranks of other divisions. The war ended a year after conscription had been imposed, but its effects were felt for a long time, not least in national politics, where the Liberal Party could claim that it had been Quebec's champion in a time of need.

## ENEMIES WITHIN

The Wartime Elections Act revealed another source of tension for a nation at war: the people whose former homeland was in enemy territory. In 1914, there were about half a million people in Canada who had been born in, or traced their origins to, Germany, Austria-Hungary, or the Ottoman Empire. Many of the hundred thousand enemy aliens—that is, people who still held citizenship in enemy countries—had arrived in the decade before the outbreak of war. As we have seen in chapter 4, some Canadians were apprehensive about the number of immigrants pouring into Canada in the early years of the twentieth century. This uncertainty turned into outright hostility under wartime pressures. Shortly after war was declared, rumours began to fly about an invasion of Canada by German Americans, and newspaper editors cried sabotage at the slightest provocation.

At first, the government was reluctant to bow to public hysteria. Enemy force reservists who attempted to return home were detained, but no further action was taken against enemy aliens. Within months, the official mood began to change. Enemy aliens in urban centres were forced to register with police authorities and were forbidden to carry arms. Those who lacked "the means to remain in Canada" were interned as prisoners of war and required "to do and perform such work as may be ... prescribed." Ultimately, over eighty-five hundred enemy aliens were interned, including over three thousand Canadian citizens, in twenty-four camps scattered across the country.

Major General Sir William Otter, a legendary veteran of the Fenian engagements of 1866, the Northwest Rebellion of 1885, and the South African War, was appointed director of Canadian internment operations. In the early months of the war, efforts to intern enemy aliens were directed less at potential saboteurs than at unemployed men, many of them Ukrainian labourers, whose presence in Canadian cities was profoundly resented by the long-time inhabitants. Otter initially established internment camps in northern Ontario and Quebec—Petawawa, Kapuskasing, and Spirit Lake—out of the way of nervous civilians. Between 1915 and 1917, some nine hundred men worked for six days a week at twenty-five cents a day, clearing land and building roads in several national parks. Others were contracted to private corporations to work as miners or farm labourers, but only after labour shortages put an end to the need to pursue "a patriotic preference for Canadian labour."

The facilities varied considerably. In Amherst, Nova Scotia, the Malleable Iron Works building housed a cosmopolitan group drawn from captures made in Bermuda, the West Indies, and Newfoundland as well as from foreign vessels that docked at Halifax. Its most famous inmate was the Russian communist leader Leon Trotsky, who apparently spent his short time there in 1917 trying to radicalize his fellow inmates. Elsewhere old forts, immigrant sheds, and exhibition buildings were commandeered into service to house internees. In Vernon, British Columbia, a comparatively well-appointed camp catered largely to the German immigrant elite who were living on the West Coast at the outbreak of the war.

Inevitably, tensions developed over disciplinary codes and labour demands imposed on prisoners. In the fall of 1917, the inmates at Kapuskasing refused an order to chop wood for the winter, resulting in an investigation of the conditions prevailing in the camp. The prisoners were eventually forced to comply not only because authorities in Germany wrote a note approving of such tasks as chopping wood, but also because guards at the camp became more "vigilant" in their pursuit of those who violated the rules. "I think that they have had enough of strikes and that prisoner being shot by a sentry the other day has made them realize what they are up against," Lieutenant Colonel W.E. Date informed Otter in November.[5] In all the camps, a total of six prisoners were killed by gunshot and four wounded in the course of their internment. Over a hundred others were confined to mental institutions and another hundred died in confinement, mostly of tuberculosis and pneumonia.

While it could be argued that the internees were prisoners of war and that their treatment fell well within the standards set by the 1907 Hague Convention, the reality was that men in camps such as Kapuskasing and Banff were discriminated against on the basis of class as well as culture. Wealthy German officers and civilians, who were

*Internees at their compound located in Castle Mountain in Banff, July 1915.*

Glenbow Archives, Millican Collection/ NA1870-6

interned in camps such as the one in Vernon, lived under much better conditions, with their families, servants, and a rich social life. For the men who were required to work in the national parks, there was a real sense that the prisoners were ineligible for the rights and privileges set aside for "real" Canadians. Throughout the war, historian Bill Waiser points out, Dominion Parks Commissioner J.B. Harkin was "forever extolling the virtues of the national parks system and how these special places would provide much-needed sanctuary and salvation when the guns finally fell silent. Sadly, the vision did not apply to the aliens. In making the

wonders of Banff, Jasper, Yoho, and Mount Revelstoke more accessible, the internees had known only exhaustion, suffering, fear, and devastation." [6]

In some respects, harassment of people who traced their origins to enemy countries was even worse than official sanctions and internment. Universities fired German professors, judges threw cases brought by alien plaintiffs out of court, and angry mobs attacked businesses owned by Germans and Austro-Hungarians. Even people whose families were deeply rooted in Canada, such as the Germans of Lunenburg County, Nova Scotia, and Waterloo County, Ontario, felt the wrath of wartime prejudice. In an effort to demonstrate their patriotism, the citizens of Berlin, Ontario, changed the name of their city to Kitchener in 1916, while people in Lunenburg County claimed their origins to be Dutch rather than German in the 1921 census.

Following the Bolshevik Revolution in the fall of 1917, radicals became the focus of attention in Canada. Pushed by an increasingly hysterical public, led by organizations such as the Toronto Anti-German League, the Union government cracked down on groups suspected of harbouring political dissidents. It issued an order-in-council making it an offence to print or possess any publication in an enemy language without a licence from the Secretary of State. "Foreign" organizations, including the Industrial Workers of the World, were banned as were meetings in which enemy languages were used. In British Columbia, tensions ran high when socialist labour leader "Ginger" Goodwin was shot by police constable Dan Campbell in 1918, ostensibly because Goodwin was evading the draft.

People who espoused pacifist views also found themselves subject to harassment by those who resented anyone who refused to fight. Acrimonious debates over the commitment to the war effort tore apart friendships, families, and organizations.

Nellie McClung recalled in 1945:

> The fall of 1914 blurs in my memory like a trou-
> bled dream. The war dominated everything. Some
> of my friends were pacifists and resented Canada's
> participation in the war of which we knew so lit-
> tle.... Chief among the Empire's defenders among
> the women was Miss Cora Hind. Her views were
> clear cut and definite. We were British and we
> must follow the tradition of our fathers. She would
> have gone herself if women were accepted. Miss
> Hind saw only one side of the question and there
> were times when I envied her, though I resented
> her denunciations of those who thought otherwise.
>
> The old crowd began to break up, and the good
> times were over.[7]

The views of journalist Cora Hind contrasted
dramatically with those of Francis Marion Beynon,
who lost her job as a columnist for the *Grain
Growers' Guide* during the war because she refused
to alter her pacifist views. She was not alone in
being driven from her comfortable prewar world.
In 1918, J.S. Woodsworth resigned from the
Methodist Church because it could no longer
tolerate his pacifist stance and social gospel
views that leaned too far to the left. Groups
such as the Mennonites and Hutterites, whose
religious convictions included a rigorous pacifism,
found themselves subject to both official and
unofficial sanctions in a country that increasingly
defined citizenship by the extent of one's military
participation.

## A White Man's War

Prejudices based on gender and race in large measure determined who could participate in the fighting. While women might keep the home fires
burning and serve behind the lines as nurses, there
was never any real thought given to allowing them
to be combatants in the fullest sense. Women, it
was believed, were too weak and emotional to stand
the rigours of battle and, in any event, it was men's
role to protect them. While women had been
struggling for entry into many avenues of public

life, few were interested in becoming soldiers.
However, many, especially the wives and girl-
friends of men serving in the forces, were keen to
go overseas, but they were systematically turned
down by military authorities. A few, such as the
Yukon's Martha Black, managed to get to Great
Britain at their own expense. There they worked as
volunteers in hospitals and other service institutions. As well, most of the more than three thousand women who joined the Canadian Army
Nursing Service went overseas. Forty-seven died
on duty, and many received distinguished service
awards, including Matron Ethel Ridley, who was
invested a Commander of the Order of the British
Empire for her work as principal matron in France.

The reasons for excluding "visible" minorities
from military service were more complex. For
many people, the notion of a racial hierarchy of
intelligence and ability led to the view that non-
whites would make inadequate soldiers. Others
were more paranoid in their thinking. If "the races"
got a taste of killing white men, where might their
martial energies ultimately be focused? Still others
felt uncomfortable fighting next to people unlike
themselves, and commanders argued that the efficiency of their unit would be compromised if racial
minorities were admitted.

Like other aspects of decision making, it took
some time for policy to be set with respect to the
recruitment of racial minorities. Only aboriginal
peoples were specifically denied admission to the
army from the outset, on the spurious grounds that
"Germans might refuse to extend to them the privileges of civilized warfare." Not widely publicized,
the directive was ignored by some militia officers,
who had wide discretion over whom to accept into
their unit. Throughout the war, officials repeatedly
insisted that there was no "colour line," but when
visible minorities offered their services, they were
invariably turned down by militia officers. Fifty
blacks from Sydney, Nova Scotia, who arrived at
the recruitment office were advised: "This is not
for you fellows, this is a white man's war."[8]

Canada's visible minorities, like white soldiers, were motivated by a sense of patriotism and
a yearning for adventure, but they also believed
that participation in the war would help them to

*Commanded by white officers, the No 2. Construction Battalion included blacks
from across Canada as well as 145 African Americans who crossed the border to participate
in the war. The battalion was attached to the Canadian Forestry Corps,
a labour unit whose job was to support the men fighting at the front.*

The Black Cultural Centre for Nova Scotia

improve the status of their people. So determined were they to be accepted that, in the face of rejection by recruitment offices, they formed their own segregated units and offered their services. On the West Coast, the Canadian Japanese Association enlisted 227 volunteers who drilled at their own expense. The crisis in recruitment helped to crack the wall of racial prejudice. In the fall of 1915, the directive against Canadian Indians was lifted, and thereafter they were recruited for the 114th Battalion and accepted into other units. African Canadians faced a more difficult battle, but they had champions in the Conservative Party from the Maritimes, including the prime minister. In April 1916, with Borden presiding, the Militia Council decided to form a black labour battalion headquartered in Nova Scotia. By the summer of 1916, Japanese men who had received basic training were admitted to eleven different battalions. Chinese men were also grudgingly accepted. When conscription was imposed, Natives and Asians were exempted because they were disenfranchised, and little effort was made to recruit black conscripts. In all, about thirty-five hundred Indians, over a thousand African Canadians, and several hundred Chinese and Japanese Canadians served in the Canadian forces.

Prejudice did not stop once they were in the army. Units composed of visible minorities were likely to be shunted into forestry and construction activities, and they were segregated whenever possible from whites. African Canadians were segregated on ships and in camps, and even had to wait for the creation of a separate "coloured" YMCA for their evening entertainment. Nor did their service in the war change their status once they returned home. It had remained a white man's war to the end, and the service of visible minorities was largely forgotten in accounts of the war effort.

## THE HALIFAX EXPLOSION

For all their problems at home and losses on the front, Canadians were relatively lucky as the belligerents went. Their territory was not invaded, and German submarines inflicted only limited damage on transports and fishing vessels in Canadian waters. Only once were Canadians offered a taste of what it was like to have their world devastated by the horrors of war. At 9:04 on the morning of 6 December 1917, the French munitions ship *Mont Blanc*, laden with explosives, collided with the Belgian relief ship *Imo* in Halifax harbour, producing one of the largest explosions in human history up to that time. Over sixteen hundred people were killed outright, another nine thousand were injured—including two hundred blinded by flying glass—and twenty thousand were left without adequate shelter for the coming winter. Homes, factories, train stations, churches, and a great sweep of harbour facilities disappeared in the blast or the subsequent fires and tidal wave that engulfed the city.

Already stretched to the limits by the demands placed on a busy wartime port, the citizens of Halifax were overwhelmed by the disaster. Makeshift mortuaries, hospitals, and shelters were set up in surviving churches, schools, and rinks, while people wandered aimlessly about the smoking rubble looking for lost loved ones. For weeks after the disaster, advertisements in local papers testified to the dislocation suffered by families.

> The owner of the baby girl about 2 months old which was handed to a young lady on Gottigen Street, being previously picked up on Almon Street by a soldier, in a pasteboard box covered with an older child's check coat, can get the same by applying at 1461 Shirley Street.

> Missing. Donald Cameron. Answers to Donnie, 4 1/2 years, fair hair, dark grey eyes. Wore red sweater or night gown. Was moved on first ambulance from Roome Street on Thursday morning. Father anxious.

> Would the soldier who rescued the baby from unconscious woman's arms on Longard Road the morning of the explosion return the baby to its parents, 9 Longard Road. [9]

As soon as word of the tragedy got out, help poured in from surrounding communities, from other provinces, from Ottawa, from Newfoundland, and eventually from around the world. The people of Massachusetts, where so many Maritime-born Canadians lived and worked,

were particularly generous. A Massachusetts–Halifax Relief Committee was established to raise donations and, in conjunction with the American Red Cross, dispatched a train equipped with medical personnel and supplies to the crippled city. Within days of the explosion, Colonel Robert Low, who had designed the camp at Valcartier, was on the job overseeing the construction of temporary accommodation on the South Common, around Citadel Hill, and anywhere else he could find space. Sir John Eaton, President of the T. Eaton Company, arrived in Halifax with his own train, food, sleeping car, staff, and medical unit. In Eaton's clothing store and supply depot, his staff handed out building materials and other necessities free of charge to anyone with a requisition signed by a pastor or relief committee official. Some $30 million, over half of it from the federal government, was provided to help Halifax and its sister town Dartmouth, which had also suffered from the blast, to recover from the devastation.

Once people were sorted out and the debris cleared away, officials settled down to impose order on the chaos caused by the blast. The progressive impulse was implicit in much of what was done. In January 1918, under the War Measures Act, the federal government established the Halifax Relief Commission to take charge of relief, medical care, and reconstruction. The commission decided to create a new town in the north end of the city, designed by urban planner Thomas Adams, who was in the employ of the Canadian Conservation Commission. To the marvel of visitors and residents alike, ten parallel blocks containing 326 houses, shopping facilities, boulevards, and green spaces rose out of the ashes of the explosion in the north-end suburb of Richmond Hill. The homes were built of hydrostone, a type of cement block moulded under pressure, which was manufactured in a factory built especially for the purpose. Known thereafter as the Hydrostone district, the neighbourhood proved to be the only enduring monument to the garden city dreams of the Halifax Relief Commission. Other development projects fell victim to dwindling resources and flagging idealism.

The gap between the progressive ideal and

*The Acadia Sugar Refinery before
and after the explosion.*

tion service, improving the milk and water supply, and overhauling municipal sanitation. While these were worthy objectives, they were compromised by vested interests and personality conflicts as well as by the high-handedness of commission officers. Their narrow "professional" vision of what constituted public health nearly lost the city a number of valuable social services, including the Victorian Order of Nurses.

The tension between labour and capital in Halifax was also heightened in the aftermath of the explosion. As part of its mandate, the Halifax Relief Commission had extraordinary powers to determine wages and working conditions for the projects it sponsored. The commission refused to recognize unions or to enter into collective bargaining, claiming that it was important that "a large amount of work be carried on at one time, so that the materials can be purchased more cheaply, and houses—particularly those of the less expensive class—be standardized and money saved."[10] Under such conditions, organized building trades in the city watched with growing concern as the commission paid more than the going rate for building materials and professional services and then violated its own wage rates.

As ten thousand workers connected with the building trades flooded the city competing for wages and living space, the Halifax Trades and Labour Council, which served as an umbrella organization for craft unions in the city, struggled to maintain "family wages" and the definition of skills, but often failed to do so. The commission's construction team worked ten to twelve hours a day, seven days a week, with no overtime rates. Cavicchi and Pegano, a railroad contracting firm from Montreal that employed twelve hundred unskilled labourers, came under particular criticism from local labourers, but they nevertheless stayed. When bricklayers held out for union wages, the commis-

the imperfect reality yawned in other aspects of the community response to the disaster. When the Halifax Relief Commission stepped in, the team from Massachusetts turned its attention from relief to helping the city to build a public health infrastructure. The explosion had focused attention on the high rate of infant mortality and tuberculosis in Halifax, problems that local health officials agreed should be addressed in any reconstruction effort. In 1918, the Massachusetts–Halifax Relief Commission sent public health expert Victor G. Heiser to report on conditions in Halifax. Heiser proposed building two new health centres, increasing laboratory facilities, developing a house visita-

sion decided that it would build its new garden community with hydrostone.

On 1 May 1919, two thousand men in the building trades conducted the largest strike ever seen in the port city. Two weeks later, the Trades and Labour Council began organizing a city-wide sympathy strike. Although the dispute over wages and hours was sent to arbitration in June, it marked a new stage in labour organization in Halifax. Workers were radicalized by what they saw as unfair treatment in the aftermath of the explosion. As a result, many of them threw their support behind the Nova Scotia Federation of Labour and its political arm, the Nova Scotia Labour Party, both founded in 1919.

After the explosion, there was widespread pressure to lay the blame on someone. People of German and French extraction were the most likely scapegoats in wartime Canada. In the days immediately following the disaster, rumour spread that the collision in the harbour had been the work of German saboteurs. One story had it that German spies had murdered the captain and the pilot of the *Imo* and engineered the collision. By the time a commission of inquiry, known as the Wreck Commission, began its work under Justice Arthur Drysdale, most people in Halifax, including Drysdale, were disposed to lay blame on the captain and pilot of the French ship, *Mont Blanc*, who had miraculously escaped injury, rather than the dead captain of the badly wrecked Belgian relief ship. Despite evidence that the harbour commission's safety regulations left much to be desired and that the *Imo* was as much to blame as the *Mont Blanc*, the Wreck Commission concluded that "the pilot and the master of the steamship *Mont Blanc* were wholly responsible for violating the rules of the road." Surprisingly, Drysdale also sat in judgement in the case that the owners of the *Mont Blanc* filed against the owners of the *Imo* but, not so surprisingly, he handed down a similar verdict. When the case was appealed to the Judicial Committee of the Privy Council, blame was assigned equally for the collision.

There were other sadly predictable developments. For many years before the explosion, Mi'kmaq living in Turtle Cove on the Dartmouth side of the harbour had been fighting against encroachment on their lands by their white neighbours. Turtle Cove took the full brunt of the blast. Although the Department of Indian Affairs had promised the residents of Turtle Cove reserve lands elsewhere if they agreed to relocate, the promise was conveniently forgotten in the aftermath of the explosion. A few years later, only five Mi'kmaq remained in Turtle Cove, the rest either killed or dispersed to other areas of the province, most with little compensation for their losses.

## CANADA ON THE WORLD STAGE

Borden's willingness to pursue an all-out war effort despite the opposition in Quebec owed much to his faith that Canada would emerge from the First World War with new international status. From the beginning, he pressed British authorities to give the dominion a voice in war planning. Borden argued passionately that Canadians would be unwilling to make greater sacrifices if they were not given a chance to affect policy at the highest level, but the British coalition government under H.H. Asquith continued to treat Canada as a colony.

Throughout the war, Canada had a London-based champion in Max Aitken, who had been elected as a Conservative to the British House of Commons in 1910. Aitken was a leading figure in the political manoeuvring that made David Lloyd George prime minister in late 1916, and, for his efforts, Lloyd George had Aitken elevated to the peerage. Under the new prime minister, who knew that the war was going badly and wanted Canadian help, the attitude in the British cabinet changed instantly with respect to both military policy and consultation with Canada and the other dominions of the empire. In 1917, he called an Imperial War Conference and created the Imperial War Cabinet—the British War Cabinet with dominion representation. These bodies met in 1918 as well, elevating Canada's status in the empire and giving Borden a huge amount of information and the opportunity to express his views. Nonetheless, the British remained firmly in control of their empire's war effort.

The United States entered the war against Germany in 1917. Canada had been instrumental in defending British policies to Americans who were suspicious of British imperialism and angered by the violation of the freedom of the seas represented by the British blockade of Germany. In 1918, with Britain otherwise preoccupied, the Canadians turned to the Americans for help to defend the East Coast of Canada from German raids. This "first North American joint defence initiative was short lived, designed solely to meet a specific emergency. The Americans had appeared to give grudgingly; the Canadians accepted the help, but cautiously."[11] It was for Borden another lesson in the importance of self-reliance: Canadians were going to have to do more on their own.

The presence of fresh American troops provided a shot in the arm for war-weary allied forces. By August 1918, the tide had turned. The final Hundred Days leading to the armistice on 11 November 1918 began with the battle of Amiens, spearheaded by Canadian troops. The Canadian Corps played a major role in bringing Germany to its knees in the last days of the fighting, but the cost was great: over thirty thousand casualties. But at least the bloody war was over.

Canada was represented in the British Empire Delegation to the Paris Peace Conference and separately signed the Versailles Treaty with Germany, the first time Canadians had signed a multilateral treaty. There would also be membership for Canada and other dominions in the new League of Nations, established to keep the peace, and the International Labour Organization, designed to maintain international labour standards. Despite these accomplishments, Canada had a long way to go before it would fully emerge as a nation in its own right.

Divided on how to pursue the war they had joined so naively, Canadians were equally divided on the meaning of their commitment to the international security system embodied in the League covenant. In a curious about-face, the United States refused to become a member of the League of Nations, even though it was American president Woodrow Wilson who had proposed the idea. Canada faced the new body awkwardly—enjoying the international prestige that membership brought, playing a valuable role in the league's social and humanitarian work, but rejecting the idea that the security of one member was the responsibility of all the other members.

## DEMOBILIZATION AND RECONSTRUCTION

The task of bringing back over three hundred thousand combatants and reintegrating them into civil society was almost as difficult as fighting the war. In October 1917, the government formed a cabinet committee on reconstruction and a few months later created a new Department of Soldiers Civil Re-Establishment to oversee the problems of demobilization. Its minister, Senator James Lougheed, was charged with responsibility for the Board of Pension Commissioners, the Soldiers' Land Settlement Scheme, hospital treatment and vocational training for the returned men, and the re-employment of munitions workers. Under Lougheed, the new department began building hospitals, nursing homes, and sanatoria and helped to establish programs to retrain the disabled. In 1919, a new Department of Health took over many of the responsibilities formerly handled by the provinces and volunteers.

What the cabinet did not predict, though it should have, was the rising tempers of soldiers when they were left hanging around Europe and Great Britain following the signing of the armistice. The lack of suitable transport and the inability of Canada's rail lines to carry more than twenty thousand troops a month from the nation's only major ice-free winter ports—Halifax and Saint John—created an explosive situation. In March, discontent among Canadian soldiers stationed in Wales burst into violent protest when a black guard arrested a white soldier and placed him under a "coloured" escort. White soldiers attacked their black compatriots, and in the ensuing mêlée five people were killed and twenty-seven injured. More riots followed in May. Determined to rid themselves of the troublesome Canadians, the British managed to find extra shipping capacity, and most Canadians were home by July.

The Great War Veterans' Association (GWVA), founded in Winnipeg in 1917, emerged as the voice of the former members of the CEF. At the war's end, the organization was dominated by able-bodied men who demanded their rights and would brook no opposition from Conservative ministers. This blunted any expectation by the government that they would have a ready-made voting bloc to guarantee victory in the 1921 election. By 1925, the GWVA was amalgamated with a number of other smaller organizations into the Canadian Legion, which was more cautious and non-partisan in its approach.

The long-term costs of helping returned men and their families was immense. In 1920, more than sixty-five hundred men were still in hospital. Over twenty thousand parents, wives, and children of dead soldiers qualified for pensions in 1925. As

*Veterans wait to disembark the* **Olympic** *at Halifax at the end of the war.*

National Archives of Canada/PA22996

health problems surfaced, the number of people qualifying for disability pensions rose from nearly forty-three thousand in 1919 to seventy-eight thousand in 1933. In the interwar period, the total cost of these and other programs for veterans ranked second after the national debt in government expenditures, with accumulated costs of over one billion dollars by 1935.

The costs of reconstruction helped to convince the government to demobilize its armed

forces as quickly as possible. Only three warships, two submarines, and the Royal Naval College survived from the larger wartime military establishment. The infant airforce was reborn in 1920 but only because of assistance from Great Britain and the United States. As before 1914, the militia absorbed the bulk of the defence budget, but there would be no massive standing army in Canada as a testament to the nation's role in the Great War.

## WHAT BRAVE NEW WORLD?

Many Canadians, particularly those who had long been committed to the reform of their society, believed that the war offered an unprecedented opportunity for national regeneration. In the crucible of conflict, reformers argued, old apathy and materialism would disappear and a better nation would emerge. A flood of publications asked contemporaries to take up the war's challenge of creating a just society: Nellie McClung's *In Times Like These* (1915), J.O. Miller's *The New Era in Canada* (1917), William Irvine's, *The Farmers in Politics* (1918), William Lyon Mackenzie King's *Industry and Humanity* (1918), Salem Bland's *The New Christianity* (1920), J.T.M. Anderson's *The Education of New Canadians* (1920), and Stephen Leacock's *The Unsolved Riddle of Social Justice* (1920). As usual, Leacock was one of the most articulate advocates for the reformed society that he felt could be achieved if governments would only agree to exercise the same powers for peace and prosperity as they had for war and reconstruction. "Put into the plainest prose," Leacock wrote in *The Unsolved Riddle of Social Justice*, "we are saying that the government of every country ought to supply work and pay for the unemployed, maintenance for the infirm and aged, and education and opportunity for the children." Nor was Leacock reluctant to draw lessons from wartime financing: "The finance of the war will be seen to be a lesson in the finance of the peace," he concluded. "The new burden has come to stay." [12]

Although French Canadians were generally far less optimistic about postwar prospects, reform-minded Catholics also developed a progressive social critique. Activists like Father Joseph Archambault, author of *La Question sociale et nos devoirs de catholiques* (1917) and the founder of the Catholic-action magazine *Semaine sociale*, pointed to the poverty, the class conflict, and the secularism that needed solutions if French Canada was to survive and prosper.

For many Canadians, the new era of liberal democracy offered potential for major reform. The Union government in 1918 followed up the Wartime Elections Act with legislation that gave the federal franchise to women on the same basis as men. During the war, the wall of opposition to female suffrage collapsed: in 1916, the three Prairie provinces adopted female suffrage, followed by Ontario and British Columbia in 1917, and Nova Scotia in 1918. Although New Brunswick extended the vote to women in 1919, they were not allowed to hold public office in that province until 1935. Prince Edward Island granted women the vote in 1922, and Newfoundland in 1925, but the latter based its legislation on British policy, which gave the vote to women over the age of twenty-five not, as for men, twenty-one. By 1920, most of the property and income restrictions placed on voting rights had also been swept away. After 1922, only status Indians, Asians in British Columbia, women in Quebec, and conscientious objectors, including Mennonites and Hutterites, were denied the right to vote.

Women's suffrage advocates had the pleasure not only of seeing the franchise question largely resolved, they also saw the beginning of an era in which programs specifically designated "women's issues," such as prohibition, mother's allowances, and minimum-wage legislation, were addressed. By 1920, allowances for destitute mothers were available in Manitoba (1916), Saskatchewan (1917), Alberta (1919), British Columbia (1920), and Ontario (1920). Under the provisions of the War Measures Act, the federal government implemented full prohibition in 1918, and following the war all provinces except for Quebec and British Columbia maintained the policy, at least for a few years. Alberta, in 1917, was the first jurisdiction to pass a minimum-wage law for women, a policy adopted during the 1920s by all provinces except New Brunswick and Prince Edward Island.

Women were slow to become directly involved in politics. Only four women out of 632 candidates ran in the 1921 federal election, and only one—Agnes Macphail, running on a Progressive ticket in Grey County, Ontario—won a seat. In 1918, a group of Ontario women from the National Equal Franchise Union attempted to form a non-partisan Women's Party, but it was opposed by western women, and the idea quickly floundered. The maternal feminist perspective made it difficult for women, whose first duty was to their families, to take up politics in a systematic way. For most women, the franchise served primarily as a means of pressing politicians to pass reform legislation, not as a means of creating "more work for mother." The National Council of Women developed a policy of adopting a Canadian Women's Platform to identify issues to be pursued through the established political parties. In 1920, the platform included demands for equal pay for equal work, the female minimum wage, and political equality of the sexes. Party organizations successfully resisted attempts to integrate women fully into their activities, much to the disappointment of some suffrage leaders who had hoped that the vote would transform Canadian political life.

Suffragists were not alone in being disillusioned by the failure of the war to usher in a major transformation in society. Higher profits for a few were accompanied by low wages, repressive working conditions, and a spiralling cost of living for many. Desperate to mobilize resources for war and with few close ties to labour, governments did little to rectify abuses. The great influenza epidemic of the winter of 1918–19 further dampened morale. It killed as many as fifty thousand Canadians—almost as many as died in the trenches—leaving citizens everywhere reeling with shock. In Labrador, half of the population succumbed to the flu. Such disasters contributed to a rising tide of discontent that swept the nation when the war ended.

Domestic conflicts may have developed in response to specific Canadian conditions, but they did not develop in isolation. The Bolshevik Revolution in Russia and the rising tide of socialist and communist protest in Europe and the United States inspired many Canadians, just as it terrified Canadian politicians and capitalists. When Borden dispatched Canadian troops in 1918–19 as part of a combined allied endeavour to put an end to the Russian Revolution, the labour movement in Canada protested what they saw as yet one more instance of state support for a system that privileged only the rich and powerful.

Unhappy as it might be with the Union government, the labour movement was also deeply divided. Conservative eastern craft unionism took control of the Trades and Labour Congress at the 1918 convention, but the Western Labour Conference held shortly thereafter in Calgary broke with TLC policies of conciliation and restraint. Those attending the conference resolved to create a single industrial union, the One Big Union (OBU), to challenge conservative unionists, hostile employers, and unsympathetic governments. Unlike the anti-electoral IWW, now deemed an illegal organization, the leadership of the fledgling OBU included many socialists who saw strike action as only one arm of class struggle and electioneering as its complement. But before the fledgling OBU could hold its founding convention, its strike philosophy had an unanticipated dry run.

On 15 May 1919, the Winnipeg Trades and Labour Council called a general strike following the breakdown of negotiations between management and labour in the metal and building trades in the city. At stake were the principle of collective bargaining and better wages and working conditions. Although only twelve thousand of Winnipeg's workers belonged to a union of any kind, about thirty thousand workers joined the strike within hours of the call for action. They included telephone operators and department store clerks who had waged successful wartime strikes and hoped to consolidate their gains by working to strengthen the labour movement as a whole. Winnipeg's strike sparked a series of general strikes of varying lengths across the country. Although these strikes were ostensibly held in support of the

Winnipeg workers, local grievances, such as the ones in post-explosion Halifax, came to the fore everywhere. Some Canadian leaders were convinced that they had a revolution on their hands.

Internal divisions and lack of resources had caused most of the strikes to come to an end within a month. The Winnipeg strike was the longest, stretching from 15 May to 26 June. While its leaders made every effort to keep it orderly, agreeing to have essential services such as milk delivery continue throughout the strike, it faced formidable obstacles. Opponents of the strike, drawn mainly from employer and professional groups in the city, organized a committee to crush the strike and discredit its leadership. Insisting that the strike was Bolshevik-inspired, the Citizens' Committee of One Thousand refused to let the issue of employees' right to collective bargaining become the sole focus of the debate.

When it became apparent that the city's police supported the strikers, the committee influenced the mayor in having the entire force replaced by people unsympathetic to the strike. With encouragement from the anti-strike forces, the federal government sent the Royal North West Mounted Police to Winnipeg, allegedly to maintain order. On 21 June—a day that became known as Bloody Saturday—the Mounties attempted to disperse war veterans holding an illegal demonstration in support of the strike. The demonstrators refused to leave and the police fired a volley of shots into the crowd. By the end of the day, two men were dead and many other protesters were injured.

Following the confrontation, strikers were arrested by the score. Included among those jailed were two Winnipeg aldermen and a member of the Manitoba legislature. Recognizing the state's determination to crush the strike, those leaders who had not yet been imprisoned capitulated on 26 June. Winnipeg would remain a class-divided city for generations to come. Its working-class residents north of Portage Avenue were now as separated politically as they were culturally from the wealthier citizens in the city's south end.

The federal government moved quickly to pass laws that would make radical protest difficult,

## BLOODY SATURDAY

Labour and capital viewed the events of 21 June 1919 in Winnipeg in entirely different ways. Following is the official strikers' view of the events of that afternoon as reported in **Strike Bulletin**, the newspaper published by the Strike Committee.

One is dead and a number injured, probably thirty or more, as a result of the forcible prevention of the "silent parade" which had been planned by returned men to start at 2:30 o'clock last Saturday afternoon. Apparently the bloody business was carefully planned, for Mayor Gray issued a proclamation in the morning stating that "Any women taking part in a parade do so at their own risk." Nevertheless a vast crowd of men, women and children assembled to witness the "silent parade."...

On Saturday, about 2:30 p.m., just the time when the parade was scheduled to start, some 50 mounted men swinging baseball bats rode down Main Street. Half were red-coated

R.N.W.M.P., the others wore khaki. They quickened pace as they passed the Union Bank. The crowd opened, let them through and closed in behind them. They turned and charged through the crowd again, greeted by hisses and boos, and some stones. There were two riderless horses with the squad when it emerged and galloped up Main Street. The men in khaki disappeared at this juncture, but the red-coats reined their horses and reformed opposite the old post office.

Then, with revolvers drawn, they galloped down Main Street, turned, and charged right into the crowd on William Avenue, firing as they charged. One man, standing on the sidewalk, thought the mounties were firing blank cartridges until a spectator standing beside him dropped with a bullet through the head. We have no exact information about the total number of casualties, but these were not less than thirty. The crowd dispersed as quickly as possible when the shooting began.

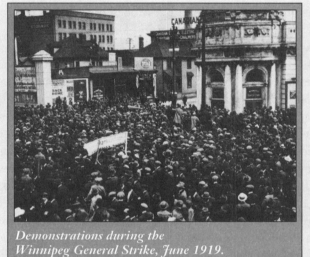

*Demonstrations during the Winnipeg General Strike, June 1919.*
Provincal Archives of Manitoba

if not impossible. Section 98 of the Criminal Code, passed in the House on 7 July, outlawed any organization whose professed purpose was to bring about "governmental, industrial or economic change" by force. Penalties for membership in such an organization included a maximum twenty-year jail sentence. Even attending a meeting, advocating the principles, or distributing the literature of such an organization could result in charges under section 98. With the "red scare" motivating much of the government's policy after 1919, many Protestant middle-class reformers retreated from their earlier idealism for fear of being targeted for harbouring politically unacceptable views.

Like the differences that increasingly separated French and English Canada, a heightened awareness of class division was a long-term legacy of the First World War. Left-wing parties benefited from such divisions. In 1921, J.S. Woodsworth, who was imprisoned for his role as editor of the strike newspaper in the latter days of the Winnipeg General Strike, was elected to represent Winnipeg's working-class north end in Parliament as a member of the Independent Labour Party. Some veterans of the strike would join the Communist Party of Canada when it was formed clandestinely in 1921.

The Labour and Communist parties were not

the only expression of political diversity that followed in the wake of the war. In 1916, the Canadian Council of Agriculture developed the Farmers' Platform, which included a call for free trade; graduated income, inheritance, and corporation taxes; nationalization of railway, telegraph, and express companies; and reform of the political process to eliminate the problems created by patronage, corruption, and centralized party discipline. Farmer candidates ran in the 1917 election on the Union ticket, but they were not converted to the Conservative cause. When exemption from conscription for farmers' sons was cancelled in 1918, some five thousand farmers marched on Ottawa in protest. In the same year, the Farmers' Platform was fleshed out and rechristened the New National Policy.

It was not long before such protest was reflected in party politics. In Ontario a coalition of Farmer and Labour party candidates under the leadership of E.C. Drury won the election in 1919. The success in the Ontario provincial election and the support for farm candidates in Prairie constituencies encouraged efforts to form a party to fight on the national level. In the final months of 1919, the National Progressive Party came into being under the leadership of Thomas Crerar, a member of Parliament from Manitoba who had been invited into the Union cabinet as a representative of the farmers.

The Liberal and Conservative Parties came

out of the war much altered but not entirely obliterated by the experience of Union government. When Laurier died in 1919, he was replaced as party leader by William Lyon Mackenzie King, a former minister of labour who claimed to personify the progressive spirit of the age. King was determined to win back the alienated Progressives—"Liberals in a hurry," he would come to call them—while retaining the party's strength in Quebec. Borden, exhausted by the war, withdrew from politics, leaving his successor, Arthur Meighen, the impossible tasks of running the divided country and pulling the Conservative Party together to fight a postwar election.

## CONCLUSION

Anyone surveying the political scene on the New Year's Eve ushering in the 1920s must have wondered what kind of revolution was taking place. So much had changed since 1911, the last time that Canadians had voted in a peacetime election. With the enfranchisement of women, the potential electorate had doubled. So, too, had the number of political parties. Many voters in the next federal election would have the opportunity to choose Progressive, Labour, or various independent candidates instead of solely Liberals or Conservatives. As we will see in the next chapter, almost a third of Canadians would do so.

## CONSCRIPTION

### A Historiographical Debate

Why was conscription introduced? Was it a military necessity? Did its introduction signal Canada's desire to assert itself in international affairs or did it reflect subservience to Britain? Did its proponents carry the 1917 election by deliberately employing anti-French-Canadian messages? Historians of conscription have offered varied answers to these questions and, perhaps not surprisingly, much of the division has been between francophone and anglo-

phone historians.

According to one perspective, political pressure from English Canada forced the government's hand. Borden was "responding to the will of the English-speaking majority," write the authors of the authoritative history of Quebec in this period.[13] English-Canadian historians agree that there was pressure on the government for conscription, but they note that the government was aware that English Canadians were divided on the issue and feared that conscription might lose votes for a government already in difficulties.[14] Borden and his key ministers, they argue, imposed conscription because of British pressure for a greater Canadian commitment to the war effort. Moreover, Borden's own conviction that Canada should do more left the government few options when voluntary recruitment failed to meet the government's targets for fighting men.

From this viewpoint, conscription was a military necessity. Military historian A.M. Willms claims that, proportionate to its population, Canada before 1917 had contributed fewer military recruits than the other white-settler dominions. More recruits were necessary because of the heavy casualties of war.[15] French-Canadian historians have argued that this interpretation accepts the Allied view that a peace treaty was not negotiable. Robert Rumilly's biography of Henri Bourassa stresses the view that negotiations were possible if both sides gave up the idea that there had to be a clear victor.[16]

Rumilly and other French-Canadian historians have generally accepted Bourassa's view that no great principles were at stake in the war, but English-Canadian historians have rejected the view that Canada simply subordinated itself to British imperialism. Ramsay Cook, explaining the support for conscription by *Winnipeg Free Press* editor, John W. Dafoe, suggests that many English Canadians who fought for greater Canadian autonomy from Britain believed the war was being fought over "cherished values" of democracy and not from motives of "sycophantic colonialism or aggressive imperialism."[17] The government's embrace of the view that this was a battle for "Canadian liberty and autonomy" is noted in a recent history of the First World War that emphasizes Borden's insistence on Canadian involvement both in war planning and in shaping the postwar world.[18]

How did the government win the election that allowed it to impose a measure it deemed necessary in this battle for "liberty?" Most historians agree that the Wartime Elections Act did not respect the liberty of all citizens, but there is less agreement about the extent to which the government resorted to ethnocentric appeals in its attempts to overcome anglophone divisions about the fairness of imposing conscription. Roger Graham, who wrote a biography on the influential cabinet minister and later prime minister Arthur Meighen, claims that the government attempted to avoid having the election contribute to national disunity.[19] French-Canadian historians dismiss this claim, noting that the whole purpose of conscription was to assuage English-Canadian opinion that French Canadians were not doing their share.[20] Some anglophone historians also disagree with Graham's suggestion that the government took the high road in the election of 1917. Note J.L. Granatstein and J.M. Hitsman: "The Union Government campaign, founded on the Military Service Act and the War Time Elections Act, deliberately set out to create an English-Canadian nationalism, separate from and opposed to both French Canada and naturalized Canadians. No other conclusion can be drawn from this election campaign, one of the few in Canadian history deliberately conducted on racist grounds."[21]

## NOTES

[1] Quoted in Desmond Morton and J.L. Granatstein, *Marching to Armageddon: Canadians and the Great War, 1914–1919* (Toronto: Lester and Orpen Dennys, 1989), 5–6

[2] Robert Craig Brown and Ramsay Cook, *Canada: 1896–1921: A Nation Transformed* (Toronto: McClelland and Stewart, 1974), 239

[3] Daphne Read, ed., *The Great War and Canadian Society: An Oral History* (Toronto: New Hogtown Press, 1978), 100

[4] Desmond Morton, *A Military History of Canada* (Edmonton: Hurtig Publishers, 1990), 136

[5] Joseph A. Boudreau, "Interning Canada's 'Enemy Aliens,' 1914–1919," *Canada: An Historical Magazine* 2, 1 (Sept. 1974): 23

[6] Bill Waiser, *Parks Prisoners: The Untold Story of Western Canada's National Parks, 1915–1946* (Saskatoon: Fifth House Limited, 1995), 47

[7] Cited in Alison Prentice et al., *Canadian Women: A History* (Toronto: Harcourt Brace Jovanovich, 1988), 207

[8] Cited in James W. St G. Walker, "Race and Recruitment in World War I: Enlistment of Visible Minorities in the Canadian Expeditionary Force," *Canadian Historical Review* 70, 1 (March 1989): 1–26

[9] Janet F. Kitz, *Shattered City: The Halifax Explosion and the Road to Recovery* (Halifax: Nimbus, 1989), 82

[10] Suzanne Morton, "The Halifax Relief Commission and Labour Relations during the Construction of Halifax, 1917–1919" in *Workers and the State in Twentieth Century Nova Scotia*, ed. Michael Earle (Fredericton: Acadiensis Press, 1989), 54

[11] J.L. Granatstein and Norman Hillmer, *For Better or for Worse: Canada and the United States to the 1990s* (Toronto: Copp Clark Pitman, 1991), 69

[12] Stephen Leacock, *The Unsolved Riddle of Social Justice*, cited in Alan Bowker, ed., *The Social Criticism of Stephen Leacock* (Toronto: University of Toronto Press, 1973), 140–41

[13] Paul-André Linteau, René Durocher, and Jean-Claude Robert, *Quebec: A History, 1867–1929* (Toronto: Lorimer, 1983), 524

[14] See, for example, J.L. Granatstein and J.M. Hitsman, *Broken Promises: A History of Conscription in Canada* (Toronto: Oxford University Press, 1977), 67

[15] A.M. Willms, "Conscription 1917: A Brief for the Defence" in *Conscription 1917*, ed. Ramsay Cook, Craig Brown, and Carl Berger (Toronto: University of Toronto Press, 1969), 1–14

[16] Robert Rumilly, *Henri Bourassa: La Vie publique d'un grand canadien* (Montreal: Les Éditions Chantecler, 1953), 544

[17] Ramsay Cook, "Dafoe, Laurier and the Formation of the Union Government" in *Conscription 1917*, 15–38

[18] Morton and Granatstein, *Marching to Armageddon*, 145

[19] Roger Graham, *Arthur Meighen*, vol. 1, *The Door of Opportunity* (Toronto: Clark, Irwin, 1960), 194-95

[20] Linteau, Durocher, and Robert, *Quebec*, 524

[21] Granatstein and Hitsman, *Broken Promises*, 78

## SELECTED READING

Borden's administration is discussed in R. Craig Brown, *Robert Laird Borden*, 2 vols. (Ottawa: Carleton University Press, 1969); Robert Craig Brown and Ramsay Cook, *Canada, 1896–1921: A Nation Transformed* (Toronto: McClelland and Stewart, 1974); and John English, *The Decline of Politics: The Conservatives and the Party System* (Toronto: University of Toronto Press, 1977).

The military experience of the war is described in G.W.L. Nicholson, *Canadian Expeditionary Force, 1914–1919* (Ottawa: Queen's Printer, 1964), and *Canada's Nursing Sisters* (Toronto: S. Stevens, 1975); Desmond Morton and J.L. Granatstein, *Marching to Armageddon: Canadians and the Great War, 1914–1918* (Toronto: Lester and Orpen Dennys, 1989); Michael L. Hadley and Roger Sarty, *Tin-Pots and Pirate Ships: Canadian Naval Forces and German Sea Raiders, 1880–1918* (Montreal: McGill-Queen's University Press, 1991); S.F. Wise, *Canadian Airmen and the First World War*

(Toronto: University of Toronto Press, 1980); Stephen Harris, *Canadian Brass: The Making of a Professional Army, 1860–1939* (Toronto: University of Toronto Press, 1988); and Duff Crerar, *Padres in No Man's Country: Canadian Chaplains and the Great War* (Montreal: McGill-Queen's University Press, 1995). External affairs are the subject of Norman Hillmer and J.L. Granatstein, *Empire to Umpire: Canada and the World to the 1990s* (Toronto: Copp Clark Longman, 1994).

On the war at home, see Daphne Read, ed., *The Great War and Canadian Society: An Oral History* (Toronto: New Hogtown, 1978); Barbara M. Wilson, *Ontario and the First World War* (Toronto: University of Toronto Press, 1977); Frances Swyripa and John Thompson, eds., *Loyalties in Conflict: Ukrainians in Canada During the Great War* (Edmonton: University of Alberta Press, 1983); and John Herd Thompson, *The Harvests of War: The Prairie West, 1914–1918* (Toronto: McClelland and Stewart, 1978). See Alison Prentice et al., *Canadian Women: A History*, 2nd ed. (Toronto: Harcourt Brace, 1996) on the experience of women during and after the war.

Works dealing with conscription include J.L. Granatstein and J.M. Hitsman, *Broken Promises: A History of Conscription in Canada* (Toronto: Oxford University Press, 1977); Ramsay Cook, Craig Brown, and Carl Berger, eds., *Conscription 1917* (Toronto: University of Toronto Press, 1969); and Paul-André Linteau, René Durocher, and Jean-Claude Robert, *Quebec: A History, 1867–1929* (Toronto: Lorimer, 1983).

The role of visible minorities is the subject of James W. St G. Walker, "Race and Recruitment in World War I: Enlistment of Visible Minorities in the Canadian Expeditionary Force," *Canadian Historical Review* 70, 1 (March 1989): 1–26; Calvin W. Ruck, *The Black Battalion, 1916–20* (Halifax: Nimbus, 1987); and John G. Armstrong, "The Unwelcome Sacrifice: A Black Unit in the Canadian Expeditionary Force" in *Ethnic Armies*, ed. N.F. Dreiziger (Waterloo, ON: Wilfrid Laurier University Press, 1990), 178–97. Internment camps are discussed in Joseph A. Boudreau, "Interning Canada's 'Enemy Aliens,' 1914–1919," *Canada: An Historical Magazine* 2, 1 (Sept. 1974): 15–27, and Bill Waiser, *Parks Prisoners: The Untold Story of Western Canada's National Parks, 1915–1946* (Saskatoon: Fifth House Limited, 1995). The Halifax Explosion is explored in Janet F. Kitz, *Shattered City: The Halifax Explosion and the Road to Recovery* (Halifax: Nimbus, 1989), and Alan Ruffman and Colin D. Howell, eds., *Ground Zero: A Reassessment of the 1917 Explosion in Halifax Harbour* (Halifax: Nimbus, 1994). Suzanne Morton discusses the Hydrostone development in *Ideal Surroundings: Domestic Life in a Working-Class Suburb* (Toronto: University of Toronto Press, 1995).

Problems relating to demobilization are discussed in Desmond Morton and Glenn Wright, *Winning the Second Battle: Canadian Veterans and the Return to Civilian Life, 1915–1930* (Toronto: University of Toronto Press, 1987). On pacifists, see Thomas Socknat, *Witness Against War: Pacifism in Canada, 1900–1945* (Toronto: University of Toronto Press, 1987). The influenza epidemic is discussed in Janice P. Dickin McGinnis, "The Impact of Epidemic Influenza, 1918–1919," *Canadian Historical Association Historical Papers* (1977): 121–40.

On worker radicalism during and after the war, see A. Ross McCormack, *Reformers, Rebels, and Revolutionaries* (Toronto: University of Toronto Press, 1977); David Bercuson, *Fools and Wise Men: The Rise and Fall of One Big Union* (Toronto: McGraw-Hill Ryerson, 1978); and James Naylor, *The New Democracy: Challenging the Social Order in Industrial Ontario, 1914–1925* (Toronto: University of Toronto Press, 1991). On the 1919 strikes, see Harry Gutkin and Mildred Gutkin, *Profiles in Dissent: The Shaping of Radical Thought in the Canadian West* (Edmonton: NeWest, 1997); David Bercuson, *Confrontation at Winnipeg: Labour, Industrial Relations, and the General Strike* (Montreal: McGill-Queen's University Press, 1990); Alan Artibise, *Winnipeg: A Social History of Urban Growth, 1874–1914* (Montreal: McGill-Queen's University Press, 1975); Paul Philips, *No Power Greater* (Vancouver: BC Federation of Labour, 1967); and Gregory S. Kealey, "1919: The Canadian Labour Revolt," *Labour/Le Travail* 13 (Spring 1984): 11–44. Works on postwar repression include Larry Hannant, *The Infernal Machine: Investigating the Loyalty of Canada's Citizens* (Toronto: University of Toronto Press, 1995); Barbara Roberts, *Whence They Came: Deportation from Canada, 1900–1935* (Ottawa: University of Ottawa Press, 1988); and Donald Avery, *Dangerous Foreigners: European Immigrant Workers and Labour Radicalism in Canada* (Toronto: McClelland and Stewart, 1979).

# 8

# THE STATE IN
# TRANSITION, 1921–1939

As the 1930s Depression descended, Ed Bates, a butcher in Glidden, Saskatchewan, found it impossible to make ends meet, so he moved his family and business to Vancouver. Again the Depression claimed the Bates family for victims and they were forced to seek relief. Denied welfare by the Vancouver authorities because of their recent arrival in that city, they attempted to get social assistance in Saskatoon, only to be told they must return to Glidden to apply for help. Too proud to return home to live on welfare, they rented a car and tried to kill themselves by carbon monoxide poisoning. Ed and his wife, Rose, survived the suicide attempt, but their son Jack did not, and they were charged with his murder. While there was no doubt that their actions had caused Jack's death, local citizens blamed the politicians, rather than the parents, for the tragedy. A defence committee was formed, and a coroner's jury found Ed and Rose Bates not guilty in the death of their son.[1]

The Bates family tragedy occurred during the Great Depression, an economic catastrophe unprecedented in its intensity. There was, to be sure, a period of serious recession and accompanying economic hardship following the war, but it was short-lived. By the mid-1920s, the Canadian economy—with the significant exception of the Atlantic region—was booming. When these relatively good times gave way to the 1930s Depression, ever-increasing numbers of people came to blame the political and economic system, rather than the individual, for widespread poverty

*Destitute family in Saskatchewan, 1934.*
Glenbow Archives/ND 3-6742

and its tragic consequences. Increasingly, too, Canadians began to demand that the state intervene to ensure that others never reached the desperate straits experienced by the Bates family.

The growth of the state at all levels—federal, provincial, and municipal—was one response to the social pressures facing Canadians after the First World War. As we shall see in this chapter, the reforms demanded by Canadian citizens were taken seriously by political leaders, though politicians were slow to act and were increasingly at odds among themselves about what should be done. The contradictions that confronted the democratic state in a capitalist economy led easily to inaction. While the politicians competing for power required the support of voters, they also had to be careful not to offend the interests of the corporate leaders who dominated the marketplace. Macdonald and Laurier had managed to survive politically by seeking compromise and accommodation among contending interests. In the interwar years, with a wider electorate and dramatic developments in the market economy, it was much more difficult to establish a consensus that would ensure political stability.

## THE MACKENZIE KING ERA

The career of William Lyon Mackenzie King sheds some light on the ways in which political leaders tried to manage the contradictory demands placed upon them. When Laurier died early in 1919, the Liberal Party had been out of power for eight years. Party organizers decided to hold a leadership convention in Ottawa to secure maximum publicity. In response to postwar labour and farmer radicalism, the Liberals adopted a platform that included the promise of state-supported old age pensions, unemployment insurance, and health care. These programs, the party declared, would form the basis of a Canadian welfare state that guaranteed all citizens a minimum level of security.

Liberal power-brokers viewed Mackenzie King as a logical candidate to convince Canadians of the party's reformist intentions while reassuring vested interests that they would not be unduly dis-

rupted. The grandson of the leader of the Upper Canadian Rebellion of 1837, King had been a prominent civil servant and served as Canada's first minister of labour in the final years of the Laurier regime. He then amassed a fortune as a consultant for American corporations attempting to dampen labour radicalism, beginning with John D. Rockefeller's coal-mining interests in Colorado. When he agreed to run for the Liberal Party leadership, wealthy Canadians, headed by the heir to the Salada Tea fortune, put together a trust fund to ensure that King's high standard of living would not suffer from his decision to enter political life.

King's blueprint for social reform could be found in his book *Industry and Humanity* (1918), in which he proclaimed, amid a welter of platitudes, that the interests of capital and labour, viewed from a long-term perspective, were one. What was necessary for the benefit of the larger society was to get both sides to recognize their common interests and to work together to find solutions. The state could contribute by mediating between labour and capital and by guaranteeing to all a minimum economic and social standard. In taking this position, King was not advocating new ideas. Such policies were already in place in Europe, where state intervention far exceeded anything contemplated in North America.

Once in power, King found excuses for not moving too quickly with a reform agenda. His career in public office suggests that he acted on social policy only when he was convinced that popular pressure gave him no other choice. Most of the time, he felt constrained by the combined pressures of big corporations, conservative elements in his party, and provincial premiers determined to protect their constitutional jurisdictions. Nonetheless, by 1945, King's government had legislated a variety of reforms, including pensions, national unemployment insurance, and family allowances. These policies served as the foundation of Canada's relatively conservative version of the modern welfare state.

King's caution in domestic policy was more than equalled on the international front. He believed firmly that national unity and Liberal Party unity—King usually confused the two—depended upon placating Quebec's anger over the imposition of conscription in 1917. To secure the trust of Quebeckers, King felt it necessary to serve notice to Great Britain that Canada would not be dragged into another war to protect imperial interests. King supported an isolationist policy for Canada in the interwar years, refusing to take a tough stand against Hitler's illegal rearmament of Germany and persecution of the Jews, and turning a blind eye when Germany, Italy, and Japan began their military assaults on independent nations. At the same time, King was quick to sense that the political mood was shifting. When Britain, whose leaders had tried for years to appease the dictators, finally went to war with Germany, King had no hesitation in accepting that Canada must fight at Britain's side.

King's contemporaries had difficulty following the twists and turns of his political thought. After his death, King became even more of an enigma when his political diaries revealed a side of the prime minister known only to his closest friends. King had planned to destroy his diaries once he had used them to write his memoirs but they survived to provide a fascinating picture of the private thoughts of a public man. In the pages of these intensely intimate documents, King is shown as a mystic, a believer in numerology, and a devoté of seances and fortune-tellers. Though politically cunning to a fault—the diaries offer conclusive evidence on this point—King's thinking was a mix of the rational and the irrational that still leaves scholars wondering what manner of man filled the position as Canada's longest-serving prime minister.

King was a bundle of contradictions: a prudish bachelor who had close relations with married women, a hard-headed realist who talked to his dog and his dead mother, an opponent of privilege who gave important cabinet and patronage posts to businessmen and party funders. Ultimately, the contradictions in his thought and actions revealed much about the ambiguities that characterized many Canadians. An incident recorded in King's diaries illustrates the point. One winter day, as the prime minister was walking near his home in Ottawa, he saw an old man who had fallen on the ice. He helped the man up and then walked him

*Mackenzie King governed the country from 1921 to 1930 and again from 1935 to 1948.*

National Archives of Canada/C9062

home. Unaware that he was walking with the prime minister, the man told King that he was a Russian Jew who had fled persecution and poverty at home and had become a wealthy department-store owner in Canada. When they arrived at the man's door, King disclosed his identity. The old man's eyes lit up with surprise, the prime minister noted in his diary. King went on to praise Canada as a country where a persecuted Russian Jew could make a fortune and be walked home by the prime minister. As an afterthought, he added that it was troubling to think that Jews like this old man had moved into the Sandy Hill area of Ottawa, and he worried that the area would be overrun with Jews.

## REGIONAL AND CLASS PROTEST IN THE 1920s

The 1921 federal election set the stage for a new era in Canadian political life. Not only were there new political parties to contend with, but the result also produced a minority government, the first in the nation's history. It came as no surprise that the Conservatives lost the election. The Union government had begun to disintegrate shortly after the armistice, with its Liberal members returning either to their old political home or to the new Progressive Party. While Arthur Meighen brought new leadership to the Conservative Party in 1920, he was not a popular prime minister. He had been involved in drawing up the legislation to impose conscription in 1917 and had taken the decision to use the Mounties against the Winnipeg strikers. Despite the fact that he represented Portage la Prairie, Manitoba, in the House of Commons, Meighen was an arch-defender of Tory high tariff policies, which were unpopular in the West. He was an easy target for all those who believed that the Borden government had allowed profiteers to benefit from the war while ordinary people suffered.

In the federal election of 1921, the Conservatives were decisively beaten, taking only 50 seats to 116 for the Liberals. The success of the Liberals in Quebec, where they won all of the province's 65 ridings, was a foregone conclusion, given the lingering hostility of Quebeckers to conscription. The real surprise on election night was the success of the Progressive Party, which had come second to the Liberals with 64 seats in Parliament. Calling for the public ownership of utilities and a speedy elimination of all tariffs, the Progressives apparently struck a responsive chord among rural residents in English Canada.

This result followed a provincial trend that began in 1919 with the election of a minority United Farmers of Ontario government supported by the province's Independent Labour Party. The following year, a Farmer–Labour coalition emerged as the opposition party in Nova Scotia. In 1921, the United Farmers of Alberta headed a majority government even though they had run candidates only in rural seats and had won just 28 percent of the popular vote. In 1922, it was Manitoba's turn to elect a government run by farmers. In all three farmer-run provinces, a healthy labour component in the legislature suggested that old-party dominance in urban and industrial areas was as unsteady as it was in the countryside. Yet, by 1939, the Progressive Party was long dead and the only remaining farmers' government was in Manitoba, where the Progressive Party had merged with the Liberals in

1928 and no longer presented itself as the voice of only one segment of the community. What happened to a movement that seemed to show so much promise in the opening years of the 1920s?

## THE PROGRESSIVE PARTY

As we have seen, farmers in the early decades of the twentieth century had become increasingly concerned that their status as the bedrock of the nation was being eroded. Frustrated by business dominance in the Liberal and Conservative Parties, many farmers found the idea of a new political party attractive. The Progressive Party arose as an attempt by the organized farm movement to unite farmers around a political program and elect members of Parliament who would speak for farmers' interests. This new political formation reflected the belief that Liberal and Conservative MPs, even when they themselves were farmers, toed the party line rather than representing their constituents.

Despite the widespread discontent in most farming communities, the Progressive Party faced real obstacles in becoming a truly national party. Its first leader, Thomas A. Crerar, had been a conscriptionist Liberal and a cabinet minister in Borden's Union government, which limited his appeal in rural Quebec. Like Canadians generally, the Progressives were divided on questions of economic restructuring. Opposition to tariffs held party supporters together, but there were strong disagreements on the merits of public control of railways, utilities, and the marketing of grain. While Crerar was a strong free enterprise, many Progressives had won elections promising their constituents to press for nationalization of the CPR and the restoration of the wartime policy of orderly grain marketing through the government-run Canadian Wheat Board.

The grass-roots character of the Progressives made it impossible to establish a national organization with control over local constituencies. At best, Progressives were a loose coalition of provincial organizations, a coalition within which the split between the radical and conservative wings made it difficult to come to an agreement on policy. On the conservative side, disenchanted imperialist Liberals, mostly from Ontario and Manitoba, focused on the party's reform agenda and rejected any notion of transforming the economic and political system. A more radical wing, based primarily in Alberta, was relatively small but highly influential within the farmers' movement. Led by Henry Wise Wood, the United Farmers of Alberta rejected the party system altogether and claimed that elected representatives should be free to vote as their constituents wished rather than forced to support the party line. Wood felt that regional and local needs had been subordinated to central Canadian business interests and called for a reorganization of Parliament so that constituencies would be based not on geography but on social class. In Wood's "group government" system, farmers, workers, entrepreneurs, and professionals would have representation commensurate with the weight of each occupational group within the population. The radical wing of the farmers' movement emphasized cooperation among individuals as an alternative to domination by capitalist monopolies. While the radicals believed that the state could play a positive role in implementing social justice, they initially regarded the cooperative movement rather than the state as the key to creating a more egalitarian society.

The women's sections of the farm organizations were particularly strong proponents of cooperation as an alternative to competition. Irene Parlby, president of the United Farm Women of Alberta (UFWA) from 1917 to 1921 and later the first female member of the Alberta cabinet, argued that rural communities could only be strong if their residents worked together to provide health, educational, and recreational facilities. Rural women throughout the West took upon themselves the task of establishing hospitals and clinics, improving local schools, and setting up community centres and theatres. Having won their battle for the vote, women's organizations used their political influence to convince governments to spend money to improve community services. The UFWA was committed not only to cooperation among farm people, but also to cooperation among all nations to end war. Joining with women's peace groups in

other regions, it called on the schools to shape curricula so that students were exposed to the values of tolerance and peaceful settlement of disputes as alternatives to bigotry and war.

Like other farm women's organizations in the West, the UFWA took up the battle for better protection of women's property rights both within marriage and during divorce. It also attempted in the 1930s to persuade the provincial government to establish family planning clinics, but it made little headway on either of these issues with the largely male UFA cabinet. The government's insensitivity to feminist demands was hardly surprising. Despite the radicalism of the UFA movement, the provincial government itself followed conventional parliamentary procedures and implemented few radical pieces of legislation. The gulf between the movement and the government bearing the UFA name grew wider over time. By the early 1930s, the UFA government was practising fiscal conservatism while the UFA organization was calling for a socialist restructuring of society.

Although Progressive MPs from Alberta remained, on the whole, committed to more democratic, participatory politics, they had little influence over the majority of Progressives, who simply wanted the Liberal Party to get rid of tariffs. First Crerar, and then his successor as party leader, Robert Forke, joined the Liberal Party when the radicals frustrated their attempts to create a traditional party machine. In an effort to lure moderate Progressives back into the Liberal fold, King lowered tariffs on farm machinery and equipment and acceded to Prairie demands to complete a rail link to the port of Churchill. King also restored the Crow rate (the favourable freight rates on grain imposed on the CPR in 1897 and later applied to all railways), which had been suspended in wartime. In the late 1920s, he capped his concessions to westerners by negotiating the surrender of federal control over the natural resources of the Prairie provinces. For many conservative Progressives, the implementation of such policies was proof positive of the success of their movement. In the 1930 election, the Progressive Party won only twelve seats, nine of them from the radical stronghold of Alberta. As a "ginger group" in the House, the remaining Progressives helped to add spice to debates on social policy, but it was clear the movement that began with so much promise in the early 1920s had run out of steam.

Within the provinces they governed, the farmers' movements appeared to follow the same economic policies as the traditional parties. The United Farmers of Ontario, unfortunate enough to be in power through a recession, proved mainly interested in cutting government expenditures. Their lacklustre performance resulted in a third-place finish when they faced the electorate in 1923. Hard-pressed to indicate what advances working people had won from the Farmer–Labour government, the Independent Labour Party also suffered an ignominious defeat. The UFA, which formed a loose alliance with the Canadian Labour Party, proved more durable, though its eventual defeat in the 1935 provincial election left both organizations without a seat in the legislature. While the UFA had a positive record in the areas of health and education in the 1920s, during the Great Depression of the 1930s, many voters thought it to be more solicitous towards finance companies than to financially strapped debtors, particularly farmers. In the final analysis, the Progressive movement lacked a coherent ideology or a blueprint for action that could sustain the party faithful in difficult economic circumstances.

## THE MARITIME RIGHTS MOVEMENT

The Progressives were already beginning to fade in the election of 1925. Nonetheless, King needed the support of the party: the Liberals had won only 99 seats in the election, compared to the Conservatives' total of 116, and a Liberal–Progressive alliance was key in enabling King to continue to govern. The election results had revealed a regionally divided nation: all but two of the twenty-four seats won by the Progressives came from the Prairie provinces, while the majority of Meighen's support had come from Ontario. In the Maritimes, Liberal popularity had reached low ebb, and this region, too, handed a majority of its seats to the Conservatives.

In the postwar period, the Maritimes faced a crisis of tragic proportions. Production declined by 40 percent between 1917 and 1921, and the recession that gripped the national economy in the early 1920s never entirely lifted from the region. Even the coal and steel industry, the much-touted basis for an industrial economy in the Maritimes, collapsed in a welter of corporate takeovers, wage cuts, and strikes. Once again the region experienced a devastating loss of population as over a hundred thousand people drifted to greener pastures to find work in the 1920s.

Meanwhile, Maritimers watched with dismay as national leaders ignored their problems, too busy, they bitterly concluded, catering to Central Canada and the West. Maritimers resented the Crow rates and the comparatively generous provincial subsidies to the western provinces. When Ottawa made huge territorial grants to Manitoba, Quebec, and Ontario in 1912, Maritime premiers opposed the policy, claiming that the wealth of these territories ought to belong to the dominion as a whole. Even more galling was the wartime policy of railway consolidation that merged the Intercolonial into the CNR and moved its head office to Toronto. Not only were jobs lost and freight rates dramatically increased, but also Saint John and Halifax were abandoned as major terminals of international trade. The hope of redressing grievances seemed hopelessly remote. As the population of the Maritimes declined relative to the rest of the nation, the political power of the region plummeted. Maritimers occupied thirty-one seats in the House of Commons in 1921, down from forty-three seats in 1882. Convinced that their interests, already largely ignored, would be shunted aside completely, Maritimers of all classes and interests came together to fight for Maritime rights.

The Maritime Rights Movement was led by business and professional interests who revived the moribund Maritime Board of Trade to bring a regional rather than a provincial perspective to bear on the problems they faced. Within the movement, Maritimers demanded larger federal subsidies, national transportation policies that took the region's needs into account, and tariff policies that offered protection for the Maritime coal and steel industry. The federal Liberal Party was the first beneficiary of Maritime discontent, taking all but six constituencies in the 1921 election. When King subsequently dismissed the concerns of his Maritime backbenchers, the region turned to the Conservative Party as a vehicle for its interests.

Nova Scotia, with its long history of protest against Confederation, took the lead in advancing the regional cause. In the June 1925 provincial election, the Conservatives, campaigning under the banner of Maritime Rights, captured all but three of the seats in the assembly, toppling a Liberal regime that had lasted an astonishing forty-three years. Premier E.N. Rhodes teamed up with Conservative premiers in New Brunswick and Prince Edward Island to bring pressure to bear on Ottawa. When the 1925 federal election resulted in another minority government, the Maritime Conservative bloc in the House of Commons found themselves almost equal in number to the Progressives and were determined to use their power to the greatest advantage.

King had difficulty holding his shaky coalition of Liberals and Progressives together. His government was defeated in June 1926 over a motion of censure relating to widespread corruption in the Customs Department. When King asked Governor General Byng to dissolve Parliament and call another election, Byng refused. Instead he asked Arthur Meighen, whose party had the most seats in the House, to form a government. As governor general, Byng had the right to determine whether any party leader could form a government that could command a working majority in the House of Commons, and he believed that Meighen deserved an opportunity to test his strength before the House was dissolved. King's claims to the contrary notwithstanding, Byng was not interfering in Canada's affairs but was responding in a responsible way to the inconclusive results of the 1925 election. Meighen's ministry lasted less than three days, making it the shortest-lived government in Canadian history, but it gave King the opportunity he needed to recoup his failing political fortunes after Meighen was forced to ask the governor general for a dissolution of Parliament.

In the ensuing election campaign, King made political hay out of Byng's refusal to accept his advice to dissolve Parliament, claiming that the governor general had violated the principle of responsible government. It is difficult to say what impact the so-called King-Byng affair had on the voters. What is clear is that King was determined to save his political hide and campaigned vigorously to win back the disaffected regions of the country. He promised a royal commission to investigate Maritime claims and drew the Progressives even closer to the Liberal fold by emphasizing his concessions to their interests and the threat posed to their goals by the high-tariff Tories. On election night, 14 September 1926, the Liberals won enough seats to give them a majority government.

Having largely pacified western and Ontario farmers and reduced the Progressives to a rump of twenty seats in Parliament, King at last turned his attention to the Maritimes. He set up the Royal Commission on Maritime Claims in 1926, naming as its head the British lawyer-industrialist, Sir Andrew Rae Duncan. Recognizing that Maritime governments were forced to tax their citizens more than other provincial governments to maintain a minimal level of services, Duncan called for a series of provincial subsidies based on need. He also recommended a revision of freight rates, assistance to the region's coal and steel industries, better ferry connections to Prince Edward Island, and improvements to port facilities at Halifax and Saint John to encourage international trade through the region.

While King appeared to embrace the Duncan Report, his government refused to fully implement its recommendations. The Maritime Freight Rates Act of 1927 helped the region's producers compete more effectively in central Canadian markets, but provincial subsidies based on need proved too hot a concept for the government to handle. So, too, was the plight of the region's fisheries, which became the subject for yet another commission of inquiry. Some assistance was provided to move Maritime coal to Quebec markets, but further aid to the coal and steel industry was deferred. As historian Ernest Forbes observes: "Unfortunately for the Maritimes, the King government turned it into a program for political pacification; only gradually would

Maritimers realize how much of the substance of Sir Andrew Rae Duncan's program had been removed in its supposed implementation."[2] Like the Progressive movement, popular agitation for Maritime rights largely dissipated in the late 1920s and proved difficult to reignite even during the Great Depression.

## POLITICAL WOMEN

For women, who were recently enfranchised, the interwar period failed to produce the results that suffrage leaders had hoped for. Only nine women sat in provincial legislatures before 1940, all of them in the western provinces, and only two won seats in the House of Commons in the interwar years. The reasons for this unimpressive showing are complex. Following the granting of suffrage, the "woman movement" lost its single focus, and women sorted themselves according to class, regional, and cultural interests. Professional women on the edge of the male-dominated public world continued to argue for equality of opportunity, especially in the context of blatantly discriminatory hiring practices, but they framed their arguments in the language of human, not women's, rights. In the interwar years, feminism and women's rights became equated with "man-hating" and the promotion of "sex wars" to such an extent that virtually every woman in public life was quick to deny any association with feminist doctrines. To embrace sexual politics was to court further exclusion from the bastions of male power and frustrate efforts to secure the equality in the public sphere that professional women sought.

Women attempting to break into formal political structures also took care not to appear to be too assertive. Although many politically active women brought a feminist perspective to their activities, they conducted themselves in cautious ways to advance their radical ends. Organizers of the mainstream parties insisted that women be absorbed and neutralized by the existing structures and beliefs, not act as agents of ideological and structural transformation. Even in left-wing parties, where women had greater access to organiza-

tional hierarchies and women's issues were frequently addressed, women were under-represented in the leadership and often found their concerns discounted.

Excluded from the inner circle of male-dominated political parties, women maintained their pre-suffrage practices of education and lobbying through their voluntary organizations and separate party committees. They continued to press for policies relating to women's rights, child welfare, prison reform, and world peace, which were still identified as women's issues. Safely tucked away in their auxiliaries, women were rarely put forward as candidates for political office.

Despite the poor electoral showing, there were some victories in the cause of women's equality. In 1929, five Alberta women were instrumental in convincing the Judicial Committee of the Privy Council that women were "persons" under the law. This right was theoretically denied them by nineteenth century legislation and in practice meant that women were excluded from appointments to the senate and a variety of other privileged bodies. The five women who pursued the case through its long battle in the courts were: Nellie McClung, the reformer, writer, and former Liberal MLA who had been prominent in the suffrage movement; writer and reformer Emily Murphy, who in 1916 had become the first woman magistrate in the British Empire; Alberta cabinet minister Irene Parlby; activist and former Alberta MLA Louise McKinney; and Henrietta Muir Edwards, who had helped to found the National Council of Women and the Victorian Order of Nurses. Despite considerable feeling that Judge Murphy should be rewarded with the post, Mackenzie King in 1930 appointed Cairine Wilson, a mother of nine children and a prominent Liberal Party organizer, as the first woman senator in Canada.

Canada's first female MP, elected in 1921, was Agnes Macphail. A teacher from Grey County, Ontario, she sat as a Progressive and soon made her mark as an outspoken defender of farmers, workers, women, and prisoners. She advocated bringing more women into political life, championed peaceful solutions to international conflicts, and won the hearts of her constituents, and

Canadians generally, with her feisty interventions in House of Commons debates. Her long career in federal politics came to an end when she was defeated in the election of 1940. By then an activist in the Co-operative Commonwealth Federation, she served as a CCF member of the Ontario legislature from 1943 to 1945 and 1948 to 1951, during which time she was responsible for the enactment of the first equal pay legislation in Canada.

*Agnes Macphail.*
National Archives of Canada/C21562

The first female MPs often secured their positions as extensions of their husbands. In 1935, Conservative candidate Martha Black was elected to keep a Yukon seat warm for her ailing husband, and, during the Second World War, Cora Casselman, the widow of the Liberal member for Edmonton East, won the by-election for her husband's riding. Dorise Nielsen, the Labour–Progressive MP for North Battleford from 1940 to 1945, was of a much different political stripe. An ardent feminist and Communist, she called for "the emancipation of women as wage earners,"[3] and a national program of publicly funded childcare. Although the Second World War increased the public role of women, greater political support was not forthcoming. In the 1945 election, Gladys Strum, the CCF candidate in Qu'Appelle, Saskatchewan, was the only woman out of the nineteen who ran to win a seat in the House of Commons.

In Quebec, women's political advance was even slower than in the rest of the country. There, the struggle for women's suffrage continued, opposed by the hierarchy of the Roman Catholic Church. Thérèse Casgrain, whose husband and father were both prominent Liberal politicians, and Idola Saint-Jean, a McGill language professor, became the leading advocates for women's suffrage in Quebec. The pressures exerted by the organized feminist movement in the province finally yielded a victory when Adelard Godbout's Liberals granted women the vote in 1940.

## FIRST NATIONS IN THE AGE OF DEMOCRACY

In the interwar years, Canada's aboriginal peoples also began to organize more systematically to reform the political structures that kept them dependent on white authorities. They faced an uphill battle. Status Indians, except those who had joined the armed forces, were still denied the franchise, and amendments to the Indian Act in 1920 gave the Department of Indian Affairs the explicit right to ban hereditary chiefdoms and other forms of Native governance.

Interference with Native governance was a long-standing grievance among status Indians. Prior to the First World War, Chief Deskadeh, a Cayuga, had begun a movement to achieve independence for the Six Nations of Grand River, Ontario. His campaign gained international attention in the early 1920s when he appealed for intervention from both the British government and the League of Nations, where several small nations supported his petition. Chief Deskadeh's campaign caused the Canadian government considerable embarrassment, but in the end it was unsuccessful. In 1924, Indian Affairs imposed an elective council on the Six Nations and banned the hereditary council. Women, who had hitherto had a veto in the selection of chiefs, had no vote on the elected council.

Another member of the Six Nations, Fred O. Loft, played a key role in the first successful effort to establish a Canada-wide aboriginal organization. The League of Indians of Canada, established in December 1918, included representatives from the three Prairie provinces, Ontario, and Quebec. Loft was a well-educated Mohawk who spent forty years in the Ontario civil service, mainly as an accountant. Married to a white woman who made a fortune in real estate in Toronto, he was well-off and determined to improve the status of Natives within Canada. Unlike the traditionalists of Grand River, he did not support independence from Canada or a total retreat from European ways. The League, under Loft's guidance, stressed the importance of improved educational opportunities on reserves and greater cooperation among Native peoples. As Loft observed, "The day is past when one band or a few bands can successfully ... free themselves from officialdom and from being ever the prey and victims of unscrupulous means of depriving us of our lands and homes and even deny[ing] us the rights we are entitled to as free men under the British flag."[4]

Despite Loft's relative moderation, the Department of Indian Affairs regarded his league as a subversive organization. Government harassment, police surveillance, and accusations of communism weakened the group, which also suffered from internal divisions. By the time Loft died in 1934, the league's Ontario and Quebec wings had already collapsed, and the Prairie branches soon succumbed as well. Nevertheless, the foundations for a pan-Canadian Indian organization had been laid.

In the Northwest Territories, the discovery of oil at Norman Wells in 1920 led to greater southern interest in the region. The federal government quickly signed a treaty, number 11, with representatives of the Dene and Métis in the region and established a council to support the Northwest Territories commissioner in his efforts to impose southern control. In the North, as elsewhere, aboriginal people would eventually claim that treaty guarantees of Native rights to hunt, fish, and trap had been violated, that they failed to receive the reserve lands promised by the treaty, and that they had been misled at the time of the original negotiations. Treaty 11 was unlike the previous ten in that a few of the people who signed it lived long enough to see their claims bear fruit. In 1976, the federal government conceded that their treaty obligations had not been fulfilled, thereby opening the door to new land claims negotiations in the Mackenzie Valley.

The federal government was slow to take responsibility for the Inuit, whose contact with southern society was mediated largely through the Hudson's Bay Company. When times were hard, it was the company that frequently made provision for their Native trappers. There was little altrusim in such a gesture, as the comments of one area manager reveal: "We must keep them alive for future profits even though we carry them at a loss till such time shall come."[5] The company continued to make decisions and implement programs for the Inuit, often with the help of federal funds, until a 1939 court decision confirmed that the welfare of the Inuit was a federal responsibility.

The federal government had considerable pressure on it to play a more direct role in promoting Native welfare. The poor health of Native peoples, often a result of extreme poverty, was a cause of growing concern, prompting humanitarian groups, church leaders, and other concerned citizens to turn to Ottawa for aid. When in the early 1940s it was revealed that the incidence of tuberculosis in the Mackenzie District was fourteen times the national average, and that the district had more than twice the average incidence of pneumonia, Roman Catholic Bishop Gabriel Breynat pleaded for government intervention. Such pleas were to find a more receptive ear in Ottawa as the war brought further changes to the North and to the federal government's role in the welfare of all Canadians.

## LABOUR POLITICS

During the 1920s, labour parties steered an uneasy course between socialism and reform. Several provincial labour parties espoused gradual nationalization of major industries and greater labour control of the workplace, but the struggle for immediate reforms for workers—minimum wages for women, improved workers' compensation, federal unemployment insurance—absorbed most of the time of elected Labour representatives. At the national level, the Labour Party elected few candidates during the 1920s, and only the popular J.S. Woodsworth was able to hold his seat for the entire decade.

Within the labour movement, craft union leaders had reasserted their supremacy and forestalled the advance of industrial unions. The increased conservatism of labour was partly a result of state repression following the Winnipeg General Strike, but it was also reinforced by the postwar recession. The major industrial unions that survived, such as the United Mine Workers (UMW) and Amalgamated Clothing Workers, became increasingly cautious in their practices. In the case of the UMW, this conservatism resulted in temporary breakaway movements in the Cape Breton and the Alberta coal fields, but produced no major shift in mainstream labour politics.

A marked contrast to this trend was the Communist Party of Canada (CPC). Organized furtively in a barn outside Guelph in 1921, the CPC included many of the nation's most committed labour radicals. Although the party never enrolled more than thirty thousand members at any time in its history, Communist leadership in the coal fields, garment shops, hard-rock mining, and among northern Ontario bushworkers brought a spirit of militancy to groups either ignored or poorly represented by established unions. Immigrant unskilled labour, particularly Ukrainians and Finns, formed the backbone of

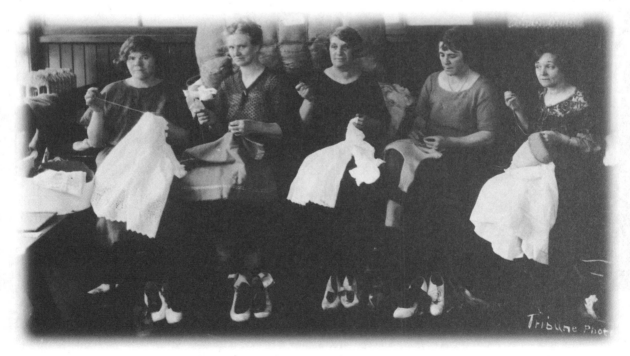

*Women's Labour League members in Winnipeg gather relief parcels for striking Cape Breton coal miners.*
Provincial Archives of Manitoba/ N13141

Canada's Communist Party. Recognizing that women in the workforce were potentially important to the movement, the CPC established the Women's Labour Leagues to educate and organize women.

Communist doctrines appealed to labour leaders such as Scottish immigrant J.B. McLachlan, whose organizational work among the coal miners of Cape Breton during a 1909–10 strike had led management to blacklist him. When he urged coal miners to conduct a sympathy strike in support of Sydney steelworkers in 1923, he was removed from his position as district president of the UMW by John L. Lewis, the American president of the UMW. Convicted in court of seditious libel, McLachlan spent a few months in prison before returning to Cape Breton in 1924 to edit the *Maritime Labour Herald*.

In the 1920s, the coal and steel industries in the Maritimes reeled under the pressures of declining markets, incompetent management, and labour unrest. A protracted and bitter strike among Cape Breton coal miners in 1925 focused widespread attention on the troubled island. As the appalling living conditions of the miners and their families became more widely known, there was a great outpouring of sympathy across the country. Even miners in the Soviet Union sent assistance, adding fuel to the rumours that Cape Breton miners were influenced by communism. When Progressive member of Parliament Agnes Macphail visited the conflict-ridden area, she found a situation, she claimed, that would make her adopt views more radical than any she detected among the starving miners.

## THE BENNETT YEARS, 1930–1935

In 1929, most Canadians began to experience what Maritimers had come to know well in the 1920s—economic depression. The crash of the New York stock market in October 1929 precipitated a collapse of the global market economy, and threatened to topple every political regime that failed to make an adequate response to the misery faced by the mounting number of unemployed. Slow to grasp the seriousness of the situation, King was an easy target for Labour MPs J.S. Woodsworth and A.A. Heaps, who demanded in the House that the government "take immediate action to deal with the question of unemployment." The Conservatives joined in the attack, causing King to lose his temper. He might, he said, be prepared to give some support to Progressive governments in Manitoba and Alberta, but he would not give any Tory government so much as "a five-cent piece."

The "five-cent piece speech" became the theme of Conservative candidates stumping the country in the July 1930 campaign, and, under their new leader Richard Bedford Bennett, the Conservatives won a resounding victory, carrying 137 seats to 91 for the Liberals, 12 for the Progressives, and 3 for

*Lawren Harris, 1885-1970,* **Miners' Houses, Glace Bay,** *c 1925. This grim representation of life in a mining town in 1921 depicts the miners' lives and work as one. The pollution over the town and the rows of identical, stark-looking homes combine to make the miners' town look much like the underground of a coal mine.*

oil on canvas 107.3 x 127 cm Art Gallery of Ontario, Toronto. Bequest of Charles S. Band Toronto, 1970

Labour. King was luckier than he realized at the time. With the nation sinking under the weight of the Depression, it was the Conservatives who would become associated with hard times, and the Liberals who would be waiting in the wings to pick up the pieces in 1935.

Born in 1870 in Albert County, New Brunswick, R.B. Bennett was a Tory's Tory. He was proud of his alleged Loyalist roots, his Methodist values, and his rise to prominence from humble origins. After teaching to put himself through Dalhousie Law School, he moved west to take a position in the Calgary law office of Senator James A. Lougheed. He rose to partnership through hard work and determination, making his fortune through real estate deals, wise investments, and powerful clients such as the CPR. In 1911, he won the Calgary seat in the House of Commons and was one of a small number of Conservatives able to win a seat in the West in the 1925 and 1926 elections. This helped to make him an appealing candidate at the Conservative Party's first leadership convention, held in Winnipeg in 1927. Prior to this time, party leaders had simply been seconded by the inner circle of the party.

Like King, Bennett was a bachelor and a self-made man, and he was prone to delivering boring speeches, but the similarities stopped there. Bennett had enormous energy and, unlike King, could never be accused of inaction. Eager to make good on his election promise to address the problems created by the Depression, he called a special session of Parliament soon after taking power. The government introduced the Unemployment Relief Act to provide $20 million—an unprecedented sum—to help people get back to work and also embarked on a program of tariff increases designed to protect languishing Canadian industries from foreign competition. It was not enough. Bread lines lengthened, prices continued to plummet, and municipal and charitable organizations collapsed under the weight of the demands placed upon them. At a loss as to how to stem the crisis, Bennett resorted to desperate measures and soon found his party embattled from without and divided from within.

## PROTEST FROM LEFT AND RIGHT

### THE COMMUNISTS

In 1932, the Bennett government decided to create relief camps under military control to house the single, unemployed men who had been travelling from city to city in search of work. Single able-bodied men faced dismal prospects: employers favoured married men in their hiring practices, and many municipalities denied single people relief of any kind. From the government's perspective, these unfortunate people were a potentially explosive group who should be segregated from society until the economy improved. The transients were to be denied welfare unless they agreed to go to remote camps, where they would work for their board and receive an allowance of twenty cents per day. Although most of the men committed to the camps performed useful work, such as the construction of highways, airfields, and barracks, the isolation and lack of pay bred hopelessness. As Irene Baird's powerful novel *Waste Heritage* (1939) vividly illustrated, Communist organizers had little difficulty convincing these desperate young men to organize to demand "work and wages" and the closing of the camps.

Communism had attracted little support during the 1920s, but it thrived in the appalling conditions of Depression Canada. In the cities, Communist agitators were active in efforts to protest against injustice in welfare and housing. Their influence among the unemployed, who formed groups to express their discontent, was strong, while branches of the Communist-inspired Workers Unity League, formed in 1929, took root among miners, loggers, and garment workers.

Bennett moved quickly to suppress dissent. In 1931, the Communist Party was declared illegal and seven of its members—including its leader, Tim Buck—were imprisoned. The party was legalized in 1936, only to be banned in Quebec in 1937. Banned yet again by Ottawa in 1940, the CPC reorganized as the Labour Progressive Party. The use of state violence to protect the established order was not new in Canada, but the intensity of the repression, which included jail sentences, beatings, and, for those who were not Canadian citizens, deportation, reached a new level in the hysteria fostered by the Depression.

While there were several tragic instances in the 1930s of strikers being killed by the police, the clash between the authorities and the victims of the Depression that gained the most national attention occurred in Regina in 1935. Relief camp workers, fed up with their lot, were enthusiastic recruits to the Relief Camp Workers Union (RCWU) organized by the Workers Unity League. In April 1935, the RCWU led nearly half of the seven thousand relief camp inmates in British Columbia on a strike for work and wages. The strikers converged on Vancouver, where they conducted orderly demonstrations that brought much sympathy from

the public, but little concrete action from authorities. Early in June, twelve hundred of the strikers boarded freight trains heading east. Picking up support along the way, they planned to converge on Ottawa and put their demands directly to the prime minister.

The On-to-Ottawa trek, as it became known, quickly attracted the nation's attention. Concerned with the momentum that the trek was gaining, Bennett called out the RCMP to stop the demonstrators in Regina. Predictably, the RCMP's attempts to disperse the strikers resulted in violence. One constable was killed and hundreds of strikers and constables were injured in the mêlée that ensued. The next year, Mackenzie King abolished the relief camps, which by that time had provided temporary homes and education in radical politics to about 170 000 Canadians.

## LIFE IN THE RELIEF CAMPS

Despite their unpopularity, relief camps were run efficiently by the Canadian military and offered many single, unemployed men their only chance for a nutritious meal and medical care. Boredom was a common complaint in most camps, but the men often made the most of their meagre resources. In some Ontario camps that were close to towns, inmates organized boxing and wrestling matches that townsfolk paid to watch. Funds collected from these events and the occasional charitable donation were used to provide radios, reading material, and sports equipment. The men made their own checkerboards and asked local farmers to lend them sets of horseshoes. Living in primitive bunkhouses, the camp inmates ate three ample military-style meals a day but complained

*Communists and socialists led marches of unemployed men and women demanding better treatment of those unable to find work and more efforts on the part of the state to create work. In 1935, the United Married Men's Association marched in Calgary, carrying a banner that read, "We stand behind 12,000 on relief."*
Glenbow Archives/NA 2800-12

bitterly about the monotony of the food.

While the Communists found eager recruits in many of the camps, protest was not always politically inspired. Camp conditions were sometimes intolerable, and, with no other recourse, the men resorted to direct action. In Ontario's largest camp, Lac Seul, for example, men clearing timber along the shoreline suffered from blackflies in the summer, extreme cold in the winter, and isolation and poor food much of the time. The men knew their rights and refused to work during a snowstorm and struck when camp administrators gave them less tobacco than the rules allowed. Chinese workers, who were segregated from others in the camp, struck in 1934 when they had their food rations cut.

Communist effectiveness in organizing the unemployed and industrial workers during the Depression failed to translate into electoral success. Most Canadians remained cool to socialist alternatives, and few saw the repressive Soviet Union, the model state espoused by the CPC, as a society that Canada should emulate. Fewer still wished to emulate fascist Italy or Nazi Germany, where dictators Benito Mussolini and Adolf Hitler were producing another kind of revolution.

## THE EXTREME RIGHT

National pride led many German and Italian Canadians to support the dictators who had seized power and seemingly restored national dignity in their native countries. While few people supported the use of violence to bring fascism to Canada, coteries of fascists came together in most major Canadian cities and in some small towns. Their leaders were primarily of British or French descent, and their followers were drawn from all classes and cultures.

Hitler's glorification of violence, white supremacy, and hatred of Jews, Communists, and homosexuals inspired Canadian Nazis to fight pitched battles with Communists and union groups and to make efforts to keep Jews off beaches and away from other public places. In Western Canada, anti-communist Ukrainian nationalist organizations sympathized with the racial exclusiveness and militarism of the Nazis, conveniently ignoring Hitler's estimation of the Slavs as an inferior race fit only to be slaves to the "Aryan" race. In Quebec, the Nazis claimed to represent the last stand of Roman Catholicism against the forces of decadence, and conservative religious leaders in the province turned a blind eye to fascist attempts to use the church to promote racism and anti-Semitism.

The ambivalence of Quebec's Roman Catholic leaders towards fascism reflected international trends. Alarmed by rising secularism, the militancy of labour movements, and the strength of parties on the left, many Roman Catholics found comfort in the state repression and heightened sense of nationalism advocated by the fascists. Abbé Lionel Groulx tapped into this trend, calling for Quebec to become an independent state where the Roman Catholic clergy would rule over a purified race of French Canadians. He and his followers urged people to reject secular pursuits such as gambling, drinking, and watching Hollywood movies, to boycott Jewish stores, and to refuse to read liberal-leaning newspapers such as Montreal's *La Presse*. While Groulx's ideas attracted some support from the francophone middle class, the majority ignored the nationalist and fascist campaigns, blending their Catholic beliefs with secular practices and support for reformist currents within Catholicism.

The racism of the extreme right was the ultimate expression of a heritage of several centuries of European imperialism in which claims of racial superiority played an important role in justifying the conquest of non-Europeans. In North America, no organization has been more identified with racism than the Ku Klux Klan (KKK), the secretive, violent brotherhood of hooded white men who took up the cause of white supremacy in the American South after the Civil War. The Klan was active in Canada in the 1920s and early 1930s, though details of its operations remain sketchy. With few blacks to terrorize, the Canadian Klan became a Protestant extremist organization with Catholics as its target. The Klan called for an end to non-Protestant immigration and for deportation of Roman Catholics born outside Canada. In targeting Roman Catholics, the Klan echoed the traditional concern of the Orange Order which continued to be the major organization of Protestant pride in Canada.

With a membership of between ten thousand and fifteen thousand in Saskatchewan in the late 1920s, the KKK exercised influence within the provincial Conservative Party, which led a coalition government from 1929 to 1934. Klan pressures contributed to the government's decision to end French-language instruction in the early grades of school and to dismiss nuns teaching in public schools. In 1931, E.E. Perley, a Conservative MP from Saskatchewan, informed R.B. Bennett that only Protestants should be appointed to the Senate from Saskatchewan. He wrote Bennett in 1931: "Possibly you are aware that the Ku Klux Klan is very strong in this province and no doubt was a great silent factor both in the provincial and in the last federal election, in favour of the Conservatives. They are very much worked up over the fact that one of the first major appointments is to go to the

*The Ku Klux Klan in Saskatchewan.*
National Archives of Canada/PA87848

Roman Catholic Church, and it certainly will do us a great deal of harm."[6] Fortunately, only a minority of Canadians believed that the Depression could be ended, and further economic crises averted, by deporting or persecuting Catholics, Jews, and Communists.

## THIRD PARTIES

With as much as one-third of the nation facing destitution by 1932, many Canadians looked to new political parties to find a solution to their problems. The Co-operative Commonwealth Federation, Social Credit, and the Union nationale were all born in the Dirty Thirties, each with its own formula for preventing capitalist boom-bust economic cycles.

## THE CCF

The Co-operative Commonwealth Federation (CCF), formed in 1932, enjoyed modest success in the 1930s. Unlike the Union nationale and Social Credit, it formed no governments during the Depression decade, and fewer than one voter in ten cast a ballot for the CCF in 1935. Yet the CCF ultimately proved influential. In 1944, under the leadership of Tommy Douglas in Saskatchewan, the CCF elected the first democratic socialist government in North America and served as the forerunner of the New Democratic Party, founded in 1961.

The CCF was a democratic socialist party formed as the result of a decision by the small contingent of Labour and Progressive MPs to capitalize on grass-roots pressure to unite the disparate left-wing labour and farm organizations in the country. It inherited the often contradictory traditions of labourism, socialism, social gospelism, and farm radicalism. Early election results demonstrated that, outside of industrial Cape Breton, the CCF had taken root mainly in the West. By 1939, it formed the opposition in British Columbia, Saskatchewan, and Manitoba, and was poised for greater successes in the future.

Led by J.S. Woodsworth, a Winnipeg Labour MP, the CCF rejected both capitalism and the revolutionary rhetoric of the Communists. The CCF's manifesto, adopted at the party's Regina convention in 1933, proclaimed the possibility of a parliamentary road to socialism, and recommended state planning as the best route to social justice. Like other political platforms, the Regina manifesto reflected a compromise among the party's constituents. It called for government or cooperative control of major industries and state intervention in the marketplace, but it also promised not to nationalize land, and, indeed, would have as a goal the preservation of family farms. At the same time, socialists were assured that the CCF's ultimate goal was an egalitarian nation. After outlining a set of public-spending measures to get the unemployed back to work, the manifesto ended on a radical note: "No C.C.F. Government will rest content until it has eradicated capitalism and put into operation the full programme of socialized planning which will lead to the establishment in Canada of the Co-operative Commonwealth." [7]

*J.S. Woodsworth in 1935. While the CCF leader won a great deal of respect from Canadians, his party was vilified by the mainstream media and made only minor electoral inroads before the Second World War.*

National Archives of Canada/C3940

## SOCIAL CREDIT

Not all western Canadians who rejected the mainstream political parties turned towards socialism for a solution to economic ills. When popular Alberta radio evangelist William "Bible Bill" Aberhart began in 1932 to inject "social credit" into his weekly radio broadcasts, he found a receptive audience. Aberhart adapted doctrines espoused by a British engineer, Major C.H. Douglas, to Alberta conditions and built on traditional provincial suspicion towards central Canadian financial institutions. Claiming that the Depression had been caused by the failure of the banks to print enough money so that consumer spending could match industrial production, Aberhart offered a blueprint for getting monetary policy back on track. To many free enterprisers, disillusioned by the severity of the Depression, Aberhart's nostrums proved appealing. If only the banks could be forced to supply consumers with money, they believed, prosperity could be restored.

Social credit meant that governments would replace financial institutions as the vehicle for deciding how much money should be in circulation and in whose hands. It claimed to offer a scientific formula to determine the shortfall in purchasing power, advocating that the government simply credit all citizens equally with a share of this shortfall to keep the economy healthy. Aberhart attempted unsuccessfully to convince the UFA government in Alberta to embrace social credit ideas such as the social dividend and the just price. Under the former, the state would boost purchasing power by issuing money to all adults, while state regulation of prices would ensure that social dividends were not eaten away by price-gouging business people.

Aberhart turned the social credit study clubs spawned by his radio appeals into a political movement that won fifty-six of sixty-three seats in the provincial election of 1935. Once in power, he failed to deliver on his promises to issue social dividends or to control prices, and he only attempted to regulate banks and currency when a revolt by backbenchers in the party forced him to stop procrastinating. Legislation to this end in 1937 and 1938 was disallowed by the federal government and ultimately by the courts, which upheld federal jurisdiction over banking and currency. Aberhart was thus able to blame the federal government for his failure to implement his election promises and could maintain provincial support for his party with his strong stand against Ottawa.

The political leanings of Social Credit shifted over time. In 1935, many Social Credit supporters in Alberta regarded the party as quasi-socialist, promising not only money for nothing, but also a new deal for the unemployed and protection of citizens against money lenders. The government legislated moratoria on debts, earning it the eternal gratitude of many farmers. Beyond this achievement, its record was spotty. Aberhart was a prickly authoritarian who ignored popular pressure for better treatment of welfare recipients and for improved workers' compensation. Although his attempt to legislate the press to print government propaganda was struck down by the courts, it revealed the anti-civil libertarian tendencies of the Social Credit movement.

By the time of Aberhart's death in 1943, the Social Credit Party had become a right-wing organization with a relatively restricted membership in which religious fundamentalists and monetary cranks loomed large. The party leaders, always receptive to conspiracy theories, began to believe that bankers, communists, socialists, and unionists were all part of an international conspiracy to suppress the human freedom that only Social Credit philosophy could create and protect. A section of the party was convinced that the Jews were the glue that stuck this strange alliance together. Under Ernest Manning, the premier of Alberta from 1943 to 1968, the party rejected such bigotry and purged itself of influential anti-Semites. The Manning government, flush with oil royalties, built schools and roads while practising fiscal conservatism, with little hint of the party's early radicalism.

## UNION NATIONALE

In Quebec, the reform movement resulted less from popular pressure than from clerical responses to the 1931 papal encyclical *Quadragesimo anno*, which supported state intervention to achieve social justice. The Jesuit-sponsored École sociale populaire, an organization that propagated church teachings, assembled representatives of lay Catholic organizations, including unions, caisses populaires, and professional groups, to produce a document on desirable social reforms in line with the pope's thinking. In 1933, they published *Le Programme de restauration sociale*, a program of non-socialist reforms including government regulation of monopolies, improved working conditions in industry, a system of farm credits, and a variety of social insurance measures. The program suggested that if regulation proved insufficient to lower prices, the state might have to set up companies in certain sectors in competition with private industry.

The business-oriented Liberal regime of Louis-Alexandre Taschereau proved resistant to reform. In frustration, more progressive Liberals, led by Paul Gouin, formed a breakaway party, the Action libérale nationale. Gouin, like many liberal Roman Catholics, believed that *Quadragesimo anno* pointed the way to a progressive society in which the church regarded the state as an ally in improving the lives of ordinary people rather than as a competitor in the provision of services. Maurice Duplessis, a Trois-Rivières lawyer who led the province's moribund Conservative Party, sensed a political opportunity and formed an electoral alliance with the renegade Liberals. In 1935, the rechristened Union nationale contested the provincial election, with *Le Programme de restauration sociale* as its platform and with its two component parties maintaining organizational autonomy.

Disillusionment with the long-governing Liberals produced a close result: forty-eight Liberal and forty-two Union nationale seats. Shortly after the election, the Union nationale was able to capitalize on evidence of government corruption and nepotism to force Taschereau's resignation. The hastily formed new government, forced to call an election in 1936, was badly mauled by the Union nationale, which made corruption rather than reform the theme of its campaign. Duplessis outmanoeuvred Gouin to take full control of the Union nationale, submerging its two founding parties into a new organization under his personal control and becoming the new political chief of the province.

In power, the Union nationale delivered only on its promises to help farmers with cheap loans and programs to settle the unemployed in remote (and generally infertile) areas of the province. The coal, gasoline, and bread companies, whose prices the 1935 Union nationale program promised to control, faced no regulation while the power companies, which the Union nationale suggested might be socialized, remained in private hands and without additional regulation. Employers, not labour, received a sympathetic ear from the government. In 1937, Duplessis demonstrated how far he would go in repressing dissent when he passed the Padlock Act. Designed to suppress communism, the act was frequently invoked to intimidate any labour organization that the government considered undesirable.

Duplessis attempted to win popular support with a strong rhetorical assertion of Quebec nationalism and opposition to federal interference in the province. Rejecting the view that the federal government must expand its programs to cope with an increasingly industrial society, he clung tightly to the provincial compact view of Confederation.

Duplessis told the Royal Commission on Dominion-Provincial Relations established in 1937, "Under our federal system, each province, within its own jurisdictions, constitutes an autonomous state, enjoying all the prerogatives of a sovereign state without any subjection to the federal power."[8]

Such views echoed the perspective of Ontario's Liberal premier, Mitchell Hepburn. Though he and Duplessis ultimately parted ways on the question of how Canada should react to the outbreak of war in Europe, the two men collaborated closely on several issues. These included an unsuccessful attempt to convince Ottawa to allow hydro-electric exports and a successful bid to prevent Mackenzie King from introducing a national unemployment insurance bill after the Bennett legislation for such a program had been overturned by the courts.

The emergence of third parties demanding

*Maurice Duplessis and Mitchell Hepburn, the two central Canadian premiers, worked together for several years, resisting federal social programs and economic regulation. While both men were economic conservatives, their motives for opposing the federal government differed in important respects. Hepburn wanted to avoid a redistribution of wealth away from the country's richest province, while Duplessis was leery of any proposals that might threaten the French-speaking, Catholic character of Quebec.*

National Archives of Canada/C19518

reform and the explosion of militancy on the part of the unemployed in Canada in the 1930s made reform necessary if the capitalist system were to be preserved. Prime Minister R.B. Bennett gave back-handed credit to the Canadian Communist Party's general secretary for influencing the Conservative government to initiate its ill-fated New Deal reforms of 1935: "Tim Buck has today a very strong position in the province of Ontario and he openly demands the abolition of the capitalist system. A good deal of pruning is sometimes necessary to save a tree and it would be well for us in Canada to remember that there is considerable pruning to be done if we are to save the fabric of the capitalist system."[9]

## From Laissez-Faire to Welfare

Nothing disappeared as quickly during the 1930s as support for the liberal notion of laissez-faire. Suddenly unable to find work, people blamed profit-seeking capitalists for their plight and no longer found the ethos of "free" enterprise so captivating. Even business people abandoned their rugged individualism when faced with personal bankruptcy and the failure of their private cartels to hold the lines on prices. Everyone turned to governments to save them from their problems, proposing marketing boards, central banks, public works, easy money—anything to put order and sanity back into the faltering industrial economy.

Beginning tentatively during the 1930s and then more confidently in the following decade, the federal government began to expand the scope of its operations and emerged as an important player in the national economy. Expansion of state power occurred in all countries undergoing increased industrialization, but the particular configuration of state institutions and policies varied depending upon the strength of contending social forces. In Britain, for example, where the Labour Party had become an important political force before the First World War, unemployment insurance had been introduced in 1911 and a massive public housing program was put in place after the war.

Despite much talk of reform in Canada during the First World War, there was little federal response in the early postwar years. Veterans were eligible for land grants and for pensions if their wounds made them incapable of working. For the citizenry in general there was only a small program of public housing. Labour exchanges were established to help job-seekers, but there was no federal assistance for those unable to find work. Pressed by Progressive and Labour MPs, the Liberals established a means-tested old age pension program in 1927. The pension was available to women and men over the age of seventy who were deemed to be destitute by their provincial government. The costs of the pension were shared by the federal and provincial governments. While the provinces gradually joined the program in the 1930s, they all had tough rules for eligibility, with the poverty-stricken Maritime provinces proving particularly tight-fisted. Pensioners received a maximum of twenty dollars per month, too little to live on if one had no other resources.

Beginning in the West in 1916, provincial governments established mothers' allowances to assist widows with children. This social program was an important concession to the women's movement in Canada, but its detailed regulations reflected a conservative gender ideology. Only "virtuous" mothers were eligible—that is, widows and, in some provinces, wives of men unable to support their families for medical reasons. Never-married, single mothers need not apply. Even deserted wives were excluded on the grounds that it might encourage men to leave their families if they knew that the state would lend a helping hand to those they had deserted. Like old age pensions, mothers' allowances were too small to keep a family above a bare subsistence level. Despite the continuing social value placed on mothers staying home to raise their children, and the complete lack of affordable day care, governments took little responsibility for keeping single-parent families, even those headed by widows, from poverty. Governments, however, would not be allowed to ignore the plight of the poor when the 1930s Depression threw tens of thousands of able-bodied men out of work.

# PUBLIC HEALTH BEFORE MEDICARE

In the wake of the Spanish flu epidemic of 1918-19 and wartime concerns about the fitness of potential troops, the scope of public health activities was expanded. A federal Department of Health was established in 1919 to work with the provinces in such areas as tuberculosis, sexually transmitted diseases, "feeblemindedness," and child welfare. Its main achievements in the 1920s were a national network of venereal disease clinics and a national educational program on childcare.

Provincial public health programs were expanded, and public health nurses were appointed in many provinces to deal with the medical health concerns of outlying areas where there were few doctors. Such programs made a difference. In Quebec, in the first two months of 1937, rural counties with health units reported an infant mortality rate of 86.2 per thousand while counties without health units had a rate of 118.6. The overall death rate was similarly higher in counties without public health units. Even in Ontario, the wealthiest province, only a third of the provincial population in the 1930s lived in areas with well-organized public health services. Reports from visiting public health nurses often portrayed a hopeless state of affairs. In 1921, the provincial nurse's report on the eastern Ontario town of Rockland, population three thousand, noted:

The town was in an unsanitary condition, there being no sewage system, no water filtration, no clean or adequate milk supply, no paved streets, no street lighting. Public health teachings were unknown and under these conditions there could be little else than sickness, distress and high death rates. Employment was provided for the majority of men in the town by the lumber mills but the families in all homes were so large that one wage earner had difficulty in providing proper food and clothes for the children. [10]

In such circumstances, it is perhaps not surprising that 75 of the 160 children born in Rockland in 1920 had died before their first birthday. As cities provided safe water supplies, better sanitation services, and medical facilities that rural and small-town governments could not afford, the gap between town and country widened (see figure 8.1). It was hardly surprising, then, that rural dwellers complained about the minimal government provision of medical services to citizens. Via the Farm Radio Forum, farm people discussed the question of a national health scheme, noting in 1943,"The government sponsors the TB testing of cattle, pays for loss and has blood testing every year free of charge. What about humans?" [11]

The province with the lowest infant mortality rate in rural areas in 1943 had had the country's highest rate before the First World War: Saskatchewan. The explanation for the change appears to be that, in the interwar period, much of rural Saskatchewan had implemented a "municipal doctor" scheme, in which the municipality hired and paid doctors. With medical care prepaid through property taxes, people were less constrained by economic considerations from seeing the doctor. Doctors, who in other provinces often left rural areas when they realized how few of their patients could afford to pay medical bills, were attracted by the stability of income that the municipal doctor plan provided.

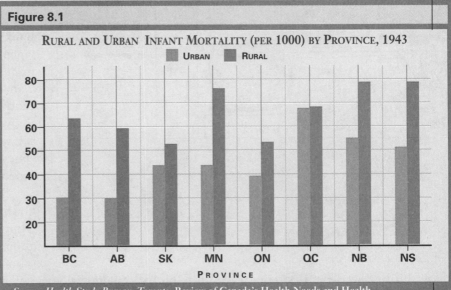

**Figure 8.1**

RURAL AND URBAN INFANT MORTALITY (PER 1000) BY PROVINCE, 1943

■ URBAN  ■ RURAL

*Source: Health Study Bureau, Toronto,* Review of Canada's Health Needs and Health-Insurance Proposals *(Toronto, 1945)*

## BENNETT'S NEW DEAL

Not immune to the mounting pressures for action, Bennett was reluctant to embark on policies that defied the free enterprise values that he and his party's backers shared. His first instinct was to turn to the traditional Tory nostrum: the tariff. Bennett promised to create jobs by raising tariffs as a means of forcing Canada's trading partners to sue for mercy. While "blasting" his way into foreign markets proved an inadequate response to the immediate crisis, as a policy it had some redeeming features.

*R.B. Bennett's tariff policy,*
*as viewed by cartoonist Arch Dale.*

Winnipeg *Free Press*, 14 April 1931

Britain was the first country to respond to Bennett's initiative. Long a proponent of free trade, Great Britain in the 1920s began to restore protectionism, finally abandoning free-trade ideas

altogether when the Depression threatened its agricultural population with destitution. It was, therefore, a policy coup for Bennett when Britain agreed to preferential treatment for Canadian apples, lumber, wheat, and a variety of meat and dairy products at the Imperial Economic Conference held in Ottawa in 1932. The agreement did little to help Canada's floundering manufacturing sector or the devastated wheat economy, but it was welcome news to apple growers in Nova Scotia, lumbermen in British Columbia, and Ontario's beef and dairy farmers. In 1935, the United States began its retreat from high tariffs when it signed a comprehensive trade treaty with Canada, the first since 1854.

There was also pressure on the government to manipulate the money supply as a means of stimulating the economy. Bennett resisted most of the "soft money" proposals that circulated during the decade but did provide relief to hard-pressed farmers through the Farmers' Creditors Arrangement Act. As banking practices became increasingly restrictive, there was widespread agreement that Canada needed a central bank, like the Bank of England or the Federal Reserve Bank in the United States, to convince the public that someone was in control. In 1934, the Bank of Canada Act made provision for a central bank. Its major function, in the words of the preamble to the act, was "to regulate credit and currency in the best interests of the economic life of the nation."

The bank's first governor, Graham Towers, was recruited from the Royal Bank at the astounding salary of $30 000 a year (about twenty times the average industrial wage). Towers pursued a policy of modest growth in the money supply in order to cut interest rates and stimulate the economy. Bankers' commitment to "sound money" was too strong for him to undertake bolder efforts to make credit available to most Canadians. Although the economy was flat as a pancake, conservative economists and bankers worried that an increase in the money supply would result in an unacceptable level of inflation.

Responding to pressing problems relating to wheat exports, municipal funding, and housing, Ottawa pumped money into the economy through programs established under the Prairie Farm Rehabilitation Act, the Municipal Improvement Assistance Act, and the Dominion Housing Act. The federal government also passed the Natural Products Marketing Act, providing a legal framework for marketing boards, and created the Canadian Wheat Board to manage the sale of Canada's most troubled staple. Given the magnitude of the crisis, it no longer seemed wrong to fix prices and regulate output in the farming sector.

Nor was the notion of a government-sponsored social security system so steadfastly resisted. In 1935, R.B. Bennett, facing widespread criticism and an imminent election, introduced legislation to regulate hours of work, minimum wages, and working conditions, and to provide insurance against sickness, industrial accidents, and unemployment. Many voters were less than impressed with Bennett's proposals. What good were social insurance programs to those who had no jobs and were therefore ineligible to make a claim? And would these measures ever be passed into legislation? By pronouncing on matters that the BNA Act deemed to be under provincial control, it was a foregone conclusion that most of Bennett's New Deal would be declared unconstitutional.

## THE 1935 ELECTION

Whatever his motives, Bennett received few benefits from his conversion to social security. He not only lost the 1935 election, but also watched his party split into warring factions. One revolt was led by trade and commerce minister H.H. Stevens in response to public outrage against the apparent callousness of big corporations in the face of widespread human misery. In 1934, Stevens headed a parliamentary committee established by the

government to investigate the gap between what producers were receiving and what consumers were required to pay for food, clothing, and other necessities of life. Testimony in the committee hearings revealed damning evidence that big meat-packing companies, such as Canada Packers, made huge profits while farmers who raised the cattle and hogs had been paid "ruinous" prices. Similarly, seamstresses who did piecework for big department stores were paid a few pennies for dresses that sold for $1.59 at Eaton's or Simpson's. When Bennett resisted taking the captains of industry to task for their exploitative policies, Stevens resigned and established the Reconstruction Party. While the party of "the little man" won only one seat—its leader won his Vancouver riding—it split the Conservative vote in constituencies from Nova Scotia to British Columbia. King, also resisting pressure to adopt new policies for new times, campaigned under the slogan "King or chaos," and won the largest majority of his political career.

As had been predicted, much of Bennett's New Deal was declared unconstitutional, and even marketing boards were deemed by the courts to be a matter for provincial rather than national legislation. King resisted appeals for dramatic action. In typical King fashion, he had the situation studied, appointing a National Employment Commission to investigate and recommend policy on unemployment and relief, and a Royal Commission on Dominion–Provincial Relations as a means of resolving the constitutional impasse. Only time would tell if Ottawa could introduce legislation to expand its role in the social and economic lives of Canadians.

## THE KEYNESIAN REVOLUTION

The general drift of economic thinking during the 1930s was towards economic planning and government intervention as a means of solving the problem of boom and bust cycles. Although a variety of experts came forward with solutions to the economic crisis, the most influential was British economist John Maynard Keynes. His book, *The General Theory of Employment, Interest, and Money*

(1936), became the bible of a new generation of academics, politicians, and bureaucrats attempting to understand the causes of, and solutions for, the Great Depression. Arguing that rigidities in the capitalist system prevented the laws of supply and demand from functioning in practice as they were outlined in classical theory, he advised that the state play a stabilizing role by increasing expenditures, lowering taxes, and inflating the money supply during the downside of the business cycle. In this way, he maintained, depressions would be less severe and recovery more immediate. If the policies were reversed once the economy was moving again, he argued, there was no need to fear that such actions would produce either runaway inflation or an intolerable level of public debt.

Proponents embraced Keynes's "counter-cyclical" proposals as a middle way between increasingly polarizing positions on economic policy. Less radical than the solutions of Marxian economists, who advocated the complete abolition of the capitalist system, Keynesian economics was more purposeful than the prescriptions of laissez-faire liberals who remained true believers in self-adjusting economic forces. In the Keynesian economy, governments could play a larger role in economic planning, but capitalism would continue to be the driving force of economic development. Surely this was the best of all possible worlds.

During the Depression, Keynes was read by only a few Canadians and understood by even fewer. One of his Canadian disciples was W.A. Mackintosh of the Department of Finance, who embraced a conservative version of Keynesian ideas that emphasized the timing of public works to coincide with economic downturns. For most Canadians, however, "pump-priming" activities had credibility not because of economic theories but because of the tangible successes of Franklin D. Roosevelt, the flamboyant president of the United States. His New Deal, introduced during his first administration (1933–37), captured the imagination of people all over the world. Impressed by New Deal programs to encourage public works, cultural development, and a more humane workplace for Americans, Canadians demanded that their government spend its way out of the Depression too.

## TOWARDS AN INDEPENDENT CANADA

In the interwar years, Canada and other dominions in the British Empire finally achieved the legal right to independent status. Mackenzie King, influenced by Quebec's hostility to Canadian involvement in European politics, took a lead along with Ireland and South Africa in demanding that the dominions be recognized as independent nations. In a series of meetings during the 1920s, the foundations were laid for a new British Commonwealth of self-governing nations to replace the old British Empire of dependent colonies, though a clear distinction was drawn between the self-governing white dominions and Britain's formal colonies in Asia and Africa. By the Statute of Westminster, passed by the British Parliament in 1931, Canada and the other dominions were given full legal freedom to exercise their independence in domestic and foreign affairs. While Canadian autonomy was not complete—amendments to the BNA Act still had to be approved by the British Parliament, and the Judicial Committee of the Privy Council remained the final court of appeal—the Statute of Westminster paved the way to complete independence for Canada in foreign affairs.

In the interwar years, Canada was a full member of the League of Nations, but the League was beset by problems, with many of its leading members unwilling to surrender authority to an international body. The ambivalence of League members ensured an ineffectual response to the aggressive behaviour of Japan, Germany, and Italy in the 1930s. When Walter Riddell, Canada's representative at the League, called for stronger measures against Italy after its invasion of Ethiopia in 1935, he was told by Ottawa to change his position: Canada had no interest in the fate of Ethiopia.

Canada was equally unwilling to provide any formal aid to the Spanish republic when its armed forces, led by General Franco, who was supported by German and Italian arms, overthrew the country's elected government during a bloody three-year civil war (1936-39). Some twelve hundred Canadians fought as volunteers for the republic,

## MACKENZIE KING ON ADOLF HITLER

Although he believed in democracy and civil liberties, King was charmed by Hitler and his thuggish colleagues when he made his one official trip to Nazi Germany in June 1937. The Nazis, he confided in his diary, had created social peace and even followed some of the ideas he had laid down in **Industry and Humanity**. Later, in 1938, King recorded his thoughts on Adolf Hitler in his diary:

I am convinced he is a spiritualist—that he has a vision to which he is being true—His going to his parents' grave at the time of his great victory—or rather achievement—the annexation of Austria was most significant—I read aloud from Gunther's **Inside Europe**, concerning his early life—his devotion to his mother—that Mother's spirit is I am certain his guide and no one who does not understand this relationship—the wor-ship of the highest purity in a mother can understand the power to be derived therefrom —or the guidance. I believe the world will yet come to see a very great man—mystic in Hitler. His simple origin & being true to it in his life—not caring for pomp—or titles, etc., clothes—but reality—His dictatorship is a means to an end—needed perhaps to make the Germans conscious of themselves—much I cannot abide in Nazism—the regimentation-cruelty-oppression of Jews—attitude towards religion, etc., but Hitler ... the peasant—will rank some day with Joan of Arc among the deliverers of his people, & if he is only careful may yet be the deliverer of Europe. It is no mere chance that I have met him, & von Ribbentrop & Goering & the others I did—it is part of a mission I believe.[12]

but their government regarded them with suspicion and the Roman Catholic hierarchy in Quebec was openly sympathetic to Franco and the fascists. Canada made no official protest when Hitler annexed Austria or invaded and dismembered Czechoslovakia. Even after Germany invaded Poland and imposed a murderous regime, Mackenzie King suggested to the British government that he try to mediate between the Allies and Nazi Germany.

Though King's main goal in pursuing isolationist policies was to maintain Canadian unity, he was, like many British and French politicians, also motivated by anti-communism. Hitler's anti-communism appealed to capitalists and aristocrats throughout the world who were terrified by the level of frustration and anger expressed by workers and the unemployed during the Depression. Although the violent tactics of Hitler, Mussolini, and Franco were troubling, they guaranteed the survival of the industrial order.

## CONCLUSION

Canadians emerged from the interwar years with few political illusions. Although Canada had become a player in its own right on the international stage, the game of global politics was a dangerous one that threatened to engulf Canadians in another world war. Nor did Canada's new international status do anything to inspire a new national identity. Canadians were divided as never before along class, regional, and cultural lines, and many had abandoned the old two-party system to support new political parties that promised to address these interests. If there was cause for hope, it was that all parties professed to seek a solution to the problem of poverty in the midst of plenty and to make Canada a better place for all Canadians. Time would tell whether such democratic idealism would survive as the new values of the age of mass consumerism.

## POPULISM, RIGHT AND LEFT

*A Historiographical Debate*

The Co-operative Commonwealth Federation and Social Credit are sometimes seen as polar opposites, but not all scholars view them in this manner. Some point to the similarity in origin of these movements: both had urban roots but found a mass audience among Prairie farmers; both claimed a national platform but focused on regional and provincial strategies for political change; neither had an important base outside Western Canada in the 1930s. Both parties were populist—that is, they claimed to be people's movements against the interests of the entrenched political and economic elites who dominated the country.

The CCF's populism was directed against all big capitalists, while Social Credit's populist attack targeted only financial institutions. The CCF may therefore be described as a "left-wing populist" movement because it identified farmers' interests with workers' interests against the interests of big business. Social Credit may be described as "right-wing populist" because it was suspicious of unions and suggested that workers and farmers had interests in common with capitalists other than bankers.

But were these two parties very different in practice? Some scholars say yes.[13] When the CCF assumed office in Saskatchewan in 1944, it nationalized auto insurance and the distribution of natural gas and established a provincial intercity bus company. By contrast, the Alberta government denounced all state ventures in the economy. The CCF pioneered universal free hospital and medical care insurance in Saskatchewan; the Social Credit regime in Alberta insisted that medical care schemes must be voluntary and must involve some direct payment for services by subscribers to prevent abuse of the program. The CCF passed labour legislation that favoured union organization in Saskatchewan, while Social Credit produced a labour code that made unionization difficult. Welfare recipients were subjected to mean-spirited treatment in Alberta, but received some sympathy in Saskatchewan.

Despite these contrasts, many scholars believe that the gap in performance between the CCF in Saskatchewan and Social Credit in Alberta has been exaggerated.[14] They claim that the farm programs of the two governments were similar and that, whatever philosophical differences existed between them, both governments spent lavishly on health, education, and roads. The provincial takeovers in Saskatchewan are held to have had a negligible impact on overall private ownership and direction of the provincial economy.

The claims of the two sides are difficult to adjudicate in part because the Alberta government, awash in oil revenues by the 1950s, had a vastly superior financial base compared to its Saskatchewan counterpart. It could afford to spend extravagantly, all the while deploring the tendencies of governments generally to spend more than they earned. Nonetheless, left-wing critics of Alberta Social Credit suggest that the poor in Alberta were largely passed over in the orgy of public spending. Their point of comparison is usually Saskatchewan, which they allege had more humanitarian social policies. Left-wing critics of the Saskatchewan CCF suggest that, in office, that party attempted to appease powerful elite interests at the ultimate expense of the poor.

## NOTES

1  James Struthers, *No Fault of Their Own: Unemployment and the Canadian Welfare State, 1914–1941* (Toronto: University of Toronto Press, 1983), 83–84

2  Ernest R. Forbes, *Maritime Rights: The Maritime Rights Movement, 1919–1927: A Study in Canadian Regionalism* (Montreal: McGill-Queen's University Press, 1979), 181

3  *Montreal Gazette*, 30 June 1943

4  Donald B. Smith, "Fred Loft and the Future of the First Nations: A Report on Work in Progress" (unpublished paper)

5  Arthur J. Ray, "Periodic Shortages, Native Welfare, and the Hudson's Bay Company, 1670–1930" in *Out of the Background: Readings on Canadian Native History*, 2nd ed., ed. Ken S. Coates and Robin Fisher (Toronto: Copp Clark, 1996), 97

6  E.E. Perley to R.B. Bennett, 6 Jan. 1931, R.B. Bennett Papers, National Archives of Canada

7  Programme of the Co-operative Commonwealth Federation adopted at the First National Convention held at Regina, Sask., July 1933

8  Canada, Royal Commission on Dominion-Provincial Relations, *Hearings* (1938), 8129

9  Alvin Finkel, *Business and Social Reform in the Thirties* (Toronto: Lorimer, 1979), 92

10  Cynthia R. Comacchio, *"Nations Are Built of Babies": Saving Ontario's Mothers and Children, 1900–1940* (Montreal: McGill-Queen's University Press, 1993), 166

11  Health Study Bureau, Toronto, *Review of Canada's Health Needs and Health-Insurance Proposals* (Toronto, 1945), 41

12  King Diaries, 17 March 1938, as quoted in Joy Esbery, "Friend or Foe: King and Hitler" in *Reappraisals in Canadian History: Post-Confederation*, ed. A.D. Gilbert, G.M. Wallace, and R.M. Bray (Toronto: Prentice-Hall, 1992), 395

13  The view that there are sharp differences between Social Credit's performance in Alberta and the CCF performance in Saskatchewan is defended in Alvin Finkel, *The Social Credit Phenomenon in Alberta* (Toronto: University of Toronto Press, 1989), 202-13, and Walter D. Young, *Democracy and Discontent: Progressivism, Socialism and Social Credit in the Canadian West* (Toronto: McGraw-Hill Ryerson, 1978). On the general distinction between left and right variants of populism, see John Richards, "Populism: A Qualified Defence," *Studies in Political Economy* 5 (Spring 1981): 5–27.

14  The best case for the convergence in the behaviour of the two parties in office is made in John F. Conway, "To Seek a Goodly Heritage: The Prairie Populist Responses to the National Policy" (PhD diss., Simon Fraser University, 1978). Peter R. Sinclair argues that the Saskatchewan CCF had lost its early radicalism before winning office. See "The Saskatchewan CCF: Ascent to Power and the Decline of Socialism," *Canadian Historical Review* 54, 4 (Dec. 1973): 419–33. An opposite view is found in Lewis H. Thomas, "The CCF Victory in Saskatchewan, 1944," *Saskatchewan History* 28, 2 (Spring 1975): 52–64.

## SELECTED READING

On the political history of the interwar period, general works include: John Thompson and Alan Seager, *Canada, 1922–1939: Decades of Discord* (Toronto: McClelland and Stewart, 1985); Ian Drummond, Robert Bothwell, and John English, *Canada, 1900–1945* (Toronto: University of Toronto Press, 1987); Douglas Owram, *The Government Generation: Canadian Intellectuals and the State, 1900–1945* (Toronto: University of Toronto Press, 1986); Larry A. Glassford, *Reaction and Reform: The Politics of the Conservative Party Under R.B. Bennett, 1927–1938* (Toronto: University of Toronto Press, 1992); and J.W. Pickersgill, ed., *The Mackenzie King Record*, vols. 1–3 (Toronto: University of Toronto Press, 1960–70).

On Western protest, see David Laycock, *Populism and Democratic Thought in the Canadian Prairies, 1910–1945* (Toronto: University of Toronto Press, 1990); Alvin Finkel, *The Social Credit Phenomenon in Alberta* (Toronto: University of Toronto Press, 1989); W.L. Morton, *The Progressive Party in Canada* (Toronto: University of Toronto Press, 1950); Vernon C. Fowke, *The National Policy and the Wheat Economy* (Toronto: University of Toronto Press, 1957); David R. Elliott and Iris Miller, *Bible Bill: A Biography of William Aberhart* (Edmonton: Reidmore, 1987); L.H. Thomas, ed., *The Making of a Socialist: The Recollections of T.C. Douglas* (Edmonton: University of Alberta Press, 1982); Seymour Martin Lipset, *Agrarian Socialism: The Co-Operative Commonwealth Federation in Saskatchewan* (Berkeley: University of California Press, 1971); Kenneth McNaught, *A Prophet in Politics: A Biography of J.S. Woodsworth* (Toronto: University of Toronto Press, 1959); Allen Mills, *Fool for Christ: The Political Thought of J.S. Woodsworth* (Toronto: University of Toronto Press, 1991); and Ronald Liversedge, *Recollections of the On-to-Ottawa Trek* (Ottawa: Carleton University Press, 1973). On the internment camps, see Laurel Sefton MacDowell, "Relief Camp Workers in Ontario During the Great Depression of the 1930s," *Canadian Historical Review* 76, 2 (June 1995): 205–28.

On political developments in the Atlantic region, important works include Ernest R. Forbes, *Maritime Rights: The Maritime Rights Movement, 1919–1927* (Montreal: McGill-Queen's University Press, 1979); E.R. Forbes and D.A. Muise, eds., *The Atlantic Provinces in Confederation* (Toronto: University of Toronto Press, 1993); David Frank, ed., *Industrialization and Underdevelopment in the Maritimes 1880–1930* (Montreal: McGill-Queen's University Press, 1979); Robert J. Brym and R. James Sacouman, eds., *Underdevelopment and Social Movements in Atlantic Canada* (Toronto: New Hogtown, 1979); Gary Burrill and Ian McKay, eds., *People, Resources and Power: Critical Perspectives on Underdevelopment and Primary Industries in the Atlantic Region* (Fredericton: Acadiensis Press, 1987).

On Canadian communists, see Ian Angus, *Canadian Bolsheviks* (Montreal: Vanguard, 1981); Ivan Avakumovic, *The Communist Party in Canada: A History* (Toronto: McClelland and Stewart, 1975); and William Beeching and Phyllis Clarke, eds., *Yours in the Struggle: The Reminiscences of Tim Buck* (Toronto: NC Press, 1977). On the national CCF, see Walter Young, *Anatomy of a Party: The National CCF, 1932–61* (Toronto: University of Toronto Press, 1969); Norman Penner, *From Protest to Power: Social Democracy in Canada 1900–Present* (Toronto: Lorimer, 1992); and William Brennan, ed., *Building the Co-operative Commonwealth: Essays on the Social Democratic Tradition in Canada* (Regina: Canadian Plains Research Center, 1984). On women in the CCF and the Communist Party, a critical account is Joan Sangster, *Dreams of Equality: Women on the Canadian Left, 1920–1950* (Toronto: McClelland and Stewart, 1989). A biography of a major woman founder of the CCF is Terry Crowley, *Agnes Macphail and the Politics of Equality* (Toronto: Lorimer, 1990). Provincial CCF histories include Nelson Wiseman, *Social Democracy in Manitoba: A History of the CCF–NDP* (Winnipeg: University of Manitoba Press, 1983); and Gerald L. Caplan, *The Dilemma of Canadian Socialism: The CCF in Ontario, 1932–1945* (Toronto: McClelland and Stewart, 1973). On intellectuals and the left, see Michiel Horn, *The League for Social Reconstruction* (Toronto: University of Toronto Press, 1980). On the extreme right, see Martin Robin, *Shades of Right: Nativist and Fascist Politics in Canada, 1920–1940* (Toronto: University of Toronto Press, 1991), and Esther Delisle, *The Traitor and the Jew: Anti-Semitism and Extreme Right-Wing Nationalism in Quebec from 1929 to 1939* (Montreal: R. Davies Publishing, 1993).

On Quebec political developments, see Paul-André Linteau, René Durocher, Jean-Claude Robert, and François Rocard, *Quebec since 1930* (Toronto: Lorimer, 1991); Andrée Lévesque, *Virage à gauche interdit: les communistes, les socialistes, et leurs ennemis au Québec* (Montreal: Boréal Express, 1984); Conrad Black, *Duplessis* (Toronto: McClelland and Stewart, 1979); Bernard L. Vigod, *Quebec Before Duplessis: The Political Career of Louis-Alexandre Taschereau* (Montreal: McGill-Queen's University Press, 1986); and Herbert F. Quinn, *The Union Nationale* (Toronto: University of Toronto Press, 1979).

On the development of the welfare state, see James Struthers, *The Limits of Affluence: Welfare in Ontario, 1920–1970* (Toronto: University of Toronto Press, 1994) and his *No Fault of Their Own: Unemployment and the Canadian Welfare State, 1914–1941* (Toronto: University of Toronto Press, 1981); Raymond B. Blake and Jeff Keshen, eds., *Social Welfare Policy in Canada: Historical Readings* (Toronto: Copp Clark, 1995); James G. Snell, *The Citizen's Wage: The State and the Elderly in Canada, 1900–1951* (Toronto: University of Toronto Press, 1995); Cynthia R. Comacchio, *"Nations Are Built of Babies": Saving Ontario's Mothers and Children, 1900–1940* (Montreal: McGill-Queen's University Press, 1993); and Alvin Finkel, *Business and Social Reform in the Thirties* (Toronto: Lorimer, 1979).

On foreign policy developments, see Norman Hillmer and J.L. Granatstein, *Empire to Umpire: Canada and the World to the 1990s* (Toronto: Copp Clark, 1994), and B.J.C. McKercher and Lawrence Aronson, eds., *The North Atlantic Triangle in a Changing World: Anglo-American-Canadian Relations, 1902–1956* (Toronto: University of Toronto Press, 1996).

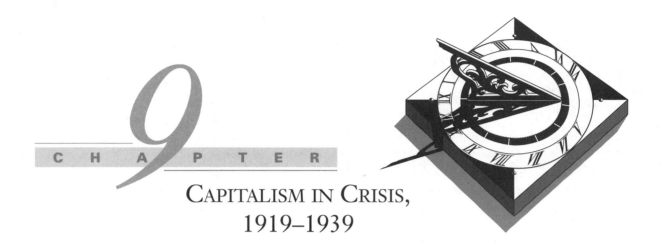

# CHAPTER 9

## CAPITALISM IN CRISIS,
## 1919–1939

DURING THE CHRISTMAS SEASON ONE Depression year, an Eaton's saleswoman witnessed throngs of little girls admiring Shirley Temple dolls. Priced at between nine and sixteen dollars, the dolls cost a month's income for a family on welfare.

> Some used to come at opening time and just stand there looking at those pink-cheeked, golden-haired lovely Shirley Temples. Little faces, they needed food. You could see a lot who needed a pint of milk a day a thousand times more than they needed a Shirley doll. They'd stare for hours. We tried to shush them away, but it didn't do any good.... This, mind you, went on day after day, day after day, until some of the [sales]girls thought they would go crazy. One [clerk] had a crying fit over just that, those hundreds of poor kids who would never own a Shirley Temple in a hundred years. They were lucky if they had breakfast that morning, or soup and bread that night.[1]

This moving account of would-be juvenile consumers speaks volumes about Canada in the interwar years. With its creation of desire through advertising in the modern media, corporate capitalism touched most people, including children. In the 1920s, many ordinary Canadians began to acquire some of the dazzling array of goods that improved technologies made available, but there was too little money in the hands of consumers to find purchasers for all the products that the industrial system produced. In the 1930s, production consequently fell and so did the number of jobs. The unemployed and underemployed seemed to be everywhere. In this chapter, we will look at the causes of the crisis and discuss its impact on Canadian society.

## RIDING THE ECONOMIC ROLLER COASTER

As the second industrial revolution based on the internal combustion engine, resource development, electrical power, and new chemical processes worked its way through the economy in the interwar years, Canadians experienced both the best of times and the worst of times. A prolonged postwar recession gave way to recovery in the second half of the 1920s only to be followed by the Great Depression of the 1930s. Nonetheless, as table 9.1 indicates, the long-term tendency away from primary industries, particularly farming and fishing, continued in the interwar period. While secondary industry held its own, employment and investment growth was concentrated in the tertiary or service

**Table 9.1**

PERCENTAGE SECTORAL DISTRIBUTION OF
THE GROSS NATIONAL PRODUCT, 1920–1940

| Year | Primary | Secondary | Tertiary | Other |
|------|---------|-----------|----------|-------|
| 1920 | 26.6 | 29.7 | 35.3 | 8.4 |
| 1930 | 15.9 | 26.1 | 52.3 | 5.7 |
| 1940 | 17.6 | 26.9 | 45.7 | 9.8 |

*Source: William L. Marr and Donald Paterson,* Canada: An
Economic History *(Toronto: Gage, 1980), 22*

sector. These trends resulted in continued migration from rural to urban areas, and transformed the lives of many Canadians.

Automobiles, the symbol of the modern age, offer a good example of how the economic sectors evolved. By the 1920s, a few Ontario cities had cornered the lion's share of the employment created in the manufacture of cars. However, every city and most towns across Canada had car dealerships, gas stations, repair shops, auto insurance firms, and tire shops. Since Canada's roads were still too primitive to make a cross-country tour anything more than a gruelling marathon, the public demand for better roads led provincial governments to construct hard-surfaced highways along much-travelled routes. Taxes levied on gasoline and cars helped to finance the ribbons of asphalt that cost even more to build and maintain than railway lines. Governments began to employ an army of workers to build and maintain roads and highways, to license drivers and cars, and to police the motorways. No longer tied to train routes, restaurants and cabins appeared along busy highways to cater to the motoring public. Tourism developed to new levels and required more service workers, many of them on a seasonal basis.

The phenomenon of new technologies creating more tertiary jobs than manufacturing work was repeated in many sectors. While a small number of workers were

required to produce radios, many more were employed selling radios, working for radio stations, or producing advertising for this popular medium. Motion picture technology created few manufacturing jobs in Canada, but movie houses sprang up even in small towns, employing projectionists, popcorn sellers, ushers, and piano players. In the late 1920s, the arrival of talking movies created unemployment for piano players but raised the number of movie houses and movie goers to new heights.

The selling of products also created employment, even if the growth of department stores and the arrival of supermarkets reduced the number of corner stores. Along with bigger stores came bigger advertising budgets, and advertising not only employed people directly, but also made possible the expansion of the staffs of radio and newspaper offices. Department stores and other large retailers such as People's Credit Jewellers made extensive use of credit to lure customers. Unlike small neigh-

*Clerical employment expanded in the postwar period as the service sector grew. As this photograph (circa 1919) of the main office of the Great West Life Assurance Company in Winnipeg illustrates, some of the new clerical employees were women. While office hierarchies reserved senior administrative posts and better salaries for men, an increasing number of women found employment as secretaries, stenographers, and file clerks.*

Great-West Life Assurance Co. Archives

bourhood stores and shops, chain stores usually did not know their customers, and they established credit departments to investigate credit worthiness of applicants for store accounts. In major cities, credit companies cooperated to establish credit clearing bureaus. Finance companies, which often charged extortionate rates, were formed to lend money to those eager to consume but regarded as poor credit risks by banks and retailers. Men could find employment as credit collectors and "repo men," repossessing goods when consumers could no longer make their payments. In the modern age, money made the world go around, and a complex world it was too.

## The Turbulent Twenties

After the armistice, the Union government moved quickly to reduce state involvement in the economy. Defence spending was slashed and pressures to create welfare programs were largely resisted. Although veterans received some consideration, the government took the position that it was up to market forces to make up for the slack resulting from the transition to peacetime conditions. When the Liberals came to power in 1921 they, like their predecessors, focused on reducing the deficit accumulated during the war rather than on stimulating the economy.

Between 1920 and 1924, a persistent recession, marked by double-digit unemployment rates, gripped the country. Eventually the market turned around in most regions and occupations, and the recovery over the next five years was sufficiently robust that the Canadian economy in the 1920s recorded a higher rate of growth than in the previous decade. The roaring success of the American economy, which was increasingly dependent on foreign markets and resources in this period, encouraged investment in Canada. As in the first two decades of the twentieth century, much of the growth in the Canadian economy came from the staples of wheat, pulp and paper, minerals, and hydro-electric power. Automobiles and electrical appliances were the leading manufactured products, while the service sector continued its steady

rise to undisputed dominance, accounting for over half of the GNP by 1930.

Apart from government indifference, several factors made the transition from a wartime to a peacetime economy a difficult one for Canadians. Export markets, which absorbed over one-third of the value of Canadian output between 1916 and 1918, contracted sharply. In 1920, near-drought conditions in the southern Prairies and a precipitous drop in wheat prices spelled disaster for the wheat economy. Protectionist sentiment in the United States led to increased tariffs, which were particularly hard-felt in Canada. In 1921, manufacturing, construction, and transportation industries stagnated, and the GNP dipped an ominous 20.1 percent.

As the effects of the slump reverberated throughout the economy, companies went bankrupt at an unprecedented rate, unemployment rose sharply, and migration to the United States increased dramatically. Even banks were brought to their knees, resulting in desperate mergers and the messy collapse in August 1923 of the Home Bank with its seventy branches. Besieged by angry petitioners, Ottawa agreed to pay $3 million in compensation to depositors of the Home Bank. In 1924, the federal government created the office of Inspector General of Banks as a step towards restoring confidence in the badly shaken banking system.

From its trough in 1922, the economic barometer began to rise, and by 1924 the clouds of recession had lifted. Massive investment in old and new staple industries in response to foreign demand, and often with foreign capital, helped to spur the recovery. As in the prewar era, the exploitation of Canada's farming, forest, and mining frontiers was made possible through technological advances. During the 1920s, tractors became more common on Canadian farms, airplanes served as a valuable aid to mineral exploration, and the selective flotation process proved an effective way of separating base and precious metals from compound ores.

As markets for wheat in Britain and Europe began to return to their earlier buoyancy, Prairie farmers expanded their acreage, and immigration to the West resumed. Between 1925 and 1929, the Prairie provinces brought nearly 24 million hectares under cultivation, produced an average of over 400 million bushels of wheat annually, and supplied 40 percent of the world's export market. After three decades of expansion, the wheat economy was a complex network of growing, harvesting, and marketing mechanisms. Farmer-owned cooperatives competed with private corporations to market the grain and secure the best prices on volatile world markets.

Encouraged by orderly marketing procedures established during the war, western farmers in the 1920s experimented with a system of wheat pools. Producers agreed to sell their wheat to a common pool and share the returns, rather than gamble individually on the Winnipeg Grain Exchange. With high prices in the late 1920s, the system worked well, and just over half of the wheat crop was sold through co-ops in 1929. When markets glutted and prices fell during the Great Depression, neither pools nor private companies could save farmers from ruin.

The most spectacular new staple industry of the 1920s was pulp and paper. Following the abolition of the American tariff on imported newsprint

## ENVIRONMENTAL CATASTROPHE: THE MYTH OF HUSBANDERS OF THE SOIL

The misery of the farmers of the southern Prairies during the Depression provides one of the enduring images of the decade. Southern Saskatchewan, southeastern Alberta, and southwestern Manitoba turned into a dust bowl where farmers' attempts to grow their cereal crops were mocked by drought, dust, and wind. "The Wind Our Enemy," by Anne Marriott, gave poetic voice to the farmers' disillusionment with nature's attack on their livelihood.

Prairie farmers liked to think of themselves as husbanders of the soil. Arguably, though, at the root of the farmers' problems was a futile attempt to dominate the natural environment rather than to respect its limitations. Dryland farmers ignored warnings from government experts about the dangers of one-crop farming, presuming that science and new technologies could conquer all obstacles. With wheat prices rising in the 1920s, farmers opted for short-term financial gains rather than for the longer-term security that might come from diversification of crops and from animal husbandry.

A disastrous drought from 1917 to 1921, accompanied by an invasion of grasshoppers, was followed by frequent and devastating attacks of rust and smut. Sawflies, cutworms, and wireworms caused millions of dollars of damage annually to repeatedly sown cropland. In Saskatchewan alone, 57 percent of all homesteaders were forced to abandon their land between 1911 and 1931. By that time, there were few traces of the buffalo landscape that had characterized the region in the mid-nineteenth century. Natural predators had been eliminated or reduced to small populations, and the vegetational composition was changed by cattle and horses overgrazing on fenced-in ranches.

*Duststorm of the 1930s.*
Glenbow Archives/NA-2496-1

The monoculture of wheat had transformed the environment and farmers' language testified to their view that this transformation represented "progress." As historian Barry Potyondi notes: "The everyday terminology of the farmers depreciated the value of the natural world and hinted at the artificiality of their intrusion: 'cultivated' crops and 'tame' grass replaced 'wild' hay; machinery replaced horsepower; 'correction' lines replaced ancient trails that followed natural contours. This was a collision of natural and human forces on a grand scale, legislated into being and mediated by science and technology." [2]

in 1913, Canadian output grew from 402 000 tons in 1913 to 2 985 000 in 1930, making Canada the world's largest producer of newsprint. The meteoric rise of the industry was capped during the 1920s when pulp and newsprint began to rival King Wheat as Canada's most valuable export. Much of the investment in pulp and paper came from the United States, which continued to absorb the bulk of the output. Although pulp and paper operations were scattered from Nova Scotia to British Columbia, over half of the productive capacity was located in Quebec, where abundant and accessible forest resources, cheap labour, and attractive power rates attracted capital. The demand for pulp and paper breathed new life into the forestry industry of the Ottawa, St Maurice, Saguenay, and Miramichi Rivers, and animated declining communities such as Liverpool, Nova Scotia, and Kapuskasing, Ontario.

Unplanned growth in the newsprint industry resulted in cutthroat competition and unstable market conditions. The Big Three—the International Paper Company, Abitibi Power and Paper, and the Canadian Power and Paper Company—together with the Little Three—Backus-Brooks, St Lawrence Paper, and Price Brothers—controlled 86 percent of Canada's newsprint industry, but were unable to bring order to the market. Between 1920 and 1926, the price of newsprint dropped from $136 to $65 a ton. In 1927–28, newsprint producers tried to control output, allocate tonnage, and set prices, but the American-based International Paper Company defied such efforts, offering to supply the Hearst newspaper interests at $7 to $10 per ton below cartel prices. In December 1928, Quebec's premier Louis-Alexandre Taschereau travelled to New York to persuade the big interests not to undermine the industry that was so crucial to the economy of his province. By threatening to "change the timber duties overnight," rebating to the mills who lived up to the agreement, he managed to secure a $5 per ton increase, but the International Paper Company persisted in its breakaway pricing policies. During the Depression, newsprint dropped below $40 a ton, causing chaos in the industry.

As in pulp and paper development, Quebec also surged ahead in electrical generating capacity. By the early 1930s, Quebec accounted for nearly 50 percent of Canada's electrical energy. Private capitalists in Quebec developed power primarily for industrial purposes: in 1933, 96.5 percent of the province's capacity was devoted to industry, compared to 82.6 percent in Ontario. Other provinces lagged far behind Quebec and Ontario, although British Columbia had huge hydro potential and, together with the Yukon, produced nearly 10 percent of Canada's hydro-electrical power. Because of the availability of abundant hydro-electric resources, Canada became the site of aluminum manufacture. Bauxite from the West Indies was imported to Quebec where intensive electrolysis isolated aluminum for industrial use. By the 1930s, the Aluminum Company of Canada, originally established in 1902 as a subsidiary of an American corporation, had emerged as the world's second largest aluminum producer, its new reduction plant in Arvida, Quebec, one of the marvels of Canada's industrial age.

During the 1920s, Canada's mining frontier continued to attract investment. The rich gold and copper ores in the Abitibi region of Quebec around Rouyn-Noranda were developed by a Toronto-based corporation, Noranda Mines. In 1927, Hudson Bay Mining and Smelting, a creation of the Whitney syndicate of New York, began to work the copper-zinc ores near Flin Flon, Manitoba. New uses for nickel in the appliance and automobile industry, as well as in the Canadian five-cent piece, kept Sudbury booming. In 1928, a merger ensured that Inco (Canada) controlled 90 percent of the world nickel market. The demand for gasoline and oil products rose quickly with growing sales of automobiles. Canada's largest petroleum company, Imperial Oil, a subsidiary of the American corporate giant Standard Oil, expanded its operations in Turner Valley, Alberta. By 1925, Alberta oil fields accounted for over 90 percent of Canada's petroleum output, but only 5 percent of Canadian consumption was supplied by Canadian wells. The rest was imported from the United States, the Caribbean, Latin America, and Borneo.

In the manufacturing sector, what economists

call consumer durables—automobiles, radios, household appliances, and furniture—were the big success story of the 1920s. Since Ontario had the largest number of consumers, it is perhaps not surprising that most of the companies producing consumer durables were located in that province.

Most of Canada's independent automobile manufacturers were left in the dust by the Big Three American firms—Ford, General Motors, and Chrysler—which controlled two-thirds of the Canadian market. High tariffs on imported cars encouraged the American giants to establish branch plants to supply the Canadian market as well as the British Empire, in which Canada had a tariff advantage. By the 1920s, Canada's automobile industry was the second largest in the world, and exports accounted for over one-third of its output. The spectacular growth of Oshawa, Windsor, and Walkerville, where the assembly plants of the big automobile manufacturers were located, was proof enough of the significance of "the great god Car." Between 1920 and 1930, the number of cars jumped from one for every twenty-two Canadians to one for every 8.5. Ford's economical Model T was particularly popular until GM's Chevrolet managed to capture the fancy of consumers in the late 1920s.

At its pre-Depression height in 1928, automobile manufacturing employed over sixteen thousand people directly, and many more in parts and service. The burgeoning industry gobbled up iron, rubber, plate glass, leather, aluminum, lead, nickel, tin, and, of course, gasoline. In 1926–27, the federal government reduced tariffs on automobiles in an effort to bring down prices, and it introduced Canadian content rules to encourage more parts manufacturing in Canada. Despite the uncertainty introduced by such policies, the Big Three and their parts suppliers continued to maintain a vigorous trade. Thus, transportation remained an important component of industrial growth, with automobiles rapidly gaining on trains as the leading sector in the transport industry.

The electrical appliance industry was another area of postwar growth. Radios were particularly popular but so, too, were washing machines, toasters, electric ranges, and vacuum cleaners. Like the automobile, household appliances were falling in price during the 1920s, coming increasingly within reach of the middle-class consumer. Canadian General Electric and Westinghouse were the giants of appliance manufacturing, and during the decade Hoover, Philco, and Phillips became household names. Only a few Canadian-owned companies, such as Moffatt and Rogers Majestic, managed to carve out a niche for themselves in the rapidly expanding appliance market. Whether wholly Canadian owned or American branch plants, Canadian companies drew most of their product designs and production technologies from the United States. A notable exception was the "batteryless" radio, capable of running on alternating current, developed by Toronto-born Edward Samuel Rogers in 1927.

In the new age of consumerism, wholesaling, retailing, banking, and insurance expanded as never before, while the paperwork associated with corporate enterprise kept offices growing. Spurred by the power of advertising and by low prices achieved through mass purchases, chain operations grabbed over 20 percent of the Canadian retail market by the end of the 1920s. In the variety-store business, chains accounted for an astounding 90 percent of sales. Indeed, chains became the symbol of consumer society, promoting mass taste and uniformity in culture. Eaton's invested in chain operations, and outlets of such American companies as Woolworth, Kresge, and Metropolitan stores could be found on the main streets of most Canadian towns. In the grocery business, Dominion and Safeway became prominent names. Direct sales by such companies as Imperial Oil, Kodak, and Singer also became a feature of the retailing scene in the 1920s.

The impressive growth in some consumer durable, service, and staple industries masked problems in other areas of the Canadian economy. In the Atlantic provinces, farming and fishing were crippled by falling prices. Market gardening remained a lucrative activity near large urban centres, but farmers and fishers who depended on international markets faced stiff competition, soft markets, and the constant threat of exclusionary tariffs. Primary producers across the country exper-

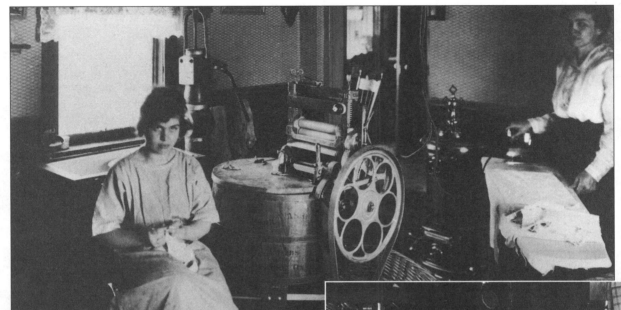

*A modern kitchen in 1921.*

Ontario Hydro/HP 1043

imented with cooperative marketing organizations and attempted to improve their efficiency by investing in new machinery, but they were always at the mercy of market forces over which they had little control. The frustration of Prince Edward Island farmers is revealed in the following tongue-in-cheek account, published in the Charlottetown *Patriot*, in March 1928:

> Potatoes are seeds that are planted and grown in Prince Edward Island to keep the producer broke and the buyer crazy. The tuber varies in colour and weight, and the man who can guess the nearest to the size of the crop while it is growing is called the "Potato Man" by the public, a "Fool" by the farmer, and a "Poor Businessman" by his creditors.

> The price of potatoes is determined by the man who has to eat them, and goes up when you have sold and down when you have bought. A dealer working for a group of shippers was sent to Boston to watch the potato market, and after a few days' deliberation, he wired his employers to this effect: "Some think they will go up and some think they will go down. I do too. Whatever you do will be wrong. Act at once." [3]

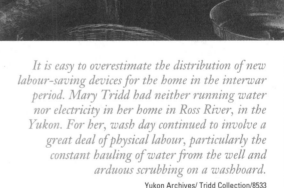

*It is easy to overestimate the distribution of new labour-saving devices for the home in the interwar period. Mary Tridd had neither running water nor electricity in her home in Ross River, in the Yukon. For her, wash day continued to involve a great deal of physical labour, particularly the constant hauling of water from the well and arduous scrubbing on a washboard.*

Yukon Archives/ Tridd Collection/8533

Having invested labour and capital in an attempt to improve their efficiency, farmers and fishers could no longer retreat into comfortable subsistence to ride out hard times. Nor would they want to. Like everyone else in the modern age, they longed for the comforts and advantages that the

## RUM RUNNING

One of the occupations that supplemented the incomes of both rich and poor in the interwar years was "rum running." With the United States committed to a rigorous policy of prohibition between 1920 and 1933, Canadians, especially in provinces where prohibition laws had been lifted or where they were imperfectly enforced, could not resist the opportunity to make big money in the illicit alcohol trade that flourished south of the border. Canadian liquor entered the United States at remote check points, by boat, by air, and even over the ice during the winter.

The Maritime provinces were particularly well-situated to supply the eastern seaboard with liquor. Much of the booze was legally produced in Montreal and Toronto

for export to Saint Pierre and Miquelon. From there, Maritime fishing vessels carried it legally to "rum row," just outside the American twelve-mile limit, where it awaited fast motor launches of the American crime syndicates who smuggled it into the country. By 1925, half the Lunenburg fishing fleet was reputedly engaged in the rum trade.

It was during the prohibition era that Canadian distillery owners such as Samuel Bronfman laid the basis for a thriving Canadian export industry and vast personal fortunes. In an effort to stop clandestine activities and to tap some of the wealth generated by the liquor trade, most provincial governments quickly abandoned prohibition and assumed direct control over the sale of alcohol.

---

new consumer society offered. If they could not get them by farming and fishing, then they would become part of the stream of labour moving into the city. Nearly a million Canadians moved to the United States in the turbulent twenties.

Primary producers were not the only ones who faced uncertainty in the 1920s. In many of the industries that defined the first phase of the Industrial Revolution, including railways, coal, and iron and steel, atrophy had set in. Canada's two national railways embarked on an orgy of spending on branch lines, steamships, and hotels, piling up debts when they should have been retrenching to meet the fast-developing competition from automobiles. When retrenchment finally came and the demand for rails and rolling stock decreased, the iron and steel industry languished. Only the Hamilton-based companies Stelco and Dofasco, fattened by the demands of the nearby automobile industry, survived the 1920s unscathed. Algoma and the new Montreal-based holding company for the Maritime iron and steel industries, BESCO, were dependent on railway orders and faced trying times. Their managers were unable or unwilling to make the investments necessary to retool their operations for the second industrial revolution. BESCO was a particularly ill-fated corporation. Under the presidency of Roy "the Wolf" Wolvin,

BESCO initiated a series of layoffs, wage reductions, and production cutbacks that brought industrial Cape Breton to the brink of civil war. At the same time, over half of the rolled steel used in the manufacture of consumer durables in the 1920s was imported. The crisis in iron and steel, in turn, reduced the demand for coal. Since the Ontario-based companies increasingly purchased their coal from the United States, the share of the market held by Canadian coal producers fell from 50 to 40 percent during the 1920s.

A few Canadians made fortunes by riding the waves of opportunity in the interwar years, but the economic transition brought only hardship to many. Historian Michiel Horn suggests that during the interwar period "it is likely that more than half of the Canadian people were never anything but poor."[4] In 1929, the average wage of $1200 per year was $230 below what social workers estimated a family required to live above poverty level. The "roaring twenties" did not even purr for many Canadians, but worse was yet to come.

## THE DIRTY THIRTIES

The problems experienced in a few industries and in some regions in the 1920s became the concern of everyone from 1929 to 1933. Although Canadians had become accustomed to economic cycles, there was nothing in the past to compare to the Great Depression of the 1930s. Capitalism had finally met its Waterloo, or so it seemed, and no one was in a position to stop the suffering caused by collapsing export markets, falling prices, and widespread unemployment. As businesses failed, banks teetered on the brink of collapse, and even the federal government faced insolvency, everyone asked the same question: What had happened to precipitate such a calamity?

The crash of the New York stock market on 29 October 1929 signalled the beginning, but was not the cause, of the Great Depression. A symbol of the underlying problems in the international economy, the crash reflected the shaky foundations upon which the prosperity of the period from 1924 to 1929 had been based. That foundation was the unprecedented productivity made possible by new technologies and continuing reorganization of corporate practices. Since investment in the production of more commodities only made sense if there were people to buy them, the purchasing power of consumers was of critical importance to the success of the industrial sector. Studies now show that in most countries the income of the working class lagged far behind the availability of new goods. In the United States, for example, the Brookings Institute estimated that productivity increased by 40 percent in the boom of the 1920s, but workers' wages rose only 8 percent while profits soared by 80 percent. Moneys not distributed as profits often went into new investments and, for a time, before inventories piled up, speculators bid up the price of stocks in expectation of continued economic growth. With stock issues largely unregulated by the state, a variety of countries witnessed gigantic sales of stocks that had been pushed far beyond their real worth by profit-seeking speculators. Such business practices, when they became publicly known in 1929, scared many investors away from the stock market.

Although Americans led the way in the speculative frenzy, Canadians were not far behind. The country's richest capitalist, Sir Herbert Holt, had made an attempt in 1928 and 1929 to effect a merger of all the Canadian-owned pulp and paper companies in the country. The resulting company, Canada Power and Pulp, with assets of $60 million, issued debentures of $160 million, confident of its ability to turn around the bidding down of newsprint prices and thereby substantially increase the value of its assets. But holdout companies ruined the prospective monopoly's plans even before the Depression had begun. The company was insolvent by the early 1930s. Little wonder that investors grew cautious about moving their money out of savings accounts into stocks and bonds over which there seemed to be no public regulation.

Trade with other countries offered the possibility of finding consumers abroad for items that home markets could not afford, but the 1920s was a period of global overproduction. There were no international bodies that could orchestrate a slowdown in production in the 1920s or ease the fall in production in the 1930s. The United States, the one country with the economic clout to assume a leadership role in the international economy, was unwilling to do so. As panic set in, the United States followed tight-money policies that squeezed not only its own borrowers, but also international borrowers dependent on American loans. Once the global downward spiral started, it took on a life of its own. Prices dropped dramatically and then dropped again and again, as producers tried to convince someone to buy their products. Governments reacted by erecting high tariff barriers against imports.

Canada was especially hard hit by the Depression. Its small and open economy was buoyed by exports of primary products, which the world now decided it no longer needed. Because the American market had played such an important role in the expansion of the 1920s, the collapse of the American economy could only mean disaster for its major trading partner. To make matters worse, in 1930 the American Congress legislated the highest tariff barriers in the country's history. But that was only the beginning. Competition from Argentine and Australian wheat, a problem throughout the 1920s, became increasingly serious in the 1930s as wheat prices dropped to their lowest in over a century. As the price of basic foods eroded, the market for fresh and salt fish collapsed. Automobile sales dropped to less than a quarter of their 1929 level, the contraction of the empire market compounding a shrinking domestic demand. By 1933, the value of Canada's exports was less than half what it had been in 1929. Although export volumes resumed their earlier levels by the late 1930s, values remained below the inflated 1929 figure (see table 9.2).

actually fired from their jobs, ostensibly to provide more work for men supporting families. During the Depression, the average wage in the clerical "pink-collar" sector, where women predominated, dropped below the average wage in the male-dominated "blue-collar" sector. In manufacturing, the wages of women workers were about 60 percent of men's wages in 1939.

Minimum wages for women workers in various economic sectors had been legislated in most provinces during the 1920s. The wage floors were generally well below the minimum level required for a woman to support herself, reflecting the reigning patriarchal view that women in the workforce ought to be living in their parents' home and biding their time until marriage when they would leave the labour force and be financially supported by their husbands. Even the minimum wage was not always enforced: waitresses in Edmonton restaurants had to strike in 1935 to force their employers to pay the modest minimum wages that Alberta law prescribed for their jobs.

**Table 9.2**

### PERCENTAGE SECTORAL DISTRIBUTION OF THE GROSS NATIONAL PRODUCT, 1920–1940

|  | 1926 | 1929 | 1933 | 1937 | 1939 |
|---|---|---|---|---|---|
| GNP* | 5152 | 6134 | 3510 | 5257 | 5636 |
| Exports* | 1261 | 1152 | 529 | 997 | 925 |
| Farm income* | 609 | 392 | 66 | 280 | 362 |
| Gross fixed capital formation* | 808 | 1344 | 319 | 809 | 746 |
| Automobile sales (thousands) | 159 | 205 | 45 | 149 | 126 |
| Common stock prices (1935–39=100) | 200.6 | 203.4 | 97.3 | 122.4 | 86.1 |
| Unemployment (thousands) | 108 | 116 | 826 | 411 | 529 |
| Unemployment (percent of labour force) | 3.0 | 2.8 | 19.3 | 9.1 | 11.4 |
| Cost of living index (1935–39=100) | 121.7 | 121.6 | 94.3 | 101.2 | 101.5 |
| Wage rates (1949=100) | 46.1 | 48.5 | 41.6 | 47.3 | 48.9 |
| Corporation profits ($ millions pre-tax) | 325 | 396 | 73 | 280 | 362 |

millions, current dollars

Source: Michael Bliss, Northern Enterprise: Five Centuries of Canadian Business
Toronto: McClelland and Stewart, 1987, 418–19

With companies collapsing, and those that survived firing workers, unemployment reached unprecedented levels. The two national railways alone laid off 65 000 employees in the first four years of the Depression. Although unemployment figures are elusive for this period, nearly 20 percent of the labour force was officially classified as unemployed in 1933, the worst year of the Depression. Many more Canadians were underemployed, working part time and in menial jobs that did not utilize their skills and training. Since rural poverty and underemployment were never measured by statistical analyses, it is impossible to quantify the exact level of misery that prevailed outside the cities.

As had always been the case in Canada, seasonal unemployment added greatly to the poverty of working people. Hidden unemployment was rife in the 1930s as women were forced into unwanted retirement and, in the case of married women,

During the Depression, some people profited while others suffered. For example, Gray Miller, chief executive officer of Imperial Tobacco, earned $25 000 a year, at the same time that clerks in the company's United Cigar Stores earned as little as $1300 a year for a fifty-four-hour week. The Depression also benefited people on fixed incomes, such as bondholders and recipients of insurance payments, and those who were able to find full-time employment. Prices fell more rapidly than hourly wages, but it was no mean feat to get enough hours of work to make this differential meaningful. In the manufacturing sector, administrative and supervisory staff did well, receiving salary reductions substantially below the reduction in the cost of living.

Although it had the potential to do so, the tax system did little to alleviate the imbalance in incomes that occurred within the marketplace. The rates of corporate and personal income taxes had been reduced in the 1920s, with the result that only 130 000 Canadians in a population of about 10 million paid federal income taxes in 1929. During the Depression, the minimum income above which income tax was charged fell from $3000 to $2000 per year for married individuals and to $1000 for single people. These changes produced 300 000 income-tax-payers in 1939. Direct taxes remained low, and indirect taxes, such as the tariff and sales taxes, collected from the poor as well as the rich, accounted for over two-thirds of federal tax collections by the end of the 1930s. The provinces, starved for cash, began to introduce modest personal and corporate income taxes.

In cities, the unemployed were dependent upon social assistance, or "relief," from the municipal authorities. Rates varied across the country, but everywhere they were low, and dozens of regulations existed to restrict funds to recipients deemed morally worthy. Reflecting long-standing beliefs that the destitute were responsible for their own plight, municipal councils tended to adopt the view that the unemployed could not budget for themselves. Most municipalities gave vouchers for food and rent to married men, usually with strict rules about what food could be purchased. Single men, if they were deemed eligible at all, were usually required to use their vouchers to get food in communal feeding halls and shelter in hostels.

Both the low rates of relief and the demeaning regulations provoked mass demonstrations and relief strikes across the country, which often met with success in convincing councils to treat the

unemployed less parsimoniously. For example, in Saskatoon in 1932, a sitdown strike by forty-eight women and their children at city hall ended after two days when the council agreed to their demands to: reduce the amount of money that relief recipi-

*Soup kitchen in Edmonton, 1933.*
Glenbow Archives/ND3 6523 B

ents had to pay back when they found work; close the relief store where social assistance recipients were segregated as shoppers; and limit the powers of bureaucrats regulating relief.

While the lives of all unemployed people were grim, gender and race determined how grim. Most cities made no provision for single unemployed women without dependants, or for never-married women with dependants. In November 1930, the Vancouver relief rolls included 4513 married men and 5244 single men. Only 155 women were on city relief, and they appear to have been mainly widows and deserted wives with dependants. Charity organizations were left to establish a women's hostel in the city. Reforms came gradually, mainly in response to a concerted campaign by the Women's Labour League and the Unemployed Women and Girls Club. At various times in 1933, the city provided milk to women with babies, relief for ill single women, medical care for pregnant women, clothing allowances for married women and their children, and assistance to needy Japanese and Chinese families. Asian and African Canadians were more likely to be denied relief than their European-origin counterparts among the unemployed. In British Columbia, the relief rates for Asian-origin recipients were set at half the rate for whites. In Calgary, only a spirited campaign by the Communist Party resulted in the city's destitute Chinese citizens becoming eligible for social assistance.

In the first four years of the Depression, per capita income dropped sharply (see table 9.3). Saskatchewan, staggering under the double assault of the collapse of the wheat economy and massive crop failures, experienced the greatest descent in income. Drought plagued the southern Prairies for most of the decade and raised fears that the region might swirl away with the dust storms that characterized the hot, dry summers. Gophers, which flourished in this climate, provided food for many poor families. Government bounties on gopher tails also provided many a child with pocket money. In every western province, the decline in staple exports had devastating consequences. Saskatchewan's net farm income—that is, receipts minus costs of operation—was a negative figure

| Table 9.3 | | | |
|---|---|---|---|
| PER CAPITA INCOME BY PROVINCE, 1928–29, 1933 | | | |
| Province | 1928–29 | 1933 | Average decrease (%) |
| British Columbia | $594 | $314 | 47 |
| Ontario | 549 | 310 | 44 |
| Alberta | 548 | 212 | 61 |
| Saskatchewan | 478 | 135 | 72 |
| Manitoba | 466 | 240 | 49 |
| Quebec | 391 | 220 | 44 |
| Nova Scotia | 322 | 207 | 36 |
| New Brunswick | 292 | 180 | 39 |
| Prince Edward Island | 278 | 154 | 45 |

*Source:* Rowell-Sirois Report, *Book 1*, Canada: 1868–1939

from 1931 to 1933. Without federal relief, there would have been mass starvation or mass migration away from rural Western Canada during the Depression.

The Maritime provinces could ill afford to sink any lower, but they did. Dependent on primary industries and international trade, the Maritimes, like the Prairies, faced a genuine crisis in the 1930s. Even their major source of relief—outmigration—was closed as Maritimers who fell on hard times elsewhere returned home during the Depression, reversing a trend that had dominated the region for half a century. The Depression highlighted the underdeveloped state of municipal and social services in the Maritime region as well as the utter inadequacy of the region's rapidly shrinking tax base. Unable to find the money to participate in federal cost-sharing programs to help the destitute, the region's governments were responsible for some of the most mean-spirited relief policies in the nation. Unemployed miners in Cape Breton received less than a dollar a week to feed their families, and in New Brunswick, officials prosecuted relief recipients who produced a child out of wedlock. Without the aid of relatives, neighbours, and charitable organizations, many of the region's dependent citizens—estimated at more than 12 percent of the popula-

*The decline in prosperity of western farmers was symbolized by the "Bennett buggy," a motor car that a farm family could no longer afford to operate in the conventional way. Hitched to a horse, it became an old-fashioned wagon.*

Saskatchewan Archives Board/ R-A19945

tion in 1933—would have succumbed to starvation. As it was, an untold number of people on relief died because hospital services were denied them until they were too far gone to be cured.

## NEWFOUNDLAND ON THE ROCKS

The Depression proved fatal for Newfoundland's long-standing efforts to preserve its relative political independence of Britain. Although successive governments after the First World War attempted to use the state apparatus to encourage a stable fishery and a more diversified economy, the edifice of responsible government collapsed in a haze of debt and scandal in 1933.

Prospects looked different in November 1919 when Richard Anderson Squires became premier. Squires's Liberal Reform Party allied with William Coaker's Fishermen's Protective Union to form a coalition government in which Coaker was responsible for fisheries policy. In an effort to help the outport fishing economy, Coaker set minimum market prices for cod and penalties for exporters who attempted to undersell. He also established a government-controlled fish-culling system, with trade agents hired in foreign markets. In 1921, the regulations were repealed because exporters simply ignored them. The fisheries failed to make the transition to an industrial economy, with results that would prove disastrous.

Although Newfoundland already carried a heavy debt load from earlier railway construction and the financing of its war effort, Squires borrowed more money. He used it for projects designed to make Newfoundland a more attractive site for investors as well as to oil his party's patronage machine. Because of postwar inflation, the interest rates on borrowed money were relatively high. The government was successful in 1923 in reaching an agreement with Newfoundland Power and Pulp to develop a paper mill at Corner Brook, but the Squires government collapsed in scandal in 1923. The next five years were mainly years of retrenchment. In 1927, the Judicial Committee of the Privy Council decided in Newfoundland's favour in the long-standing border dispute between

Labrador and Quebec, but it was one of only a few bright spots in a difficult decade.

Depressed as the Newfoundland economy was in the 1920s, it was devastated by the collapse of international markets for resources in the 1930s. With 98 percent of its exports coming from the fish, forestry, and mineral sectors, Newfoundland was unable to keep up payments to its mainly British creditors and at the same time provide minimal social assistance to a growing population of destitute citizens. Squires was elected premier again in 1928 and had few answers when the Depression resulted in the country's insolvency. In August 1932, a demonstration of unemployed workers in St John's deteriorated into a riot that gutted the legislature and forced Squires to call an election. The United Newfoundland Party, led by Frederick Alderdice, won an overwhelming victory, but it had no solutions to the financial crisis. In desperation, the government turned to Britain for help.

Britain established a commission of inquiry into the colony's future. Headed by a Scottish peer, Lord Amulree, the commission recommended the suspension of Newfoundland democracy and the handing over of power to a British-appointed commission of government headed by a governor. While humiliated, the members of the House of Assembly felt that they had no choice but to acquiesce. The commission of government, which came into operation in February 1934, brought an injection of British funds to pay off interest on debts, and began programs to encourage cooperatives and a cottage hospital system in the outports. Nevertheless, the loss of local democracy demonstrated the vulnerability of the once-proud dominion to the ravages of economic depression.

## HANGING ON BY THE FINGERNAILS

The Canadian economy managed to weather the crisis, but it experienced some difficult moments. In September 1931, Canada's dollar began dropping in relation to American currency, and the New York capital market refused to make any more Canadian loans. Since corporations and governments at all levels borrowed in New York, the situation was critical. In October, three big Montreal brokerage firms went into receivership when panicky American creditors called in their loans. Sun Life, Canada's largest insurance company, and most of Canada's investment and brokerage firms were on the verge of bankruptcy. Forced to declare their real profit-and-loss positions, many Canadian corporations would have had to admit insolvency. Most were not called upon to do so, agreeing among themselves, with government approval, to accept the paper value of their increasingly worthless assets. To pay its bills, the federal government resorted to wartime precedents of borrowing money from the public. A National Service Loan of $150 million—oversubscribed by $72 million—helped to pull Canada through the crisis. Ottawa also came to the rescue of the provincial governments, most of which were deeply in debt.

The path to economic recovery in Canada proved to be long and difficult. By 1934, in tandem with the United States, the economic cycle had begun to edge upward, and most economic indicators showed a slow but steady rise until 1938, when the spillover of a sharp American recession brought them tumbling down again. Unemployment still hovered around 11 percent in 1939, although GNP had almost regained the levels of the late 1920s. Rearmament in Britain, which created a market for Canadian minerals, aided the process of recovery. Only with the demand created by the Second World War did the economic clouds finally lift entirely.

The "self-regulating" aspects of free enterprise manifested themselves in the speed with which various industries recovered from the Great Depression. While most entrepreneurs were slow to gamble on new investment, the automobile industry rebounded quickly. Radio stations, cinemas, and oil and gas companies showed steady growth, especially in the second half of the 1930s. When the price of gold was artificially raised from $20 to $35 during the Depression, mining companies had little difficulty attracting investors. Ontario and British Columbia were the main beneficiaries of the gold-mining boom, but many provinces—and the territories—experienced their

own gold rushes in the 1930s. Discoveries of the mineral pitchblende near Great Bear Lake made Eldorado Gold Mines one of the success stories of the Depression. The source of radium used in the treatment of cancer, pitchblende also contains uranium, initially considered a useless by-product of the mining process.

The Great Depression served as a serious shock to western capitalism. It did not, however, dislodge that system; nor did it seriously impede its momentum. In many respects, the liberal economists were right: the downward swing cut out the economic deadwood and let the strongest survive. By the end of the 1930s, a handful of huge corporations dominated most of Canada's productive capacity. Nevertheless, as the Depression ran its course, many Canadians came to the conclusion that survival of the fittest was not the best policy by which to run a nation. A new social contract was necessary to create an economic order in which everyone was guaranteed at least the bare necessities for survival. In 1938, the National Employment Commission issued a report advocating unemployment insurance as a means of preventing the kind of insecurity experienced by wage earners during the Great Depression. This suggestion had the support of both organized labour and reform-minded business people such as Arthur B. Purvis, who chaired the commission. Similarly, the Royal Commission on Dominion–Provincial Relations (more often cited by the names of the men who chaired it, Newton Rowell and Joseph Sirois) recommended that Ottawa assume greater control over economic and social policy. By the time that the Rowell–Sirois report was submitted in 1940, the Second World War had become the focus of public attention, and the powers that the commission recommended were temporarily made possible under the War Measures Act.

## TRADE UNIONS IN THE INTERWAR PERIOD

Part of the reason that some industrialists began to accept the need for the government to play a more active role in the economy was that working people had become more demanding. Without major reform, it was becoming increasingly less likely that social peace could be achieved. Huge demonstrations of the unemployed and violent strikes by workers trying to limit wage cuts and speed-ups rocked many communities in the 1930s and convinced even the most conservative Canadians that change was necessary.

In 1918, about 378 000 workers were estimated to be enrolled in unions but the long recession that followed the war reduced union memberships by about 130 000 over the next six years. With courts recognizing the right of employers to use blacklists against union "agitators," and to force workers to sign pledges not to join unions, there was only a slow recovery in membership in the "roaring" half of the twenties, and there were more losses in the early thirties. As the economy picked up in the late thirties, the numbers of unionists begin to return to wartime figures, but as late as 1939, union members represented only 17.3 percent of the labour force.

Numbers do not tell the whole story. During the Depression, a new militancy developed among Canadian workers. In the United States, workers began to join a brash new federation of industrial unions, the Congress of Industrial Organizations (CIO), which soon also had branches in Canada. Many of the early CIO organizers in Canada were Communists who had been activists in the Workers Unity League (WUL). Although the WUL was small in relation to the major Canadian union federation, the Trades and Labour Congress, it is estimated that strikes inspired by league leadership accounted for half the labour stoppages of the early 1930s.

The CIO played a role in convincing Nova Scotia's Liberal premier, Angus L. Macdonald, to pass Canada's first legislation requiring union recognition and compulsory bargaining. When the CIO and local union organizations in Cape Breton signed up 90 percent of the employees at the Sydney steel plant in 1936, DOSCO management refused to bargain. Union leaders lobbied Macdonald and other members of the Nova Scotia cabinet. With an election approaching, the government passed the desired legislation, permitting a flurry of organizing activity throughout the province.

Mitch Hepburn, Ontario's Liberal premier from 1934 to 1943, was not as open to accommodation as his Nova Scotian counterpart. When the CIO-inspired United Auto Workers (UAW) called a strike in 1937 against General Motors in Oshawa, the union brought four thousand workers onto the streets—and demands from Hepburn that Ottawa send in the RCMP or the army. King's government resisted provoking the strikers by such a move, but Hepburn refused to stay out of the struggle. He organized a special police force which quickly became dubbed "Hepburn's hussars" or "the sons of Mitches." Afraid that things would get out of hand, General Motors instructed its Canadian managers to negotiate an agreement with the UAW.

In the same year, violence erupted in Peterborough when men and women employed by the city's two Dominion Woolens plants participated in a CIO-led strike. The determination of the police, particularly the Ontario Provincial Police, to help the employer to keep the plants running with strikebreakers led to clashes with the striking workers. "Dorothy," one of the women arrested during the conflict, was surprised by the state's vilification and repression of people who were simply struggling for better pay. Interviewed a half century later, she recalled:

> I remember being on picket line. That's all I was doing, I was really surprised how wild [the police] were.... The chief of police came and grabbed me from behind with fingernails in my neck—you could see the marks. I was trying to kick out at him: I couldn't figure out why he was picking on me. He shoved me under the gate.... By that time I was crying and ... started to run out.... Another girl came to rescue me from Chief Newall, and they threw her in [to the paddywagon] too. They made us go to city jail and we had "a bit of a trial."... The chief of police charged me with throwing pepper in his face, and I never even had any pepper.[5]

In 1939, on orders from the American Federation of Labor, CIO affiliates were expelled from the craft-dominated Trades and Labour Congress. Undeterred, they joined a group of Canadian controlled unions to form the Canadian Congress of Labour (CCL). The unions were biding their time. Only the high rate of unemployment gave employers and the state so much power to prevent willing workers from unionizing. When and if the economy ever turned around, the unions would be ready to assert themselves.

In Quebec, the Confédération des travailleurs catholiques du Canada (CTCC) continued to be a strong force within the labour movement. Associating strikes with socialism, church leaders believed that international unions were promoting an adversarial model that pitted class against class. In practice, the Catholic unions and many of the priests associated with their operations soon came to the view that workers needed the weapon of the strike to deal with those intransigent employers who could not otherwise be persuaded to treat their workers fairly. Equally important in influencing the outlook of the CTCC was the fact that Catholic workers proved wary about leaving strong international unions to join a local Catholic union. Only concrete successes in extracting good contracts from employers could persuade them that it was worth giving the Catholic union a try.

In both the Catholic and international trade union movements in the province, male organizers and male workers predominated. There were some significant exceptions. During the Depression, Madeleine Parent and Lea Roback began lifelong careers as dedicated union organizers and political activists. Parent was a middle-class francophone Catholic who was denounced by her church for her "unladylike" profession. Roback, the daughter of Jewish storekeepers, was moved by communist convictions and braved both anti-Semitism and sexism to fight for social justice for Montreal workers.

In Newfoundland, as in Canada, the Depression provided a spur to union organization. The Newfoundland Lumbermen's Association was formed in 1935 by twelve thousand loggers to fight for a just piece rate for the wood that they cut. Railway clerks unionized, and when both their employer and the commission of government refused to recognize the union, they took their case to Britain, which granted recognition of their

rights as workers. In 1937, the Newfoundland and Labrador Federation of Labour (NLFL) was formed. The product of this new militancy, the NLFL campaigned for an end to child labour, the implementation of a five-day, forty-hour week, and improvements in mine inspection and workers' compensation.

Labour in Western Canada, particularly in mining communities, remained militant in the interwar period. Although the One Big Union was largely undermined by state repression and internecine conflicts, western Canadian workers continued to prove receptive to radical labour leadership. In the 1930s, the communist-led Workers Unity League spearheaded strikes among New Westminster sawmill workers, Vancouver Island loggers, and fishers on the Skeena and Nass Rivers. The popularity of the CCF and the militancy of the relief camp workers attest to the continued strength of radicalism among working people in the West, but repression limited labour's gains in the region. The RCMP were used to suppress strikes such as the Estevan coal miners' strike in 1931, during which three miners were killed.

## MAKING ENDS MEET

Ordinary Canadians who lived through the interwar period experienced a bumpy ride economically. While the second half of the 1920s gave many Canadians a taste of the good life, most faced unemployment, a reduction in income, or outright destitution in the 1930s. People spent their savings, if they had any, and then were forced to make ends meet the best way they could. Despite the availability of a means-tested old age pension, many elderly Canadians suffered terribly. This letter, written by a man from New Brunswick to R.B. Bennett in 1935, suggests the depths of their despair:

Dear Sir

I am writing you a few lines to ask if you will be kind enough to let me know the Law of the Direct Relieved, I am an Old man of 73 years old cant hardly help myself nearly cripple of both hands and my wife 68 years old I went to see the man who is appointed to give the Relieved this morning and I had a hard time to get $3.00 worth I got a bag of flour and a gallon of Paraphine oil I couldn't not get no tea nor anything else long as we cant get no tea we will have to eat that bag of flour with cold water indeed it is a hard way to live so long in the party conservative and to be used that way. [6]

Much of the pressure to make do was borne by housewives who had little recourse once the family breadwinner was out of work. As one Saskatchewan woman explained to Bennett in 1933: "I really dont know what to do. We have never asked for anything of anybody before, We seem to be shut out of the world altogether we have no telephone Radio or newspaper. For this last couple of years we have felt we could not afford to have them." Nor could this woman afford underwear for her husband who worked outside in the cold Saskatchewan winter: "I have patched and darned his old underwear for the last two years, but they are completely done now." As a last resort, she wrote to the prime minister to ask him to "send for the underwear in the Eaton order made out and enclosed in this letter," a request to which the prime minister acceded. [7]

Many of those who came of age in the 1930s considered themselves members of a lost generation, destined to scrounge for a living while rich men like R.B. Bennett and William Lyon Mackenzie King ran the government to suit themselves and their well-heeled friends. For younger Canadians, the trauma of not being able to find a job created a sense of economic insecurity that never went away. The desperation is captured in the following letter from an Ontario boy to Bennett:

Dear Sir

I am just a lad out of school and looking around for a job, and can't find one. I am sixteen years of age. My father left us twelve years ago and we haven't heard from him since and mother has worked out until this winter and now I am the only one in the family that is old enough for to do any work. We have hardly any good clothes nothing but patches and no stockings and we haven't any money to get anything to wear. I have only one sister, 2 brother

and mother and I am asking will you be so kind as to give us enough money to get some stockings and clothes I thank you

Yours truly
Hugh McKinnon [8]

Some people, as this notice in a Toronto newspaper suggests, simply gave up the struggle: "The death of James C. Grant, 22, unemployed bookkeeper, and member of the Toronto Flying Club, who jumped 1500 feet from the wing of an aeroplane Saturday night after bidding a smiling farewell to his instructor, Flight Lieutenant Ralph Spadbrow." [9]

For children, the economic problems experienced by their parents often created tensions that left their mark. One wonders what happened to the three enterprising young people from Saskatchewan who wrote letters to Bennett: [10]

Dear Sir

I would be real pleased to be wearing a ball suit if you sent me one. My sizes are as folllows, Chest 34, Waste 32, size 7 shoes and a cap size 22 inches. I am 5 ft 8 in and am 14 years old. The colors I would like it are Black trimmed with white and a P on the front. I am hopping to receive it by the third of June because we are going to play at a picnic. Thanking you in advance.

Yours truly
Sean Kelly

Dear Sir

I am a girl thirteen years old, and I have to go to school every day its very cold now already and I haven't got a coat to put on. My parents can't afford to buy me anything this winter. I have to walk to school four and a half mile every morning and night and I'm awfully cold every day. Would you be so kind to send me enough money ... so that I could get one.

My name is
Edwina Abbott

Dear Mr. Bennett,

I have heard mamma and daddy talk about you so much, and what a good man you are. I am a little boy eight years old and I'm in Grade III at school. I've wanted a little red wagon to hich my dog to for so many years, but daddy has no money. Please, Mr. Bennett would you send me enuff money to buy my wagon. Thank you so much.

Your very good friend,
Horace Gardiner

Sean, Edwina, and Horace each received five dollars in the mail from the prime minister, but charity was no answer to the economic crisis facing the nation as a whole.

While Canadians everywhere felt the effects of the Depression, and made common cause against the capitalist system that had let them down, they disagreed in a typically Canadian way on the specific source of their miseries. Westerners concluded that the problem started with the big financiers "in the East" who inadvertently staged a market collapse in their efforts to grab ever larger profits. In the real East, Maritimers held "Upper Canadian" capitalists responsible for their plight. Among francophones, the English-dominated "trusts" were the villains. Capitalists blamed politicians and workers, both of whom returned the charges with interest. In the desperate climate of the 1930s, regional, class, and cultural divisions flourished, as people looked for someone to blame for the plight of the nation.

## CONCLUSION

In the interwar years, Canadians did their best to survive the economic roller coaster, but they were beginning to lose faith in a capitalist system that destroyed human beings in its uncontrolled drive to satisfy the laws of supply and demand. While Canadians voted for new parties and experimented with state intervention, their leaders rejected a total overhaul of either the political or the economic system. Politicians hung on grimly, hoping that the pendulum would swing back and the good times would return.

## WHAT CAUSED THE GREAT DEPRESSION?

### A Historiographical Debate

"Why did the capitalist economy between the wars fail to work?"[11] asks historian Eric Hobsbawm. In particular, why did the Great Depression of the 1930s occur, and why did it take a murderous war to end it?

Canadian historian Michael Bliss provides the standard conservative view of the origins of the Depression, one that blames governments rather than capitalists for the breakdown of the market economy. According to Bliss, the Great Depression was not the result of a "business foul-up": it was not, as socialists like to suggest, a "crisis of capitalism"—though it certainly became a crisis *for* capitalism. Rather, it was an international crisis, rooted in the deep dislocations caused by the Great War of 1914–18 and its aftermath, then made worse by the nationalistic attempts of governments to shelter their own producers at foreigners' expense.[12]

Bliss's perspective echoes the views of historians who believe that attempts to force Germany to pay for the economic losses of victor nations in Europe prevented economic recovery. For many scholars, the main culprit was the United States. American financiers, they argue, had made huge wartime loans at high interest rates to France and Britain, and the need to repay these loans caused these countries to deal harshly with Germany. However, during the boom of the twenties, Germany was making "reparations" payments to the victors, and France and Britain were repaying their American loans. So something besides the dislocations created by the war must have been at work by 1929 to destroy the underpinnings of the economy. For Bliss, and for others who take this perspective, high tariffs, which created havoc for international trade, were at least part of that something else. From the Canadian point of view, such an explanation is particularly compelling since Canada was, more than most countries, dependent on foreign markets for its natural products.

A variant of the view that blames political rather than economic actors for the Depression focuses on the overwhelming power of the United States in the economy after the First World War. When Britain had dominated the world economy before the war, it had an interest, as a trading nation, in ensuring that the world economy was stable. Trade for the United States, while lucrative, represented only a small proportion of its GNP, and its political authorities had no interest in interfering with the operations of lenders to ensure that global stability was maintained. In the late 1920s, American lenders, whose role in the global economy was crucial, reduced the availability of credit to foreign borrowers, with their government refusing to intervene. [13]

Of course, it can be argued that these failings of American lenders constitute a "business foul-up." From the point of view of socialists and many Keynesians, the existing framework of capitalism, rather than short-sighted behaviour of politicians, was the culprit in bringing on the economic collapse of 1929. From their point of view, the lenders and high-tariff governments were simply reacting to the underlying economic problem, rather than causing it. That problem was the lack of sufficient demand for the products that could be produced. As Eric Hobsbawm writes of the 1920s, "What was happening, as often happens in free market booms, was that, with wages lagging, profits rose disproportionately and the prosperous got a larger slice of the national cake. But as mass demand could not keep pace with the rapidly increasing productivity of the industrial system in the heyday of Henry Ford, the result was over-production and speculation. This, in turn, triggered off the collapse." [14]

Conservatives argue that the Depression lingered until the war because governments would not lower tariffs and let the free market correct the rigidities that had produced the Depression. For left-wing theorists, like Hobsbawm, the Depression lingered because the underlying inequalities that ensured that more could be produced than distributed remained in place. In any case, such theorists usually question how free the market of this period really was. Monopolistic and oligopolistic concentrations of wealth, often involving transnational corporations, meant that in many, perhaps most, industries, little real competition existed.

## NOTES

[1] Cited in Veronica Strong-Boag, *The New Day Recalled: Lives of Girls and Women in English Canada, 1919–1939* (Toronto: Copp Clark Pitman, 1988), 13

[2] Barry Potyondi, "Loss and Substitution: The Ecology of Production in Southwestern Saskatchewan, 1860–1930," *Journal of the Canadian Historical Association*, n.s., 5 (1994): 235

[3] *Patriot*, 26 March 1928, cited in Ruth A. Freeman and Jennifer Callaghan, "A History of Potato Marketing in Prince Edward Island, 1920–1987" (prepared for the Royal Commission on the Potato Industry, April 1987)

[4] Michiel Horn, ed., *The Dirty Thirties: Canadians in the Great Depression* (Toronto: Copp Clark Pitman, 1972), 14

[5] Joan Sangster, *Earning Respect: The Lives of Working Women in Small-Town Ontario, 1920–1960* (Toronto: University of Toronto Press, 1995), 178

[6] L.M. Grayson and Michael Bliss, eds., *The Wretched of Canada: Letters to R.B. Bennett, 1930–1935* (Toronto: University of Toronto Press, 1971), 111

[7] Ibid., 53–54

[8] Ibid., 136

[9] Ibid., 185

[10] Ibid., 25, 56, 180

[11] Eric Hobsbawm, *Age of Extremes: A History of the World, 1914–1991* (New York: Pantheon, 1994), 97

[12] Michael Bliss, *Northern Enterprise: Five Centuries of Canadian Business* (Toronto: McClelland and Stewart, 1987), 412

[13] This interpretation of the cause of the Depression is emphasized in Charles P. Kindleberger, *The World in Depression, 1929–1939* (London: Allen Lane, 1973)

[14] Hobsbawm, *Age of Extremes*, 100

## Selected Reading

Many of the works mentioned in chapters 7 and 8 have important information on the interwar economy. Works with a focus more exclusively economic are mentioned here. On the 1920s, see Tom Traves, *The State and Enterprise: Canadian Manufacturers and the Federal Government, 1917–1931* (Toronto: University of Toronto Press, 1979); Ian Macpherson, *Each for All: A History of the Cooperative Movement in English Canada, 1900–1945* (Ottawa: Carleton University Press, 1979); and Trevor J. Dick, "Canadian Newsprint, 1913–1930: National Policies and the North American Economy" in *Perspectives on Canadian Economic History*, ed. Douglas McCalla (Toronto: Copp Clark Pitman, 1987).

On the economy during the Depression, see Douglas Owram, "Economic Thought in the 1930s: The Prelude to Keynesianism," *Canadian Historical Review* 66, 3 (Sept. 1985): 344–77; A.E. Safarian, *The Canadian Economy in the Great Depression* (Ottawa: Carleton University Press, 1970); Ian M. Drummond, *British Economic Policy and the Empire, 1919–1939* (London: Allen and Unwin, 1972); Ian M. Drummond and Norman Hillmer, *Negotiating Freer Trade* (Waterloo, ON: Wilfrid Laurier University Press, 1989); Gillian Creese, "The Politics of Dependence: Women, Work and Unemployment in the Vancouver Labour Movement before World War II" in *British Columbia Reconsidered: Essays on Women*, ed. Gillian Creese and Veronica Strong-Boag (Vancouver: Press Gang, 1992), 364–90; Robert Bothwell and William Kilbourn, *C.D. Howe: A Biography* (Toronto: McClelland and Stewart, 1980); E.R. Forbes, "Cutting the Pie into Smaller Pieces: Matching Grants and Relief in the Maritime Provinces during the 1930s" in *Challenging the Regional Stereotype: Essays on the Twentieth-Century Maritimes* (Fredericton: Acadiensis Press, 1989).

On the labour movement, see Ian Radforth, *Bushworkers and Bosses* (Toronto: University of Toronto Press, 1987); Craig Heron, *Working in Steel* (Toronto: McClelland and Stewart, 1988); Joan Sangster, *Earning Respect: The Lives of Working Women in Small-Town Ontario, 1920–1960* (Toronto: University of Toronto Press, 1995); Irving Abella, *Nationalism, Communism, and Canadian Labour* (Toronto: University of Toronto Press, 1973); Bryan D. Palmer, *Working-Class Experience: Rethinking the History of Canadian Labour, 1800–1991* (Toronto: McClelland and Stewart, 1992); Michael Earle, ed., *Workers and the State in Twentieth-Century Nova Scotia* (Fredericton: Acadiensis Press, 1989); and John Manley, "Canadian Communists, Revolutionary Unionism, and the 'Third Period': The Workers' Unity League, 1929–1935," *Journal of the Canadian Historical Association*, n.s., 5 (1994): 167–94.

# CHAPTER 10

## MASS CONSUMER SOCIETY AND THE SEARCH FOR IDENTITY, 1919–1939

Hell! - FIRST IT'S THE
bloody foreman, then
the boss, and now
you.
All you think of
is to run off to those
movie joints and cry yourself
sick over Valentino.

But when it comes to the
fellows in the shop,
you don't fall for us.
—We don't put
axle-grease on our hair,
and we wear oil-soaked
work shirts.[1]

This male worker's poetic lament, published in the Communist Party newspaper, *The Worker*, in 1927, demonstrates the frustration some men felt with the masculine ideal that prevailed in the mass media during the interwar years. Few men had opportunities to live in the manner of matinee idols such as Rudolph Valentino. Although this unhappy poet may not have recognized it, equally few women could afford to look or behave like Hollywood "vamps" such as Theda Bara. Yet the images that prevailed in Hollywood movies, New York radio shows, popular recordings, and glossy magazines had a profound influence on interwar society. Some individuals opposed the impact of Hollywood movies on social values because, like the poet quoted above, they felt that this created unattainable ideals. Others, including most church leaders, were shocked by the attack on their beliefs about how society should be organized. No matter where one stood on the cultural trends, almost everyone had an opinion on jazz, the flapper, and the Model T Ford, all harbingers of a new age of mass culture.

The commercial media focused on the good life, with men and women free to indulge the whims of the moment. Defying the sexual and social taboos of the prewar period, many women wore shorter skirts, bobbed their hair, and displayed a devil-may-care attitude. Men returning from the war set the tone for a more cynical and worldly view of life than had prevailed in prewar Canada. Having faced death in the trenches of Europe, they were unwilling to put up with the petty conventions that characterized polite society in a more innocent age.

Notwithstanding the new trends, Canadians in the interwar years also experienced prohibition, poverty, and a domestic ideal in which gender roles were rigidly prescribed, if somewhat modified by notions of companionate marriages and smaller families. These were familiar features of Canadian life, with roots stretching back to at least the mid-nineteenth century. If nothing else, the period from 1919 to 1939 was fraught with contradictions. This chapter focuses on social and cultural life in this period, as Canadians lived through the early years of mass consumer society and juggled traditional values with the often contradictory messages that the new media embodied about what it meant to be a "modern" man or woman.

## THE COMMUNICATIONS REVOLUTION

In the interwar years, the isolation of even the remotest rural regions of the nation was shattered by new developments in communication. Radio made its first appearance in Canada in 1920. Twenty years later, three Canadian households in four owned a radio. Radio was introduced in North America by electrical companies. Having manufactured receiving sets, they began to broadcast programs to sell these appliances. Ten years after radio's introduction, Canada had over sixty stations, many owned by electrical retailers or newspapers, which depended upon advertisers for revenue. In this way, radio, like other media in the interwar years, became the handmaiden of corporate enterprise, selling its products and dreams to a largely uncritical and unsuspecting audience.

In the early days of radio, the United States dominated the North American airwaves. Most of the early Canadian radio stations had weak signals that were easily drowned out by stronger American programming beamed across the border. A decade after the advent of radio, over 40 percent of Canadians still had access to only American stations. Several metropolitan stations in Canada, unwilling to finance Canadian programming, affiliated with the major American radio networks, thereby gaining the lucrative privilege of broadcasting popular American shows to Canadians from within Canada. Only a few Canadian programs, most notably religious shows, were cheap enough to produce profitably. Alberta's premier, "Bible Bill" Aberhart, with his *Back to the Bible Hour*, was

one of many radio preachers with a large audience in Canada.

Fears that unregulated radio would contribute to the Americanization of Canadian culture sparked the formation of the Canadian Radio League. Dedicated to the creation of a Canadian version of the state-owned British Broadcasting Corporation, the league popularized the slogan that, in broadcasting, Canadians had the choice between "the state or the United States." In 1928, Prime Minister Mackenzie King responded to pressure for government regulation of radio by creating a royal commission to advise on the future control, organization, and financing of broadcasting. Sir John Aird, president of the Bank of Commerce, chaired the commission. His 1929 report called for a public broadcasting company to own and operate all radio stations and to build seven stations across the country.

In 1932, the Privy Council awarded exclusive control over radio to the federal government, and Prime Minister R.B. Bennett established the Canadian Radio Broadcasting Commission, which in 1936 was reorganized as the Canadian Broadcasting Corporation (CBC). While private stations were not banished, as Aird had recommended, the CBC would have control over their operation. The CBC's own stations were given a mandate to foster "a national spirit" and "interpret national citizenship." Like the railways, radio communication was seen by the government as a vehicle for strengthening national unity. The early years of CBC broadcasting were disappointing to those who supported state-controlled radio. Because of Depression parsimony, the early CBC stations had limited budgets with which to prepare programs that would lure Canadian radio listeners away from such popular American shows as *Amos 'n' Andy*, the *Jack Benny Show*, and *Burns and Allen*.

The radio also strengthened the hold of the American recording industry, which had taken root in Canada before the war. New York's Tin Pan Alley and Nashville's Grand Ole Opry became the centres of production for popular music. In Halifax, nearly one in ten households in September 1923 owned a recorded version or the sheet music of "Yes, We Have No Bananas," the latest song sensation. The new music spawned jazzy dance steps such as the Charleston which were popular with the young, though shocking to their elders.

Canadians also watched American movies. After the First World War, movies had become a favourite pastime for Canadians of all social classes. The average Canadian went to twelve movies per year in 1936. For children and teenagers in urban centres, the number was much higher. A 1933 study in Edmonton and Calgary suggested that over a third of all students in grades six to ten watched at least one movie a week, with another one in five seeing at least two movies a month. Most of these movies were made in Hollywood. Even newsreels and cartoons, which theatres screened before the main attraction, tended to be American imports.

Marginalization of the Canadian film industry was apparent by the early 1920s as major American studios came to dominate the distribution as well as production of films. In 1923, Famous Players bought out the Allen company, the major chain of Canadian theatres that had started with a cinema in Brantford, Ontario, in 1906. When a Combines Investigation Act report on the film industry was released in 1930, it revealed that Famous Players distributed about 90 percent of all feature pictures shown in Canada. Nonetheless, the report concluded that Famous Players was not a "combine" under Canadian law: it did not collude with others to forestall competition in its industry because it controlled too much of the industry to combine with anyone!

Without a major feature film industry in Canada, talented actors flocked south. Oscar-winning Canadian actors Mary Pickford, Marie Dressler, Norma Shearer, and Walter Huston were acclaimed for their Hollywood careers. Fabulous incomes and glamorous lifestyles were the reward for success in Hollywood, and few could resist the dream of becoming a movie star. One young Canadian actor was an exception to this rule. In the 1930s, Deanna Durbin of Saint Boniface, Manitoba, became a child star second in popularity only to Shirley Temple. Rejecting the artificiality of Hollywood, she left show business in her late teens to live in France, shunning requests from

journalists to discuss her post-celebrity life.

More than any other cultural medium, movies defined the material desires of mass consumer society. The silver screen shaped individual fantasies, established clothing and hairstyles, and encouraged new patterns of leisure and recreation. Because so many of the movie plots centred on romance, they also educated people on sex roles and sexuality. Until his sudden death in 1926 at the age of thirty-one, Rudolph Valentino was the screen's first great romantic hero. The lines of loyal fans at his funeral stretched for eleven blocks, indicating that movie stars commanded the attention of people in much the same way that monarchs and political leaders had in an earlier age.

Canadian politicians recognized that film was a powerful medium. In 1923, the federal government established a Motion Picture Bureau to coordinate the film activities of its various departments. In the late 1930s, King asked British film producer John Grierson to investigate the government's film policy. His report led to the creation of the National Film Board (NFB) in May 1939, with a mandate to interpret Canada to Canadians and to the larger world. Quickly swept up in producing wartime propaganda, the NFB thrived under Grierson, who was appointed its first commissioner in October 1939. The NFB emerged from the war as one of the largest film studios in the world with a staff of nearly eight hundred people and more than five hundred films to its credit.

Magazines also helped to establish Canadian standards of taste and behaviour, which were increasingly being defined in the United States. In 1925, it was estimated that American magazines outsold their Canadian counterparts by eight to one. R.B. Bennett responded to pressure from Canadian publishers for protection from foreign competition by slapping a hefty tariff on American magazines in 1931. Within four years, Canadian magazine sales had risen 64 percent, while American magazine sales in Canada had fallen 62 percent. General interest magazines such as *Maclean's*, *Liberty*, and *Chatelaine* were major benefactors, along with magazines aimed at rural Canada. After King returned to power, tariff protection fell victim to trade agreements, and

## THE DIONNE QUINTUPLETS

The five girls born to a poor rural francophone couple on 28 May 1934 in Corbeil, Ontario, illustrate the impact of show business on Canadian society. They also reveal the increasing power of the state and medical experts in the lives of Canadian families. From the moment they were born, Annette, Emilie, Yvonne, Cecile, and Marie Dionne were famous. The media immediately focused on what was indeed a remarkable event—the birth and survival of quintuplets. Almost as quickly, the state removed the infants from the care of their parents, who were already raising five older children. Two months after their birth, the Ontario government placed the girls under the control of a local board of guardians and moved the babies to a specially equipped hospital so their upbringing could be overseen by Dr Allan Roy Dafoe, who had delivered them. He and other medical practitioners monitored the babies' every movement. Only after a long battle, which enlisted the aid of the Roman Catholic Church and Franco-Ontarian nationalists, were the girls restored to their outraged parents.

It was little wonder that everyone wanted custody of the quints. The girls were a major economic asset: they had endorsements of over $1 million, were the subjects of Hollywood films, and became a major tourist attraction —three million curiosity seekers flocked to view them from behind a one-way screen. The girls never recovered from their first traumatic years and felt little bond with their parents or older siblings after their return to the family home. Emilie died in a convent in 1954, and the four survivors recorded their unhappy stories in **We Were Five** (1965). In 1995, the survivors charged that their father had sexually abused them, offering yet another wrinkle to their tragic story.

Much energy has been expended studying the lives of the quints. In recent years, the scholarly focus has been less on the complicated facts of the case than on the broader ramifications of public interest in the products of this "freak" event. The willingness of the state, the media, the medical profession, and even their own family to exploit the girls, provides a fascinating glimpse into the values of the modern age, as do the more recent revelations by the surviving quints of their own private hell growing up in mid-twentieth-century Canada.

---

American magazines regained their former market share.

Although newspapers remained largely Canadian owned, most of the foreign news in all but a few dailies was produced by American press services. The *Canadian Annual Review* complained in 1922 that not only were Canadians reading foreign news items with American biases, but also that stories about Canadian participation in European events displayed appalling inaccuracies. There were a few bright spots in this grim press picture. *Canadian Forum*, a magazine founded in 1920 in Toronto, offered a Canadian and progressive perspective on national issues, though it did not have a wide circulation. In the 1930s, the *Winnipeg Free Press*, owned by the Sifton family and edited by John Dafoe, fought a lonely but consistent battle to awaken western Canadian readers to the horrors of Nazi Germany.

Except for establishing the CBC, interwar governments made little attempt to ensure greater Canadian content in the popular media. Their focus instead was on censoring what they felt was unsuitable material, particularly in the movies. Quebec's censorship board, following the prompting of the Catholic Church, snipped not only sexual scenes but also depictions of burglaries, gambling, divorce, suicide, or unpatriotic behaviour. Other provincial boards were scarcely more liberal. Alberta's board would not allow the screening of pictures that depicted seduction of women, adultery, abortion, venereal disease, or too much violence or drunkenness. In 1922, it condemned movies for "being 'too sensuous,' 'grossly suggestive,' 'immoral,' 'very offensive,' and 'vulgar' as well as for portraying a 'suggestive sex story,' 'a story of a vampire,' 'the life of an immoral woman,' 'a burlesque on clergymen,' and 'a burlesque on missions.'" [2]

## SEXUALITY AND RESPECTABILITY

Demands that movies show only wholesome activities reflected wider concerns about a moral breakdown in society. Church leaders, in particular, found modern culture, with its hedonism, violence, and secular values, profoundly disturbing. In an effort to counter these trends, traditionalists began to reaffirm the long-standing moral conventions that sex was only acceptable if it was heterosexual, confined to married couples, and not engaged in too frequently. They also railed against drinking, smoking, swearing, and gambling, all popular activities on the screen and in the trendy nightspots of interwar Canada.

While there were few penalties for heterosexual men who violated this moral code, women risked their reputations if they became sexually available "flappers." The "working girl" was increasingly accepted as a permanent feature of the economic system, but women in the public sphere were expected to maintain their "respectability" at all costs. In the interwar years, the courts in some jurisdictions still acceded to requests of families to place "promiscuous" daughters in mental institutions or reformatories. A single woman who became pregnant continued to face a dismal prospect. If they could afford to do so, pregnant unwed women tried to conceal their condition, and both public and private institutions were prepared to exploit them for their own ends.

In Chester, Nova Scotia, the Ideal Maternity Home took in unwed pregnant women—for a hefty fee. Once registered in the home, a mother was pressured to give up her child for adoption, for which the owners of the home also extracted a handsome sum from wealthy would-be parents eager to adopt a healthy white baby. Despite the profit that could be made from the adoption service, many of the babies born in the Ideal Maternity Home died. Their bodies were packed in empty butter boxes and hastily buried behind the home. Although the "butterbox

babies" eventually became the subject of local scandal, the desperation surrounding modern motherhood that the home symbolized was experienced by many Canadian women in the interwar years.

In Montreal or Quebec City, unmarried pregnant women could give birth at the homes for unwed mothers run by the Sisters of Miséricorde. Women who took this option were hidden from society and required, after giving birth, to work in the home for several months as penance and as a way of paying for their care. Few could afford to raise their children, and most left them to be adopted. Over a third of the children died in the home during their first year, mostly from preventable diseases. Both the mothers and the nuns who operated the homes knew that "illegitimacy" would dog these children for as long as they lived. A sister wrote to the grandfather of one of the children left to the hospital's care in 1934: "Dear Sir: We regret to say that the baby born to E.C. is dead. Thank God for this great favour." [3]

In the interwar period, birth control information became more readily available to much of the population and the birth rate continued its steady decline (see figure 10.1). Defying the 1892 law that forbade the provision of birth control information, advocacy groups and a few birth control clinics, beginning with one in Hamilton in 1932, let people

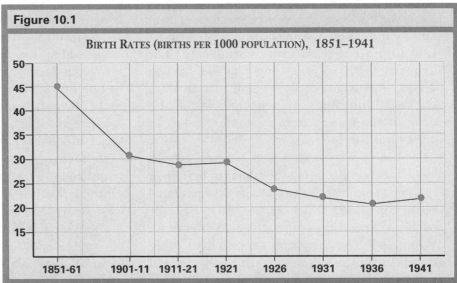

**Figure 10.1**

BIRTH RATES (BIRTHS PER 1000 POPULATION), 1851–1941

*Source: Wayne W. McVey Jr. and Warren E. Kalbach*, Canadian Population *(Toronto: Nelson, 1995), 268, 170*

know how unwanted pregnancies could be avoided. Women's organizations such as the United Farm Women of Alberta argued that having smaller families would allow women to have more satisfying lives and to devote more time and resources to each child. In most families and cultures in Canada, this view became widely accepted.

In 1936, birth control advocates won an important legal victory in an Ottawa court room. Dorothea Palmer, a field worker for the Parents' Information Bureau (PIB), was found not guilty of violating the law because her provision of birth control information to working-class people in Ottawa was clearly done for the public good. The PIB was a birth control advocacy organization sponsored by Kitchener-based industrialist A.R. Kaufman, who hired nurses to provide birth control information and to arrange for the distribution of contraceptives to women in many parts of the country. Although his goal seems to have been specifically to limit the fertility of the "lower classes"—the PIB began as a service to workers laid off from Kaufman's own factory—he was a key figure in the birth control movement in Canada. Largely because of the resolute resistance of Quebec and the Roman Catholic Church, the federal government declined to make birth control devices legal.

A darker side of the birth control movement was the idea that the human race would be improved if people who were physically and mentally inferior to some defined standard were sterilized to prevent them from reproducing. The extreme lengths to which eugenics was taken in Nazi Germany eventually discredited such ideas, but in the interwar years, eugenics was widely debated and viewed as an acceptable policy by many Canadians.

Women who were victims of sexual assaults were often wary of using the courts to have their assailants punished. If there was any suggestion of sexual impropriety in her life, the trial could easily be turned against the victim rather than the rapist. Women who laid complaints against rapists risked disbelief and ostracism within their communities. If most women did not pursue legal remedies after sexual assault, they often focused their efforts to seek redress into more traditional channels. For instance, immigrant women in western farming communities were sometimes so intimidated by their assailants and lack of knowledge of English that they failed to report their assault to the police. Nevertheless, if their families and neighbours found out about the incident, they often pressured the assailant into making monetary restitution to the family of the victim. Such a solution reflected Old World attitudes that sexual crimes, like other crimes punishable by imprisonment in Canada, should be treated more like civil offences.

## The Burden of Respectability

The desire to be seen as respectable rather than rough encouraged most women to accept the view that sex should be confined within marriage and to condemn as immoral women who transgressed this norm. Yet respectability had more than just a sexual dimension. Women wished to be seen as good mothers and frugal housekeepers who maintained clean homes for their families and attended to their husbands' needs. Similarly, men wanted to be seen as good providers who turned over enough wages to their wives to allow their family to live decently. When the Depression made it impossible for many men to sustain their breadwinning roles, it caused great distress. Some men in this position became hopelessly depressed, others committed suicide, and a great many deserted the family that they no longer had the money to maintain.

Even during the roaring twenties, perhaps half of the population would have been hard-put financially to fully meet the ideal of respectability. A letter written by a Mrs Richards to her landlord, the Halifax Relief Commission, in 1926, illustrates the efforts of women to cling to an image of respectability even when extreme poverty was the central fact of their lives. In begging for time to make up back rent, she argued that her husband's limited income made it "pretty hard to be respectable a[nd] to keep up under the conditions we are living." This family of six had one bed, where the father and three of the children slept while the mother and the baby slept on a mattress with a broken spring. There was too little money for food or fuel, but Mrs Richards made plain: "I'm not going on the streets to earn money to pay back rent. I'll go to prison first." Her father-in-law had offered to help only if she put the older children in an orphanage and threw out her husband to live common-law with him. "I'm an Englishwoman and I'd not touch one cent of money belonging to that man," wrote Mrs Richards. Her concluding sentence described the lives of many women in Canada in the interwar period: "I'm trying to live a[nd] pay my way a[nd] keep respectable a[nd] I cannot do any more." [4]

Not every man or woman made respectability his or her first goal. Many young people certainly gave their elders cause for concern by engaging in premarital sex, drinking to excess, and cruising their parents' automobiles down the main streets of town with little regard for speed limits. Middle-class parents were shocked to find that some of their own children were adopting a live-fast, love-hard, die-young philosophy that they associated with the working class. Ironically, it was generally members of the working class who were so desperately trying to stake their claim to respectability in the interwar years.

For those without pretensions to respectability, there were ways to get by that often involved the complicity of their social betters, who were clients for their services. An ambitious young man might turn to making moonshine, running gambling dens, or pimping for prostitutes. For women, almost the only alternative to destitution was prostitution. Emily Murphy, a police magistrate in Edmonton from 1916 to 1931, regularly encountered the destitute women who sold their bodies, and risked their lives in the process. Writing to reformer Nellie McClung in 1930, she described one tragic end to the life of a prostitute:

> I have just been trying to identify a young half-breed girl at the undertaker's who died in a store here from haemorrhage.... She had been round the city, I believe, serving the taxis, and here she is at the end of the road, and no one knows her name. She had a heart——a lovely crimson heart—and some roses tattooed on her arm. Poor child! "Only

a half-breed." I'd like to tell the world some of the things I know about "superior men"—but I've just got to keep the heartbreak of it all to myself. [5]

Although Murphy used this case to demonstrate the unfairness of the double standard, most women accepted this aspect of patriarchal society, and social values in general, protesting only when they faced desperate straits.

Divorce remained uncommon in the interwar period. According to the 1931 census, fewer than eight thousand people were legally divorced in Canada. Most desertions of homes involved men leaving their wives. While some women left abusive husbands, sometimes taking the children with them, most accepted the economic logic that fleeing simply plunged the family into permanent poverty. The judicial system continued to be unsympathetic to most women's accusations of battering, and it was even more unsympathetic to claims from children that their fathers or other relatives had abused them.

The most celebrated case of child abuse in this period occurred in Quebec. On 12 February 1920, Aurore Gagnon of Fortierville, Quebec, died at the age of ten, a victim of neglect and physical abuse by her father, Télesphore Gagnon, and her stepmother, Marie-Anne Houde. The parents were brought to trial and convicted of murder. While the father was sentenced to life in prison, the stepmother was condemned to hang because testimony from neighbours and family members suggested that she had been instrumental in the beating and torture of the child. The Prisoners' Welfare Association took up Houde's case and succeeded in having her sentence commuted to life in prison. While Gagnon was released within five years of being sentenced, Houde spent most of the rest of her life in the Kingston Penitentiary and was released just a year before her death from cancer in 1935. Meanwhile, the story of *l'enfant martyre* became the subject of gossip, books, plays, and films, and in the 1990s was the subject of a documentary aired on the Quebec network TVA. As historian Peter Gossage points out, the story became the vehicle for popular notions about wicked stepmothers:

The courtroom drama, the newspaper accounts, the novels, the film: all served to transmit negative stereotypes about women who married widowers and took on the task of raising their children. Like the fairy stories of an earlier time, these stories exploited widely held prejudices about stepmothers. In so doing they articulated dominant ideologies of family life, essentially by holding up for public condemnation an inverted example of the prescribed maternal role.[6]

## MOTHERHOOD IN THE MODERN AGE

Mothers in the interwar years became the particular focus of a campaign to reform child-rearing practices, which hitherto had differed widely depending on family, class, and cultural standards. With the advent of mass circulation magazines and government-sponsored child welfare departments, "scientific" advice on how to be a better mother proliferated. "Old-fashioned" methods and "maternal instinct" came under harsh criticism. In 1932, the *Canadian Home Journal* noted: "The trouble is that the home today is the poorest run, most mismanaged and bungled of all human industries.... Many women running homes haven't even the fundamentals of house management and dietetics. They raise children in the average by a rule of thumb that hasn't altered since Abraham was a child."[7]

Experts increasingly intruded in the nursery, with middle-class families leading the way in embracing new methods of bringing up baby. In the mid-1920s, Montreal and Toronto became the centres for research on children. Funded by the Laura Spellman Rockefeller Foundation and the Metropolitan Life Insurance Company, two nursery schools were established to study children. McGill University's Day Nursery closed in 1930, but St George's School for Child Study (later the University of Toronto Institute of Child Study) became world famous under Dr William Blatz for its pioneering work on child development. By the late 1920s, St George's School accepted a select group of students into a three-year program of child study. They, in turn, spread the new scientific approach to mothering across the nation.

While one of the major goals of the reformers was to reduce infant mortality through better hygiene, dietary practices, and prenatal care, there was also a tendency to medicalize motherhood. Women were encouraged to consult doctors once they became pregnant, have their babies in hospitals rather than at home, and submit their children to a strict disciplinary regime, monitored by doctors. In an age before state-funded medical care, such a route to motherhood was too costly to pursue for many women, and was not always in the best interest of mother and child. Nevertheless,

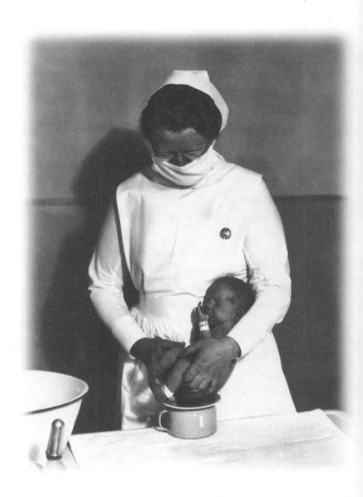

*Child care experts opined that regimentation was best for both mother and baby. Such advice was reflected in attempts to "toilet train" infants almost immediately after birth.*

National Archives of Canada/PA803178

more and more women accepted professional advice on how to bear and raise their children. In 1926, the first year for which statistics are available, only 17.6 percent of births took place in hospitals; by 1960, that figure had increased to 94.6 percent.

Views about raising children departed dramatically from the prewar period. Reflecting new notions of behavioural science pioneered by American psychologists, families were encouraged to teach their children good habits from an early age by establishing fixed schedules for every activity. Detailed charts indicating the correct times for feeding, sleeping, elimination, and bathing were included in most of the advice literature pressed on anxious mothers. At its height, the trend towards regimentation reached absurd lengths that included the injunction to begin toilet training at the age of two weeks. "If the time and place are always the same and the mother shows her approval of the first successes," one 1943 pamphlet opined, "the baby will soon learn what is expected of him."[8] Following the Second World War, more permissive approaches to child rearing were adopted, but for children born in the interwar period, such as the Dionne quintuplets, the idea that a baby was "a little machine" made life difficult for those whose parents subscribed to the advice of experts.

## HOUSING CANADIANS

It was not necessary for a family to own its own home to be deemed respectable. About two-thirds of all urban households were renters; in Montreal, four families in five rented. By international standards of the period, Canadians were relatively well housed, enjoying better sanitation standards and sewerage and drainage facilities than Europeans and experiencing less overcrowding. The averages, however, hid class and racial differences in the

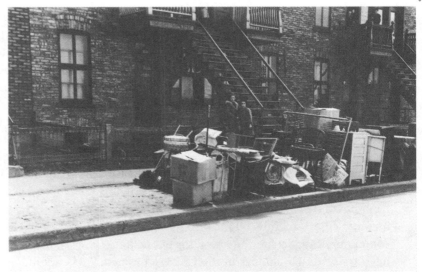

*Tenants being evicted in Montreal during the Depression.*

accommodation available to Canadians.

During the Second World War, a committee headed by Queen's University economics professor C.A. Curtis produced a detailed picture of the shelter available to Canadians. Curtis concluded that 10 percent of existing dwellings in Canada were beyond repair and should be demolished. Another 25 percent required major repairs. Using the assumption that a four-person nuclear family ought to have at least two bedrooms and a kitchenette, Curtis concluded that one dwelling in five was overcrowded. Most Canadians, he noted, paid too much rent relative to their incomes and the poorer they were, the more likely they were to be getting little value for their rent money.

The poor and the wealthy continued to live in different areas of the same cities, with the wealthy enjoying better sewerage and drainage and access to municipal parks. Substantial differences in infant birth weight and mortality bore witness to unequal prospects. In 1921, the infant mortality rate for Montreal's well-to-do suburbs of Outremont and Westmount was less than 6 percent. In contrast, that of west-end working-class districts was over 20 percent. Tuberculosis claimed hundreds of lives in that year, with the working-class districts predictably suffering the highest death rates.

Although Curtis ignored ethnicity as a factor

in determining housing conditions, it also had a bearing on the issue. Land titles often had restrictions that kept non-whites as well as Jews and sometimes eastern Europeans out of new developments. French Canadians and eastern European immigrants were far more likely than Anglo-Canadians to be living in overcrowded conditions. In terms of accommodations, visible minorities fared the worst, being easy targets for prejudiced realtors. Natives on reserves lived in unheated shacks without sanitation or sewerage and suffered from high rates of preventable diseases as a consequence. The Vancouver Housing Association, a community organization pressing for public housing, observed that families in the Chinese business quarters east of Dewdney Street had poor accommodation and that single Chinese males lived in crowded, poorly lit, poorly ventilated boarding houses. This should have come as no surprise since the British Columbia government gave Chinese men an accommodation voucher worth twenty cents, while white men's vouchers were worth sixty cents. More affluent members of the Chinese community often took in their destitute countrymen. The Yip family, for example, even leased a large building on Canton Avenue from the city and converted it to a shelter for homeless older Chinese men.

In the age of the expanding automobile industry, suburban developments proliferated outside major Canadian cities. Suburbs offered white middle-class Canadians the possibility of living in quiet, low-density communities away from noisy workplaces and gave them homes and yards large enough that they could emulate elite lifestyles that mass advertising suggested were within their reach. The Depression brought suburban expansion to an abrupt end, but suburbia was still held out as the best place to live for upwardly mobile Canadians.

Whether they lived in suburbs, the inner city, or in farmhouses, Canadians of the interwar period were influenced by the new domestic ideal propagated in the media. This ideal suggested that the home, rather than institutions such as the church and community hall should be the major centre for entertainment. Radios, gramophones, and fine furnishings were necessary accoutrements for the

home. As "labour-saving devices," such as electric stoves, vacuum cleaners, and washing machines began to replace servants, wives increasingly did all their own housework, often in isolation from other women. Men were expected to spend less time at public places than they once had, and more time with their families. Some Canadians paid outrageous rents because they placed so great an emphasis on having an accommodation that could approximate the goals of the new cult of domesticity.

## WOMEN, WORK, AND THE FAMILY

Work did not always mean the same thing to men and women. Aside from the obvious distinction industrial society makes between unpaid work in the home, done largely by women, and work in the paid labour force, there were differing attitudes towards waged work itself. These attitudes, notes historian Joy Parr, were reinforced by the different socialization that girls and boys received:

> Through waged work, boys learned manliness; they mastered disciplines and discriminations, ways of appraising their work and one another, which they would practice through their adult lives; varied though these ways of being manly were, they shared one trait: they were lessons males alone might learn. Girls did not learn womanliness through their paid employment. Their experience of waged work ... was important in their growing into womanhood because it became them to remain under the protection of male kin while they waited for their life's work, in marriage and outside the market, to begin.[9]

Many young women from rural areas enjoyed the escape to the city. As their diaries and letters attest, they went to movies, dances, and shops with friends they had met at work and in boarding houses. However, their work lives were rarely glamorous. Before the Second World War, most were primarily underpaid store clerks, office workers, and domestics. Immigrant women whose first language was not English fared worse than their English-speaking counterparts. They were clustered in occupations such as sewing for extremely low piece rates and in minimum-wage jobs as cleaners and launderers.

Women's work was central in establishing a sense of community in small towns or in local neighbourhoods of larger cities. New single-industry towns, such as Powell River, BC, and Gagnon, Quebec, were springing up as "suburbs in the wilderness," designed to attract a core group of stable family men as employees. Management believed that such workers would be less prone to mobility and strikes than an earlier generation of single male workers. While most of the men worked in the town's main industry, their wives took up the challenge to establish community facilities. A woman who arrived in Flin Flon, Manitoba, in 1926 when the town was still a bush camp, later recalled, "Without women this town would be nothing. Women organized the community centre, the schools, the hospital.... But most important, women were wives and mothers. They kept the house, raised the children right.... Women looked after the home and that's what makes this town great. It's a family town."[10]

In cities such as Halifax, Moncton, Hamilton, and Ottawa, female single parents headed one home in six. Most of these women were widows, although many were deserted and a few had never been married. Without husbands, women had little alternative but to join the paid labour force. If their children were young, this often meant placing them in orphanages since there were few day-care facilities, and reliable, affordable child-minders were not easy to find. In many orphanages, over half the children had at least one parent, but work lives and strict orphanage rules limited the time that a single mother was able to spend with her children.

Rose and Edith Biscun were nine and six respectively when their widowed mother, a Russian immigrant, placed them in the Winnipeg Jewish Orphanage in 1931. For the next five years, until their mother remarried and they went to live with her and their stepfather, they saw their mother only a half-day each week. She worked in a shmata (clothing) factory six days a week. Only Sundays and occasional holidays afforded the possibility of a family get-together. Children in single-parent families enjoyed fewer educational opportunities than in two-parent families because income from their labour was needed to help the family get by. In Halifax in 1931, 25 percent of children aged fifteen to nineteen were in school; for children of widows, the corresponding figure was 12 percent.

## RURAL LIFE

In the interwar period, Canada is best described as half urban, half rural. As late as 1921, a majority of Canadians lived in communities of less than twenty thousand people, and even in 1941, over 44 percent of Canadians were rural residents (see table 10.1). During the Great Depression, three of every ten Canadians lived on a farm. Most farmers were commercial farmers, depending on the sale of their produce to buy farm implements and consumer goods. When hard times descended, they were proud of their ability to survive by subsistence farming, an option not available to most city-dwellers. This was particularly true for farmers in the fertile belts of southern Ontario, Quebec, and the Maritimes. Although farmers on the southern Prairies sometimes moved to cities and towns to seek work or relief, many farmers' sons and daugh-

**Table 10.1**

### URBAN PERCENTAGES OF POPULATION FOR REGIONS AND PROVINCES, 1901–1941
#### (PEOPLE IN CITIES OF 20 000 OR OVER)

|  | 1901 | 1911 | 1921 | 1931 | 1941 |
|---|---|---|---|---|---|
| Canada | 34.9 | 41.8 | 47.4 | 52.5 | 55.7 |
| Quebec | 36.1 | 44.5 | 51.8 | 59.5 | 61.2 |
| Ontario | 40.3 | 49.5 | 58.8 | 63.1 | 67.5 |
| Prairies | 19.3 | 27.9 | 28.7 | 31.3 | 32.4 |
| British Columbia | 46.4 | 50.9 | 50.9 | 62.3 | 64.0 |
| Maritimes | 24.5 | 30.9 | 38.8 | 39.7 | 44.1 |

Source: *Wayne W. McVey Jr. and Warren E. Kalbach*, Canadian Population (Toronto: Nelson, 1995), 149

ters, who had been able to find work during the late twenties, returned to farms during the 1930s to wait out the Depression.

More than ever before in Canadian history, Canadians in rural areas were connected to metropolitan centres. By the late 1920s, 40 percent of Alberta farmers owned an automobile, and many made use of it to shop in the larger towns and cities. Both automobiles and catalogue shopping restricted the ability of local merchants to corner the business of farmers. As larger centres grew and offered bigger and better services, many small towns began to languish, a trend that would continue throughout the twentieth century.

In the interwar period, the farm population of Ontario and Quebec declined, but it remained stable in the Maritime provinces and increased on the Prairies. More farms were created in northern Saskatchewan and Alberta as well as in the foothills of the Rocky Mountains. These provided an alternative to unproductive areas on the southern Prairies, the driest of which were abandoned after homesteaders had made heartbreaking efforts to turn deserts into productive farmlands. Despite farm expansion in the West, the opportunity of moving up the social ladder from farm labourer to farm owner was declining. Farming was becoming more technologically involved, with the result that larger farms were necessary to make agriculture profitable. As the number of farms declined and the costs of farming increased, many farm labourers, often unmarried male immigrants, found their dreams of owning their own land dashed.

The lot of farm labourers was mixed. John Grossman was a German émigré to Jansen, Saskatchewan, in the mid-1920s. As a farm labourer, he did such unpleasant work as hauling stones and pitching hay from sunrise to sunset, complaining that his employer and the employer's sons avoided the heaviest physical labour. He also was displeased that the farm owner was so rigid that he would not let him go to Saskatoon to attend an exhibition. Other farm labourers had a happier experience. Jens Skinberg of Dalum, Alberta, a Danish immigrant in the late 1920s, was, like Grossman, disappointed when he realized that he would not be able to afford his own farm. Instead he spent his life as a farm labourer. The Danish cultural community of Dalum, including

his employer, made him feel at home, and he chose not to seek urban or industrial employment opportunities.

During the 1930s, provincial governments settled landless families who had no incomes on infertile lands where it was hoped that they could eke out a subsistence. Many of these families moved off their new lands when wartime employment made it possible for them to relocate to cities and towns. The "back-to-the-land" movement of the 1930s suggested the strength of agrarian ideology in Canada, which held that it was still possible in an industrial age for families to be rugged individualists, living off the land without the help of the state.

Successful farmers increasingly viewed themselves as independent commodity producers, more akin to small businessmen than to wage labourers. The agricultural colleges attached to the universities preached a new view of farming that had a growing appeal. The farmer, it was argued, was an intelligent businessman who studied all the relevant market factors and then decided what crops to grow, what animals to buy and sell, and what machinery he needed. Meanwhile, the farmer's wife, apart from her important work on the farm, was to provide the volunteer labour needed to ensure that a rich and wholesome social life was available to farm communities.

In the interwar years, an alternative perspective rejected the notion that the farm family was the rural equivalent of an urban middle-class household. Farmers who joined the CCF or who laboured in the cooperative movement blamed the market rather than the farmer when farm families faced bankruptcy. Radicals suggested that the banks, the farm implement companies, and speculators exploited farmers much as employers exploited workers. Many farm women were also active in the CCF and cooperative movements, campaigning as well for equal ownership of the farm property by husband and wife and for legalization of birth control. For these farm men and women, working-class people were more likely urban allies than were middle-class professionals and business owners.

## RELIGION IN A SECULAR SOCIETY

Modern society with its worldly focus posed a major challenge to all Christian churches in Canada. As we saw in chapter 5, the Industrial Age drove a wedge between Christians who were prepared to adapt to the changes taking place around them and those who were reluctant to do so. The First World War and its aftermath purged some of the radicals from the mainline churches, but this did little to protect the church from growing scepticism about religious beliefs generally or competition from conservative evangelicals who rejected the modern age entirely.

## THE PROTESTANT CHURCH

We are thankful for these and all the good things of life. We recognize that they are a part of our common heritage and come to us through the efforts of our brothers and sisters the world over. What we desire for ourselves we wish for all. To this end may we take our share in the world's work and the world's struggles.[11]

In the 1920s, this grace was spoken before meals in the home of J.S. Woodsworth, Labour politician and former Methodist minister. Woodsworth and others like him had become estranged from the mainstream churches, whose thrust following the First World War was essentially conservative. Worker radicalism prompted many middle-class Protestant ministers and activists to turn away from the social gospel's emphasis on reform and to focus instead on the improvement of individual behaviour. Some church leaders, particularly Methodists, believed that the churches should do more to create a united Canada whose values reflected British traditions. They looked with alarm at regional protest movements and efforts by minority immigrants to maintain their cultural heritage. In

December 1923, Dr W.B. Creighton, the Methodist editor of the *Christian Guardian*, told his readers that the church "do[es] not desire to have Canada filled with an unassimilated mass of people of different races and tongues and religions who would possess no common bond of union and whose presence in large numbers would undo all the work that has already been done in trying to build up the Canadian nation."[12] For Creighton and other church leaders, church union would contribute to a mighty Protestant effort to create a unified, British-inspired Canadian people embodying Protestant virtues of thrift and sobriety.

Although the merger of the Methodist, Presbyterian, and Congregationalist churches into the United Church of Canada in 1925 was motivated by lofty notions of the Christian mission in Canada, the reality was quite different. The United Church and the Presbyterian Church struggled for fourteen years to sort out their jurisdictional disputes, as a large element of the lay Presbyterian population, particularly in Ontario and the Maritimes, was more concerned with preserving its Scots and Scots-Irish cultural traditions than with pursuing the exalted goals of its ministers. Refusing to accept the merger, many Presbyterians insisted that they had the right to remain a separate denom-

*The campaigns of Protestant churches for prohibition and, later, stringent regulation of liquor sales, created a great deal of work for police forces. Here, two Saskatchewan Mounties proudly demontrate a still that they seized in the 1930s.*

Saskatchewan Archives Board/R-A7536

ination and use the churches that their ancestors had built. A particularly galling point for the Presbyterians was the removal of their name by the Act of Union that incorporated the new United Church. Finally, in 1939, the United Church relented and agreed to ask Parliament to recognize the reality that the Presbyterian Church had not disappeared.

The founders of the United Church hoped that a united Protestantism could influence legislators in such areas as temperance, censorship, Sunday observance, and gambling, but their success was limited. The prohibition issue offers a good example of the uphill battles faced by church leaders in the interwar years. After the First World War, the federal government yielded to distiller pressure, dispensed with federal prohibition legislation, and left the provinces to decide the fate of "demon rum" within their own borders. It was not long before the prohibition front began to crumble. British Columbians voted in 1920 for a government monopoly on hard liquor sales, with beer to be sold in grocery stores. Within four years, Quebec and the three Prairie provinces had restored liquor sales, though the Prairies chose to ban bar rooms and to restrict liquor consumption to private homes. In Ontario, the puritanism of the Farmer government on the temperance issue, as well as on questions such as legalizing horse racing, proved an important factor in its humiliating election defeat in 1923. Nova Scotia maintained prohibition until 1929. Only Prince Edward Island held out, finally abandoning prohibition in 1948.

Apart from attempting to influence legislators, the Protestant churches tried to maintain their hold over their congregations by providing leisure activities such as picnics, plays, and exhibitions. By the 1930s, most of the mainstream churches sponsored dances, though ten years earlier many had denounced men and women dancing cheek-to-

cheek as immoral. Observing the limited number of young people in their pews, the churches were prepared to modify their views in the hope of attracting adolescents to organized religion. Women continued to constitute the majority of active church members, but most churches resisted feminist efforts to have women ordained and elected as church elders. The United Church accepted its first female minister, Lydia Gruchy, in the 1930s, but it would be years before churches accepted more than a handful of women into their pulpits.

*"Bible Bill" Aberhart and his lieutenant, Ernest Manning, are pictured here on the campaign trail in 1940. For these two men, a political campaign was simply an extension of the work they did on radio, mixing old-time religion with Social Credit economics.*

Provincial Archives of Alberta/ A-2048

A growing minority of Canadians were unhappy with what they perceived as the decreased fervour of the established churches. Interested in neither the social gospel nor moral reform, they wanted their ministers to focus exclusively on the individual's relationship with God. The

Pentecostals and the millennialist Jehovah's Witnesses were among religious sects that grew in the interwar period. While the popularity of William Aberhart's radio evangelism helped win him the premier's chair in Alberta, many evangelists were dismayed by his attempts to wed fundamentalist religion with a politics that had a distinct flavour of the social gospel, at least in the early years of the Social Credit movement. Charismatic ministers like Canadian-born Aimee Semple McPherson, who preached from her California temple, won the hearts of those who missed the energy and conviction of old-time religion.

## THE CATHOLIC CHURCH

The Roman Catholic Church was as conservative as the major Protestant denominations on most issues of individual behaviour. While the Catholic Church refused to join in the campaign for prohibition, it was as keen as any Protestant denomination to control what Canadians could read, watch at the movies, hear on radio, or do in their spare time. The mainstream Protestant denominations cautiously endorsed the use of mechanical contraceptives to limit family size in the 1930s, but the Roman Catholic Church would only endorse the use of the unreliable rhythm method. It was also implacably against divorce.

On some political and economic issues, there was evidence of growing liberalism in the Roman Catholic Church. Cooperatives were particularly favoured by Catholic reformers. Under Father Moses Coady, the founding director of the Extension Department of St Francis Xavier University in Antigonish, Nova Scotia, attempts were made from 1928 onwards to spread cooperatives through communities dependent on farming, fishing, coal mining, and steel production. Concentrating on the Atlantic region, Coady's achievements included the United Maritime Fishermen's Co-operative (UMFC), which finally put an end to the truck system by using cooperatives to provide supplies, process the fish, and market the final product. The Acadians in the region proved particularly receptive to the call

for cooperatives. By the 1940s, the UMFC counted about forty-five hundred members and was a force to be reckoned with politically as well as economically. The Pecheurs unis du Québec, founded in 1939, followed the same principles as its Maritime counterpart.

On the whole, the Roman Catholic Church in Quebec continued to resist reform efforts. The church hierarchy distrusted the state and regarded it as a competitor. The unwillingness of Duplessis to establish state-supported social services, while raising the ire of liberals, ensured his support by the church establishment. Continued church control over educational, health, and charitable institutions was seen as a shield to protect the faithful from the temptations that secular society constantly placed before them. Defying the trends taking place around them, the Roman Catholic hierarchy resisted all efforts to foster equality for women and opposed compulsory education.

Nonetheless, many church leaders recognized that the church's position was increasingly removed from that of their francophone parishioners who were embracing North American secular values. The birth rate continued to fall in the interwar period, the percentage of workers enrolled in international unions vastly exceeded those who chose to join confessional unions, and blasphemous expressions were common in the Quebec vernacular. Church-sponsored newspapers and the independent, but very Catholic, *Le Devoir* had a combined readership vastly inferior to secular newspapers like *La Presse*. Although rural Quebec parishes might remain under the sway of the priests and nuns, six out of ten Quebeckers, including a majority of francophones, lived in cities in the 1930s. They respected the church leaders, but apparently listened to their views only when it suited them.

## EDUCATION

By the 1920s, parents who could afford to delay their children's entry into the workforce generally encouraged them to complete as many years of secondary schooling as possible. The number of jobs for which high school matriculation was a qualification increased dramatically as employers demanded a more literate workforce. The national increase in school attendance illustrates the change. In 1921, 27 percent of girls and 22 percent of boys between fifteen and nineteen attended school; twenty years later, the respective figures were 37 and 35 percent. In Ontario, the secondary school population quadrupled in the 1920s over the previous decade, though the provincial population had grown only 17 percent.

Quebec francophones, and indeed francophones generally, did not share in this trend. As late as 1926, only 6 percent of Quebec francophones attended school beyond the elementary level. While public schools across the country increasingly emphasized science and mathematics along with literature and grammar in a curriculum that responded to employers' notions of a useful education, Catholic secondary schools in Quebec taught Thomist philosophy, Latin, religion, and humanities. The Church regarded instruction in religious doctrines and religious values as more important than utilitarian, secular knowledge. It believed that too much education in non-religious subjects would lead young people away from the paths of righteousness into the murky waters of North American agnostic materialism. In the view of church leaders, elementary school was sufficient for those whose lives would be spent in honest toil as farmers, labourers, and housewives. Higher education was needed only for future priests, teachers, church administrators, and other professionals. Since the labour of older children was often necessary to ensure a sufficient income for many households or to help mothers of large families with the raising of younger children, many Quebeckers were pleased that schooling was not compulsory.

By the early forties, reformist elements within the church joined with trade unions and liberal women's organizations in recognizing the need for a better-educated citizenry. In 1943, the Liberal government of Adelard Godbout passed legislation making education compulsory for children from ages six to fifteen. By then, the wartime economic situation had created full employment for adult males, and parents were more willing than in the past to accept state intervention in an area of parental authority.

French-language instruction in public schools continued to be resisted in the predominantly anglophone provinces. Although Ontario permitted French instruction in elementary schools after 1927, the province extended French-language schools none of the planning or coordination that English-language schools enjoyed. The provincial department of education provided no curricular materials in French, and the normal schools, which trained teachers, operated solely in English. Most western and Maritime provinces either forbade or made little provision for French-language education. Only in New Brunswick was French-language education accepted without restrictions, but the province put little money into curriculum planning for the francophone schools, and the small tax base in francophone communities guaranteed an inferior French-language school system.

Poor educational opportunities and a recognition that people who spoke French were often condemned to poverty caused many francophones outside Quebec to assimilate to the anglophone culture. This meant not simply learning English, which would have been necessary in areas where the francophone population was small, but abandoning French as the home language. In 1931, the percentage of Ontarians whose first language was French but who later became primarily English speakers was reported as 22.1 percent. The rate was even higher in provinces with small francophone populations, such as British Columbia. Only in New Brunswick, with its concentrated Acadian community, was assimilation successfully resisted.

While schooling was regarded as important by nearly everyone, teaching, particularly at the elementary level, was still deprecated as a "woman's profession." Elementary school teachers in urban areas required only a year of normal school, which could be taken after high school matriculation, to be eligible to teach. In rural areas, they might be even less qualified for the classroom. Their limited training and poor salaries distinguished them from high school teachers, who were predominantly male and were more likely to have university degrees. During the Depression, as school boards ran short of cash, teachers faced not only pay cuts, but also sometimes months without any salary at all.

The problem was particularly severe in rural areas where the tax base was small. Rural teachers were single women who usually taught in one-room schools and boarded with a local family or lived in a room attached to the school. In frontier areas, both the living and working conditions were primitive. Still, many teachers enjoyed their work, appreciated the hospitality of local folk, and felt that they had more autonomy and independence than their urban counterparts of this period. Lillian Gates's description of her experience in the Cariboo in British Columbia was fairly typical: "I loved to be alone in my teacher's residence at Willow River, even if, in the winter months, sometimes at -45 degrees, I had to get up every 2–3 hours all night to keep my little wooden heater going. I loved to walk along the old logging trails, through the silent forests.... I learned to shoot, without success. The parents of my pupils supplied me with moose meat, caribou, grouse, ptarmigan and wild mushrooms."[13]

The enthusiasm for more schooling slowly extended to the postsecondary sector, but with university education generally still confined to an elite minority, provincial governments were reluctant to vastly increase spending on universities. While University of Toronto students might demonstrate in the late 1930s against spending cuts by Mitchell Hepburn's government, few ordinary people sympathized with the students' plight. More helpful than governments were private, mainly American, foundations such as Carnegie, Ford, and Rockefeller, which poured money into major universities and helped to fund the Canadian Social Science Research Council, whose grants allowed scholars outside professional facilities to conduct research.

Between 1929 and 1940, Canadian university enrolments increased from 23 418 to 37 225. Women's participation jumped from 16 to 24 percent of all enrolments, but their increase was concentrated in areas stereotyped as women's professions: nursing, household science, library science, and physical and occupational therapy. No males were enrolled in any of these areas in the 1940–41 academic year. Men predominated in professional areas that promised higher salaries and greater independence. In engineering, there were 2851 men enrolled across the country in 1920-21, but only 3 women; twenty years later, 4381 men and 13 women were studying in the discipline. Medicine and law were only slightly less solidly male preserves; education and arts were more extensively coeducational.

## MEDICAL RESEARCH IN CANADA

Canadian universities were not only teaching institutions; they sponsored research as well. At the University of Toronto, Canadians made headlines in the field of medicine when a team headed by Frederick Banting discovered insulin, a life-saving therapy for diabetes mellitus. Banting and one of his co-researchers, J.J.R. McLeod, shared the 1923 Nobel Prize for their efforts. Banting gave half of his prize money to C.H. Best, who was a key researcher on the investigative team.

At McGill University's Medical Museum, Maude Abbott's authoritative cataloguing of the types of congenital heart disease led to the eventual development of surgical therapies for its treatment. Surgical intervention saved the lives of countless "blue babies" whose fate in earlier years had been almost certain death. Although Abbott was recognized as one of the world's leading authorities in her field, McGill never promoted her beyond the level of assistant professor.

In 1934, Wilder Penfield established the Montreal Neurological Institute, which rapidly became internationally renowned for its research, teaching, and treatment related to diseases of the nervous system. Penfield established the "Montreal procedure" for the treatment of epilepsy and was a tireless student of the brain, which he argued was the most important unexplored field of scientific inquiry.

Women were rarely hired as professors outside the departments offering training in "women's professions." Moreover, the positions of female faculty were never as secure as those of men. When the University of Alberta had to lay off a classicist during the Second World War, they chose to force the retirement of the distinguished scholar Geneva Misener rather than to dismiss any of her junior colleagues, who were all "family men."

In the interwar years, women seeking educational challenges or career training became an important part of the audience for adult education programs. Several universities established extension programs aimed first at rural areas and eventually at the non-university population of the cities. E.A. Corbett, who led the University of Alberta's Faculty of Extension in the 1920s and 1930s, felt that his mission was to promote high culture in rural areas. He encouraged local drama productions, and his department lent films, classical music recordings, and books to groups and individuals. Under his leadership, the Faculty of Extension established a radio station to provide educational and cultural programs throughout the province and a summer drama program that later evolved into the Banff School of Fine Arts. McGill and the University of British Columbia established programs along Corbett's model in the 1920s and 1930s. A rather different blend of education and social activism characterized the Extension Department at St Francis Xavier University under the energetic leadership of Moses Coady.

Adult education was not restricted to the universities. At the turn of the century, Frontier College had been founded by Alfred Fitzpatrick, a Nova Scotia-born Presbyterian minister, to provide basic education to workers, particularly immigrants. It flourished in the interwar years as university students flocked to work sites on the industrial frontier to teach those who otherwise would have had little hope of receiving any formal education. Trade unions and political parties of the left also ran schools for their activists in an attempt to counter the information dispensed by the media, which the left viewed as tools of the capitalist class.

# CULTURE AND LEISURE

## ART AND LITERATURE

A better-educated public provided an increasing market for Canadian literature, art, drama, and music, despite the overweening influence of American popular culture. With the support of voluntary groups, churches, universities, and corporations, Canadians produced a vibrant, if fragile, culture and a critical audience. Debates in the media about issues such as the relative merits of the Group of Seven, the growing American control of radio programming, and the necessity for censorship brought the politics of culture to a wide audience.

The creation of the Canadian Authors' Association (CAA) in 1921 testified to a new sense of national identity among Canadian writers. At its largest, it had eight hundred members and a French-Canadian branch. It sponsored an annual book week and encouraged sales of the works of Canadian authors. As in the prewar period, Canadian writers produced little that was genuinely innovative. Montreal poet F.R. Scott was highly critical of the uninspired outpourings of national sentiment by the members of the CAA, satirizing them in his poem "The Canadian Authors Meet" (1927):

O Canada, O Canada, Oh can
A day go by without new authors springing
To paint the native maple, and to plan
More ways to set the self-same welkin ringing.

Quebec novels of the interwar period maintained the idealization of the land evident in earlier works. However, there was a recognition by writers such as Ringuet (Philippe Panneton) and Claude-Henri Grignon that the traditional Quebec was disappearing and could not be restored. In Montreal, a group of anglophone poets made social criticism the focus of their works. Dorothy Livesay, F.R. Scott, A.M. Klein, Miriam Waddington, and Louis Dudek were major figures in this movement for social realist works.

English-Canadian social realism approached themes such as sexuality, repression of women, and psychological blackmail in such classic Prairie novels as Martha Ostenso's *Wild Geese* (1925), several works by Frederick Philip Grove, and Sinclair Ross's *As for Me and My House* (1941). Too bleak for contemporary tastes, Ross's novel only received the recognition it deserved in the 1960s. The instinct for survival and resistance during the Depression was celebrated in Irene Baird's *Waste Heritage* (1939), while class strife was the subject of Grove's *The Master of the Mill* (1944). In the 1930s, Hugh MacLennan embarked on a project to chronicle Canadian identity. His first published novel, *Barometer Rising* (1941), which focused around the Halifax Explosion of 1917, was widely acclaimed for its insights into the Canadian colonial mentality.

In the interwar years, many Canadian painters were in revolt against conventional subject matter and styles. Emily Carr, who by 1914 had largely given up painting due to lack of both moral and financial support, resurfaced in the late 1920s to become one of Canada's most renowned artists. Her work was enriched by Native art forms and themes. Abstract and non-objective painting made tentative, if not particularly popular, debuts in Canada prior to the Second World War. Inspired by American and French artists, abstract painters used objects or natural scenes as a base for producing paintings that often bore no direct resemblance to the original object. Non-objective painters began not with objects but with pure imagination to produce their art. Russian-born painter Paraskeva Clark of Toronto raised eyebrows with her cubist-inspired paintings, which owed a debt to experiments by Soviet artists in the early years after the revolution. Paris continued to have a great influence, particularly among artists in Montreal. Returning from Paris in 1940, Alfred

Pellan became the first of many francophone artists to demonstrate the influence of Picasso and other cubists.

During the Depression years, realism crept back into art. Works such as Leonard Hutchinson's woodcut *Protest*, Miller Brittain's paintings of

*Emily Carr, 1871–1945*, **A Haida Village**, *circa 1929.*
Oil on canvas 82.7 x 60.7 cm; McMichael Canadian Art Collection; Gift of Dr. and Mrs. Stern, Dominion Gallery, Montreal; 1974.18.1

unemployed longshoremen in Saint John, and Carl Schaefer's watercolours of rusting agricultural machinery in the fallow fields of southern Ontario are poignant reminders of the economic dislocation facing many people in this difficult decade. Following the policies set by Franklin Roosevelt's government in the United States, business and gov-

## IN EXILE FOR HIS ART:
## BRION GYSIN OF EDMONTON

Artists interested in radical art forms often decided that there was no future for them in Canada. An example is Brion Gysin, a painter and writer who became famous in Europe but remained unknown in Edmonton, where he had grown up. He was born in wartime Britain to Canadian parents, but his soldier father died shortly after he was born. His mother eventually moved to Edmonton, where Brion went to school from the age of five to sixteen. His mother then sent him to an English public school, and he never returned to live in Canada. An atheist, homosexual, and avant-garde artist, he found little to hold him in the repressive atmosphere of Edmonton, though his mother felt abandoned by his decision to remain in Europe. In the 1930s, just beginning a long and important artistic career, Gysin gained attention for his surrealist work in Paris. Despite his obvious contempt for the Canadian Prairies, Gysin painted a series of illusionist desert landscapes that were inspired in part by his memories of Alberta.

ernment commissioned work from Canadian artists. For example, Charles Comfort painted eight murals for the Toronto Stock Exchange while Miller Brittain produced two murals for the University of New Brunswick's Beaverbrook Gymnasium.

The success of Carr and Clark, among other women artists, demonstrated that in artistic areas where their entry was not explicitly barred, some determined women could penetrate the barriers of social prejudice. In other fields, such as architecture, women were excluded completely. Esther Marjorie Hall, Canada's first woman architect, earned her architecture degree from the University of Toronto in 1920. Returning to her native Edmonton, she was denied the right to register by the Alberta Association of Architects. The Farmers' government, influenced by Canada's first woman Cabinet minister, Irene Parlby, finally passed legislation in 1925 making registration automatic for any graduate of a recognized faculty of architecture. This meant that Hall was theoretically able to practise her craft, but the hostility of the architects' professional body made it difficult for her to find clients. During the Depression, she was simply unable to make a living and moved to Victoria with her parents.

Many of the works of sculptor Frances Loring were architectural in nature. In the interwar years, she was commissioned to design public monuments as well as several war memorials across the country, including one for the Law Society of Upper Canada in Osgoode Hall in Toronto. Along with her lifelong companion, fellow sculptor Florence Wyle, Loring was a founding member of the Sculptors' Society of Canada and worked to promote the acceptance of women within the artistic community.

Perhaps the most deeply influential art of the period was produced by the Group of Seven. More popular than the new experimental art, it contributed to a nature-based Canadian nationalism.

*Frank Carmichael, 1890-1945,* **Northern Tundra**, *1931.*
oil on canvas 76.4 x 91.6 cm; McMichael Canadian Art Collection; Gift of Col. R.S. McLaughlin, 1968.7.14

Painting scenes all over the country, A.Y. Jackson remained particularly faithful to the group's original work. Arthur Lismer became educational supervisor of the Art Gallery of Ontario and built upon his earlier landscapes. Some members of the group were drawn to more experimental ideas: in particular, Lawren Harris's work became more abstract. Fred Varley was named head of the Department of Drawing and Painting at the Vancouver School of Art in 1926. He was drawn to Oriental art and, through Emily Carr, also discovered Native art. Anthropomorphism permeated later Varley works, such as *Snow People*, and in 1938 he went North to sketch the landscapes and people of the Arctic. Despite the fact that individual members of the group went their separate ways, the impact of their original project was enormous.

## MUSIC AND THEATRE IN THE INTERWAR YEARS

Film and radio reduced the audience for the vaudeville shows that had been popular before the First World War, and many of the old music halls were turned into cinemas. Although movies posed a major threat to touring theatre troupes, community theatre groups flourished. In 1933, the first Canadian Drama Festival was held in which community theatre groups competed for prizes in acting, directing, design, and production after a series of regional run-offs. This remarkably successful annual event stimulated amateur theatre all across the country.

Radio and records increased the audience for live bands, particularly dance bands, and a variety of nightclubs sprang up in Canadian cities between the wars. While visiting "hit parade" artists attracted the largest audiences, there was a market for full-time and part-time jazz and "swing" musicians in every city. Guy Lombardo and His Royal Canadians became famous in the United States in the 1930s for their broadcasts from New York's Roosevelt Grill on New Year's Eve. For those who shared the growing passion for country music, the United States also offered opportunities. Wilf Carter drifted across the border in the 1930s and,

as Montana Slim, was soon being beamed into Canadian homes on American airwaves.

North American trends also influenced francophone Quebec, where Marie Travers, known as La Bolduc, became Quebec's first successful recording artist. A gifted child born to English parents in the Gaspé town of Newport, she played a number of musical instruments and composed songs, the first of which were recorded in 1927. Her songs, such as "La Cuisinière," "La Servante," and "La Grocerie du coin," focused on themes of daily life and the material difficulties faced by ordinary people. Although her witty and, for the times, naughty lyrics earned her the disapproval of the church, she was wildly popular among francophone Quebeckers, who listened to her on the radio and flocked to buy her records.

The classical music tradition was strengthened in Canada by the creation of Schools of Music at the University of Toronto (1918), McGill (1920), and Laval (1922). With the founding of symphony orchestras in Toronto, Montreal, and Vancouver, professional classical musicians had an outlet for their talents. As with popular music, imported music dominated the radio waves, but a few Canadian composers managed to gain an audience for their work. As in other areas of the arts, musicians struggled to give expression to unique Canadian images and motifs in their work. Claude Champagne's *Suite Canadienne* and Ernest MacMillan's *Two Sketches for Canadian Strings*, which incorporate themes from folk music, have become Canadian classics.

## THE INVENTION OF TRADITION

In the 1920s, Canadians began reflecting on the rapid changes that had occurred in the post-Confederation period. In doing so, they often viewed the past through a romantic haze, inventing traditions, imagining golden ages, and creating identities that may never have existed quite as they came to be described. The National Museum of Canada, created by an Act of Parliament in 1927, symbolized this new interest in the past, as did the establishment of the Historic Sites and Monuments

Board in 1919. Upon the advice of the board, the government began to designate national historic sites across the country. Most of the sites recognized by the board in the interwar years related to military and political developments in the nation's past. Strongly influenced by the reconstruction of colonial Williamsburg in Virginia in the 1920s, the government embarked on its own reconstruction projects, beginning with a replica of Champlain's habitation at Port Royal, Nova Scotia, in 1939.

Perhaps reflecting their pride in the longest-settled regions of the country, many Maritimers and Quebeckers eagerly embraced historical approaches to identity creation. Pioneers in the pre-Confederation period were increasingly depicted as happy folk, living in farming and fishing communities untouched by the materialism of the industrial age. In the 1920s, researchers began seeking out the descendants of the folk still living in the "traditional" way, claiming to find in these people the essence of regional identities.

The "cult of the folk" sold well to consumers of culture and tourism in the modern age. In Nova Scotia, many of the symbols of provincial identity—Peggy's Cove, the Bluenose, and the Scottish bagpiper at the border—emerged in the interwar years. Meanwhile, a coterie of creative writers, calling themselves the "song fishermen," idealized the rural values of the past, which they felt were fast slipping away in a tide of modern values. Since many of the song fishermen were highly educated and actually lived and worked in the United States much of the time, their view of the Nova Scotia "folk" was highly modern in its conceptualization and shaped to appeal to contemporary consumers. Historian Ian McKay underlines the contradictions embodied in the cult of the folk: in upholding their premodern, quaint, therapeutic otherness, he argues, it was simultaneously drawing the folk into the commercial and political webs of modern society. [14]

The cult of the folk led to a new appreciation of folklore. In the Maritimes, Helen Creighton embarked on a lifelong career collecting Nova Scotia folk songs and stories. At the National Museum of Canada, Rhodes scholar Marius Barbeau collected traditional songs, texts, and arti-

facts of French Canadians and Native peoples. His first loyalty was to his Quebec homeland, which he concluded had preserved folk traditions reaching back to the middle ages. In his work with the Tsimshian in British Columbia, Barbeau collected stories about an ancient migration from a distant homeland, convincing him that they had journeyed from Asia. Barbeau founded the Archives de folklore at Laval University and helped to make ethnology and folklore an academic pursuit in twentieth-century Canada.

The folk themselves were not always amused by the process through which they became cultural artifacts. For example, in 1927, Frank Parker Day, one of the Maritime-born song fishermen who lived in the United States, published *Rockbound*, a thinly disguised novel about the people on Ironbound Island off the south shore of Nova Scotia. The Ironbounders, who welcomed the university English professor into their homes, felt misrepresented and betrayed by his portrait of them. On 20 February 1929, the "Offended Citizens of Rockbound" published a letter in the Lunenburg *Progress-Enterprise* offering evidence that they were not the "ignorant, immoral and superstitious" people portrayed in the novel. "Our island boasts three teachers and there isn't a child who cannot read and write," the Ironbounders proudly stated. Why, they asked, had "Mr Day put such a ridiculous book on the market, belittling the inhabitants of his native province, and those who befriended him?" The Ironbounders, of course, knew the answer to their rhetorical question. Mr Day, they concluded, might "accumulate quite a bit of money from his enterprise." [15]

## SPORTS IN THE MODERN AGE

In the interwar years, interest in professional sporting events increased among all social classes. Hockey's claim to be the national sport was cemented as indoor stadiums, artificial ice, and expansion of the National Hockey League to American cities gave the game new prominence. The Montreal Forum opened in 1924, followed by Maple Leaf Gardens in Toronto in 1931. Not only sports stars, but also sports commentators became household names, most notably Foster Hewitt, whose play-by-play during radio and television hockey broadcasts, starting in 1931, entertained generations of Canadians. Although a few hockey superstars earned a sensational $10 000 a year during the 1920s, the average wage in the NHL was $900, a poverty wage if it was the only income a hockey player could claim. After the legendary Ottawa Senators, winners of four Stanley Cups, were forced to fold in 1934 as unemployment reduced the potential audience for professional hockey, the only Canadian teams in the NHL were the Montreal Canadiens and the Toronto Maple Leafs. Still, all four American teams in the league had a majority of Canadian-born players. Although the NHL dominated the hockey world, smaller-city leagues with semi-professional players continued to draw crowds throughout the period.

Baseball remained a popular participant sport. In Halifax, six teams from working-class neighbourhoods composed the Twilight League, which held games three days a week. As many as two thousand spectators attended some games. Softball was also popular. In 1923, the Ontario Amateur Softball Association was formed, the first association in the world for this increasingly popular sport. There was also professional baseball in Canada: Quebec had a semi-professional provincial baseball league and both Montreal and Toronto had teams in the International League headquartered in the United States.

The sports world was still a largely male preserve, but women continued to make inroads. In 1928, Fanny Rosenfeld, a Russian-born Canadian Jew, returned from the Amsterdam Olympics with a silver medal in the 100-metre dash. She had also been lead runner for the gold-medal relay team and was Canada's leading woman broad jumper and discus thrower. Esther Catherwood won the gold medal in the high jump in 1928 as well, setting an Olympic record in the process. In the 1930s, champion swimmer Phyllis Dewar won four gold medals at the British Empire Games, a feat that was not surpassed by another Canadian until 1978. While hockey and football were regarded as inappropriate sports for "ladies," softball was acceptable for women as long as they remained in amateur leagues. In basketball, the Edmonton Grads continued their remarkable career throughout the interwar period. When the Grads disbanded in 1941, they left a record that has yet to be equalled, winning 93 percent of their games and forty-nine out of a possible fifty-one domestic titles.

## SERVICE ORGANIZATIONS

Spurred by increased urbanization and shorter work weeks, voluntary organizations proliferated in the interwar years. Churches, fraternal associations, and the militia continued to provide Canadian men with opportunities to bond on the basis of religious, ethnic, or patriotic inclinations. While trade unions also organized their own class-related social activities, middle-class businessmen were increasingly involved in community-service organizations such as the Rotary Club, Kiwanis, Gyros, and the Elks, which had no ethnic or religious affiliation. These clubs raised funds for local facilities such as libraries, swimming pools, community halls, and parks, participated in parades to boost community spirit, and supported community groups such as the Boy Scouts.

Women remained active in both mixed-sex and women's church groups and continued their enthusiasm for secular voluntary organization in the interwar years. Women who had university degrees founded the Canadian Federation of University Women in 1919. Initially focused on women's role in social reform and the prevention of war, the CFUW became involved in a wide range of charitable activities and supported, through their scholarship program, the next generation of female scholars. In 1930, the Canadian Federation of Business and Professional Women's Clubs was organized to convince the business community's leaders that better training and fairer treatment for women were ultimately in the interest of business. In Ontario and Nova Scotia, black women established clubs that organized cultural programs, studied African-Canadian history, and worked for better local race relations. Women also

**Table 10.2**

| CANADA'S POPULATION (IN THOUSANDS), 1911–1941 | | | | | |
|---|---|---|---|---|---|
| Year | Natural increase | Immigration | Emigration | Net migration | Population |
| 1911–21 | 1349 | 1592 | 1360 | 233 | 8 788 |
| 1921–31 | 1486 | 1198 | 1095 | 103 | 10 377 |
| 1931–41 | 1242 | 149 | 262 | - 112 | 11 507 |

*Source: David C. Corbett*, Canada's Immigration Policy: A Critique *(Toronto: University of Toronto Press, 1957), 121*

generally led the Canadian Home and School (or Parent–Teacher) Associations that mushroomed in the 1920s.

## POPULATION

By 1941, Canada's population was over 11 500 000. Immigration reached a high point during the late 1920s but was reduced to a trickle during the Depression (see table 10.2). Although Canada still gave preferential treatment to immigrants from Britain and the United States, the federal government bowed to pressure from railway companies, manufacturers, and farmers—all facing labour shortages—and opened the doors to wider European immigration after the First World War. They were firmly closed again in the 1930s. Even those trying to help Jewish refugees flee Hitler's genocide could not convince those who administered immigration policy to pry them open. Only four thousand Jews were admitted to Canada between 1933 and 1939. Canada was not alone in its exclusionary policies. In 1939, the *St Louis*, a ship bearing 907 German Jews, was refused permission to land anywhere in North or South America. "The line must be drawn somewhere," a senior official in the Canadian Immigration Department declared, as the *St Louis* returned its desperate cargo to the death camps of the Third Reich.

Most of the population growth in the 1930s came from natural increase and from Canadians returning home from the United States. As the Depression settled into the North American economy, many Canadians working south of the border lost their jobs. Those who had not taken out American citizenship were, therefore, subject to deportation. Canada adopted a similar policy with the result that twenty-eight thousand immigrants were officially deported between 1930 and 1935. Immigrants could be expelled for a number of stated reasons: criminality, medical causes, being a public charge, or for "other civil causes," a euphemism for radicals and union organizers.

Canadians were generally healthier than they had been in earlier generations, and life expectancy was on the rise. The average Canadian boy born in 1931 could expect to live 60 years, while the average girl had 62.1 years ahead of her. Better nutrition, preventive medicine, and reduced infant mortality helped to increase life expectancy over the course of the twentieth century. Native people, however, survived only half as long as other Canadians, testimony to the dire poverty in which they continued to live.

The slow-growth provinces—the Maritimes, Manitoba, and Saskatchewan—saw little change in their ethnic distribution during this period. Despite its significant Acadian minority, the Maritimes continued to be dominated by people of British origin. Saskatchewan and Manitoba saw significant immigration from Southern and Eastern Europe, as they had before the First World War. Southern Ontario, which had been largely an Anglo-Celtic preserve before 1920, became home to tens of thousands of southern and eastern European immigrants whose numbers would grow even more dramatically in the decades following the Second World War.

Some of those entering Canada in the 1920s were fleeing religious persecution at home. Between 1922 and 1930, over twenty thousand Mennonites arrived from the Soviet Union, sponsored by the Canadian Mennonite Board of

Colonization in cooperation with the CPR. Most of them settled on farms in Saskatchewan and Manitoba, reliving the harsh lives of earlier generations of settlers. By 1941, there were over a hundred thousand Mennonites in Canada, despite the fact that, in the 1920s, almost eight thousand had left the country for Latin America to protest the imposition of unilingual education in the Prairie provinces. They feared that failure to educate their

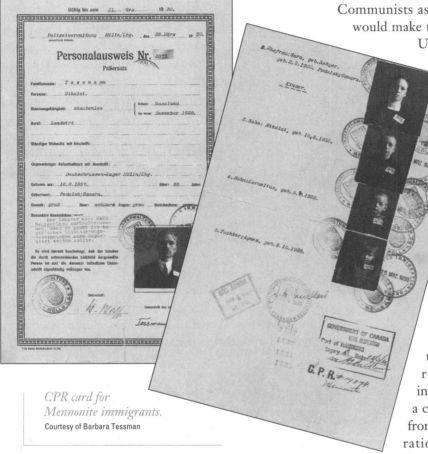

*CPR card for Mennonite immigrants.*
Courtesy of Barbara Tessman

children in German would expose them to secular influences from the larger society. For the Mennonites, fears of secularism ran deep. Many Mennonites had abandoned their local communities for city life. While most of these émigrés still identified with their religion of origin, they also embraced secular urban values. In this they joined most Canadians, leaving the churches in a quandary as to how to assert the primacy of spiritual values over consumerism.

For some Canadians, the connections with their former homelands meant as much or more than their ties to the larger Canadian society. Ukrainian-Canadian politics of the interwar period makes little sense if it is disassociated from the debate about the future of the Ukraine. While radicals supported the Soviet Union, conservative Ukrainians demanded the release of their homeland from the clutches of the Communists. Rival nationalist groups battled one another as well as the Communists as they fought over which dictator would make the best leader for an independent Ukraine.

Chinese Canadians often regarded their situation in Canada as hopeless. The Exclusion Act of 1923 made it impossible for men working in Canada to bring their families from China, and unemployment, especially during the Depression, often meant that they could not afford to send money to their families in their homeland. Many decided to return home, some accepting Vancouver City Council's offer of a free one-way ticket to China, on condition that they agreed never to return to Canada. The Japanese invasion of China in 1937 resulted in a cessation of shipments of foodstuffs from China to Canada, making preparation of traditional meals in Chinatowns extremely difficult. Worse, communications between China and Canada were cut off, leaving Chinese Canadians without knowledge of the fate of their loved ones back home.

The Japanese in Canada were also caught up in the web of international developments. Since most were second-generation Canadians, known as Nisei, they spoke English and shared the liberal democratic outlook of their white contemporaries. Nevertheless, they continued to face discrimination in educational and job opportunities and were subject to growing hostility as Japan began its military assault in Asia. An articulate minority among the Nisei formed voluntary associations to discuss their mutual problems and founded English-language newspapers such as *The New Canadian*, which was established in 1938. In doing so, they drove a

*Blood woman curing beef.*
National Archives of Canada/NA13-1-48

wedge between themselves and their elders who clung to the language and traditions of their Japanese homeland.

## CANADA'S NATIVE PEOPLES

Canada's Native peoples had no foreign homeland upon which to fix their gaze when oppression in Canada seemed relentless. Poverty could be extremely harsh in the North, where "the most consistent features of northern society were limited growth, federal government neglect, dependence on a small number of mines, a vibrant fur trade and a bicultural society." [16] The "vibrant fur trade" meant that trappers from the south overtrapped, ignoring exclusive Native rights to hunt in certain territories.

While aboriginal hunters could still generally get by, the Inuit who were drawn into the whaling industry off Herschel Island in the western Arctic suffered massive epidemics and then technological displacement. The population began to rise only in the 1930s, as Native peoples began to develop immunities to European diseases. In the south, population decline, residential schools, and battles over land rights continued to be the order of the day.

After the federal government transferred to the Prairie provinces jurisdiction over their natural resources in 1930, thousands of Native peoples were arrested for violating provincial fish and game laws. In their efforts to consolidate control over the land, the provinces ignored treaties with the federal government that had granted hunting and fishing rights in traditional Native territories.

While Indians might find their treaty rights ignored by both federal and provincial jurisdictions, the Métis had no treaty rights and lived under appalling conditions. In Alberta, a provincial commission established in 1934 to investigate conditions among the Métis heard shocking medical evidence suggesting that the group, still victims of intense discrimination, was facing extinction. As much as 90 percent of the Métis population was infected with tuberculosis; paralysis, blindness, and syphilis were also rampant. The province respond-

*These Métis trappers at their winter camp in the foothills of the Rockies eked out a bare living for their efforts.*
Glenbow Archives, Brady Collection/ PA 2218-985

ed in 1939 by establishing six Métis colonies where schools and health care were provided, but no attempt was made to give these colonies a real economic base. In Saskatchewan and Manitoba, the Métis were almost completely ignored by their provincial governments during the interwar period.

## CONCLUSION

With hindsight, it is easy to see that interwar Canada was a society in transition. Older ways rubbed uneasily against the new mass culture and its commercially oriented values. Attracted by American movies, records, magazines, and radio programs, Canadians struggled to establish their own national culture, but it was an uphill battle. The threat of a larger North American culture was balanced by identities that were regional, local, and political. For cultural minorities, the sense of belonging to smaller groups was equal to or greater than their identification with Canada as a whole. The Depression exposed class and gender differences that had been easier to minimize in the better economic times of the 1920s. With the outbreak of the Second World War in September 1939, Canada's fragile unity would again be tested. Could the nation rise above its internal divisions to fight a common enemy?

---

# THE FARMING COMMUNITY

## A Historiographical Debate

The farming community of the interwar years was anything but unified. While some farmers saw themselves as allies of the working class, others increasingly viewed themselves as middle-class business people. Historians also take opposing sides on the issue. In the classic work *The National Policy and the Wheat Economy*, by economist Vernon Fowke, Prairie farmers are presented as a rather uniform group of individuals oppressed by national tariff and railway policies.[17] C.B. Macpherson's study of the Social Credit movement, *Democracy in Alberta*, presents a similar though less sympathetic view of the farmers of that province. Macpherson portrays farmers as "independent commodity producers" who were, in fact, dependent upon market forces over which they exercised little control. Still, as individuals who owned modest farmsteads and employed few labourers, their self-image did not allow them to identify with the cause of working people.[18]

Other historians present the farming community as more diversified and call into question the notion of "independent commodity producers." David McGinnis indicates that off-farm labour was required by most farmers in the interwar period to make ends meet; they might view themselves as independent commodity producers, but this perspective was largely an illusion.[19] Jeffery Taylor argues that false views of farmers' true position were not accidental but in large part were the creation of agricultural colleges and other institutions in Canadian society that shaped the view that farmers held of themselves.[20] The Manitoba Agricultural College, for example, rejected the older language of agrarianism in which farmers joined workers as an exploited producing class whose problems were the result of greedy monopolists. Instead, its professors encouraged farmers to see themselves as scientific managers of a producing property who could, if they behaved intelligently, make market forces work to their advantage.

John Herd Thompson notes that many farmers employed labourers on a seasonal basis and that they often proved to be very harsh employers.[21] In a study that focuses on farm labourers, Cecilia Danysk details the increasing stratification of the farm community in the interwar period. As the costs of farming soared, only the farmers who developed large land holdings could survive. The lifestyles of these farmers were quite different from those of farmers who eked out a living from small homesteads. They were even more at variance with the lives of farm labourers.

While farm labourers had once been a group composed both of men saving money to buy their own farms and of transients who did not remain for long on the Prairies, the number of permanent farm labourers was on the rise in the interwar period because the cost of getting into farming had become prohibitive. [22]

## Notes

[1] Quoted in Suzanne Morton, *Ideal Surroundings: Domestic Life in a Working-Class Suburb in the 1920s* (Toronto: University of Toronto Press, 1995), 151

[2] Rebecca Priegert Coulter, "Patrolling the Passions of Youth" in *Edmonton: The Life of a City*, ed. Bob Hesketh and Frances Swyripa (Edmonton: NeWest Press, 1995), 160

[3] Andrée Lévesque, "Deviant Anonymous: Single Mothers at the Hôpital de la Miséricorde in Montreal, 1929–1939," *Historical Papers/Communications Historiques* (1984): 178

[4] Morton, *Ideal Surroundings*, 41–2

[5] Faye Reineberg Holt, "Magistrate Emily Ferguson Murphy" in *Edmonton*, 148

[6] Peter Gossage, "La marâtre: Marie-Anne Houde and the Myth of the Wicked Stepmother in Quebec," *Canadian Historical Review* 76, 4 (Dec. 1995): 596

[7] Cited in Katherine Arnup, *Education for Motherhood: Advice for Mothers in Twentieth-Century Canada* (Toronto: University of Toronto Press, 1994), 32

[8] Ibid., 92

[9] Joy Parr, *The Gender of Breadwinners: Women, Men, and Change in Two Industrial Towns 1880–1960* (Toronto: University of Toronto Press, 1990), 186

[10] Cited in Meg Luxton, *More than a Labour of Love: Three Generations of Women's Work in the Home* (Toronto: Women's Press, 1980), 29

[11] Quoted in Vera Fast, "The Labor Church in Winnipeg" in *Prairie Spirit: Perspectives on the Heritage of the United Church of Canada in the West*, ed. Dennis L. Butcher et al. (Winnipeg: University of Manitoba Press, 1985), 242

[12] Cited in Mary Vipond, "Canadian National Consciousness and the Formation of the United Church of Canada" in *Prophets, Priests, and Prodigals: Readings in Canadian Religious History, 1608 to the Present*, ed. Mark G. McGowan and David B. Marshall (Toronto: McGraw-Hill Ryerson, 1992), 169

[13] Cited in Paul J. Stortz and J. Donald Wilson, "Schools, Teachers and Community Influence in North-Central British Columbia," *Histoire sociale/Social History* 26, 52 (Nov. 1993): 267

[14] Ian McKay, "Helen Creighton and the Politics of Antimodernism" in *Myth and Milieu: Atlantic Literature and Culture, 1918–1939*, ed. Gwendolyn Davies (Fredericton: Acadiensis Press, 1993), 16

[15] Gwendolyn Davies, "Frank Parker Day's Rockbound" in *Studies in Maritime Literary History* (Fredericton: Acadiensis Press, 1993), 174

[16] Kenneth Coates, *Canada's Colonies: A History of the Yukon and Northwest Territories* (Toronto: Lorimer, 1985), 100

[17] Vernon C. Fowke, *The National Policy and the Wheat Economy* (Toronto: University of Toronto Press, 1957)

[18] C.B. Macpherson, *Democracy in Alberta: Social Credit and the Party System* (Toronto: University of Toronto Press, 1962)

[19] David McGinnis, "Farm Labour in Transition: Occupational Structure and Economic Dependency in Alberta, 1921-1951" in *The Settlement of the West*, ed. Howard Palmer (Calgary: University of Calgary, 1977), 174–86

[20] Jeffery Taylor, *Fashioning Farmers: Ideology, Agricultural Knowledge and the Manitoba Farm Movement, 1890–1925* (Regina: Canadian Plains Research Center, 1994)

[21] John Herd Thompson, "Bringing in the Sheaves: The Harvest Excursionists, 1890–1929," *Canadian Historical Review* 59, 4 (Dec. 1978): 467–89

[22] Cecilia Danysk, *Hired Hands: Labour and the Development of Prairie Agriculture, 1880–1930* (Toronto: McClelland and Stewart, 1995)

## SELECTED READING

On the media in Canada during the interwar years, see Mary Vipond, *The Mass Media in Canada* (Toronto: Lorimer, 1989), and *Listening In: The First Decade of Canadian Broadcasting* (Montreal: McGill-Queen's University Press, 1992). On the Dionne quintuplets, see the articles in the special issue of *Journal of Canadian Studies* 29, 4 (Winter 1995).

The interwar period for women is studied in detail in Veronica Strong-Boag, *The New Day Recalled: Lives of Girls and Women in English Canada, 1919–1939* (Toronto: Copp Clark Pitman, 1988); Andrée Lévesque, *Making and Breaking the Rules: Women in Quebec, 1919–1939* (Toronto: McClelland and Stewart, 1994); Joan Sangster, *Earning Respect: The Lives of Working Women in Small-Town Ontario, 1920–1960* (Toronto: University of Toronto Press, 1995); Suzanne Morton, *Ideal Surroundings: Domestic Life in a Working-Class Suburb in the 1920s* (Toronto: University of Toronto Press, 1995); Frances Swyripa, *Wedded to the Cause: Ukrainian Canadian Women and Ethnic Identity, 1891–1991* (Toronto: University of Toronto Press, 1993); Ruth A. Frager, *Sweatshop Strife: Class, Ethnicity, and Gender in the Jewish Labour Movement of Toronto, 1900–1939* (Toronto: University of Toronto Press, 1992); Karen Dubinsky, *Improper Advances: Rape and Heterosexual Conflict in Ontario, 1889–1929* (Chicago: University of Chicago Press, 1993); and Cynthia R. Comacchio, *"Nations Are Built of Babies": Saving Ontario's Mothers and Children 1900-1940* (Montreal: McGill-Queen's University Press, 1993). Varying experiences of men and women in the workforce and the home are discussed in Joy Parr, *The Gender of Breadwinners: Women, Men, and Change in Two Industrial Towns 1880–1950* (Toronto: University of Toronto Press, 1990), and Thomas Dunk, *It's a Working Man's Town: Male Working-Class Culture in Northwestern Ontario* (Montreal: McGill-Queen's University Press, 1991). On housing, see Michael Doucet and John Weaver, *Housing the North American City* (Montreal: McGill-Queen's University Press, 1991), and Jill Wade, *Houses for All: The Struggle for Social Housing in Vancouver, 1919–1950* (Vancouver: UBC Press, 1994).

Religious developments are discussed in David B. Marshall, *Secularising the Faith: Canadian Protestant Clergy and the Crisis of Belief, 1850–1940* (Toronto: University of Toronto Press, 1992); Robert K. Burkinshaw, *Pilgrims in Lotus Land: Conservative Protestantism in British Columbia, 1917-1981* (Montreal: McGill-Queen's University Press, 1995); Royden K. Loewen, *Family, Church, and Market: A Mennonite Community in the Old and New Worlds, 1850–1930* (Toronto: University of Toronto Press, 1993); Michael Gauvreau, *The Evangelical Century: College and Creed in English Canada from the Great Revival to the Great Depression* (Montreal: McGill-Queen's University Press, 1991); Terrence Murphy and Gerald Stortz, eds., *Creed and Culture: The Place of English-Speaking Catholics in Canadian Society, 1750–1930* (Montreal: McGill-Queen's University Press, 1993); N. Keith Clifford, *The Resistance to Church Union in Canada, 1904–1939* (Vancouver: UBC Press, 1985); and John S. Moir, *Enduring Witness: A History of the Presbyterian Church in Canada* (Toronto: Presbyterian Church of Canada, 1987). James Gray's *Booze: The Impact of Whiskey on the Prairies* (Toronto: New American Library, 1972), and Angus McLaren and Arlene Tigar McLaren, *The Bedroom and the State: The Changing Practices and Politics of Contraception and Abortion in Canada, 1890–1980* (Toronto: McClelland and Stewart, 1986) treat issues that caused endless difficulties for churches.

On cultural developments in the Atlantic provinces, see Ian McKay, *The Quest of the Folk: Antimodernism and Cultural Selection in Twentieth-Century Nova Scotia* (Montreal: McGill-Queen's University Press, 1994) and Gwendolyn Davies, ed., *Myth and Milieu: Atlantic Literature and Culture, 1918–1939* (Fredericton: Acadiensis Press, 1993). On British Columbia, see Patricia E. Roy, *A History of British Columbia: Selected Readings* (Toronto: Copp Clark Pitman, 1989). On the Prairies, social histories of the period include Cecilia Danysk, *Hired Hands: Labour and the Development of*

*Prairie Agriculture, 1880–1930* (Toronto: McClelland and Stewart, 1995); Jeffery Taylor, *Fashioning Farmers: Ideology, Agricultural Knowledge and the Manitoba Farm Movement, 1890–1925* (Regina: Canadian Plains Research Center, 1994); and Don Wetherell and Irene Kmet, *Useful Pleasures: The Shaping of Leisure in Alberta, 1896–1945* (Regina: Canadian Plains Research Center, 1990). Quebec's social evolution is detailed in Paul-André Linteau, René Durocher, and Jean-Claude Robert, *Quebec since 1930* (Toronto: Lorimer, 1983), and Susan Mann Trofimenkoff, *Action Française: French-Canadian Nationalism in Quebec in the 1920s* (Toronto: University of Toronto Press, 1975). The Canadian North is analysed in Kenneth Coates, *Canada's Colonies: A History of the Yukon and Northwest Territories* (Toronto: Lorimer, 1985).

Children's experiences during this period are described in Neil Sutherland, "'We Always Had Things to Do': The Paid and Unpaid Work of Anglophone Children Between the 1920s and the 1960s," *Labour/Le Travail* 25 (Spring 1990): 105–41. On higher education, important works include A.B. McKillop, *Matters of Mind: The University in Ontario, 1791–1951* (Toronto: University of Toronto Press, 1994); Paul Axelrod, *Making a Middle Class: Student Life in English Canada During the Thirties* (Montreal: McGill-Queen's University Press, 1990); Paul Axelrod and John G. Reid, eds., *Youth, University and Canadian Society: Essays in the Social History of Higher Education* (Montreal and Kingston: McGill–Queen's University Press, 1989); and G.A. Rawlyk, ed., *Canadian Baptists and Higher Education* (Montreal: McGill-Queen's University Press, 1988).

On art history for the period, see J. Russell Harper, *Painting in Canada: A History*, 2nd ed. (Toronto: University of Toronto Press, 1977), and Ann Davis, *The Logic of Ecstasy: Canadian Mystical Painting, 1920–1940* (Toronto: University of Toronto Press, 1992). On sports, see Colin Howell, *Northern Sandlots: A Social History of Maritime Baseball* (Toronto: University of Toronto Press, 1995), and Ron Hotchkiss, "'The Matchless Six': Canadian Women at the Olympics, 1928," *The Beaver* 73, 5 (Oct.–Nov. 1993): 23–42.

On Native peoples, see J.R. Miller, *Skyscrapers Hide the Heavens: A History of Indian–White Relations in Canada* (Toronto: University of Toronto Press, 1989), and Murray Dobbin, *The One-and-a-Half Men: The Story of Jim Brady and Malcolm Norris, Métis Patriots of the Twentieth Century* (Vancouver: New Star Books, 1981). On Chinese Canadians, see Denise Chong, *The Concubine's Children: Portrait of a Family Divided* (Toronto: Viking, 1994). On immigrant experiences, see Donald H. Avery, *Reluctant Host: Canada's Response to Immigrant Workers, 1896–1994* (Toronto: McClelland and Stewart, 1995); John E. Zucchi, *Italians in Toronto: Development of a National Identity, 1875–1935* (Montreal: McGill-Queen's University Press, 1990); Paul Voisey, *Vulcan: The Making of A Prairie Community* (Toronto: University of Toronto Press, 1988); and Lubomir Luciuk and Stella Hryniuk, eds., *Canada's Ukrainians: Negotiating an Identity* (Toronto: University of Toronto Press, 1991).

# CHAPTER 11
## CANADA'S WORLD WAR, 1939–1945

O N 16 JULY 1945, SCIENTISTS AND OTHER observers gathered in bunkers near Los Alamos, New Mexico, one of the locations where work on the top-secret Manhattan Project had been carried out. At its peak, the Manhattan Project employed six hundred thousand people based at thirty separate sites. Dr J. Robert Oppenheimer headed the team of international scientists who had brought the world to this fateful day. When the first atomic bomb—nicknamed "Fat Man" because of its shape—exploded, with a force of over 15 000 tonnes of TNT, it produced a huge mushroom cloud and outshone the sun. Oppenheimer, perhaps more than anyone, understood the significance of that day's event. Overwhelmed by the bomb's frightening power, he recalled the words from the sacred Hindu text, the *Bhagavad Gita*: "I am become death, Destroyer of Worlds."

The atomic bomb was the culmination of the powers unleashed by science, technology, and industrial enterprise that characterized the modern age. It was not by chance that Canadians had a part to play in the Manhattan Project. Rich in uranium, a necessary ingredient of atomic energy, Canada was essential to the successful production of nuclear weapons. Early in the Second World War, a team of British, European, and Canadian

scientists under the umbrella of the National Research Council had begun working on aspects of the atomic energy puzzle in laboratories based in Montreal. The Canadian government agreed to make uranium resources available for American atomic research, and a Combined Policy Committee consisting of three Americans, two British, and one Canadian—Minister of Munitions and Supply C.D. Howe—was established to oversee the international effort. Chalk River, Ontario, was chosen as the site of Canada's first nuclear reactor. In September 1945, the facility was up and running but, by that time, Oppenheimer's team in the United States had already made history. Two of their bombs had been dropped on Japan in August 1945.

Canadians had hoped that the Great War would be the war to end all wars, but it was not to be. Under Nazi leader Adolf Hitler, who came to power in 1933, Germany adopted a fascist program for the reconstitution of its "homeland," which included destroying other nations and cultures. Italy's fascist leader, Benito Mussolini, gravitated towards Hitler, especially after Britain and France had tried to thwart Mussolini's plans for an Italian empire in Africa. In 1938, Germany annexed Austria and then gobbled up Czechoslovakia.

Italy annexed Albania in the spring of 1939, while in August Hitler signed a non-aggression pact with the Soviet Union under Joseph Stalin, freeing the way for the depredation of their mutual neighbour, Poland. In the Pacific, the Japanese had long been running roughshod over China. On 3 September, two days after Hitler had invaded Poland, Great Britain and France declared war on Germany. One week later, on 10 September, Canada joined the war against the Nazis.

Even more than the First World War, this war was an easy one for most Canadians to see as a struggle between good and evil. It was also a difficult war to avoid. In 1924, Canada's delegate to the League of Nations, Senator Raoul Dandurand, boasted that Canada lived in a "fireproof house, far from inflammable materials," but with submarines, fast surface warships, and long-range aircraft capable of spanning great distances in a short time, every country in the world was becoming vulnerable. Indeed, it was the Japanese bombing of Pearl Harbor on 7 December 1941 that finally jarred the United States out of its own isolationism and into the war.

## CANADA'S WAR

As in 1914, the Canadian government invoked the War Measures Act to ensure that it had all the powers it needed to fight an all-out war. Also, as in the First World War, the cabinet was initially slow to mobilize the nation's military and economic might. This policy earned King some harsh criticism from Premier Hepburn of Ontario, among others, but it helped to reassure Quebeckers that this would be Canada's war, not one in which Canada's wartime policy would be dictated by Great Britain. Early in 1939, prompted by his Quebec lieutenant, Ernest Lapointe, and doubtless by the Conservative Party's similar pledge, King had promised Quebec that his government would not impose conscription for overseas service in the event of war. It was a pledge that he would have occasion to repeat in two elections held in the early months of the conflict.

After war was declared, Quebec premier Maurice Duplessis hoped to gain an easy victory

for his government by calling a snap election and making Canada's wartime involvement the major issue in the campaign. Quebec's ministers in King's cabinet threatened to resign if Duplessis won. Fearing that without its Quebec contingent, the cabinet might well renege on King's promise not to impose conscription, a majority of Quebeckers elected the provincial Liberal Party, led by Adélard Godbout, to office. Hepburn's stinging criticisms of Ottawa's failure to pursue an all-out war effort prompted King to dissolve Parliament in January and call a national election for March 1940. Campaigning on a policy of voluntary enlistment, the Liberals won a resounding victory, taking over 51 percent of the popular vote and 184 out of 245 seats in the House of Commons.

King was shrewd or just plain lucky to have gone to the polls when he did. In April 1940, Hitler's forces struck down Denmark and Norway and then conducted a *blitzkrieg*, literally a lightning war, through the Netherlands, Belgium, and France. The surrender of France early in June, and the evacuation of the British Expeditionary Force from Dunkirk, raised fears that Great Britain might also be defeated. Would an invasion of Britain come soon, and would North America be next? As Great Britain's largest surviving ally, Canada was suddenly forced to consider a much larger contribution to the war effort than King and his cabinet had originally envisaged. The government moved swiftly to enact the National Resources Mobilization Act (NRMA), which provided for the conscription of soldiers for home defence and state control of economic resources.

As the war dragged on, pressures from army commanders, from within cabinet, from opposition members, and from many Canadians caused King to re-evaluate his position on conscription. He decided to call a national plebiscite on 27 April 1942, which asked Canadians for a "yes" or "no" vote on whether the government should be released from its pledge not to impose conscription for overseas service. While overall 64 percent of Canadians voted "yes," at least 85 percent of Quebec francophones demanded that King honour his original promise. King continued to resist imposing conscription, but even the threat of it was enough to spark the formation of the Bloc populaire canadien, another nationalist political party in Quebec, and for the return of the ardently anti-conscriptionist Union nationale to power in a 1944 provincial election.

*The provincial wing of the Bloc populaire was led by André Laurendeau, a young journalist shown here speaking in Montreal before the 1944 election.*

Centre de Recherche Lionel Groulx/P2-B302

King did everything in his power to avoid conscription, including firing his defence minister, J.L. Ralston, who, King felt, was overly committed to the army's position on the matter. In a last-ditch effort to make voluntary enlistment work, Ralston was replaced in November 1944 by General A.G.L. McNaughton, an artillery commander in the First World War and King's choice in 1939 to command the army overseas. He had been "eased out" of his position as overseas commander, and he proved unable, as minister of national defence in the fall of 1944, to secure the voluntary enlistments he had promised to provide. To top it off, he lost a by-election in Grey County, Ontario. In the Second World War, as in the First, Canadians would face overseas conscription.

In late November 1944, the government passed an order-in-council allowing the armed forces to dispatch sixteen thousand NRMA men for duty overseas. Commonly called "Zombies"—a word made fashionable in Hollywood as an African-Caribbean reference to men who had no souls—NRMA men were not pleased about this turn of events. Demonstrations followed King's announcement, although such actions were never disclosed in the media, whose war reporting was subject to censorship. In Terrace, British Columbia, NRMA men seized an anti-tank gun to defend themselves against officers who were trying to send them overseas; in London, Ontario six hundred men of the Oxford Rifles went absent without leave; and in Drummond, Quebec, two thousand civilians attacked RCMP and military police who were sent to hunt down deserters. Eventually, thirteen thousand NRMA men were sent overseas. As in the First World War, conscription strengthened the credibility of Quebec nationalists and added to feelings of betrayal among French Canadians without doing much to help the war effort. However, unlike Borden and the Conservative Party, King avoided the backlash from Quebec in the subsequent election because it was clear that he had done nearly everything humanly possible to avoid conscription.

French-Canadian enlistment in the Second World War was significantly higher than in the First World War. Nineteen percent of the volunteers for overseas service were French Canadians, compared to 12 percent in the earlier war, and about 37 percent of the men called up for home defence were French Canadians. Like their English-Canadian counterparts, French Canadians who enlisted in the early stages of the war often did so to seek adventure. Most simply wanted employment. Eventually, the wartime economy led to a labour shortage, and recruitment became more difficult.

Overall Canadian participation in the war was impressive: nearly 1.1 million men and women joined the forces, including 100 000 in the NRMA, from a population estimated at 11.5 million in

1941. Most served in the army, although about 250 000 joined the Royal Canadian Air Force, and nearly 100 000 joined the Royal Canadian Navy. Over 42 000 died in service, including more than 17 000 members of the RCAF, which suffered the highest proportion of casualties. Over 54 000 more were wounded or injured. As in the First World War, Canadians were relatively lucky. The total dead and wounded in the Second World War reached a staggering 55 million. Many were civilians, killed by bombs, invading armies, or concentration camp personnel. The USSR alone lost 20 million people; and six million Jews were slaughtered by the Nazis.

Although only men participated in combat, 50 000 women served in the Canadian armed forces. As in the First World War, women were eager to participate and began volunteering their services as soon as war was declared. The military establishment was reluctant to accept them but, in the face of manpower shortages and the British example, it finally relented to the extent of creating separate female auxiliaries in the various branches of the armed services. In 1941, the army created the Canadian Women's Army Corps (CWAC), while the air force organized the Women's Division of the RCAF. The navy followed suit in 1942 with the Women's Royal Canadian Naval Service (WRENS). In all, the WRENS enlisted 7126 women, the CWAC 21 642, and the RCAF (WD) 17 467. There were also 4439 nurses in the Canadian Nursing Service. One nurse and three members of the RCAF (WD) were killed in action.[1]

The women faced a great deal of sexism, but their services were essential to the war effort. Initially slotted into jobs as nurses, clerks, secretaries, drivers, stretcher bearers, and cooks, they gradually took on less traditional roles such as mechanics, truck drivers, technicians, and spies. While their usefulness was never really questioned, their morality was. The double standard that prevailed in civilian life was cruelly highlighted in a military setting. As a result, rumours

spread about the lax morals of women in the military, especially in the CWAC, who were alleged to have more "illegitimate" children and venereal disease than civilian women. Men were allowed, indeed encouraged, to vent their sexual energies; women, quite clearly, were not. Nor did women receive the same pay and benefits as their male colleagues, even when they performed the same job. Women complained about their unequal status, and the National Council of Women took up their cause, but the pay gap, while narrowed, was never completely eliminated.

The military was careful to keep the women's divisions separate and subordinate to those of the men. Margaret Eaton achieved the highest rank of any woman in the services when, in April 1944, she was made Acting Colonel and Director-General of the CWAC. As historian Ruth Roach Pierson points out, the thirty-one-year-old Eaton had the right family background to help her secure the

*A member of the WRENS operating direction-finding equipment in New Brunswick, 1945.*

National Archives of Canada/ PA142540

respect and confidence of the National Defence Headquarters:

> She came from the Timothy Eaton family and, when first approached to become an officer of the CWAC, had demurred on the grounds that her only qualifications were that she "knew the best night clubs in London and hunted with the best packs." But after her promotion to the position of the Director-General, CWAC, it was precisely her high social standing, as she herself observed, that put her in such a "strong position *vis-à-vis* the boys": it was difficult for the male officers, no matter how high their title, to pull rank on her. The top ones, she recalled, never addressed her as colonel but rather always as Miss Eaton.[2]

When the war ended, all three women's services were abandoned.

## DESCENT INTO WAR

Just before the surrender of France in June 1940, Italy entered the war, greatly increasing the pressure on British armed forces in the Mediterranean and North Africa. With the benefit of French air bases, Hitler's Luftwaffe conducted a destructive blitz on London and other British cities beginning in the summer of 1940. Had the Germans followed up their bombardment with an invasion, it is anybody's guess what the outcome would have been, but no invasion came. Instead, Hitler conducted a devastating U-boat campaign against Allied shipping in the Atlantic, and in June 1941 he turned his army on his erstwhile ally, the Soviet Union. The United States entered the war against Germany as well as Japan at the end of the year, but it took time for its presence to be felt. Meanwhile, Japan destroyed the Far East fleets of both the United States and Britain, defeated the British and Australians in Malaya and Singapore, and captured the American army in the Philippines. In June 1942, Japanese forces occupied islands in the Aleutian chain of Alaska.

It is in this context that two incidents in the war, one in Hong Kong and the other in British Columbia, must be understood. In December 1941, two battalions of Canadian troops, totalling nearly two thousand men, were involved in an effort to defend the British colony of Hong Kong against the Japanese. Almost three hundred Canadians lost their lives and another seventeen hundred were taken prisoner. Mistreatment in prison camps in Hong Kong and as forced labour in Japanese mines killed nearly three hundred before the end of the war. At the time and later, there was much criticism of political and military leaders for allowing Canadians to get involved in such a hopeless campaign.

In February 1942, two months after Japan's attack on American territory at Pearl Harbor, President Franklin Roosevelt announced that, by reason of military necessity, persons of Japanese ancestry were to be removed from the Pacific Coast of the United States. A few days later, the Canadian government also decided that it would remove nearly twenty-two thousand people of Japanese ancestry—nearly three-quarters of whom had been born in Canada or were naturalized Canadians—from the coastal areas of British Columbia. Their homes, businesses, and personal property were placed under the "protection" of the federal government, and it came as a shock when they were informed, in January 1943, that the government had begun to auction off their property and belongings.

Ottawa had no evidence about the disloyalty of Japanese Canadians, other than suspicions about a few individuals who were already well-know to the local RCMP. Moveover, no one was ever charged with treason. Yet Mackenzie King's government suspended the civil liberties of the entire Japanese-Canadian population until 1949.

The long-standing racist attitudes of British Columbians towards Japanese Canadians, coupled with the hysteria created by the war, made it difficult for the federal government to pursue a more humane policy. About seven hundred men who had expressed support for a Japanese victory or had protested too vigorously against Ottawa's repressive policies, were legally interned in a prisoner-of-war camp in Angler, in northern Ontario. Women, children, the old, and the sick were unofficially interned in abandoned mining towns in the interior

*Japanese-Canadian internees packing to leave for camps in the interior of British Columbia.*
Tak Toyota/National Archives of Canada/ C046350

of British Columbia. Able-bodied men were separated from their families and sent to work in road camps in the province. Families who wished to remain together were shipped to sugar beet farms in Alberta and Manitoba. Among the children removed from their homes in 1942 were David Suzuki, the future scientist, and Joy Kogawa, whose 1981 novel, *Obasan*, dealt with her family's internment.

Beginning in May 1945, all Japanese Canadians were forced to choose between deportation to war-devastated Japan or relocation east of the Rockies. To make deportation a more attractive option, Ottawa offered money and free passage to those persons who were destitute or too elderly or infirm to begin life again in Eastern Canada. Nearly four thousand of the community's most vulnerable were shipped out to Japan between May and December 1946. Starving and desperate in postwar Japan, some of the deportees tried to return to Canada, but found a mountain of bureau-

cratic red tape blocking their re-entry. It was not until the 1980s that the Canadian government officially acknowledged its mistreatment of Japanese Canadians during the war and provided compensation to surviving members of the community in recognition of their suffering.

In Europe, the war continued to go badly for the Allies. Although the German army was stalled in its drive to Moscow, Allied efforts to create a division in France ended in dismal failure. An ill-conceived landing on French beaches at Dieppe in August 1942 left 907 Canadians dead and almost 2000 prisoners. Only in the Middle East was there good news. In November at El Alamein, the British Eighth Army finally broke through the German and Italian lines, forcing General Erwin Rommel and his hitherto seemingly invincible Africa Korps into retreat. At the same time, the Russians were fighting the Germans to a standstill at Stalingrad. A staggering 850 000 Germans and their Italian, Hungarian, and Rumanian allies lost their lives in the campaign. In December, the 80 000 survivors surrendered. The war had reached a turning point.

By 1943, the Canadian Army Overseas in Britain had expanded to a full field army, the 1st Canadian Army, with two corps, three infantry and two armoured (tank) divisions, and a wide array of additional formations and support units. Aside from the disastrous Dieppe raid and some smaller operations, the army stood guard in Britain until the liberation of Western Europe began with the

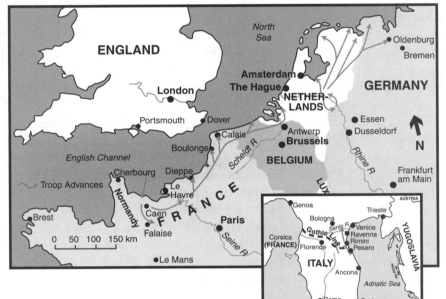

**Map 11.1** *The European Front, 1944-45—Italian Campaign and Northwest Europe Campaign.*

Allied invasion of Sicily and then mainland Italy in the summer of 1943. The 1st Canadian Infantry Division took part in these operations, which became increasingly difficult as the Allies pushed up the boot of Italy against fortified lines the Germans had established in the mountainous terrain. During December 1943, in appalling conditions amid winter rains, the 1st Division lost over twenty-three hundred men killed or wounded in bitter fighting for the town of Ortona, on the Adriatic coast. In early 1944, the Canadian presence in Italy expanded, playing a key role in breaking through the strongly defended approaches to Rome.

Meanwhile, there had been a massive build-up of forces in Britain for the invasion of France, at Normandy, on 6 June 1944. Among the initial assault force was the 3rd Canadian Infantry Division. Over a hundred warships of the Royal Canadian Navy formed part of the naval forces that cleared mines, kept enemy warships and submarines at bay, landed troops, and provided gunfire support to the soldiers struggling ashore. The huge air armada that forced back the Luftwaffe and saturated the German defences with bombs included many squadrons of the Royal Canadian Air Force. During the following weeks, the 1st Canadian Army, under the command of Lieutenant-General H.D.G. Crerar, crossed to France. The push inland from the beaches was a slow-moving, brutal campaign, with the Germans concentrating their strongest armoured forces in the British–Canadian sector. By the last week in August, two German armies had been destroyed, with some 400 000 casualties, but the Canadians also paid heavily, with 5000 dead and over 13 000 wounded, some of the heaviest losses of any Allied formation.

After the defeat of the main German forces in Normandy, the 1st Canadian Army moved up the coast of the English Channel, clearing strongholds. The culmination of these operations was a bitter five-week battle in October and early November, which, in the end, opened the Belgium port of Antwerp. The port was essential to maintain the supplies of all the Allied armies in northwest Europe, but was opened at the price of over six thousand Canadians killed or wounded.

The significant role the Royal Canadian Navy had played in the Normandy assault was only a small part of that services's work. In 1944–45, it also provided the lion's share of the escort forces for the north Atlantic convoys that sustained Britain and the invasion force. The RCN helped to protect British waters against the still-strong German U-boat force, joined in offensive strikes at German naval bases in Norway, and contributed escort ships to convoys that supplied the Russian forces through the Arctic port of Murmansk.

These achievements did not come easily. At the outbreak of the war, there were only six destroyers, a handful of small minesweepers, and no more than thirty-five hundred personnel in the RCN. The plan was to increase this force gradually, primarily for the protection of Canadian waters. The fall of France in 1940 changed this idea and forced Canada into crisis naval development. With access to French ports, the Germans were able to keep increased numbers of U-boats at sea, and by the end of 1940, concentrated "wolfpacks" of U-boats slaughtered merchant ship convoys. In response to Britain's urgent appeal in May 1941, the Royal Canadian Navy rushed the small corvettes, intended for coastal defence, into high-seas service to provide anti-submarine escort for convoys between Newfoundland and British waters. At the same time, programs to build corvettes and other anti-submarine vessels in Canada were accelerated and expanded, and recent recruits hurried to sea before they were properly trained.

The entry of the United States into the war brought U-boats streaming into Canadian and American coastal waters in January 1942. Because the Americans were woefully short of anti-submarine vessels, the RCN had to maintain its Newfoundland force, while defending Canadian waters and also helping the Americans on their east coast and in the Caribbean. Although the RCN was generally effective in protecting Canadian waters, it was of little effect in the Gulf of St Lawrence, where deep waters gave every advantage to the U-boats. Two small warships and nineteen merchant ships were sunk in the gulf and in the lower reaches of the St Lawrence River. Among them was the Sydney–Port-aux-Basques ferry, which went down in October 1942 with the loss of 237 lives.

During late 1942, the expanding U-boat force was able to assemble the largest wolfpacks yet to attack convoys between Newfoundland and Ireland. Convoys sailing under the protection of Canadian escorts suffered some of the heaviest losses and, in all, twelve hundred Canadians in the Merchant Marine lost their lives when their ships were sunk. In early November 1942, a convoy bound for the United Kingdom lost fifteen of its forty-two merchant ships. In response to such losses, the routes of three of the four Canadian mid-Atlantic escort groups were changed in early 1943 so that they could use British base facilities to get improved equipment and some advanced training.

Other measures to improve the RCN's escort organization gradually came into effect. The British turned over additional destroyers to the Canadians so that these powerful ships could reinforce the little corvettes. In April 1943, Rear-Admiral L.W. Murray, RCN, at Halifax, became commander-in-chief of the Canadian Northwest Atlantic theatre. He was the only Canadian to command an Allied theatre of war. Soon thereafter, the Allies allocated to the RCAF bombers that could effectively provide support to convoys across the whole breadth of the Atlantic. During the last two years of the war, the RCN and RCAF greatly increased their already large responsibilities for convoy protection in the North Atlantic. The benchmarks of their success were the thousands of ships and tens of millions of tonnes of cargo that safely reached port under Canadian protection.

Soon after war was declared, Canada agreed to play host to the British Commonwealth Air Training Plan (BCATP), whereby Canadian and other allied pilots and air crews would be trained for the war effort. Canada was an ideal location for the program because it had ample space beyond the range of enemy aircraft and was close to vital American aircraft industries upon which the success of the war in the air depended. Because it would allow him to fight the war from Canada, Prime Minister King initially hoped that the BCATP could be the major component of the war effort. This thinking was shattered by the invasion of France, but the BCATP was nevertheless one of Canada's most successful contributions to the Allied victory. At its height, it employed over 100 000 ground crew at 231 sites across the country. In total, the program trained over 130 000 pilots, navigators, flight engineers, and other aviation specialists, representing almost half the total air crew supplied by Great Britain and the Commonwealth for the war effort.

Another successful joint venture with the British and Americans was Ferry Command, which was responsible for delivering planes built in North America to Britain. In 1939, the idea of flying planes across the Atlantic rather than sending them by ship was denounced as visionary nonsense by most officials in the British Air Ministry. Fewer than a hundred successful transatlantic flights had been made since the first one in 1919. To the sur-

rian Carl A. Christie, "one of the most spectacular achievements of the war."[3]

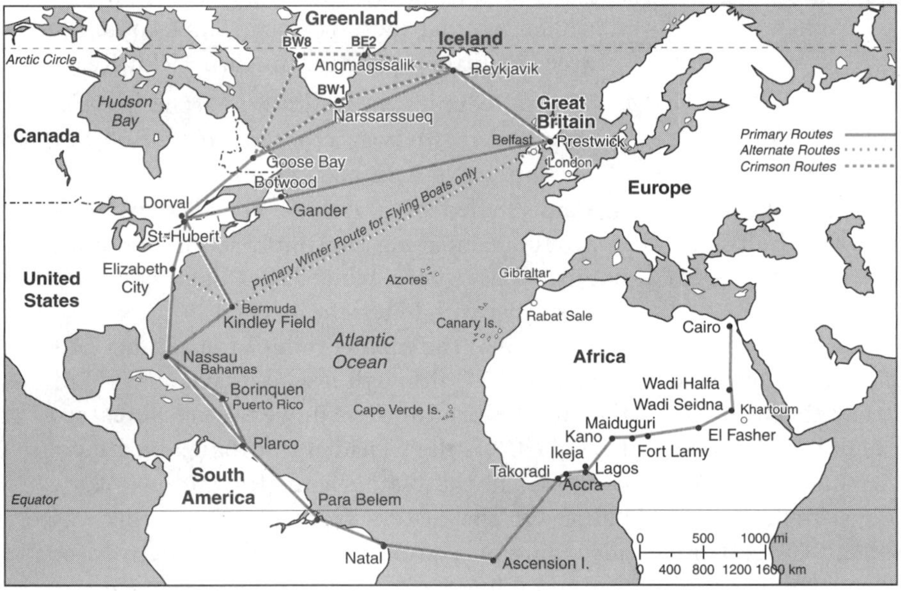

A much more controversial operation in which Canada played a major role was the Allied bomber offensive against Germany. From its bases in northeastern England, the Royal Air Force's Bomber Command maintained a "second front" against German cities in an effort to disrupt industrial production and reduce German morale. Because the targets in these attacks were often city centres or residential districts, rather than industrial areas, critics claim that the campaign was neither efficient nor effective and that it was immoral to boot.

The German economy proved more elastic than Allied planners had foreseen. By a greater rationalization and geographic dispersal of industry, the Germans were able to increase war production despite the apparently devastating effects of the bombing. Allied bombing, it can be argued, spurred the Nazis to greater productivity, just as the bombing of London in 1940 made the British determined to carry on. It was not until the final months of 1944 that the production of war material began a rapid decline. Allied bombing forced the Germans to employ over half a million workers in repairing the bomb damage and almost a million men to operate the Flak defences around their cities, person-

**Map 11.2** *Principal routes flown by Ferry Command, 1940-45.*

nel that could otherwise have ben used in factories or on the battlefield.

Allied bomber attacks killed 560 000 Germans and injured even more, most of them men over military age, women, and children. Until the final twelve months of the war, Bomber Command lacked the electronic and navigational aids that were needed to hit precise industrial targets. Even when more precise attacks became possible, the

prise of many sceptics, both the idea and the planes flew, due in large measure to the energy of Lord Beaverbrook, who, as minister of aircraft production after May 1940, supported the project. Based in Montreal, Ferry Command flew nearly ten thousand aircraft from enlarged or newly created air bases such as Gander and Goose Bay to Great Britain. Over five hundred people lost their lives in Ferry Command, but it was, in the words of histo-

*Target photo of an Allied bomber raid over Münster, Germany.*
National Archives of Canada /C44062

RAF chose to continue with area raids directed against German civilians. Morton and Granatstein argue that Bomber Command was doing what it set out to do—hit back at Germany, whose Luftwaffe had killed over thirteen thousand civilians in London and other British cities.[4]

As for the wisdom of the British air marshals who oversaw the bombing offensive, the evidence is mixed. There is little doubt that the head of Bomber Command, Sir Arthur Harris, was a single-minded individual, but his views on the strategic importance of air power to the war effort were shared by other Allied commanders. Nor is there any question that the bombing offensive was pressed in spite of the high casualty rates among the bomber crews themselves. Only one airman in three survived a thirty-mission tour of duty in 1942.

Loss rates continued to rise the following year when the Canadian government convinced the Air Ministry to form an RCAF group—Group No. 6—in Bomber Command. As a junior group, 6 Group—which eventually totalled fourteen squadrons—was assigned inferior aircraft and equipment and was stationed in the Vale of York,

farther from their targets than any other group in England. The results were predictable. From 5 March to 24 June 1943, 6 Group lost a hundred aircraft, morale sagged, and an increasing number of missions were aborted or failed to reach their objective.

In February 1944, as the costly Battle of Berlin was drawing to a close, Air Vice-Marshall C.M. McEwan was appointed to bring his professional energy to bear on 6 Group. Better training, new aircraft, and a reprieve from missions in Germany while Bomber Command supported the Normandy invasion brought improvement. By the end of 1944, No. 6 Group boasted the highest accuracy and the lowest casualty rate of any group in Bomber Command. Such achievements, however, do little to counter the critics who argue that the money and manpower committed to Bomber Command would have been much better spent on the understaffed and poorly equipped convoy service, or in maintaining army ranks so that conscription could have been avoided. But fighting wars is always easier with hindsight.

By 1943, the momentum of the conflict had clearly shifted, although it would take much hard fighting before the Axis powers were defeated. Early in 1945, the Canadians in Italy joined their comrades in the Netherlands for the final campaign. On the eastern front, the Red Army was advancing on Germany, while the western front was crumbling fast under Allied assault. Overrun from all sides, and with their leader dead by his own hand, the Germans surrendered on 5 May.

The war in the Pacific dragged on for three more months and became the occasion for another embarrassing incident for the navy. When Canada agreed to provide support for a final drive against Japan, the crew members of the HMCS *Uganda*, already in Okinawa, refused to participate, on the grounds that the war with Germany was over and they had not enlisted to fight Japan. Since only volunteers were authorized for the Pacific front, the

## WAR ARTISTS

During the First World War, Lord Beaverbrook had commissioned artists to record Canada's war effort. It was the first large official commission for Canadian artists. Men with well-established reputations, such as Maurice Cullen, and promising unknowns, such as David Milne, were hired for the task. So, too, were four men who would later become associated with the Group of Seven: A.Y. Jackson, Frederick Varley, Arthur Lismer, and Franz Johnston.

In 1943, the war art program was reactivated, and artists were commissioned into the three divisions of the armed services. For the first time, female artists were included to document

*Alex Colville*, Tragic Landscape, *1945.*
Canadian War Museum

women's contribution: painter Molly Lamb eventually received a lieutenant's commission in the CWAC; Pegi Nicol MacLeod painted many aspects of the women's forces; Paraskeva Clark and Alma Duncan recorded women's work in the war industries. Artists captured on canvas some of the worst horrors of the war. Charles Goldhamer painted RCAF flyers at a plastic surgery hospital in England; Aba Bayefsky and Alex Colville had the difficult job of documenting the Belsen concentration camp. Confronted with a larger-than-life situation, Canadian war artists produced some of their finest, if most disturbing, work during the war.

---

men claimed they were not obliged to fight and they had the right to come home. Before the *Uganda* reached Canadian shores the war had come to an abrupt halt following the dropping of atomic bombs on Hiroshima and Nagasaki on 6 and 9 August. On 14 August, the Japanese surrendered.

## THE BUSINESS OF WAR

"It drives one mad to think that any old Canadian boor, who probably can't even find Europe on the globe, flies to Europe from his super-rich country which his people don't know how to exploit, and here bombards a continent with a crowded population," Joseph Goebbels, Hitler's minister of propaganda, complained in his diary on 3 March 1943. Goebbels had some reason to be concerned. By 1943, Canada was turning out fighter planes, pilots, and bombs at a rate few could have imagined in 1939. The sad irony of war was recognized by peo-

ple other than Joseph Goebbels. What Canadians seemed unable to do in peacetime they did with surprising ease during the Second World War: they produced their way out of the Great Depression.

On the surface, the Second World War had much the same impact as the First World War on the Canadian economy. It pulled the nation out of an economic slump, expanded production in all sectors of the economy, and dramatically increased export sales. On closer inspection, it was obvious that the country that declared war on Germany in 1939 was vastly different from the one that rode to war on Britain's coat-tails in 1914. First, the experience of the Great War had taught some lessons about the need for tighter controls on a wartime economy. The system of planning, rationing, taxation, and wage and price controls imposed by the federal government in the early stages of the Second World War prevented the devastating inflation that had seriously disrupted the economy during the First World War.

Second, the federal government, following a decade of increasing intervention in the economy, was better equipped to coordinate a major war effort. Under the guidance of a sophisticated cadre of civil servants, economic policy was centralized and orchestrated to achieve desired ends. From April 1940, the Department of Munitions and Supply, run like a commando unit by its energetic minister, C.D. Howe, was given sweeping powers. With the help of members of Canada's business community who were seconded to Ottawa, Howe expanded existing industries, created new ones, and focused the total resources of the country on the successful prosecution of the war.

The federal government's role in the war economy was pervasive. In its twenty-eight Crown corporations, the government produced everything from synthetic rubber to airplanes. In 1943, Ottawa suspended the operations of the Winnipeg Grain Exchange and made the Canadian Wheat Board the exclusive international sales agent for the nation's precious wheat crop. Under the auspices of the Wartime Prices and Trade Board, an army of controllers, regulators, and troubleshooters fanned out across the country allocating output, rationing consumer purchases, and cutting through red tape. During the course of the war, the number of federal civil servants more than doubled, from 46 000 in 1939 to 116 000 in 1945. Ottawa would never return to its prewar size and sleepy pace.

In the First World War, federal spending represented about 10–15 percent of the GNP. By 1944, Ottawa's expenditures accounted for nearly 40 percent of the GNP, which translated into the sum of $4.4 billion. All this was accomplished without resorting to the massive foreign borrowing that had characterized public policy during the earlier war. Extensive taxation of both corporate and personal incomes, the sale of Victory Bonds, and the careful regulation of the money supply through the Bank of Canada enabled Canadians to finance their own war.

Despite the impressive record, Canada's wartime economy encountered both short- and long-term problems. Before the war, Canada balanced its trade deficit with the United States by selling a surplus in its trade with Britain. Sterling was converted into dollars and the deficit easily covered. Once locked in a life-and-death struggle with Germany, Britain imposed exchange controls, which included restrictions on the convertibility of sterling into dollars. As Britain's wartime purchases in Canada escalated, and Canada came increasingly to depend on the United States for war supplies, Canadians were left with the daunting prospect of having a huge surplus of sterling and a crippling deficit in American currency.

In an effort to deal with the crisis, Ottawa established stringent exchange controls, which were monitored by a Foreign Exchange Control Board. The dollar was pegged at 90.9 cents in relation to American currency, and imports were permitted only under licence. By 1940, restrictions were placed on travel to the United States, and an embargo was imposed on the importation of a long list of commodities from countries outside the sterling bloc. Although Britain released gold and American dollars to the tune of $248 million for Canadian purchases in 1940, the Canadian trade deficit with the United States continued to mount alarmingly.

There was little Canada could do to solve the problem. During the interwar years, Canadian and American industry had become so integrated that virtually everything Canada produced included American components. Canadian automobile manufacturers imported parts from their parent companies; Stelco's furnaces were fuelled by coal from Pennsylvania; and mining companies required complex machinery manufactured in the United States. With over 30 percent of Canada's wartime output consisting of components imported from the United States, the nation's war effort would be compromised unless some solution was found to the exchange crisis. The problem was eventually solved when the United States entered the war in December 1941. By that time, North America was already functioning as a unit in defence production, and the problem for Canada became too much, rather than too little, American exchange.

The Second World War tended to reinforce rather than alter the geography of the Canadian economy. Before the war, Canadian industrial capacity was concentrated in Central Canada. Wartime production was initially expanded in existing industries, and virtually all of the plants built and operated by the government were located in the industrial heartland of the country. There were some notable exceptions. Winnipeg became a centre for munitions and communications industries. Adjacent to Alberta's oil and natural gas reserves, Calgary was the obvious site for nitrogen and high octane fuel production. So important was oil to modern warfare that a Crown corporation, Wartime Oils, was created to develop Canada's oil potential. Vancouver sprouted a Boeing aircraft factory and a modern shipbuilding industry. New military bases quickened the economic pace in communities from Summerside to Esquimalt, while such projects as the Ferry Command to Britain brought development to the northern territories and Newfoundland. As the economy reached its full productive capacity, Ontario's industrial output actually declined slightly relative to the other Canadian provinces, but the war demonstrated that industry, whether fuelled by private or public enterprise, had a tendency to concentrate in the St Lawrence heartland.

It was clear to those on the losing end of the wartime investment boom that political rather than strategic interests often governed economic decisions. There was no obvious reason, for example, why the constituency of Digby–Annapolis–Kings in Nova Scotia became the location for two military bases other than that its member of Parliament was Finance Minister J.L. Ilsley. Similarly, the languishing Algoma Steel Corporation in Sault Ste Marie, which had the support of northern Ontario's C.D. Howe, fared better in the race for contracts than the equally languishing Dominion Steel and Coal Corporation based in Cape Breton. Because H.R. MacMillan, chair of Wartime Shipping Limited, took a special interest in British Columbia, shipbuilding facilities were developed on the West Coast. They proved useful when the Pacific war moved into high gear in 1942. For the most part, however, decisions relating to shipbuilding and repair were notoriously ill-conceived. Even British officials failed to understand why the ice-free ports of Halifax and Saint John were treated as secondary to Montreal, which was ice-bound during the winter and whose narrow access was infested with German U-boats. The failure to develop repair facilities in the Maritime provinces not only consolidated regional disparity but also seriously impeded the effectiveness of the Canadian navy.

Traditional attitudes towards labour were called into question by the wartime experience. When war was declared, those involved in military recruitment and wartime production could draw upon a pool of over half a million unemployed Canadians. Many more gladly left their uninspiring jobs for better prospects in the armed forces or work relating to the war. By 1941, the labour pool had dried up, and a shortage of workers was looming. In 1942, the government embarked upon a campaign to recruit women into the paid labour

*The Toronto Transit Commission offered women drivers full rates during wartime labour shortages.*

TTC/14906

*Day care was a problem for mothers who took jobs in the paid labour force. This Mi'kmaq woman brought her child with her to the Pictou shipyards in 1943.*

National Archives of Canada/ PA116154

force. Before the war, only 21 percent of women between the ages of fifteen and sixty-five worked outside the home and, of these, only 4 percent were married. At first only unmarried women between the ages of twenty and twenty-four were recruited, but by 1943 all women, married or single, with or without children, were strongly encouraged to do their patriotic duty. In Quebec and Ontario, a government-sponsored day-care system offered support for a handful of mothers. The number of women in the workforce increased from 638 000 in 1939 to over a million by 1944, some 255 000 of whom were engaged in what were defined as war industries. Like the women in the military, civilian women were paid less than the men whose jobs

they assumed. When the war ended, the day-care facilities were closed and women "retired" from their paid positions, except, of course, from the clerical, teaching, and nursery jobs that they had dominated before the war.

## CONTROLLING THE ENEMY WITHIN

As in the First World War, the Canadian government kept a close watch on enemy aliens and others perceived as potential troublemakers. The Defence of Canada Regulations, which came into effect a week before Canada declared war, gave the government sweeping powers to curb freedom of expression, arrest anyone who might threaten public safety or recruitment efforts, and intern enemy aliens. While the evacuation of Japanese Canadians was the biggest operation taken under wartime regulations, a number of other groups also experienced the heavy hand of government control.

Among the first targets were members of political organizations associated with enemy nations. In the early days of the war, the RCMP, the organization in charge of public security, arrested 358 known supporters of Nazi organizations and sent them to camps at Petawawa and Kananaskis. Another sweep occurred after the fall of France and the entrance of Italy into the war, netting over 850 more. Canada's official Nazi party, the National Unity Party, was banned in June 1940. Not only enemy aliens were affected by this crackdown. The leaders of the National Unity Party, including Quebec-born Adrien Arcand and eleven other officials, were interned immediately. By the end of the war, twenty-seven other party members who had neither German nor Italian links had been incarcerated.

While Germany and Italy were admittedly the enemy, other groups targeted by the RCMP had less impressive credentials. On 4 July 1940, the Canadian government passed an order-in-council declaring the Jehovah's Witnesses illegal. The order made seven thousand Canadian Jehovah's Witnesses subject to surveillance and arrest, while their meeting halls and property were handed over to the Custodian of Enemy Property. The treatment of the Jehovah's Witnesses, like the evacuation of the Japanese, is an example of how prewar prejudices are acted upon in wartime contexts. Because the Witnesses criticized the Roman Catholic Church, they were especially loathed by Cardinal Villeneuve, who appealed to Justice Minister Ernest Lapointe to curb their activities. Lapointe, eager to maintain the Catholic hierarchy's support for the war effort, promptly had the ban issued and enforced. Although there was some criticism of this action, it was not until 1943, two years after Lapointe's death, that Jehovah's Witnesses were allowed to practise their faith openly.

Several prominent Canadians were also directly affected by the wartime hysteria. Camillien Houde, the mayor of Montreal, spoke out against the National Resources Mobilization Act in August 1940 and was promptly arrested and interned. University of Toronto history professor Frank Underhill did not face internment, but he almost lost his job after making unpopular comments on the Canadian–American Permanent Joint Board of Defence. Freedom of speech and association was clearly in question in the summer of 1940.

Even refugees were treated with suspicion by the RCMP, officials in the immigration department, and other members of the government. In total, Canada took in only about thirty-five hundred refugees from enemy countries between 1939 and 1945. Quebec's opposition to Jewish immigration contributed to Ottawa's reluctance to respond generously to Britain's request that Canada admit German and Austrian refugees, many of them anti-Nazi Jews who had been rounded up during the war. Jewish refugees were initially put in prison camps with German prisoners of war. Although they were eventually housed separately, many of them remained under guard in rough internment camps. Not even reports, widespread by 1943, of Nazi extermination camps changed official or public sentiment. In the fall of 1943, Maurice Duplessis publicly charged that there was a conspiracy between Jewish organizations and the federal government to place a hundred thousand Jewish refugees in Quebec. He called for a moratorium on large-scale immigration because of the

undesirable effect it would have on Quebec.

The treatment of refugees became a major concern of the Canadian National Council on Refugees (CNCR), whose president was Senator Cairine Wilson. Under pressure from the CNCR, the government passed an order-in-council in December 1943 releasing enemy alien refugees from internment and granting them one-year permits to stay in Canada. The CNCR tried to find work for these unfortunate people, many of whom were well educated and eventually made major contributions to their adopted country as scientists, university professors, and artists.

Anti-war dissidents were another group that came under surveillance during the war. Since the Communist Party spoke out against the war, it was outlawed in June 1940, and 133 of its leaders were arrested. The ban on the Communist Party remained in effect until the end of the war, but most of the Communist internees were released after Hitler invaded the Soviet Union in 1941. In addition to such political dissidents, an estimated 12 000 Canadians, most of them Quakers, Mennonites, and the Brethren in Christ, declared themselves conscientious objectors. Many of them were required to work in rural camps or factories; those who refused such placements were kept at labour camps, which were in effect internment camps.

Over the course of the war, the lives of thousands of people were affected by the workings of the security forces. In total, over 100 000 enemy aliens were registered and 647 interned during the war. Another 1776 men, many of them Canadian citizens, were interned to prevent them from "acting in any manner prejudicial to the public safety or the safety of the state." During the war, twenty-five temporary and permanent internment camps were in operation at one time or another. The largest camps, built to house up to ten thousand inmates, were located at Medicine Hat and Lethbridge.

While fewer people were interned during the Second World War than the First, Germans and Italians not subject to arrest nevertheless faced hostility and economic harassment from nativist Canadians. For example, Antonio DiSippio, a naturalized Allied veteran of the First World War and a member of the Canadian Legion, was ruined when an Ontario government official maliciously cancelled his liquor licence.

No internees were deported after the war. Although the Canadian government planned to deport the Japanese evacuees, the legality of the policy was called into question. By the time the courts handed down their decision, Canadians and much of the world were beginning to adopt a new attitude towards cultural minorities and refugee populations.[5]

## THE WELFARE STATE

Almost as soon as the war started, Canadians began to worry about the nation's postwar agenda. Memories of the Great Depression and of the major recession that had followed the First World War caused many to believe that the end of this war would usher in another period of hard times. Government planning of the economy during wartime, including price controls and rationing, had resulted in a higher standard of living for ordinary people. Why, they asked, could governments not continue such a role with the same success in peacetime? Joseph Levitt, a soldier who later became a history professor, summed up the thinking of many people at the time: "The propaganda of the thirties had always been that the government had no money, couldn't do anything about it, and that's the way things were. But the war taught people a lot. It was a matter of common sense and simple to understand that if the government could find money for war, then they could find it for peace."[6]

The two major parties appeared at first to ignore such concerns, but they would soon change their tunes. Having followed a reformist path from 1935 to 1940, the Conservatives elected Arthur Meighen as their leader in 1941. Meighen had led the Conservative Party from 1920 to 1927 and was identified primarily as a man who supported conscription and Britain, not social insurance programs. In early 1942, Meighen sought a parliamentary seat in a by-election in the supposedly safe Conservative riding of York South. King, who

feared Meighen's pro-conscription campaign, decided not to run a Liberal candidate, leaving the CCF to challenge Meighen. The CCF had won only eight seats in 1940 and appeared to be no threat to the federal Liberals. Throughout the by-election, Meighen talked of the need to impose conscription; the previously unknown CCF candidate, Joseph Noseworthy, spoke of the need to plan employment and insurance programs for the postwar era. The majority of constituents liked his message. Meighen's defeat and subsequent resignation as Conservative leader had repercussions throughout the political system. By the end of 1943, a Gallup poll revealed that slightly more Canadians would vote CCF than Tory or Liberal.

Reform-minded Conservatives argued that the country could not be allowed to fall to the socialists. In 1942, they sponsored a symposium in Port Hope, Ontario, to prepare for a more progressive approach to policy. Later that year at a leadership convention in Winnipeg, the Conservatives chose John Bracken, the Liberal–Progressive premier of Manitoba, as national leader. The delegates at the convention also adopted a platform that went beyond Bennett's New Deal to embrace universal pensions, medical insurance, equality for women, and union rights. At Bracken's insistence, the party changed its name to "Progressive Conservative" in the hope of shedding its reactionary image.

Despite attempts to steal its thunder, the CCF advance continued. In 1943, the party captured thirty-four seats in the Ontario legislature and became the official opposition in a house shared with thirty-eight Conservatives, fifteen Liberals, and two Communists. Provincial Conservative leader George Drew, who was no friend of socialists or their policies, was obliged to promise a comprehensive social security program in an attempt to blunt the CCF advance. Meanwhile, in Saskatchewan, the CCF under the leadership of the dynamic Tommy Douglas won the 1944 provincial election. Douglas capitalized on the popular policies of the CCF and the widespread disenchantment among Saskatchewan farmers with Ottawa's price controls on grain.

The shift in public opinion towards the left

## TOMMY DOUGLAS

Born in Scotland in 1904, Tommy Douglas immigrated with his family to Winnipeg in 1919, where he witnessed the General Strike. After serving as a printer's apprentice, he decided, in 1924, to enter the Baptist ministry. He attended Brandon College for six years where he was exposed to social gospel teachings. Following his ordination in 1930, he moved to Weyburn, Saskatchewan, where he witnessed first-hand the suffering of farmers during the Depression. He soon became deeply involved in politics, establishing a local association of the Independent Labour Party in

*Tommy Douglas.*
National Archives of Canada/C036 220

1931 and attending the founding convention of the CCF. In 1935, he was elected to the House of Commons and soon developed a reputation as a skilful and witty debater. He resigned his seat to lead the CCF to victory in Saskatchewan in 1944 and remained premier of the province until he resigned in 1961 to become leader of the federal New Democratic Party. Under his leadership, Saskatchewan earned a reputation for innovative and efficient government. Indeed, Douglas pioneered many of the social welfare programs that would eventually be implemented in other provinces of Canada.

was not unique to Canada. In Great Britain, voters rejected wartime leader Winston Churchill and his Conservative Party in 1945, electing a Labour government to preside over postwar reconstruction. A report published in Britain late in 1942 by Sir William Beveridge, a distinguished social planner, argued for a government-sponsored social security system from the cradle to the grave. It was a blueprint for social change that would have a major impact on developments in Canada.

Ever vigilant of trends that might undermine his power, King decided the time had come to implement reforms to which his party had nominally been committed since the national convention in 1919. The government had introduced a national unemployment insurance program in 1940, but it was a cautious initiative. An insurance plan rather than a welfare scheme, the program required earners and employers to make contributions to a fund from which employees could draw if they were laid off work. Since everyone expected that hard times would return when the war ended, such compulsory savings were considered wise planning. Contributions to the unemployment insurance fund helped to dampen wartime inflation by drawing money out of the pockets of consumers

in a period of rapid growth, presumably to be spent when hard times returned.

As it was initially designed, unemployment insurance covered only a small proportion of the labour force, and even that unequally. Some exemptions, such as farm labourers, were testimony to the influence of special interest groups. Other exemptions reflected patriarchal notions of women's place in the economy. Married women were excluded from coverage: few people regarded a married women's job loss as of consequence to the woman or her family. Domestic work, still a frequent occupation for single women, was exempt from coverage. By gearing the size of benefits to the wages earned and by tying eligibility to weeks of continuous work, the program also discriminated against low-wage and part-time workers.

There were many Canadians who felt that Ottawa's plans to stabilize the economy should go beyond insurance policies for a small proportion of the labour force. In March 1941, the Department of Health, which had responsibility for veterans, established a Committee on Reconstruction. It included representatives from business, labour, and universities, and was chaired by Cyril James, principal of McGill University. When the committee became too imaginative in its approach, it was superseded by a more conservative committee under Dr William MacIntosh from Queen's University. Nevertheless, James and his colleagues captured the attention of Canadians with a report eventually known by the name of its principal author, Leonard Marsh. A McGill economist, Marsh brought his CCF sensibilities and the insights of the Beveridge Report to the problems of reconstruction. The Marsh Report argued that full employment should be a major goal of the postwar industrial state; to that end, the government and the whole society should play a role in ensuring that people found work, remained healthy, and were properly fed, housed, and educated. Although the cost of programs such as universal old age pensions and family allowances was high, Marsh implied that the cost of not having such programs was even higher. Social programs, the report argued, "are not money lost," but "investments in morale and health, in greater family stability,... in human productive efficiency."

Conservative critics were appalled by such thinking. In 1944, Charlotte Whitton, one of Canada's leading social workers, wrote a book entitled *The Dawn of an Ampler Life* in which she argued that Marsh's schemes would make Canadians dependent on the state, destroy initiative, and encourage the feeble-minded to procreate. King's finance minister, J.L. Ilsley, was also reluctant to embrace the Marsh proposals. Where on earth would the government get the money to implement them, he wondered? Proponents of the new social programs responded that changes to the taxation system were critical to the success of the welfare state. During the war, individuals and corporations paid taxes at unprecedented levels. If such tax levels could be carried over into peacetime, a national social safety net just might be possible.

The biggest problem facing the federal government in the long run was the constitution. In the interwar years, the Judicial Committee of the Privy Council had struck down some of Ottawa's most progressive legislation because it violated the provisions of the BNA Act, which stipulated that the provinces had jurisdiction over social policy.

Before it could proceed with a national unemployment insurance program, the federal government had been obliged to secure an amendment to the BNA Act. The King government had established a Royal Commission on Dominion—Provincial Relations in 1937 to explore ways of reforming the constitution to permit the federal government to intervene directly in the field of social welfare. When the proposals of the royal commission were unveiled in 1940, they were strongly opposed by the premiers of Ontario, Alberta, and British Columbia, who refused to concede their taxation powers so that the federal government could establish a national policy to create full employment and social services. Ottawa might impose the income and corporate taxes it needed to run the war, but the provinces were less likely to accept such policies in peacetime.

Most Canadians were unconcerned about constitutional niceties. They wanted reform. At a meeting of the National Liberal Federation in September 1943, the party followed the CCF and the Progressive Conservatives in adopting a platform supporting social security. King moved quickly to establish three new departments—Reconstruction, National Health and Welfare, and Veterans Affairs—to preside over the government's postwar planning. His administration introduced family allowance legislation, by which mothers of children under sixteen received a monthly stipend. The first cheques, amounting to between five and eight dollars per child, were sent out in 1945. Universal old age pensions and state-supported health care were postponed after a majority of the cabinet, led by Ilsley, decided that it was premature to press ahead with these measures. Nevertheless, the idea of the welfare state, nurtured by the suffering of the Depression and the seemingly spectacular success of wartime planning, survived the crises that produced it.

In the last two years of the war, the government focused on policies that would help cushion the shock of returning to peace. It passed a National Housing Act to generate construction, established an Industrial Development Board to help companies retool for peacetime production, created a Veterans' Charter to provide benefits for

*In the North, family allowance cheques often came in the form of food and supplies issued at Hudson's Bay Company stores.*

S.J. Bailey/ National Archives of Canada/PA164744

council advocated that management recognize unions and engage in collective bargaining with them, but it gave no legislative teeth to this injunction. Many employers still tried to ignore unions. For example, in 1941 Dominion Steel and Coal refused to recognize a local of the Steelworkers' Organizing Committee, forerunner of United Steelworkers of America, even though 93 percent of the workforce in its Montreal mill had signed union cards. In the following year, labour alienation reached new heights as the federal government helped gold mine operators in Kirkland Lake, Ontario, keep unions out of their mines, first by using conciliation to delay a strike and then by refusing to intervene as the miners and their wives walked picket lines.

those who served in the war, and developed policies to help primary producers survive the transition to peacetime markets. In all, the government appropriated $3.12 billion for reconstruction, an incredible sum even today. These policies went some distance in helping the Liberals to ward off the CCF threat and to prepare the party for victory in the 1945 election.

## LABOUR AND THE STATE

Another reason for the Liberal government's success in fending off socialism was its official recognition that the state could no longer ignore the demands of trade unions. Its position had been otherwise when the war began. The Industrial Disputes Investigation Act, found to be unconstitutional in 1925 when applied to industries outside federal jurisdiction, was vastly extended under the War Measures Act to allow the government to use conciliation to avoid strikes. A 1940 order-in-

Workers were no longer prepared to submit silently to the dictates of government and hostile managers. Industrial and craft unions took full advantage of improved wartime employment conditions to organize workers who were no longer afraid of being fired for union activities. In highly mechanized industries, including steel production, automobile manufacturing, electrical parts production, meat packing, and the pulp and paper industry, skilled male workers, generally of Anglo-Canadian background, led the drive for industry-wide unionism. The refusal of some companies to accept the unions formed by the democratic votes of their workers resulted in strikes and work slowdowns. In 1943, Canadian workers engaged in over four hundred strikes involving more than two hundred thousand workers. King had taken note of the fact that in a 1943 by-election, the Canadian Congress of Labour had poured personnel and funds into the CCF's campaign. Eager to keep war industries functioning smoothly and his political popularity high, King felt compelled to act.

In February 1944, Order-in-Council PC 1003 ushered in a new era of labour policy in Canada. The order guaranteed workers the right to organize and to bargain collectively, established procedures for the certification and compulsory recognition of trade unions, defined unfair labour practices, and created an administrative apparatus to enforce the order. Designed initially as a war measure, PC 1003 was popular with workers and gave them hope that they would be able to carry the gains they had made during the war into the peacetime workplace.

The move to accommodate labour and a massive anti-socialist campaign by business interests helped to reduce support for left-wing parties. In the spring of 1945, the Conservative Party in Ontario won a majority of the seats in a provincial election that reduced the CCF to eight seats and third place in the provincial legislature. On 11 June, the CCF won only 28 of 245 seats in the federal election, with 15 percent of the popular vote. Although they received a reduced parliamentary majority, the Liberals were given a mandate to govern the country in peacetime. King had proven his ability to stay in the middle of the political road, no matter what direction that road took.

## THE NEW WORLD ORDER

King also presided over a government that took a new road in international affairs. Even more obvious in retrospect than at the time, the Second World War reinforced Great Britain's long decline from its dominant role in world affairs. Its mantle passed to the United States. During the Second World War, Canada moved closer to the Americans, economically, politically, and militarily. Critics such as the distinguished scholar Harold Innis, who taught political economy at the University of Toronto, would later claim that in this period Canada moved from "colony to nation to colony" in its efforts to maintain good relations with the superpower living next door—that is, that it had achieved independence from Britain only to lose it to the United States.

As Hitler's armies erased national borders with ease, King had recognized that Canada was increasingly dependent on the United States for its defence. American president Franklin Roosevelt was equally conscious of this fact and was afraid that Canada's involvement in the war made the whole North American continent vulnerable to the fascist dictators. In August 1940, Roosevelt invited King to meet him at Ogdensburg, New York. As a result of their meeting, a Permanent Joint Board on Defence was established to prepare for mutual assistance in defence of North America. The notion of permanency gave King few qualms, and the board was established without prior reference to Parliament. In the crisis atmosphere of the late summer of 1940, few people in Canada voiced any objection.

The United States also made adjustments to its wartime policies to ensure that Canada's economy would not suffer unduly. Early in 1941, the American Congress empowered the president to have manufactured "any defense article for the government of any country whose defense the President deems vital to the defense of the United States." These articles he could "sell, transfer title to, exchange, lend, lease, or otherwise dispose of" to the governments involved. In March 1941, a Lend-Lease arrangement was concluded between the United States and Britain. As originally drawn up, Lend-Lease, which made available $7 billion for the purchase of equipment and supplies in the United States, excluded Canada. This "oversight" was rectified at another meeting between Roosevelt and King at Hyde Park, New York, in April 1941. The Americans would increase purchases in Canada and would charge many of the components bought by Canada in the United States to the British account, thereby helping to solve the balance of payment difficulties. King told Parliament that the Hyde Park declaration "involves nothing less than a common plan for the economic defence of the western hemisphere," and "the enduring foundation of a new world order."[7] King was given to rhetorical exaggeration, but in this instance he was strikingly prophetic. Valuable wartime arrangements as they were, Ogdensburg and Hyde Park were less important in themselves than as symbols of an intimate Canadian–American relationship that was becoming a dominant fact of life for Canada.

Once the United States officially entered the war, Canada no longer figured very prominently in American calculations. While King hated to be taken for granted, he had to accept that Canada was

*When British prime minister Winston Churchill and American president Franklin Roosevelt met in Quebec City in 1943, Mackenzie King was on hand for a photo opportunity.*

National Archives of Canada/ C31186

a minor player in a world of superpowers. The United States resisted Canadian efforts to have a military mission in Washington to learn more about American military strategy. The United States also protested loudly when Canada quietly supported the successful efforts of Charles de Gaulle's Free French forces to seize St Pierre and Miquelon—two French islands off the coast of Newfoundland—from the Vichy government. Despite American demands, King refused to attempt to dislodge de Gaulle's forces because he suspected Vichy—the pro-German government in that part of France unoccupied by the Nazis—of

using the islands as a base from which to report to the Germans on Allied convoy movements.

Canadians took the practical route and developed what became known as the functional principle in wartime planning. When Canadian interests were at stake, they would insist on having a voice in determining international policy. This approach was most clearly expressed in the words of Hume Wrong, a senior officer in the department of External Affairs in 1942: "The principle ... is that each member of the grand alliance should have a voice in the conduct of the war proportionate to its contribution to the general war effort. A subsidiary principle is that the influence of the various countries should be greatest in connection with those matters with which they are most directly concerned."[8] Canadians used such arguments to win a seat on the Allied Combined Food Board, which allocated food resources for the war effort, and with less success in pressing for a seat on the United Nations Relief and Rehabilitation Administration, which was designed to distribute aid to liberatedcountries. A newly activist, internationalist foreign policy was on the rise, even though the always cautious Mackenzie King carefully watched his flock of ambitious officers at the Department of External Affairs lest they commit Canada to too much international responsibility.

The American presence loomed large as the war dragged on. Roosevelt had arranged for American bases in Newfoundland, still a dependency of Great Britain, but one in which Canada had a considerable interest and which Canada had agreed to protect for the duration of the war. When the Japanese occupied the Aleutian Islands in the summer of 1942, the United States, with Canada's permission, built an overland route through Canada to Alaska. The Alaska highway was a marvel of American efficiency. Between March and October 1942, civilian workers and seven engineer regiments, together totalling eleven thousand people, began carving a highway from Dawson Creek, British Columbia, to Big Delta,

Alaska, a total of over twenty-two hundred kilometres, at a cost of nearly $150 million. To ensure oil supplies, the Americans built the Canol pipeline from Whitehorse in the Yukon to Norman Wells in the Northwest Territories. The Americans also developed northern staging routes of rough airstrips to transport bombers and fighter planes to Europe and the USSR. By 1943, there were 33 000 Americans working in the Canadian North.

King and officials in the Department of External Affairs were troubled by the American invasion of Canada's northern territories. In an effort to establish sovereignty over the area, and to reduce Canada's balance of American dollars, the government announced in December 1943 that the United States was to be paid in full for all permanent military installations built by the Americans in Canada. Canada ultimately paid $123.5 million for twenty-eight airfields, fifty-six weather stations, and a variety of other facilities. In 1943, the Canadian government decided to upgrade its diplomatic presence in Washington. The Canadian legation took on embassy status, and Leighton McCarthy, the Canadian minister to the United States, became an ambassador, the first Canadian diplomat to hold that rank.

Cooperation more than conflict characterized Canadian–American relations throughout the war. At the American request, Canadians agreed to participate in the expedition to dislodge the Japanese from the Aleutians in 1943, and Canadians adopted American army organization for the sixteen thousand Canadian Army Pacific Forces assembled for the final campaign against the Japanese in 1945.

The new world order that was put in place after the Second World War was largely dominated by American policy. In the spring of 1945, meetings were held in San Francisco to establish the United Nations, an organization designed to replace war with negotiation as a vehicle for settling international disputes. Although Canadian diplomats had their own ideas about the economic structures that should govern the postwar world, they went along with American plans for the International Monetary Fund and the World Bank. Only time would tell whether this blueprint for peace and prosperity would be any more successful than the one put in place by the League of Nations following the Great War.

The prospects for a peaceful postwar world were not good. When the war in Europe came to an end, the leaders of the Soviet Union, Great Britain, and the United States met in Potsdam, Germany, in July 1945 to discuss how to manage the peace process. It was a different group of leaders than had met to plot strategy during the war. Joseph Stalin was the only constant player. Franklin Roosevelt had died in April 1945, succeeded by his vice-president, Harry Truman. Britain was in the process of holding an election even as the Potsdam conference was in progress. A Labour victory meant that Clement Attlee replaced Winston Churchill at the bargaining table. The conference revealed the growing tension between the Soviet Union and the West, tension that ultimately led to the partition of Germany and to the Cold War that was to characterize international relations for decades to come.

## DEMOBILIZATION AND POSTWAR RECONSTRUCTION

In Canada, the people planning demobilization during the Second World War were determined not to repeat the mistakes that created the unrest following the Great War. Planning for postwar reconstruction began almost as soon as the war began. In January 1940, the government created the General Advisory Committee on Demobilization and Reconstruction under Great War veteran H.F. McDonald. A new department of Veterans Affairs was established in 1944 to help soldiers make a successful transition to civilian life. The Veterans' Charter of the same year offered veterans more generous benefits than those available in 1919, including a gratuity of $752.3 million to help them get re-established. In 1942, the government passed an act requiring companies to rehire veterans in their former jobs under conditions "not less favourable" than if they had never enlisted. Nearly 200 000 veterans benefited from this injunction, and only four charges were brought against uncooperative employers under the

Reinstatement Act. A slightly smaller number, about 150 000, had their entry into the labour market postponed for several years by the provision that helped veterans to attend university or college. Others took up land offered by the Veterans' Land Act and settled into farming.

While it was all well and good to plan for the end of the war, victory in Europe brought the predictable problem of getting the forces home. Repatriation went faster than expected, but nothing could solve the problem of too few ships for too many soldiers. In theory, repatriation followed a point system allowing those with the longest service and who were married to come back first, with ex-prisoners of war, the wounded, and service women being given top priority. In practice, there were problems and unrest. The worst disorder took place in Aldershot, in England, in July 1945, when Canadian forces erupted in a two-night riot. By the end of 1945, only half of the nearly 350 000 Canadians in Europe were home. A division of 25 000 troops and eleven air force squadrons was committed to the occupation of Germany. When few Canadians volunteered for this tour of duty, Canada informed the Allied Command that it would pull its forces out of Germany by the spring of 1946.

Most of the ships arriving from Europe docked at Halifax, which did its best, under difficult circumstances, to welcome "the boys" home, but not before for VE day (victory in Europe) celebrations blew the city apart. As news of the German surrender spread, Haligonians closed their offices, stores, and restaurants, while throngs of service people and civilians celebrated in downtown streets. Seamen were free to come and go, but there was nothing for them to do. Even their canteen at the naval dockyard HMCS Stadacona closed at 9:00 pm. With the city closed down as well, the inevitable occurred. Liquor stores were looted, a tram trashed, and chaos reigned in the streets of Halifax.

This should have been the end of the affair, but it was not. As a victory parade was forming up the next morning over three thousand sailors and a contingent from other services poured into the city to continue their looting rampage. Neither the naval patrols nor the city police were strong enough to keep the peace, and Rear-Admiral Murray was at a loss as to how to restore order among his men. The two-day riot caused $5 million worth of damage and left civilians and military authorities pointing fingers at each other for causing the fracas. In the inquiry following the riot, 41 soldiers, 34 sailors, and 19 airmen were among the 211 indicted for offences. Murray was relieved of his command because of the affair, and the navy took most of the blame for the damage.

While officials professed surprise at the extent of the rampage, conditions had been ripe for just such an incident. The population of Halifax had doubled during the war, although goods were still rationed on the basis of the 65 000 people counted in the 1941 census. With the shortage of consumer goods, living space, and recreational facilities, tensions between civilians and service personnel mounted. Halifax's problems were discussed several times in the war cabinet, and plans were formulated to move out people who were not essential to the war effort, but no action had been taken. The pent-up frustrations were unleashed on VE day.

Among those returning on the big ships from Europe were 44 886 war brides (only a few war husbands) and their 21 358 children. In addition,

**Table 11.1**

| MARRIAGES, DIVORCES, AND BIRTHS IN CANADA, 1939–1948 | | | |
|---|---|---|---|
| **Year** | **Marriages** | **Divorces** | **Births** |
| 1939 | 106 266 | 2073 | 237 991 |
| 1940 | 125 797 | 2416 | 252 577 |
| 1941 | 124 644 | 2462 | 263 993 |
| 1942 | 130 786 | 3091 | 281 569 |
| 1943 | 113 827 | 3398 | 292 943 |
| 1944 | 104 656 | 3827 | 293 967 |
| 1945 | 111 376 | 5101 | 300 587 |
| 1946 | 137 398 | 7757 | 343 504 |
| 1947 | 130 400 | 8213 | 372 589 |
| 1948 | 126 118 | 6978 | 359 860 |

*Source: F.H. Leacy, ed.,* **Historical Statistics of Canada** *(Ottawa: Minister of Supply and Service, 1983), cited in Desmond Morton and J.L. Granatstein,* **Victory 1945** *(Toronto: HarperCollins, 1995), 119*

there were 414 child maintenance orders served on Canadians by authorities in Britain. The vast majority of war brides were British, although Canadians soldiers also married Dutch, Belgian, French, Danish, Italian, and German women. Once in Canada, the war brides faced a difficult adjustment, to new families, new communities, and a new country. Some, such as Betty Oliphant, divorced their husbands but ended up staying in Canada anyway. Oliphant became the founder of the National Ballet School.

As in the First World War, the reestablishment of family life was difficult for many veterans. The number of marriages and births increased after the war but so, too, did divorces. For many of the veterans, it was impossible to pick up the threads of civilian life. One wife described the difficulties that arose because she had tried to hide the problems faced by the family while her husband was overseas:

> I don't know what to make of Jim, I'm sure. I've tried to be a good wife to him and keep things going here at home, but now he's back and you'd think I'd done everything wrong. Of course, it was a shock to him finding us in a place like this—I never let on in my letters, you know, just told him we'd moved. I knew it would worry him. Well, that's all right now and we're moving to a better place next month. But the way he carried on when he saw little Gloria wearing glasses—you'd think it was my fault she has to have them. She's worn them six months now and we're all used to it, but to hear Jim talk she would never have needed them if he'd been here to look after things.[9]

As the men returned home and women were forced out of their wartime jobs, families were encouraged by state and business propaganda to establish homes in the suburbs and raise their children in one of the world's luckiest democracies. Most Canadians, it appears, did what they were told.

Much of the responsibility for establishing Canada's postwar economy on a peacetime footing fell on the shoulders of C.D. Howe, who was appointed minister for reconstruction in 1944. With his usual energy, he set about reducing rationing, converting war industries to peacetime purposes, and re-establishing Canada's export sales.

Canada's merchant marine was scrapped, and most Crown corporations were closed down or sold. To meet fifteen years of pent-up civilian demand, companies were given tax breaks to get their factories producing consumer goods. The loss of overseas markets was in part compensated for by sales made possible under the Marshall Plan. When it looked as if communism might sweep war-torn European countries, the United States agreed in 1947 to a generous aid program to help them restore their capitalist economies. Canada was included in the Marshall Plan purchases and as a result sold a billion dollars worth of its products overseas by 1950. With policies such as these, Canada managed to weather the adjustment to peacetime production reasonably well. Instead of the postwar slump predicted by many economists, Canada experienced growth, its GNP rising from $11.8 billion in 1945 to $18.4 billion in 1950.

Canada was not spared the wave of strikes that followed the First World War. In 1945 and 1946, proportionately more time was lost in strike activity than in 1919. A major strike was conducted at the Ford Motor plant in Windsor in 1945, and a national steel strike shut down plants in Sault Ste Marie, Hamilton, and Sydney in 1946. The results of arbitration at Ford and the willingness of federal and provincial governments to enshrine the principles of PC 1003 in postwar legislation helped to prevent the stand-off between labour and capital that characterized the aftermath of the Great War. With the legal and administrative apparatus in place, the way was paved for organized labour to join big business and big government in the three-cornered power structure of modern corporate capitalism.

## CONCLUSION

Canada came out of the war a different country from the one that went into it in 1939. With a stronger federal state and the beginnings of a social welfare system, the nation was in a position to avoid returning to the misery experienced during the Depression. The booming economy seemed to hold its own in a peacetime context. In comparison to the devastated cities and countrysides of Europe

*Waving "the flag" to celebrate victory over Japan, 14 August 1945.*

Alberta Provincial Archives/G 1293

and Asia, Canada was an untouched utopia and the destination of choice for many European refugees. Even racial and ethnic tensions that surfaced during the war seemed to be replaced by the increasingly popular concept of human rights. While many hotels and restaurants still refused to serve blacks and Asians, the owners of these establishments faced the prospect of being taken to court for discrimination. Ontario and Saskatchewan in 1945 became the first provinces to adopt human rights codes that banned many forms of discrimination in hiring and accommodation.

Canadians were also assuming a new place among the nations of the world. Although not a major power like Great Britain or the United States, Canada began to embrace the term "middle power," a small nation no more, and one with an expanding role to play in international affairs. It was also a country in the process of creating its own identity independent from the British Commonwealth. In 1946, Secretary of State Paul Martin introduced a bill, passed the next year, to establish a distinct Canadian citizenship, since up to that point Canadians still carried British passports. There was also some discussion in the media about adopting a Canadian flag—Canadians still waved the Red Ensign, the Union Jack, and even the Stars and Stripes during victory celebrations. Clearly issues of Canadian identity were on the agenda as Canada entered the atomic age.

## ORIGINS OF THE WELFARE STATE

*A Historiographical Debate*

Social scientists generally agree on the various factors contributing to the evolution of the welfare state in Canada, but the relative weight of these factors is in dispute. In identifying the groups pressing for the creation of federal social insurance programs, scholars list the following: the unemployed; business groups; municipalities and provinces; liberal churches; and elements within the state bureaucracy. They also note the support of key politicians. Is there evidence to suggest that one group more than another left its mark on the kind of welfare state that emerged in Canada? The contours of the debate can be understood by looking at how scholars explain the emergence of an unemployment insurance program in 1940.

Alvin Finkel has suggested that pressure from big business was largely responsible for producing an unemployment insurance program.[10] According to Finkel, business people felt that unemployment insurance would help prevent public finances from being besieged by unplanned expenditures when unemployment rose. Business leaders wanted the scale of payments to be modest so that people would be encouraged to find work. They also wanted the cost to be borne by working people themselves rather than by companies or the government. To a considerable degree their views prevailed in the program that was introduced in 1940.

James Struthers argues that this scenario is too one-sided, suggesting that popular pressures, both from the unemployed and from liberal-minded citizens, generally played a role in securing unemployment insurance.[11] Some argue that the business community, though divided, was largely opposed to unemployment insurance. According to sociologist Carl Cuneo, unemployment insurance was an example of the state implementing reforms to save capitalism from itself. By providing a social safety net for workers, the state helped to prevent widespread social unrest that might lead to revolution and the total destruction of the market economy.[12]

Still others stress the role of specific politicians. R.B. Bennett's need to appear reform-minded before the 1935 election is often mentioned.[13] Since Bennett had promised unemployment insurance as early as 1931, it is not surprising that it emerged as an item in his "New Deal" package of reforms in 1935. J.L. Granatstein attributes Mackenzie King's reintroduction of unemployment insurance in 1940 to his desire to plan for expected postwar unemployment.[14] Struthers

also sees the war as the major catalyst for the welfare state. "When King finally pushed for speedy passage of the Unemployment Insurance Act, it was out of his own fear of post-war unrest," Struthers argues. "No one expected that veterans or unemployed war workers would queue up meekly in front of local relief offices. In the final analysis it was war and not the depression which destroyed the poor-law heritage."[15]

Most scholars concede the degree to which the state bureaucracy shaped the character of Canada's unemployment insurance program. While admitting that a variety of forces caused politicians to accept the need for some form of social insurance, political scientist Leslie Pal suggests that a state-centred, rather than society-centred, perspective explains the character of the program itself. In its formative years, he argues, unemployment insurance became grounded in administrative logic when it came to determining contributions, benefits, duration, and coverage. Whereas employee groups tended to view unemployment insurance in terms of rights, and employers saw it in terms of costs and theeffect on the labour supply, officials were preoccupied with administrative feasibility, actuarial soundness, and strict insurance principles. This led to a similarity of views between employers and officials, particularly on the abuse question, but this similarity was coincidental in that the official view was arrived at independently. It was not the result of "pressure."[16]

When examined from the perspective of gender, there is also a remarkable coincidence of views between the state bureaucrats, business men, and union leaders on the treatment of female workers under the unemployment insurance program.[17] Indeed, as Ruth Pierson has pointed out, neither progressives nor conservatives, labour nor management, organized to defend the right of married women workers to receive fair compensation when they lost jobs.

## NOTES

[1] Enlistment and casualty figures vary widely. The figures cited in this chapter are taken from Desmond Morton and J.L. Granatstein, *Victory 1945: Canadians from War to Peace* (Toronto: HarperCollins, 1995), 19.

[2] Ruth Roach Pierson, "Canadian Women and Canadian Mobilization During the Second World War," *Revue internationale d'histoire militaire* 51 (1982): 198

[3] Carl A. Christie, *Ocean Bridge: The History of RAF Ferry Command* (Toronto: University of Toronto Press, 1995), 3

[4] Morton and Granatstein, *Victory 1945*, 41

[5] The statistics cited in this section are drawn from David Lee, "Emergency Government Powers in Canada in the Twentieth Century" and Elizabeth Vincent, "Internment Camp B/70 Ripples, New Brunswick" in *Agenda Papers*, Vol. 3, Historic Sites and Monuments Board, 25, 26 Nov. 1994, 987–1041 (unpublished).

[6] Cited in Morton and Granatstein, *Victory 1945*, 114

[7] J.L. Granatstein and Norman Hillmer, *For Better or for Worse: Canada and the United States to the 1990s* (Toronto: Copp Clark Pitman, 1991), 147

[8] Cited in Morton and Granatstein, *Victory 1945*, 234

[9] Cited in J.D. Ketchum, "Home Won't be Heaven, Soldier" in *The Good Fight: Canadians and World War II*, ed. J.L. Granatstein and Peter Neary (Toronto: Copp Clark, 1995), 419

[10] Alvin Finkel, *Business and Social Reform in the Thirties* (Toronto: Lorimer, 1979)

[11] James Struthers, *No Fault of Their Own: Unemployment and the Canadian Welfare State, 1914–1941* (Toronto: University of Toronto Press, 1981)

[12] Carl J. Cuneo, "State, Class and Reserve Labour: The Case of the 1941 Canadian Unemployment Insurance Act," *Canadian Review of Sociology and Anthropology* 16 (May 1979): 147–70

[13] See, for example, Larry A. Glassford, *Reaction and Reform: The Politics of the Conservative Party under R.B. Bennett, 1927–1938* (Toronto: University of Toronto Press, 1992)

[14] J.L. Granatstein, *Canada's War: The Politics of the Mackenzie King Government, 1939–1945* (Toronto: Oxford University Press, 1975)

[15] Struthers, *No Fault of Their Own*, 213

[16] Leslie Pal, *State, Class and Bureaucracy: Canadian Unemployment Insurance and Public Policy* (Montreal: McGill-Queen's University Press, 1975), 109

[17] Ruth Roach Pierson, "Gender and the Unemployment Insurance Debate in Canada, 1934–1940," *Labour/Le Travail* 25 (Spring 1990): 77–103

## SELECTED READING

On Canada's wartime experience, see Norman Hillmer, Robert Bothwell, Roger Sarty, and Claude Beauregard, eds., *A Country of Limitations: Canada and the World in 1939* (Ottawa: Canadian Committee for the History of the Second World War, 1996); J.L. Granatstein and Desmond Morton, *A Nation Forged in Fire: Canadians in the Second World War* (Toronto: Lester and Orpen Dennys, 1989); J.L. Granatstein and Peter Neary, eds., *The Good Fight: Canadians and World War II* (Toronto: Copp Clark, 1995); W.A.B. Douglas, ed., *The RCN in Retrospect, 1910–1968* (Vancouver: UBC Press, 1982), and his *The Creation of a National Airforce* (Toronto: University of Toronto Press, 1968); Brereton Greenhous et al., *The Crucible of War, 1939–1945* (Toronto: University of Toronto Press, 1994); Marc Milner, *North Atlantic Run: The Royal Canadian Navy and the Battle for the Convoys* (Toronto: University of Toronto Press, 1982); Roger Sarty, *The Maritime Defence of Canada* (Toronto: Canadian Institute for Strategic Studies, 1997); C.P. Stacey, *Six Years of War* (Ottawa: Queen's Printer, 1955), *The Victory Campaign* (Ottawa: Queen's Printer, 1960), and *Arms,*

*Men and Governments: The War Policies of Canada, 1939–1945* (Ottawa: Queen's Printer, 1970); G.W.L. Nicholson, *The Canadians in Italy, 1943–1945* (Ottawa: Queen's Printer, 1957); Terry Copp and Bill McAndrew, *Battle Exhaustion: Soldiers and Psychiatrists in the Canadian Army, 1939–1945* (Montreal: McGill-Queen's University Press, 1990); Daniel Dancocks, *The D-Day Dodgers: The Canadians in Italy, 1943–1945* (Toronto: McClelland and Stewart, 1992); J.L Granatstein, *The Generals: The Canadian Army's Senior Commanders in the Second World War* (Don Mills, ON: Stoddart, 1993); and Carl A. Christie, *Ocean Bridge: The History of RAF Ferry Command* (Toronto: University of Toronto Press, 1995). On women's participation at home and abroad, see Ruth Roach Pierson, *"They're Still Women After All": The Second World War and Canadian Womanhood* (Toronto: McClelland and Stewart, 1986).

On political developments at home during the war, see J.W. Pickersgill and D.F. Foster, *The Mackenzie King Record*, vols. 1 and 2 (Toronto: University of Toronto Press, 1960, 1968); Reg Whitaker, *The Government Party* (Toronto: University of Toronto Press, 1977); Douglas Owram, *The Government Generation: Canadian Intellectuals and the State, 1900–1945* (Toronto: University of Toronto Press, 1986); J.L. Granatstein, *Canada's War: The Politics of the Mackenzie King Government, 1939–1945* (Toronto: Oxford University Press, 1974); Robert Bothwell and William Kilbourn, *C.D. Howe* (Toronto: McClelland and Stewart, 1979); Leonard Marsh, *Report on Social Security for Canada 1943* (Toronto: University of Toronto Press, 1945); Gary Evans, *John Grierson and the National Film Board, 1939–1945* (Toronto: University of Toronto Press, 1984); and E.R. Forbes, "Consolidating Disparity: The Maritimes and the Industrialization of Canada during the Second World War," *Acadiensis* 15, 2 (Spring 1986). For a discussion of labour policy during the war, see Bryan Palmer, *Canadian Working-Class History: Character of Class Struggle* (Toronto: McClelland and Stewart, 1986); Irving Abella, *Nationalism, Communism and Canadian Labour* (Toronto: University of Toronto Press, 1973); and Laurel Sefton MacDowell, "The Formation of the Canadian Industrial Relations System during World War II," *Labour/Le Travailleur* 3 (1978).

The treatment of minorities is the subject of Norman Hillmer, Bohdan Kordan, and Lubomyr Luciuk, eds., *On Guard for Thee: War, Ethnicity, and the Canadian State, 1939–1945* (Ottawa; Canadian Committee for the History of the Second World War, 1988); Irving Abella and Harold Troper, *None Is Too Many* (Toronto: Lester and Orpen Dennys, 1982); Daniel Dancocks, *In Enemy Hands: Canada's Prisoners of War, 1939–1945* (Edmonton: Hurtig, 1983); Marjorie Wrong, *The Dragon and the Maple Leaf: Chinese Canadians in World War II* (Toronto: Dundurn Press, 1994); and Tom Socknat, *Witness Against War: Pacificism in Canada, 1900–1945* (Toronto: University of Toronto Press, 1987).

Security and intelligence are the subject of John Bryden, *Best-Kept Secret: Canadian Secret Intelligence in the Second World War* (Toronto: Lester, 1993); Gregory S. Kealey and Reg Whitaker, eds., *RCMP Security Bulletins: The War Series*, 2 vols. (St John's: Canadian Committee on Labour History 1989, 1993); and Larry Hannant, *The Infernal Machine: Investigating the Loyalties of Canada's Citizens* (Toronto: University of Toronto Press, 1995).

On Newfoundland in this period, see Peter Neary, *Newfoundland and the North Atlantic World, 1929–1949* (Montreal: McGill-Queen's University Press, 1988), and the useful synthesis by James K. Hiller, "Newfoundland Confronts Canada, 1867–1949," in *The Atlantic Provinces in Confederation*, ed. E.R. Forbes and D.A. Muise (Toronto: University of Toronto Press, 1993).

On the Japanese evacuation, see Ken Adachi, *The Enemy that Never Was* (Toronto: McClelland and Stewart, 1976); Ann Gomer Sunahara, *The Politics of Racism* (Toronto: Lorimer, 1981); W. Peter Ward, *White Canada Forever: Popular Attitudes and Public Policy toward Orientals in British Columbia* (Montreal: McGill-Queen's University Press, 1978); and Pat Roy et al., *Mutual Hostages: Canadians and Japanese During the Second World War* (Toronto: University of Toronto Press, 1989).

On foreign policy during the war, see James Eayrs, *In Defence of Canada*, vol. 2: *Appeasement and Rearmament* (Toronto: University of Toronto Press, 1965); Stanley Dziuban, *Military Relations Between Canada and the United States, 1939–1945* (Washington: Office of the Chief of Military History, Dept. of the Army, 1959); and two books by J.L. Granatstein and Norman Hillmer: *For Better or For Worse: Canada and the United States to the 1990s* (Toronto: Copp Clark Pitman, 1991) and *Empire to Umpire: Canada and the World to the 1990s* (Toronto: Copp Clark Longman, 1994).

War's end is described in Desmond Morton and J.L. Granatstein, *Victory 1945: Canadians from War to Peace* (Toronto: HarperCollins, 1995). On the Halifax riots of 1945, see Graham Metson, *An East Coast Port: Halifax at War, 1939–1945* (Scarborough: McGraw-Hill Ryerson, 1981); and Stanley Redman, *Open Gangway: The (Real) Story of the Halifax Navy Riot* (Hantsport, NS: Lancelot Press, 1981). The experience of the war brides is described in Joyce Hibbert, *The War Brides* (Toronto: Peter Martin Associates, 1978).

Farley Mowat has produced two evocative memoirs of his wartime experience: *The Regiment* (Toronto: McClelland and Stewart, 1973) and *And No Birds Sang* (Toronto: McClelland and Stewart, 1979). See also Barry Broadfoot, *The Veterans' Years* (Toronto: Douglas and McIntyre, 1985); Murray Peden, *A Thousand Shall Fall* (Stittsville, ON: Canada's Wings, 1979); and E.L.M. Burns, *General Mud* (Toronto: Clarke Irwin, 1970). Heather Robertson offers a fine sampling of Canada's war art in *A Terrible Beauty: The Art of Canada at War* (Toronto: Lorimer, 1977).

3

# REINVENTING CANADA, 1945–1997

# T I M E   L I N E

| | |
|---|---|
| **1945** | • Gouzenko revelations |
| **1946** | • Special joint committee of House and Senate reviews Indian Act |
| **1947** | • Marshall Plan; GATT Agreement; oil strike at Leduc, Alberta, begins western oil boom |
| **1948-57** | • Louis St Laurent's Liberals form government in Ottawa |
| **1949** | • Creation of NATO; Newfoundland joins Canada; Asbestos strike |
| **1950-53** | • Korean War |
| **1951** | • Universal old age pension approved by Parliament |
| **1952** | • Atomic Energy of Canada created; first Canadian television stations begin operation |
| **1954** | • Canada joins International Control Commission for Indochina; NATO proclaims a nuclear-centred strategy; St Lawrence Seaway agreement |
| **1956** | • Suez Crisis; pipeline debate in Parliament |
| **1957** | • Murdochville strike; hospitalization insurance and equalization grants approved by Parliament; Canada Council created |
| **1957-63** | • John Diefenbaker serves as prime minister |
| **1958** | • Canada signs NORAD agreement; Board of Broadcast Governors established |
| **1959** | • Defence Production Sharing Agreement; Newfoundland loggers' strike; opening of St Lawrence Seaway; cancellation of AVRO Arrow development |
| **1960** | • Contraceptive pill first introduced; Lesage Liberals win Quebec election |
| **1961** | • New Democratic Party created |
| **1962** | • Canada launches Alouette 1; medicare implemented in Saskatchewan; liberalization of Immigration Act |
| **1963** | • Major powers sign a nuclear test ban treaty; nuclear weapons for Canada debated in federal election |
| **1963-68** | • Lester Pearson leads a minority Liberal government in Ottawa |
| **1965** | • Lester Pearson criticizes American policy in Vietnam; Canada and Quebec Pension Plans established; Canada's new flag proclaimed; Auto Pact signed |
| **1966** | • Canada Assistance Plan introduced |
| **1967** | • Centennial celebrations; Expo '67 in Montreal; Further liberalization of Immigration Act |
| **1968** | • Parti québécois formed; formation of National Indian Brotherhood; national medicare implemented |
| **1968-79** | • Pierre Elliott Trudeau serves as prime minister |
| **1969** | • Official Languages Act; reform of Criminal Code relating to homosexuality, abortion, and birth control; White Paper on Indian policy released |

| | |
|---|---|
| **1970** | • Report of the Royal Commission on the Status of Women; October Crisis; War Measures Act proclaimed |
| **1971** | • Canada Development Corporation established |
| **1972** | • United Nations Conference on the Human Environment; National Action Committee on the Status of Women created |
| **1973** | • OPEC oil embargo sparks an "energy crisis" |
| **1974** | • Foreign Investment Review Agency created |
| **1975** | • Creation of Petro-Canada; Alberta Heritage Trust Fund established; James Bay Native land settlement signed |
| **1976** | • Parti québécois forms Quebec government |
| **1977** | • Established Programs Funding replaces block funding for medicare and postsecondary institutions; Berger report on Mackenzie Valley Pipeline released |
| **1979-80** | • Joe Clark heads federal government |
| **1980** | • Announcement of National Energy Program; Quebec referendum rejects sovereignty-association |
| **1980-84** | • Pierre Trudeau serves as prime minister |
| **1981-82** | • Major global recession |
| **1982** | • Constitution Act proclaimed |
| **1984** | • John Turner is prime minister from June to September; Brian Mulroney's Conservatives win federal election; Bhopal disaster |
| **1984-93** | • Brian Mulroney's Conservatives govern Canada |
| **1985** | • Macdonald Commission report; Alberta Microchip Centre established |
| **1987** | • Meech Lake Accord approved unanimously by premiers; Reform Party established |
| **1988** | • Canada and the United States sign a free trade agreement |
| **1989** | • Ottawa establishes Canadian space agency; Audrey McLaughlin becomes first woman to lead federal political party |
| **1990** | • Meech Lake Accord dies; Bloc québécois created; major recession begins in Canada |
| **1992** | • North American Free Trade Agreement signed; Charlottetown Accord defeated in national referendum; collapse of the east coast cod fish stocks |
| **1993** | • Kim Campbell becomes briefly Canada's first woman prime minister; Jean Chrétien's Liberals win federal election |
| **1995** | • "No" side wins a slim victory in second Quebec referendum on sovereignty |
| **1997** | • Chrétien's Liberals win federal election |

In the half century following the Second World War, Canada emerged as one of the world's great industrial nations, with all the benefits and problems associated with its new status. Wealth continued to be unequally distributed, but the state assumed increasing responsibility for ensuring the basic welfare of all Canadians. No longer tied to the apron strings of Great Britain, Canadians developed a stronger sense of their own identity. The arts flourished, buoyed by the new prosperity and government grants. As the centennial of Confederation approached, many Canadians felt that they, at long last, had something to celebrate, and Ottawa hosted a birthday party worthy of a great nation. Yet the country's survival remained at risk, threatened both by a sovereignty movement in Quebec and by the overwhelming impact of the United States on Canadian economic, political, and cultural life. The Cold War, which periodically threatened to become hot in the 1950s and 1960s, helped to impress the American view of the world on the consciousness of Canadians. After 1975, the Cold War began to thaw, and by 1989 communism was on the run. By that time, the challenges of the global corporate economy had locked Canada into a continental embrace and a mean-spirited approach to public policy that left many Canadians worried about what the new millennium had in store for them.

# CHAPTER 12

## REDEFINING LIBERALISM: THE CANADIAN STATE, 1945–1975

An exchange of letters between a prominent Canadian businessman and a socialist, feminist member of Parliament in 1972 revealed a great deal about the poles of political debate in postwar Canada. Taking exception to a speech in Parliament by Grace MacInnis, New Democrat MP for Vancouver-Kingsway, Eric Harrington, president of Canada Vickers Ltd., wrote, in part:

> Could you please tell me what on earth "day centres" of which you claim we need 130 000 and "family planning centres" of which you claim we need 700 have to do with "equal rights for women?"

> Surely family planning and day-care centres for children are purely a family responsibility and a personal matter and don't have a damn thing to do with equal rights.

> Please all of you, stay out of our family affairs and our bedrooms, leave our children alone and do some planning that might help the economy, the unemployment situation and a hundred other more important problems on which to date you have been ineffectual.[1]

MacInnis replied pointedly:

> The fact that you can believe that family planning and day care centres for children are purely a family responsibility and a personal matter, indicates very clearly that you enjoy an income standard where you and those who surround you are well able to handle such matters from your own resources. Such, I regret to have to tell you, is not the case for a very large percentage of the Canadian people.[2]

With the war over and memories of the Great Depression very much alive, Canadians developed a much greater sense of entitlement than they had felt in earlier periods. A decent income, quality medical care, pensions, childcare, a minimum standard of housing: none of these were seen as rights of citizenship before the war. Rather they were goals that individuals could set for themselves and work to attain in the marketplace. Scarred by the economic devastation of the 1930s and impressed by their government's ability to plan for war, Canadians were increasingly won over to the argument that planning for peacetime purposes could prevent another depression. Having made sacrifices during six long years of war, Canadians believed they had won the right to a large measure of social security and the state was seen as the principal vehicle for providing that security and making life better for all citizens.

This chapter traces the changing role of the Canadian state in the period from 1945 to 1975, a period often described as embodying a "postwar liberal consensus." The liberalism of this consensus was very different from the traditional liberalism of the prewar period. Liberalism had tended to mean freedom from the intervention of the state: it embodied such principles as freedom of trade, freedom of speech, and freedom of worship. The new liberalism, while confirming support for such goals, emphasized freedom from want. Recognizing that it was the marketplace that created inequalities in the distribution of wealth, the postwar consensus held that state intervention, rather than being the enemy of liberalism, was its essence, provided that the state limited its intervention to the economic sphere. As the Harrington–MacInnis exchange demonstrates, there was much debate about the limits of that sphere. Indeed, beneath the surface, the old liberalism and the new remained at odds about how, if at all, a state intervening to produce greater equality could be reconciled with a free-enterprise economy.

While the term welfare state is often used to describe the programs that were meant to give cradle-to-grave security to citizens, the term is elusive. Supporters of the new liberalism defined the welfare state as the broad set of programs by which the state ensured a guaranteed minimum income and social opportunities for all citizens as a matter of right. Minimum wages and programs for employment creation, farm subsidies, and public education were included in the definition; so, too, were universal programs, such as medical insurance, and narrower programs, such as social assistance and old age pensions, that targeted certain groups. Opponents of an expansion of state intervention for the purpose of redistributing wealth put a different spin on the welfare state. They often focused on social assistance and unemployment insurance—programs that provided money to able-bodied people without jobs—in contrast to less controversial forms of state aid, such as education for the young and pensions for the old. Programs such as unemployment insurance, they claimed, robbed people

of initiative, cost too much money, and led to too much government involvement in people's lives.

## FEDERAL PARTIES AND LEADERS

Recognizing the widespread appeal of new social programs, both the Liberals and the Conservatives embraced the welfare state in the federal election of 1945. With the established parties promising them full employment and an array of new social programs, most Canadians saw no need to take a chance on the radical and inexperienced CCF.

Before the Second World War, the Liberal and Conservative Parties were both patronage machines controlled by business interests and elite professional groups, but their programs had different emphases. The Liberals were continentalists and, however marginally in practice, were disposed to support free trade and a foreign policy independent of Britain. The Conservatives were imperialists who, at least in theory, distrusted the Americans and sought greater empire trade and imperial unity in foreign policy. After the war, the empire quickly dissolved and Britain became a marginal player in international affairs, while international trade agreements largely removed the tariff as an issue in Canadian politics. The result was that, for a generation, there was little to differentiate the two major political parties in Canada. Both supported the basic premises of the Cold War, which, as we will discuss in chapter 13, led to closer continental ties in foreign and defence policy. Both favoured the cautious addition of social programs to appease public demands for social security. Neither was willing to condone a degree of state intervention that might alarm private investors. Personalities and regional interests, rather than overarching ideologies, determined the public image of the main parties. As first radio and later television became the major source of images and information for voters, party leaders attempted to project themselves as visionaries rather than as spokespersons for a particular ideology or cohesive program.

The Liberal victory in the 1945 election, though narrow, demonstrated that most Canadians judged the government's war effort favourably and put their faith in Mackenzie King's programs to prevent a postwar depression. King, however, remained a fiscal conservative, unwilling to sponsor a great deal of social experimentation. In 1948, King stepped down as prime minister and was succeeded by Louis St Laurent. Before entering public life during the war, St Laurent had been a successful lawyer who held a string of corporate directorships in Montreal. Pleased with their increased prosperity through much of the 1940s and 1950s, Canadians gave St Laurent resounding election victories in 1949 and 1953, during which time his avuncular style earned him the affectionate nickname "Uncle Louis." St Laurent was less suspicious than his predecessor of Canadian entanglements in foreign affairs and generally shared the American view of international events.

*John F. Kennedy, Governor General Georges Vanier, John Diefenbaker, Jacqueline Kennedy, and Olive Diefenbaker, Ottawa, 1961.*

National Archives of Canada/ PA154665

Support for the Liberals was weakened in 1956 when the government invoked closure on debate in the House of Commons over its controversial bill to support a private gas pipeline. Eventually tiring of the arrogance that twenty-two years in power seemed to have imparted to the Liberals, Canadians shifted their allegiance towards the Conservatives. John Diefenbaker formed a minority Conservative government in 1957 and then went on in 1958 to win the biggest electoral majority held by any government in Canada's first century—208 out of 256 seats.

Diefenbaker was a successful Saskatchewan lawyer with a burning ambition to succeed in politics. As a member of Parliament since 1940, he had become one of the more prominent figures in his party but had twice failed to win contests for national leader. After Conservative leaders John Bracken and George Drew had both failed

to defeat the Liberals, the party turned to the ambitious Saskatchewan MP. Sixty-one when he assumed his party's leadership in 1956, Diefenbaker was a powerful orator and liked to champion the cause of the underdog. His denunciation of the Liberal old age pension as too small, his call for a huge spending program to open up Canada's North, and his willingness to grant subsidies to the economically challenged Atlantic provinces demonstrated that the postwar Conservative need not be a fiscal conservative. His pursuit of closer trade and foreign policy ties between Canada and Britain suggested that old-style Tory imperialism might not be dead, but in practice he could not divert trade to Britain or remake that country into an independent player on the international scene. Despite his eventual defiance of the Americans on nuclear weapons policy, Diefenbaker and his cabinet appeared to waffle on most issues and to represent little ideological difference from the Liberals they had defeated.

Lester Pearson became Liberal leader shortly before the 1958 election that so humbled his party. A long-time bureaucrat in the Department of External Affairs, Pearson was deputy minister when his old boss, St Laurent, became prime minister and asked him to join the government as minister of external affairs. He remained at that post until the defeat of the Liberals in 1957. In that year, he won the prestigious Nobel Peace Prize for his role in helping to diffuse the Suez Crisis in 1956 and seemed the obvious choice to lead the Liberals when St Laurent retired.

As leader of the opposition, Pearson recommitted his party to implementing social programs that it had promised in 1945 but never fully delivered. Pearson formed minority governments in 1963 and 1965, dependent on support from the New Democratic Party, the successor of the CCF. The brief Pearson period would prove to be the heyday of social reform in twentieth-century Canada, with medicare capping a series of new programs designed to provide Canadians with a social safety net. By the time he left office, Pearson could boast that he had taken the reins of power in a country whose social programs were similar to those of the United States and in five short years had left the Americans in the dust.

Pierre Trudeau, elected Liberal leader and then prime minister in 1968, had the image of a reformer. The son of a Montreal millionaire, Trudeau was an intellectual and world traveller who had few real jobs to place on his résumé before he entered politics in the 1965 federal election. A one-time socialist and editor of the liberal but anti-nationalist Quebec journal *Cité Libre*, Trudeau was associated with progressive causes in his home province. He maintained this image in the federal arena. As justice minister from 1965 to 1968, he was responsible for legislation that removed the

*Pierre Elliot Trudeau.*
National Archives of Canada/ C25000

label of criminality from homosexual relations, liberalized divorce laws, and made abortion legal under some circumstances. Largely unknown to the Canadian public before he faced a Liberal leadership convention in 1968, Trudeau captured the public imagination with his promise to create a "just society." Cosmopolitan and debonair by Canadian political standards, he projected an image of a vigorous, trendy, forward-looking leader. The spellbound media lapped it up, and Trudeaumania was born. While leadership had always been an issue in Canadian politics, in the 1968 election (and many thereafter), it would overshadow substantive issues. In his sixteen years of government, Trudeau consolidated existing social and regulatory programs and proved responsive to new social forces within Canadian society. Nevertheless, the wave of reform that characterized the Pearson years ebbed as the economy slowed down in the early 1970s.

Throughout the thirty years under study, third parties played a role in the nation's politics. The CCF, at the top of the polls for part of the Second World War, was forced to accept third-party status at war's end. Reduced to an eight-member rump in Parliament in the Diefenbaker sweep of 1958, the CCF joined forces with organized labour in 1961 to create the New Democratic Party (NDP). Both the postwar CCF and the NDP were more moderate versions of the CCF that had been born in the Depression. In an attempt to shake off slanderous Cold War allegations that linked the party with communism, the CCF largely abandoned its commitment to public ownership. Instead, it favoured private enterprise, regulated by a strong state that was able to control the direction of the economy and implement extensive social programs and progressive taxation to redistribute wealth. Despite its third-party status, the CCF-NDP had a significant impact on policy. Both of the old-line parties assumed that if they did not implement the social programs demanded by Canadians, they could lose votes to the socialist upstart.

On the right of the political spectrum, Ernest Manning, the Social Credit premier of Alberta from 1944 to 1968, was apprehensive about the federal Conservative Party's embrace of the liberal postwar consensus. In the 1960s, he called for a realignment of Canada's political parties in which the Conservatives and Social Credit would unite to provide a truly conservative alternative. The unpopularity of such an idea was obvious during the 1967 Conservative leadership race to replace John Diefenbaker. The two leading candidates, Robert Stanfield and Duff Roblin, the former premiers of Nova Scotia and Manitoba, were both liberal-minded and had expanded the role of the state in the lives of residents of their respective provinces. Stanfield's early championing of the idea of a guaranteed annual income made him at least as liberal as most of the Liberal ministers he faced as leader of the opposition in the federal Parliament from 1967 to 1976.

Social Credit had faded as a force in federal politics in English Canada by the 1960s, but the Créditistes, the Quebec wing of the party, carried twenty-six of seventy-four federal seats in that province in the 1962 election. Although few believed that inflation of the money supply, the party's prescription for society's ills, was a panacea, many working-class and rural Québécois, dissatisfied with the traditional parties, regarded the Créditistes as a legitimate avenue of protest. The charismatic leadership of Réal Caouette and resentment against the power of the big banks over people's lives helped the Créditistes to make their breakthrough.

## PROVINCIAL POLITICS

The CCF-NDP governed Saskatchewan from 1944 to 1964 and pioneered hospital insurance and medicare in that province. NDP governments elected in Manitoba in 1969, Saskatchewan in 1971, and British Columbia in 1972 were responsible for a degree of social experimentation well exceeding that in the other provinces.

Social Credit's power base was also provincial. Its Alberta bastion was not successfully assaulted before Peter Lougheed's Conservatives upset thirty-six years of continuous rule in 1971. In 1952, Social Credit, led by the charismatic W.A.C. Bennett, began a twenty-year reign in British Columbia. In the postwar period, Social Credit, while maintaining its obsession with the power of financiers, was largely a right-wing party even more hostile to socialists than to bankers. Though the governments of Alberta and British Columbia embraced the new state interventionism in practice, their leaders denounced Canada's leftward drift.

In Quebec provincial politics, Duplessis's Union nationale provided a conservative administration until the death of *le chef* in 1959. Despite attempts by his successors to provide a more progressive face for the Union nationale, Quebec voters elected the Liberals in 1960 and 1962. That party proved both reformist and nationalist, but the pace of reforms left many behind, and the Union nationale was returned to office one last time in 1966. Thereafter, Quebec politics would polarize between the federalist Liberals and the sovereignist Parti québécois, formed in 1968.

Politics in the Atlantic provinces mirrored national politics: indistinguishable reform-minded Liberal and Conservative Parties differentiated in the public mind by the personalities of their lead-

*Ellen Fairclough was MP for Hamilton West from 1950 to 1963 and, in 1957, became the first woman to serve in the federal cabinet.*

City of Ottawa Archives/CA19893

ers. With the lowest standard of living in the country and a shrinking proportion of seats in the House of Commons, Atlantic Canadians felt that they had little choice other than to be allied to a national party that could throw some policy and patronage crumbs their way. Even in industrial Cape Breton, politics took a conservative turn in the 1950s. Meanwhile, the region's political leaders began cooperating across party lines to pressure Ottawa for policies that would lift the region from its economic doldrums. Atlantic premiers lobbied for special regional subsidies and development projects that would jump start their economies. Although their tactics brought some concessions, the region continued to lag behind the rest of the nation.

Ontario politics seemed the most predictable, with the Conservatives in power without interrup-

tion from 1943 to 1985, usually with a comfortable majority of seats in the legislature. While the CCF-NDP had only the most marginal success electing federal MPs in Ontario, the party usually had a thriving presence in the provincial legislature. The ruling Conservatives were sometimes called "Red Tories" because of their willingness to spend lavishly on education and health. While the government was prepared to spend money on programs that clearly benefited the middle class, it was more conservative on issues that involved the poor or working people. Despite the province's wealth, the government was no more eager than administrations in far poorer provinces to give social assistance recipients an income that would lift them out of poverty. Trade unions complained that the Tories were pro-business in areas such as minimum wage legislation and environmental regulation. Nonetheless, the level of state intervention seemed to satisfy a voting majority, whose attendance at the polls was increasingly assured by a well-funded, efficiently run party, referred to by supporters and opponents alike as the "Big Blue Machine."

## NEWFOUNDLAND ENTERS CONFEDERATION

Newfoundland's entry into Confederation serves to illustrate the impact of both the welfare state and the Cold War on post-war developments. While Canada's social programs proved enticing to many Newfoundlanders, the demands of the Cold War made Canada more eager than ever to accept the new province. Both Britain and the United States encouraged Canada to offer attractive terms to Newfoundland, which sat astride the sea lanes of the North Atlantic, and therefore played an important role in Cold War strategy.

In June 1946, Newfoundlanders elected delegates to a convention to determine their future political arrangements. Thirteen years of commission government meant that democratic traditions were rusty but old political divisions remained as vital as ever. While some people, especially in the outports, favoured Confederation with Canada, others, including many leaders of the Roman Catholic Church and the merchant community,

## SYMBOLS OF INDEPENDENCE

In the period after 1945, Canada moved quickly to break many ties that smacked of colonial subordination. The Canadian Citizenship Act of 1947 enabled immigrants, for the first time, to become citizens of Canada, as opposed to "British subjects." Shortly afterwards, Canada's Supreme Court became indeed supreme in legal matters, as appeals to the Judicial Committee of the Privy Council in Great Britain were abolished. In 1952, Vincent Massey became the first governor general to be named by the government of Canada rather than by the British government. He was also the first native-born Canadian to hold the post.

The flag debate of 1964 showed that some Canadians, particularly former prime minister John Diefenbaker, were unhappy with the severing of symbolic ties with Great Britain. The Pearson government proposed a distinctive Canadian flag with the maple leaf as the symbol of the nation. Diefenbaker's unsuccessful counter-proposal was a new flag that incorporated the Union Jack and the fleur-de-lys as a way of paying tribute to Canada's "two founding peoples." Such a proposal ignored not only Native peoples, but also the increasing numbers of Canadians whose origins were neither British nor French.

wanted Newfoundland to return to the status of a separate dominion with responsible government. Still others wanted to retain the commission government.

At the convention, Joey Smallwood emerged as the principal proponent of joining Canada. Journalist, trade unionist, and farmer, the colourful Smallwood promised escape from the old dominion politics and a better material life within Confederation. Not only would trade with Canada—which had grown dramatically during the war—continue to expand, but also economic uncertainty would be forever banished by the social safety net provided by family allowances, unemployment insurance, and old age pensions. St John's merchants presented a rather different picture of the Confederation option, suggesting that the fisheries and trade policies of the once-proud dominion would be controlled by foreign politicians.

When the convention failed to reach a consensus, it was decided that a referendum should be held to determine popular opinion. Newfoundlanders, like their convention delegates, remained divided, casting 44.6 percent of their votes in the 3 June 1948 referendum for responsible government, 41.1 percent for Confederation, and 14.3 percent for retaining the commission government. A second referendum on 2 July removed the commission government option and resulted in a less-than-convincing 52.4 percent in favour of

Confederation with Canada. Soon afterwards, the terms of union were finalized and on 31 March 1949, Newfoundland became the tenth province of Canada, rounding out the nation from the Atlantic to the Pacific. Smallwood's Liberals won the first provincial elections in May 1949 and he remained premier of Newfoundland until forced to resign in January 1972 after the Conservatives, under the leadership of Frank Moores, finally toppled "the only living Father of Confederation."

## POLITICS AND REPRESENTATION

The federal Parliament and provincial legislatures remained largely the privileged arena of wealthy white males of British and, in the case of Quebec, French extraction. The upper levels of the civil service were staffed with men from the same backgrounds. As the period progressed, there were slight gains for groups outside this dominant circle. In 1951, Thérèse Casgrain became leader of the Quebec CCF. While Grace MacInnis was the only woman in Parliament from 1968 to 1972, five women were elected in 1972 and eight in 1974. A few women held cabinet posts, beginning with Ellen Fairclough, who was appointed by John Diefenbaker. After Lester Pearson appointed Judy LaMarsh to cabinet, Pauline Jewett, a Liberal backbencher who was a well-known political scientist, indicated that she would be proud to serve in cabinet as well. Pearson replied that she would make a good minister but that LaMarsh had no intention of retiring. The implication was clear: one token woman per cabinet was the quota.

Not all politicians came from French or English backgrounds. Diefenbaker was partly of German-Canadian extraction, as was Ed Schreyer, who became Manitoba's first NDP premier in 1969. Herb Gray was appointed by Pierre Trudeau to cabinet, becoming the first Jew to hold such a position; Dave Barrett, the first NDP premier of British Columbia, was also of Jewish descent. The successes of ethnic immigrants were especially noticeable at the civic level. Steven Juba served as mayor of Winnipeg for two decades, William Hawrelak was mayor of Edmonton for several terms during the 1950s to the 1970s, and Nathan Phillips, who was Jewish, served as mayor of Toronto. Visible minority Canadians fared less well and were rarely elected to legislatures or to Parliament. Dave Barrett's cabinet included one Native, and his caucus included two African Canadians. One of these was Rosemary Brown, who won 37 percent of the ballots for the NDP federal leadership in 1974 in a contest with Ed Broadbent.

## SHAPING THE WELFARE STATE

The postwar welfare state had an inauspicious start. Shortly after the 1945 election, Mackenzie King called the Dominion–Provincial Conference on Reconstruction. The federal government's Green Book of proposals prepared for the conference called for comprehensive national programs to take care of the old, the sick, and the unemployed. Declaring unemployment a problem that the federal government must handle, the Green Book also included support for public works to coincide with economic downturns. To fund these costly endeavours, Ottawa suggested it would require exclusive rights to income and corporate taxes and to succession duties. The provinces, led by Ontario and Quebec, argued that they could not surrender all major taxes and still fulfil their responsibilities. After meeting with the provinces over a period of nine months, the federal government announced

that the talks had collapsed.

By this time, the conservative forces in Canadian society had rallied to try to limit federal social reforms. The social radicalism of the Depression and the war had jarred many pro-business groups, such as the Canadian Chamber of Commerce, into supporting a degree of social reform, but they reverted to conservative positions once the predicted postwar depression failed to materialize. The country could not afford to implement a variety of social programs at once, such critics argued, warning that if corporate taxation were to be the source of revenues for welfare, private investment would quickly dry up. The Canadian Medical Association, a wartime supporter of national prepaid medical insurance, recognized that a return to depression conditions, in which even middle-class Canadians could not pay their doctors, was unlikely. It increasingly supported private, doctor-controlled medical insurance schemes and rejected a state medicare program.

## THE ORIGINS OF MEDICARE

While physicians argued that doctor-controlled and voluntary private insurance schemes were preferable to a state program forcing all doctors and patients to enrol, national public opinion had long been against them. In 1944 and again in 1949, 80 percent of Canadians indicated their approval of a federal health plan that would cover complete medical and hospital care for a monthly flat rate. Governments initially rejected the call for universal medical and hospital insurance, but took steps to improve medical services. They put more money into hospitals, and most provinces paid medical bills for the poorest of the poor. In 1957, a hospital insurance program with costs shared by the provincial and federal governments was implemented.

Prosperity allowed more people to consult doctors and to access hospital services, but prosperity was uneven. The regional distribution of medical personnel paralleled regional patterns of wealth distribution. Although Canadians collectively had one doctor to serve every 938 people in 1959, much more favourable ratios were found in

Ontario, British Columbia, and Alberta. In Newfoundland, there was only one doctor for every 2190 residents. The gap in dental services, which were generally deemed inadequate everywhere in the country, was more extreme—one dentist to every 2400 British Columbians but only one for every 11 000 in Newfoundland; if St John's and Corner Brook were excluded, the figure for dental care in the province was one dentist for every 30 859 people.

The lack of local medical services caused the Newfoundland Federation of Labour to mock the slogans on the posters that Ontario public health organizations sent around to schools:

> "Brush your teeth three times a day and see your dentist twice a year" say posters in the school. The dentist is 150 miles away.

> "Fight cancer with a checkup and a cheque." The checkup means a trip by coastal boat to a doctor with no training or equipment to diagnose cancer.

> "Prize your eyes" says the CNIB. But on the coast of Labrador or at the head of Bay d'Espoir, there has never been an eye specialist, not even in transit.[3]

By 1960, almost half of Canadians had purchased private medical insurance, but most plans covered only diagnostic and curative services, and not dental care, prescription drugs, preventive services, or mental health care. Given the level of poverty in Atlantic Canada, it is not surprising that coverage in that region was 50 percent less than for the country as a whole. In the Prairie provinces, coverage was much lower in rural areas than in cities.

John Diefenbaker established a Royal Commission on Health Services in 1961. Its report, submitted to the Pearson government in 1964, called for a universal medicare scheme embracing hospital, physician, dental, and prescription costs. The Liberals made medicare an issue in the 1965 election and, on their return to office, announced what was to be the first stage of a national health insurance program.

While to some extent a response to the royal commission, the government's action also owed

much to the province of Saskatchewan, which had introduced medicare in 1962. The province had persisted with its legislation, despite a strike by its doctors. To encourage compliance, the government gave in to demands that physicians receive fees for service rather than salaries and that medical treatment continue to be dispensed from physicians' offices rather than from community health clinics integrating the services of a variety of health professionals.

The federal plan added physician care and the services of some non-physician specialists to the earlier federal-provincial hospital insurance scheme. Ottawa would share costs with the provinces if provincial programs adhered to four principles: universality of coverage; coverage of most medical treatment; portability of benefits; and provincial administration. Although every province except Saskatchewan and British Columbia criticized the federal plan, by 1970 all provinces had established programs embodying the four federal principles.

## WELFARE REFORM

While the jewel in the crown of the Pearson social programs was universal medicare, there were other significant reforms as well, beginning with the introduction of the Canada Pension Plan, an earnings-related pension, in 1965. Recognizing that it was impossible to live on the old age pension alone, and that many pensioners had no other resources, Pearson introduced the Guaranteed Income Supplement in 1966. Low-interest loans for postsecondary students also made their appearance in 1966. The Canada Assistance Plan (CAP) of the same year built upon the 1956 cost-sharing agreement on welfare and assured all Canadians of the right to receive social assistance. CAP established national guidelines that provinces were obliged to incorporate in their welfare programs in order to receive federal assistance.

There is no doubt that CAP produced improvements in the lives of poor Canadians. Marion Dewar, executive director of the Canadian Council on Children and Youth and former mayor of Ottawa, recalled in 1990:

> When I was nursing with the Victorian Order of Nurses in the early 1960s, it was a very different society from the one we live in today. We gave bedbaths to elderly people living in cold rooms, or living with relatives who refused to feed them. I particularly recall one woman who had suffered a stroke. She had lost her ability to speak. I went in once a month to see her at first. Each visit she clutched my uniform and pointed to her mouth. I realized she was hungry. I started going in two or three times a week. I would bring her soup and feed her. When government assistance became available, she went to live in a nursing home....
>
> In those days welfare was granted to those persons whom local politicians decided to give it to. If you were a young person out of work, very often having run away from an abusive home, you could be refused welfare. If you were a juvenile, you could

be sent to one of the "reform schools," in some of which, we are hearing today, the young people were abused.[4]

## CANADA'S WELFARE STATE IN PERSPECTIVE

How did Canadian efforts in the social policy arena compare with those of other countries? Critics of big government point to the rapid increase in Canadian social expenditures. According to the Organization for Economic Co-operation and Development (OECD), the cost rose from 12.1 to 21.7 percent of gross domestic product from 1960 to 1981. Less publicized was the modest extent of government spending on social programs relative to other OECD countries, including some of the world's most competitive trading nations. West Germany had the OECD's largest per capita social expenditures in 1960, and yet it continued to post the greatest productivity

### A WELFARE FAMILY

The new social welfare programs made a difference in the lives of many families. The Jackson family of Toronto serves as an example. A young couple with five children, the Jacksons came to the attention of the welfare authorities when the Juvenile Court received word of the destructive behaviour of their son Richard, age four and a half. The court referred the boy to the Hospital for Sick Children, which, in turn, suggested that Richard spend part of his day at the Victoria Day Nursery.

Social workers who visited the Jacksons found the parents "plagued by ill health, marital strife, debts, and the demands of five children." Discouragement had created an abusive atmosphere, and the parents had all but given up hope that they could successfully raise their brood. The social workers were able to use state funds to intervene in a variety of ways. Medical attention was arranged for Mrs Jackson, who suffered from rheumatic heart disease. While she recovered, a homemaker was provided to help with the housework. Childcare was arranged for the periods when Mrs Jackson needed to visit doctors. The Jacksons were given counselling about budgeting and Mrs Jackson was advised to find

part-time work. As for Richard, his behaviour quickly improved in the day nursery, and he was able to attend regular school classes a year later. "After two years, this family, once about to fly apart, was functioning adequately on its own."[5]

From a conservative perspective, this family might be said to have lost its independence to a group of meddling employees of the state. From a radical perspective, it was a victim of inadequate wages and the lack of guaranteed medical provisions and universal day care. From a feminist perspective, the social workers might be criticized for having focused mainly on changing Mrs Jackson's behaviour, leaving this frail woman to eventually take responsibility again for all of the household work, as well as working outside the home. Nevertheless, the social workers believed that they had made the dysfunctional Jackson family a functioning unit within the existing social framework, and that, given the resources, they could perform the same task with thousands of other "problem families." What the Jacksons themselves thought of all this, we simply do not know.

gains of any OECD country. Sweden, Italy, Austria, and the Netherlands, all successful in global trade, also exceeded Canada in growth and volume of social expenditures.

Pensions are a case in point. By 1981, Canada devoted less of its GDP to public pensions than any other industrialized country. The Canada Pension Plan had, from the beginning, kept rates low to appease private insurance companies. Even with the Guaranteed Income Supplement, pensioners could not maintain a decent standard of living unless they had other income. Private pensions failed to make up the difference: among western

| Table 12.1 |
| :--- |

### SOCIAL EXPENDITURES BY COUNTRY
(PERCENTAGE OF GROSS DOMESTIC PRODUCT)

| Country | 1960 | 1981 |
| :--- | :--- | :--- |
| Belgium | 17.0 | 38.0 |
| Netherlands | 16.3 | 36.1 |
| Sweden | 14.5 | 33.5 |
| Germany | 20.5 | 31.5 |
| Italy | 16.5 | 29.1 |
| Denmark | 10.2 | 29.0 |
| Austria | 17.9 | 27.9 |
| Ireland | 11.7 | 27.1 |
| Norway | 11.7 | 27.1 |
| United Kingdom | 13.9 | 24.9 |
| France | 13.4 | 23.8 |
| Canada | 12.1 | 21.7 |
| United States | 10.9 | 21.0 |
| New Zealand | 13.0 | 19.6 |
| Australia | 10.2 | 18.6 |
| Japan | 8.0 | 17.5 |

*Source: OECD Bulletin, no. 146 (Jan. 1984). Reprinted in Andrew Armitage, Social Welfare in Canada: Ideas, Realities and Future Paths, 2nd ed. (Toronto: McClelland and Stewart, 1988), 22*

democracies, only the United States had less private pension protection than Canada. In 1980, 44 percent of paid workers in Canada had private pension plan coverage. By contrast, 90 percent of workers in Sweden, 80 percent in France, 60 percent in West Germany, and 50 percent in Britain enjoyed such coverage. The lowest-paid workers were most likely to have no pension coverage at all. While only 9.4 percent of Canadians earning under $7500 in 1979 had pension plans, 76.4 percent of

those earning over $30 000 had coverage. Lack of portability of most plans meant that many workers nominally covered by pension plans would never collect from them. It was not surprising, then, that Statistics Canada reported in 1980 that 27 percent of seniors lived on "limited incomes" and that the percentage for elderly women was even higher.

The Canadian version of the welfare state generally treated women less fairly than men. Canadian pensions, which were calculated on the basis of individual earnings, penalized women on two fronts: first, women workers earned on average far less than men; second, many women withdrew completely from the labour force to raise their children. Unemployment insurance policy was also discriminatory. Men could leave jobs for any reason and, if they had worked the required number of weeks, collect unemployment insurance, provided they demonstrated that they were making reasonable efforts to find new work. Women who quit or were forced to leave a job during a pregnancy or after giving birth were deemed ineligible to collect unemployment insurance, even if they were looking for work. Women's organizations and the labour movement successfully campaigned to have this exclusion lifted.

In contrast, the Canada Assistance Plan was less discriminatory. It made state assistance, however modest, available to all women without male partners, including single and divorced mothers, rather than leaving provinces and municipalities the right to determine which "undeserving" women did not qualify for welfare. But "man-in-the-house" rules persisted in most jurisdictions, and a woman could be cut off social assistance if it was discovered that a man was spending the night at her house. In Ontario, volunteers from charitable organizations carried out surveillance of the moral behaviour of mothers' allowance recipients. Welfare rights groups protested the assumption that suggested a man must be providing economic support to a woman who was his sexual partner, but the rules for assistance changed only slowly.

The 1970 *Report of the Royal Commission on the Status of Women* argued that a major barrier to women's economic equality was the lack of affordable day care. Women were assigned the responsi-

## DAY CARE AND THE NEW LIBERALISM

Speaking to the Canadian Chamber of Commerce in October 1946, Laura Hardy, president of the National Council of Women of Canada, stated: "As women, we want to live in a Canada in which we can raise our children in our own homes and in the schools of our choice, not in public institutions under the guidance of the State."[6] Hardy did not oppose the federal government's withdrawal of funds from day-care centres at the end of the Second World War. Her organization, while supporting a woman's right to work, tended to believe this right did not apply to married women with young children. In this, the council spoke for most Canadians. A Gallup poll in 1960 indicated that 93 percent of Canadians opposed the idea of mothers of young children working outside the home; ten years later, 80 percent remained opposed.

For both economic and personal reasons, many married women with children worked outside the home. The old liberalism dictated that the state should not intervene in a family's decision about how to care for children, but the new welfare state liberalism suggested that the government had an obligation to ensure affordable, quality day care for children of working parents. In practice, in the 1950s, only Ontario had developed systematic licensing of day-care centres; only Ontario and British Columbia had modest programs of subsidized dayhomes. Even in these two provinces, most working parents relied on private arrangements for childcare.

Studies by women's groups and social agencies pointed to the inadequacies of such haphazard arrangements. Forced by economic desperation to work, yet unable to find affordable and reliable childcare centres, women sometimes left very young children with abusive, neglectful, or alcoholic caregivers. Social policy researchers documented a variety of cases of children warehoused in quarters infested with parasites, in facilities without toys or play areas, and in spaces so cramped that closets became sleep areas. In the first four months of 1979, ten babysitters in Calgary were charged in unrelated incidents with sexual attacks on young children.

Immigrant families often kept school-age children home to look after younger siblings. A disturbing number of children, including pre-schoolers, spent much of the day alone. Social workers and women's groups maintained that it was time to stop arguing about whether it was desirable that mothers work, recognize that many were working, and insist that the state assist them to find quality, affordable day care.

Speaking before the Royal Commission on the Status of Women, the president of the Kingcrest Business and Professional Women's Club in Vancouver related the circumstances of one family. In order to buy a house, both parents were working, and their two preschoolers were briefly left alone each day. The mother had commented that the entire family, "even the little children," were cooperating so that the family would not be forced to live in a cramped apartment with no yard for the children to play in. As the club president told the royal commission, "With great anguish in my heart, I walked away but those words never left me. 'Even the little children cooperate,' why couldn't our government, I thought?"[7]

Such sentiments had only a modest impact on public policy. After the mid-1960s, several provincial governments began to provide childcare subsidies for the neediest families, but the provinces proved as unwilling as the federal government to fund universal, public day care. While none of Canada's political parties made childcare a priority, some parties were more sympathetic than others to the issue. When Social Credit was voted out of office in British Columbia in September 1972, twenty-six hundred children received subsidized day care in the province. By the end of 1973, the new NDP administration was providing subsidies for ninety-five hundred children.

bility for childcare, but had little government support, except for family allowances, whose value over time had been eroded by Ottawa's failure to peg rates to inflation. If a mother of young children worked outside the home, she generally found that the costs of good private childcare were prohibitive. The royal commission concluded: "Parents require supplementary help, and society may legitimately be called upon to contribute to community services for its younger generation. The equality of women means little without such a programme, which should include ... day-care centres."[8]

In some countries, notably Sweden and France, state programs of free day care for all children had contributed to dramatic reductions in the rates of poverty for single mothers and fairer distribution of income between men and women. The royal commission recommended a more modest national program funded in part by user fees geared to income. Concern about rising social costs and a general indifference to gender equality led most governments to shelve this recommendation from the commissioners.

## HOUSING POLICY

While discussions about the cost of state-sponsored social programs tended to assume that the poor were the main recipients, this was not always the case. In 1954, a government body, the Canadian Mortgage and Housing Corporation (CMHC), hoping to encourage more private initiative, agreed to guarantee mortgages from private financial companies. To reduce the potential for default, CMHC limited its loan guarantees to middle-and-upper-income Canadians. Little government aid was available to renters, despite campaigns by trade unions, women's groups, and the Canadian Legion. Although the beginnings of state-subsidized senior citizens' housing were in evidence by the late 1950s, few public housing units were built for families before the 1960s.

In the 1960s, provincial governments begrudgingly admitted that the market economy would not adequately house all Canadians. The Ontario Housing Corporation was established in 1964; by 1972, it managed fifty thousand units of public housing, including units purchased on the private market as well as publicly built developments. Other provinces had similar, if less ambitious, programs. Federal funds made available to the provinces for social housing on a cost-sharing basis were not fully tapped, except by Ontario, and by Manitoba once the NDP came to power in that province. Most of the public-housing developments built in the 1960s and 1970s were notable for overcrowding, cheapness of construction, and lack of green space. Residents created committees to complain about pipes that froze every winter, inadequate heating systems, and cracking plaster.

Their homes were a stark contrast to suburban houses whose mortgages were guaranteed and subsidized by state funds. Yet the former, not the latter, were referred to as "welfare housing."

## THE PROVINCES AND THE NEW LIBERALISM

The provinces extended their social welfare policies in areas other than public housing. The new liberalism required of provincial governments that they make social services and educational opportunities available on a more equitable basis throughout the province rather than allowing local councils and school boards to determine what services their area could afford. Provinces provided funds for new schools, universities, hospitals, and highways. Provincial bursaries allowed bright children from lower-income families to attend universities.

To allow poorer provinces to provide education, health, and social services comparable to those in the wealthier provinces, generous equalization payments were built into the tax system in 1956. All provinces received per capita grants from Ottawa based on the average revenues of the two wealthiest provinces, British Columbia and Ontario. The percentage of federal corporate and personal income taxes that was rebated to provinces rose gradually from a mere 5 percent just after the Second World War to 24 percent by the early 1960s. Federal cost-sharing programs and grants enriched provincial coffers but created the threat of federal interference. Alberta's Social Credit government, for example, objected to federal insistence that it stop charging user fees for hospital care if it wished to be eligible for its full grant under the hospital insurance scheme.

At the same time, the Atlantic provinces, the losers in the liberal consensus, had little choice other than to become dependent on federal largesse. University of Toronto economist Harold Innis, writing to the premier of Nova Scotia, Angus L. Macdonald, in 1946, had noted prophetically: "I have always felt that these various devices for full employment implied grave dangers for the Maritimes in that full employment is apt to mean prosperity on the St Lawrence and the continued steady drain of population and revenues from the Maritimes."[9] The truth of that statement was confirmed in the ensuing decade. In 1958, the federal government established subsidies in the form of Atlantic Provinces Adjustment Grants in recognition of the region's difficult position. The three Maritime provinces benefited absolutely from this transfer of moneys, but Newfoundland approached the grant from a different perspective. Having entered Confederation in 1949 with a special subsidy to keep its services equal to those of the Maritime provinces, it soon became just one of four poor provinces with claims on Ottawa.

Transfer payments were not the only federal schemes to help the have-not provinces. Ottawa also implemented a variety of targeted development programs. For example in the early 1960s, the government passed the Agriculture Rehabilitation and Development Act, which poured money into rural areas to improve efficiency in the development of local resources and to create alternative employment in depressed regions.

Both the federal and provincial governments attempted to lure industries into depressed provinces as well as to the poorer regions of wealthy provinces. Unwilling to have the state itself take an entrepreneurial role, governments searched for private investors upon whom they could lavish government funds in return for promises to establish new industries. The major recipients of regional assistance grants were corporations. The 1960 federal budget allowed firms double the normal tax advantage for capital expenditures if they located in areas designated as slow growth. In the 1960s and 1970s, garment firms that set up what amounted to low-wage sweatshops in rural areas of Manitoba, for instance, received a dizzying array of federal, provincial, and municipal subsidies. These

included grants to introduce new technologies, "forgivable loans" from the federal government, federal wage subsidies, tax concessions, government-paid training for employees, subsidized hydro-electricity rates, and reduced tariffs on fabrics. Despite such programs, business leaders took great exception to federal NDP leader David Lewis's remarks in the 1972 federal election criticizing "corporate welfare bums."

With its floundering economy, Atlantic Canada pursued several notable development programs, most to little effect. In Nova Scotia, millions of dollars were lost in efforts to establish a heavy-water plant in Glace Bay and an electronics company in Stellarton. Both communities had been seriously affected by the decline in the coal industry that had previously sustained them, but the new industries failed to take root. Millions of dollars were poured into New Brunswick premier Richard

**Map 12.1** *Canada, 1949.*

Hatfield's pet project to build a luxury automobile, the Bricklin, but that company, too, went into receivership. In Newfoundland, Premier Smallwood attracted a variety of entrepreneurs willing to gamble with taxpayers' money, but few of his industrial ventures paid off. An oil refinery at Come-by-Chance that had been opened with great fanfare in October 1973—the *Queen Elizabeth II* was chartered at a reported fee of $97 000 a day for the occasion—went bankrupt within three years.

Regional assistance incentives generally failed in their stated objectives: they served to maintain rather than change the relative distribution of wealth in the country. State-subsidized private enterprise seemed no better a model for economic development in the peripheral regions of the country than unaided free enterprise. In the end, it was easier to make the Atlantic region a dependant of Ottawa—fully half of the region's income was derived from federal transfer payments by 1975—than to spend the funds necessary to make the region more economically viable.

The failure of regional development programs encouraged Atlantic Canadians to fight to at least hold on to what they already had. The citizens of Sydney, with help from Cape Bretoners generally, campaigned tirelessly to prevent their steel mill from closing down in the mid-1960s when it was abandoned by DOSCO. Federal and provincial governments agreed to keep both the steel mill and DOSCO's coal mines at Glace Bay in operation under the auspices of the Cape Breton Development Corporation (DEVCO), which was also charged with seeking ways to diversify Cape Breton's declining industrial base.

Other provinces pursued policies to attract industrial development to their jurisdictions. Ontario stepped up existing infrastructure programs, ensuring that the transportation system and provincial training programs met industrial requirements. In most other provinces, economic development agencies were established with a mandate to pursue new industries. These agencies advertised to prospective industrialists the extensive federal and provincial incentives available to them. Agencies such as the Manitoba Development Fund and the investment arm of the Quebec Pension Plan offered competing incentives to companies thinking of building new plants or moving existing ones.

Alberta was a latecomer to the view that give-aways should be used to attract new industries. The Social Credit administration preferred to use Alberta's low-tax regime as a means of encouraging diversification, but the results were meagre. Conservative premier Peter Lougheed called for a more aggressive approach, arguing that Alberta's prosperity would be short-lived if oil and gas revenues were not used to diversify the economy to prepare for the era when these resources would be depleted. In 1975, his government created the Heritage Trust Fund, into which a portion of oil royalties was committed to provide moneys to stimulate new economic activity. Saskatchewan's NDP government followed a different tack, buying shares for the state in private companies in order to encourage economic development. It was responsible for establishing a steel-manufacturing firm in Regina, but the province's limited resources, relative to the Heritage Trust Fund, restricted achievements of these kinds.

The energy-producing provinces responded bitterly when the federal government attempted to increase its revenues from oil and gas developments in the wake of the huge increases in oil prices undertaken by the Oil and Petroleum Exporting Countries (OPEC) after the Arab–Israeli war of October 1973. They were equally resistant to federal intervention to shield Canadian consumers from the price shocks, particularly when many of those consumers were businesses located in Central Canada. Ottawa cited its constitutional control over taxation and interprovincial and international trade to justify policies that it claimed were for the good of Canadians as a whole. Resource policy was added to a roster of western grievances against the federal government, including monetary policy, the promotion of bilingualism, the introduction of the metric system, and indifference to the plight of farmers.

"Fed bashing" became important to political success in Western Canada, particularly in Alberta and Saskatchewan. But not everyone in the region believed that provincial rights advocates spoke for the average westerner. John Conway expressed a view common on the left in the region when he noted that Alberta premier Lougheed "bash[ed] the 'feds' and [won] overwhelming mandates while ignoring the fact that his provincial economy is the near-private reserve of the multinational oil companies."[10] Ironically, while Lougheed and the other premiers of Western Canada and the Atlantic region accused the federal government of following policies that virtually negated provincial development strategies in favour of central Canadian economic development, the province most alienated from Ottawa *was* in Central Canada: Quebec.

## QUEBEC AND THE FRENCH-CANADIAN NATION

### MODERNIZATION AND NATIONALISM

The new liberalism almost guaranteed a collision between Ottawa and Quebec City. While Ottawa insisted that the federal government play a large role in all areas of social and economic development, Quebec resisted all federal involvement in areas of provincial jurisdiction. For example, Duplessis, under pressure from nationalist intellectuals, spurned over $200 million in federal moneys earmarked for Quebec universities. Nationalists feared that federal funding might lead to interference in university affairs within Quebec.

Determination to resist federal encroachments increased during the Quiet Revolution ushered in by the election of Jean Lesage's Liberals in 1960. Quebec underwent dramatic social changes in the 1960s as its francophone population, particularly in the cities, embraced the secular values of the rest of North America. Nationalists in the province expected their provincial government to follow policies that reflected a new liberal consensus and at the same time to ensure that the national identity of Quebec's majority was preserved within the Canadian Confederation.

Changes within the Roman Catholic Church helped to precipitate a rising tide of reformism within Quebec. In the mid-1960s, Pope John XXIII convened the Second Vatican Council, which emphasized greater simplicity in church ceremonies and democratic participation in church governance. This new approach reinforced reformist forces already at work in the Quebec church and ensured that the church would not use its institutional power to block social reforms proposed by the Lesage government.

Although no conscious plan shaped the policies of Lesage, his overall goal was to promote economic development in Quebec under francophone control. This meant a significant expansion of the role of the state. One of the leading exponents of the new *étatisme* in Lesage's cabinet was René Lévesque. He waged a successful campaign for the province to nationalize all private hydro companies, making Hydro-Québec a monopoly. With the state in control of hydro-electricity, strategies that fulfilled nationalist goals of economic development, including the hiring of francophone managers and engineers in massive power projects, could be more easily implemented.

Another major provincial initiative was the establishment of the Quebec Pension Plan in 1965 in response to the creation of the Canada Pension Plan. Lesage argued that a separate plan was needed to provide Quebec with an investment fund to encourage secondary industries and to build the infrastructure required to exploit natural resources. Over time, the fund would be used to give the province minority shares in companies, allowing it to push those companies to invest in Quebec and to increase their francophone representation.

Quebec's desire to run its own social programs soon led to confrontation with Ottawa. In their determination to prevent the federal government from using funding arrangements to control areas of provincial responsibility, provincial leaders in Quebec created a dilemma for the reform-minded Pearson Liberals. Their solution was to allow Quebec, or any other province for that matter, to opt out of a federal program, retaining its share of funding as long as it established a similar provincial program with the moneys. In practice, only Quebec availed itself of this option. When Pierre Trudeau became prime minister in 1968, he rejected the opting-out principle and announced that provinces that pulled out of future federal programs would not be reimbursed.

As the Quiet Revolution worked its way through the fabric of Quebec society, a growing number of Quebeckers became sovereignists—supporters of a sovereign Quebec nation-state. While their opponents called them separatists, to emphasize that they wished to break up the country, the sovereignists or *indépendantistes* chose to emphasize the creative aspect of their goals. Resistance by the Trudeau government and most English-Canadians to the de facto special status that Quebec had begun to develop in the Pearson period strengthened the hand of sovereignists in Quebec.

A major breakthrough for the sovereignty forces came in 1968 when René Lévesque left the Liberals and cobbled together an alliance of nationalist forces to create the Parti québécois (PQ). By the mid-1970s, the PQ platform was sovereignty-association—the creation of a separate Quebec state with the maintenance of close economic links with Ottawa. Such a state, it was argued, could negotiate with Ottawa *égal à égal*. It was an interesting notion, but its flaw, as both federalists and supporters of complete sovereignty argued, was that it assumed that the nine remaining provinces and two territories of Canada would be interested in establishing a special economic relationship with a sovereign Quebec and would be willing to let the federal government represent them in negotiations with Quebec. The perception in the Atlantic and western provinces that Quebec, along with Ontario, already controlled the federal government made such a development improbable.

## The Move to Official Bilingualism

The federal government was not standing idly by as Quebec drifted outside of the Canadian Confederation. In 1963, the Pearson government established a Royal Commission on Bilingualism and Biculturalism under co-chairs André Laurendeau and Davidson Dunton. The commission confirmed that there was a strong relationship between poverty and French unilingualism in Canada. It also revealed that the rate of assimilation of French Canadians outside Quebec and northern New Brunswick was so alarming as to support Quebec nationalist claims that something had to be done to prevent the disappearance of French

culture in North America. Pierre Trudeau, who distrusted Quebec nationalism, or "tribalism" as he called it, was determined to make francophones feel *chez nous* throughout the country.

In 1969, Parliament passed the Official Languages Act, an attempt to put French on an equal footing with English throughout the federal government. The bill created an official languages commissioner responsible for ensuring that federal departments served the public equally well in both languages. A significant percentage of new hirings required that successful applicants be functionally bilingual, and large numbers of existing unilingual civil servants (usually anglophones) were given second-language instruction. In Trudeau's mind, one of the benefits of bilingualism in the civil service was that it would advertise to young educated Québécois that they need not look only to their own province for employment opportunities.

Through the 1970s, the federal government tried to expand the use of French across the country by providing funds to support French-language schools, French immersion programs for anglophones, and organizations for francophones outside Quebec. Even earlier, provincial governments had lifted long-established restrictions on the use of French as a language of instruction in schools. More Canadians than ever before were becoming bilingual, but the success of these programs in strengthening either the French community or national unity was debatable. Francophones outside Quebec complained that economic realities in most of the country still forced them to become proficient in English to get well-paying jobs. Moreover, the lack of francophone cultural facilities meant that they had to rely on English-language institutions. Although Radio-Canada could be accessed on radio and television throughout much of the country, the centralization of its production in Montreal meant that francophones outside Quebec played little role in shaping its programming. Many of them found the Quebec orientation of Radio-Canada's news programs so pronounced that they turned to English-language stations, which had more local content. As for the Official Languages Act, the Fédération des francophones hors Québec reported pessimistically in 1978 that it had "only slightly, not to say imperceptibly, contributed to the development of Francophone communities outside Quebec." [11]

Encouraged by developments in Quebec, federal support for bilingualism, and the momentum of the times, Acadians in the Atlantic region experienced their own quiet revolution. The number of Acadians continued to grow in the postwar period, but the rate of assimilation to anglophone culture was high. It soon became clear that, unless Acadians developed institutions and policies to address their needs, they would disappear as a cultural group. As in Quebec, education was identified as a key to maintaining cultural identity. Acadians throughout the Maritimes pushed for more French-language instruction in their schools and for institutions of higher learning to prepare their children for the new opportunities of the service economy.

In New Brunswick, sheer numbers made the Acadians a force to be reckoned with. Confrontations with Moncton's anglophone mayor, student sit-ins at the Université de Moncton, and a well-attended Day of Concern over unemployment in January 1972 brought attention to Acadian demands for programs that would protect their culture and improve their economic condition. In the fall of 1972, New Brunswick Acadians founded the Parti acadien, whose goal was to create a separate province of Acadie in the northeastern section of New Brunswick. New Brunswick became Canada's only officially bilingual province, its status declared in 1969 and confirmed in the Constitution of 1982.

Opposition to official bilingualism ran deep in English Canada, though polls suggested majority support. While many middle-class families were placing their children in immersion programs, other Canadians resented the notion that they had to speak French in order to get federal jobs. In popular thinking, particularly in Western Canada, all civil service jobs had become bilingual, the only people wanted for bilingual jobs were francophones, and most federal grants were going to Quebec, the spoiled child of Confederation. Sporadic acts of separatist terrorism added to the image of a province where respect for non-francophone

Canadians had collapsed.

## THE OCTOBER CRISIS

Resentment against francophone militancy reached new heights during the October Crisis, which erupted in the fall of 1970. On 5 October, James Cross, the British trade commissioner in Montreal, was kidnapped by members of the Front de libération du Québec (FLQ). Five days later, Pierre Laporte, the Quebec minister of labour and immigration, was abducted by another cell of the FLQ. Although consisting of only a few dozen members, the FLQ had been active since 1963 in pursuing its goals of revolutionary change in Quebec.

*Protest in Ottawa following proclamation of the War Measures Act, October 1970.*

National Archives of Canada/ PA126347

Associated with over two hundred bombings between 1963 and 1970, the FLQ had targeted such bastions of privilege as McGill University, the home of Montreal mayor Jean Drapeau, and the Montreal Stock Exchange.

The success of the Liberal Party, led by Robert Bourassa, in the provincial election of April 1970 disgusted the FLQ, as it did many nationalists in Quebec. From their perspective, the outcome was due to the anglophone business community and federalists who did everything in their power to steal victory from the PQ. By daring to seize a representative of the British Crown and a Liberal cabinet minister, the FLQ was hitting at the heart of the establishment.

In return for release of the hostages, the kidnappers demanded, among other things, the freeing of FLQ members who were imprisoned or detained and the broadcasting of the group's manifesto. The manifesto was read on Radio-Canada following the Cross kidnapping, but when the FLQ struck a second time, politicians in Quebec City and Ottawa decided to take strong action. On 16 October, the federal government proclaimed the War Measures Act under which it banned the FLQ, suspended civil rights, and imposed martial law on the nation. This was only the third time in the twentieth century that the War Measures Act had been invoked, and on the two previous occasions Canada had been at war with foreign powers.

The act played little, if any, role in the apprehension of the revolutionaries and the release of the trade commissioner in early December. It may well have precipitated the murder of Laporte, whose body was found in the trunk of an abandoned car on the night of 17 October. Yet most English Canadians and, initially, most francophones accepted claims by Trudeau and Bourassa that the FLQ was planning a full-scale insurrection that had to be nipped in the bud. Ironically, the use of the act to detain over 450 people, most of whom were never charged with any offence, became another example for Quebec nationalists of the injustice imposed by an English-dominated Parliament. In reality, all francophone members of Parliament voted for the War Measures Act. The sixteen MPs who voted against it—fifteen New Democrats and one Conservative— were all anglophones.

## THE "SPECIAL STATUS" DEBATE

Though Robert Bourassa worked closely with the federal government to destroy the small revolutionary separatist movement, he and Trudeau often disagreed about how to react to the growing parliamentary movement for sovereignty. Trudeau defended the existing distribution of powers between the provinces and the federal government and rejected requests from Quebec for special status as the homeland of a French-Canadian nation. Wishing to appease nationalist sentiment, Bourassa followed his predecessors in calling for Quebec City to have absolute control in a variety of areas, particularly social programs, communications, and immigration.

Bourassa's determination to gain ground in the area of the constitutional division of powers frustrated Trudeau's attempts to achieve his most cherished objective. Like several of his predecessors, Trudeau wanted to patriate the Canadian constitution—that is, to end its life as a creature of the British Parliament. In the past, the prime ministers who supported patriation had reason to believe that Britain would accept a request to hand control of the constitution to Canadians only if all the provinces had agreed with the central government on an amending formula. In 1964, Lester Pearson came close to success. Jean Lesage, wishing to repay Pearson for agreeing to the "opting-out" principle, indicated at a federal–provincial conference that Quebec would accept an amending formula that did not give the province a veto over constitutional changes. A storm of protest from nationalist intellectuals convinced him to withdraw his support. At a federal–provincial conference in Victoria in 1971, Trudeau offered Bourassa the veto that had eluded Lesage. Faced with an increasingly popular Parti québécois, Bourassa spurned the prime minister, warning that Quebec would not support patriation until it was given extra powers. In particular, Bourassa wanted Pearson's "opt-out" principle to be applied to all social programs, present and future, for which federal funds were provided. Trudeau refused and was generally scathing in his comments about the Liberal premier of Quebec thereafter.

Bourassa's language legislation also appalled the prime minister. In 1974, the Quebec legislature passed Bill 22, a law that made French the only official language in Quebec and promoted its use in the workplace. All children were to be educated in French unless their parents were Canadian-born anglophones. Immigrant children wishing to enrol in English-language schools would have to pass a language test. Unilingual English signs were banned. Quebec anglophones criticized the bill for infringing on civil liberties. For nationalist francophones, the legislation did not go far enough in restricting the use of English. They believed that the collective rights of a people, in this case, the francophone Québécois, outweighed the individual rights of those who wished to choose their language of business and school without interference by the state. The nationalists argued that such individualism threatened the national existence of the Québécois.

Given the city's unique demography, Montreal was one of the centres of resistance to Bill 22. While over four-fifths of Quebeckers had French as their first language, on Montreal Island the ethnic French constituted little more than 60 percent of the total population. This proportion had held fairly constant for over a century. It was the remaining 40 percent that had experienced the greatest change since Confederation. In 1871, people of British origin accounted for 38 percent of Montreal's population; only 2 percent of the population was of neither French nor English extraction. By 1971, allophones constituted 23 percent of Montrealers, and only 16 percent of the city's population was of British descent. It was often these allophones who resisted enrolling their children in French schools.

## INTERNATIONAL RELATIONS AND THE NEW LIBERALISM

If the new liberalism was reflected in federal social welfare programs and the Quiet Revolution in Quebec, it was also evident in international affairs. Most of Canada's leaders wanted the nation to play a role on the world stage. The image that Canada attempted to project was that of a peacekeeper and benevolent donor in the area of foreign aid. Like its American counterpart, the Canadian government subscribed to the view that poverty in the Third World was the result of "underdevelopment" rather than the effects of colonialism and a vastly uneven distribution of wealth. While the old liberalism might have argued that the untrammelled marketplace, left to its own devices, would bring development to these nations, the new liberalism recognized the need for non-market intervention to encourage the process. Foreign aid would allow the governments of these countries to build the infrastructure, including transportation systems and schools, necessary to encourage industrial development and agricultural improvement.

In 1950, Canada was one of the signatories of the Colombo Plan, meant to provide assistance to former British colonies in Asia as they gained their independence. Over the next two decades, aid was extended to Commonwealth nations in other parts of the world, to francophone Africa, and, in 1970, to Latin America. The Canadian International Development Agency (CIDA) was established in 1968 to coordinate the nation's foreign aid efforts. CIDA increased publicity as well as expenditures in the area of foreign aid, and reports of Canadians assisting Third World countries to build modern highways and improve crop yields became more common. In the early 1970s, Canada committed itself to spending 0.7 percent of its gross domestic product on foreign aid, but by the end of the decade such expenditures had barely reached 0.4 percent. By then, the economic buoyancy that had led to the original promise had disappeared, and the government was less willing to tax citizens or incur debts to support development in other nations.

Critics of the foreign aid program questioned not only its lack of generosity, but also its heavy reliance on "tied aid": countries received funds on condition that they spent specified amounts of their grants to acquire Canadian goods or services. This discouraged the development of indigenous technologies and competencies on the part of recipient nations.

Canada was perhaps more successful in its role as international peacekeeper. In 1956, Canadian diplomacy was responsible for finding a solution to the Suez Crisis when British and French troops attacked Egypt following its nationalization of the Suez Canal. Canadians were proud of the role they played in the Suez Crisis, particularly after Minister of External Affairs Lester Pearson won the Nobel Peace Prize for his efforts in defusing the potentially explosive situation. Canada was a member of the United Nations Emergency Force that kept the peace between Egypt and Israel from 1956 until 1967, when Egyptian President Gamal Abdel Nasser expelled the UN forces. Among other hot spots where Canadian peacekeepers served were the Congo (now Zaire), Yemen, and Cyprus.

## CONCLUSION

At the Canadian Chamber of Commerce's annual convention in September 1965, J.M. Keith, vice-chair of the organization's executive council and president of Imperial Tobacco Company of Canada, had a grim message for delegates. Reporting on a survey on public attitudes towards economic issues, Keith commented: "Although the great majority of the public profess to believe in the principle of free enterprise, they, paradoxically, very strongly favour measures which could function to destroy the very foundation upon which the system is built." Indeed, "the desire for extensive programmes of social welfare" was so "broadly and strongly rooted in the public mind" that "it is doubtful whether such deeply rooted feelings can be altered."[12]

This "deeply rooted" sense of entitlement was fairly new in Canadian history. While poverty and disease had been widespread before the Second World War, particularly during the Depression, the prevailing view was that it was up to the individual and the family to set aside money in good times to tide family members through periods of unemployment, sickness, or old age. Charitable agencies were the next line of defence. Only when all else had failed could an individual or family call upon the state for help, and such help was usually meagre and demeaning. Mass privation during the Depression followed by the good times aided by government intervention in the economy during the war convinced most Canadians that a return to the old values of self-reliance was unthinkable.

The state was given the responsibility of finding ways of balancing the ordinary citizen's sense of entitlement to social programs with the business community's sense of entitlement to low taxes. In the first three decades following 1945, there was sufficient economic growth to allow governments to provide general satisfaction to both groups. Indeed, the major confrontations over social programs in this period were less likely to be between citizens' or business groups and the state than between federal and provincial leaders. The federal government's desire to control the development of the welfare state posed particular challenges vis-à-vis Quebec. The increasing array of social programs—and the ensuing federal-provincial struggle for control—only seemed to stimulate claims for the need for self-determination in Quebec.

As we have seen in earlier chapters, the Canadian state had always intervened to some extent to shelter Canadians from market forces and to stimulate a national economy. But the prewar liberal philosophy, which stressed individual liberties, suggested that the state should intervene as little as possible in the marketplace. In the postwar period, the new liberalism recognized that freedom from want, once regarded as within the reach of hard-working individuals, was not guaranteed, and that the state had the obligation to remove some services, such as health care, from the marketplace altogether. The state also had the responsibility to determine a minimum level of income for all citizens rather than leaving charitable organizations to look after the destitute.

The state's expansion in the postwar period was not limited to social programs. As the next three chapters show, the state played an integral role in most areas of economic and social life in postwar Canada.

# THE DEVELOPMENT
## OF QUEBEC NATIONALISM

*A Historiographical Debate*

What have been the causes of growing sentiment for sovereignty in Quebec since the 1960s? Political scientist Kenneth McRoberts offers one of several theories rooted in economics to explain this phenomenon. The Quiet Revolution, he argues, raised francophone hopes that they would take over the levers of economic power in the province and experience a measurable increase in their standard of living. When this failed to occur, the upwardly mobile professional middle classes were particularly offended. They provided the impetus for the Parti québécois as well as movements that preceded its founding.[13] A somewhat more radical view is provided by sociologist Marcel Rioux, who argues that Quebec francophones identified with the movements for decolonization in the Third World and wished to end their own colonial status. According to Rioux, the Quebec francophones were an ethnic group relegated to working-class status and therefore gradually began to develop the view of themselves as an ethnic class that must break free not only from the Canadian Confederation, but also from the capitalist ethos that pervaded anglophone North America.[14]

Several authors have challenged the view that the educated middle class and indeed francophones generally failed to benefit from the reforms of the Quiet Revolution. Historian Ramsay Cook, comparing incomes of male workers in Montreal, notes that the spread of average earnings between francophones and anglophones fell from 51 percent in 1961 to 32 percent in 1970 and 15 percent in 1977.[15] Economists François Vaillancourt and Pierre Saint-Laurent demonstrate that increased public employment for francophones has accounted for much of the decline in the income gap between the two linguistic groups.[16]

Political scientist Mary Beth Montcalm argues that it is the very economic success of the francophone middle classes that has impelled them towards the creation of their own nation. Comparing Quebec separatism with similar breakaway nationalist movements in Belgium, France, Spain, and Britain, she argues that the rise of middle-class groups with distinct ethnic identities has been a common catalyst for modern separatist movements. It is not economic anxiety, but rather the wish of such groups to establish an ethnic state in their own image that motivates such movements. Thus, Montcalm sees cultural goals rather than economic ones as the primary motivation of the Quebec sovereignty movement.[17]

Political scientist André Bernard goes further, suggesting that the struggle to preserve the French language united Quebec secessionists, regardless of social class:

> The French language ... is a fundamental characteristic of the French-Canadian nation, but it is also more than that. It is the symbol of identity for French Canadians as a group, the rallying force among them, their pride and their wealth. It has an appeal which compares to no other group characteristic. In the last analysis, it is what French Canadians fight for. In this light, the idea of a unilingual French-speaking people in the territory populated and dominated by French Canadians is more a reflection of ideology than a formula prompted by narrow economic interests. [18]

## NOTES

1  National Archives of Canada, MG 32, C 12, Grace MacInnis Papers, vol. 19, File "Women, Status of, 1972," J. Eric Harrington, president, Canada Vickers Ltd., to MacInnis, 9 May 1972

2  Ibid., MacInnis to Harrington, 18 May 1972

3  Canada, Royal Commission on Medical Services, brief presented by the Newfoundland Federation of Labour, Oct. 1961

4  Quoted in Canadian Council on Social Development, "Canada's Social Programs Are in Trouble" (Ottawa: CCSD, 1990), 5

5  Archives of Ontario, Ontario Welfare Council papers, F 837, box 48, "Day Care Paper, 1965," Address by Freda Manson, Ontario Welfare Council, 17 Feb. 1965

6  Quoted in Alvin Finkel, "'Even the Little Children Cooperated': Family Strategies, Childcare Discourse, and Social Welfare Debates, 1945–1975," *Labour/Le Travail* 36 (Fall 1995): 105

7  Ibid, 112

8  *Report of the Royal Commission on the Status of Women in Canada* (Ottawa: Information Canada, 1970), 261

9  Harold Innis to Angus L. Macdonald, 17 Jan. 1946, Public Archives of Nova Scotia, Angus L. Macdonald Papers, MG 2, Box 898

10  J.F. Conway, *The West: The History of a Region in Confederation* (Toronto: Lorimer, 1983), 228

11  La Fédération des francophones hors Québec, *The Heirs of Lord Durham: Manifesto of a Vanishing People* (Toronto: Burns and MacEachern, 1978), 70

12  National Archives of Canada, MG 28, 111, 62, vol. 4, 36th Annual Meeting of the Canadian Chamber of Commerce, *Addresses*, J.M. Keith address, 29 Sept. 1965

13  Kenneth McRoberts, *Quebec: Social Change and Political Crisis*, 3rd ed. (Toronto: McClelland and Stewart, 1988), 173–208

14  Marcel Rioux, *Quebec in Question* (Toronto: Lorimer, 1971)

15  Ramsay Cook, "Quebec's New Quiet Revolutionaries" in *Canada, Quebec and the Uses of Nationalism*, (Toronto: McClelland and Stewart, 1986), 87–104

16  François Vaillancourt and Pierre Saint-Laurent, "Les déterminants de l'évolution de revenu entre Canadien anglais et Canadien français," *Journal of Canadian Studies* 15, 4 (Winter 1980–81): 69–74

17  Mary Beth Montcalm, "Quebec Nationalism in a Comparative Perspective" in *Quebec: State and Society in Crisis*, ed. Alain Gagnon (Toronto: Methuen, 1984), 45–58

18  André Bernard, *What Does Quebec Want?* (Toronto: Lorimer, 1978), 45

## SELECTED READING

Key works that deal broadly with postwar national political developments include: Ian Drummond, Robert Bothwell, and John English, *Canada Since 1945: Power, Politics and Provincialism*, rev. ed. (Toronto: University of Toronto Press, 1989); J.L. Granatstein, *Canada, 1957–1967: The Years of Uncertainty and Innovation* (Toronto: McClelland and Stewart, 1986); Robert Chodos, Rae Murphy, and Eric Hamovitch, *The Unmaking of Canada: The Hidden Theme in Canadian History Since 1945* (Toronto: Lorimer, 1991); Reginald Whitaker, *The Government Party: Organizing and Financing the Liberal Party of Canada, 1930–1958* (Toronto: University of Toronto Press, 1977); Norman Penner, *From Protest to Power: Social Democracy in Canada 1900-Present* (Toronto: Lorimer, 1992); William Brennan, ed., *Building the Co-*

*Operative Commonwealth: Essays on the Social Democratic Tradition in Canada* (Regina: Canadian Plains Research Center, 1984); John English, *The Life of Lester Pearson*, vol. 2, *Worldly Years* (New York: Alfred A. Knopf, 1992); Stephen Clarkson and Christina McCall, *Trudeau and Our Times* (Toronto: McClelland and Stewart, 1990); John G. Diefenbaker, *One Canada: Memoirs of the Right Honourable John G. Diefenbaker* (Toronto: Macmillan, 1975); Denis Smith, *Rogue Tory: The Life and Legend of John G. Diefenbaker* (Toronto: McFarlane Walter & Ross, 1995); and Lester B. Pearson, *Mike: The Memoirs of the Right Honourable Lester B. Pearson* (Toronto: University of Toronto Press, 1972).

Provincial political histories dealing with this period include: Roger Graham, *Old Man Ontario: Leslie Miscampbell Frost* (Toronto: University of Toronto Press, 1990); Allan Kerr McDougall, *John P. Robarts: His Life and Government* (Toronto: University of Toronto Press, 1986); Nelson Wiseman, *Social Democracy in Manitoba: A History of the CCF-NDP* (Winnipeg: University of Manitoba Press, 1983); Raymond B. Blake, *Canadian at Last: Canada Integrates Newfoundland as a Province* (Toronto: University of Toronto Press, 1994); James Hiller and Peter Neary, eds., *Twentieth Century Newfoundland: Explorations* (St John's: Breakwater, 1994); David Mitchell, *W.A.C. Bennett and the Rise of British Columbia* (Vancouver: Douglas and McIntyre, 1983); Alvin Finkel, *The Social Credit Phenomenon in Alberta* (Toronto: University of Toronto Press, 1989); Verner Smitheram et al., *The Garden Transformed: Prince Edward Island, 1945–1980* (Charlottetown: Ragweed, 1982); Margaret Conrad, "The Atlantic Revolution of the 1950s" in *Beyond Anger and Longing: Community and Development in Atlantic Canada*, ed. Berkeley Fleming (Fredericton: Acadiensis Press, 1988), 55–96; Thomas H. McLeod and Ian McLeod, *Tommy Douglas: The Road to Jerusalem* (Edmonton: Hurtig, 1987); and Della Stanley, *Louis Robichaud: A Decade of Power* (Halifax: Nimbus, 1984).

Studies of postwar Quebec include: Paul-André Linteau, René Durocher, and Jean-Claude Robert, *Quebec Since 1930* (Toronto: Lorimer, 1991); Kenneth McRoberts, *Quebec: Social Change and Political Crisis*, 3rd ed.(Toronto: McClelland and Stewart, 1988), René Lévesque, *Memoirs* (Toronto: McClelland and Stewart, 1986); Alain Gagnon, *Quebec: State and Society in Crisis* (Toronto: Methuen, 1984); John Saywell, *The Rise of the Parti Québécois, 1967–1976* (Toronto: University of Toronto Press, 1977); Dale C. Thomson, *Jean Lesage and the Quiet Revolution* (Toronto: Macmillan, 1984); William Coleman, *The Independence Movement in Quebec, 1945–1980* (Toronto: University of Toronto Press, 1984); and Michael Behiels, *Prelude to Quebec's Quiet Revolution: Liberalism Versus Neo-Conservatism, 1945-1960* (Montreal/Kingston: McGill-Queen's University Press, 1985).

On the views of Quebec's most noted federalist, see Pierre Trudeau, *Federalism and the French Canadians* (Toronto: Macmillan, 1977); *Against the Current: Selected Writings 1939-1996* (Toronto: McClelland and Stewart, 1996); and *Towards a Just Society: The Trudeau Years* (Markham, ON:Viking, 1990). Among useful works on francophones outside Quebec are Richard Wilbur, *The Rise of French New Brunswick* (Halifax: Formac, 1989); la Fédération des francophones hors Québec, *The Heirs of Lord Durham: A Manifesto of a Vanishing People* (Toronto: Gage, 1978); Sally Ross and Alphonse Deveau, *The Acadians of Nova Scotia: Past and Present* (Halifax: Nimbus, 1992); and Georges Arsenault, *The Island Acadians, 1720–1980* (Charlottetown: Ragweed Press, 1989).

Federal–provincial relations are discussed in David Milne, *Tug of War: Ottawa and the Provinces Under Trudeau and Mulroney* (Toronto: Lorimer, 1986), and Garth Stevenson, *Unfulfilled Union: Canadian Federalism and National Unity*, 3rd ed. (Toronto: Gage, 1988). On federal–provincial relations in the social welfare area, see Keith Banting, *The Welfare State and Canadian Federalism*, rev. ed. (Montreal: McGill-Queen's University Press, 1987).

Among useful works on the evolution of the welfare state more generally, see Dennis Guest, *The Emergence of Social Security in Canada*, rev. ed. (Vancouver: UBC Press, 1985); Andrew Armitage, *Social Welfare in Canada*, 2nd ed. (Toronto: McClelland and Stewart, 1988); Allan Moscovitch and Jim Albert, eds., *The Benevolent State: The Growth of Welfare in Canada* (Toronto: Garamond Press, 1987); John C. Bacher, *Keeping to the Marketplace: The Evolution of Canadian Housing Policy* (Montreal: McGill-Queen's University Press, 1993); James Struthers, *The Limits of Affluence: Welfare in Ontario, 1920–1970* (Toronto: University of Toronto Press, 1994); James Snell, *The Citizen's Wage: The State and the Elderly in Canada, 1900-1951* (Toronto: University of Toronto Press, 1996); and Raymond B. Blake and Jeff Keshen, eds., *Social Welfare Policy in Canada: Historical Readings* (Toronto: Copp Clark, 1995). On day care, see Laura Johnson and Janice Dineen, *The Kin Trade: The Day Care Crisis in Canada* (Toronto: McGraw-Hill Ryerson, 1981); and Alvin Finkel, "'Even the Little Children Cooperated': Family Strategies, Childcare Discourse, and Social Welfare Debates, 1945–1975," *Labour/Le Travail* 36 (Fall 1995): 91–118.

# 13

## C H A P T E R

# THE AMERICAN DREAM: CANADA AND ITS SOUTHERN NEIGHBOUR, 1945–1975

IN APRIL 1965, PRIME MINISTER LESTER Pearson, addressing students at Temple University in Philadelphia, cautiously advocated that the American government temporarily cease bombing North Vietnam in an effort to seek diplomatic solutions in Indochina. Meeting Pearson afterwards, American president Lyndon Johnson grabbed him by the shirt collar and shouted, "You pissed on my rug!"

With this experience in mind, the Pearson government approved a report prepared by two veteran ambassadors, one American, one Canadian, in July 1965, calling on the two countries to avoid public criticism of one another. The Merchant-Heeney report indicated that disagreements should be aired only through diplomatic channels.

Pearson never uttered another indictment, however cautious, of American policy in Indochina. As he commented in an interview in 1967: "We can't ignore the fact that the first result of any open breach with the United States over Vietnam, which their government considers to be unfair and unfriendly on our part, would be a more critical examination by Washington of certain special aspects of our relationship from which we, as well as they, get great benefit."[1] In other words, Canada's close economic relations with the United

States had to be considered when the Canadian government set its foreign policy.

It might, in any event, have been hypocritical for Canada to protest American behaviour in Vietnam, and do no more. Under the Defence Production Sharing Agreement of 1958, Canadians had the right to bid for military contracts on an equal basis with Americans. When anti-war protesters in Canada criticized Ottawa for allowing arms sales to the Americans for use in Vietnam, Treasury Board president Edgar Benson observed that unemployment in Canada would rise if the government stopped the arms trade.

Benson was certainly correct. In the late 1960s, an estimated 125 000 Canadian jobs were tied to armaments production. Largely because of the Vietnam War, arms sales were 56 percent greater in 1965 than they had been in 1964; by 1972, American defence procurement in Canada, much of it war-related, was worth $226 million. Firms such as Canadian Acme Screw and Gear, Canadian Marconi, Litton Systems, and Valcartier received large contracts for shells, military aircraft, and radio relay sets while metal mining companies such as INCO received record orders for minerals required in defence production. The impact of the war on Canada's economy went well beyond the sale of arms and minerals. With the American economy enjoying a war-induced boom, other exports to the United States, such as lumber for constructing homes and office buildings, also soared.

In the postwar years, the United States was not only Canada's major trading partner; it also was the source of many of Canada's cultural values. Canadians read American books, watched American-produced television programs, listened to American popular music, and had more respect for American political leaders, such as Dwight D. Eisenhower and John F. Kennedy, than they had for their own elected politicians. The Vietnam War (1965–75) and an increasing awareness of the downside of the American Dream eventually caused Canadians to develop some ambivalence about their powerful southern neighbour, but the United States continued to provide the benchmark against which Canadians, and many other western nations, measured their successes and failures.

## THE COLD WAR

Canadian foreign policy, economic development, and cultural change were all connected to some degree in the thirty years following the Second World War. This was the era of the Cold War, in which capitalist democracies were pitted against the communist states, competing for resources, trade, and political allies throughout the world. Their fierce ideological battles tended to create a simplified view of the political and economic options available to nations on either side of the communist–capitalist divide. Increasingly enthralled by the American mass entertainment industry, most Canadians embraced both the cultural values espoused by the United States as leader of the "free world" and the economic opportunities created by the expanding American military. The politics of the Cold War are therefore a good place to start examining the complex relations between Canada and the United States after 1945.

The Soviet Union had been a valued member of the anti-Nazi forces during the Second World War. Its troops did the lion's share of the front-line fighting and dying and it lost almost as many citizens as all other combatants combined. After the war, Soviet leaders insisted upon friendly governments in Central and Eastern Europe and upon maintaining the presence of Soviet troops in the nations of the region. After all, they argued, Germany had easily descended upon the Russian Empire in the First World War and the Soviet Union in the Second World War because the countries separating the two nations were weak. Only a Soviet military presence in the "buffer states" would calm Soviet fears of another German invasion.

The western countries, particularly the United States, rejected this reasoning and insisted on the right to military and economic independence of the countries in Central and Eastern Europe. Economic aid for the war-shattered Soviet Union was made dependent on Soviet willingness to withdraw troops from Eastern Europe and to open the markets of those countries, as well as the Soviet Union itself, to western investment. The Soviets responded by tightening the screws on Eastern Europe, replacing democratically elected postwar coalition governments with communist-dominated regimes subservient to the Soviet state. Each side then declared that the other was bent on world domination.

In dramatic contrast to its isolationism in the interwar years, the United States became the champion of international activism. Its chief policy goal, trumpeted in classrooms, from the pulpit, and in the media, was the containment of communism at home and abroad. Yet both sides tried to avoid a direct confrontation—a "hot war"—instead limiting themselves to virulent rhetoric and to support for either pro-Soviet or pro-western forces in localized conflicts.

Soviet agents seemed to be everywhere, including Ottawa. In September 1945, Igor Gouzenko, a cypher clerk in the Soviet Embassy, revealed to the Canadian government that a Soviet spy ring had been in operation in Canada throughout the war. Given Canada's close involvement with research relating to the atomic bomb, this was perceived as a serious matter, and arrests were followed by increased security within the government—and increased mistrust of the Soviet Union. Despite the evidence of the spy ring, most External Affairs officials, while appalled by dictator Joseph Stalin and his police-state apparatus, regarded American claims concerning Soviet intentions in foreign policy as vastly exaggerated. Publicly, however, Canada supported American views, determining that a less partisan approach would not serve Canadian interests.

The Permanent Joint Board on Defence, established during the Second World War, remained in operation to coordinate the defence policies of the two nations. Although the Canadian government balked at the board's suggestion that the two nations mesh their defence forces, Canada was increasingly drawn into American defence strategy. In 1949, Canada became a founding member of the North Atlantic Treaty Organization (NATO), a military pact that included the United States and Britain as well as continental western European nations. Canada had insisted on formal acknowledgement that NATO's goal was economic, as well as military, integration, but the organization soon became primarily an American instrument for coordinating the defence policies of its allies.

In 1950, Canada agreed to contribute troops to the United Nations forces sent to hold the line against communism in Korea. Following the Second World War, Korea had been divided into two zones: North Korea, under the supervision of the Soviet Union, and South Korea, under the control of the United States. The two zones were slated for amalgamation but were frozen in their antagonistic divisions by the Cold War. When troops from North Korea invaded South Korea in June 1950, the United States manoeuvred the United Nations into

sending a peacekeeping force into the region. Canada worked behind the scenes to restrain its aggressive allies as UN troops under American General Douglas MacArthur, having driven the communists out of South Korea, entered North Korean territory. This foray led to a military response from China, and the war grew in length

*Personnel of the 25th Canadian Infantry Brigade preparing machine gun position in Korea, 1951.*

National Archives of Canada/NA112639

and intensity. It finally came to an end in 1953, with Korea seemingly permanently divided. In total, about twenty-five thousand Canadians participated in the hostilities, and three hundred lost their lives.

As it had during the Second World War, Canada's economy boomed during the Korean conflict. By contrast, the two Koreas, both controlled by ruthless dictators, experienced economic devastation and the loss of millions of lives.

## THE NUCLEAR ISSUE

Meanwhile, Canada and the United States were pouring billions of dollars into an elaborate defence system to protect North America from a Soviet air attack. Between 1949 and 1957, three radar defence systems, including the Distant Early Warning (DEW) Line, were built. The DEW Line stretched from Alaska to Baffin Island and did much to open the Canadian North to southern influences. Cooperation on this project helped pave the way for the North Atlantic Air Defence Treaty (NORAD), which produced a unified air command for North America. Negotiated by the Liberals under St Laurent, the NORAD agreement was formally signed by the Progressive Conservative government in 1958, indicating the wide degree of consensus in Canada in support of close Canadian-American cooperation in defence matters.

America's exclusive possession of nuclear weapons from 1945 to 1949, followed by a decade of clear nuclear superiority over the Soviet Union, encouraged American political leaders to enunciate a policy of "deterrence": the Americans threatened to use nuclear weapons against communist states if they intervened in other countries' affairs. In 1954, NATO members, hoping to avoid the expense of large conventional armed forces, adopted nuclear deterrence as the mainstay of their defence strategy. Although a nuclear war, once begun, would be difficult to contain, NATO decided to build up stocks of "tactical" nuclear weaponry—intermediate-range weapons designed for battle in a particular region—as opposed to "strategic" weapons designed for a full-scale nuclear war. In December 1957, in line with this NATO policy, Canada agreed to play a role in surveillance of possible military strike plans by the communists. In 1959 and 1960, Canada ordered a variety of aircraft and missiles meant to help serve this objective. Canada also agreed to permit storage of American nuclear weapons at Goose Bay and Harman air force bases, which, though on Canadian territory, were controlled by the Americans. In 1958, Canada received a reward for its close cooperation with American defence policies: the Defence Production Sharing Agreement, which guaranteed that Canadians would benefit from the industrial potential of military production for the Cold War.

## SUPPORTING DEMOCRACY?

At the same time that Canada was forging military alliances and profiting from war industries, its leaders were also cultivating an image as peacemakers in a war-torn world. Canada's ability to play this role depended to a large extent on toeing the line drawn by the United States. If vital interests of the Americans were at stake, the Canadian peacekeeping role was invariably compromised. This was the case in policy relating to Vietnam, a tiny Asian nation that, like Korea, had the misfortune of becoming one of the hot spots in the Cold War.

A French colony since the nineteenth century, Vietnam emerged from the Second World War with a powerful nationalist movement led by French-educated communist Ho Chi Minh. In 1954, France was forced to recognize communist control over the northern half of Vietnam and ceded South Vietnam to anti-communist Vietnamese landlords and businessmen. Negotiations in Geneva that year produced an accord calling for reunification of North and South Vietnam after elections to be held in 1956. An International Control Commission (ICC) with Canada, Poland, and India as its members, was established to monitor the implementation of the provisions of the Geneva accord. The Americans, aware that the communists would win national elections, forced a delay to give the pro-American South Vietnamese regime a chance to establish its credentials. Such plans foundered as the regime unleashed a reign of terror, murdering suspected communist sympathizers and uprooting peasant villages. By the 1960s, the Americans' goal was to maintain the partition so that South Vietnam could remain non-communist.

The ICC members rarely proved neutral in their observations. Poland seemed able to see only South Vietnamese violations, while Canada tried to counter Poland by focusing exclusively on violations by the North Vietnamese. A report in 1962

## CANADIAN WORKERS AND COLD WAR POLITICS: THE CASE OF THE SEAMEN'S UNION

Between 1949 and 1962, as many as ten thousand Canadian seamen lost their right to work. Their names are lost to history, but their victimizer became famous and, later, notorious. He was Hal Banks, an American union organizer who oversaw a reign of terror on the waterfronts of the nation.

Banks owed his rise to power to anti-communist paranoia and Cold War cooperation between Canada and the United States. Banks's involvement with Canadian unions came about in response to a request by both Ottawa and Washington for American union assistance in addressing, in the words of one American labour leader, "a serious problem of Communist subversion in the Canadian maritime industry."[2]

The communists were the leaders of the Canadian Seamen's Union (CSU), a national union whose leaders won popular acclaim among Canada's seamen as fighters for workers' rights. When attempts to convince the workers to reject these leaders failed, the Canadian government, collaborating with the Americans, brought Banks into the country, conveniently ignoring a criminal record that made him ineligible for immigration to Canada. The two governments feared that a communist-led union would call strikes at the behest of the Soviets and would interrupt shipments to North America's allies.

The government, the shippers, and the Trades and Labour Congress (TLC) were all aware that Banks's Seafarers International Union (SIU) did not represent Canadian workers. The TLC, a federation mainly of affiliates of American unions, at first denounced the American union but soon buckled under pressure from the American Federation of Labor. For a decade, the government, the shippers, and even the unions said nothing as Banks made a mockery of the notion of union representation. Only when he began to raid other unions did organized labour react. Pressure from the Canadian Labour Congress forced Ottawa to investigate the SIU, uncovering a corrupt and violent union leadership. Charges were laid against Banks, and he was found guilty of ordering the savage beating of Captain Henry Walsh, a leader of the mates' guild that opposed SIU representation. But Banks fled the country, and the American authorities failed to extradite him.

Government, business, and much of organized labour demonstrated rather contradictory values throughout the Banks affair. They agreed to decertify the CSU, claiming that it was undemocratic even after it won government-supervised certification votes in the face of stark anti-communist propaganda campaigns by the shippers. Then they toasted Banks as an exemplar of democratic values, ignoring the fact that he was fleecing his members and casting out of the industry thousands of former CSU members as well as thousands of SIU members who resisted his leadership.

prepared by Canada and co-signed by India, desperate for American goodwill because of border wars with China, was regularly produced by American officials during their undeclared war in Indochina (1965–75) to demonstrate North Vietnamese atrocities. Though Canada provided weapons to the Americans and "humanitarian" aid to the South Vietnamese, its leaders claimed to be neutral in the conflict. In 1981, however, documents released by two New Democrat MPs revealed that the Canadian and American defence departments collaborated to test chemical defoliants that the Americans used in Vietnam.

Ottawa supported the general direction of American foreign relations, claiming that Canada wished to encourage the development of non-communist, democratic regimes around the world. In practice, it was not a government's democratic character, but rather its support for western investment and trade that became the criterion for American and NATO approval. Fascist Spain and Portugal were included in NATO. In Asia and throughout Latin America, the United States supported a variety of thuggish regimes. To Canada's embarrassment, many of these regimes were installed with American support by overthrowing democratically elected governments that struck the United States as too leftist or too nationalist. Yet there was silence from Ottawa as repressive military dictatorships overthrew a string of democratic

Diefenbaker decried American interference in a Canadian election and finally made the commitment to reject nuclear weapons for Canada. His unpopular government went down to defeat by Lester Pearson's Liberals, who had abruptly changed their position on the nuclear question following the missile crisis. Once in office, the Liberals followed through on their commitment to the controversial nuclear warheads. Pearson's secretary of state for external affairs, Paul Martin, suggests in his memoirs that it was important for the Pearson government to restore harmonious relations between the governments of Canada and the United States. "One of the functions of Canadian diplomacy has been to ensure that the United States will always harbour a special regard for Canada."[4]

When Pierre Trudeau came to power in 1968, he talked of a reassessment of Canada's NATO and NORAD commitments. In the early 1970s, plans were announced to gradually cut Canada's NATO troops in Europe by half, but its NORAD commitment remained unchanged. The obsolescence of the nuclear warheads available to the Canadian forces allowed Trudeau to return Canada to its earlier status as a nation without nuclear weapons. While Trudeau supported the campaign to slow down the arms race, he continued to support the policy of nuclear deterrence.

Trudeau attempted to move away from the Americans on several issues. In 1970, two years before the Americans took the same step, he recognized the People's Republic of China, rejecting the fiction that the defeated anti-communist forces compelled to retreat to Taiwan in 1949 remained the legitimate government of all of China. The prospect of increased trade with this poor but populous country motivated Canada to ignore the continued American hostility towards the People's Republic. In 1973, the Trudeau government agreed only reluctantly to participate in the International Commission of Control and Supervision established to implement the terms of a North

Vietnamese–American ceasefire. Despite American pressure, Canada left the commission after six months, lamenting its ineffectiveness.

## CONTINENTAL ECONOMIC INTEGRATION

The nuclear industry demonstrates how good the Cold War was for business. The development of the atomic bomb and the nuclear reactor stimulated the Canadian uranium market. Because of the strategic importance of the element, the Canadian government had nationalized Canada's major uranium mining company, Eldorado Mining and Refining, in 1944. Following the war, Eldorado served as a marketing agency for all private Canadian uranium companies, selling most of the Canadian output at fabulous prices to the United States Atomic Energy Commission. In 1952,

**Table 13.1**

### PERCENTAGE OF FOREIGN CONTROL OF SELECTED CANADIAN INDUSTRIES, 1939–1973

| Industry | 1939 | 1948 | 1958 | 1968 | 1973 |
|---|---|---|---|---|---|
| Manufacturing | 38(32)* | 43(39) | 57(44) | 58(46) | 59(44) |
| Petroleum and natural gas** | – | – | 73(67) | 75(61) | 76(59) |
| Mining and smelting | 42(38) | 40(37) | 60(51) | 68(58) | 56(45) |
| Railways | 3(3) | 3(3) | 2(2) | 2(2) | 2(2) |
| Other utilities | 26(26) | 24(24) | 5(4) | 5(4) | 7(4) |
| Total† | 21(19) | 25(22) | 32(26) | 36(28) | 35(26) |

*Numbers in brackets indicate percentage controlled by American residents
**Petroleum and natural gas combined with mining and smelting to 1948
†Total includes merchandising, not shown separately

Sources: F.H. Leacy, ed., *Historical Statistics of Canada*, 2nd ed. (Ottawa: Statistics Canada, 1983), Series G 291-302; John Fayerweather, *Foreign Investment in Canada: Prospects for National Policy* (Toronto: Oxford University Press, 1974), 7

another Crown corporation, Atomic Energy of Canada (AECL), was created to develop peaceful uses for atomic energy, in particular the Candu reactor, which was sold internationally. Ontario was the first province to enter an agreement with

**Table 13.2**

### DESTINATION OF DOMESTIC EXPORTS
(EXCLUDING GOLD), 1946–1975 (IN MILLIONS OF DOLLARS)

| Area | 1946 | 1955 | 1965 | 1975 |
|---|---|---|---|---|
| United States | 884 | 2548 | 4840 | 21 074 |
| United Kingdom | 594 | 768 | 1174 | 1 795 |
| Japan | 1 | 91 | 316 | 2 130 |
| Other west European | 189 | 261 | 626 | 2 347 |
| Other American | 202 | 216 | 433 | 1 583 |
| Centrally planned (communist) economies | 91 | 12 | 418 | 1 049 |
| Other | 312 | 363 | 717 | 2 571 |
| Percentage of exports to U.S. | 38.9 | 59.8 | 56.8 | 64.7 |

*Source: F.H. Leacy, ed.,* Historical Statistics of Canada, *2nd ed. (Ottawa: Statistics Canada, 1983), Series G 401-407*

The postwar economic boom gave the United States a powerful incentive for ever-closer economic and political relations with Canada. The Paley Commission established by President Truman in 1951, noted in its report, tellingly entitled *Resources for Freedom*, that the United States was fast running out of the raw materials required to fuel its military and civilian economy. Where better to invest than in the vast friendly hinterland to the north? During the 1950s and 1960s, American investment poured into Canada.

## INDUSTRIAL INTEGRATION

AECL to build nuclear power stations, and the first demonstration plant at Rolphston came into operation in 1962. With major finds at Beaverlodge and Blind River in Northern Ontario, Canada supplied a third of the world's military and civilian uranium requirements in the 1950s. Eldorado Nuclear, Rio Tinto–Rio Algom, and Dennison Mines became both literally and figuratively some of Canada's hottest companies, while Uranium City, Saskatchewan, and Elliot Lake, Ontario, were added to the pantheon of boom towns on Canada's resource frontier.

The shift in economic dependence from Britain to the United States had proceeded gradually from the time of Confederation. By the turn of the century, the United States had overtaken Britain as Canada's major trading partner, and in the interwar period most Canadian companies controlled from outside the country were in American hands. Close wartime and postwar relations between the two countries simply accelerated long-term trends. By Canada's centennial year, over a third of its industrial assets were foreign-controlled, with the Americans alone owning 28 percent of Canadian industry (see table 13.1). Three-quarters of the nation's imports came from its southern neighbour to whom it shipped two-thirds of its exports (see tables 13.2 and 13.3).

## OTTAWA AND ECONOMIC NATIONALISM

**Table 13.3**

### ORIGIN OF CANADIAN IMPORTS, 1946–1975
(IN MILLIONS OF DOLLARS)

| Area | 1946 | 1955 | 1965 | 1975 |
|---|---|---|---|---|
| United States | 1387 | 3331 | 6045 | 23 641 |
| United Kingdom | 137 | 393 | 619 | 1 222 |
| Japan | – | 37 | 230 | 1 205 |
| Other west European | 14 | 143 | 514 | 2 074 |
| Other American | 164 | 409 | 548 | 1 802 |
| Centrally planned (communist) economies | 5 | 8 | 59 | 234 |
| Other | 134 | 246 | 618 | 4 537 |
| Percentage of imports from U.S. | 75.3 | 72.9 | 70.0 | 68.1 |

*Source: F.H. Leacy, ed.,* Historical Statistics of Canada, *2nd ed. (Ottawa: Statistics Canada, 1983), Series G 408-414*

## THE GORDON REPORT

Canadians were ambivalent about this transformation in their economic relations. They had long courted American capital investment and had boasted about the success of the tariff in encouraging American companies to locate north of the forty-ninth parallel. Now the degree of American control of Canada's economic destiny began to take on sinister overtones. In 1955, the Canadian government appointed a Royal Commission on Canada's Economic Prospects to inquire into and report on the long-term prospects of the Canadian economy. Chaired by Walter Gordon, a partner in one of Toronto's major accounting firms, the commission expressed concern over the impact that American branch plants and the high degree of foreign investment were having on the Canadian economy. Branch plants typically hired American managers, devoted little attention to research and development, and remitted a high percentage of their profits to foreign investors. Built to serve only a Canadian market, branch plants often operated inefficiently and were restricted by head office from export opportunities. The high level of foreign investment in Canada contributed to Canada's growing balance of payments problem as capital flowed out of the country in the form of interest and dividends. If Canadians hoped to create a balanced economy and let their manufacturing sector reach maturity, it would be necessary to curtail American influence. The commissioners urged the government to exercise closer control over the activities of foreign companies operating in Canada and suggested that foreign corporations be required to employ more Canadians in senior management positions, include Canadians on their boards, and sell an "appreciable interest" in their equity stocks to people in the country where they did their business.

While nationalists supported policies that limited American control of the Canadian economy, classical economists, represented by University of

*Chrysler plant in Windsor, Ontario, 1954 (above) and ESSO station, circa 1950.*
*American corporations seemed omnipresent in the postwar Canadian economy.*

National Archives of Canada/NA112635

## VIEWS OF FOREIGN OWNERSHIP

In the 1950s and 1960s, Canada's political and business leaders expressed conflicting views regarding the benefits of foreign ownership of Canadian industries. The following excerpts provide a hint of the flavour of the debate.

> With an enormous area still of almost virgin country to be opened, Canadians need and welcome foreign investments and with their own healthy stake in the national development they have no fears of any domination.
>> —G.K. Sheils, president of the Canadian Manufacturers Association, in the **Financial Post**, 1953

> The free and unhampered flow of foreign investment into Canada has brought so many benefits to this country that it certainly is entitled to a fair and unbiased hearing from the Canadian people.

> ... If one allows for Canadian investment abroad and the use of foreign resources as a percentage of net capital formation, it turns out that not more than 6 per cent of Canadian investment in the postwar world depended on foreign resources.

> ...Canada's economy has been growing at such a rapid rate that the role of foreign investment in relation to our productive capacity has diminished and will continue to do so.
>> —C.D. Howe, minister of trade and commerce, in the House of Commons, 1956

> No other country in the world with something like our relative state of development has ever had such a degree of foreign domination, or even one half or one quarter the degree of foreign domination. Canada is being pushed down the road that leads to loss of any effective power to be masters in our own household and ultimate absorption in and by another.
>> —James Coyne, president of the Bank of Canada, to the Canadian Chamber of Commerce, 1960

> During the two-and-one half years I held that office [minister of finance], the influence that financial and business interests in the United States had on Canadian policy was continually brought home to me. On occasion, this influence was reinforced by representations from the State Department and the American Administration as a whole. It was pressed by those who direct American businesses in Canada, by their professional advisors, by Canadian financiers whose interests were identified directly or indirectly with American investment in Canada, by influential members of the Canadian civil service, by some representatives of the university community, and by some sections of the press.[6]
>> —Walter Gordon, **A Choice for Canada**, 1966

Toronto economist Harry Johnson, argued that economic nationalism was a "narrow and garbage cluttered cul-de-sac."[5] Canada, and Canadian workers in particular, he maintained, would benefit from the removal of all restrictions to trade and foreign investment. Only by remaining open to global economic trends could the Canadian economy function at optimal efficiency and therefore provide the best jobs and highest incomes. The free trade option elicited a considerable following among business people and politicians in the early 1960s, but the only tangible result was the Auto Pact of 1965. The pact, which created an integrated continental market for automobiles and auto-

mobile parts, included quotas for Canadian production, making it more an example of "managed trade" than unfettered free trade.

The Diefenbaker government made a few attempts to respond to the growing view that Americans exercised too much power in the Canadian economy. It introduced tax incentives for Canadian-based industries, and incurred the wrath of the United States by trading with communist countries such as Cuba and the Soviet Union.

The Pearson government appeared at first willing to go further than their predecessors. Lester Pearson named his long-time friend Walter Gordon minister of finance. Gordon set out to use legislation to implement some of the nationalistic ideas set out in the 1957 report of the royal commission he had chaired. Gordon's first budget was a highly controversial one. Included among a variety of nationalistic proposals was a 30 percent "take-over tax" on the sale of publicly held Canadian companies to foreigners. Although Gordon was forced by an angry business community and American government pressures to abandon the tax, his economic nationalism was gaining significant popular support. In 1964–65, Gordon introduced legislation to protect Canadian banks, insurance companies, and other financial services from foreign control, and steps were taken to reduce American dominance of the Canadian media. Gordon tweaked the beaks of too many powerful business people, and his cabinet influence had been reduced by the time he resigned as finance minister in late 1965. Nevertheless, Pearson agreed to a Gordon proposal to establish a Task Force on the Structure of Canadian Industry to examine whether it really mattered who owned industry in Canada. Gordon's choice for its head was a respected economist, Mel Watkins of the University of Toronto.

## THE WATKINS REPORT

Although Watkins was once a critic of economic nationalism, his investigation of Canadian–American economic relations converted him to a different view, and his report, appearing in 1968, was tougher than the Gordon report eleven years earlier. Watkins attempted to torpedo the common view that, whatever the impact on Canada's sovereignty, American investment was helping to create a more dynamic, efficient economy than Canadians could build on their own. The view that Canada remained short of capital and needed foreign investment was branded by Watkins as a myth. Canada's investors abroad, had they kept their money at home, could have reduced the need for foreign capital by half.

The task force painted a picture of a branch-plant manufacturing economy geared to serving the Canadian market alone, leaving international markets to the plants headquartered in the United States. While defenders of the American branch plants pointed with pride to the large number of corporations operating in Canada, Watkins charged that having a Canadian "miniature replica" of an American industry was irrational and further minimized Canada's economic competitiveness. Watkins argued that a few firms working at full capacity, focusing on international as well as national markets, and spending money to apply the latest technologies, would better serve the national interest.

A much-debated document, the Watkins report was released at a time when nationalistic sentiment was strong and misgivings about the United States were growing. An organization calling itself the Committee for an Independent Canada was formed to rally support for the demands of the task force for legislation to encourage Canadian investment and research and to curb foreign ownership. At a 1969 party convention, the Waffle group within the New Democratic Party won one-third of the votes for a resolution that called for public ownership of industry to replace foreign private ownership. Watkins, once a liberal internationalist, became a leader of this socialist and nationalist group. He argued that private market forces left on their own had made Canada an economic colony of the United States and only a democratic socialist strategy could empower Canadians to determine their economic fate collectively.

Two further government-sponsored investigations on the foreign-ownership issue followed the Watkins report. While both produced reports more moderate in tone, they confirmed the task force's conclusion that the federal government should be promoting greater Canadian ownership of the economy.

## ECONOMIC NATIONALISM IN THE 1970s

Despite Pierre Trudeau's scepticism about economic nationalism, his government enacted several of Watkins's recommendations. The Canada

Development Corporation (CDC) was created in 1971 to encourage Canadian ownership and management in vital sectors of the economy. In 1974, the Foreign Investment Review Agency (FIRA), under the direction of Herb Gray, was established to screen proposals for foreign takeovers of existing Canadian businesses.

There was also federal intervention in one of the industries where the Americans exercised greatest control in Canada: petroleum. In late 1973, the federal government created Petro-Canada, a Crown corporation with a broad mandate to develop a Canadian presence in the petroleum industry. It was a task that earlier Canadian governments had shunned. There were campaigns in the 1950s by independent petroleum companies for an oil pipeline from Montreal to Alberta that would replace a developing north–south energy grid with an east–west one. But the industry's dominant company in Canada, Imperial Oil, was controlled by Standard Oil of New Jersey, which also had large investments in Venezuela and the Middle East. Standard Oil's marketing strategy collided with the nationalist goals of the independent producers. Lacking an infrastructure that could provide reliable data on the industry, the federal and Alberta governments relied on Imperial for information and advice and therefore rejected the independents' plans as impractical.

Not surprisingly, the federal government's tentative entry into the petroleum industry was greeted with hostility by the American oil giants. It was not the only source of friction between the United States and Canada over oil. American oil companies operating in Alaska claimed the right to have their supertankers travel across the Arctic passage to transport their product to eastern American markets. Canada argued that such voyages would violate Canadian sovereignty and adversely affect the fragile northern environment. Although the government did not protest when the American tanker *Manhattan* carried several cargoes across the Arctic in 1969 and 1970, it passed the Arctic Waters Pollution Prevention Act to protect its northern coast. The Nixon administration's hostility suggested confrontation would occur if Canada attempted to enforce this legislation, and the

Canadian government chose rather to campaign at the United Nations for "law of the sea" legislation that would give Northern countries greater control over their coastlines.

The Nixon administration made matters difficult for opponents of economic nationalism in Canada by establishing the Domestic International Sales Corporation (DISC) in August 1971. DISC used the tax system to further encourage American multinational firms to export from their American facilities to the detriment of their branch plants. The legislation also imposed a temporary import surcharge of 10 percent. Although this was not the first time that Americans had pursued a policy of economic nationalism, it was the first time since the Second World War that Canadians were not exempt from such measures. Trade policy in the United States, once largely made in the offices of the secretary of state with a sharp eye on Canada as a strategic ally, moved to economic departments concerned mainly with protecting American jobs.

Such policies in the United States coincided with a growing concern about what the character of Canada's imports and exports said about the country's economy. Exports, which made up a quarter of GNP, consisted largely of unprocessed and semi-processed products. By contrast, Canada's imports were mainly manufactured goods. While the Americans imported only 10 percent of the manufactured products they consumed, Canadians imported 36 percent.

Following Nixon's announcement, Trudeau's minister of external affairs, Mitchell Sharp, issued a statement that committed Canada to what became known as the "Third Option" in Canadian foreign policy. Option one, maintaining Canada's present relationship with the United States, had been tried and found wanting. Option two, closer integration with the Americans, was clearly impossible in the age of Nixon. Option three, reduction of Canada's vulnerability to American actions by expanding global political and economic links, seemed the obvious choice. Diplomatic efforts to expand Canada's trade with other nations bore some fruit, but Canada remained overwhelmingly dependent on the American economy for its imports and exports.

## CONTINENTALISM AND THE PROVINCES

Federal efforts to control American investment in Canada often met a hostile response from the provinces. In the postwar period, as American resource demands increased, north–south economic linkages became more important to several provinces than east–west links. Since the provinces had constitutional jurisdiction over resources and could earn important economic rents from their development, they increasingly resisted the use of the federal power over trade and taxation to shape patterns of resource exploitation. Alberta governments, both Social Credit and Conservative, were particularly resistant to any "discriminatory" treatment of foreign capital, arguing that the rise of their province from have-not to have status in the postwar period was largely the doing of the giant American energy corporations.

Before the war, the federal government had disallowed provincial efforts to secure long-term contracts to sell hydro-electricity to the Americans. In the postwar period, the combination of American and provincial pressures gradually led the federal government to abandon its policy that hydro should be harnessed mainly for national needs. The American Northwest could not meet its own power needs, and the United States negotiated a treaty with Canada to develop dams on the Canadian side of the Columbia River in British Columbia. These would provide flood control as the Americans produced more hydro-electricity on the American Columbia. The original treaty between the two countries agreed to return to Canada half of the power generated on the American side, but Premier W.A.C. Bennett of British Columbia preferred to sell that power to the Americans and to use the Peace River to generate British Columbia's power needs.

Yielding to pressure from British Columbia, the federal government negotiated a protocol that included commitments to sell power to the western American states. Canada ratified the Columbia River Treaty and Protocol in 1964. Soon Manitoba was signing long-term deals with the Americans to deliver power from the province's North. Native peoples were removed from thriving communities along northern rivers so that giant power projects could meet the dual needs of American consumers and the provincial treasury. Cree and Inuit of northern Quebec suffered the same fate in the 1970s when the Quebec government began its ambitious James Bay project to meet not only provincial power needs but also considerable demand from the state of New York.

## AMERICANIZATION OF CANADIAN CULTURE

Although the Canadian government was slow off the mark in attempting to regulate American-dominated resource and manufacturing industries, it was quicker in recognizing the danger posed by American cultural industries. Concerns about the overwhelming American influence on Canadian culture, particularly in anglophone Canada, led to the creation in 1949 of a royal commission to study national developments in the arts, letters, and sciences. Headed by Vincent Massey—scion of the farm-implements giant Massey-Harris, wealthy Liberal Party backer, and former Canadian high commissioner to Britain—the royal commission recommended government programs to stimulate the arts. In the 1950s, the federal government responded by establishing the Canada Council and other bodies to dispense modest funds to the nation's writers, painters, musicians, and scholars. The result was that, while profitable popular culture remained Americanized, there was a strengthening of the Canadian presence in literature, music, and art.

When television made its commercial appearance after the Second World War, the federal government decided to grant licensing power over the new medium to the CBC's board of governors. The CBC was to establish a television network and initially would be given a monopoly over Canadian TV. By 1960, nine CBC stations and thirty-eight affiliates were on the air. While the stations gave over much of their prime time to American shows such as *I Love Lucy* and *The Ed Sullivan Show*, CBC-TV also produced Canadian dramas and variety shows that provided an outlet for many Canadian actors, musicians, and entertainers. *Front Page Challenge*, a sedate guess-the-name-in-the-news show, was introduced in 1956 and remained on the air until 1995 with the same host, Fred Davis, and with original panelist Pierre Berton still in harness. *Country Hoedown* introduced a generation of country music entertainers, notably Tommy Hunter, and *Don Messer's Jubilee*, which was first aired in 1959, earned a devoted following. While American sitcoms and teleplays proved more popular than their Canadian equivalents, *The Plouffe Family*, a teleplay focusing on the lives of a working-class Montreal family, was a huge success in both its French and English versions.

In 1958, the federal government responded to pressure from private broadcasters to end the CBC monopoly over television. Many Canadians wanted more American offerings and resented the geographical unfairness that allowed Torontonians to tap into a variety of Buffalo stations while Winnipegers and Edmontonians had only the CBC. Under new legislation, private channels became eligible for licences, and a Board of Broadcast Governors (BBG) was set up to license radio and television stations. After the first private stations went on the air, featuring almost non-stop American entertainment, nationalist pressures forced the BBG to establish a 55 percent Canadian content guideline in the 1960s. Cheaply produced game shows, modelled on American programs, were the private stations' answer to the rule, and hopes that content regulations would stimulate a viable Canadian television production industry were largely unrealized.

While most television shows, whether produced in Canada or the United States, constituted light entertainment, they also embodied a set of conservative social values and stereotypes. "Family shows," including *Father Knows Best* and *Leave It to Beaver*, extolled middle-class patriarchal families in which father earned the money while mother cared for the household. A woman's purpose in life was presented in innumerable commercials that explained how, by purchasing the advertised products, a housewife could fulfil herself and be the envy of neighbours by staying young and attractive

while keeping a spotless house with impeccably well-groomed and well-nourished inhabitants.

American content and American models were evident in other areas of mass culture besides television. In response to the competition from "the tube," radio stations turned their attention from drama and comedy to music. Most of that music was recorded in the United States. Movies were overwhelmingly American. The average Canadian went to eighteen movies per year in 1950 before television caused a drop in movie attendance. In 1953, 74.6 percent of the feature films that were distributed in Canada originated in the United States, 16.9 percent in France, and 5.8 percent in Britain. There was only one Canadian film in movie houses that year. Nonetheless, the government resisted imposing quotas on Hollywood movies, instead entering an agreement with the major studios to include mentions of Canada in American feature films.

Canadian entertainers continued to seek success in the larger American market, and their reputations among the home folk were enhanced when they achieved it. Former CBC newsman Lorne Greene was lionized for his role as the patriarch of the Ponderosa ranch in television's *Bonanza*. A variety of Canadian recording artists, including the Crewcuts, Paul Anka, the Diamonds, the Guess Who, and Anne Murray, topped the American charts at various times. Johnny Wayne and Frank Shuster, about to lose their Canadian television series, were renewed after American audiences cheered their comic portrayal of Julius Caesar's murder on *The Ed Sullivan Show* in May 1958.

## THE NATIONALIST RESPONSE

The government provided some assistance to Canadian film-makers and recording artists. Tax breaks and subsidies were given to producers of Canadian films, and in 1970 the Canadian Radio-television and Telecommunications Commission introduced regulations requiring radio stations to ensure that no fewer than 30 percent of the records they played were of Canadian origin. While these measures were not without effect, the next several decades would confirm that anglophone Canadians preferred to spend their money on American movies and American as well as British recordings. American culture's hold on the mass market would not easily be dislodged.

By the early 1970s, much of English Canada's artistic community had become ardent Canadian nationalists. Cultural icons such as authors Pierre Berton and Farley Mowat, poet Earle Birney, and artist Harold Town were prominent members of the Committee for an Independent Canada. Celebrated novelist and poet Margaret Atwood wrote *Survival* (1972), an outline of the development of Canadian literature that attempted to find a distinct Canadian identity in the resilient, if often cheerless, characters who peopled national writing. Not every successful Canadian author applauded such developments. Mordecai Richler, one of Canada's best-known authors both at home and abroad, argued that cultural nationalism would result in mediocre work and that Canadians should be willing to have their work judged by international standards. Like many Canadians who were not of British descent, Richler suspected that Canadian nationalism was a plot by white Anglo-Saxon Protestants to impose their version of a national identity on immigrant groups who had their own complex identities of which being Canadian was but one component.

The French-Canadian artistic community, particularly in Quebec, was largely estranged from the new assertive cultural nationalism of English Canada. Its members had, for the most part, joined in the movement for Quebec sovereignty and they felt that their language saved the Québécois from the onslaught of American culture so visible in the rest of the country.

The bombarding of Canadians with American messages disquieted some Canadian scholars, particularly the country's most celebrated political economist, Harold Adams Innis. In a number of essays, collected in *Empire and Communications* (1950) and *The Bias of Communications* (1951), Innis suggested that media empires in the United States were shaping the thinking of people the world over. Democratic discussion was being diverted by the limited number of individuals who controlled access to information. As historian Mary Vipond observes, Innis's "thesis has provided the theoretical groundwork for contemplation of one of the central paradoxes of Canadian history: how technology in general and communications technology in particular have acted as a double-edged sword that simultaneously facilitates the promotion of national unity and serves as the highway on which the culture of another nation rides into our homes."[7]

Universities themselves came under criticism from Canadian nationalists in the 1960s for their policies to cope with the large enrolments of baby boomers. Most universities had hired a significant number of foreign, mainly American, academics, many of whom ignored Canadian topics in their teaching and research. In 1972, the Association of Universities and Colleges of Canada established a commission to study and make recommendations on the state of university scholarship and teaching relating to Canada. Chaired by Thomas H.B. Symons, the founding president of Trent University, the commission concluded in its two volume report, entitled *To Know Ourselves*, that students were much more interested in learning about Canada than professors were in teaching about it. Indeed, the commissioners maintained that no country in the world spent so little time studying itself. The Symons report was hotly debated, but it ultimately helped to convince the federal government to establish programs to encourage Canadian studies and to pass legislation giving preference to qualified Canadians in university hiring. Canadian universities in the late 1960s and early 1970s also acceded to student pressures to expand their offerings in the literature and history of the country.

## FROM RED BAITING TO STUDENT REBELLION

The American impact on Canadian thinking was complex. Not only were imported messages increasingly filtered through nationalist lenses, but also American society itself was dynamic, and the messages that it transmitted through mass culture changed over time. One dramatic example is the shift from the repressive atmosphere of the early

Cold War to the radicalism that prevailed during the student and anti-war movements of the late 1960s.

The Cold War was, in part, an ideological battle, and its participants, hoping to impose their values on other countries, would not countenance defeat on the home front. The Soviets and their allies crushed dissent ruthlessly. Although western countries claimed that they were champions of freedom of expression and association, their behaviour often indicated otherwise. In the United States the House Committee on Un-American Activities (HUAC) had harassed communists since the 1930s, but the anti-communist campaign in 1950 became identified with one man—Senator Joseph R. McCarthy of Wisconsin. He used the HUAC to investigate a wide spectrum of American citizens, including government bureaucrats, university professors, and popular entertainers. He finally over-reached himself when he began launching an investigation into possible subversion in the American army in 1954. By that time, many institutions had begun their own witch-hunts, and many blacklisted people found themselves out of a job. In one of the most controversial court cases of the twentieth century, Americans Ethel and Julius Rosenberg were convicted of passing atomic secrets to the Soviet Union and hanged in 1953.

McCarthyism in Canada was less virulent than in the United States, but it infected Canadian institutions nonetheless. Anti-communism became a key ingredient in immigration policy. While restrictions on former Nazis were lifted to the point where the RCMP complained that war criminals were being admitted to Canada, no such tolerance was extended to communists and ex-communists. Communists were not only deported and kept out as permanent immigrants, they were even prevented from visiting Canada. The federal government attempted to root radicals out of the civil service. After all, it was just such people who had handed information to Soviet Embassy officials about nuclear research during the Second World War. Homosexuals, regardless of their political beliefs, were excluded on the grounds that Soviet agents might blackmail them into becoming spies by threatening to disclose their sexual orientation.

In such an environment, the civil libertarian argument that individuals ought to be judged by their actions and not their beliefs or associations was rejected out of hand.

Communists and communist sympathizers who had been democratically chosen to head unions were denounced so stridently in the media and by their non-communist union opponents that the state confidently persecuted them and, in some cases, destroyed their unions. In 1946, Maurice Duplessis jailed Kent Rowley and Madeleine Parent, organizers for the Trades and Labour Congress local of textile workers in Valleyfield. In British Columbia, the Labour Relations Board refused to certify the communist-led Woodworkers Industrial Union of Canada as bargaining agent for locals wishing to secede from the American-dominated Industrial Woodworkers of America (IWA). The provincial police then joined with employers to break strikes by this "illegal" union. The breakaways were forced to rejoin the IWA, whose American leadership had purged communists from leadership roles in both the United States and Canada.

Communists and ex-communists faced constant surveillance and harassment. Roscoe Fillmore, active from the early 1900s with the socialists and communists, was a prominent horticulturalist in Nova Scotia. Although he gave up his membership in the communist Labour Progressive Party in 1950, years later the RCMP was still following him to horticultural conferences and filing reports, complete with licence plate numbers, on the cars stopping by the Fillmore Valley Nursery on summer weekends. RCMP agents even spied on the funerals of Fillmore's comrades, sitting in the back row, noting the names of those attending.

The suicide of veteran Canadian diplomat E.H. Norman in Cairo in 1957, after repeated but unsubstantiated charges that he was a Soviet agent, demonstrates the tragic side of McCarthyism. Lives could be ruined if individuals were suspected of being communists or even of being soft on communism. Members of peace groups, such as the Women's International League for Peace and Freedom, founded in 1915, also suffered from red baiters, who smeared anyone who opposed them.

In such an atmosphere, those leery of the Cold War philosophy or of particular actions that flowed from such a philosophy generally kept their mouths shut. In both Canada and the United States, fundamental criticism of foreign policy or of red baiting was rare.

This reticence changed dramatically in the 1960s. The civil rights and anti-war movements in the United States sparked an extensive student movement that questioned everything about American society. By the end of the decade, movements for black power, feminism, gay liberation, Native rights, and Third World liberation challenged fundamental notions about American society. Young Canadians were influenced by this awakening of dissent, to the dismay of many of their elders. Ironically, Canadian social critics, while borrowing ideas liberally from their American counterparts, were likely to assert the need for greater independence from the Americans.

## CONCLUSION

The shadow of the Americans cannot be ignored in any discussion of Canadian development following the Second World War. As the world's most powerful nation in the age of the atomic bomb and instantaneous communications, the United States exerted an influence even greater than France or Great Britain in earlier eras of Canadian history. Many Canadians accepted this reality without much concern, but others were troubled by the spectre of American domination.

In 1965, George Grant wrote *Lament for a Nation*, in which he explored the career of John Diefenbaker, whose government, some people believed, had been brought down in 1963 by the hostility of the Kennedy regime. Grant pointed out the self-defeating character of the well-meaning nationalism of John Diefenbaker. On the one hand, Diefenbaker genuinely wanted Canada to develop outside of the shadow of the Americans. He sought to focus on Canada's links with the British Commonwealth to provide a counterweight to the overwhelming influence of the United States in the nation's economic and political life.

On the other hand, according to Grant, Diefenbaker, while sometimes defiant of the Americans, shared their fundamental values. He accepted the supremacy of the marketplace over the state, and of individual acquisitiveness over collective goals. Canadians generally, lamented Grant, shared Diefenbaker's contradictions. They had embraced American social values, all the time protesting that they wished to be a sovereign people. Yet their materialistic pursuits had turned them into a people who had integrated their economy and their foreign policy with that of the Americans and who consumed what the American entertainment industry served them.

Writing in 1970, historian Donald Creighton, like Grant a conservative who lamented Canada's fascination with the United States and its break with British ties, had a withering description of the Canadians of the postwar period: "They had permitted their government to turn its back on their past and to repudiate their history; and in the bankruptcy of their own national philosophy, they turned instinctively to the nearest creditor, the United States.... Imitation and plagiarism had become deep-seated Canadian instincts; economic and political dependence had grown into a settled way of life."[8]

While Grant and Creighton were pessimistic about Canada's ability to resist absorption into the American Empire, there were clearly a variety of Canadians who believed that the battle for an independent economy, a made-in-Canada foreign policy, and for a more assertive Canadian cultural nationalism was still worth waging. Certainly by 1975, the year the Americans were defeated in Indochina, gains had been made on all three fronts. Many Canadians believed that, with the American Empire in decline and the Cold War waning, Canada could slowly extricate itself from a web of entanglement weaved especially tightly in the early postwar period.

# VIETNAM: WHAT ROLE DID CANADA PLAY?

## A Historiographical Debate

As we have seen, Canada prided itself on its image as a peacemaker in international relations. But in instances where American interests were at stake, how successful was Canada in fulfilling this role? Was Ottawa able to strike an independent course, or did it take its cue from the Americans?

There is considerable debate about Canada's role inside the International Control Commission, which was originally established in the 1950s to monitor the Geneva Accord for the resolution of conflict in Indochina, and about Canada's larger role in the war in Indochina. With its American neighbour pitted against the North Vietnamese communists, how neutral an observer could Canada be?

Political scientist James Eayrs's *Indochina: Roots of Complicity*, as the title suggests, views Canada as "complicit" in pushing the American point of view within the ICC. Though he deals with only the first three years of the Commission's existence (1954–57), Eayrs demonstrates that Canada quickly established a partisan stance within the ICC. Apart from faithfully supporting American positions, Canada's commissioners developed the habit of reporting confidential information to the Americans. Put less delicately, Canada betrayed its trust and acted as a spy for the United States.[9]

Douglas Ross suggests in his book *In the Interests of Peace* that the Eayrs text lacks nuance. While conceding that Canada's focus in the ICC was on North Vietnamese violations, he points out that Canada was trying to counter Poland's one-sided attacks on South Vietnam. Ross argues that Canada joined the ICC in order to influence the course of events in Indochina and Canadian diplomacy urged moderation upon the Americans in their prosecution of the war, although the strength of militaristic forces in the United States limited the impact of such counsel.[10]

Political scientist Victor Levant disputes most of Ross's account. *His Quiet Complicity* emphasizes that, in 1962, Canada joined India in preparing a report on North Vietnamese violations of the Geneva Accord, which the Americans used to justify increasing their scale of intervention in Indochina. Using American State and Defence Department records, he argues that Canada was well aware of American plans to bomb North Vietnam and was willing to use its diplomats as intermediaries for the Americans to deliver threats to the North Vietnamese government.

Levant, in contrast to Ross, focuses on the economic gains made by Canadian business from the war in Vietnam. He rejects the view that the Canadians were acting on orders from the United States government or out of fear of that government's retaliation if Canada behaved independently. Rather he argues that the shared views of the elites of the two countries led Canada's political leaders to support the main lines of American policy. Canada's leaders were supporters of international capitalism and wanted to see the defeat of the Vietnamese communists at any cost.[11]

*So Many Worlds*, the second volume of Paul Martin's autobiography, which Levant brands "a classic example of historical amnesia and political double-talk,"[12] denies that Canada's role in Vietnam was partisan. Martin maintains that Canada worked tirelessly to arrange for ceasefires and to have the two warring sides arrive at a compromise, but that, ultimately, the Canadians were unable to achieve much due to the rigidity that characterized the two factions. While Martin's autobiography concedes that good political relations with the Americans could translate into special consideration on economic questions, he ignores this connection in his discussion of Canada's behaviour regarding Vietnam.[13]

## NOTES

[1]  Kari Levitt, *Silent Surrender: The Multinational Corporation in Canada* (Toronto: Macmillan, 1970), 2–3

[2]  Cited in William Kaplan, *Everything That Floats: Pat Sullivan, Hal Banks, and the Seamen's Unions of Canada* (Toronto: University of Toronto Press, 1987), 181

[3]  The term *Third World* was coined to differentiate the poorer countries of the world from the wealthier industrialized nations. The First World consisted of the western powers plus Japan. The Second World comprised the Soviet Union and its satellites in Eastern Europe. Self-determination suggested the right of the peoples of these poor nations to choose their own future without undue influence from outside powers. Though decolonization proceeded rapidly from 1945 onwards, most of the newly independent nations found that in practice they were forced to become economic vassals of either the West or the Soviets.

[4]  Paul Martin, *A Very Public Life*, vol. 2, *So Many Worlds* (Toronto: Deneau, 1985), 389

[5]  Harry Johnson, *The Canadian Quandary* (Ottawa: Carleton University Press, 1963), 11–12

[6]  Quoted in Philip Resnick, *The Land of Cain: Class and Nationalism in English Canada 1945-1975* (Vancouver: New Star Books, 1977), 79, 102, 114, 115

[7]  Mary Vipond, *The Mass Media in Canada* (Toronto: Lorimer, 1989), 131

[8]  Donald Creighton, *Canada's First Century, 1867–1967* (Toronto: Macmillan, 1970), 356

[9]  James Eayrs, *In Defence of Canada*, vol. 5, *Indochina: Roots of Complicity* (Toronto: University of Toronto Press, 1983)

[10]  Douglas Ross, *In the Interests of Peace: Canada and Vietnam, 1945–1973* (Toronto: University of Toronto Press, 1983)

[11]  Victor Levant, *Quiet Complicity: Canadian Involvement in the Vietnam War* (Toronto: Between the Lines, 1986)

[12]  Ibid., 297

[13]  Martin, *So Many Worlds*, chap. 13

## SELECTED READING

Surveys and books of essays dealing with a cross-section of the issues discussed in this unit include: Robert Bothwell, *Canada and the United States: The Politics of Partnership* (Toronto: University of Toronto Press, 1992); Edelgard E. Mahant and Graeme S. Mount, *An Introduction to Canadian-American Relations*, 2nd ed. (Scarborough: Nelson, 1989); Norman Hillmer, ed., *Partners Nevertheless: Canadian–American Relations in the Twentieth Century* (Toronto: Copp Clark Pitman, 1989); Allan Smith, *Canada: An American Nation? Essays on Continentalism, Identity and the Canadian Frame of Mind* (Montreal: McGill-Queen's University Press, 1994); and Philip Resnick, *The Land of Cain: Class and Nationalism in English Canada, 1945–1975* (Vancouver: New Star, 1977).

Canada's aims and roles throughout the Cold War are discussed in Norman Hillmer and J.L. Granatstein, *Empire to Umpire: Canada and the World to the 1990s* (Toronto: Copp Clark Longman, 1994); J.L. Granatstein and Norman Hillmer, *For Better or for Worse: Canada and the United States to the 1990s* (Toronto: Copp Clark Pitman, 1991); Denis Smith, *Politics of Fear: Canada and the Cold War, 1941–1948* (Toronto: University of Toronto Press, 1988); James Eayrs, *In Defence of Canada*, vols. 4 and 5 (Toronto: University of Toronto Press, 1980, 1983); George Ignatieff, *The Making of a Peacemonger* (Toronto: Penguin, 1985); Ernie Regehr and Simon Rosenblum, eds., *Canada and the Nuclear Arms Race* (Toronto: Lorimer, 1983); Denis Stairs, *The Diplomacy of Constraint: Canada, the Korean War and the United States* (Toronto: University of Toronto Press, 1974); Douglas Ross, *In the Interests of Peace: Canada and Vietnam, 1945–1973* (Toronto: University of Toronto Press, 1985); and Victor Levant, *Quiet Complicity: Canadian Involvement in the Vietnam War* (Toronto: Between the Lines, 1986). On the domestic Cold War, see Reginald Whitaker and Gary Marcuse, *Cold War Canada: The Making of a National Insecurity State, 1945–1957* (Toronto: University of Toronto Press, 1994); Reginald Whitaker, *Double Standard: The Secret History of Canadian Immigration* (Toronto: Lester and Orpen Dennys,

1987); Len Scher, *The Un-Canadians: True Stories of the Blacklist Era* (Toronto: Lester, 1992); Roger Bowen, *Innocence Is Not Enough: The Life and Death of Herbert Norman* (Vancouver: Douglas and McIntyre, 1986); and Nicholas Fillmore, *Maritime Radical: The Life and Times of Roscoe Fillmore* (Toronto: Between the Lines, 1992).

On the relationship between the Cold War and Canadian–American economic relations, see Melissa Clark Jones, *A Staple State: Canadian Industrial Resources in Cold War* (Toronto: University of Toronto Press, 1987), and J.L. Granatstein and Robert Cuff, *American Dollars and Canadian Prosperity* (Toronto: Samuel-Stevens, 1978). On Canadian–American economic relations from 1945 to 1975 more generally, useful sources include: Mel Watkins et al., *Foreign Ownership and the Structure of Canadian Industry*, Report of the Task Force on the Structure of Canadian Industry (Ottawa: Ministry of Supply and Services, 1968); Ian Wahn et al., *Eleventh Report of the Standing Committee on External Affairs and National Defence Respecting Canadian–American Relations* (Ottawa: Ministry of Supply and Services, 1970); Herb Gray et al., *Foreign Direct Investment in Canada* (Ottawa: Ministry of Supply and Services, 1972); Kari Levitt, *Silent Surrender: The Multinational Corporation in Canada* (Toronto: Gage, 1971); and H.G. Johnson, *The Canadian Quandary* (Ottawa: Carleton University Press, 1977). The politician most associated with Canadian economic nationalism of this period, Walter Gordon, is the subject of Denis Smith, *Gentle Patriot: A Political Biography of Walter Gordon* (Edmonton: Hurtig, 1973).

On American cultural impact on Canada, see George Grant, *Lament for a Nation* (Ottawa: Carleton University Press, 1983); Mary Vipond, *The Mass Media in Canada* (Toronto: Lorimer, 1989); Paul Rutherford, *When Television Was Young: Primetime Canada, 1952–1967* (Toronto: University of Toronto Press, 1990); and Frank Peers, *The Public Eye: Television and the Politics of Canadian Broadcasting, 1952–1968* (Toronto: University of Toronto Press, 1979).

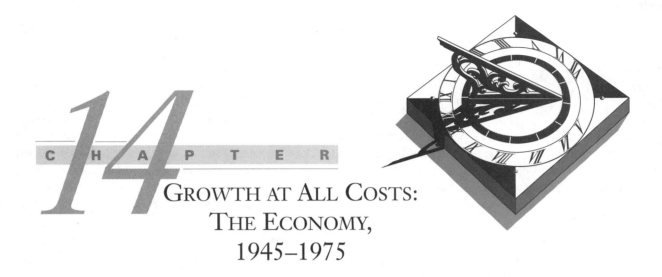

# CHAPTER 14
## GROWTH AT ALL COSTS: THE ECONOMY, 1945–1975

IN 1964, COMINCO BEGAN OPERATING A LEAD-zinc mine in the Northwest Territories, creating an instant community that was named Pine Point. About $100 million of federal money was lavished on the project, which included not only developing a townsite, but also building new highways, hydro-electricity plants, and a railway to haul minerals to waiting markets. By 1975, about eighteen hundred people, mainly white, lived at Pine Point, about five hundred of whom were employed by the mine. Their high wages and modern homes were evidence of the good lives that many Canadians were able to carve out for themselves in the long period of prosperity that began during the 1940s and lasted for over three decades.

Forty miles west of this new town created by business and government was the long-established Native community of Fort Resolution. Its view of the economic benefits of the mine was rather different than Cominco's. Speaking to a federal inquiry established in 1974 to determine whether oil and gas pipelines should be built across the Mackenzie Valley, Mike Beaulieu of Fort Resolution indicated why many Native northerners resented the presence of development-minded resource companies in their midst:

> We, the Dene people, do a lot of hunting and trapping and fishing. Our hunting has decreased a lot due to the construction of the highway, the building of the mine, and the increase of the people from the South.... Our traditional grounds are slowly being overtaken by these [mine] employees. There is virtually no benefit to be spoken of from the mine.[1]

The impact of the Pine Point mine on the environment and on Native peoples provides an example of the other side of the equation of the unprecedented economic growth that characterized the period from 1945 to 1975. Dramatic improvements in overall living standards were accompanied by environmental degradation, uneven distribution of the new wealth, and destruction of many communities. This chapter traces the economic history of the period when the American dream of unlimited prosperity became a realistic goal for many Canadians, but an unattainable—even undesirable—illusion for others.

## THE GOVERNMENT'S POSTWAR STRATEGY: THE WELFARE AND WARFARE ECONOMY

At the end of the Second World War, the federal government rejected radical demands for public ownership and extensive state regulation of the economy. Led by the Department of Finance and the Bank of Canada, Ottawa proposed that a combination of expanding the money supply and incurring government deficits in times of unemployment would be sufficient to prevent another depression. Reconstruction Minister C.D. Howe's White Paper on postwar reconstruction, presented to Parliament in April 1945, set the tone for the government's strategy: "The Government will be prepared in periods when unemployment threatens to incur the deficits and increases in the national debt resulting from its employment and income policy whether that policy in the circumstances is best applied through increased expenditures or reduced taxation."[2] The private sector would continue to operate companies, price goods, and make investment decisions.

Even this moderate Keynesianism shocked economic conservatives. Traditional economic theory held that large government deficits and accumulating debt would produce uncontrollable inflation because banks, having loaned most of their money to the state, would have little left over for private borrowers. In 1945, the federal debt alone was one-and-a-half times the nation's gross national product. Despite scepticism on the part of Mackenzie King, the government did not lose its nerve. Spending was increased rather than decreased and the Bank of Canada expanded the money supply to finance much of the debt.

The Canadian government moved quickly to rid the private sector of wartime price controls and to privatize most of the twenty-eight public corporations that had been established to produce goods required for the wartime effort. Still, social policy commitments and, in the 1950s, military spending, ensured growing state expenditures. Measured in *macroeconomic* terms—that is, the performance of the economy as a whole, with special emphasis on growth in output and productivity—the new government strategy worked well.

Immediately after the war, production slowed, exports contracted, and, with the winding down of the Wartime Prices and Trade Board, inflation reared its ugly head. The federal government kept the economy moving with tax incentives to industry and programs targeted at veterans, the private-housing market, and municipalities. Soon, consumer demand, fuelled by a decade and a half of depression and denial—and a well-orchestrated advertising campaign honed on wartime propaganda techniques—picked up the slack. Industries geared for war hardly skipped a beat as plants were quickly converted from producing troop carriers, uniforms, bombs, and barracks, to making cars, clothes, appliances, and housing materials. Emerging from the war with shiny new plants and equipment (some of them purchased at fire sale prices from the federal government), the Canadian business community continued its orgy of investment in capital stock until 1957.

Canadian officials may have been leery of wartime controls, but they were enthusiastic about the level of multilateral trade that had developed during the war. Since Canada's economic prosperity depended on a healthy export trade, trade liberalization became a cornerstone of Canadian postwar foreign policy. In November 1947, Canada signed the General Agreement on Tariffs and Trade (GATT), which bound its twenty-three signatories to consultation aimed at reducing trade barriers. Ironically, the intent of the agreement was immediately compromised in Canada by a series of restrictive trade measures announced by Finance Minister Douglas Abbott. Another exchange crisis precipitated by a binge of postwar spending on American products forced the government to reimpose import controls and secure a $300 million loan from the American Import-Export Bank. By 1949, controls were being lifted again, foreign investment resumed, and exports began to rise. The cyclical upswing was reinforced by massive military spending, sparked by the escalating Cold War.

Between 1949 and 1953, defence expenditures

rose from 16 to 45 percent of the federal budget, and a new ministry was created to orchestrate the business of war. C.D. Howe became the minister of defence production, and in this guise he continued to play godfather to the business community. With well over a billion dollars spent annually on defence in the 1950s, every aspect of the Canadian economy was shaped by military considerations. As late as 1960, when defence had slipped back to a quarter of federal budgetary expenditures, military purchases accounted for 89 percent of the shipments in the aircraft industry, 41 percent in electronics, and 21 percent in shipbuilding. Research and development in both Canada and the United States was increasingly related to defence priorities. Strategic stockpiling by the American military led to large-scale purchases of Canadian primary products, particularly minerals. In the United States, the term *military-industrial complex* was coined to describe this new era of defence-induced growth. It was equally applicable to Canada.

Contrary to the philosophy espoused in C.D. Howe's White Paper in 1945, federal planners failed to tailor their policies to cyclical swings. Ottawa ran budget surpluses for most of the years between 1949 and 1956, but they were not sufficiently large to offset private investment or the ambitious spending by provincial and municipal governments. In the heady atmosphere of postwar prosperity, politicians and the public came to believe that both welfare and warfare could be accommodated. Their treasuries fattened by higher personal and business taxes, governments at all levels spent money at an unprecedented rate, investing in infrastructure (roads and electrical power facilities) and building up social capital (schools and hospitals). In cooperation with provinces and private industry, the federal government became involved in several megaprojects, including the Trans-Canada Highway, the St Lawrence Seaway, the Trans-Canada Pipeline, and Beechwood Power. The decision to build the seaway, completed in 1959, had been debated for several decades before Canada and the United States signed an agreement in 1954 to jointly fund the project. Its purpose was to enlarge the canals and develop the power potential along the inland

waterway. Nearly thirty-eight hundred kilometres from Anticosti Island to Lake Superior, the seaway was an impressive engineering and construction feat that cost the Canadian government over a billion dollars.

With the booming economy, the unemployment rate for 1956 was only 3.2 percent, the lowest rate for the rest of the century, though double the rate of most western European countries that year. Wages increased faster than prices throughout the postwar decade. The government's debt as a proportion of gross national product halved during the decade because, while the government was spending more, a wealthier population was paying more taxes. With unemployment low, the unemployment insurance fund bulged. Output between 1946 and 1956 increased by 5.3 percent a year and consumption by 5.1 percent.

In 1957, the economic bubble burst: the American economy went into recession, and the Canadian economy, so closely integrated with that of its southern neighbour, followed suit. By 1958, the rate of unemployment was twice its 1956 level.

## ECONOMIC GROWTH IN THE FABULOUS FIFTIES

While the new economy was constrained by considerations of welfare and warfare, the direction of economic development in the 1950s bore a marked resemblance to the trends of the 1920s. Spectacular growth occurred in construction, consumer durable, staple, and service industries, while innovation and mass marketing sustained a high level of productivity.

Much of the productivity was stimulated by technological innovation leading to new product lines. Although many innovations such as synthetic fibres, plastics, and pesticides had been stimulated by wartime needs, others, including televisions, the self-propelled combine harvester, and the snowmobile, had been developed prior to the war but became commercially viable only in the improved postwar economic climate. In the iron and steel industry, the basic oxygen furnace, introduced in 1954, improved efficiency. Metropolitan Life installed elephantine computers in their offices in 1956, at the same time that the Department of National Revenue decided to enter the electronic age. Developments in the chemical industry revolutionized agriculture and sparked massive forest spraying programs. Homemakers even used DDT to rid their houses of annoying insects. The pharmaceutical industry could hardly keep up with the demand for new products, including such miracle drugs as penicillin and polio vaccines.

| Table 14.1 | | | |
|---|---|---|---|
| CANADA'S ECONOMIC GROWTH, 1945–1976 | | | |
| Year | GNP* | GNP in 1971 dollars* | GNP per capita in 1971 dollars* |
| 1945 | 11 863 | 29 071 | 2400.81 |
| 1951 | 21 640 | 35 450 | 2530.52 |
| 1956 | 32 058 | 47 599 | 2959.95 |
| 1961 | 39 646 | 54 741 | 3001.48 |
| 1966 | 61 828 | 74 844 | 3739.40 |
| 1971 | 94 450 | 94 450 | 4379.17 |
| 1976 | 191 031 | 119 249 | 5195.02 |

*millions of dollars

Source: F.H. Leacy, ed., Historical Statistics of Canada, 2nd ed. (Ottawa: Statistics Canada, 1983), tables A1, F 13, F 15

Attempting to anticipate consumer demands and to take advantage of government largesse, entrepreneurs weaved and darted from one opportunity to another, building up corporate empires at a dazzling rate, succeeding in one venture, failing in another, moving fast enough to avoid bankruptcy and public criticism. H.R. MacMillan graduated from his wartime duties to put together MacMillan-Bloedel in 1953, one of the largest forestry companies in the world, with integrated timber reserves, sawmills, and shipping operations. E.P. Taylor, another of Howe's wartime recruits, engineered his investment firm, Argus Corporation, into one of North America's major conglomerates, with controlling interest in everything from Canadian Breweries and Orange Crush to Massey-Ferguson and Domtar. The Bronfmans used their commanding position in the distilling industry to create their own investment companies. In New Brunswick, K.C. Irving constructed an empire based on oil, timber, and communications that would make him one of the richest men in the world.

## FARMING AND FISHING

In the postwar period, marketing boards revolutionized farming in Canada by establishing quotas, setting prices, and defining market boundaries. A larger percentage of farm products was destined for canning and, increasingly, freezing. Such novelties as the potato chip and the TV dinner gobbled up the output of Canadian farms. Farms became larger and could increasingly be viewed as full-fledged business enterprises, part of a delicately balanced network of production, processing, and marketing required to feed an increasingly urbanized North American society. Giant American corporations such as Hostess Foods, Stokely Van Camp, Swift's, and Swanson's competed with domestically based processors such as McCains, Aylmer, E.D. Smith, and Schneider's for the produce of Canadian farms. Increasingly too, corporations established vertically integrated operations by growing the crops required for their processing plants.

The crops in demand in the marketplace were changing. During the war, federal subsidies encouraged Prairie farmers to diversify their output. Oats, barley, and flax soon became as important as wheat to western producers. Although the volume of postwar wheat sales was maintained through special agreements with Britain, the price of wheat remained low on international markets throughout the 1950s, discouraging further expansion of the wheat economy. A similar transformation occurred in the Annapolis Valley where farmers were paid to uproot their apple orchards and concentrate on other fruits as well as vegetables, poultry, and dairy products for a domestic rather than a British market.

The transformation of the east coast fishing industry in the postwar decade paralleled that of agriculture. As European markets for saltfish disappeared, sales of fresh and frozen fish were increasingly geared to an oversupplied North American market. At the same time, technology revolutionized productivity in the fisheries. The stern trawler, introduced on the Grand Banks in the 1950s, could harvest 180 000 kilograms of fish in a two-week period. In 1953, Britain built the *Fairtry*, a factory freezer trawler with unsurpassed fishing power. Within a decade there were fourteen hundred trawlers of various shapes and sizes engaged in the Bank fishery, netting an unprecedented 2.6 million metric tonnes of fish.

## RESOURCE INDUSTRIES

Impressive growth also occurred in mining and hydro-electric power generation, benefiting from North American military requirements as well as from the demands of the booming North American economies. Private companies developed copper deposits at Murdochville on the Gaspé Peninsula, lead-zinc-copper ores in the Dalhousie–Bathurst region of New Brunswick, and potash in Saskatchewan. In 1949, a consortium of six American steel companies and two Canadian resource groups formed the Iron Ore Company to bring the vast deposits on the Ungava–Labrador border into production. The company built a 570-kilometre railway from Sept-Îles to the new resource town of Schefferville and were enthusiastic about improvements to the St Lawrence–Great Lakes transportation system so that ores could easily be moved to mills in the industrial heartland of North America.

Canada's energy resources seemed to know no bounds in the postwar period. On 3 February 1947, Imperial Oil's Leduc No. 1 well, near Edmonton, struck oil, and ten days later five hundred Albertan dignitaries were invited to the official production test. Once the geological base of Alberta's vast oil

reserves was understood, oil discoveries became regular fare. From 1945 to 1960, Alberta's annual production of crude petroleum increased by a factor of sixteen while natural gas production increased tenfold. Saskatchewan also made promising finds of energy resources during this period.

In the early 1950s, four corporate giants, Imperial, Shell, Texaco, and British American dominated the Canadian oil and gas industry. Gulf Oil entered the picture when it bought out British American in 1956. The last integrated Canadian-owned oil company, Canadian Oil, which operated the White Rose chain of service stations, was taken over by Shell in 1952. Canadians remained active on the production side of the industry, through such companies as Pacific Petroleums, Home Oil,

*Oil well at Leduc, Alberta, 1947.*

Imperial Oil Archives

Husky, and Hudson's Bay. With world oil and gas prices remaining low—less than $2 a barrel in the mid-1960s—the big problem for Canadian producers was to find a market for their abundant product.

By 1952, pipelines in which Imperial Oil was a major shareholder funnelled oil from Alberta either to Vancouver or through Wisconsin to Sarnia, Ontario. Canadian-owned Westcoast Transmission Company's thousand-kilometre pipeline was completed to Vancouver in 1951. In 1956, the Canadian government entered an agreement with an American company, Trans-Canada Pipelines, to build a gas pipeline from Alberta to Montreal. In addition to a generous loan to the company, Ottawa agreed to create a Crown corporation to build the uneconomical section of the pipeline through northern Ontario. Predictably, it was C.D. Howe who, as minister of trade and commerce, backed the ambitious project and demonstrated his government's arrogance by having closure imposed on the vigorous parliamentary debate that the project incited. Although ownership of Trans-Canada gradually fell into Canadian hands, an American consortium including Trans-Canada eventually built a larger line south of the Great Lakes. The United States absorbed about half of the Canadian output of oil and gas, but cheap imports of crude oil from the Middle East kept the industry lean until the early 1970s.

Ontario, with its state-owned hydro plants, seaway, and nuclear power stations, and Alberta, with its burgeoning energy industry, set a high standard for other provinces to follow. Yet follow they did. Newfoundland premier Joey Smallwood convinced British and European capitalists to develop the mighty Churchill Falls in Labrador, while New Brunswick premier Hugh John Flemming wrung $30 million out of the federal government to help him complete his Beechwood Power complex on the St John River. Nova Scotia put its energies into developing coal-generated thermal power plants. In the early 1950s, Alcan built a huge generating station at Kemano, British Columbia, to supply its $450 million aluminum smelter at Kitimat. Social Credit premier W.A.C. Bennett was determined to make his province rich by developing the potential of the Rocky Mountain Trench and the Columbia River. Saskatchewan's socialist premier, Tommy Douglas, with generous subsidies from Ottawa, planned an ambitious power-generating project on the South Saskatchewan River.

## THE POSTINDUSTRIAL ECONOMY

The increasing importance of communications in determining the pace of economic change in the second half of the twentieth century led analysts to coin the terms Information Age and Postindustrial Age to describe the phenomenon. While industrial and service industries remained significant players in the economy, communications technology, represented by computers and satellites, contributed to quantum leaps in productivity and subjected people to revolutionary changes. As new commodities, new production techniques, and new social values burst on the scene, products and approaches considered crucial to the Industrial Age were regularly threatened with obsolescence. Constant adaptation became necessary for economic survival.

## COMMUNICATIONS

Since information was the key to diffusing and controlling technological innovation, communications technology—itself subject to breathtaking innovation—determined the pace and direction of the postindustrial economy. With the development of satellite and space communications in the late 1950s and 1960s, signals could be transmitted around the world in a split second. Computers were linked to telecommunications systems in the early 1970s, permitting vast quantities of information to be sent over telecommunications networks. Marshall McLuhan's much talked about "global village" had become a reality, or so it seemed.

Canadians have been closely associated with new developments in communications for at least two reasons. First, because of Canada's tremendous size, improvements in communication have been important in welding the nation together. Governments, recognizing this fact, have usually worked in partnership with private enterprise to develop better communications networks. Second, because of its economic relationship with Britain and the United States, Canada has had easy access to technological innovations. Telegraph, telephone, and radio networks appeared in Canada as soon as the inventions on which they were based became practical. It is therefore not surprising that Canadians were among the first people in the world to experiment with the communication technologies that defined the Information Age. In 1958, Canada's television network, stretching from Victoria to Sydney, was the longest in the world. Canada also established cable-television systems more quickly than other nations. When Alouette I was launched on 29 September 1962, Canada became the third nation in space after the Soviet Union and the United States. With its Anik (the Inuit word for "brother") series launched in the 1970s, Canada led the world in the use of satellites for commercial communications. It was the first nation to establish a digital data network for computer users.

## COMPUTERS

Virtually every human activity has been altered in some way by computer technology. For this reason, the computer, like the steam engine, electricity, and the internal combustion engine, is considered a *transforming* technology, one that cuts a swath across all sectors of the economy and leaves massive political and social upheaval in its wake. Computer technology helped to send people to the moon, revolutionized the office, and automated manufacturing processes.

The initial research on computers was conducted in Britain and the United States. During the Second World War, British scientists sequestered at Bletchley Park used primitive computers to crack German codes. Soon after the war, the Americans

*Founder of the Centre for Culture and Technology at the University of Toronto, Marshall McLuhan contended that communications technologies defined the shape and scope of institutions and values—in McLuhan's words "the medium is the message."*

National Archives of Canada/PA133299

began using computers to increase the accuracy of new guns and missiles. Canada's first entry into the computer age was UTEC, developed by scientists at the University of Toronto between 1947 and 1951. A massive structure that filled a whole room, UTEC was powered by electric tubes, over-heated quickly, and experienced more down time than computing time. In 1952, the University of Toronto purchased a British-made computer.

Had innovation stopped with the first generation of computers, the computer revolution would have been stillborn, but the invention of the transistor in 1949 transformed the whole field of electronics. The replacement of vacuum tubes with solid state transistors—ultimately made of chips of silicon sand—allowed computers to become smaller, more reliable, and less expensive to build and operate. Integrated circuitry, developed in 1958, led to further miniaturization. By 1968, a single silicon chip could hold 256 bits of random access memory (RAM), more than the first generation of computers could cram into a large room. Within another decade, Apple, a microcomputer company based in California, was selling desktop computers to the technology-fixated consumer.

Once the commercial potential of the computer was realized, IBM and other big multinational corporations soon dominated the field. A Canadian-based corporation, Northern Electric (later renamed Northern Telecom), eventually carved a niche for itself by producing telephone equipment and switching devices for a global telecommunications market. Nevertheless, Canada's trade deficit in electronic goods reached $850 million in 1973 and continued to rise quickly in the years that followed. The vast quantities of capital invested by the United States and Japan in computer technology made it difficult for nations such as Canada to compete successfully in the latest race for economic supremacy.

## THE SERVICE ECONOMY

In the Postindustrial Age, seven out of ten Canadians in the labour force were employed in providing services rather than producing goods. Sectors such as transportation, communications, retail and wholesale trade, finance, real estate, education, health and welfare, recreation, personal services, food, and accommodation created new jobs that replaced employment in the goods-producing primary and secondary sectors of the economy.

One of the most obvious features of Canada's service economy was the growth of government

## AMERICAN FAST FOOD AND THE SERVICE INDUSTRY

The fast-food industry was one example of an American-dominated service industry that made its entry into Canada in the postwar period. Franchise operations, such as Colonel Sanders' Kentucky Fried Chicken, Burger King, and, after 1968, McDonald's, defined the eating-out experience for teenagers and for two-income families who sought occasional relief from having to prepare a meal.

Ester Reiter worked at a Toronto Burger King in the early 1980s and interviewed fellow employees as part of a thesis project. Each Burger King is operated by a franchisee who pays Burger King's Miami headquarters a large fee for the right to operate a firm with the Burger King name and every outlet is required by Miami to follow unswervingly the procedures laid out in the **Manual of Operating Data**. "Burger King University" in Miami trains managers so that they know how to implement these procedures uniformly. Headquarters is linked by computer to each franchise and monitors performance daily. The result is that the "Burger King experience" is the same for workers and customers whether one is in New Orleans or in Halifax. For employees what this means is a rigid work schedule in which the time allowed to take an order, prepare a specific item, or to get the food to the customer is measured in seconds.

Reiter's fellow workers were teenagers, often working part-time, and immigrant women for whom better jobs were unavailable. Few liked the work, which paid minimum wage, and many felt like robots, waiting for their breaks in the "crew room" for a chance to listen to rock music and talk about plans for the weekend. On the job, "hamburgers are cooked as they pass through the broiler on a conveyor belt at a rate of 835 patties per hour. Furnished with a pair of tongs, the worker picks up the burgers as they drop off the conveyor belt, puts each on a toasted bun, and places the hamburgers and buns in a steamer. The jobs may be hot and boring, but they can be learned in a manner of minutes." [3]

*While their labour force participation continued to expand, women, such as these typists at the Dominion Bureau of Statistics, worked in traditional, poorly paid occupations.*

C.Lund/National Archives of Canada/PA133212

spending. The expansion of government services meant a plethora of new jobs. Government spending, which had accounted for only 5 percent of GNP in 1867, had risen to 30 percent by 1960 and increased still further as the major social programs of the 1960s were introduced. By 1985, it reached an astounding 48.2 percent of GNP. Nearly half of government expenditure was on goods and services; the rest involved transfer payments, which moved private income from one group of citizens to another (including old age pensions, veterans' allowances, family allowances, medical care, farm subsidies, regional development programs, and incentives to business). The federal share of GNP rose only marginally after 1960, but the provinces' share doubled as their responsibilities grew rapidly. Although governments produced a wide range of primary and secondary goods, most of their expenditures fuelled the service sector of the Canadian economy.

The trend towards urban concentration, typical of the Industrial Age, was consolidated by the service economy. While goods-producing industries were often located near resources, most tertiary industries required a large pool of nearby clients for their services. Nevertheless, the trend to urbanization began to slow down in the 1970s as people moved away from congested city cores and monotonous suburbs to rural "exurbia." Commuting to work in the cities from exurban homes became a way of life for an increasing number of Canadians. To improve their tax bases, many city councils expanded their boundaries into exurbia, becoming vast, sprawling administrative units. Metropolitan growth increased the size and power of Canada's major cities, making Canada little more than a cluster of city states and their economic hinterlands. In 1971, three out of four Canadians were classified as urban dwellers.

While Canadians generally exported more than enough primary goods to balance the manufactured goods the country imported, there was a disturbing growth in the deficit in Canada's "service account." The two most important items in the service account were business services and travel. When branches of such widely patronized multinational corporations as Century 21, McDonald's, and Midas Muffler remitted funds to head office to cover the costs of administration, advertising, product development, and research, they contributed to Canada's service account deficit.

The growth of the service sector was one of the major factors contributing to the influx of women into the paid labour force. Prior to the Industrial Revolution, women performed many of the services essential to survival. As services moved from the domestic economy into the market economy, women often moved with them. Domestic work as a paid occupation declined under the impact of household appliances in the twentieth century, but teaching, nursing, secretarial, clerical, and cleaning jobs remained dominated by women. With the expansion of the service economy in the second half of the twentieth century, women's paid employment increased dramatically. Overall, women's labour force participation in Canada increased from 23.4 percent in 1953 to 48.9 percent in 1979, while the male participation rate fell from 82.9 percent to 78.4 percent during the same period. Despite their increasing participation in the labour force, in 1971 women with full-time jobs made on average less than 60 percent of what men with full-time jobs earned. Women were also far more likely than men to be employed in part-time work.

## END OF THE ECONOMIC MIRACLE

Spurred by government spending and technological innovation, the Canadian economy continued its spectacular rate of economic growth until the mid-1970s. Unit labour productivity, a measure of the efficiency of the labour force, had tripled since the end of the war, due largely to technological and administrative changes, and workers received some benefits from the increased productivity. In 1975, the incomes of working Canadians were twice as great in constant dollars as incomes in 1945. While the cost of living had tripled, wages and salaries had increased sixfold. Average family income had more than doubled, since the number of two-income households had dramatically increased. Higher taxation ate up much of the increased income, but, because of new social programs, Canadians in 1975 had far less need than earlier generations to set aside money for health purposes and for old age.

But dark clouds were on the horizon. The American government had been unwilling to raise taxes to offset expenses associated with the unpopular Vietnam War. Allowing the economy to overheat, it then made a fruitless attempt to reduce inflation by cutting spending and tightening credit. American unemployment increased, and the government responded with trade restrictions, which

had repercussions for Canadian trade and therefore Canadian rates of employment and inflation.

While the debate raged about how Canada should respond to the twin evils of unemployment and inflation, the OPEC oil price shocks late in 1973 seemed to knock the stuffing out of western economies, which had relied throughout the post-war boom on cheap energy. In 1974, though unemployment was a manageable 5.3 percent, inflation stood at 14.5 percent. One year later inflation was down to 9.9 percent, but unemployment had reached a postwar high of 6.9 percent. The combination of high unemployment and high inflation, unseen in the postwar period, was labelled *stagflation*, a short form for stagnation plus inflation.

## THE DEBATE OVER CONTROLS

A political debate ensued about how to combat this economic phenomenon. In the August 1974 federal election, Conservative leader Robert Stanfield called for wage and price controls. Prime Minister Trudeau won re-election after vigorously opposing such massive state intervention in the economy. In October 1975, Trudeau reversed himself, announcing a three-year program of controls. Trudeau's economic policies to deal with stagflation proved contradictory. Government spending increased substantially in accordance with Keynesian prescriptions for a stagnating economy but, beginning in 1975, the money supply was severely restricted. Tight money policies were also implemented by the United States and most governments in Europe in an effort to control inflation. If the three decades that followed the war had been characterized by a focus on maintaining high levels of employment and providing easy credit, the years that followed would be notable for the state's focus on price stability and decreasing interest in unemployment.

The shift occurred in large part because the business community, concerned about profit margins, began to abandon the postwar consensus on economic policy. Owners and managers of major firms complained that unions, emboldened by low rates of unemployment and generous unemployment insurance benefits, were forcing employers to pay wage increases that hurt profits. Recognizing that corporate complaints were rejected by the public as self-interested propaganda, Canada's largest firms sponsored a number of right-wing economic research institutes in the 1970s. The Fraser Institute in British Columbia and the C.D. Howe Institute in Ontario, among others, could present a pro-employer line as the product of supposedly disinterested research. The media uncritically reported their claims that tight money policies had to be adopted to slow down the Canadian economy in the short run to stop inflation and create long-term stability. Downplayed in such reports was that tight-money policies would create a higher rate of unemployment.

## THE COSTS OF GROWTH

Following the Second World War, government policy and economic activity was focused on bringing every Canadian into the modern age. Subsistence survival by farming, fishing, and hunting was deemed unworthy, and rural life, unless fully commercialized, experienced a rapid decline. As a result, many communities became ghost towns, while cities experienced unprecedented growth.

Most Canadians moved voluntarily from their rural communities to urban centres where they had better access to jobs and services, but there were exceptions. In Newfoundland, families in outport communities had to be encouraged by government grants to move to anticipated "growth centres." Inuit in the Arctic were often reluctant to be relocated from their traditional communities to "northern suburbs,"[4] where they were expected to live under government surveillance. In both cases, the move failed to live up to its promise. The housing and sanitary conditions in communities created by the state for the Inuit were appalling. Even had they been better, the fact remained that people had been uprooted to live in communities where it was difficult to make a living. Similarly, outport Newfoundlanders found few jobs in the communities where they were encouraged to relocate.

The transformation from subsistence to consumer society was evident in the incorporation of the Inuit into the North American economy through their painting and sculpture, which had become popular in the art market in southern climes. It was equally evident in the experience of a vacationing antique dealer who in a short period in the late 1950s bought twelve hundred spinning wheels in rural areas of Cape Breton.

## FARMING

While the new corporate giants in the food industry prospered, farmers as a whole did not share in postwar prosperity. Grain prices rose only marginally from 1945 to 1972, though the years from 1973 to 1975 were a boon to the relatively few farmers who were left. In Saskatchewan, where a majority of the population still farmed in 1941 and earned most of their income from harvesting grains, the farm population fell over the next thirty years from 514 677 to 233 792. Those who remained had larger farms that were more diversified, but federal farm subsidies and income from off-farm jobs provided the greater part of their

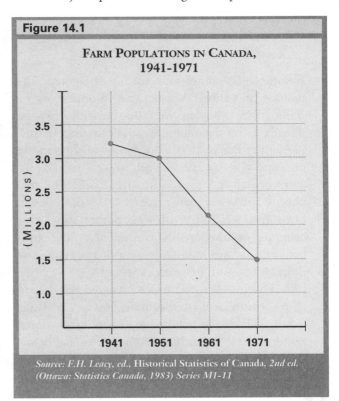

**Figure 14.1**

**FARM POPULATIONS IN CANADA, 1941-1971**

Source: F.H. Leacy, ed., *Historical Statistics of Canada*, *2nd ed.* (Ottawa: Statistics Canada, 1983) Series M1-11

livelihood. Except in British Columbia, where the number of fruit and vegetable growers fell relatively modestly, similar patterns prevailed across the country. Prince Edward Island witnessed the most change as costs of production for its major farm products, particularly potatoes, increased well out of proportion to rising prices to consumers: the size of farms doubled and the farm population fell from almost 144 000 in 1941 to under 27 000 thirty years later. The nation had lost a third of its farming population between 1951 and 1961 and then lost a third again by the 1971 census. Over one Canadian in four lived on a farm at the end of the Second World War. Thirty years later, fewer than one in fifteen farmed.

Those who left farms often did so unwillingly, bowing to economic circumstances that forced them to abandon a cherished way of life and communities where they had roots that often spanned many generations. Those who stayed watched as village or town businesses closed for lack of customers, and as schools, community centres, ethnic halls, and other institutions were centralized further afield for economic reasons.

## FISHING COMMUNITIES

Fishing communities were equally devastated. The magnificent trawlers that came to dominate the Banks fishery sealed the fate of inshore fishers. Their catches dwindling because of excessive fishing on the Banks, they were forced to concentrate on more valuable species such as scallops and lobsters, which in turn became depleted. The real choice for most inshore fishers was between becoming a labourer on a corporate trawler or changing occupations. Not surprisingly, the number of Canadians in the Atlantic fishery declined by nearly 40 percent between 1951 and 1961.

The federal government seemed helpless to stop the uncoordinated exploitation of the Banks fishery, which was still defined as an international resource. In 1949, an International Commission for the Northwest Atlantic Fisheries was created, but it had no authority to bind its membership to comply with conservation measures. Nor was the law of the

sea, formulated over three hundred years earlier by the Dutch jurist Hugo Grotius, of much value in regulating the new uses of the ocean. Interest in resources in and under the ocean finally led the United Nations to institute the Law of the Sea Conference. At conference meetings in 1958 and 1960, Canadian officials demanded that nations be given the right to control ocean activities within twelve miles of their shores. In 1964, Canadians made a unilateral declaration of a twelve-mile limit, which remained in effect until the two-hundred-mile limit was established by the third Law of the Sea Conference in 1977.

As the fisheries developed into a modern industry, cooperative fishing organizations founded prior to the war lost control of processing and marketing structures. During the 1950s and 1960s, large domestic and foreign corporations, including National Sea Products (Halifax), Booth Fisheries (Chicago), Atlantic Fish Processors (Toronto), and B.C. Packers (Toronto) emerged as integrated trawling and processing firms selling mainly through Boston, New York, and Chicago. The east coast fishery, like its west coast counterpart, became part of the continental corporate universe. Most fishers earned a wage rather than being self-employed. In 1956, the remaining poverty-prone self-employed fishers became eligible for unemployment insurance.

## WORKING CONDITIONS

Industrial workers benefited more from the economic growth of the post-1945 period than farmers and fishers. In some industries, working conditions improved noticeably. Ontario's lumber industry, finding it difficult to retain workers in an economy with low unemployment, replaced logging camps—once notorious for their crowded, cold, and poorly maintained bunkhouses—with suburban-like accommodations. In other industries, however, employers reckoned that highly paid workers would put up with unsafe or unhealthy conditions. In the mining industry, for example, innovations such as scooptrams meant back injuries and respiratory problems for nickel miners; while the remote-controlled vehicles could have been enclosed to prevent their operators from bouncing about and inhaling diesel fumes, the mining companies resisted the expense that this would entail. The United Steelworkers vividly described the work environment of the mines before an Ontario government commission on the mining industry in 1978. After noting the large numbers of accidents and deaths in mines, the Steelworkers pointed to such hazards as:

> immense pressures from underground rock that is frequently described as "solid" but which in fact is constantly in varying states of flux and change; total absence of natural light; working with heavy equipment which for the most part is designed for maximum efficiency, and not for the protection of workers using it; the use of high explosives, high noise levels, air concussions, etc.,... hygiene, sanitary and health dangers arising from dusts, gases, fog, oils, deep holes, falling rocks (loose), runs of muck (broken ores), slippery and unsure footing, and in some instances (as in Elliot Lake) ionizing radiation. [5]

Machines that improved productivity posed problems not only for worker safety, but also for the preservation of jobs. During the postwar boom, the proliferation of technology created more jobs than it made redundant. But by the 1970s, the net impact of technology on employment prospects appeared to be negative. Microprocessors, first introduced in 1971, displaced blue-collar workers by controlling systems that automatically cut boards, stitched seams, and assembled parts. White-collar jobs, particularly those dominated by women, were even more in jeopardy as file clerks, keypunch operators, and other low-paid workers found their jobs automated and no new positions available. "The chip" devalued the work of many women. As Heather Menzies has argued, "Cashiers are deskilled by the transfer of price information and change calculation into the memory and processing components of the cash register. Like the weaver in the industrial factory, the cashier valued for good price memory and arithmetic efficiency is no longer needed; the cashier becomes a highly replaceable unskilled worker."[6]

Many workers who lost their jobs proved ill-equipped to take up the other jobs that were available, thus becoming victims of "structural unemployment." Most unemployed coal miners, for example, lacked the skills to be computer programmers; nor could farmers be readily transferred to jobs in health care industries. Although training programs were implemented to address the problem of structural unemployment, they failed to produce the skilled labour force required in Canada's postindustrial economy. Indeed, many of Canada's most highly trained workers were immi-

*Workers in fluorspar mine,*
*St Lawrence, Newfoundland.*

National Archives of Canada/PA130784

grants. After 1967, Canada's immigration laws sub-stituted educational and occupational biases for ethnic ones, in an effort to attract skilled workers to the jobs expanding in the Information Age.

## GROWTH AND THE ENVIRONMENT

Of all the costs of economic growth, the impact on the biosphere that supports life is no doubt of greatest importance in the long term. Yet consider-ations of the impact of uncontrolled economic development on the environment were far from uppermost in the minds of most Canadians in the period of postwar prosperity. Only gradually did the fear take hold that industrial countries were pursuing an economic course that would lead to environmental disaster for future generations.

The atomic bomb was the culmination of the powers unleashed by science, technology, and industrial enterprise that characterized the modern age. While the development of the bomb caused many people to reconsider the notions of science as neutral and scientists as servants of historical change, it did not translate into a general scepti-cism about scientific and industrial progress. The long-term consequences of industrial pollutants received little attention, even though polluted air, undrinkable water, and scorched landscapes had been associated with factory production since the early days of the Industrial Revolution.

The age of innocence came to an abrupt end in 1962 when American scientist Rachel Carson published *Silent Spring*. In her highly publicized book, Carson provided stunning revelations about the dangers posed by the "tide of chemicals born of the Industrial Age." Rivers and oceans, the air and soil, animal and human species, she argued, were being rapidly destroyed. Lest Canadians should consider their pristine environment immune from such dangers, she singled out the "Rivers of Death" created in New Brunswick and other forested areas of Canada where aerial pesticide-spraying pro-grams begun in the 1950s were more effective in killing fish than their intended target, the spruce budworm. "We stand now where two roads diverge," Carson concluded. "The road we have

long been travelling is deceptively easy, a smooth superhighway on which we progress with great speed, but at its end lies disaster. The other fork of the road offers our last, our only chance to reach a destination that assures the preservation of our earth."[7]

As the environmental movement gained momentum, public and private institutions began to alter their behaviour. The Soviet Union, Britain, and the United States signed an agreement to ban atmospheric testing of nuclear weapons in 1963, and industries built higher smokestacks to diffuse their polluting emissions. Consumers contributed to the environmental cause by avoiding the use of chemical-laden detergents, foods laced with pesti-cides, and leaded gasoline. Despite such well-meaning efforts, the environmental problem would not go away. Scientists discovered that polychlori-nated biphenyls (PCBs), a family of highly toxic chemicals used in electrical equipment, continued to poison the food chain after their use had been discontinued. No one knew how to dispose of the hazardous waste from nuclear power plants. Even the emissions released into the atmosphere by tall smokestacks came back to earth hundreds of kilo-metres away as acid rain and snow, which ravaged lakes and forests.

A United Nations Conference on the Human Environment met in Stockholm in 1972 to discuss the decaying state of the planet. Chaired by a Canadian, Maurice Strong, the conference pro-duced a declaration of environmental rights and established a program to fund and coordinate investigations into environmental problems. In the same year, the study *Limits to Growth* reported the findings of scientists who used sophisticated com-puter modelling techniques to investigate the "predicament of mankind." They maintained that accelerated industrialization, rapid population growth, increased agricultural consumption, deple-tion of renewable resources, and environmental deterioration threatened the very future of civiliza-tion. If the planet were to continue to support life, the report concluded, a "sustainable state of global equilibrium" must become an urgent priority. A similar message was conveyed by E.F. Schumacher, a German-born economist and progressive thinker,

*Disposal of toxic waste is a major problem facing the industrialized world.*

whose book *Small Is Beautiful: The Study of Economics as if People Mattered* became an instant best-seller when it was first published in 1973. Canadian scientist David Suzuki helped to focus public attention on environmental issues through his CBC television series "The Nature of Things."

Suzuki worked and lived in British Columbia, a province that epitomized the triumph of economic growth over environmental concerns. Social Credit, which governed British Columbia from 1952 to 1972 and again from 1975 to 1991, did little to stop the environmental degradation wrought by resource companies. Preferring short-term prosperity, they seemed indifferent to lax reforestation policies and agricultural land lost to industrial development and urban sprawl. As late as the 1980s, only a third of logged land in British Columbia was being reforested. Studies of pulp mills in the province decried a record of poor control over effluents, which seeped into rivers and lakes. Waste coal from strip-mining operations in the East Kootenays fouled the Elk River Valley's

creek system, and the stench in cities such as Prince George challenged company claims that they used the best pollution-dissipating equipment.

Perhaps the group of Canadians that suffered most from the "growth at all costs" philosophy were the aboriginal people. Although Native peoples fought in the courts to stop megaprojects that would harm the ecology of their traditional hunting and fishing territories, their concerns were largely brushed aside by the larger society. Hydroelectric projects, mines, pulp and paper mills, and new transportation systems displaced Native peoples or jeopardized their traditional ways of life. In the 1950s, Native settlements along the St Lawrence were flooded when the seaway was built. Effluent from the Reed paper mill made it unsafe for Natives in the area to fish in the English–Wabigoon River system near Kenora. Not only was their major food supply affected, but also the tourism that had made the reserves outside Kenora relatively prosperous and which depended on good local fishing dried up. Moreover, mill operators rarely hired Native labour. Thus, for Native peoples in the area, chronic unemployment accompanied environmental degradation.

## ECONOMIC DISPARITY

From the 1960s onwards the public was increasingly concerned about protecting the environment, but governmental policy was slow in coming. One of the reasons why politicians and business leaders were reluctant to put environmental protection ahead of economic growth was that growth had been the Conservatives' answer to the socialist call for a more egalitarian distribution of wealth. If the pie kept getting bigger, even if there was no change in its distribution, the poor would be relatively better off and therefore would be unlikely to demand radical changes in the economic structure.

Notwithstanding the egalitarian rhetoric underlying the nation's democratic institutions, postwar Canada remained a highly stratified society. Economic cycles might come and go, but the structure of inequality remained hauntingly familiar. In postindustrial Canada—as in the pre-industrial and industrial periods of Canadian history—age, class, ethnicity, gender, and geography remained important factors in determining how one fared in the quest for economic well-being.

In 1965, John Porter published *The Vertical Mosaic*, an impressive analysis of stratification in Canadian society. Porter showed that ethnicity and class in Canada were closely interrelated and that an economic elite of less than a thousand men—most of them of British background, Protestant in their religious affiliation, and graduates of private schools—dominated the Canadian economy. Even in Quebec, where over three-quarters of the population was French in origin, anglophone elites controlled the economic structures. Studies con-

ducted for the Royal Commission on Bilingualism and Biculturalism revealed an ethnic hierarchy in Quebec that included francophones among the poorest of Quebeckers. Only Italians and Native peoples in Quebec had a lower per capita income than French Canadians in 1961. The Quiet Revolution did much to improve the status of francophones both in Quebec and elsewhere in the country. In contrast, visible minorities, especially Indians, Métis, Inuit, and African Canadians, remained at the bottom of the economic scale.

Women also figured prominently in the ranks of Canada's economically disadvantaged. Until the 1960s, it was perfectly legal to state a preference for either men or women in job advertisements. "Help Wanted, Male" and "Help Wanted, Female" did much to stream men and women into different occupations. Commonly, "women's jobs"—secretaries, sales clerks, food servers, childcare workers—were those with the lowest pay. Professional and technical occupations followed a similar pattern. Women dominated the relatively poorly paid occupations of dental assistant, occupational therapist, and librarian. By contrast, in 1971, less than 5 percent of dentists and lawyers and just over

*Native dwellings contrast sharply with houses in Fort George, Quebec, 1973.*

John Flanders/National Archives of Canada/PA130854

10 percent of physicians were women. Even within the same occupation, women were paid less than men. In 1970, female janitors earned just 58.5 percent of the wages of male janitors; female secretaries earned 57.4 percent of the income of their male counterparts; and women who operated sewing machines could expect to make 63.6 percent of the wages of a male operator.

## DISTRIBUTION OF INCOME

Despite growth and change in the Canadian economy since the Second World War, the overall distribution of income remained remarkably static, as figure 14.2 indicates. Obviously, the welfare state did little to redistribute wealth, although it prevented an even greater concentration of wealth. In the Information Age, the old, young adults, visible minorities, and single parents and their children figured prominently in the lowest quintile, highlighting the significance of age and marital status in determining income distribution.

Because government transfer programs were too modest to lift individuals out of poverty, Canadians looked to economic growth as the panacea that would allow everyone to enjoy some of the fruits of prosperity. The Economic Council of Canada, an advisory group to the government on economic planning, calculated in 1961 that 27 percent of Canadians received incomes low enough to qualify them as poor. Eight years later, the federal government, using the same measures, announced that poverty had been cut in half. Academic studies suggested that growth of the economy accounted directly for half of the decline, while the increase in the number of two-income families, indirectly also related to economic growth, accounted for much of the rest.

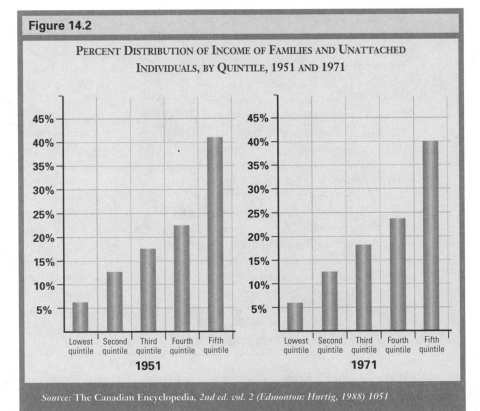

**Figure 14.2**

PERCENT DISTRIBUTION OF INCOME OF FAMILIES AND UNATTACHED INDIVIDUALS, BY QUINTILE, 1951 AND 1971

*Source:* The Canadian Encyclopedia, *2nd ed. vol. 2 (Edmonton: Hurtig, 1988) 1051*

## POVERTY AND THE REGIONS

Whether the national economy was booming or in recession, certain provinces and regions of provinces lagged well behind the national average. Southern Ontario generally prospered far more than the rest of the country, while northern Ontario suffered high rates of unemployment and poverty, particularly in Native areas. Even within southern Ontario, there were large pockets of poverty in the southeast. Montreal had a vibrant mixed economy, but northern Quebec and the Gaspé experienced grinding poverty even during economic upswings. In wealthy Alberta and British Columbia, northern residents, especially Natives, had little to show for the resource boom that created high average incomes in their provinces. The Atlantic region, Saskatchewan, and Manitoba con-

## THE WORKING POOR

The prosperity of the average Canadian in the early 1970s often hid from view the lives of millions who were just scraping by. Despite the common view that poverty was generally limited to people on social assistance, most poor households included one or more individuals who held a job. Journalist Sheila Arnopolous provided a glimpse into the lives of some of these people in a series of articles in the **Montreal Star** in 1974. Her focus was on immigrants from the Caribbean, Latin America, India, Pakistan, Greece, Portugal, and Italy who worked in Montreal. Some were illegal immigrants—it was estimated in the late 1970s that one hundred thousand illegal immigrants worked in Canada, generally in sweatshops in Montreal and Toronto. Intimidated by the threat of discovery and deportation, they often had to accept work at less than the legislated minimum wage. While legal immigrants did not share the fear of deportation, they often spoke little English or French and were desperate for work, so they rarely demanded that authorities enforce minimum wage laws. Many such workers laboured under conditions reminiscent of the nineteenth century, with workdays of thirteen hours and subsistence pay. Noted Arnopolous, "They man the clanging textile and clothing factories which line St. Lawrence and Park. They clean toilets in glittering high-rises, wash dishes in grimy restaurant kitchens, pull switches and operate machinery in fuming plastics and chemical factories, abattoirs, machine shops." [8]

Far from urban industrial sites, farmworkers also often laboured under conditions and rates of pay that few Canadians were aware existed in their prosperous society. Excluded from minimum-wage protection, immigrant orchard workers in British Columbia and Ontario and Native sugar-beet pickers in Manitoba worked long hours for negligible pay and slept in miserable accommodations provided by the employers. Many farmworkers were illegal immigrants; still others were contract workers for the growing season and were required to return home to Latin America or the Caribbean once the harvest was over. Canada apparently wanted their labour power, but did not want them as citizens.

stituted the country's have-not provinces, dependent on equalization grants to provide reasonable levels of service to their citizens, but unable to provide the economic diversification that would create more jobs. The bias of federal fiscal and monetary policies towards the more populous and wealthy regions did not help matters. How, for instance, could the bank rate be set to meet the needs of the lagging Atlantic region when the central Canadian economy was facing inflationary pressure?

## TAXATION AND THE DISTRIBUTION OF WEALTH

If the distribution of wealth remained largely unchanged despite extensive welfare measures introduced in the postwar period, an assessment of the taxation system helps to explain why. Before the war, most working Canadians earned less than the minimum income required before personal income tax had to be paid. After the war, the tax exemption was not increased to take into account the rate of inflation, and most workers became income taxpayers. Apart from increasing "direct taxation," ordinary Canadians also faced increases in a variety of "indirect taxes" such as sales taxes and property taxes. A "hidden tax" levied on manufacturers based on the sales of their products was also absorbed by consumers. Corporate taxes, once presented as a temporary wartime measure, were given permanent status in 1949. But taxes on profits were ameliorated by generous capital cost (depreciation) allowances and, for many firms, by a variety of loopholes. Dividend holders received a 10 percent tax credit in recognition of dividends forgone because of corporate tax assessments, and in 1953 that credit was doubled.

The Diefenbaker government, criticized for overtaxation both by ordinary Canadians and by business, established a Royal Commission on Taxation in 1962. Diefenbaker chose Kenneth Carter, former president of the widely respected tax-study organization, the Canadian Tax Foundation, to head the commission. Carter was a senior partner in one of Canada's leading firms of chartered accountants, a firm that had dealings with many of the country's largest companies. Yet his commission's report would bring little comfort to the corporate elite. Concluded the commissioners: "The present system does not afford fair treatment for all Canadians. People in essentially similar circumstances do not bear the same taxes. People in essentially different circumstances do not bear appropriately different tax burdens." [9]

Commission studies of the incidence of all forms of taxation revealed that the poorest Canadians paid proportionately more taxes than well-off citizens, while the wealthiest Canadians paid barely more in taxes than modest income earners. While about a third of all income earned in the country was paid out in taxes, the group earning under $2000 lost 60 percent of their income to taxes. Indirect taxes—all applied without reference to income—ate up most of the little income of the poor. By comparison, the richest 5 percent of Canadians—those who earned over $10 000 per year—lost 38 percent of their income to taxes.

Carter recommended that indirect taxation be substantially reduced and that the base for personal and corporate income tax be broadened by removing most loopholes. As one journalist summed up the philosophy of the report, "a buck is a buck," and all income should be taxed much the same. The poor would be compensated through the tax system by the institution of a "negative income tax"—that is, a payment from the government to individuals whose incomes were too low to support a decent standard of living.

The Carter recommendations, released in 1966, took the Pearson government by surprise. Faced with a barrage of lobbying by industry, the government proved unwilling to take major steps in the taxation arena. In the early 1970s, the Trudeau government made a half-hearted attempt at tax reform, taxing most capital gains at half the rate of other income and increasing income exemptions so as to remove the poorest citizens from the tax rolls. But negative income taxes were rejected, and most of the exemptions of rich individuals and corporations remained on the books. Indeed, the federal government abandoned estate taxes in 1972, leaving the provinces to decide how to tax the wealth of

individuals who had died. Alberta immediately announced that it would have no death tax at all, and by the end of the decade the other provinces had been forced to follow its lead as the rich threatened to relocate to provinces without taxes on estates. The taxes that they would not collect from the estates of the rich had to be collected elsewhere. From the mid-1960s, provincial governments, desperate for new sources of revenue, and unwilling to increase corporate taxes for fear that business would move away, began to introduce sales taxes, despite Carter's evidence of their disproportionate impact on the poor. The limited impact of Carter's recommendations demonstrated the overwhelming influence of the corporate elite in Canadian political and economic decision making.

## THE TRADE UNION MOVEMENT

The trade union movement was the most vocal opponent of the corporate agenda in the postwar period. Although legislation recognized the right of workers to organize, the Industrial Relations Disputes Act of 1948, which applied to federal workers, and its provincial equivalents, also attempted to co-opt union leaders into the planning mechanisms of corporations and governments. Under all the new labour laws, workers found their rights to negotiate limited to wages and narrowly defined working conditions. Unions were expected to enforce contracts and to keep their members in line. Decisions to reduce the size of the workforce, to speed up production, or to use hazardous materials in the workplace were generally not covered by contracts, and union leaders were obliged to inform their members that strikes or slowdowns meant to force management to reconsider these issues would not be tolerated. Even when management appeared to violate a contract, workers were not allowed to strike. Instead they had to use often drawn-out grievance procedures to seek redress. Employers generally found that "management's right to manage" had been preserved.

When better wages and working conditions could not be won at the bargaining table, unionists could use the weapon of the strike. Wartime wage freezes created pent-up demands for increases at war's end. Many working-class families had fared well in wartime because of overtime pay and two salaries. A resurgence of patriarchal arguments that women should return to their homes so that men could find jobs, aided by discriminatory hiring and firing policies, caused the number of married women in paid work to decline precipitously. Their husbands, if they worked in the mass-production industries, then demanded "family wages," which they believed employers could well afford to pay. In 1946 and 1947, about 240 000 workers struck for a total of almost seven million workdays. Automobile, steel, rubber, textile, packing, electrical manufacturing, forestry, and mining companies all felt the sting of such action. Average wages rose from 69.4 cents per hour in 1945 to 91.3 cents per hour in 1948.

Women, who were generally not members of unions, did not share in the wage gains. In 1948, the Retail, Wholesale, and Department Store Union (RWDSU), supported by the Canadian Congress of Labour, initiated a three-year drive, headed by Eileen Talman, to organize Toronto's Eaton's store. The company pulled out all the stops to oppose the union, linking unions with communism, raising wages just before the vote on unionizing took place, and warning part-time workers that unionism would cost them their jobs. When only 40 percent of the workers supported affiliation with the RWDSU, the CCL leadership, almost exclusively male, concluded that women were too passive to unionize and ceased its attempts to organize sectors dominated by female labour. Such stereotypical views were being exploded in Quebec where women endured a bitter and ultimately successful strike at Dupuis Frères department store in 1952 to win better pay and working conditions. Members of the increasingly secular Confédération des travailleurs catholiques du Canada, these women were a harbinger of things to come in postwar Quebec.

## ACHIEVING UNION RIGHTS

Quebec workers who struck were well aware that the provincial government often came to the armed defence of strike-bound employers. In 1949, workers in the town of Asbestos, unwilling to delay a strike until a government-appointed board of arbitration reported on their grievances, struck so that the company would not have time to stockpile asbestos before the inevitable walkout. During the five-month strike, the workers faced a large contingent of provincial police who protected replacement workers hired by the company. Many strikers were arrested or beaten in clashes with the police.

The brutal state response to the strike galvanized considerable resistance to the Union nationale. Liberal and liberal-nationalist intellectuals, including future prime minister Pierre Elliott Trudeau, were increasingly united on the need to defeat Duplessis and to protect workers' interests. Even within the church, there were dissenters against Duplessis's heavy-handed tactics. Rank-and-file clergy who supported the Asbestos strikers briefly had a champion in Archbishop Charbonneau of Montreal, but his ecclesiastical superiors transferred him out of the province. The Roman Catholic Church had played a long-standing role in mediating labour conflict in Quebec, but its rigidity during the Asbestos strike destroyed that role forever.

It was not only in Quebec that striking workers were confronted by police. In November 1945, the Ontario government sent provincial police and reinforcements from the RCMP into the gates of the Ford plant at Windsor to end a five-week-old strike. The strikers responded by blockading the plant with cars. The federal government appointed Justice Ivan Rand to mediate the conflict. The major issue was the *closed shop*, or compulsory union membership for employees. Rand successfully proposed a formula for union membership: in a bargaining unit where a majority voted to join a union, employers must collect union dues from all members of the unit, but individuals could formally apply to have their dues sent to a designated charity rather than the union. A less happy ending greeted the loggers of Newfoundland who struck in 1959, only to have Premier Joey Smallwood use the RCMP to enforce his decision to decertify the International Woodworkers' Association as the bargaining agent of the loggers. Three people died during this violent strike.

Opposition by employers to unions meant that the rate of unionization of private sector workers stalled after the 1950s. By contrast, public sector workers increasingly were unionized. Because women were heavily concentrated in the lower echelons of the public service, four-fifths of Canada's new unionists from 1966 to 1976 were women. Women in the "caring" professions, such as nursing, social work, and teaching, also questioned the stereotype that "women's work" was mainly community service rather than remunerative professional labour. At times consciously feminist, at times not, these women gradually recognized that their work was undervalued and that their working conditions required improvement. No longer deterred by arguments that it was unladylike to organize, women who had the opportunity to do so unionized at a rapid rate. Strikes of teachers, social workers, and of civil servants, unheard of before the 1970s, began to become commonplace by the end of the decade. "We are not Florence Nightingales," United Nurses of Alberta president Margaret Ethier proclaimed as Alberta's nurses "walked the bricks" during an illegal strike in 1979, the first of three such strikes by the province's nurses in an eight-year period.

The strike was increasingly being used as a weapon in Quebec as well: in 1960, there were 38 strikes in the province; in 1975, there were 362. The province's Catholic unions formally ended their affiliation with the church in 1960, organizing the Confédération des syndicats nationaux (CSN). The CSN played a major role in the Common Front formed by Quebec public sector unions in 1972, conducting general strikes to improve the position of the lowest-paid public sector workers, most of whom were women. The Common Front provoked much opposition. The Bourassa government invoked legislation to end the labour disruption, jailing the heads of Quebec's three largest labour federations when they encouraged their members to defy back-to-work orders. Several conservative unions, alienated by the CSN's embrace of such militant tactics, broke away to form the Centrale des syndicats démocratiques.

Apart from seeking gains for workers through collective bargaining, labour also looked to formal politics for legislated changes that would improve working environments. Since 1961, organized labour had been formally linked to the NDP, but many members wanted their unions to do more than back a political party. Unionists also participated in women's, peace, environmental, and gay rights activities. In Quebec, supporters of sovereignty pressed successfully to have the unions take an active role in nationalist campaigns. Political activism created tensions. British Columbia's woodworkers were often at odds with environmentalists inside and outside the union movement; feminist campaigns for affirmative action upset many male workers who still believed in the "family wage" and the sex-typing of work roles that this concept implied.

## CONCLUSION

The three decades of prosperity that followed the Second World War led many commentators to believe that a working compromise had been reached between private profit making and a fair distribution of social wealth. In striking this balance, the state played an important role in the economy, directing funds towards needy individuals and towards companies to attract investment. Governments in Canada argued that they had sufficient economic powers to ensure that private economic decision makers, foreign and national, were forced to respect the public interest.

Measured by purchasing power, most Canadians had never been so well off. Yet millions remained on the outside of the new consumer society, looking in. Women, while working for wages for longer periods than prewar generations, received far less income than men. If they were the sole support of children, they were more likely to live below the poverty line than above it. The state had introduced a variety of social measures that redistributed wealth, but the workings of the market economy and the taxation system counterbalanced these measures. That left only economic growth to create some degree of affluence for all.

By the 1960s, it was clear that uncontrolled economic growth was damaging not only to the continuance of many communities, but, to the global environment. Moreover, the delicate and perhaps illusory consensus that informed state policies regarding the economy was coming unstuck by 1975. For almost thirty years, there had been economic growth combined with low unemployment and low inflation. Now employers were becoming

increasingly incensed as their restive work forces, no longer intimidated by the threat of unemployment, demanded a larger share of the corporate pie. Unemployment remained stubbornly high, but it no longer seemed to be a primary focus of government policy.

## CAUSES OF AND SOLUTIONS FOR STAGFLATION

### A Historiographical Debate

Why did the so-called Keynesian policies that promoted over a quarter of a century of unprecedented economic prosperity prove inadequate in the early 1970s to prevent stagflation—a combination of increasing inflation and rising unemployment? Some scholars argue that changes in the labour market made rising unemployment inevitable and that government efforts to stem the growth in unemployment simply caused inflation to balloon, without significantly affecting unemployment rates. Others argue that governments did not do enough to control both unemployment and inflation.

In their text on the Canadian economy, economist Kenneth Norrie and historian Douglas Owram argue that higher unemployment was caused by a combination of factors. Technological change reduced industry's labour requirements just as more women and younger workers were entering the labour market. They also maintain that workers were able to quit their jobs and take advantage of generous unemployment insurance benefits. Governments, Norrie and Owram argue, vainly tried to counter these factors by expanding the money supply and increasing state expenditures, hoping these policies would create economic growth and produce more jobs. Such policies proved counterproductive because they increased the rate of inflation and made employers hesitant to borrow money. Policy makers failed to recognize

that what economists called the non-accelerating inflation rate of unemployment (NAIRU) had risen—in plain English, that more people had to be unemployed if a market-oriented economy was to be maintained.[10] This monetarist analysis advocated restricting the money supply, which would force governments to spend less. If governments did not increase either money supply or spending to create jobs, employers would have an incentive to keep wages down, and fear of unemployment would force workers to accept this new state of affairs.

Some post-Keynesian economists have argued that the monetarist solution to stagflation meant a return to the economic thinking that preceded the Great Depression. Taken to its logical extreme, it would recreate the conditions that produced the economic catastrophe of the 1930s. These economists reject the view that a higher rate of unemployment was a natural outgrowth of changes in the structure of the economy and that expansionary economic policies necessarily led to unacceptable levels of inflation. They denounce the NAIRU as technical gibberish designed to make higher unemployment and lower wages appear as inevitable, rather than as an outcome of particular public policies. Economist Pierre Fortin, studying the economies of industrialized countries from 1960 to 1985, disputed the assertion that low rates of inflation were necessary for increases in economic productivity. He found that some countries with low inflation had weaker economic growth than countries with relatively high inflation.[11]

Economist Harold Chorney observed that Keynes had always been sceptical that low unemployment and low inflation could be achieved without substantial state economic intervention. In the postwar period, the fear of returning to Depression conditions had caused employers and unions to make compromises that made such intervention less necessary. With the postwar compromise in tatters by the early 1970s, it was up to governments to take a clearer stand on how wealth was to be distributed. According to Chorney, post-Keynesians advocated either wage and price controls or a tax-based system that penalized those deemed to be causing inflation as an alternative to the monetarism espoused by the anti-Keynesians.[12]

## NOTES

[1] Mr Justice Thomas R. Berger, *Northern Frontier, Northern Homeland: The Report of the Mackenzie Valley Pipeline Inquiry* (Ottawa: Minister of Supply and Services Canada, 1977), 1:123

[2] Canada, Department of Reconstruction, *Employment and Income with Special Reference to the Initial Period of Reconstruction*, Sessional Paper no. 90, 12 April 1945

[3] Ester Reiter, "Life in a Fast-Food Factory" in *On the Job: Confronting the Labour Process in Canada*, ed. Craig Heron and Robert Storey (Montreal: McGill-Queen's University Press), 317–18

[4] Frank James Tester and Peter Kulchyski, *Tammarniit (Mistakes): Inuit Relocation in the Eastern Arctic, 1939–1963* (Vancouver: UBC Press, 1994), 7

[5] Quoted in Wallace Clement, *Hardrock Mining: Industrial Relations and Technological Changes at INCO* (Toronto: McClelland and Stewart, 1981), 227–28

[6] Heather Menzies, *Computers on the Job: Surviving Canada's Microcomputer Revolution* (Toronto: Lorimer, 1982), 56

[7] Rachel Carson, *Silent Spring* (Boston: Houghton Mifflin, 1962), 244

[8] Sheila Arnopolous, "Immigrants and Women: Sweatshops of the 1970s" in *The Canadian Worker in the Twentieth Century*, ed. Irving Abella and David Millar (Toronto: Oxford University Press, 1978), 204

[9] Canada, *Report of the Royal Commission on Taxation*, Vol. 1, *Introduction, Acknowledgements and Minority Reports* (Ottawa: Queen's Printer, 1966), 1

[10] Kenneth Norrie and Douglas Owram, *A History of the Canadian Economy* (Toronto: Harcourt Brace Jovanovich, 1991), 602

[11] Linda McQuaig, *Shooting the Hippo: Death by Deficit and Other Canadian Myths* (Toronto: Viking, 1995), 138

[12] Harold Chorney, "The Economic and Political Consequences of Canadian Monetarism" (paper presented to the British Association of Canadian Studies Annual Meeting, 1991)

## SELECTED READING

In addition to titles cited in chapters 12 and 13, works covering postwar economic developments include: Kenneth Norrie and Douglas Owram, *A History of the Canadian Economy* (Toronto: Harcourt Brace Jovanovich, 1991); Harold Chorney, *The Deficit and Debt Management: An Alternative to Monetarism* (Ottawa: Canadian Centre for Policy Alternatives, 1989); David A. Wolfe, "The Rise and Demise of the Keynesian Era in Canada: Economic Policy, 1930–1982" in *Modern Canada 1930–1980s*, ed. Michael S. Cross and Gregory S. Kealey (Toronto: McClelland and

Stewart, 1984); and Robert M. Campbell, *Grand Illusions: The Politics of the Keynesian Experience in Canada, 1945–1975* (Peterborough, ON: Broadview Press, 1987). On taxation debates, see Canada, *Report of the Royal Commission on Taxation* (Ottawa: Queen's Printer, 1966); John N. McDougall, *The Politics and Economics of Eric Kierans: A Man for all Canadians* (Montreal: McGill-Queen's University Press, 1993), chap. 6; and J. Harvey Perry, *A Fiscal History of Canada: The Postwar Years* (Toronto: Canadian Tax Foundation, 1989).

Growing concern for the environment and uncontrolled technological innovation is discussed in Chad Gaffield and Pam Gaffield, eds., *Consuming Canada: Readings in Environmental History* (Toronto: Copp Clark, 1995); Rachel Carson, *Silent Spring* (Boston: Houghton Mifflin, 1962); *Limits to Growth: A Report for the Club of Rome's Project for the Predicament of Mankind*, 2nd ed. (New York: Universe, 1974); and E.F. Schumacher, *Small Is Beautiful: The Study of Economics as if People Mattered* (New York: Harper and Row, 1975). Donald Savoie discusses the economic implications of regionalism in *Regional Economic Development: Canada's Search for Solutions* (Toronto: University of Toronto Press, 1986). Thomas Berger's report for the Mackenzie Valley Pipeline Inquiry, *Northern Frontier, Northern Homeland*, rev. ed. (Vancouver: Douglas and McIntyre, 1988) offers a classic statement on Native dilemmas over the development ethic, as do Mel Watkins, ed., *Dene Nation: The Colony Within* (Toronto: University of Toronto Press, 1977), and the texts on Canada's First Nations by Arthur Ray, J.R. Miller, and Olive Dickason. On the impact of hydro-electric projects on Native communities and the environment more generally, see James Waldram, *As Long as the Rivers Run: Hydroelectric Development and Native Communities in Western Canada* (Winnipeg: University of Manitoba Press, 1988), and Sean McCutcheon, *Electric Rivers: The Story of the James Bay Project* (Montreal: Black Rose Books, 1991). On Natives and the economy, see also Dianne Newell, *Tangled Webs of History: Indians and the Law in Canada's Pacific Coast Fisheries* (Toronto: University of Toronto Press, 1993).

Works with extensive coverage of regional economic developments include: Gerald Friesen, *The Canadian Prairies: A History*, rev. ed. (Toronto: University of Toronto Press, 1987); Rennie Warburton and Donald Coburn, eds., *Workers, Capital and the State of British Columbia* (Vancouver: UBC Press, 1987); Patricia Marchak, *Green Gold: The Forest Industry in British Columbia* (Vancouver: UBC Press, 1983); and Gary Burrill and Ian McKay, eds., *People, Resources and Power in Atlantic Canada: Critical Perspectives on Underdevelopment and Primary Industries in the Atlantic Region* (Fredericton: Acadiensis Press, 1987).

# 15

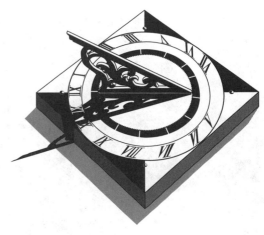

CHAPTER

## COMMUNITY
## AND NATION,
## 1945–1997

HELEN BURGESS HAD SEPARATED FROM HER husband and was working to support herself and her two children when she wrote a desperate letter to Prime Minister Mackenzie King in June 1947. The Toronto woman was a victim of the critical urban housing shortage that had resulted from a virtual halt in residential construction during the Depression and Second World War. While urban populations increased, the quantity and quality of available accommodation deteriorated. Wrote Burgess:

> I make clear a week $26.09. Out of this I have to live, pay rent for one little room, street car fare and personal expenses. I had to send my little children to an orphanage as I couldn't keep them with me in a room as nobody will give you a room if you have children. Now please would you help me, tell me what I should do in order that I could have my babies with me. My heart is breaking for them as I need them and want them with me. I miss them terribly and they miss me too.[1]

Helen Burgess would have found incomprehensible the scorn that intellectuals would pour on the new suburbs that sprang up after the Second World War. For most working families in 1945, five rooms plus a small yard where children could play seemed an unattainable ideal. Within two decades, such homes had materialized for many Canadians.

Despite the persistence of poverty for a large minority of Canadians, the promise of abundance appeared to be within the reach of a majority not long after the war's end. Depression and war had forced delays in purchasing appliances and gadgets, but consumers in the 1950s earned the wages necessary to buy—usually on time payments—automobiles, televisions, refrigerators, and washing machines. Consumption became, arguably, the major pastime of society, and status was bestowed on individuals increasingly on the basis of the goods they owned.

Materialist values permeated society at every level. Not surprisingly, there was also a sharp reaction among those who believed that unbridled individualism and acquisitiveness were destroying community and spiritual values. Indeed, despite the homogenizing impact of the American dream, diversity and difference flourished in postwar Canada. Ethnic organizations expanded in an increasingly polyglot society; suburban community groups involved in myriad activities appeared within months of the establishment of new suburbs; and churches continued their traditional ministrations of their flocks and often took on new social roles as well. New social movements from feminism and

*This postwar float encouraged women to think of themselves as consumers and ornaments.*
Provincial Archives of Alberta/BL 2021/1

environmentalism to Native and gay rights gradually emerged. This chapter provides an overview of the changing character of daily life in Canada in the half century following the Second World War.

## POPULATION

Canada's population increased from about twelve million in 1945 to twenty-nine million in 1995. "Now we are twenty million," announced Bobby Gimby's "Canada," a popular patriotic hit record during the 1967 centennial. The baby boom of the postwar period, which boosted populations throughout the industrialized world, was part of the story. Women had limited their pregnancies during the Depression and the war, but the relative security of the postwar period encouraged couples over the next two decades to marry young and have families of four children and more. At the peak of the baby boom in 1959, the fertility rate of women in their childbearing years was about 50 percent greater than it had been in 1941.

Immigration was the other major factor in Canada's population explosion. From 1946 to 1962, almost 1.8 million new immigrants came to Canada. Early postwar immigrants were primarily European; only 4 percent came from Asia and Africa, and many of these were white South Africans and Israelis. Overseas offices of the Department of Immigration were confined to Europe, as were visa offices, and the minister of citizenship and immigration enjoyed substantial discretionary power in granting entry. Such practices made specific legislated interdictions unnecessary. Initially, there was some resistance to opening doors to immigrants from countries that were Canada's enemies during the Second World War. About 10 000 Germans and 20 000 Italians were permitted entry from 1946 to 1950, but the explosion in labour needs led to acceptance of 189 705 Germans and 166 397 Italians from 1951 to 1957.

As the economic boom of the 1960s began, it became clear that Western Europe, back on its feet after postwar rebuilding, would no longer produce the steady stream of immigrants required to support Canada's economy. Since the well-educated technical and professional people that Canada most wanted would not be available in the required numbers, immigration regulations were changed to open the door to skilled people, as well as the domestics whom wealthy Canadians desperately wanted, from regions other than Europe and the United States. Revisions of the Immigration Act in 1962 and again in 1967 reduced the colour bias that once kept Canada's gates largely closed to non-whites. People from the Caribbean and Asia in particular took advantage of Canada's changing immigration policy. While recent immigrants, as a group, had once been relatively poor compared to other Canadians, in the 1980s and 1990s the aver-

| Table 15.1 | | | | | | |
|---|---|---|---|---|---|---|
| A GROWING POPULATION, 1941–1991 | | | | | | |
| Period | Population increase | Births | Population increase due to births | Net immigration | Population increase due to immigration | Population at the end of period |
| 1941–51 | 2141** | 1972 | 92.1 | 169 | 7.9 | 13 648 |
| 1951–56 | 2072 | 1473 | 71.1 | 594 | 28.9 | 16 081 |
| 1956–61 | 2157 | 1675 | 77.7 | 482 | 22.3 | 18 238 |
| 1961–66 | 1777 | 1518 | 85.4 | 259 | 14.6 | 20 015 |
| 1966–71 | 1553 | 1090 | 70.2 | 463 | 29.8 | 21 568 |
| 1971–76 | 1425 | 934 | 65.5 | 491 | 34.5 | 22 993 |
| 1976–81 | 1350 | 978 | 72.4 | 372 | 27.6 | 24 343 |
| 1981–86 | 1011 | 988 | 97.7 | 23 | 2.3 | 25 354 |
| 1986–91 | 1754 | 985 | 56.2 | 779 | 43.8 | 27 108 |

*All population figures in these tables are in thousands.
**Excludes Newfoundland

*Source:* Canada Year Book, *1994, 113*

age immigrant in the labour force earned more than Canadian-born workers. The averages masked the poverty of some immigrant groups, but they demonstrate the extent to which the immigrants, often having superior job credentials to the Canadian-born, succeeded in their new country. Among the poorer groups were refugees from Indochina and Latin America fleeing persecution and ethnic discrimination in their war-torn countries.

By 1991, immigrants of European origin accounted for slightly more than half of all Canadians born outside the country, while Asians accounted for a quarter of immigrants, about double their percentage just a decade earlier. That year, three of every five new Canadians arriving in the country were of Asian or African origin, with the remaining two coming in almost equal numbers from the rest of the Americas and from Europe.

The federal government reduced immigration levels to below 100 000 per year in response to the recession of 1982, but they were allowed to rise once the economy rallied. During the recession of the early 1990s, smaller cuts in immigration levels were made as it became clear that Canadians were having too few children to maintain the population through natural increase alone. More effective contraception and changing social values produced a

*Events such as the Chinese dragon parade celebrate the cultural diversity of Canadian society.*

Vancouver Public Library/79795-A

huge decline in the birth rate from 28.3 newborns per 1000 population in 1959 to 15.7 in 1976. Demographers suggest that each Canadian woman on average would have to produce 2.1 children each for the population to remain stable over the next generation; in 1990, it was forecast that they would bear only 1.8 children.

The dramatic decline in infant deaths since the beginning of the century meant that, in 1990, only 7.9 infants per 1000 failed to reach their first birthday. Better nutrition, preventive medicine, and the use of antibiotics increased not only infant survival but life expectancy more generally. Children born in 1961 could expect to live ten years longer than children born in 1931, and children born in 1991 another five years more. By the latter date, life expectancy was seventy-four years for men and nearly eighty-one years for women. Wealthy Canadians still tended to live longer than the poor, and Native peoples had a shorter life expectancy than non-Natives. Although infectious diseases in Native communities were less common than in earlier periods, and medical care facilities and personnel were more accessible, poverty-related diseases such as tuberculosis were not eradicated. Despair produced disastrous rates of alcoholism and drug addiction, leading to an array of health problems.

## CHANGING SOCIAL MORES

For the majority of Canadians, education levels and income increased, and so too did material expectations. Many Canadians lived in consumer heaven, even if it meant lifelong indebtedness. Statistics Canada reported that in 1990, three-quarters of all households had automatic washing machines, clothes dryers, and cable television, and two-thirds had microwave ovens, VCRs, and tape recorders. Sixteen percent had home computers. While fewer homes in poorer regions had all this gadgetry, the spread of high-tech products was on the increase everywhere.

The nuclear family, consisting of a husband, a wife, and several children, remained the ideal for most Canadians, but with each census, it accounted for a noticeably smaller proportion of households. Divorce laws were liberalized in 1969, allowing more unhappy marriages to be dissolved and increasing the number of single-parent households. The effectiveness of "the Pill," which was widely prescribed in the 1960s, allowed women the option of delaying childbirth or of not having children at all. Reflecting somewhat greater tolerance of homosexuality, same-sex couples "came out" in unprecedented numbers. Common-law marriages, once associated with the poorer classes, became popular across the economic spectrum, particularly among young adults. Divorce and remarriage substantially increased the number of "blended" families, which might include a couple's biological

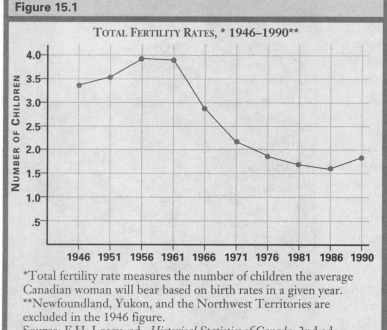

**Figure 15.1**

### TOTAL FERTILITY RATES, * 1946–1990**

*Total fertility rate measures the number of children the average Canadian woman will bear based on birth rates in a given year.
**Newfoundland, Yukon, and the Northwest Territories are excluded in the 1946 figure.
Source: F.H. Leacy, ed., *Historical Statistics of Canada*, 2nd ed., (Ottawa: Statistics Canada,1983); Series B1-14 *Canada Year Book*, various years.

*The relative roles played by natural increase and immigration could vary a great deal from one census period to the next. Birth rates and rates of immigration and emigration together determined how fast the population would grow.*

children as well as each partner's offspring from earlier marriages. Developments in reproductive technology further blurred notions of family. Surrogate mothers, egg donors, sperm donors, and processes such as *in vitro* fertilization, sex predetermination, and embryo screening made reproductive practices increasingly complex and raised fundamental ethical questions about the bounds of medical science.

The baby boomers tended to embrace more liberal social values than their parents had. Children of a prosperous and media-dominated age, they fostered an ever-changing youth culture characterized at first by rock music and blue jeans,

and later by premarital sex, mind-altering drugs, unisex clothing and hairstyles, and political protest. The changes were most evident among middle-class teenagers enrolled in expanding liberal arts programs at universities, but they had their impact throughout the postwar generation. Even at the conservative University of Alberta, where only 1 percent of students in residence had used drugs in 1965, fully a quarter of residence students in 1971 had experimented with illegal drugs, usually marijuana. Police arrested more than fifteen hundred people in Alberta for cannabis possession in 1971, more than the number of arrests for this act in the entire country just four years earlier.

## WHO IS FIT TO HAVE A BABY?

The high birth rate from 1945 to 1960 reflected both the prosperity of the period and the high value that most Canadians placed on the domestic ideal that was portrayed in American television shows such as **Leave It to Beaver**. But not every woman was a potential June Cleaver, and society and the state continued to frown upon women who had children out of wedlock. In Quebec, thousands of "illegitimate" Catholic children were placed in homes for the feeble-minded, regardless of their actual intelligence, to hide them from society. At least until the late 1950s, single mothers in Canada were denied mothers' allowances, thus virtually ensuring that they had to give their children up for adoption.

Single mothers were not the only Canadians deemed unworthy to have children. People labelled mentally unfit were also discouraged from reproducing. According to popular psychology of the period, the offspring of such people would grow up to become criminals. The province of Alberta has a particularly shameful history of enforcing such eugenicist policies. From 1929 to 1972, the provincial Eugenics Board ordered the sterilization of 2822 "mentally defective" people. The board interpreted this category broadly: it included, among others, some adult sexual offenders, young women whom the board determined to be promiscuous or potentially promiscuous, and school-age children whose parents could not cope with them and whose intelligence appeared to be less than average. Such children, who were placed in the Provincial Training School for Mental Defectives in Red Deer, ranged from those requiring around-the-clock care

to others who were quite able to feed and dress themselves but who scored poorly on the intelligence tests venerated by educational psychologists of the period.

Most of the men and boys ordered sterilized by the board were vasectomized, but some sexual offenders were castrated. Several boys with Down's syndrome had one testicle removed so that the medical director of the training school could have laboratory specimens for a study of the causes of the condition. Girls in the school were routinely sterilized at puberty. Among them was Leilani Muir, an inmate of the school from 1955 to 1965. An abused child at home, Muir suffered developmental delays and scored only sixty-four on an IQ test. School officials told her that she was to have her appendix removed, but during the appendectomy, for which there were no medical grounds, her Fallopian tubes were tied. Muir left the school when she was twenty-one and later moved to Victoria where she worked as a waitress and was twice married and divorced. At the age of forty-five, after her mother finally informed her of the sterilization, she sued the provincial government. In 1996, the Court of Queen's Bench awarded Muir $750 000 in compensation, but the provincial government failed to issue a formal apology. In a final victory, Leilani Muir confronted Alberta premier Ralph Klein at a shopping mall during the 1997 provincial election campaign. The premier gave her a personal apology for the injustice she had suffered as a result of the policies of earlier Alberta governments. Meanwhile, there were hundreds of other cases of involuntary sterilization before the Alberta courts.

Surveys among Canadian young people showed that by the mid-1960s, a majority of university students were sexually active; a decade later the same was true for high school students. The widespread availability of contraceptives meant that fear of pregnancy became a less important reason for unmarried people to avoid sex. Parental claims that sex outside of marriage was a sin had less and less resonance for young people growing up in a culture that bombarded them with sexual images. Most young people, in any case, were not hedonistic: sexual relationships tended to be monogamous, and sex was rarely dissociated from romantic love.

The "sexual revolution" was complex, especially for young women. Many complained that they felt compelled by peer pressure to have sex with their boyfriends. Looking back, some women felt that the sexual revolution was "scripted by men for men's benefit" and that it exploited women.[2] Many young women experienced coercion that went far beyond social pressure to be sexually active. Some men began to insist that the women they date provide sexual services, using physical force when a woman was reluctant to consent to sex. Although the term *date rape* would not come into use for another generation, sex forced on women by men of their acquaintance seems to have become more common in this era when many men assumed women were on the pill and ready for casual sex. To the extent that women were able to choose their partners, many experienced the new sexual morality as a form of liberation, freeing them from the compulsory same-sex monogamy that had earlier characterized socially acceptable sexual relations.

## EDUCATION

In an increasingly urbanized society, the illiterate, self-educated, and those lacking formal training found fewer employment prospects. Both technology and the increased concentration of business ownership limited the opportunities of those who simply learned a trade as an apprentice. Increasingly, most Canadians perceived formal education as the key to success in an uncertain world. In the 1950s, a high school diploma was essential for all but the least skilled, lowest paying jobs. By the 1980s, employers expected university degrees or college diplomas for many junior positions. Corporations came to have an ever larger direct and indirect impact on the character of education programs, as faculties attempted to woo students with promises that a particular course of study would lead to a job.

Over half of Canadians had nine grades or less of schooling in 1951. By 1986, fully 95 percent of Canadians aged fifteen to twenty-four had completed more than nine grades. University degrees, once limited to a numerically negligible, if extremely influential, elite, became commonplace. The number of Canadians with university degrees multiplied by ten from 1951 to 1986. Initially, men constituted most of the new graduates. Certain fields such as engineering, law, and medicine were male bastions, while schools of social work and nursing had a largely female clientele. From 1987 onwards, more women than men earned undergraduate degrees. In 1990, three in ten doctorates went to women, twice as many as in 1975.

Both employer and popular pressures played a large role in convincing governments to make the large outlays necessary to provide most Canadian children with a solid formal education. An opinion poll conducted for the Social Credit Party in Alberta in 1956 found that the major area in which Albertans wished to see more government action was education. A subsequent provincial royal commission on education reported that the effectiveness of schools was limited by poorly paid and underqualified teachers, crowded classrooms, and a narrow curriculum. The commission heard from the Canadian Petroleum Association, manufacturers, and chambers of commerce that there must be "a reduction in pupil-teacher ratios in classrooms, more and better qualified teachers, better materials of instruction, greater efforts to capitalize on the interests of pupils as means of raising the general level of academic attainment, for the purpose of equipping more young people for job efficiency in the age of machines."[3] The appeal of such views led Alberta's premier, Ernest Manning, then campaigning in the 1959 provincial election, to pledge $350 million in new education spending over five years. Other provinces, while not able to spend as generously as Alberta, also substantially increased their education grants in the 1950s and 1960s. Throughout rural areas, the one-room schoolhouses where poorly paid, inadequately trained young women taught eight grades gave way to modern, centrally located facilities. For many rural residents, the creation of consolidated school divisions was a mixed blessing because it removed local control over schools and created the need for daily bussing of children, sometimes over long distances.

By the 1970s, most public school boards across the country required that new teachers hold at least a university degree in education to be considered for a teaching position. Powerful teachers' associations in every province had won professional wages for teachers, sometimes using strikes or the threat of strikes to achieve their demands. Teachers, parents, politicians, and business people endlessly debated the best ways to educate children as citizens and future employees. For the most part, schools became more humane, as corporal punishment and rote learning gave way to child-centred education and attempts to encourage critical thinking. Critics charged that children graduated from twelve or more years of schooling less knowledgeable about the basics of reading, writing, and arithmetic than earlier generations of high school graduates.

The enthusiasm for more schooling slowly extended to the postsecondary sector. Between 1944 and 1947, university enrolment doubled as a result of generous federal grants to veterans wishing to pursue university educations. Federal grants to universities, recommended by the Massey Commission in 1951 and quickly implemented by Ottawa, also gave a boost to institutions that were receiving only modest funding increases from the provinces. Demands from the growing group of high school graduates and their parents led the provinces to loosen their purse strings in the 1960s, and new universities such as York in Toronto, Simon Fraser in Burnaby, and the University of Regina were opened. Some affiliated colleges, such as United College in Winnipeg and Brandon College, became full-fledged universities. Church-affiliated universities, particularly important in

postsecondary education in the Maritimes, became more secular and began to rely mainly on governments for their revenues.

## EDUCATION IN QUEBEC

Educational changes were perhaps most dramatic in Quebec. In 1960, there were only twenty seminaries, sixty boys' secondary schools, and twenty girls' schools whose certificates permitted students to enter the Catholic universities. While 11 percent of anglophones in the province between the ages of twenty and twenty-four attended universities, only 2.9 percent of francophones in that age group did so. Not only was the number of graduates from Catholic secondary schools poor in relation to the graduates from the province's Protestant system, but also critics persistently complained that the Catholic curriculum was antiquated. For boys, education still focused on classical thought; for girls, the system taught above all else "preparation for family life, the beauty of the home, its virtues, and its unique position in society."[4] The teachers in Quebec's Catholic schools were less educated than the teachers in the Protestant system. Among Protestant teachers in 1960, 30 percent had university degrees and 57 percent had more than twelve years of schooling; among Catholic teachers, the figures were 10 percent and 33 percent.

Dissatisfaction with the conservative, clerically run educational institutions of Quebec revealed itself in the phenomenal success of *Les Insolences du Frère Untel* (*The Impertinences of Brother Anonymous*), which was published in 1960. Written by Brother Jean-Paul Desbiens, it was a stinging indictment of Quebec education by someone within the ranks of the Roman Catholic Church. The Lesage government appointed a commission to examine the state of Quebec education and make recommendations for improvement. Although the commissioners decided that schools should remain organized along religious lines, they recommended that the state play a larger role in administration and curriculum development.

In 1964, for the first time since 1875, the provincial government established a Ministry of

Education, with Desbiens as one of the officials. Under the guiding hand of Education Minister Paul Gérin-Lajoie, new curricula were introduced to bring Quebec schools in line with education systems in the rest of North America. The ministry set up a network of secular junior colleges, or CEGEPs, to provide postsecondary vocational and academic training. Between 1960 and 1970, enrolment in Quebec's secondary schools rose 101 percent, college enrolments rose 82 percent, and university enrolments rose 169 percent.

The creation of the Centrale de l'enseignement du Québec, a militant teachers' union, out of the old Catholic teachers' association, reflected the continued secularization of education—and unions—in Quebec. Leaders of the new union issued manifestos inspired more by Marx than by Jesus and easily overwhelmed the rapidly declining numbers of priests and nuns in their ranks who clung to traditional Catholic positions. Nevertheless, conservatives could still mobilize the support needed to win school board elections, for which voter turnout was notoriously low, and they fought off attempts to formally deconfessionalize the school system. In this goal, they had the support of Protestant boards, which believed that the dual system defended anglophone rights and the superior schools developed by the wealthier non-Catholic community. Despite its continued existence, few Catholic teachers supported the confessional system, and most taught little differently than teachers in the public schools.

Increased funding for education at all levels was supplemented by nationalist-inspired language legislation. Bourassa's Bill 22 (which was discussed in chapter 12) was followed by the Parti québécois's Bill 101, which, among other things, permitted only Quebec-born anglophones to educate their children in English. All of these policies reflected a key goal of the Quiet Revolution: *rattrapage*, or a catching-up by Quebec to North American economic standards and a catching-up by Quebec francophones to the incomes earned by the province's anglophones. Although Quebec's distinct cultural identity remained and indeed deepened from the 1960s onwards, Quebeckers also increasingly identified with North American

social values. The suburban ideal by then had become central to these values.

## CITIES AND SUBURBS

### SUBURBANIZATION AND ALIENATION

Demands for more and better housing were common in a generation that had weathered the Great Depression by sharing living space and deferring the purchase of goods. The media, particularly the advertising they carried, portrayed the suburbs as a world of quiet, privacy, modern appliances, and fine furnishings, a world to which many urban residents aspired. Government-guaranteed mortgages, veterans' housing grants, and consumer credit brought it into the purview of a widening group. Little consideration was given to European models of apartment buildings around central shopping and entertainment courts. Canada, after all, was a relatively unpopulated country with a vast territory. The solution favoured by developers, governments, and much of the population was the extension of major urban areas outwards to create suburbs with easy access to the urban centres where jobs awaited.

The new suburbs increased the costs of urban administration. New roads had to be built and maintained for the cars that became indispensable to suburban life. Utility lines and sewers had to be built in the new areas and public transportation provided. More police and firefighters were required, and each new area had to be given its own schools, if pupils were not to be bussed to large, centrally located institutions. In the prosperous fifties, the municipalities received some of the funds for such developments from property tax increases and levies on the residents of the new suburbs. They also successfully pressured provincial governments to establish grants to municipalities for construction projects, to increase school grants, and to take over all or most of the costs of looking after indigents.

In most cases, new suburbs initially lacked

shopping areas, community centres, theatres, taverns, sport complexes, and other recreational areas. Residents found entertainment in the city centre and friendship via workplace, church, and community organizations that only sometimes were located within their new subdivisions. Many suburbanites and, indeed, increasing numbers of Canadians generally either sought privacy or had it thrust upon them in anonymous settings that brought the term "community" sharply into question. Television replaced community events. Supermarkets, department stores, and malls eventually replaced neighbourhood shops where customers and merchants all knew each other.

Women experienced this new privatization most directly, sometimes with devastating psychological consequences. Men in paid work often had a sense of camaraderie with fellow workers and certainly had time away from their homes. Many women who worked only in the home lacked any feeling of connectedness with a world beyond their families. For those who were well educated, a sense of uselessness was often most acute. Some upper-middle-class housewives suffered from what American feminist Betty Friedan, in her groundbreaking book *The Feminine Mystique* (1963), called "the problem that has no name." Some women, particularly if their children were older or if kin were available to act as child minders, sought refuge in paid work, while others focused their energies on voluntary activities that sought to transform the suburban community into something approaching the richness of more established urban locations. Some developed various nervous disorders for which a male-dominated medical profession prescribed tranquilizers that often created long-term addiction and left the underlying problems unresolved.

Older children, too, often fared poorly in suburban environments where public recreational spaces were few. A report of the Social Planning Council of Metropolitan Toronto in the 1970s described the dilemma:

Suburban youth are expected to act as adult consumers....While the market influences youth to consume, it creates an environment which does not enable them to meet some of their basic needs, needs for belonging, needs for social contact....When young people transcend the framework of home and neighbourhood and move out into the larger suburban community they come up against the stark reality that they are almost alone in seeking public forms of community life.[5]

Not all women remember the suburbs as a negative experience. Women developed community leagues that organized recreation for children as well as adults, and many formed close friendships with neighbours and shared shopping and childcare. Toronto suburbanite Anne Lapp recalled fondly: "Nearly all of us had small children and it was a daylong job keeping them out of the mud and excavated house sites.... It was like a small village and we knew almost everyone." For some, the similarity between homes that caused critics to label suburbs as bleak dens of conformity proved an advantage. Another Toronto suburban dweller noted: "We baby sat for each other. The houses were identical so the babies didn't make strange. Everyone knew where the bathroom was. We rigged intercoms across the driveways. We reported fast delivery trucks."[6]

## HOUSING STANDARDS

While the idealized images of suburbia were middle class, many postwar neighbourhoods on the urban fringe were shantytowns. Tarpaper shacks in Villes Jacques Cartier on Montreal Island, unserviced homes in Bridgeview on the British Columbia lower mainland, and shacks without water or sewer facilities, garbage collection, or street lighting outside St John's demonstrated that many suburbs had greater problems than middle-class angst. Residents of these instant slums were unable to find accommodation in urban cores, where established housing disappeared as office towers and apartments for the middle class encroached upon residential neighbourhoods. As we saw in chapter 12, public housing programs developed slowly. It was not for lack of success of early experiments. Toronto's Regent Park, Canada's first large-scale public housing development, was completed in 1947 and, eleven years later, a study suggested that its twelve hundred families—low-income people whose former neighbourhoods were plagued by crime, alcoholism, poor health, and school absenteeism—had established a relatively peaceful, healthy neighbourhood. While residents complained of a lack of recreational facilities and of the bureaucratic management of the project, their lives had improved as a result of their relocation to roomy rowhouses with excellent sewage and sanitary services.

Opportunities to find decent housing varied particularly dramatically between regions, with Atlantic Canadians, Natives, Northerners, and Gaspésiens, for example, far less likely to live as well as people in southern Ontario. While less than one in ten new homes built in Ontario in the early 1960s lacked either a furnace or a flush toilet, over four in ten built in Atlantic Canada during that period lacked one or both of these amenities.

By the 1970s, the core areas of many cities had become rundown. Slumlords refused to maintain their properties and city governments controlled by suburban councillors funnelled municipal funds away from the downtown areas. While tenants formed organizations to demand stricter implementation of municipal housing standards and more funding for public housing, homeowners called for improved municipal services. Some middle-class people had a different view of how conditions in the core areas could be improved. They supported programs for "redevelopment," which often meant little more than levelling existing homes and replacing them with fancier houses that only the well-off could afford. This was the fate of the historic but poor Rossdale area of Edmonton. Where the basic architectural structures were sound, as in Cabbagetown in downtown Toronto, slumlords renovated homes to meet the tastes of affluent Torontonians who preferred to live close to their offices and the city's night life. In other cities, poor districts were transformed into chic shopping areas, such as Osborne Village in Winnipeg. Increasingly, the poor were forced to live further from the urban core. With each census, the number of urban residents who lived outside the historic boundaries of the major cities

increased. In some cities, particularly Toronto, Vancouver, and Victoria, sky-high prices in the city proper made home ownership and even apartment rentals difficult for those without substantial incomes.

## The Immigrant Experience

If the postwar suburbs often appeared colourless, the established areas of cities were often reinvigorated by the huge influx of immigrants. The majority of the postwar immigrants settled in cities, and by the 1990s the initial destination of over half of all immigrants to Canada was Greater Toronto, Montreal Island, and Greater Vancouver. Although many would eventually move to the suburbs and prosper, newcomers initially concentrated in older areas of the cities, creating Little Italies, Little Budapests, and Little Jerusalems. The colourful, multilingual storefronts, the smells of a variety of cuisines, and the preference for streets and cafés over privatized living transformed cities like Vancouver, Montreal, and Toronto into cosmopolitan metropoles.

Early postwar male immigrants were usually blue-collar workers, and the jobs they were able to obtain generally paid poorly. Their wives often had little choice but to seek work, even if they had young children. Maria Rossi's experience was not atypical. In November 1956, she and her daughter arrived in Toronto. Her husband had emigrated one year earlier from their southern Italian peasant farm. The family rented a basement flat in the home of another Italian émigré family, and Maria spent her first few days in Canada buying cooking utensils and observing the annual Santa Claus parade. Four days after her arrival she began work as a steampress operator at a local laundry. For the next twenty years she worked continuously in a variety of low-paying jobs including sewing, cooking, and cashiering.

Poverty initially left many immigrants with little money or time for joining and participating in ethnic organizations, but within a generation most immigrant groups had spawned dozens of organizations, from community centres to businessmen's clubs and from sports teams to charities. In the meantime, the private cafés and clubs within an ethnic organization provided entertainment for immigrants, especially men. Women, when freed from housework, childcare, and paid work, were generally active in community-based churches. Political organizations also abounded in ethnic communities. Ukrainian-Canadian politics had long been dominated by the struggle between supporters of the Soviet Union and adherents of an independent Ukraine. With eighty thousand Ukrainians—mainly anti-communists—arriving in Canada in the early postwar period, the nationalists, who enjoyed financial and ideological support from the Canadian government, came to dominate Ukrainian-Canadian organizations. Their activities helped to publicize famines, induced by Soviet collectivization policies in the 1930s, that had taken the lives of millions. Zionism, in the prewar period the interest of only one faction of Canadian Jewry, became a uniting cause in the aftermath of the Nazi Holocaust.

Immigrants wanted their children to learn English and to succeed in their new homeland, but they also wished to preserve their home languages and cultural practices. By the 1960s, ethnic groups were more assertive about preserving their cultural heritage. Federal bilingualism and biculturalism programs led minority ethnic groups to lobby for federal and provincial grants for what became known as multiculturalism. In 1971, Prime Minister Trudeau appointed a secretary of state for multiculturalism. The federal government and the provinces with the greatest ethnic mix began to fund ethnic organizations and festivals as well as heritage-language instruction in the schools.

Ethnic diversity helped to mute the prejudices that were once so prevalent in Canada, schools made a special effort to make students aware of the problems created by prejudice, and opinion surveys indicated the growth of tolerance among Canadians. Still, discrimination in employment, housing, and other areas continued to face many non-whites. Although human rights legislation in the 1970s ameliorated the situation somewhat, it could not eliminate racism and bigotry from Canadian society.

## ASIAN-CANADIAN COMMUNITIES

When Hing Chang, an exceptional student, decided to leave her Vancouver high school in the late 1940s to go to business college, her principal was supportive, but he admitted that college training, a ticket to success for white Canadians, would not help Hing find a job. His top Chinese-Canadian graduates had faced discrimination in their job searches and had been unable to secure good positions.

Before the 1970s, Chinese Canadians had good reason to feel embattled in Canadian society. Their communities were close to downtown and viewed with contempt by urban redevelopers. Two-thirds of Toronto's Chinatown was bulldozed in the 1960s to build a new city hall. In Vancouver, city by-laws eroded the distinct character of Chinatown. As author Denise Chong, daughter of Hing Chang, recalled:

> Vancouver's city council enacted bylaws to sanitize the squalor and ordered commerce off the sidewalk—gone were the squawking chickens in cages, the barbecued pork and duck that once hung for the customer's perusal. The gambling dens that used to be my grandmother's livelihood and entertainment had also disappeared; the last one had been padlocked long ago by city police. Now when we went to Chinatown, I couldn't help but feel, as its walls seemed to close in, that we were walking through the debris of my mother's past.[7]

After Canadian recognition of the communist government in Mainland China, new Chinese immigrants began to arrive in Canada, reinvigorating the Chinese-Canadian community and eventually giving it enough clout to resist the redevelopers. Educational institutions and major employers gradually became less racist, opening new opportunities for more Chinese Canadians. In the 1980s and 1990s, wealthy Hong Kong residents, skittish about the impending return of their city to the Chinese government in 1997 after a century of British control, were actively courted by the Canadian government because of the capital and expertise they promised to inject into the country.

Beginning in the late 1960s, professionally trained South Asians, particularly from India and Pakistan, were also in demand by some Canadian companies. In contrast, East Indian immigrants without university degrees were often ghettoized in low-wage, supposedly unskilled factory jobs. Sociologists found that South Asian women workers were confined, in many factories, to the lowest-paying and most difficult tasks on the worst shifts. South Asians also provided much of the farm labour force in British Columbia, picking pesticide-sprayed crops without protective clothing or masks, and living in converted barns without running water or electricity.

Vietnamese and other Indochinese immigrants, often "boat people" fleeing either political repression or economic hardship, began arriving in Canada in the late seventies. While many prospered in their new home, the rate of unemployment among Canadians of Vietnamese descent in the early nineties was double the Canadian average. Violent youth gangs in the Vietnamese community reflected the presence of an underclass for whom racism made the future appear quite bleak. Middle-class Vietnamese resented the media spotlight on the gangs and the limited attention paid both to those who were succeeding despite the odds and to the conditions that caused some youth to turn to gangs.

## AFRICAN CANADIANS

African Canadians, like their American counterparts, faced particularly deep-seated racism, and in the postwar period they organized to fight its vicious effects. In Nova Scotia, blacks fought for their rights through the Nova Scotia Association for the Advancement of Coloured People (NSAACP), founded in 1945. In 1946, the NSAACP raised money to help Viola Desmond fight segregation in movie theatres. Desmond, a Halifax beautician, was arrested in a New Glasgow theatre for sitting downstairs rather than in the balcony to which blacks were usually restricted. She was thrown in jail and fined for attempting to

defraud the government of one cent in amusement tax—seats in the balcony were less expensive than those downstairs. Sentenced to thirty days in jail or a $20 fine, she paid the money but appealed the decision. Although the case was thrown out on a technicality, the incident resulted in so much negative publicity that such discriminatory laws were soon abandoned. Nevertheless, African Canadians in Nova Scotia faced dismal prospects. A report prepared for the National Council of Women of Canada in the 1950s on the position of women in Nova Scotia observed that African-Canadian women—and men—had few job opportunities in that province, which was home to over 30 percent of Canada's black population in 1961.

Elsewhere, discrimination on the basis of race was also common and was even upheld by the courts. In 1949, the Appeal Court of Ontario ruled that there was nothing legally wrong with a clause in property deeds that barred Jews and blacks from buying property in Beach O'Pines near Sarnia. In Dresden, Ontario, where blacks made up 17 percent of the town's two thousand people in 1950, restaurants, poolrooms, and barber and beauty shops refused patronage from non-whites. Although black organizations, particularly in Nova Scotia, struggled against the most blatant forms of discrimination, particularly segregated facilities, they were unable to break down the racist attitudes that kept many of them in the ranks of the underclass. Apart from discrimination in the job market, African Canadians could expect to live in poorer housing and receive less schooling than whites.

Encouraged by the black power movement in the United States, African Canadians in the 1960s became more assertive in their struggle against discrimination. A new generation of black leaders, many of them recent immigrants from the West Indies and Africa, refused to accept second-class citizenship, challenging the moderate approach of the early postwar leaders, who were usually associated with African-Canadian church congregations. Numbers contributed to a greater community confidence. From 1955 to 1961, only 4219 Caribbean immigrants were allowed to enter Canada. Some were professionals or skilled workers in such demand by the labour market that gov-

*Africville in the 1960s.*

Bob Brooks/Public Archives of Nova Scotia

ernments relaxed racist restrictions on immigration. Almost half were domestics who entered under the Caribbean Domestic Scheme, which was meant to maintain Canada's imperial trade and investment ties with the region and to supply wealthy households with a source of cheap domestic labour. By contrast, there were 140 000 West Indian immigrants to Canada from 1971 to 1981, with two-thirds settling in Ontario. Their concentration in southern Ontario allowed them to establish a rich institutional cultures, including social clubs, newspapers, Toronto's annual Caribana festival, and anti-racist organizations. Nonetheless, a detailed study of race relations in Toronto published in 1985 suggested that at least 10 percent of the white population of Metro Toronto was deeply racist and that the colour bar to a variety of jobs remained firm.

The plight of blacks in Nova Scotia received international attention when the city of Halifax decided to demolish Africville. Located on the shores of Bedford Basin, Africville had been home to Halifax's black population since the middle of the nineteenth century. The community had been shamefully neglected by the city authorities, who had provided no water, sewerage facilities, or garbage collection to its homes and had located the municipal dump nearby. In 1961, city council decided to remove the four hundred citizens of Africville to make way for an industrial development on the site. Residents' protests were ignored; most whites and even a few blacks argued that urban renewal was a necessary prelude to a better future for all Haligonians. Although many residents were compensated for their property and offered alternative housing, they resented not being fully consulted, and they feared the loss of community that would result from the relocation.

In the wake of the demolition of Africville, the Black United Front (BUF) was founded in 1968 to intensify the struggle for change. A visit to Halifax by Stokely Carmichael, a leading African-American militant, served as a catalyst for the new organization. In an effort to defuse what appeared to be a growing militancy among blacks in Canada—a student protest against racism at Sir George Williams University (now Concordia) ended in the destruction of the university's computer system—the federal government offered to fund BUF and other black organizations.

Beginning in the late 1960s, provincial human rights legislation, backed up by human rights commissions with powers to investigate and prosecute cases of clear discrimination on the basis of race, sex, or religion, demonstrated a greater desire on the part of authorities to reduce systemic racism in Canada. Canadians became quite complacent about racism, comparing their society favourably to that of their southern neighbours, where race relations often boiled over into violence. Such self-satisfaction began to evaporate in the early 1990s. A series of police shootings of unarmed blacks in Montreal and Toronto led to accusations that many police officers were racists who stereotyped all blacks as criminals. Neo-Nazi skinheads—largely unemployed white male youths—attacked non-whites of Asian and African origin and desecrated Jewish cemeteries. Intolerance had its violent side, even in Canada.

A small group of neo-Nazis infiltrated the Canadian Airborne Regiment, and several suspected racists were inexplicably among the troops sent by the armed forces for peacekeeping in Somalia in 1992–93 when that country was torn apart by civil war. During that operation, three unarmed civilians were shot, allegedly for trying to steal from the Canadian compound, and Somali teenager Shidane Arone was tortured to death. The military claimed that the documented racists were not the men responsible for the killings, but they failed to explain why individuals known by the military to be right-wing extremists were sent to Somalia and indeed why they were admitted to the armed forces in the first place.

## NATIVE PEOPLES FIND A VOICE

The group of Canadians that probably felt the sting of intolerance the most was not an immigrant group—it was Canada's first peoples. In 1946–48, a special joint committee of the House and Senate reviewed the Indian Act. Its report demonstrated that the old assimilatory goals were to continue, although there would be some reforms. In 1951, ineffectual bans on the potlatch and sun dance were lifted. Elected band councils could make decisions in areas that traditionally concerned municipal governments, but Indian Affairs could overrule these decisions. Beginning in the 1950s, the provinces began to enfranchise Natives, and status Indians were finally granted this token of citizenship by the federal government in 1960.

By this time, Native peoples, like many other subordinate groups, were becoming increasingly militant in their pursuit of fairer treatment. Movements for decolonization in Africa and Asia in the postwar period provided a stimulus to action among oppressed peoples within the developed world, while the general militancy of the 1960s prompted aboriginal Canadians to argue that they

had waited long enough for justice and would increasingly take matters into their own hands.

A catalyst for action by treaty Indians was the unveiling of the Trudeau government's White Paper on Indian policy in June 1969. Ottawa planned to relinquish Native lands while at the same time removing Indians' special status, dismantling the Department of Indian Affairs, and having the provinces assume responsibilities for services to Native people. The Indian response to the White Paper was overwhelmingly negative. The National Indian Brotherhood (NIB), which was formed in 1968 to speak for treaty Indians, led the resistance, claiming that Indians wanted self-government and not the assimilation implied in becoming ordinary citizens of the provinces. Native groups argued that aboriginal peoples had a right to reassert their cultures so long suppressed by government and church policies. The White Paper, if implemented, would be a final nail in the coffin for Native peoples, a policy of cultural genocide. Surprised at the vehemence of Native reaction, the Trudeau government withdrew the White Paper but offered no framework for negotiating Native demands for self-government.

During the 1970s, pressures from the NIB—the name was changed to the Assembly of First Nations in 1982—and provincial associations led the government to gradually give Native peoples the responsibility for their own education. After 1973, it became increasingly common for Native children to attend local schools controlled by their band councils, particularly in the elementary grades; but many reserves had little success in convincing Ottawa to build high schools nearby so that their children were not forced either to bus several hours a day or to live in towns away from the reserve. Although the residential education system was phased out in the 1960s and 1970s, its scars remain. In 1990, the head of the Manitoba Association of Chiefs, Phil Fontaine, made a public issue of claims that had frequently been heard privately: Native children in residential schools had been victims of violence, including sexual abuse, at the hands of members of religious orders as well as lay teachers.

The marginalization of Native adults often resulted in family problems in which children were innocent victims. Native parents who, as children, had been forced to attend residential schools, and had thus been deprived of a continuing relationship with their parents, had no role models for parenting. Though many families struggled to provide caring environments for their offspring, many children grew up in abusive situations. On remote reserves, glue-sniffing and other forms of dependency on mind-numbing drugs became common among Native children, with a high number of drug-related deaths. The suicide rates among Native teenagers and even pre-teens were alarming. Native groups increasingly demanded that traditional cultural practices, once suppressed by governments and churches, be restored so that Native children could grow up with positive images of their culture.

Native people who left the reserves for towns and cities were rarely assimilated into the larger society. Undereducated and faced with discrimination, many succumbed to lives in urban ghettos marked by poor housing, poverty, and drunkenness. Indian and Métis Friendship Centres and Native-run addiction programs helped to rescue some from the worst aspects of city life, but, for the most part, aboriginal leaders reckoned that reserves offered their people a better opportunity to live in prosperity and preserve their cultural inheritance.

## NORTHERN FIRST NATIONS

Not all Native peoples had the option of living on reserves. The Mackenzie Valley Indians of the North had no reserves, while neither the Yukon Indians nor the Inuit had signed treaties with the federal government. Such a situation made northern Native peoples particularly vulnerable to the burgeoning development in the postwar North. Native peoples of the Yukon and Northwest Territories were particularly vocal in rejecting the oil and natural gas pipelines proposed in the 1970s to fuel southern Canada as well as the United States with energy. While some of the Métis of the Northwest Territories supported a pipeline as a source of jobs, a large percentage joined the Indians of the region to declare the existence of a Dene nation seeking independence within the framework of Canadian Confederation.

The Dene had supporters in the white community, particularly from sections of the Roman Catholic Church. By the 1960s, Canada's churches—both Catholic and Protestant—had begun to reverse their centuries-old position that Native cultures were inferior and that the goal of white missionaries ought to be assimilation of Native peoples into mainstream Canadian culture. The churches generally did not resist Native demands for an end to residential schools and for schools on reserves to be run by Natives. Greater Catholic liberalism was reflected in the incorporation of Native ceremonies into Catholic rituals and the establishment of the Anishanabe Spiritual Centre at Espanola in Ontario. In the late 1980s and early 1990s, both the United Church of Canada and the Oblate Order of the Catholic Church formally apologized to First Nations peoples for having been agents of imperialism. Catholic social justice advocates, inspired by liberation theology—the notion that the church, in keeping with the teachings of Christ, ought to support the struggles of the poor and the outcast—were increasingly vocal in their support for Native demands for autonomy and land rights. In the North, the Oblate missionary René Fumoleau led an effective campaign to publicize the case of the Dene against pipeline advocates.

The Trudeau government, which supported the proposed pipeline projects, appointed Justice Thomas Berger, a former leader of the New Democrat Party in British Columbia, to study the impact of a pipeline in the Mackenzie Valley on local residents and the environment. Berger proved sympathetic to the Dene and Inuit who stressed the extent to which they still subsisted on local resources. They made clear their desire to hold off major developments until their land claims had been settled and they were in a position to negotiate with potential investors rather than having the Canadian government impose projects upon them. Although the government accepted Berger's call for a halt to pipeline developments for a decade, it was slow in pursuing comprehensive land-claims settlements for the North and providing aid to bands seeking to establish local businesses under

Native control.

It was not until 1984 that the Inuit of the Mackenzie Delta received a land settlement—242 000 square kilometres—and the Yukon Indians reached an agreement with Ottawa in 1988. In November 1992, the Inuit of the eastern Arctic accepted a negotiated deal that provided them with 350 000 square kilometres of subsurface mineral rights. At the same time, they voted for partition of the Northwest Territories, with the eastern Arctic to become a separately administered territory called Nunavut (meaning "the people's land" in the Inuktitut language). Within Nunavut's boundaries, 17 500 of the approximately 22 000 residents were Inuit, and many of them saw Nunavut's creation as a bold experiment in Native self-government.

*Berger Commission hearings in the Northwest Territories.*
Northern News Services Ltd.

## Land Claims and the Legal System

Outside the territories, the federal government proved even slower to settle land claims made by Indians who lacked treaties or reserves as well as by treaty Indians who claimed more territory than the government had allotted them. In 1995, there were about five hundred outstanding claims, and only three or four per year were being settled. Saskatchewan Indians, for example, claimed that over four hundred thousand acres of reserve land

had been illegally taken from them before 1914. Many Indians experienced frustration as their land claims bogged down in bureaucracy and the courts, and militancy became more common. One of the first confrontations occurred in 1974 when Indians occupied Anicinabe Park in Kenora, claiming that the park, like much of Kenora, belonged to the Native peoples.

The provincial government of British Columbia had resisted Native treaties, and Ottawa had done little to protect aboriginal peoples when their lands were seized by the province for industrial and urban expansion. Gradually things began to change. In 1985, the Supreme Court of Canada awarded the small Musqueam band $10 million in compensation for Indian Affairs duping them into granting an unfair golf course lease on their land. But many Native people, rather than hoping for monetary compensation after their resources were depleted and their traditional lifestyle was destroyed, began to actively resist developers, even if it meant breaking the law. In the late 1980s, in various parts of British Columbia, Native peoples clashed with loggers whose activities were despoiling traditional aboriginal lands. In 1991, the provincial government, responding to growing Native militancy, agreed to negotiate land issues. If there was any optimism that such negotiations would go smoothly, it dissipated later that year when Judge Allan McEachern issued his decision on the Gitksan-Wet'suwet'en land claim. The judgement reflected long-standing Eurocentric biases and showed the tremendous distance between the two parties.

Pent-up frustrations were evident across the country in the 1990s. In northern Alberta, the Lubicon Cree, who had been waiting for a reserve for over fifty years, forcibly kept out oil companies wanting to drill on disputed territories. Supported by environmentalists, the Temagami Indians in

Ontario tried to prevent logging on their territories. The Cree of northern Quebec threatened both court action and sabotage if Quebec proceeded with a second James Bay hydro-electric project. Nova Scotia Mi'kmaq pursued their hunting and fishing rights against an unsympathetic provincial government and used an investigation into the wrongful conviction of a young Mi'kmaq, Donald Marshall, to expose the racism they faced on a daily basis. In Manitoba, the Public Inquiry into the Administration of Justice and Aboriginal People was sparked by two tragic deaths: the conspiracy of silence that followed the murder of Helen Betty Osborne in The Pas in 1971 and the shooting of an unarmed Native leader, John Joseph Harper, in Winnipeg in 1988. The inquiries in Manitoba and Nova Scotia, as well as a royal commission in Alberta, concluded that all components of the legal system, from the police through the judiciary, exhibited prejudice against Native peoples.

In the 1990s, some Native peoples resorted to armed confrontations over the right to occupy land. The most sensational conflict occurred in the summer of 1990 between the Quebec Provincial Police and Mohawk Warriors at a reserve near Oka, Quebec. The violent clash left one police officer dead and created a stand-off that provoked Canadian military intervention. The Warriors, who ran gambling casinos and smuggling operations at other reserves, were controversial among the Mohawk, but the issue they chose was not: the town of Oka wished to develop a golf course on lands the Mohawk regarded as sacred. While denouncing the Warriors as terrorists, the federal government was forced to buy the disputed land to make it available to the Indians, but the solution appeared to be a pragmatic reaction to confrontation rather than magnanimity towards Native peoples.

In some cases, militants were suspicious of the elected aboriginal leaders. When Ovide Mercredi, grand chief of the Assembly of First Nations, attempted to act as a conciliator between the British Columbia government and armed Natives demanding recognition of their title to lands near Gustafsen Lake, the leaders of the protests denounced him as a collaborator with the white governments that oppressed Native peoples.

*Ronald Cross, also known as Lasagna, was a prominent Native figure in the Oka crisis. The media suggested that he had ties with the Mafia and that he was a Vietnam War veteran fixated on violence. In fact, the Mohawk Warrior had no connections with organized crime and had never served in the armed forces of any nation. For his part in his people's resistance at Oka, Cross received a five-year sentence for criminal assault.*

Canapress Photo Service/Tom Hanson

## NATIVE WOMEN

Under the Indian Act, Indian women who married white men lost their treaty status, as did their children, even though Indian men could marry white women without a similar loss of status for themselves or their children. In the early 1970s, Native women formed two organizations—Indian Rights for Indian Women and the National Native Women's Association—to campaign against such discriminatory treatment. They were supported in their efforts by non-Native women's groups. Together they persuaded the federal government to remove the offending section from the act in 1985. Subsequently, some Indian leaders blocked the return to reserves by women who had lost their status. Sometimes they argued that these women and their children were not Indian enough, either culturally or in their bloodlines. More generally, they charged that the federal government had done nothing to add to the land base of overcrowded reserves to make reintegration of these women and their families possible without creating hardship for existing residents.

Native women often charged that white imperialism had eroded women's traditional influence in Native communities. Men's power on reserves, they argued had been buttressed by state assumptions that viewed men as the natural leaders of the community and the main source of family support. In an atmosphere of hopelessness, alcoholic or drug-dependent Native men struck out at their wives and children. Studies of remote reserves indicated a pattern of physical and sexual abuse in which girls and women were the main victims. On some reserves, almost every woman had been the victim of sexual abuse, usually by a family member, before she reached adulthood. Native women organized support groups and healing centres and demanded that elected band councils implement programs to counsel men who had abused women and to protect their potential victims. Although male band leaders were often resistant to such pressures, there were increasing numbers of successful groups and programs.

## RECOVERING COMMUNITY

In the early 1970s, almost every adult resident of Alkali Lake, a Shuswap community of four hundred people in the British Columbia interior, was an alcoholic. Phyllis Chelsea and her husband, Andy, were typical. He had been in hospital on several occasions for kidney trouble after binge drinking, and Phyllis had required medical care twice after Andy had beaten her while in a drunken stupor. One evening, after again drinking heavily, Phyllis stopped to pick up her children at their grandmother's house. There she was confronted by her eldest daughter, then only seven, who refused to go home, accusing her parents of being violent drunks. Phyllis was shocked and resolved to stop drinking immediately. Andy was initially unwilling to follow her example until, one day, he was deeply struck by the many bruised, hungry faces among local children on the way to school, a reflection of the effects of alcohol on families in the community.

The Chelseas began to spread their anti-alcohol message zealously on the reserve. They persuaded the band council to make treatment for alcoholism a condition for receiving financial help. They and their converts looked after the children of reserve residents who had enrolled in Native treatment programs. As people sobered up, it soon became clear that alcohol was a symptom, not the primary cause, of the degradation of many Native people. The extent of sexual abuse that had occurred at the Catholic-run St John's Mission residential school near Williams Lake gradually became public. Sexual abuse had, in turn, become common in the households of Alkali alcoholics. Healing circles became crucial in allowing people to overcome the shame that had caused generations of local residents to seek comfort in drunkenness. By the early 1980s, Phyllis Chelsea could point proudly to a community in which 95 percent of the adults were sober and where children attended a new school built by the band and where elders "came to share prayers, pipe ceremonies, and songs in Shuswap," thus renewing the traditional culture that had all but died out in the wake of poverty, abuse, and despair. [8]

## THE WOMEN'S MOVEMENT

Native women were not alone in questioning their position in postwar Canadian society. Women from all regions, classes, and ethnic groups increasingly challenged sexual stereotypes, and some women, joined feminist organizations to fight for full equality. Some groups espoused a liberal feminist perspective, encouraging governments, businesses, and community organizations to involve women equally with men at all levels of decision making. Other more radical groups claimed that female representation in institutions was not enough; the institutions themselves had to change, as did the behaviour of both men and women.

During the 1950s, with its cult of domesticity, it would have been hard to predict that movements challenging every assumption of patriarchy would soon emerge. Yet even in that decade women, had begun to question social structures that made women subordinate to men.

Although they participated more than ever in paid work, women found that their employment options were limited and that their pay was deflated by notions that women's wages were "pin money," unlike the wages of a male "breadwinner." In reality, financial necessity motivated most women workers.

Liberalization of divorce laws and the flight of men from family obligations increased the number of self-supporting women. By the 1980s, one marriage in three ended in divorce. From the 1971 to the 1981 census, the number of single-parent families jumped from 477 525 to 714 005, of which 85 percent were headed by women. In 1979, 40 percent of women workers were separated, divorced, or widowed: most of these women who had children at home were sole providers. In both 1975 and 1987, the National Council on Welfare reported that 59 percent of adults living in poverty were women. In the early 1990s, a majority of single-parent households headed by women had incomes below the poverty line. This statistic was in stark comparison with countries such as France, where only 15 percent of such households lived on poverty incomes, and Sweden, where the comparable fig-

ure was 5.5 percent. In those countries, government policies focusing on retraining and finding work for single mothers, along with free day care, were clearly effective, but governments in Canada generally resisted pressure for such sweeping programs.

While employers and families required women's paid work, social institutions adapted slowly to accommodate the needs of women workers. Despite their new responsibilities, women found that there were virtually no formal arrangements for childcare. Moreover, both single and married women returned from work to find the housework waiting. The "double day" of housework and paid work often left women even less leisure time than their mothers had enjoyed, although their wages sometimes allowed them to purchase labour-saving devices, prepared foods, and off-the-rack clothing. Neither at home nor at work did they receive recognition for their contribution. Society did not view housework as "real" work, and those women who worked outside the home were confronted with low wages, paternalism, outright harassment, and lack of opportunity for advancement.

Individual reactions to the obstacles facing women slowly coalesced into political action. In Quebec in 1966, Thérèse Casgrain, a leading figure in the provincial NDP and the peace group Voice of Women, helped to found the Fédération des femmes du Québec (FFQ), an umbrella group of women's organizations, to fight for women's rights. In English Canada, women's groups, galvanized by leaders such as Laura Sabia, president of the Canadian Federation of University Women, and *Chatelaine* magazine editor Doris Anderson, pressured Ottawa for action. Supported by the FFQ, English-Canadian women's groups formed the Committee for the Equality of Women whose tactics convinced the Pearson government, spurred by outspoken cabinet minister Judy LaMarsh, to create the Royal Commission on the Status of Women. Established in 1967 and chaired by journalist Florence Bird, the commission served as a catalyst to focus complaints from women of every social class in Canada. The National Action Committee on the Status of Women (NAC), an umbrella organization for the many women's groups springing up across the country, was created in 1972. It lobbied governments to ensure that the commission's recommendations—which included calls for reform in education, employment, immigration, criminal and family law, and childcare—would not simply gather dust.

Perhaps no other issue raised by the royal commission provoked more controversy—both among the commissioners and within the larger society—than abortion. The debate polarized between those who demanded the complete removal of abortion from the Criminal Code and those who sought a ban on all abortions, sometimes making exceptions where a pregnancy endangered the woman's life. The pro-choice group stressed a woman's right to control her own body, while anti-abortionists claimed that a fetus was a living person from the moment of conception, and that its right to life outweighed a woman's right to reproductive self-determination. After the relaxation of the abortion law in 1969, access to abortion was uneven across the country, leading the Supreme Court to rule in 1988 that the law, which required an abortion to be approved by a three-doctor panel, violated the guarantees in the Charter of Rights and Freedoms of equal rights for all Canadians. After the court decision, Parliament grappled unsuccessfully with this divisive issue. Meanwhile, the anti-abortionists became increasingly militant, picketing abortion clinics and harassing patients. In 1992, a bomb blast destroyed the Toronto clinic run by Dr Henry Morgentaler, a tireless crusader for women's right to safe abortion. Two years later, a Vancouver doctor who performed abortions was shot by an anti-abortionist.

As the women's movement evolved, it identified and brought to public attention problems that had previously been overlooked. One such subject, virtually ignored even by the royal commissioners, was that of violence against women. Sexual assaults, battering, physical and sexual abuse of children, and sexual harassment in the workplace had generally been regarded as private problems and were often not taken very seriously by the authorities. Indeed, when NDP MP Margaret Mitchell rose in the House of Commons to speak on the issue of wife battering in May 1982, she was greeted with laughter and disparaging remarks from some of her fellow MPs. Such insensitivity shocked many Canadians and helped to bring the issue into focus. Another event that galvanized action on violence, not only against women, but in Canadian society more generally, was the Montreal Massacre. On 6 December 1989, a deranged young man fatally shot fourteen female engineering students at the École Polytechnique in Montreal while shouting his hatred of feminists. In the wake of this tragedy, women's groups continued to press for battered women's shelters, rape crisis centres, counselling for abusers and their victims, and increased court charges and convictions for rapists, batterers, and harassers. Government action proved slow in coming, and what few programs were available were often among the first victims of fiscal restraint in the debt-conscious nineties.

## DIVERSITY WITHIN THE WOMEN'S MOVEMENT

In the 1990s, the women's movement faced challenges from within. Women living in poverty and minority women argued that the movement had for too long been a white middle-class enclave overly concerned with issues relating to professional advancement for women. Increasingly, the feminist movement was called upon to raise the issues that affected less-privileged women and to give women of colour important roles as decision makers and spokespersons. NAC president Judy Rebick brought the language of class and race into the feminist movement. She insisted that the movement work to prevent the exploitation of domestics, who were largely visible-minority immigrant women, and pursue not just equal pay for equal work, but equal pay for work of equal value—a concept that would weigh traditional female jobs against men's jobs that required about the same education and skills. Some women vented their displeasure with the radical turn of the women's movement when Sunera Thobani was named Rebick's successor in 1993. Of East Asian background, Thobani was the first visible-minority president of NAC, and her election signalled both a continuation of the radicalism of the Rebick period and a symbolic commitment on NAC's part to respond positively to the demands of visible-minority women in the organization. NAC's Women's March Against Poverty and the election of Joan Grant-Cummings, an African Canadian, to replace Thobani in 1996 indicated that the organization would continue to address issues affecting poor and minority women.

*Women's March Against Poverty, Ottawa, 1996. Standing to the right of the banner, then NAC president, Sunera Thobani.*

Canadian Women's Movement Archives/Morisset Library/University of Ottawa

Conservative feminists were also often uncomfortable with vocal lesbians in the movement. Until homosexuality was legalized in 1969, lesbians were rarely public about their sexual orientation. Although lesbian networks had operated in larger cities, they focused on social support rather than political lobbying. Increasingly, lesbians came out of the closet and attacked "compulsory heterosexuality," the pervasive social and cultural images that extolled heterosexual relations as the only acceptable sexual option. In company with gay men, they called for an end to discrimination in such areas as adoption and spousal benefits.

## A Culture of Protest Emerges

The women's movement emerged in the context of increasing dissent within Canadian society in the 1960s. Canada, of course, had a long tradition of protest movements, including the Native rebellions of 1870 and 1885, the general strikes of 1919, and the movements of the unemployed of the 1930s. Social justice groups did not disappear after 1945, but for two decades they were relatively inactive and almost completely ignored by the media.

Expanded university campuses spawned movements for greater democratization of society beginning with the university itself. In the 1960s, the "New Left," a loose grouping that embraced a socialist vision of society but rejected the authoritarianism and puritanism of traditional Marxism as well as the gradualism of social democracy, was transplanted from the United States to Canada. Students for a Democratic University and like-minded groups arose on most campuses to demand that students be more involved in university decision making and that courses have a more "critical perspective" on social problems. Sizeable numbers of New Left adherents found political homes in the left-wing Waffle group within the NDP or, in Quebec, on the left-wing of the Parti québécois.

## The Environmental Movement

Leaders of the new social movements were often quite skilled at getting attention from the Canadian media. An environmental organization, Greenpeace, was particularly astute at focusing public attention and creating controversy. In 1970, a small group of American and Canadian activists in Vancouver created Greenpeace to protest nuclear testing at Amchitka, in the Aleutian Islands. Publicity generated by the fledgling organization prompted the Americans to abandon their tests. Buoyed by its initial success, Greenpeace conducted dramatic non-violent protests to raise the profile of other environmental issues, among them French nuclear testing in the South Pacific, the slaughter of whales and dolphins, the clubbing of baby seals for fur coats, and the dumping of nuclear and other toxic wastes in lakes and oceans.

*Oil drilling protest in Victoria, B.C., staged by Greenpeace.*

© Heinz Ruckemann, Greenpeace

By the mid-1970s, branches of Greenpeace had mushroomed throughout the world, and Greenpeace protesters popped up everywhere, precipitating incidents for the television cameras. Helium-filled balloons emblazoned with "End the Arms Race" were released in the Soviet Union, and Greenpeace crews intervened between harpoon-throwing Soviet whalers and their intended catch. In 1985, a Greenpeace member was killed by a bomb planted on the Greenpeace flagship *Rainbow Warrior* by French agents attempting to stop a "peace flotilla" protesting nuclear tests on Mururoa Atoll.

While many people were angered by Greenpeace tactics, no one could deny the organization's effectiveness. The Newfoundland seal hunt was abandoned, the save the whales campaign brought reforms to the whaling industry, and, following the bombing of the *Rainbow Warrior*, the French minister of defence resigned. By the mid-1980s, Greenpeace was an international organization with its headquarters in Amsterdam, but it retained a strong contingent of Canadian members, many of whom could remember when it operated on a shoestring budget with one leaking boat.

At the century's end, the environmental movement in Canada consisted of hundreds of local movements organized to deal with environmental issues generally or with a specific environmental problem. Victories were rare but the environmental movement created a greater public sensitivity around issues such as air and water pollution, endangered plant and animal species, rainforest destruction, acid rain, and ozone destruction.

## GAY RIGHTS

The gay rights movement also proved effective in its efforts to persuade Canadians that sexual orientation should be a matter of individual choice rather than state dictation. Before the late sixties, the state regarded homosexuality as a crime, the major churches pronounced it a sin, and the medical profession branded it a psychological disorder requiring such treatment as aversion therapy. Gay civil servants, RCMP officers, and members of the armed forces were fired as a matter of policy, and gay men—but not lesbians—were barred from immigration to Canada. Despite such repression, an underground homosexual culture flourished. Lesbians and gay men created social networks that included clubs where they could socialize without fear of prosecution.

Gays campaigned to convince politicians, doctors, and church leaders that they were not deviants and that sexual preference was a matter of individual conscience. In an atmosphere of growing concern for civil liberties, some progress was made. Reforms to the Criminal Code in 1969 removed some of the legal restrictions against homosexual relations between consenting adults, and sexual preference was removed as a criterion for immigration in 1977. The Parti québécois added sexual orientation to Quebec's human rights code and, by 1996, many other provinces also prohibited discrimination on the basis of sexual preference. The federal government promised to follow suit as early as December 1992, but first the Conservatives and then the Liberals failed to deliver on their promise. The limits of public acceptance of equality for homosexuals were demonstrated in 1994 when the NDP government of Ontario failed to pass a bill that would have removed discrimination in such areas as adoption rights.

Intolerance against homosexuality sometimes manifested itself in violence. Homophobic thugs beat up and in some cases killed gay men. In the 1980s, Toronto's gay newspaper, *The Body Politic*, was slapped with obscenity charges, while police raids on gay bars and bathhouses indicated a con-

tinued willingness to harass gays in the name of public morality. The arrest of three hundred men in a February 1981 bathhouse raid in Toronto became a focal point for gay organizations

*AIDS awareness campaign poster.*
Canadian AIDS Society

demanding legal protection from police harassment.

The spread of AIDS—Acquired Immune Deficiency Syndrome—provided a daunting challenge to the gay community, whose male members initially formed the majority of the victims of the disease. AIDS organizers developed support systems for persons infected with AIDS and educational campaigns to slow the spread of the disease. They also pressured governments to increase funding to community groups and medical research to fight AIDS.

Gay activists of the 1990s were often more militant than their counterparts a generation earlier. In contrast to the repression of earlier days, activists celebrated gay culture. Gay Pride Days became annual events in many cities, with the Gay Pride parade in Toronto attracting more than a hundred thousand participants and spectators. No longer confined to the closet, gays and lesbians published newspapers and magazines, founded bookstores, established theatre companies, and made films and wrote books dealing with gay lifestyles and concerns. Activists won court battles that gave same-sex partners benefits similar to heterosexual spouses. After legal challenges, the Canadian Army agreed in 1992 to end long-standing policies against homosexuals. Gays won the right to be ordained ministers in the United Church, but the Roman Catholic Church joined evangelical Protestants in continuing to denounce homosexuality, along with abortion and divorce, as threats to the traditional family.

## ORGANIZATIONS OF THE POOR

The new culture of protest among the young middle class in the 1960s encouraged a revival of lobbying organizations among working people and the poor. By the 1970s, hundreds of groups representing tenants, welfare rights advocates, single mothers, the unemployed, and other categories of the poor and powerless were organized. These groups provided emotional support and empowered individuals to make collective demands upon government to improve their lot. Demonstrations at provincial legislatures, city halls, and sometimes the homes of slumlords brought increased media attention to those who lived destitute lives within a prosperous society. Thousands attended a conference of poor people's organizations in Ottawa in 1971 that led to the creation of a national poverty organization to fight for a guaranteed annual income and other legislation that would benefit the country's poorest citizens. In Quebec, where both nationalist sentiment and social grievances spurred tens of thousands to join community groups, there was a close alliance between grass-roots move-

ments and the powerful trade unions. "Social animators," often university-educated facilitators paid by the unions, mobilized citizens and provided a link between the protests of radical baby boomers, organized workers, and the poor.

Work in such organizations led many of the underprivileged to recognize their problems as public or social issues resulting from the operations of the economic system rather than as primarily individual troubles resulting from personal inadequacies. So, for example, the Unemployed Citizens' Welfare Improvement Council of Greater Vancouver demonstrated against provincial legislation in 1970 that would have required welfare recipients to work for municipalities as a precondition for receiving welfare. They were hardly on the defensive as they made their views known to the government:

> We demand a recognition of the right to the necessities of life as being separate from the right to work.
>
> We demand it be recognized that people must have the right to refuse jobs which have no future, which do not meet union conditions and which lack adequate pollution control devices—without fear of cut-offs and other punitive action.
>
> We demand an immediate implementation of the guaranteed annual income tied to the fluctuations of the cost of living. For the present time we consider $200 per adult and $60 per dependent child to be the minimum adequate sum.[9]

None of the above demands were met, but the province did quietly drop the proposed legislation that sparked the demonstration.

Not all such campaigns were successful. In general, where the interests of developers and community groups representing the poor clashed, the developers won. The "skid row" residents of Vancouver, for example, failed in their efforts to stop their eviction as their province and city prepared for Expo 86. Most of the ten thousand targetted residents, who lived in small hotel rooms without cooking facilities, were single elderly men, many disabled, with poverty-level incomes. When the Expo site was announced in 1981, the Downtown Eastside Residents' Association organized a campaign to prevent mass evictions by landlords seeking to take advantage of tourist opportunities. Nevertheless, over a thousand people were evicted, some of them several times. People with wheelchairs ended up in second-floor rooms of hotels without elevators. After Expo, the situation was even worse. The "revitalization" of the eastside, much praised by businesses, removed two thousand affordable housing units to make way for parking lots, high-rise office towers, and luxury condominiums.

## RELIGION IN A SECULAR AGE

Such social injustices sparked a 1983 document prepared by the Canadian Conference of Catholic Bishops' Social Affairs Commission. Entitled *Ethical Reflections on the Economic Crisis*, the bishops' manifesto challenged the social values that determined government and business policies in Canada. The bishops set forth the ethical priorities that they wanted governments to follow: "The needs of the poor have priority over the wants of the rich; the rights of workers are more important than the accumulation of machines or the maximization of profit; the participation of the marginalized takes precedence over an order that excludes them."[10] With unemployment in double digits, the bishops called on the government to focus on policies that would create jobs rather than continuing to emphasize the battle against inflation, as the business community urged.

The leaders of the Anglican and United Churches praised the Catholic bishops for their stand. But within all three churches, there were major divisions on the question of whether religious institutions should take positions on secular political questions such as the economy and, if so, how radical such positions should be. While the Quebec bishops united behind the Social Affairs Commission's statement, Cardinal Gerald Emmett Carter, the archbishop of Toronto, publicly disassociated himself from the manifesto. He echoed in

milder form the views of his friend, right-wing businessman Conrad Black, that the bishops knew nothing about economics and should stick to more narrowly defined spiritual matters. In all churches, much of the hierarchy identified with the business leaders, whose corporate sponsorship was essential to the churches' charitable work. By the end of the 1980s, the limits of the churches' social justice movement were demonstrated by the decision of the Roman Catholic and Anglican Churches to take no position on the Canadian–American Free Trade Agreement and the mildness of the United Church's public opposition to the deal.

The issues confronting the churches in the period after 1945 were not entirely new, but the era of mass society and rampant consumerism posed unique challenges. While most Canadians continued to believe in God, there was a growing minority who were agnostics or atheists. Believers were increasingly unlikely to be church attenders, and they told pollsters that they, not their ministers, made the moral decisions that shaped their lives. Many Christians saw their church merely as a Sunday social obligation.

Leaders of the Protestant churches increasingly tried to find enough common ground to allow for the union of their denominations. This ecumenism spread to meetings between Protestant groups and the Roman Catholic Church, with the goal of reuniting Christians into one big organization. Many mainstream Christians could not distinguish the beliefs of their church from those of other Christian denominations. Regardless of whether the differences that separated them from other denominations were minor, many believers wanted to maintain the separate identity of their churches.

## THE PROTESTANT CHURCHES

The churches faced a great deal of internal soul-searching as they tried to make the Gospels relevant to people's lives in an industrial society. While some people were abandoning organized religion, claiming their church was not addressing social issues, fundamentalist Protestant denominations, with an otherworldly orientation, were gaining memberships. In the 1950s and early 1960s, the mainstream Protestant denominations tried to strike a balance in their views, supporting social programs such as medicare while staking out more conservative ground on other issues, opposing homosexuality, abortion, divorce, and jobs for married women.

Ironically, while they opposed greater social opportunities for women, the Protestant churches offered them opportunities to demonstrate leadership skills in social and charitable activities as well as in missionary roles. The United Church, the largest Protestant church, reported 401 757 members in its Women's Auxiliary and Women's Missionary Society in 1955. In keeping with their notions of distinct gender roles, the churches generally reserved their paid positions and their senior decision-making bodies for men. The Presbyterian Church set up a committee on the role of women in the church in the 1950s and found little support for ordination of women or even election of women elders.

By the 1970s, the mainstream Protestant churches, influenced by the growing women's movement, which had a strong component within the churches, began to change their views on gender roles both within society and within the church. While progress, particularly in the ordination of women, occurred slowly—the Anglican Church agreed to ordain women in 1976—the churches joined with other social groups in calling for state-subsidized quality day care and for greater economic equality between the sexes. Others supported community groups active in combatting child abuse and violence against women.

Church members had their own political and moral views and were usually only comfortable with the church taking public positions when these positions accorded with their own. The ordination of women divided social conservatives from liberals and feminists, but even sharper divisions occurred in the United Church when it decided, through a democratic process, to allow the ordination of homosexuals. Homophobes, who claimed to find evidence in the scriptures that God would not agree with this decision, proved to be immovable in

their resistance to gay clergy.

## THE ROMAN CATHOLIC CHURCH

From the early 1960s, the Catholic Church was undergoing its own struggles and soul-searching, as liberal trends in Rome played themselves out in an institution with an extremely conservative history. Liberal elements preached "the preferential option of the poor" and were likely to support the ordination of women and the relaxing of celibacy requirements. They offended conservatives who stressed the need for the church to concern itself with both the rich and the poor and to respect the God-given hierarchy of the church. Congregations increasingly failed to heed the pronouncements of that hierarchy on moral issues. Despite the church's frequently reaffirmed ban on the use of contraceptives, the birth rate among Catholics failed to rise above the rate for non-Catholics. Quebec, though nominally overwhelmingly Catholic, had the country's lowest birth rate by the 1970s. Pollsters found that most Catholics, like most Canadians generally, supported a woman's right to abortion, despite the official position of their church.

Fewer Catholics were going to church at all. In Montreal, church attendance had been more than halved in just one decade. Despite reforms designed to appeal to the secular generation, the church had difficulty recruiting enough priests and nuns to minister to their congregations. In 1946, there were two thousand new priests in Quebec; in 1970, only a hundred. Sisterhoods, the mainstay of the religious work force, were deserted as jobs opened up for women in the paid labour force and feminist ideology challenged the church's teachings on the role of women. Though Protestant churches gradually opened their ministries to women, the Roman Catholic Church successfully resisted movements from within to end its long-standing practice of maintaining an all-male celibate priesthood.

New challenges to celibacy and to arrogant church hierarchies deemed increasingly out of touch with social concerns were common in the wake of child-abuse scandals that rocked the church in the late eighties and nineties. In Newfoundland, an inquiry heard sad testimony of sexual abuse and violence directed towards boys at the Mount Cashel orphanage, run by the Christian Brothers. It became clear, in the course of the inquiry, that not only the church, but police and civil servants had either ignored or attempted to cover up evidence of the abuse. Many of the faithful were disillusioned by the church's response to Mount Cashel and other similar cases.

## THE RELIGIOUS MAKE-UP OF CANADA

While the percentage of Canadians who identified themselves as Catholics rose 1 percent from 1951 to 1991, Protestant denominations accounted for 15 percent fewer Canadians in 1991 than forty years earlier. Much of the decline was accounted for by the increase in Canadians who followed no religion. Even among those who claimed to be Christians, there were many people who were attracted to New Age religions, spiritual movements with an affinity to Oriental and ancient New World religions.

For traditional Catholics and Protestants, Canada's evolution as a multicultural country began to pose new issues. Was Canada really a "Christian" country? As new Canadians of non-Christian faiths protested that public schools were requiring their children to participate in Christian ceremonies, many school boards agreed to take the religion out of Christmas and to end such practices as prayers and Bible readings in the school. The growing number of atheists and agnostics similarly applied pressures upon schools and other public institutions to end religious observances.

## CONCLUSION

Throughout the post-Confederation period, there has been a shift in Canada from rural living, characterized by relatively self-sufficient primary production, towards an urban, industrial society in which market forces shape relations among individuals. In such a society, there is continuous tension between the marketplace ideology that defines citizens as consumers of products, interested mainly in individual and household accumulation, and human need for identity and contact with a broader community. For some, the extensive organization of community groups in the suburbs has recreated a sense of belonging. Others have sought to find a sense of community with others on the basis of ethnicity, gender, political perspectives, sexual orientation, or religious affiliation. While this has produced a Canadian society that is pluralistic, it is debatable whether it has contributed to a society that is tolerant or one in which most citizens feel a real sense of belonging to a large national entity.

**Table 15.2**

| RELIGIOUS AFFILIATIONS OF CANADIANS (IN PERCENTAGES) | | | |
|---|---|---|---|
| **Religious organization** | **1911** | **1951** | **1991** |
| Roman Catholic | 39.4 | 44.7 | 45.7 |
| United Church | — | 20.5 | 11.5 |
| Anglican | 14.5 | 14.7 | 8.1 |
| Presbyterian | 15.6 | 5.6 | 2.4 |
| Lutheran | 3.2 | 3.2 | 2.4 |
| Baptist | 5.3 | 3.2 | 2.5 |
| Pentecostal | — | 0.7 | 1.4 |
| Other Protestant* | 17.3 | 2.5 | 7.9 |
| Eastern Orthodox | 1.2 | 1.2 | 1.5 |
| Jewish | 1.0 | 1.5 | 1.2 |
| No religion | 0.4 | 0.4 | 12.4 |
| Other | 2.0 | 1.4 | 2.8** |

* Includes Methodists and Congregationalists for 1911; Adventists, Churches of Christ, Disciples, and Salvation Army for 1951 and 1991, along with smaller groups.
**Includes Muslims, 1 percent; Hindus, 0.6 percent; and Buddhists, 0.7 percent.

*Source*: Canada Year Book, *1994, 123*

# CONSUMERISM AND LOSS OF COMMUNITY

The transformation of everyday life in the twentieth century has been the subject of studies by scholars in several disciplines. Many questions have been raised: Did increased prosperity bring greater freedom of choice or simply more sophisticated manipulation of average people? Did suburbanization destroy an earlier sense of community or recreate it in a richer environment? Did the triumph of corporate capitalism result in the creation of a value system that encouraged status seeking, or was social and family life insulated from the values that dominated marketplace relations?

These are broad questions that go beyond the history of a single nation. Yet, as historian Paul-André Linteau suggests, in a study of Canadian suburbanization, historians have avoided making broad generalizations, concentrating instead on the "specificity" of individual cases.[11] Suburbanization in Canada, notes Linteau, has not been accompanied by the same degree of destruction of inner-city life as in the United States; nor has racism been as powerful a motive impelling white folk away from the urban core.

Nonetheless, Linteau accepts that, on many dimensions, the notion of the "North American city" is applicable to Canada because the patterns of urban and suburban development have been similar in both countries. Political economist Harold Chorney goes further, claiming that in the modern period, there has been a decline in community in cities throughout North America and Europe. Everywhere, lured by a social ethic that emphasizes isolation and privacy in the design of neighbourhoods, transportation systems, and shopping areas, people have become less conscious of belonging to a definable geographical community.[12] Throughout this century, argues Chorney, conservative social planners have emphasized the need to reduce

workers' collective solidarity in order to maintain social peace in the interests of the elites.

American historian Stuart Ewen, among others, has traced the growing privatization of life, and the focus on consumer satisfaction, to sophisticated attempts by industry to create markets for a range of products. His history of American advertising demonstrates the extent to which, in an age of mass communication, social values can be shaped by sophisticated manipulators of human emotions.[13]

Feminist historian Dolores Hayden reminds us that alternative visions of community have contended with the developers' creation of the suburb, which generated privacy. In the United States, in particular, "proposals for community kitchens, laundries, dining halls, kitchenless houses and feminist cities"[14] enjoyed considerable support, especially among women, early in the century. For Hayden, the modern suburb as it evolved worked especially against the interests of women, stranding them in their houses as consumers of the goods that the media told them they must accumulate in order to be good mothers and the envy of their anonymous neighbours.

The opposing argument to this "community-centred" literature suggests that the new consumer products of this century have lightened women's burden and, with the automobile, given them a mobility that earlier generations of women could never have imagined. The suburban housewife's participation in volunteer activities in a myriad of community groups is used as evidence against the notion that women who lived in the suburbs became atomized and unable to participate in the world beyond the front doors of their homes.[15] Above all, opponents of the pessimistic view of increased commodification of culture have insisted that the alternatives to a capitalism keyed to creating insatiable consumer demands were untenable. The older communities of the inner cities, where the street provided endless human contact and encouraged empathy and cooperation, were also cesspools of overcrowding and disease. The communist alternative represented by the Soviet Union, in which most citizens lived in apartment buildings and had to share many facilities, was marked by individual powerlessness and minimal satisfaction of consumer demands. But if Chorney, Ewen, and Hayden are correct, there were once other alternatives to all of these models, and their defeat owed as much to the organized opposition of the powers-that-be as to their unpopularity with the masses.

## NOTES

[1] National Archives of Canada, Mackenzie King papers, vol. 421, June 1947, pp. 382096–99

[2] Myrna Kostash, "Dissing Feminist Sexuality," *Canadian Forum*, Sept. 1996, 16

[3] Cited in Alvin Finkel, *The Social Credit Phenomenon in Alberta* (Toronto: University of Toronto Press, 1989), 124

[4] Kenneth McRoberts and Dale Posgate, *Quebec: Social Change and Political Crisis*, 2nd ed. (Toronto: McClelland and Stewart, 1980), 53

[5] Cited in Harold Chorney, *City of Dreams: Social Theory and the Urban Experience* (Scarborough: Nelson, 1990), 202

[6] Veronica Strong-Boag, "'Their Side of the Story': Women's Voices from Ontario Suburbs, 1945–1960" in *A Diversity of Women, 1945–1980*, ed. Joy Parr (Toronto: University of Toronto Press, 1995), 53

[7] Denise Chong, *The Concubine's Children: Portrait of a Family Divided* (Toronto: Viking, 1994), 228

[8] Dan Smith, *The Seventh Fire: The Struggle for Aboriginal Government* (Toronto: Key Porter, 1993), 57

[9] National Archives of Canada, Grace McInnis papers, vol. 4, File "Citizen Participation, 1970"

[10] Tony Clarke, *Behind the Mitre: The Moral Leadership Crisis in the Canadian Catholic Church* (Toronto: HarperCollins, 1995)

[11] Paul-André Linteau, "Canadian Suburbanization in a North American Context: Does the Border Make a Difference?" in *Cities and Urbanization: Canadian Historical Perspectives*, ed. Gilbert Stelter (Toronto: Copp Clark Pitman, 1990), 221. Studies that argue this case further are Michael A. Goldberg and John Mercer, *The Myth of the North American City: Continentalism Challenged* (Vancouver: UBC Press, 1986), and Caroline Andrew and Beth Moore Milroy, eds., *Life Spaces: Gender, Household, Employment* (Vancouver: UBC Press, 1988).

[12] Chorney, *City of Dreams*

[13] Stuart Ewen, *Captains of Consciousness: Advertising and the Social Roots of the Consumer Culture* (New York: McGraw-Hill, 1976)

[14] Delores Hayden, *The Grand Domestic Revolution: A History of Feminist Designs for American Homes, Neighborhoods, and Cities* (Cambridge, MA: MIT Press, 1981), 302

[15] A relatively positive assessment of Canadian suburbia is S.D. Clark, *The Suburban Society* (Toronto: University of Toronto Press, 1968). A nuanced attempt to demonstrate contradictory trends within suburbia is Veronica Strong-Boag, "Home Dreams: Women and the Suburban Experiment in Canada, 1945–60," *Canadian Historical Review* 72, 4 (1991).

## SELECTED READING

On baby boomers, see Douglas Owram, *Born at the Right Time: A History of the Baby Boom in Canada* (Toronto:

University of Toronto Press, 1996). On postwar education, see Paul Axelrod, *Scholars and Dollars: Politics, Economics, and Universities of Ontario, 1945–1980* (Toronto: University of Toronto Press, 1982), and Henry Milner, *The Long Road to Reform: Restructuring Public Education in Quebec* (Montreal: McGill-Queen's University Press, 1986).

Canadian suburbanization is addressed in Stanley R. Barrett, *Paradise: Class, Commuters, and Ethnicity in Rural Ontario* (Toronto: University of Toronto Press, 1994); Paul-André Linteau, "Canadian Suburbanization in a North American Context: Does the Border Make a Difference?" in *Cities and Urbanization: Canadian Historical Perspectives*, ed. Gilbert A. Stelter (Toronto: Copp Clark Pitman, 1990), 208–24, and Veronica Strong-Boag, "Home Dreams: Women and the Suburban Experiment in Canada, 1945–60," *Canadian Historical Review* 72, 4 (Dec. 1991): 471–504.

Immigration policies are analyzed in Donald H. Avery, *Reluctant Host: Canada's Response to Immigrant Workers, 1896–1994* (Toronto: McClelland and Stewart, 1995); Reginald Whitaker, *Double Standard: The Secret History of Canadian Immigration* (Toronto: Lester and Orpen Dennys, 1987); and Freda Hawkins, *Canada and Immigration: Public Policy and Public Concern* (Toronto: Institute of Public Adminstration of Canada, 1972). Among excellent works on immigrant and ethnic experiences are: Franca Iacovetta, *Such Hardworking People: Italian Immigrants in Postwar Toronto* (Montreal: McGill-Queen's University Press, 1992); Frances Swyripa, *Wedded to the Cause: Ukrainian Canadian Women and Ethnic Identity, 1891–1991* (Toronto: University of Toronto Press, 1993); Jean Burnet, ed., *Looking into My Sister's Eyes: An Exploration in Women's History* (Toronto: Multicultural History Society of Ontario, 1986); Bridglal Pachai, *Beneath the Clouds of the Promised Land: The Survival of Nova Scotia Blacks, vol. 2, 1800–1989* (Halifax: Black Education Association, 1990); and E. Wickberg, ed., *From China to Canada: A History of the Chinese Communities in Canada* (Toronto: McClelland and Stewart, 1982).

The lives of Canada's Native peoples are explored in Arthur J. Ray, *I Have Lived Here Since the World Began: An Illustrated History of Canada's Native People* (Toronto: Lester/Key Porter, 1996); J.R. Miller, *Skyscrapers Hide the Heavens: A History of Indian–White Relations in Canada*, rev. ed. (Toronto: University of Toronto Press, 1991); Pauline Comeau and Aldo Santin, *The First Canadians: A Profile of Native People Today* (Toronto: Lorimer, 1990); Geoffrey York, *The Dispossessed: Life and Death in Native Canada* (Boston: Little Brown, 1992); Kenneth Coates, *Canada's Colonies: A History of the Yukon and Northwest Territories* (Toronto: Lorimer, 1985); Boyce Richardson, *Strangers Devour the Land*, 2nd ed. (Vancouver: Douglas and McIntyre, 1991); Sally Weaver, *Making Canadian Indian Policy:The Hidden Agenda, 1968–1970* (Toronto: University of Toronto Press, 1980); J.R. Miller, *Shingwauk's Vision: A History of Native Residential Schools*, (Toronto: University of Toronto Press, 1996); and Celia Haig-Brown, *Resistance and Renewal: Surviving the Indian Residential School* (Vancouver: Arsenal Pulp Press, 1988).

On the women's movement in Canada, see the comprehensive women's histories of Canada and Quebec, by Alison Prentice et al. and the Clio Collective; Constance Backhouse and David Flaherty, eds., *Challenging Times: The Women's Movement in Canada and the United States* (Montreal: McGill-Queen's University Press, 1992); and Jeri Dawn Wine and Janice L. Ristock, eds., *Women and Social Change: Feminist Activism in Canada* (Toronto: Lorimer, 1991). On African-Canadian women, see Peggy Bristow, Dionne Brand, Linda Carty, Afua P. Cooper, Sylvia Hamilton, and Adrienne Shadd, *"We're Rooted Here and They Can't Pull Us Up": Essays in African Canadian Women's History* (Toronto: University of Toronto Press, 1994). On the changing position of women in Canada, important works include Angus McLaren and Arlene Tigar McLaren, *The Bedroom and the State: The Changing Practices and Politics of Contraception and Abortion in Canada* (Toronto: McClelland and Stewart, 1986), and Pat Armstrong and Hugh Armstrong, *The Double Ghetto: Canadian Women and Their Segregated Work*, 3rd ed. (Toronto: McClelland and Stewart, 1994).

On the environmental movement, see Mary Richardson, Joan Sherman, and Michael Gismondi, *Winning Back the Words: Confronting Experts in an Environmental Public Hearing* (Toronto: Garamond, 1993); George N. Hood, *Against the Flow: Rafferty-Almeda and the Politics of the Environment* (Saskatoon: Fifth House, 1994); and John Dyson with Joseph Fitchett, *Sink the Rainbow! An Enquiry into the "Greenpeace Affair"* (London: Victor Gollancz, 1986).

On gay liberation and AIDS organizing, see Gary Kinsman, *The Regulation of Desire: Homo and Hetero Sexualities* (Montreal: Black Rose, 1996), and David M. Rayside and Evert A. Lindquist, "AIDS Activism and the State in Canada," *Studies in Political Economy* 39 (Autumn 1992): 37–76. The state campaign against homosexuals is discussed in Daniel J. Robinson and David Kemmel, "The Queer Career of Homosexual Security Vetting in Cold War Canada," *Canadian Historical Review* 75, 3 (Sept. 1994): 319–45, and Gary Kinsman, "'Character Weaknesses' and 'Fruit Machines': Towards an Analysis of the Anti-Homosexual Security Campaign in the Canadian Civil Service," *Labour/Le Travail* 35 (Spring 1995): 133–61.

Religion in postwar Canada is discussed in Tony Clarke, *Behind the Mitre: The Moral Leadership Crisis in the Canadian Catholic Church* (Toronto: HarperCollins, 1995); Gregory Baum, *Compassion and Solidarity* (Toronto: CBC Enterprises, 1987); John Webster Grant, *The Church in the Canadian Era* (Toronto: Welch Publishing, 1988); Pierre Berton, *The Comfortable Pew: A Critical Look at Christianity and the Religious Establishment in the New Age* (Toronto: McClelland and Stewart, 1965); and Reginald Bibby, *Fragmented Gods: The Poverty and Potential of Religion in Canada* (Toronto: Irwin,1987).

# 16

## CREATING A CANADIAN CULTURE, 1945–1997

IN 1962, THE GOVERNOR GENERAL'S AWARD for Canadian literature was given to Jacques Ferron, a physician, committed socialist, and *indépendantiste*, for his *Tales from the Uncertain Country*. Ferron had practised medicine first in a fishing village in the Gaspé and then in a working-class suburb of Montreal. In 1963, he founded the Rhinoceros Party, which ran candidates who committed themselves to such planks as holding the country together with Crazy Glue and eliminating class privileges in Quebec City by flattening the Upper Town. All of the party's candidates in the 1968 federal election took the name of Lucien Rivard, a convicted drug dealer whose escape from prison in 1965 was alleged to have been abetted by bribery of federal Justice Department officials.

Like the Rhinoceros Party, the stories in *Tales from the Uncertain Country* used humour to raise serious issues. In "Back to Kentucky," for example, a Kentucky druggist serving in the American armed forces in Belgium during the Second World War marries a French-speaking Belgian woman though neither can speak the other's language. The two search for a place to live where they can each speak their own language and feel at home. "We nearly opted for Lowell in New England. Human geography evolves fast in America. Our books were already out of date: Lowell, too late. We arrived in

time in Montreal."[1] Yet in Montreal, too, they discover that the French language is threatened in the anglophone sea of North America. Unlike his linguistically challenged couple, most of Ferron's characters are francophone Québécois who are uncertain of their identity as they confront both the clerical oppression that dominated their rural past and the sterile anglophone North American culture that beckons them as the sole alternative to their former values. The tales show people trying to establish their own identity rather than allowing others to tell them how they should think and act.

While the Québécois attempt to define a new identity for themselves, in the post-Duplessis period, was compelling, Anglo-Canadians and ethnic minorities, including Canada's First Peoples, were increasingly critical of mass North American culture and of traditional conservative values. Much of Canadian literature, theatre, film, art, and music reflected efforts to establish collective identities of various groups within Canada. Some argue that this differentiated Canada's cultural production from that of the Americans, whose heroes and heroines were involved mainly in establishing their personal identities and drawing the boundaries between themselves and the larger society. This chapter describes some of the cultural production of the postwar period as well as the popular entertainments that became an important form of recreation for Canadians.

## QUEBEC'S CULTURAL REVOLUTION

Quebec's artists had begun to challenge the status quo well before the Quiet Revolution. Although the Duplessis years would later be characterized as *la grande noirceur*, or the Dark Age, they nonetheless witnessed important cultural developments. In 1948, painter Paul-Émile Borduas published *Refus global*, a rejection of the narrow world of orthodoxy

within which artists and writers were expected to work in Quebec. The manifesto resulted in his exile from the province but inspired the Hexagone Group of poets, active from 1953 to 1963, who refused to recognize the traditional boundaries of literary expression. It also became the guiding spirit of the *automatistes*, artists who believed that the painter's spirit rather than objects or the imitation of forms should shape the production of art.

Quebec's novelists of the immediate postwar years abandoned the prewar focus on rural Quebec in favour of an urban setting, reflecting the lives of most Québécois. Gabrielle Roy's *Alexandre Chevenant (The Cashier)* (1954), uses a portrayal of an unhappy Montreal cashier to depict the economic and cultural alienation of urban society. Roger Lemelin, creator of *Les Plouffes (The Plouffe Family)* (1948), dealt frankly with issues of social class in several works. Novelists such as Germaine Guèvremont in *Le Survenant (The Outlander)* (1945) attempted to demystify the rural milieu and demonstrate the ignorant claustrophobia in which many rural dwellers lived. Guèvremont and Roy as well as Yves Thériault were pioneers in including non-francophones in their novels. Roy, who grew up in St Boniface, Manitoba, wrote novels, short stories, and non-fiction articles about her childhood and her years as a teacher in the West. Her realistic works are in sharp contrast to *La Belle Bête (Mad Shadows)*, published in 1959 by a young Marie-Claire Blais. Blais blazed a trail for other Quebec novelists with her surreal novel in which both chronology and the boundary between the real and the imagined are deliberately left vague.

*Paul-Émile Borduas,* **Les carquois fleuris**, *1947. Borduas had a great influence on postwar Quebec painting. He studied at the École des Beaux-Arts in Montreal and later painted on his own in Paris. Borduas opposed all formalism in art, arguing that each painter must experiment by letting individual feeling determine both the subject and style of work.*

The Montreal Museum of Fine Arts

## URBAN POOR IN QUEBEC LITERATURE

In the 1940s, French-Canadian writers began to examine the lives of the urban poor. One of the most celebrated novels of this kind was **Bonheur d'occasion (The Tin Flute)** by Gabrielle Roy (1945). In the novel, Rose-Anna Lacasse heroically encourages her many offspring to be hopeful, despite the despair in Depression-era Saint Henri, the railway-factory slum district of Montreal where they live. Florentine, the eldest, whose work at a five-and-dime store's restaurant is the source of most of the family's income, is cold and cynical, desperately searching for any means to escape the poverty that confronts her. Her chosen vehicle, Jean Lévesque, a machinist, is equally determined to escape poverty, and he shuns the pregnant Florentine because she is a stumbling block to his aspirations. Rose-Anna nobly struggles on, but her life is one of misery, as this excerpt suggests:

> They were all old enough to go to school except little Gisèle, but Rose-Anna had been keeping them at home for several weeks, Lucille because she had no overshoes and Albert because he had a bad cold. As for little Daniel, he had been wasting away for two months now, without any outward signs of serious illness. Philippe, who had reached the age of fifteen, obstinately refused to go back to school. ...
>
> During all her married life two events were always associated with the spring: she was almost always pregnant, and in that condition she was obliged to look for a new place to live. Every spring they moved.... [T]hey reached the point where they never moved of their own volition, but because they were behind in their rent and must find something less expensive. From year to year, they looked for cheaper and cheaper lodgings, while rents went up and habitable lodgings became more and more scarce. [2]

## CULTURE AND SOVEREIGNTY

The society-wide questioning of existing structures and social values unleashed by the Quiet Revolution resulted in a flowering of Quebec culture, and the climate of nationalist pride created a strong home market for artistic expressions of every kind. Political commitment, particularly support for sovereignty, marked much of the celebrated literature of the sixties in Quebec. Hubert Aquin's stream-of-consciousness account of an imprisoned sovereignist member of a group much like the FLQ, *Prochain Épisode* (1965), won widespread acclaim. Its general theme is that, as long as Quebec remained within Confederation, it would be a colonized society in which individual francophones could find no real identity. Such ideas echoed Jacques Godbout's *Le Couteau sur la table* (*Knife on the Table*), published two years earlier. Godbout's principal character is a young francophone whose life is aimless and who becomes the lover of an equally aimless but wealthy anglophone woman; he begins to discover himself and to break from his shallow lover only after he reads of the exploits of the nascent FLQ. While they received much praise for their innovative styles, both novels reflect much of the sexism of the period: they are nationalist versions of coming-to-manhood stories, and the female characters are no more than foils for the heroes. There is a similar sense of colonial oppression of manhood in Quebec depicted in FLQ activist Pierre Vallières's autobiographical account, *Nègres blanc d'Amérique* (*White Niggers of America*) (1969). The book's central premise is that francophones in Quebec are treated as an underclass in the province, much as African Americans are in the United States, and will continue to be oppressed until they achieve sovereignty.

Nationalist literature, while written mainly by men in the 1960s, was not always insensitive to the position of women in Quebec society. In Michel Tremblay's many plays and novels, there was a focus on the ways in which domination by both the English and the church had dampened people's ability to communicate their thoughts to others or to demonstrate social solidarity. Tremblay portrayed francophone women as the main victims of a social disintegration resulting from the long suppression of independent thought in Quebec. Dysfunctional families and neighbourhoods characterize plays such as *Les Belles-Soeurs* (1968), in which relatives and friends of a Montreal woman join her in putting together books of green stamps that allow her to make certain purchases for free. While the characters utter endless statements of conventional morality, they demonstrate little willingness to listen to and empathize with each other's real concerns and, indeed, are all engaged in theft of their hostess's green stamps.

In Tremblay's plays and increasingly throughout Quebec literature in this period, characters spoke the language of the Quebec streets—called joual—rather than Parisian French. The use of joual occasioned much debate in the province. Some intellectuals welcomed the use of the real language of Quebec francophones as an assertion of nationalist pride; others claimed that joual, with its many anglicisms and pronunciations that made much of Quebec French a mystery to European visitors of French ancestry, was the product of colonialism rather than a symbol of potential liberation. Yet the street language included a rich variety of words and phrases specific to Quebec and reflective of the historic oppression of francophones. The common use of "*nous autres*," from the point of view of language purists, involved simply the superfluous use of "others" after the word "we"; for defenders of joual, it was a way in which the common people expressed their sense of solidarity as francophones against those who had kept them down. A term such as "*mange-canayen*" for rip-off artists demonstrated a similar feeling of oppression.

Even plays that eschewed the language of the street and experimental structures tended to raise political issues. Anne Hébert's *Le Temps sauvage* (1967) focused on individuals who were attempting to break with conformity to outdated conventions, the characters thinly disguised symbols of Quebec as a whole. Also in the centennial year, Gratien Gélinas, Quebec's dean of playwrights, and founder of the Théâtre de la Comédie Canadienne, wrote and produced in French and English *Yesterday the Children Were Dancing*. The play featured a confrontation between a Liberal Party activist and lawyer, Pierre Gravel, who is offered the federal justice portfolio, and his son, who is a member of a separatist organization that uses terrorist tactics. Pierre does not approve either of his son's methods or his rejection of Canada.

Nonetheless, Pierre is clearly a Quebec nationalist who believes that the status quo is untenable, and the play serves as a plea that non-Quebeckers listen to Quebec's demands for greater autonomy.

Quebec's popular music reflected the new nationalism as well. In the 1950s, francophone radio stations were largely limited to pop music from France, local attempts to copy the metropolitan sound, and standard North American English fare. Only Félix Leclerc, a Quebec nationalist whose traditional French-Canadian music also won him an audience in France, stood out as a distinctly Québécois talent. By the end of the sixties, the airwaves were dominated by home-grown talents such as Robert Charlebois, Monique Leyrac, and Pauline Julien, whose music represented an amalgam of traditional French-Canadian folk music, rock and roll, and metropolitan French music.

Gilles Vigneault became the major songwriter of the sovereignist movement. His "Mon pays" helped define the yearning of many Québécois for an independent national existence, while his "Gens du pays" became the anthem of the sovereignist movement. In the 1970s, Beau Dommage led a host of new Québécois rock groups whose music was infused not only with the language of the streets, but also with the language of nationalism. Except for a few new artists such as Paul Piché, by the late seventies there was a movement away from political themes and towards love songs. This reflected a general cultural shift in the province: although the majority of francophones under forty were nationalists to some degree, there was a popular reaction against the cultural community's preoccupation with nationalist and other political issues.

The importance of the artistic community to the nationalist cause was demonstrated during the 1980 and 1995 referenda on Quebec sovereignty. In both cases, far more members of the arts community supported the nationalist than the federalist cause. Pro-sovereignty concerts helped to reinforce the support of young francophones for Quebec nationalism. In the 1995 referendum campaign, the Parti québécois government joined poets, including Gilles Vigneault, and constitutional experts to produce the preamble to the declaration of sovereignty that the government claimed would come into effect if the supporters of sovereignty won the vote. The preamble read in part: "Because the heart of this land beats in French and because that heartbeat is as meaningful as the seasons that hold sway over it, as the winds that bend it, as the men and women who shape it ... we, the people of Quebec, declare we are free to choose our future."

## FILMS AND BROADCASTING

State subsidies, both provincial and federal, were crucial to the creation of many of the new cultural groups and products in postwar Quebec. Without state support, many new theatre groups could not have performed, and publishing houses would have been unable to take the risk of publishing many new titles. In no area was state funding more crucial than in film. The National Film Board was the pivotal player in film financing before the late 1970s, when the Parti québécois government established a provincial film board. Quebec francophones wanted to see movies in their own language and about places and events familiar to them, and locally produced movies drew large audiences. An early success was Claude Jutra's *Mon Oncle Antoine* (1971), which also drew good crowds for its English-language version. More controversial was Michel Brault's *Les Ordres* (1974), which won prizes at the prestigious Cannes Film Festival but was denounced by the federal and provincial governments as an inaccurate portrayal of the arrests and detentions during the October Crisis in 1970. Several Quebec films won critical acclaim, including films by Gilles Carle, Francis Mankiewicz, and Denys Arcand. Arcand's *Le Déclin de l'empire américain* (1986) was an international success, but most Quebec movies played to small audiences outside the province. As was the case with music, after the 1970s Quebec films had less overtly political themes. Arcand's first major film, *Rejeanne Padovani* (1973), had been a scathing indictment of government corruption in Quebec and the involvement of the Mafia at the highest levels of the province. *Le Déclin*, by contrast, though it could be viewed on several levels, was a bedroom romp that reflected

an understanding on the director's part that Quebec audiences, like North American audiences generally, wanted escapism when they went to movies.

Arcand's *Jésus de Montréal* won the Jury prize at the Cannes Film Festival in 1989 and the film-maker directed an English-language film in 1993, *Love and Human Remains*, an adaptation of a play by acclaimed homosexual playwright, Edmonton's Brad Fraser. While Arcand and a few others continued to draw large audiences in the 1990s, Quebec film-makers complained that reduced government subsidies and chain ownership of cinemas made it difficult to make French-Canadian films or find an audience for them. Increasingly, film-makers had to be content with having their movies screened on television, where they often found large audiences, rather than in movie houses.

Television in Quebec, as elsewhere in North America, became a more important medium than film, and the Quebec government followed the federal government in establishing a provincial agency in the area. Radio-Canada, the French-language CBC, joined its English-speaking counterpart in the early 1950s in branching out from radio to television. During the Duplessis years, information programs on Radio-Canada became an important source of liberal viewpoints. With its funding coming from the federal government, Radio-Canada was largely impervious to Union nationale bullying. By contrast, Quebec newspapers, fearful of losing provincial government advertising, offered little criticism of the Duplessis regime. Radio-Canada produced a number of celebrities, one of whom was René Lévesque, the future premier, who in the 1950s hosted a popular weekly information show on international events. By the late sixties, Quebec federalists accused Radio-Canada journalists of using the network to broadcast sovereignist propaganda. Both Radio-Canada and Radio-Québec, the Quebec broadcasting service established by the provincial government in 1968, provided Quebec entertainers with important outlets for their creative talents. Quebe*c téléromans* (soaps), including those with historical themes, proved immensely popular.

In the 1980s and 1990s, hundreds of thousands of francophones watched Pierre Gauvreau's *Le Temps d'une paix (Peacetime)*, a dramatization of life in Quebec from 1918 to 1930, and *Cormoran*, which highlighted political and class struggles in Rimouski during the Great Depression. Fernand Dansereau's *Le Parc des Braves* focused on the Second World War while his *Shehawek* was set in the period of Montreal's founding. Among TV series focusing on modern Quebec, several by the feminist author, broadcaster, and former PQ cabinet minister Lise Payette have been particularly successful. Her *Marilyn*, which began a long TV run in 1991, had as its protagonist a charwoman whose experiences put her in contact with people from all walks of life in Quebec.

The massive outpouring of francophone literature, movies, television shows, and recordings demonstrated the extent to which the French language insulated francophones from North American culture, but such insulation could easily be exaggerated. Most of the major American television shows, movies, and best-selling novels were available in French versions. Young people snapped up copies of the latest recordings by the Beatles or Madonna or whoever was currently on the top ten. Nonetheless, while francophones in Quebec were fascinated by North American culture, they were also determined to develop their own cultural artifacts and create a distinct space for themselves within the North American milieu. So, for example, while audiences for classical music preferred the traditional canon, they also supported local composers such as Serge Garant, Gilles Tremblay, and Micheline Coulombe-Saint-Marcoux. Québécois were happy to buy tickets for visiting circuses but were even happier to see their own internationally renowned Cirque du Soleil.

Such an environment also provided a growing audience for locally produced visual art. Quebec art reflected a variety of styles and found outlets not only in traditional commercial markets but in such novel sites as the Montreal subway system. Several women including Rita Letendre, Lise Gervais, and Marcelle Ferron, painted earthy works that demonstrated the changes that Quebec women had undergone since the Quiet Revolution.

## ANGLOPHONES AND ALLOPHONES

Quebec anglophones made significant contributions to Quebec and Canadian culture. In the 1950s, Dorothy Livesay, F.R. Scott, A.M. Klein, and Louis Dudek were key figures in Montreal-centred social realist poetry. Mordecai Richler became the best-known of the Jewish novelists of Montreal, gaining an international reputation with vivid novels based on the Jewish experience in the city, including *The Apprenticeship of Duddy Kravitz* (1959) and *St Urbain's Horseman* (1971). He also ruffled nationalist feathers with his biting humour regarding the "language police" and other products of the nationalist movement in *Oh Canada! Oh Quebec! Requiem for a Divided Country* (1992). Another product of Montreal's Jewish community, Leonard Cohen, achieved national fame as a poet and novelist and then international recognition as a composer of poetic popular-music lyrics. The playwright David Fennario spoke out for the working-class Irish in his plays such as *On the Job* (1975) and *Balconville* (1979). Fennario tried to promote solidarity of social class across the language divide as an alternative to ties based solely on language. His view was that the exploiters in Quebec spoke both languages and so did the exploited.

Non-francophones in Quebec complained that there was far less provincial money available for their cultural endeavours than there was for francophones. They interpreted the PQ's 1978 White Paper on cultural development as hostile to non-francophones and interested only in their assimilation into the dominant francophone culture; the government denied that this was its intention. Nonetheless, the "cultural communities," as the PQ referred to the multicultural mosaic of the non-francophone minority, continued to produce important cultural works.

While non-francophones might complain of their treatment by the provincial Department of Cultural Affairs, they received at least some federal help to promote their cultural endeavours. Just as Radio-Canada became a crucial institution in preserving the identity of francophone minorities outside Quebec, English-language CBC radio and television became a major source of communication and cultural production within the English-speaking communities of Quebec. The National Film Board and Canada Council were also important sources of funds for cultural production by minority groups.

## CULTURAL DEVELOPMENT IN THE "REST OF CANADA"

For obvious reasons, English-speaking Canadians were more susceptible than Québécois to the American media onslaught. There was much debate among intellectuals and artists about what, if anything, differentiated Canadian and American cultural identity. Many anglophone artists, like their francophone counterparts, struggled to define regional and ethnic identities, and the rate of cultural production in many areas of the arts was impressive.

## LITERATURE

In the late 1940s and 1950s, writers from a number of regions—including Thomas Raddall and Ernest Buckler from the Maritimes, Ontario's Morley Callaghan and Hugh Garner, and the West's W.O. Mitchell, Sheila Watson, and Adele Wiseman—were gaining a national audience. Although not prolific, Wiseman created a moving account of the experience of Jewish immigrants to the Prairies in her novel *The Sacrifice* (1956). John Marlyn in *Under the Ribs of Death* (1957) dealt with the experiences of the son of Hungarian immigrants in the north end of Winnipeg and expressed the confusion of many newcomers as they faced an environment that reviled their native cultures but denied them a firm place within the dominant Anglo-Canadian culture. Hugh MacLennan examined Canadians' conflicting social values in *Two Solitudes* (1945), which focused on English–French dualism, and in *The Precipice* (1948), which examined the impact of American culture on small-town values. Despite their didactic tone and Canadian content, MacLennan's books sold very well internationally. A unique novel for this period was *The Swamp Angel* (1954) by Ethel Wilson. Wilson made a

heroine of a woman who leaves her husband and wealthy home for a life of adventure in remote areas. Though the book met a mixed critical reception at the time, Wilson's novel would be embraced by feminists in the 1960s and afterwards.

From the 1960s on, English-Canadian literature seemed to come into its own. Margaret Laurence's novels and short stories, many peopled by the fictional characters of Manawaka, clearly a replica of her hometown of Neepawa, Manitoba, were best-sellers. Her small-town characters, searching for moral values that made more sense than the prudishness and bigotry that surrounded them, had resonance for many Canadians, and many women identified with the struggles of her female characters to defy society's stifling restraints. Not surprisingly, Laurence was influenced by Ethel Wilson, with whom she corresponded frequently. Alberta novelist Aritha van Herk was also influenced by Wilson, and her novel *The Tent Peg* (1981) represented, to some degree, a more contemporary version of *The Swamp Angel*. Alice Munro, whose short stories focused on rural Ontario, became a favourite with many Canadians. Like Laurence, she stripped away the veneer of conventional morality to look at the emotions that women experienced as they tried to find both meaning and passion in their lives. Even more clearly identified both with women's liberation and Canadian nationalism was Margaret Atwood, with her novels *The Edible Woman* (1969) and *Surfacing* (1972).

Timothy Findley's novels and short stories also had political themes, including the horrors of war, the extent of state manipulation of people's lives, and the issue of how and why people are labelled mad. Findley was Canada's leading openly homosexual writer, and some of his short stories also explored homosexual relationships. Less overtly political were the novels of Robertson Davies, which had a more psychological focus. His novels, such as *Fifth Business* (1970), won huge audiences. Mavis Gallant, a Canadian expatriate in France, was internationally respected for her brilliant short stories, dealing sometimes with Canadian themes, but more usually with the lives of expatriates like herself.

Among francophone writers outside of Quebec, the most distinguished was Antonine Maillet. In 1979, she won France's major literary prize, the Prix Goncourt, for *Pélagie-la-Charrette*, a fictional work drawing upon the theme of Acadian expulsion. An earlier work, *La Sagouine*, had gained a wide audience and provided Canadians with a fictional character as enduring as Longfellow's Evangeline.

In the last two decades, these authors have been joined by a variety of important new writers, including Indian expatriate novelist Rohinton Mistry; Sri Lanka-born Michael Ondaatje, a gifted poet and novelist; Trinidad-born Neil Bissoondath; and poet and literary social critic Himani Bannerji. Non-white authors often depicted a world in which visible-minority immigrants were in, but not of, their adopted country. In M.G. Vassanji's *No New Land* (1992), for example, the major protagonist, a Muslim Indian forced to flee from Africa, lives largely within the walls of a community composed of his fellow émigrés. They limit their contacts with the dominant community because it offers them only hostility and exploitation. Nova Scotia's black community produced two fine poets in Maxine Tynes and George Elliott Clarke. Toronto poet Dionne Brand explores the issues of sexism, racism, imperialism, and homophobia.

Native authors were also beginning to be noticed by the broader society. Thomas King's portraits of Native life in novels such as *Medicine River* (1990) and Tomson Highway's plays, including the critically acclaimed *Dry Lips Oughta Move to Kapuskasing* (1989), represented just a few of the Native attempts to bring their stories to Canadians as a whole. The Mi'kmaq found a voice in the poetry of Rita Joe. Non-Native authors also made more attempts to present rounded Native characters in their writings. Particularly notable were playwright George Ryga's *The Ecstasy of Rita Joe* (1970) and novelist Rudy Wiebe's *The Temptations of Big Bear* (1973).

Native autobiographical works also attracted some attention. In her 1973 best-selling autobiography, *Halfbreed*, Maria Campbell describes the dire poverty of her childhood in Northern Saskatchewan. While Métis traditions partly compensated for grim living conditions and racial discrimination, the death of Campbell's mother in 1952 put an end to this source of solace. Only twelve years old at the time, Maria struggled to hold together her family of seven brothers and sisters and her proud but discouraged father. She married at the age of fifteen, but the relationship quickly deteriorated. Campbell drifted across Western Canada, becoming a prostitute and drug addict in Vancouver and later doing low-paid "women's work"—cooking, waitressing, hairstyling. In the late 1960s, she became a militant Native activist in Alberta. The popularity of her account of her struggles as a Native person and a woman indicated a growing willingness of Canadians to listen to voices from the margins of society.

The increase in the production of serious literature in Canada in the postwar period was more than matched by skyrocketing sales for formula romances. In the 1950s, Harlequin was a struggling Winnipeg publisher. Its empire grew as it convinced booksellers of the vast popularity of its escapist plots, mainly among female consumers. By the late 1980s, Harlequin was selling over two hundred million books in over a hundred countries.

While Harlequin was cornering the global market on formula romances, more serious Canadian writing was also having an impact internationally. Margaret Atwood's *Handmaid's Tale* (1985) was shortlisted for Britain's prestigious Booker Prize; she was again shortlisted for *Alias Grace* in 1996. Michael Ondaatje became the first Canadian novelist to win the Booker when *The English Patient* shared this award with Barry Unsworth's *Sacred Hunger* in 1992. In 1994, Carol Shields received the Pulitzer Prize in the United States for *The Stone Diaries*. Such awards were a reflection of the growing respect with which Canadian authors were viewed.

The variety and quality of Canada's postwar literature meant that "CanLit," disdained by Canadian universities before the 1970s, became a mainstay of most English departments by the 1980s. At the same time, there was a massive increase in the production of academic works on the history, politics, and sociology of Canada, many of which were assisted by grants from the federally funded Canada Council or Social Sciences and Humanities Research Council.

The Canada Council also assisted Canadian musicians, playwrights, film-makers, painters, and dancers to various degrees. Provincial and sometimes municipal government grants to artists and artistic companies helped to solidify the identity and the tourist trade of certain cities. The town of Stratford, Ontario, demonstrated the potential for theatre in Canada when local business people launched the Stratford Festival in July 1953. Modelling their first theatre in part on Shakespearean designs, the festival's directors provided a blend of Shakespeare and other drama aimed at both the southern Ontario and tourist markets. Stratford was eventually joined by summer festivals in Niagara-on-the-Lake and Blyth, Ontario, Wolfville, Nova Scotia, and Charlottetown. In the 1980s and 1990s, a number of Canadian cities, beginning with Edmonton, established successful "fringe" theatre festivals. In Edmonton and Vancouver, the fringe festival involved the performance of hundreds of plays by local, national, and international troupes, both amateur and professional, at various venues.

## THEATRE AND FILM

Professional theatres opened in most urban centres, initially concentrating, like Stratford, on the classics. Many small-town playhouses closed down, unable to compete with better-financed theatres a short drive away. Canadian playwrights had difficulty convincing theatre directors to consider using their plays before the nationalism of the 1960s produced a sea change in directors' thinking. Radio and television offered playwrights such as John Coulter and Lister Sinclair an audience for their work. By the 1970s, many Canadian playwrights were having their works staged at major theatres, which began to intersperse Canadian fare among the classics and Broadway imports. Producing new Canadian drama became the *raison d'être* of many of the new alternative theatres, like the Touchstone Theatre in Vancouver, the 25th Street Theatre in

Saskatoon, and the Tarragon and Theatre Passe Muraille in Toronto. The Mummers' Troupe and the Mulgrave Road Co-op were the most successful of a number of alternative theatre groups in Atlantic Canada. The Mulgrave troupe, like the Company of Sirens in Ontario, used drama to raise consciousness about child abuse, wife battery, and other little-discussed problems.

English-Canadian films were generally less successful than the country's theatrical productions. In the 1970s, the federal government began to provide tax concessions to financial backers of Canadian films. This resulted in a quantitative leap in the number of films produced in the country, but few of these films were well received by either film critics or at the box office. There were some serious films with Canadian themes, including *Goin' Down the Road*, *The Grey Fox*, *Wedding in*

*Chief Dan George of British Columbia played roles in several Hollywood movies, including* **Little Big Man** *in 1971. In this movie, his character challenged the Hollywood stereotypes that helped to reinforce long-standing racist views of First Nations peoples.*

Media Services, Manitoba Department of Education

*White*, and *I've Heard the Mermaids Singing*. National Film Board documentaries continued to receive acclaim. A feminist film unit within the NFB, Studio D, was particularly successful, producing *If You Love This Planet*, an Academy Award-winning anti-nuclear documentary; *Not a Love Story*, an anti-pornography film; and *Forbidden Love*, an examination of lesbian relationships. While a few feature films such as Cynthia Scott's *The Company of Strangers*, Anne Wheeler's *Bye Bye Blues*, and Atom Egoyan's *Exotica* received distribution in theatres, on the whole cinema in Canada continued to be dominated by American products.

# ART

In art, as in theatre and literature, regional, ethnic, and gender sensibilities struggled to emerge. On the West Coast, Bill Reid was recognized for his revival of traditional Haida carving. Northwest Coast Native art influenced the work of Jack Shadbolt, a Vancouver surrealist painter, and other non-Native artists. On the Prairies, the major landscape artists included Dorothy Knowles, Wynona Mulcaster, and Ernest Lindner. The paintings of Esther Warkow of Winnipeg recalled the pre-Holocaust life of Polish Jews. In a class by himself was William Kurelek, whose work reflected his attempts to deal with a difficult childhood as a Ukrainian Canadian growing up in rural Alberta and Manitoba. His lyrical work depicted Prairie life and dealt with a variety of spiritual themes.

Film-maker and artist Joyce Wieland produced provocative works that reflected her nationalist and feminist values. Several artists from London, Ontario, among whom Greg Curnoe was best-known, created a

regional art celebrating local identity and the Canadian struggle to be free of American control. With the Maritime environment as his context, Alex Colville introduced "magic" to representional art and inspired a generation of artists, including Christopher Pratt, Mary Pratt, and Tom Forrestall.

Native artists continued to produce both ceremonial and decorative art and to carry on a modest commerce with collectors who appreciated their work. In the 1950s, Norval Morrisseau, an Ojibwa from Sand Point Reserve in Ontario, began to create paintings that incorporated the pictography of rock paintings and Ojibwa spiritual themes. This style, labelled Woodland Indian art, won applause in the white professional art community in the early 1960s and influenced the work of such celebrated artists of the 1970s as Daphne Odjig of Ontario and Jackson Beardy of Manitoba. Largely

*Jim Shirley*, **Nigger on Salmon Road.**

due to the promotional energy of Toronto artist James Houston, what is now known as Inuit art was introduced to southern buyers. Beginning in the late 1940s, he encouraged Inuit to produce their prints and ivory and soapstone carvings for market through Inuit co-operatives.

## RECORDING ARTISTS

In 1970, the Canadian Radio-television Commission (CRTC), which had been established as the regulatory agency for broadcasters, introduced regulations requiring radio stations to ensure that no fewer than 30 percent of the records they played were of Canadian origin. Although francophone stations generally exceeded that percentage, most English-Canadian stations other than CBC Radio played little music by Canadian artists. The regulation helped many Canadian musicians to establish themselves. Some artists, including Joni Mitchell, Neil Young, Bryan Adams, the Guess Who, and Anne Murray, crossed over to the American market and produced music that was largely indistinguishable from its American counterpart. In mid-1996, three female Canadian artists simultaneously had CDs in the top ten in *Billboard* magazine, the authoritative American counter of record sales. Alanis Morrisette, Shania Twain, and Céline Dion, between them, boasted sales of over forty million copies. All three artists, thanks to the CRTC, had established their credentials in Canada before coming to the attention of a mass audience in the United States.

For all the draw of foreign markets, artists such as Bruce Cockburn, Leonard Cohen, Rita MacNeil, and Gordon Lightfoot remained identifiably Canadian even when their records sold internationally. Among rock groups, the Tragically Hip and the Barenaked Ladies stood out as mavericks uninterested in finding a sound that would open American markets that matched their Canadian following. Finding a niche was not always easy for Canadian singers. Alberta's talented k.d. lang, a Canadian nationalist who nonetheless represented herself as the reincarnation of American country music legend Patsy Cline, made a brief splash in Nashville. Her open lesbianism and vegetarianism alienated the conservative establishment of country music: some radio stations in cattle country in her own province boycotted her recordings to protest

an advertisement she had made for an animal rights group in which she proclaimed "meat stinks." By the mid-1990s, lang turned to mainstream popular music, with considerable success.

The Canadian-content rule encouraged more diversity in the types of music aired by radio stations and broadcast on the video channels that appeared in the 1980s. Political tunes such as Bruce Cockburn's "Rocket Launcher" and Parachute Club's "Rise Up," which may not have been played in Canada in the period before the "Can con" rule, proved to be big sellers. Even in country music, it meant that a song such as Michelle Wright's "He Would Be Sixteen," which many American stations refused to play because it dealt with an unwed mother's memories of being forced to give up her child for adoption, became a number one hit.

Regional musicians also attracted important audiences at home and often nationally. Atlantic artists, including the Barra MacNeils, Figgy Duff, John Allan Cameron, and the Rankin Family, performed folk music with Celtic roots. Edith Butler's compositions, inspired by folk traditions became popular hits in Canada and France, while Prince Edward Island's Angèle Arsenault, after becoming known for both her folk songs with historical messages and her pop tunes, won acclaim for her revival of the songs of La Bolduc, Quebec's popular diva. Stompin' Tom Connors, who grew up in Skinners Pond, Prince Edward Island, appealed to both folk and country audiences with his working-class perspective on Canadian themes. His trademark was a pounding foot, inspired by the need to be heard above the noisy crowd. In Western Canada, artists such as Connie Kaldor, Jim Keelaghan, Spirit of the West, and Tom Russell drew on regional themes and often spoke to the lives of the disadvantaged.

In the 1990s, some Native artists gained recognition. Kashtin, two Innu performers from northern Quebec who sang in their Native language, produced a hybrid of Native music and rock and roll, and played to large audiences of both francophones and anglophones in the south. Susan Aglukark, although singing mainly in English, paid tribute to her Inuit heritage and dealt with social problems of the North. The biggest success commercially was country singer Shania Twain, who, while proud of her northern Ontario Ojibwa heritage, was intent on doing mainstream country music. Her 1995 release, *The Woman in Me*, sold over ten million copies in Canada and the United States, making it the biggest album ever by a female country artist.

While Native people wished Twain well, most Native performers were not seeking breakthroughs in Nashville. Native dance troupes performing traditional dances in ceremonial costumes performed before their own people and increasingly before white audiences as well, attempting to reproduce the dances as they had been performed by their ancestors rather than refashioning them for commercial broadcasters. There was a growing audience for dance in Canada in the postwar period generally. Canadian dance companies such as Les Grands Ballets Canadiens and the Danny Grossman Dance Company came into their own, and dancers such as Karen Kain and Frank Augustyn of the National Ballet and Evelyn Hart of the Royal Winnipeg Ballet won prestigious international competitions.

*Frank Augustyn and Karen Kain dance in the National Ballet's production of "The Sleeping Beauty."*
Andrew Oxenburg/National Ballet Archives

## HERITAGE CONSERVATION

Heritage conservation became an important means by which national, regional, and ethnic identities could be preserved. Outside of the work of the Historic Sites and Monuments Board, founded in 1919, and the National Museum, little attention had been paid before 1960 to preserving historic buildings and artifacts. An explosion of conservation and historical reconstruction activities accompanied the centennial celebrations in 1967 and continued thereafter. Such activities involved all levels of government and were carried out for a variety of reasons. Sometimes the key goal was job creation, as in the federally sponsored reconstruction of Louisbourg as a tourist attraction in Cape Breton in the early 1960s. Provincial projects such as the Acadian Historic Village in Caraquet, New Brunswick, and the Ukrainian Village outside

Edmonton represented a recognition by government of the voting power of ethnic groups. At other times projects involved attempts to invigorate decaying areas of cities, as in the conversion of dilapidated buildings on the Halifax waterfront and in Winnipeg's warehouse district into fancy shops. The Main Street program in Ontario in the late 1980s allowed smaller cities and towns to restore their downtowns to something like their former glory. In some cases, such as the remains of a Viking settlement at l'Anse aux Meadows in Newfoundland and the well preserved buildings in old Quebec City, historic sites received international recognition.

Heritage protection groups achieved many victories. In Saskatchewan, their pressure led the NDP government to proclaim a Heritage Property Act in 1980, giving both the province and the municipalities the right to designate certain sites as historical properties that could neither be torn down nor altered. Within three years, there were over two hundred municipal designations, and various old churches, schools, residences, railway stations, and town halls were saved from the wrecker's ball. The government also instituted grants for restoring and maintaining historic properties. Similar programs were soon in place throughout the country. Interest in conservation developed unevenly. While Quebec City and Victoria sought to make their core areas historical showcases, Vancouver, Calgary, Edmonton, Winnipeg, and Toronto all proved latecomers to conservation. Their city councils were more concerned with development than preservation, which they often associated with stagnation and fossilization. Yet even fossils could attract tourists, as the citizens of Drumheller learned when Alberta constructed a dinosaur museum in town. Museums, like historic sites, mushroomed after 1960, most focusing on the history of Canada or its regions.

Preservation of historic sites, as many commentators pointed out, was not quite the same thing as preservation of history. The history of preserved places and buildings was often presented in a romantic and simplified way to tourists. The thousands of visitors who parked their vehicles for a day at pretty-as-a-picture Peggy's Cove, near Halifax, learned little of the difficult lives of the fishermen and their various battles with fish buyers or banks. For all its meticulous detail in reproducing the exteriors and interiors of buildings, the Ukrainian Village outside Edmonton gave little hint of the political divisions that were important to pioneer life for the early generations of Ukrainian immigrants to Western Canada.

## PROFESSIONAL SPORTS

Postwar prosperity resulted in a larger potential audience of paying customers for professional sporting events. Hockey remained the national passion, and fans were often quite demonstrative in their feelings for their teams. In March 1955, after the legendary Maurice "Rocket" Richard of the Montreal Canadiens was suspended for the balance of the season as a penalty for brawling, fans at the Forum pelted National Hockey League president Clarence Campbell with food and then took to the streets, breaking windows and looting stores in

what many saw as a demonstration of Quebec nationalism.

In 1967, the size of the NHL doubled, but all the new teams were American. The Vancouver Canucks joined the league in 1970, and four Canadian teams, representing the cities of Ottawa, Winnipeg, Edmonton, and Quebec City, were included in the World Hockey Association, a rival to the NHL, founded in 1972. When the WHA faced bankruptcy in 1979, all of the WHA teams but Ottawa joined the NHL, and the transfer of the NHL's Atlanta franchise to Calgary increased the number of teams in Canada to seven. The Edmonton Oilers won five Stanley Cups from 1984 to 1990, and Oiler Wayne Gretzky became almost synonymous with the game. To the chagrin of most Edmontonians, Gretzky was sold to the Los Angeles Kings in 1988 by Peter Pocklington, the Oiler owner, for $18 million. It was a reminder that hockey, like most professional sports, had become big business and that a franchise belonged to an individual owner rather than to a particular city. By the mid-nineties, the cost of signing star players had forced both Quebec City and Winnipeg to concede that they could not draw the home audiences needed to sustain a professional hockey team, and their teams headed south of the border.

Football had also become big business with major signings yielding annual contracts in the millions of dollars. Earlier generations of players had made modest salaries and were wise to plan a second career for the days when most would no longer play professional football. In 1956, the Western Interprovincial Football Union and the Interprovincial Rugby Football Union had joined forces to form the Canadian Football Council, later renamed the Canadian Football League. All of the teams in the league were Canadian. By the 1990s, with the economy stagnant, fans became more hesitant to pay high ticket prices necessitated by the lucrative players' contracts and the desire of the owners to maintain their former profit levels. Though the ownership of Ontario teams was private, the Western teams were owned and operated by non-profit community organizations. An attempt to increase interest in the CFL by expansion of franchises to the United Sates in the mid-nineties flopped. American football fans proved uninterested in the Canadian version of the game. By 1996, the CFL was once again made up of only Canadian teams.

Professional baseball in Canada was represented by American major league teams in the two largest cities. The Montreal Expos had difficulties filling the stadium; baseball was never as popular as hockey among the city's francophones. The Toronto Blue Jays attracted large crowds in their home town, even though no member of the team was a Torontonian or even a Canadian. After spending almost $50 million on player salaries, the Blue Jays won the World Series in 1992 just as Canadians prepared to vote in a divisive referendum on constitutional change. Despite the resentment that most non-Torontonians hold towards that city, it was clear from the outpouring of joy across the country at the Blue Jays' wins (they won another World Series in 1993) that Canadians could be more easily united by sport than by politics.

Similar jubilation had greeted Canada's victory in the first Soviet–Canadian hockey series in 1972. Canadian coaches, players, promoters, and fans had long insisted that Canadians were the best hockey players in the world and that their unimpressive showings at the Olympics and other international amateur competitions were due to strict definitions of amateurism that excluded players in the National Hockey League. National pride was on the line when a series was arranged between the Soviets and the best Canadian players in the NHL. Paul Henderson's famous series-ending goal has come to be seen as one of the classic moments in Canadian sports history.

While professional sports teams were almost exclusively male, both female and male Canadian athletes won international honours in individualized sports. Two women received particular media attention in the early postwar period. Barbara Ann Scott won the 1948 Olympic figure-skating title and then skated professionally in ice shows. Marilyn Bell was hailed for her swimming achievements beginning in 1954 with her fifty-two-kilometre swim across Lake Ontario when she was only sixteen years old. She later went on to become the youngest swimmer to cross the English Channel and the Strait of Juan de Fuca.

Canada produced an impressive range of amateur athletes. Canadian figure skaters built on the tradition of Barbara Ann Scott and produced a long list of world champions and Olympic medallists including Donald Jackson, Barbara Wagner and Robert Paul, Karen Magnussen, Toller Cranston, Barbara Underhill and Paul Martini, Elizabeth Manley, Brian Orser, Kurt Browning, and Elvis Stojko. Speed skater Gaetan Boucher captured three medals at the 1984 Olympics. Swimmers Elaine Tanner, Victor Davis, Alex Baumann, Mark Tewkesbury, and Marianne Limpert brought Commonwealth, Pan-American, world, and Olympic medals to Canada, as did Carolyn Waldo and Sylvie Frechette in synchronized swimming. Skiers Anne Heggtveit, Nancy Greene, Ken Read, and Steve Podborski turned in winning runs on the slopes while sprinter Harry Jerome, rowers Silken Laumann, Marnie McBean, and Kathleen Heddle, gymnast Curtis Hibbert, and diver Annie Pelletier dazzled spectators at international competitions. Sprinter Donovan Bailey captured two gold medals at the 1996 Olympics, one in the hundred metres and the second as anchor for the men's relay team. High jumpers Debbie Brill and Greg Joy and pentathlon champion Diane Jones Konihowski were among notable Olympic and Commonwealth games winners in track and field events other than running.

## SPORTS AND SOCIETY

For many Canadians, the country's most inspiring athlete had never attempted to win any competition. In April 1980, Terry Fox, a twenty-one-year-old Vancouver student, who had lost a leg to bone cancer, began a run across Canada to raise funds for cancer research. After five months of running almost forty kilometres per day on his "Marathon of Hope," Fox was forced to give up his run at Thunder Bay when doctors found that the cancer had spread to his lungs. He died in June 1981, but the Terry Fox Run, an annual fund-raising event for cancer research, became one of the major participatory sports events in Canada. British Columbia wheelchair athlete Rick Hansen, inspired in part by Fox's achievement, dramatized the oft-ignored capabilities of people with disabilities by circling the globe in his wheelchair.

For Terry Fox, running was a means to a noble end but running was also big business. As in many other sports, the desire to win often lead athletes and coaches to cheat. A steroids scandal rocked Canada after sprinter Ben Johnson was stripped of a gold medal at the Seoul Olympics in 1988. In the media circus and official enquiry that followed, Canadians learned that many athletes used performance-enhancing steroids, ignoring ethical issues and endangering their personal health in order to win. Questions of amateurism that had plagued earlier international competition seemed rather quaint as sports took on a big-business atmosphere where millions of dollars in endorsements could await Olympic gold medallists. Canada's reputation in running rebounded with Donovan Bailey's convincing 100-metre win in the 1996 Olympics.

While many young Canadians dreamed of becoming sports celebrities, studies suggested their chances were best if they were Anglo-Canadian males with professional or white-collar parents. The costs involved in training athletes who could compete in national and international events excluded most working-class children. Girls faced particular challenges as sexual segregation continued to make sports a largely male preserve. Attempts by girls and women to share the same opportunities as boys were mightily resisted. In 1985, the Ontario Hockey Association barred thirteen-year-old Justine Blainey from participating on a leading boys' hockey team. Several courtrooms and thousands of dollars later, Justine got her wish in 1987, but the OHA continued to grumble that the bodychecking and slapshots of the boys' league made the inclusion of girls inappropriate. Such stereotypes prevented most girls with athletic talent from following Justine Blainey's example. A breakthrough of sorts occurred in the early 1990s when Quebec's Manon Rhéaume became the first woman in North America to play professional hockey, first with the Tampa Bay Lightning and later their minor league affiliate in Atlanta.

For many, civic identity was bound up with local sports teams. In big cities, the presence of a professional franchise was a source of pride, even if no one on the hockey, football, or baseball team was a local resident. In smaller towns, where teams were composed of local people who played in amateur leagues, sport meant more than vicarious satisfaction from the performances of highly paid professionals. The death of four young members of the Swift Current Broncos in a bus crash in 1986 was a cause for mourning in the whole community, and the team's win of the junior hockey Memorial Cup a few years later was seen as a fitting tribute to the dead boys' memory.

The Broncos were in the news again in 1997 when Sheldon Kennedy, a former Bronco who had made it to the NHL, revealed that in the late 1980s the Bronco coach had sexually abused him on hundreds of occasions. It soon became clear that Kennedy was not his only victim and that coaches for other teams had sexually abused players as well. The hockey scandal followed revelations about sexual abuse of both boys and girls in other sports, alarming parents and sports authorities at a time when more and more children were become involved in organized sporting activities.

As in other nations, sports became increasingly identified in Canada with the "national identity." In 1961, the Fitness and Amateur Sports Act was passed, which made federal funds available for sports activity. Amateur sports became more bureaucratized, presided over by paid administrators rather than enthusiastic volunteers.

Canadians in the postwar period spent a great deal of money and time as sports spectators, both at professional and children's games. What was noticeable in the 1950s was the near-absence of adults except as supervisors at the public swimming pools, skating rinks, and hockey arenas that the new prosperity allowed municipalities to erect. In the early 1970s it was estimated that 90 percent of adults did not do the minimum amount of exercise recommended for protection against heart disease and stroke. While Canadians were living longer, poor nutrition habits, lack of exercise, and smoking were ending many lives prematurely and causing many other Canadians, who survived cancer surgery, heart attacks, or strokes, to live restricted lives. Increasingly the federal government, aided by campaigns of nutritionists, physical education specialists, and physicians, encouraged Canadians to rethink their lifestyles. Urged on by a federal body called Participaction, which placed clever ads on radio and television, previously indolent Canadians took up jogging, enrolled in aerobics classes, swam, or at least took the occasional long walk. The physical fitness craze meant new business for leisure industry operators from ski hills to fitness clubs.

Anti-smoking campaigns also had an impact. By the 1990s, the intrepid smoker stood out in the snow or rain during a coffee break at most workplaces, public buildings, and halls of education. Airlines banned smoking altogether, and intercity buses, once thick with smoke, became havens for the non-smoker as well. In most cities, restaurants were divided into smoking and non-smoking sections as a result of provincial or municipal legislation. Tobacco companies' right to directly advertise their product was removed, although in 1996 the Supreme Court ruled that restrictions on tobacco advertisements were too strict. "Sin taxes," which fell on liquor as well as tobacco, made smoking less financially attractive, although the availability of cheap smuggled cigarettes from the United States eventually forced governments to reduce these taxes. The percentage of adults who smoked halved between the 1960s and the 1990s, but today young people seem to be beginning to smoke at rates similar to those that had prevailed when their parents' generation was young.

The diets of many Canadians have changed and are now more likely to meet Nutrition Canada's requirement for "balanced" eating. Consumption of red meat, one of the items that physicians linked to cardiovascular problems, fell, and the cattle industry changed breeding habits to develop leaner meats. Diet gurus and clubs were also kept busy by Canadians' increased interest in what experts told them were the ways of living longer and more healthily. Social class was a big factor in people's response to the new ideas of healthy living. Surveys suggested that the working class and the poor had less time and money to

devote to "participaction" and that, in any case, they often regarded the new opposition to smoking, drinking, and relaxation as an attack on the few pleasures in their lives.

## TELEVISION AND THE PUBLIC BROADCASTER

Whether they spent much of their time exercising or participating in the arts or not, most Canadians found a great deal of time to watch television. As we saw in chapter 13, early efforts to Canadianize this important medium largely failed. The chances of reversing Canadians' preferences for American programming worsened in the 1970s as cable companies, providing dozens of channels via satellites, began operations. The CRTC tried in the 1980s to take advantage of the success of cable by insisting that cable companies carry a number of new television channels. Both the CBC and Radio-Canada introduced all-news stations modelled on the successful American Cable News Network. The large audiences for these channels—about eight hundred thousand nightly for the major newscast on Newsworld, the English-language news channel—demonstrated that even if Canadians wished to turn to the Americans for escapist entertainment, they preferred to watch home-produced news shows. Indeed, another million English-speaking Canadians watched the evening news on the regular CBC while over two million watched news on the private CTV network. Only a minority preferred the American TV channels for their news and most of those who watched news on American stations were "news junkies" who also tuned in for news on Canadian stations. Among francophone Québécois, most everyone watched news from Canadian outlets.

How well Canadian broadcasters, including the public broadcaster, reflected the nation is debatable. CBC personality and media critic Nathan Cohen explained why a Hugh Garner script about a hydro lineman was turned down by five producers. "Finally, one of them said to me, 'What do we know about working people? You can't expect us to do plays about people we don't understand.'"[3]

The Canadian arts community faced many frustrations in trying to convince the networks, and often audiences, that they could provide worthwhile alternatives to the slick American product that dominated the weekly ratings that were so important in attracting advertisers. In the mid-1970s, the CBC drew a large audience for a series of Canadian plays directed by John Hirsch. In spite of this success, the network mysteriously refused to continue the series into a second year and gradually cut the moneys devoted to "serious" programming. The network occasionally stumbled onto a winning product like *Street Legal*, but on the whole Canadians turned to the public broadcaster for the sorts of programs they simply could not find on private television, Canadian or American: drama, dance, documentaries, and current affairs. Such programming was jeopardized by deep and repeated funding cuts under both the Mulroney and Chrétien governments. Sports fans continued to enjoy the hugely popular *Hockey Night in Canada* and other telecasts of sports shows, though channels devoted exclusively to sports, both Canadian and American, offered the CBC new competition.

CBC Radio had its own loyal following of about 10 percent of all radio listeners in Canada. After the 1970s, emphasis was placed on current affairs, with its new FM network concentrating largely on classical music. CBC radio programs such as *This Country in the Morning* and *As It Happens* became many Canadians' preferred means of learning about the country's political and cultural developments. Their respective hosts, Peter Gzowski and Barbara Frum, became media icons, with Frum departing for television in the 1980s and Gzowski, after an unsuccessful attempt to launch a television career, returning to radio to host *Morningside*. Regional programming on CBC radio also focused on current affairs and cultural production. The CBC was the main venue for recording artists whose music did not fit the pigeon-holes of mainstream radio. Its nationwide talk shows allowed Canadians to discuss serious national issues, while talk shows on privately owned stations were more likely to invite people to discuss whether American football star O.J. Simpson had murdered his wife or whether the Prince and

Princess of Wales should divorce. Budget cuts in the 1990s first reduced the regional operations of CBC Radio and eventually limited national programming as well.

*CBC radio host Peter Gzowski became one of Canada's media celebrities. His morning radio shows from the 1970s onward were broadcast nationally and featured guests from all walks of Canadian life. Gzowski announced he was retiring in 1997 as federal cuts at the CBC contributed to the cancellation of his radio program* Morningside.

Canadian Broadcasting Corporation

One area in which Canadians became a major player in both their own and the American market was children's programming. Beginning in the 1950s, CBC and, to a lesser extent, CTV produced a variety of classic children's shows such as *The Friendly Giant* and *Mr Dress-Up*, which, in contrast to some of the slick programming for children favoured by American broadcasters, relied on a minimum of props and depended upon home-spun humour for their appeal to children. Canadians also dominated the market for children's records in North America, and author Robert Munsch, whose stories of clever children besting hopeless adults appealed to every child's tastes, became one of North America's favourite storytellers. Also popular were children's poet Dennis Lee, best known for his singalong poem, "Alligator Pie," and singers such as Sharon, Lois, and Bram, Raffi, and Eric Nagler.

## MEDIA CONCENTRATION AND CENSORSHIP

The mass media, which has so great an impact on Canadian social values, has come to be controlled by fewer and fewer corporations and individuals. Concern about concentration of ownership is not new, and was reflected in the findings of the Special Senate Committee on Mass Media (the Davey Committee) in 1970. A decade later, the Royal Commission on Newspapers—the Kent Commission—reported that three chains controlled 90 percent of French-language newspapers and that another three conglomerates controlled over two-thirds of English-language papers in Canada. Since that time, the problem of concentration of ownership has only worsened. By 1996, the Southam chain, once owned by the Southam family, was effectively controlled by industrialist Conrad Black. It dominated most large anglophone urban markets outside of the Atlantic provinces and Toronto. Smaller markets had been captured by the Thomson chain, which in the 1980s also acquired the *Globe and Mail*. The *Globe* claimed to be "Canada's national newspaper" and produced regional editions in an attempt to break the perception that it was, in fact, the newspaper of Bay Street. New Brunswick's newspapers were the fiefdom of the Irving family.

Conrad Black's media empire, which included the *Financial Post* and *Saturday Night* as well as major newspapers abroad, also controlled Quebec's *Le Soleil* while two other entrepreneurs, Pierre Desmarais and Pierre Peladeau, controlled the rest of the daily press in Quebec, except for *Le Devoir*, which saw its circulation drop by half from the early 1970s to the mid-1980s. A similar concentration was evident in weekly newspapers, television stations, and radio stations.

Such media concentration, which also occurred in other western democracies, raised questions about the degree to which the media could be counted on to provide a range of points of view. In both French and English Canada, there were a variety of progressive or feminist journals, but they could not afford to produce the slick products needed to compete with the mainstream media. Media magnates claimed that consumer choice, not media concentration, determined the news product that Canadians received. In their view, the market was the best way of allocating goods and services and, since media concentration was the product of market forces, it must be producing what the public wanted.

There was somewhat more competition in the magazine industry and in book publishing, where the problem was more one of foreign control. In the 1970s, Maclean-Hunter and Southam dominated the Canadian-owned magazine industry. These two firms were the big beneficiaries of a 1976 law passed by the Trudeau government that discontinued tax deductions for advertising aimed at the Canadian market but appearing in foreign journals. Opposed bitterly by *Time* and *Reader's Digest*, American publications with huge Canadian markets, the legislation aimed at convincing Canadian advertisers to spend their dollars on media operating in Canada. The book-publishing industry faced an uphill battle in convincing provincial departments and local boards of education to purchase Canadian-produced texts rather than cheaper and glossier American ones. American and British publishers gradually absorbed some of Canada's longest-established publishers. Ryerson Press was taken over by the American firm McGraw-Hill in 1970; Copp Clark, Canada's oldest publisher, was bought first by the British firm Pitman in the 1950s and then by the conglomerate Pearson in 1985. Foreign acquisition often meant corporate "rationalization" and loss of control over publishing programs. In the 1980s, while Canadian-owned firms were responsible for most of the new textbooks that appeared in Canada, they garnered less than a third of the revenues from book sales.

While social critics complained that the big money that controlled the private media led to de facto censorship over ideas and information displeasing to the media owners, there was also formal state censorship of what Canadians could see and hear. Radicals such as French feminist Simone de Beauvoir were barred from the CBC in the 1950s due to government apprehension about their corrupting influence. Books such as *Peyton Place*, *Lady Chatterley's Lover*, and *The Tropic of Cancer* were seized by customs officials at the border. Film censorship boards existed across the country. In Alberta, a British Information Office film extolling the United Nations and condemning racism ran afoul of the anti-communist witchhunters, and popular American films *The Wild One* and *The Blackboard Jungle* were banned for not being uplifting.

Municipal library boards and school boards have also at various times banned books of clear literary merit, usually for having too much explicit sex or too many profane words. Campaigns by the religious right in Canada, influenced by the successes of the well-funded Christian right in the United States, led to book bannings as supposedly secular libraries and schools bowed to pressure from groups who claimed that certain books offended Christian sensibilities.

## CONCLUSION

In the post-war period, Canadians developed cultural and sporting industries that brought worldwide attention and praise. Much of the success of these industries was due to the efforts of governments, both through subsides and regulations to protect the Canadian market for home-grown products. With government cutbacks in the fiscally conscious 1990s, and pressure to open up cultural markets under NAFTA, Canada's artists and athletes faced new challenges. Could Canada's talent withstand the brutal competition from the American cultural industries that were well on the way to dominating the globe? As the century closed, Canadians were still not confident that the twenty-first century, culturally at least, belonged to them.

---

## WHO SPEAKS FOR A 'CULTURE'?

### A Debate

In his provocative best-seller, *Selling Illusions: The Cult of Multiculturalism in Canada*, Neil Bissoondath writes about the change in Canadian perceptions of Ben Johnson after he was stripped of his Olympic gold medal:

> Within a shattering twenty-four-hour period in Seoul, Korea, Mr. Johnson was transformed in media reports from being the Canadian who had won Olympic gold through effort to the Jamaican immigrant who had lost it through use of drugs. The only thing faster than Mr. Johnson's drug-enhanced achievement was his public demotion from "one of us" to "one of them." The exotic multicultural concept of the everlast-

ing immigrant has come to function as an institutional system for the marginalization of the individual: Ben Johnson was, in other words, a Canadian when convenient, an immigrant when not. Had he, success or failure, been accepted as being simply Canadian and not "Jamaican-Canadian," it would have been difficult for anyone to distance him in this way. [4]

Bissoondath's book makes a strong plea against the use of stereotypes, whether positive or negative, to describe cultural communities in Canada. He argues that while some individuals of a particular background wish mainly to strengthen their ethnic ties and maintain their ancestors' language and culture, others wish to assimilate to various degrees within Canadian society. If Canadian society is to be tolerant and individuals are to have options, they cannot be forced into particular boxes. While extolling multiculturalism as a goal for Canadian society, he attacks government funding for this goal, which he suggests leads to artificial fragmentation of Canadians and public support for a hyphenated Canadianism that many individual members of minority groups are, uncomfortable with. Bissoondath particularly takes issue with two groups: writers who claim that only members of a particular cultural community—especially if that community is non-white—have a right to write about that group; and those people who are quick to brand as racist whites who ignore that stricture and express a different point of view from the one prevailing within that cultural community. He defends two individuals whom he regards as prominent victims of this separatist view of cultures: Jeanne Cannizzo and June Callwood.

Cannizzo was a University of Toronto anthropology professor who served as curator for a Royal Ontario Museum exhibition of the history of Canadian missionaries in Africa. The exhibit faithfully reproduced the missionaries' racist opinions but some African Canadians, instead of appreciating Cannizzo's forthrightness in not hiding the truth about missionaries' goals and attitudes, accused her of being a racist for replicating uncritically their racist statements. Her home defaced and her classroom invaded by students who shouted her down as a racist, Cannizzo, shattered, left the University of Toronto and Canada.

Callwood was one of Canada's best-known crusading journalists and political activists when she was labelled a racist by some African-Canadian members of the Toronto arts community after a confrontation in 1989 with Marlene Nourbese Philip at a benefit for PEN, an organization that defends imprisoned writers. When Philip attempted to hand Callwood a pamphlet that accused the

Canadian section of PEN of excluding blacks from positions of authority, Callwood told her loudly to "fuck off." For Philip and her supporters, this was evidence that Callwood was a racist. But, notes Bissoondath, her friends vouched that Callwood, despite her many virtues, was often short-tempered and profane. Bissoondath rejects the view that as a white woman and therefore a woman with supposedly more privilege than Philip, Callwood should have restrained herself from swearing. He regrets that the incident forced Callwood to resign from the Writers' Union of Canada and from the board of a women's hostel, Nellie's, two institutions she co-founded.

Bissoondath scores easy points against the white liberals who have tried to argue that people like Callwood and Cannizzo are "objectively" racist because they fail to confront the privilege that their white skin has conferred upon them and the social disadvantage that others face because their skins are not white. But Philip and other writers of colour have raised some important questions in their writing about the depiction of non-whites in the larger culture and its impact on both artists of colour and people of colour generally. Philip challenges the view, expressed by many writers, including Bissoondath, that it is enough to write honestly from the heart and not to worry about the political fallout of one's writing. She observes that it is all too easy to repeat standard stereotypes about non-whites and Third World countries and thereby promote racism. Context for people's actions is all-important to her, and she criticizes authors, white and non-white, who present unsavoury black characters with no context of the colonial experience or ongoing oppression and no recognition of people's efforts to make their mark as either individuals or as members of a larger group struggling for rights for their people. [5]

Dionne Brand likewise argues that it is important for people who have been denied a voice in the past to be given the right to speak of their experience now. She claims that "cultural appropriation" of that voice by members of more privileged groups, even when they try to be sympathetic, simply leaves long-silent people still unable to say in their own words what their experience has been.[6]

Neither Philip nor Brand supports separation of the races—or the sexes—physically or culturally, as some of their opponents suggest they do. Rather they suggest that, at the present time when people of colour in Canada are struggling to define their own histories and identities, they deserve support from other members of the cultural community. Although many artists of colour have achieved public recognition in recent years, the opponents of cultural appropriation believe that these gains are still fragile and that much more must be done to encourage groups that have faced oppression in the past to tell their own stories.

## NOTES

[1] Jacques Ferron, *Tales from the Uncertain Country* (Toronto: Anansi, 1972), 100

[2] Gabrielle Roy, *The Tin Flute*, trans. Hannah Josephson (New York: Reynal and Hitchcock, 1947), 74–76

[3] Paul Rutherford, *When Television Was Young: Primetime Canada, 1952–1967* (Toronto: University of Toronto Press, 1990), 284

[4] Neil Bissoondath, *Selling Illusions: The Cult of Multiculturalism in Canada* (Toronto: Penguin, 1994), 116

[5] M. Nourbese Philip, *Frontiers* (Stratford, ON: Mercury Press, 1992)

[6] Dionne Brand, "Who Can Speak for Whom?" *Brick*, no. 46 (Summer 1993)

## SELECTED READING

On cultural identities in Canada, see William Dodge, ed., *Boundaries of Identity* (Toronto: Lester, 1992), and Neil Bissoondath, *Selling Illusions: The Cult of Multiculturalism in Canada* (Toronto: Penguin, 1994). On Quebec cultural developments, see Renate Usmiani, *Michel Tremblay* (Vancouver: Douglas and McIntyre, 1982); Gabrielle Roy, *Letters to Bernadette* (Toronto: Lester and Orpen Dennys, 1990); Guy Bouthilier and Jean Meynaud, *Le choc des langues au Québec* (Montreal: Presses de l'Université du Québec, 1972). On Canadian literature generally, see Margaret Atwood, *Survival* (Toronto: Anansi, 1972), and Northrop Frye, *The Bush Garden: Essays on the Canadian Imagination* (Toronto: Anansi, 1971). On authors writing in English, see Judith S. Grant, *Robertson Davies: Man of Myth* (Toronto: Penguin, 1994); Janice Williamson, *Sounding Differences: Conversations with Seventeen Canadian Writers* (Toronto: University of Toronto Press, 1993); Ed Jewinski, *Michael Ondaatje: Express Yourself Beautifully* (Toronto: ECW Press, 1994); and Beverly Rasporich, *Dance of the Sexes: Art and Gender in the Fiction of Alice Munro* (Edmonton: University of Alberta Press, 1990). On Native cultural assertion, see the texts by Arthur Ray, Olive Dickason, and J.R. Miller referred to in earlier chapters as well as G. Gottfriedson and R. Schneider, *In Honour of Our Grandmothers: Visions of Cultural Survival* (Penticton, BC: Theytus Books, 1994).

Histories of Canadian film include Gary Evans, *In the National Interest: A Chronicle of the National Film Board of Canada from 1949 to 1989* (Toronto: University of Toronto Press, 1991), and R. Bruce Elder, *Image and Identity: Reflections on Canadian Film and Culture* (Waterloo: Wilfrid Laurier University Press, 1989). Key works on Canadian art include *Visual Arts in Canada: Painting, Drawing, and Sculpture* (Ottawa: Canadian Heritage, 1993); Dennis Reid, *A Concise History of Canadian Painting* (Toronto: Oxford University Press, 1988); and Elizabeth McLuhan and Tom Hill, *Norval Morrisseau and the Emergence of the Image Makers* (Toronto: Methuen, 1984). On the media in Canada, see Paul Rutherford, *When Television Was Young: Primetime Canada, 1952–1967* (Toronto: University of Toronto Press, 1990); Mary Vipond, *The Mass Media in Canada* (Toronto: Lorimer, 1989); and Frank Peers, *The Public Eye: Television and the Politics of Canadian Broadcasting, 1952–1968* (Toronto: University of Toronto Press, 1979).

On heritage preservation, see C.J. Taylor, *Negotiating the Past: The Making of Canada's National Historic Parks and Sites* (Montreal: McGill-Queen's University Press, 1990); *Prairie Forum*, 15, 2 (Fall 1990), special issue on Heritage Conservation; and Ian McKay, *The Quest of the Folk: Antimodernism and Cultural Selection in Twentieth-Century Nova Scotia* (Montreal: McGill-Queen's University Press, 1994).

On sports in Canada, see Bruce Kidd, *The Struggle for Canadian Sport* (Toronto: University of Toronto Press, 1996); Richard S. Gruneau and David Whitson, *Hockey Night in Canada: Sport, Identities and Cultural Politics* (Toronto: Garamond, 1993); Ann Hall, *Sports in Canadian Society* (Toronto: McClelland and Stewart, 1991); Donald Macintosh, *Sports and Politics in Canada: Federal Government Involvement Since 1961* (Montreal: McGill-Queen's University Press, 1987); and Rick Hansen and Jim Taylor, *Rick Hansen: Man in Motion* (Vancouver: Douglas and McIntyre, 1987).

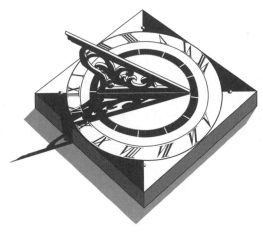

# CHAPTER 17

## CANADA IN THE GLOBAL VILLAGE, 1975–1997

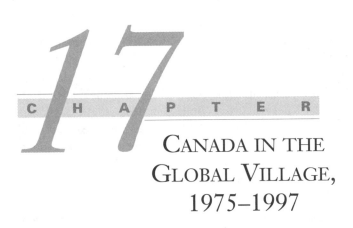

O N A SUNNY JUNE DAY IN 1995, ABOUT FOUR thousand women, most of them living in poverty, completed a ten-day trek to Quebec City to demand that politicians take action to address their dire circumstances. The women had walked twenty kilometres a day from three gathering points, staying along the way with feminist sympathizers. Along with poor women and their children across the country, they represented the largest group of victims of state policies that placed less and less emphasis on responsibility for those whose social conditions disadvantaged them in the marketplace. When the women arrived in Quebec City, the opposition Liberals refused to have anything to do with them, alleging that they were part of a separatist conspiracy to discredit Canadian federalism. Sovereignist premier Jacques Parizeau told the women that their demand for a program of social infrastructure spending could only be met when Quebec was independent from Canada. He then announced an increase in Quebec's minimum wage from $6 to $6.45 an hour, 20 percent of the increase that the marchers had demanded. Many of the protesters were understandably disappointed that their efforts to draw attention to the plight of the poor were being manipulated by politicians with their own agendas.

Four months later, Moinul Haque, whose East Indian restaurant had gone bankrupt in Toronto's stagnant economy in 1993, was admitted to hospital for surgery after his knee became infected, rendering him unable to walk. Haque, a welfare recipient, had been evicted from his rooming house after welfare cuts by a newly elected Conservative provincial government left him insufficient money to pay his rent. Unable to find another place to live, he joined the city's homeless who slept on the street, and the harsh weather led to his health problems.

About the same time, Dr Hubert Kammerer, a medical doctor who was also an activist in Friends of Medicare, a group opposing the drift towards privatizing medical services, wrote the *Edmonton Journal* about the unnecessary death of a patient whom he had recently discharged from hospital. The patient was a diabetic law professor who suffered from dementia and therefore needed home care to inject him with his insulin twice a day. Following health-care cuts in Alberta, his home-care visits were cut to twice weekly. One evening, left to take personal responsibility for his insulin, he injected himself, forgot he had done so, then re-injected himself. He died of irreversible brain damage. Dr Kammerer wrote that this was an extreme example of what "can be found in a health care system that has had too much cut out of it too quickly and is in danger of falling apart." [1]

Twenty years earlier, such incidents would have caused general condemnation of the governments that had allowed the so-called social safety-net to develop such large holes, but Canada in 1995 was generally a meaner country than it had been twenty years earlier. Its economy had suffered the ravages of several recessions, prompting the federal government to replace the postwar goals of social security and full employment with policies designed to increase global economic competitiveness through decreased government spending and reduced deficits. As part of this new national strategy, Canada entered into a comprehensive free trade agreement with the United States in 1989, which fuelled the pressure to "harmonize" social as well as economic policies on a continental basis.

Global pressures also put a severe strain on the fragile fabric of national unity. In Quebec, political independence became the goal of a growing number of nationalists. Preoccupied with the concerns of Quebec and Ontario, the federal government pursued policies that provoked western alienation and complaints from Atlantic Canada that their needs were being ignored. Class, gender, and cultural divisions cut across regional tensions and added further complexity to the problem of devising a national policy that would capture the imagination of a majority of the nation's jaded citizens.

This chapter traces the political, economic, and social developments that followed the unprecedented economic growth of the three postwar decades. The era of prosperity seemingly over, Canadians were forced to make hard choices about their social values and the direction they wished to pursue in the new millennium.

## ECONOMIC STAGNATION AND THE POLITICAL RESPONSE

The average rate of unemployment in 1976 measured over 7 percent, the first time that this had happened since 1939. In every subsequent year for the following two decades, it remained over the 7 percent mark, and from 1982 to 1985 and again from 1991 to 1994 the average reached double digits (see figure 17.1). The rules of the game of international capitalism were being rewritten and Canadian working people proved generally to be among the losers.

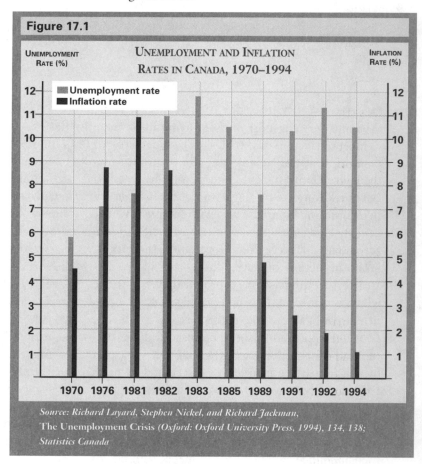

**Figure 17.1**

UNEMPLOYMENT AND INFLATION RATES IN CANADA, 1970–1994

Source: Richard Layard, Stephen Nickel, and Richard Jackman, *The Unemployment Crisis* (Oxford: Oxford University Press, 1994), 134, 138; Statistics Canada

## GLOBALIZATION

By the 1970s, the rising economic power of Japan led giant corporations in the West to believe that their postwar compromise with labour and governments was no longer workable. Rising from the ashes of the Second World War, Japan had built an extremely efficient industrial sector. The products of Japanese factories were often both cheaper and of better quality than those produced in North America and Europe. Nor did the Japanese remain content with the textiles and small consumer items that they had produced in the immediate postwar period. By the 1970s, Japanese radios, televisions, stereo equipment, appliances, computers, and cars were putting North American factories out of business. With huge markets in India, China, and other Asian nations at its doorstep, Japan was poised to become the world's economic leader in the Information Age. A close business–government alliance had promoted Japan's industrial cause, and the "Four Tigers" of Asia—Hong Kong, South Korea, Taiwan, and Singapore—benefited from similar strategies to make important strides in industrial development.

Their well-being threatened by new competitors, the energy crisis, and the environmental movement, mega-corporations began moving their production facilities to off-shore locations around the world. Developing countries, desperate for capital investment, offered cheap labour, lower taxes, and fewer corporate and environmental regulations to eat into profits. Able to transfer assets instantaneously around the world, these "transnational" corporations could defy attempts by any one government to control their activities. It was not long before corporate managers could also extract favourable conditions from governments of western nations eager to prevent jobs from being exported to other countries. Corporate taxes were cut, trade union protection reduced, environmental regulations relaxed, and social programs cut in an effort to convince corporate leaders that they were welcome.

The weakening commitment to environmental protection shattered ecologists' hopes that the world community would recognize that the future of the biosphere depended upon collective action to reduce alarming trends. Disasters such as those that occurred at Three Mile Island (1979), Bhopal (1984), and Chernobyl (1986) underscored the difficulty of controlling technology. The destruction of the ozone layer by chlorofluorocarbons (CFCs), used in aerosols, foam insulation, and super-clean-

ers for electronic equipment, was altering the world's climate and exposing the earth to the unfiltered ultraviolet rays of the sun. The rapid disappearance of tropical rain forests caused further deterioration of the atmosphere. Although the major world powers reduced their stocks of nuclear weapons in the aftermath of the Cold War, the weapons that remained were capable of wreaking irreparable environmental damage. Seemingly devoid of any sense of social responsibility, France even persisted in testing nuclear weapons in the atmosphere. With both the greenhouse effect and nuclear winter threatening the future of the planet, the limits of technology and the people who planned it were plain for all to see. A spate of international conferences resolved little because the governments whose representatives attended these meetings had become less powerful than the multinational corporations, which did not attend.

## TRADING BLOCS

Although governments increasingly capitulated to the view that corporations rather than the state should set the rules for the economy, regional trading blocs were created or strengthened in an effort to secure elusive markets and to balance the growing power of multinational corporations. The European Economic Community, created by six western European nations in 1958, expanded to include almost all of Western Europe in what became know as the European Union (EU). Members of the EU were expected to drop all tariff and non-tariff barriers against fellow members and to collectively determine protectionist trade policies with the rest of the world. Japan implemented its own protectionist policies. Canada and the United States signed the Free Trade Agreement in 1989. Three years later, the North American Free Trade Agreement (NAFTA) brought Mexico into the North American trading bloc, and plans were under way to include South American nations as well. Efforts to eliminate trade restrictions under the General Agreement on Tariffs and Trade (GATT) were hopelessly complicated by these developments.

In the 1990s, it was becoming increasingly

clear that transnational corporations had more power than most nation-states. When a recession descended in late 1981, corporations began a massive program of "restructuring" for a leaner and meaner global economy. Automating production processes, reducing the number of workers, and offering a more flexible response to changing market conditions, it was argued, would allow the fittest to survive and triumph. A wave of mergers and takeovers followed, which further concentrated economic power. By 1986, thirty-two families and nine giant conglomerates controlled over one-third of the country's non-financial assets.

## Neo-conservatism

In the new climate of corporate concentration and "downsizing," the views of American economist Milton Friedman, dismissed during the age of prosperity as right-wing fringe notions, gained ascendancy among western leaders. According to Friedman and his followers (sometimes called monetarists because of their emphasis on monetary policy), government intervention—deficit financing, tax incentives, and the expansion of the money supply—had led to rigidities and inefficiencies in western economies. The solution was to encourage efficient production to improve the *supply* of goods and services rather than to stimulate *demand* through government spending. If governments simply reduced taxes, controlled inflation, and let the private sector adjust to changing economic conditions, the global economy would right itself soon enough. Opponents of Friedman noted that such policies had been pursued before and during the Great Depression, with disastrous results, but reminders of this kind, voiced eloquently by Canadian-born economist John Kenneth Galbraith, were increasingly ignored by political leaders.

Supply-side economics inspired the policies of conservative governments in Britain under Margaret Thatcher (1979–90), in the United States under Ronald Reagan (1981–88) and in Canada under Brian Mulroney (1984–93). Although their economies were experiencing the worst dislocation since the 1930s, these leaders attempted to reduce spending on social programs, privatize government

activities, cut back the civil service, and exercise tighter control over the money supply. All argued that they had no choice. With western economies growing at a fraction of the rates they had posted in the period of prosperity, government revenues were being outstripped by expenditures. Since governments felt compelled to cut corporate taxes, and generally resisted significant increases to the individual tax rate, the result of the imbalance between revenues and expenditures was an annual deficit. Deficits compounded from year to year created large debt loads that had to be financed through loans from financiers. The consequence was that an increased portion of state expenditure went simply to repaying debts, leaving even less money to finance social programs. Many people accepted the argument that governments could not go on spending forever without taking their revenues into account. *Neo-conservatism*, the view that it was necessary to increase marketplace control over the economy and reverse the extensive state interventionism of the post-1945 period, had growing support.

Opponents of this view claimed that neo-conservatives were "neo-cons" of a different sort, deceiving the public by following contradictory policies. On the one hand, tight money policies, meant to control the inflation that easy credit allegedly encouraged, produced high interest rates. On the other hand, the debt load of governments was considerably worsened by the need to renew loans at ever higher interest rates. Similarly, claims that governments were short of revenue and therefore had no alternative but to cut social programs, were contradicted by corporate tax cuts and by government handouts to business. The link between tight money and inflation, so assiduously promoted by the monetarists, was demonstrated historically never to have existed. Similarly, it was easily shown that there was no historical merit to the argument that low inflation was necessary to produce economic growth. Deflation during the Depression had not encouraged investors back into markets where there were no obvious consumers, while the high inflation of the early postwar period had not deterred capitalists from investing in the buoyant markets that state expenditures and trade union wages had created.

Increasingly, opponents of neo-conservatism charged that high unemployment, resulting from the credit squeeze that tight money produced, was not simply an unfortunate consequence of the battle against inflation: it was the goal of the whole exercise. Such accusations gained steam from statements made by officials such as Bank of Canada governor John Crow (1987–94), who publicly opined that allowing the rate of unemployment to fall below 8 percent would produce a new round of inflation. Again, there seemed to be a deep contradiction in the stated views of neo-conservatives. They claimed that the welfare state and Keynesian economics had mollycoddled individuals, discouraging them from taking the jobs on offer. At the same time, they promoted a monetary and fiscal regime that reduced both the numbers of jobs available as well as the compensation for those unable to find work. Their ultimate belief was that increased reliance on the marketplace would produce rates of economic growth that eventually would conquer both inflation and unemployment.

## CANADIAN POLITICS AND THE FREE TRADE AGREEMENT

The Liberal Party had been the chief political beneficiary of postwar prosperity. Given credit by Canadians for implementing welfare state policies, it governed the country for thirty-two of the thirty-nine years from 1945 to 1984. It was weak in Western Canada, where competition between the right-wing Conservatives and the left-wing New Democrats squeezed out the party that was seen not so much as centrist but as central Canadian. By contrast, the party was strong in Quebec, if only because the Conservatives and New Democrats were viewed as anglophone parties. The Liberals ' selection of francophone leaders from Wilfrid Laurier and Louis St Laurent to Pierre Elliott Trudeau served to reinforce the view that the party was the most sympathetic to the interests of Quebec and francophones.

By the late 1970s, the Tories were beginning to tap the resentment among middle-class Canadians against increasing taxes and increasing state intervention. In the federal election of 1979, the Liberals were reduced to second place. But in office, the willingness of Joe Clark's Progressive Conservative minority government to allow energy price increases met with little favour outside the energy-producing provinces of Western Canada. The Progressive Conservative government's first budget was defeated by the opposition parties, forcing a second election in less than a year. In 1980, Trudeau's Liberals remained the safest bet for many Canadians. They were perceived as the party that balanced corporate and individual interests, that promoted social welfare and full-employment policies, and that resisted American control over the economy. After their humiliation nine months earlier, the Liberals once more formed a majority government.

By 1984, Trudeau was gone, and the new Liberal leader, John Turner, had a different legacy with which to contend. After almost three years of a bruising recession and increasing government deficits, Canadians were ready to change governments. Brian Mulroney, the new Progressive Conservative leader, knew how to take advantage of that desire for change. He promised Canadians that he would restore employment and reduce deficits without touching Canada's social programs, which he labelled a "sacred trust." Cynically recognizing that most Canadians had not yet been won over to the hard-hearted politics of Thatcher and Reagan, he promised Canadians gain without pain. He took advantage of a televised forum on women's issues to announce that his party would implement a national day-care program if he won the election. While he did not deliver on the promise, his willingness to make it suggested that he did not believe that the Conservatives could be elected on a program of cutting back the state's obligations.

## THE MACDONALD COMMISSION AND THE MOVE TOWARDS FREE TRADE

In 1984, Mulroney claimed that he was opposed to free trade between Canada and the United States. That issue, he suggested, had been settled in the federal election of 1911. Contrary to Mulroney's claims, the idea had been revived by the Royal Commission on Canada's Economic Union and Development Prospects. Appointed by Trudeau in 1982, with the country mired in recession, the commission was chaired by Donald Macdonald, a former Liberal finance minister. Its three-volume report, released in September 1985, one year after the election of the Mulroney Tories, argued that Canada had to maintain a flexible economy, capable of adjusting to global economic change and new technologies. Market mechanisms, rather than government intervention, the report maintained, provided the best means of ensuring a vibrant Canadian economy. To that end, free trade with the United States offered the only hope for continued economic prosperity.

The commission marshalled a broad array of evidence to support free trade. Despite attempts to pursue a "third option" of more diversified trade, especially through an arrangement with the European trading bloc, Canada's dependency on the United States had actually grown in the previous decade. Over three-quarters of Canada's exports were sold to the United States, and half of that trade was between parent companies and branch plants of multinational corporations. With over one-third of their GNP derived from foreign trade, Canadians would experience a crisis of unthinkable proportions if the flow of goods across the Canada–United States border was disrupted. The time had come to shake up the industries that remained sheltered behind the old National Policy and to lay the foundations for a New Age economy that would serve Canadians in the twenty-first century.

## The Free Trade Agreement

Mulroney ignored his pre-election statements and initiated trade negotiation with the Americans. Canada's chief negotiator was Simon Reisman, a career civil servant who had been instrumental in negotiating the 1965 Auto Pact. The Business Council on National Issues, an organization composed of the chief executive officers of the hundred and fifty leading Canadian corporations, most of them multinationals, was fully committed to free trade. The venerable Canadian Manufacturers Association, once the bulwark of the National Policy, came on side. Even the Canadian Federation of Independent Business, which represented the increasingly powerful small business community in Canada, threw its weight behind the scheme.

The details of the free trade agreement were ironed out in the fall of 1987. Tariffs on primary and manufactured goods would be eliminated over a ten-year period and free trade in services would gradually be implemented. Most non-tariff barriers to trade, such as quotas and content regulations, were also slated for elimination. Following a year of heated debate, the Mulroney government called an election on 25 November 1988 after the Liberal majority in the Senate made clear their unwillingness to ratify the agreement before the Tories had received an electoral mandate for free trade.

Leaders of the NDP, labour unions, feminists, some church groups, and a variety of nationalist coalitions opposed free trade in principle, while the Liberal Party, which waffled about the concept, rejected certain features of the actual proposal. Opponents of the free trade agreement maintained that it would allow multinational corporations to consolidate their North American operations in locations with better climates and lower wage levels than those prevailing in Canada. Jobs would be lost in the goods-producing sectors, and the wages of those remaining in the labour force would be substantially reduced. Moreover, Canada's cultural industries would be threatened, and Canadians would be forced to tailor their welfare, environmental, and regional development policies to "harmonize" with the goals of the larger economic partner. Under such pressure, Canada as a nation would surely fall apart. Nor was such a sweeping agreement necessary. Since American industry did not want to lose Canadian resources and markets, economic nationalists argued, there seemed little likelihood of the United States suddenly pulling the plug on trade with Canada.

Brian Mulroney maintained that Canada would remain a sovereign nation once the agreement was in effect. Although the government's ability to levy tariffs to protect industries would gradually disappear, the question of which state subsidies constituted unfair trade practice had yet to be negotiated between the two economic partners. He accused his opponents of "scare-mongering" when they suggested that old age pensions or medicare might be undermined by free trade. The opening of the American market to more Canadian-produced goods and services would benefit workers in the manufacturing and service sectors, he claimed. Moreover, the agreement merely furthered the work of the GATT, which had effectively removed tariffs on 80 percent of all goods produced in Canada.

If the 1988 election is taken as a referendum on the issue of free trade, its opponents won, since the Liberals and New Democrats together received over 52 percent of the total votes cast. Supporters of the agreement, the Conservatives and the fledgling Reform Party, won about 46 percent of the vote, with the remaining vote going to parties whose campaigns were mainly focused on other issues. The Liberals and New Democrats had formed no alliance in the campaign, and the large plurality of Conservative voters returned a second Mulroney majority government.

At 1:48 AM, 24 December 1988, the legislation authorizing the free trade agreement between Canada and the United States passed in the House of Commons by a vote of 141–111. Nine days and nights of stormy debate had preceded the vote. The government invoked closure four times during the session to ensure that the legislation would pass before the ratification deadline of 1 January 1989. With fewer than half of the 104 senators in the upper chamber on Friday 30 December, the free trade bill easily passed the Senate. Canada was entering a new economic era.

## THE FREE TRADE ERA

The ink was barely dry on the Free Trade Agreement when firms, beginning with Gillette, announced that they were closing all or part of their Canadian operations and centralizing their manufacturing in the United States. In every case, they insisted that their plans to vacate Canada were unrelated to the agreement and had been in place prior to its enactment. After 1 January 1989, they could move without fear that Canada would use tariff or non-tariff barriers to restrict their penetration of Canadian markets. Supporters of free trade minimized the importance of the exodus, arguing that tariffs encouraged non-competitive operations with the limited horizon of a domestic market. Canadians, they argued, should turn the companies that remained into world-class firms with markets around the globe.

The agreement securely in place, companies now also set aside their former rejection of arguments that free trade meant the end of Canadian welfare and environmental programs. Canada's welfare state and state interventionism more generally were identified as obstacles to attracting and retaining corporate investors. It could hardly be a surprise if firms, freed from the necessity of maintaining a Canadian operation, chose to locate in the country where there was less corporate taxation, trade union protection, and industrial regulation.

As a deep recession gripped Canada and all western countries in 1990, free trade promoters went on the defensive. Although the recession, which lasted for three years and was followed by a "jobless recovery," affected all western nations, it was more severe in Canada than in most other countries. Mel Hurtig, a long-time champion of Canadian nationalism, charged in his best-selling book, *The Betrayal of Canada* (1992), that, in its first two years, the free trade agreement was responsible for the loss of 264 000 manufacturing jobs as branch plants closed and new operations were located in Mexico and elsewhere. He charged that the agreement had already brought "a big decline in the standard of living of Canadians," and he predicted that "the future will be much worse ... the destruction and disappearance of our country."[2]

Supporters of the agreement accused the nationalists of blaming free trade for job losses that were the result purely of the recession. Even without the FTA, Canadians would have been victims of the restructuring and downsizing policies that were part of global economic strategy, they argued.

---

## MASSEY-HARRIS: A TALE OF CANADIAN CAPITALISM

As we have seen in earlier chapters, the agricultural machinery company founded in 1847 by Daniel Massey went from strength to strength in the late nineteenth and early twentieth centuries. The company moved from Newcastle to Toronto in 1855 and in 1891 merged with its chief competitor to become Massey-Harris, the largest company of its kind in the British Empire. By the first decade of the twentieth century, it had captured a huge share of the rapidly expanding Prairie market for farm machinery and had established branch operations in the United States. When the company ran into difficulties following the Second World War, it was reorganized under the direction of its holding company, Argus Corporation, and continued to prosper. As Massey-Ferguson, it developed a global market and reached annual sales of over $1 billion in the 1960s.

In the difficult economic climate of the late 1970s, Massey's fortunes again began to slip. Conrad Black, the ambitious young head of Argus, became chair of the troubled company in 1978, but the bottom fell out of the farm machinery market in 1980 and Argus wrote off its Massey-Ferguson shares as worthless. In an effort to save the capital and jobs that Massey represented, banks, governments, and shareholders poured $1.2 billion into the failing firm between 1978 and 1984. By 1987, when Massey-Ferguson changed its name to Varity Corp (after the Varity Plough Company, which had been acquired in 1892), it was a third of its former size, but nonetheless ranked as the forty-ninth largest firm in Canada with sales and operating revenue of $1.8 billion. Following the signing of the Free Trade Agreement, it moved its head office to the United States.

---

They had their own statistics to throw at the doomsayers, including a 16 percent increase in the volume of Canadian exports between 1989 and 1992, the continued success of the government in fighting inflation, and the drop in the value of the Canadian dollar, all of which suggested to them that the Canadian economy was making the necessary adjustments to survive in an increasingly competitive economic environment.

## THE JOBLESS RECOVERY

Although moderate economic growth had succeeded the recession, by 1995 Canada, like many western countries, could not find work for about a tenth of its labour force. Profitable businesses such as the major banks, the energy giants, and Bell Canada joined less successful employers as well as governments in reducing their workforces. Business spokespersons justified cutbacks by asserting that trade liberalization forced companies to be more competitive. That meant mergers, factory shutdowns, and the introduction of technology, particularly computerization, all of which reduced the economy's demand for labour. Robots often replaced assembly-line workers; traditional "women's jobs" vanished as voice mail and electronic mail replaced many secretaries and automated banking reduced the need for tellers. The unemployed remained out of work for longer stretches than had their counterparts even a decade earlier.

From 1989 to 1994, the after-tax income of Canadians fell 5 percent in constant dollars. While the majority of households still had a comfortable income, a growing number of Canadians were living under the poverty line. Rates of poverty had dropped gradually during the era of prosperity, but they climbed during the recessions of the early eighties and the early nineties. So, for example, while 3.5 million Canadians were classified as poor in 1987, a year of considerable economic growth, there were an additional 1.4 million impoverished Canadians just six years later. About 1.4 million children under the age of eighteen were among the poor of 1993, representing 21 percent of all Canadian children. Sixty percent of poor children lived in homes headed by single mothers, whose ability to find work or day care, never mind both, had been undermined first by the recession and then by the jobless recovery.

Women's labour force participation nonetheless continued to rise. By 1994, women made up 45 percent of the workforce, an increase of 8 percent from 1976. Fewer women believed that it was either desirable or likely that they could depend entirely on the income of a man to maintain them and their children. Men's wages and job security were on the decline, making it imperative for most families that women seek paid work. Although women increasingly unionized and fought successfully for better wages, there was still a considerable degree of inequality in income. In 1994, women working full time earned 72 percent of the incomes of men working full time. Also, far more women than men were trapped in part-time work, with the result that women's incomes overall were only 58 percent of men's.

## INFLATION VERSUS UNEMPLOYMENT

Federal economic policies, both under the Tories and their Liberal successors, elected in 1993, continued to emphasize the battle against inflation and government debt rather than the battle against unemployment. Yet high unemployment drained the federal treasury, as unemployment insurance and social assistance costs mounted, and it deprived that treasury of the income taxes that resulted from more people working. Jean Chrétien's Liberals hinted in the 1993 election that there might be some return to employment creation as a priority, but shortly after the election Finance Minister Paul Martin, a leading member of the corporate community, made clear that the new government would follow substantially the same financial policies as its predecessor. Social programs would be cut, and the Bank of Canada's monetary policies would not be fundamentally altered.

Young people were disproportionately the victims of the new unemployment. In an economy that was producing few new jobs, experienced workers were favoured over newcomers, making it difficult for the young to get a start in the labour market. In contrast to the generation of the sixties, young people in the nineties were unlikely to find well-paying manufacturing jobs after high school.

They were in a somewhat better position to find employment if they had postsecondary training, but even this proved no guarantee. Life-long employment with a single company became increasingly uncommon, and young workers often had to be content with short-term contracts followed by a new intensive job search. "McJobs" in the service industry appeared to be the fate of large numbers of people in their twenties, even if they had excellent qualifications for professional employment. While some young people beat the odds and either found good jobs in the profession for which they had trained or created their own fortune through an entrepreneurial venture, it was clear that opportunities were limited. The term *Generation X* entered the language to denote a generation whom some pessimists suggested could only live well if they remained in their parents' homes throughout their adult lives.

The decline in availability of jobs, and the governments' apparent inability to cope with a changing economy had important political repercussions. Regional alienation and Quebec nationalism fed upon the declining sense of national purpose that laissez-faire economics encouraged. Perhaps because the economic issues seemed so intractable, politicians focused their energies on finding solutions to constitutional problems.

## QUEBEC SOVEREIGNTY

At first, it might appear wrong-headed to relate Quebec sovereignty to economic issues such as the rate of unemployment or the size of federal transfers. After all, Quebec nationalism and even the sovereignty movement have a long pedigree stretching back to the conquest of 1760, passing through the rebellion of 1837 and the uproar over the hanging of Riel in 1885, to the conscription crises of 1917 and 1944. Quebec's intellectuals and artists, generally in favour of the greatest autonomy possible for Quebec within Confederation, began in the 1960s to embrace the demand for full sovereignty for Quebec, for recognition of the Québécois as a people.

Yet it is clear that popular support for sovereignty has waxed and waned with the performance of the provincial economy. In the 1966 provincial election, the two separatist parties garnered only 10 percent of the vote. At the time, the rate of unemployment in Quebec was barely 4 percent, only marginally higher than in the country as a whole. By 1970, when the fledgling Parti québécois won almost a quarter of the vote, unemployment had increased to 7 percent. Six years later, with the unemployment rate at 8.7 percent, the PQ was elected to office. Throughout the 1970s, not only had the unemployment rate risen, but the gap in the rate between Quebec and the rest of the country had widened.

It seemed more than happenstance that the PQ was defeated by the resurgent Liberals in 1985 as the recession of the early 1980s receded, or that it failed to regain power in 1989 when the Liberals called an election another recession occurred. Quebec was still suffering the effects of this latest recession when the PQ was returned to power in 1994.

The same trends were visible in both 1980 and 1995 when the PQ held its referenda on sovereignty. In 1995, high unemployment, in both absolute and relative terms, as well as federal cutbacks in transfer payments, and promises of more to come, could not help but influence Quebec's attitude towards remaining in the Canadian Confederation. Only a paper-thin majority—50.6 percent—voted to maintain the federation; moreover, for the first time, a decisive majority of francophones—60 percent—expressed the desire to have Quebec form an independent nation.

Apart from high unemployment, the major impetus for sovereignty in Quebec came from the flowering of cultural nationalism. No longer protected by an omnipresent Catholic Church and a high birth rate from assimilation into North American values, francophone Québécois attempted to create a distinct identity for themselves within a secular North American context. For the more nationalist among them, it became intolerable that the province lacked the trappings of nationhood: a seat in the United Nations, ambassadors abroad, a central bank. They claimed that the federal government's efforts to exercise control over social pro-

grams and civil rights were intended to circumvent a constitution that promoted decentralization but also to erode the ability of the people of Quebec to determine their own future.

The rest of the country was sceptical about such claims. Wasn't the prime minister invariably a Quebecker? Wasn't Quebec benefiting handsomely from its membership in Confederation? Quebec received more than its per capita share of transfer grants and of federal government contracts. Ottawa's bureaucracy, once virtually closed to French speakers, especially at senior levels, came to reflect the linguistic balance in the nation. Sovereignists argued that the poverty that federal programs were trying to compensate was itself the product of a long history of colonialism. Only by seizing their destiny in their own hands could the

*Claude Ryan and René Lévesque.*
National Archives of Canada/PA117480

Québécois become a prosperous, entrepreneurial people, no longer dependent on outsiders who, while handing them money, were trying to assimilate them.

One such attempt to seize their destiny came in 1980, with the PQ's first referendum on sovereignty-association. About 60 percent of Quebeckers —led by the province's anglophones and allophones—voted "*non*" to a question that asked for authorization for the Quebec government to negotiate political sovereignty with economic association. The outcome did not put an end to the question of Quebec's status in Confederation: even federalists in Quebec did not defend the status quo of federal–provincial relations. Claude Ryan, leader of the Quebec Liberal Party and head of the "*non*" campaign, advocated a renewed federalism that would give Quebec control over social programs and most economic policies, leaving the federal government in charge of foreign affairs, defence, and monetary policy. This was a far cry from Trudeau's advocacy of federal control in any area involving the national interest.

A 1979 federal task force on national unity, chaired by former Trudeau cabinet minister Jean-Luc Pépin and former Ontario premier John Robarts, had also advocated a "soft" federalism that would give more powers to all provinces, not just Quebec. Trudeau rejected such a decentralized vision of Confederation. From his point of view, Ottawa already housed a weak central government, and the provincial politicians who played on alienation from Ottawa were demagogues after more personal power.

*Pierre Trudeau and Queen Elizabeth II completing the patriation of Canada's constitution.*

Robert Cooper/National Archives of Canada/PA141503

## PATRIATING THE CONSTITUTION

Once the referendum was over, Trudeau announced that the federal government was tired of endless constitutional consultations with the provinces and of Quebec's inevitable vetoes of attempts to patriate the constitution. With or without provincial approval, Ottawa planned to ask the British government to place the constitution in Canadian hands. The patriated constitution would include a Charter of Rights and Freedoms and a new amending formula. If the government of either Ontario or Quebec or a majority of western and Atlantic provinces objected to an amendment, Ottawa could call a referendum where voters could effectively veto their provincial governments.

Most provinces resisted Trudeau's initiative, seeing it as a bid to weaken provincial rights. Only Ontario and New Brunswick, which had few grievances with Ottawa at the time, supported the plan. René Lévesque had the support of seven other premiers in opposing Trudeau. The eight provinces agreed to stand together in challenging the procedure in the courts. The Supreme Court ruled in September 1981 that "substantial consent," but not unanimity, of the provinces was needed for patriation. With the British prime minister, Margaret Thatcher, unwavering in her declaration that Britain would accept a request by the federal government for patriation, the premiers began to fear that constitutional reform would be achieved without the provinces winning any concessions. On 5 November 1981, nine premiers came to terms with Trudeau, leaving Lévesque to claim betrayal. The premiers of the three westernmost provinces and Newfoundland had been won over by Trudeau's agreement to strengthen provincial control over resources. In Quebec, which had lost its veto over constitutional change, Lévesque argued that he had been betrayed by the anglophone premiers and that their actions demonstrated that Quebec would never receive justice in the federal system. In fact, he had been outmanoeuvred by fellow Québécois Pierre Trudeau, whose vision of the future of Quebec in Canada stood in such contrast to his own.

## THE CHARTER OF RIGHTS AND FREEDOMS

The premiers' deal with Trudeau created the Constitution Act, 1982, which consisted of the renamed British North America Act, an amending formula, and the Charter of Rights and Freedoms. The amending formula allowed the federal government to change the constitution with the approval of the federal Parliament plus two-thirds of the provinces representing a combined population of at least 50 percent of all Canadians. Unanimous consent of all provinces as well as both houses of Parliament would continue to be required for amendments affecting representation in the House of Commons, Senate, and Supreme Court and for changes affecting the use of the French and English languages. Furthermore, a province that believed that its legislative or proprietary rights were compromised by an amendment could declare that amendment null and void within its boundaries. A province would also have the right to opt out with full financial compensation from a program established by amendment that affected educational or cultural matters. As a concession to Atlantic Canada as well as to Saskatchewan and Manitoba, section 36 of the constitution committed Canadian governments to the principle of equalization to "ensure that provincial governments have sufficient

revenue to provide reasonably comparable levels of public services at reasonably comparable levels of taxation."

The Charter guaranteed Canadians freedom of speech, association, conscience, and religion and prohibited discrimination on the basis of colour, sex, or creed. Enshrined were voting rights, rights to legal counsel, and protection against arbitrary arrest. While the courts could be used to protect various rights that governments had at times infringed in the past, there were several restrictions on Canadians' constitutional freedoms. Legislatures could place "reasonable limits" on citizens' enjoyment of their rights. Mobility rights were limited by giving provinces experiencing high unemployment the right to give existing residents preferential treatment in hiring. Provinces could also override constitutional rights by specifically exempting pieces of legislation from the Charter's reach. This clause, dubbed the "notwithstanding clause" because it allowed legislatures to assert that a law would apply notwithstanding Charter provisions, was used by Quebec to exempt all of its legislation from the Charter. The Quebec government claimed that its own human rights code protected citizens better than the federal version.

Section 28 declared that Charter rights "are guaranteed equally to male and female persons." This section owed its existence to concerted pressure from women's groups, as the proposed Charter had originally said nothing about gender equality. Effective feminist lobbying also succeeded in exempting section 28 from the override provisions of the Charter. Although equality provisions fell short of the demands of some women's groups, feminists celebrated their success in overcoming government indifference and their own disagreements to secure section 28.

Native lobbies were likewise only partially successful in pressuring for changes to the constitution. Their attempts to win the right to self-determination failed, but the Charter did acknowledge aboriginal concerns by guaranteeing that nothing in the document would affect existing treaty rights or prejudice later land settlements. A constitutional conference on Native rights was to be called within one year of the proclamation of the constitution.

For women and Native peoples, the new constitution would prove a disappointment. Early Charter decisions regarding gender rights suggested that the courts, dominated by men, were blind to the differences in social power between the sexes. In 1989, a study prepared for the Canadian Advisory Council on the Status of Women reported that "women are initiating few cases, and men are using the Charter to strike back at women's hard-won protection and benefits." [3]

Native people were no more successful. Three first ministers' conferences yielded nothing on Native attempts to win an amendment guaranteeing self-government. Seven provinces, including either Ontario or Quebec, had to be on side, and Quebec refused to consider constitutional amendments on the grounds that it had not signed the new constitution and therefore did not recognize its legitimacy. At the third conference in 1987, British Columbia, Alberta, and Saskatchewan, all with Conservative or Social Credit governments, claimed that Native demands were imprecise. They feared that their provinces' rights to control resources would be compromised by a self-government amendment. In practice, the focus of constitutional talks after 1982 was far more on the rights of provinces, especially Quebec, than it was on social justice issues.

## The Meech Lake Accord

In the 1984 federal election, Brian Mulroney had swept Quebec and was determined to cement his party's new-found respect in the province. Robert Bourassa, returned to power as Quebec premier the following year, was equally determined to win constitutional concessions that might blunt the sovereignist thrust for another generation. He presented five demands that had to be fulfilled before Quebec would sign the constitution. The first was a clause recognizing Quebec as a distinct society. The second was a Quebec veto for constitutional amendments. The remaining three would give all provinces a greater role in immigration, would allow them to remain outside any new cost-sharing programs without financial penalty, and would

have the federal government choose Supreme Court judges from lists of nominees provided by the premiers. A first ministers' conference held at Meech Lake, near Ottawa, in April 1987 tentatively approved a package that met Quebec's demands and incorporated concerns expressed by other provinces. To win support from premiers who balked at the idea of Quebec having a veto over constitutional change, Mulroney granted all provinces a veto. The Meech Lake Accord would be the first test of whether an amendment could muster the consent of the federal Parliament and all provincial legislatures. The first ministers had given themselves a three-year deadline to achieve this consent, and, to close off public debate, Mulroney announced that not one word of the document could be changed.

To Mulroney's chagrin there was a great deal of opposition to the deal. Most sovereignists and some federalists in Quebec rejected the agreement, although polls showed that the majority of Quebeckers wanted the accord to be passed. The Parti québécois leaders claimed that the "distinct society" clause was window dressing because it recognized no special powers for Quebec. Pierre Trudeau denounced the "distinct society" clause as well. He pointed out that if the clause was largely symbolic, as Mulroney sometimes suggested, it could only disappoint Quebec nationalists, who would continue making constitutional demands for more provincial powers. If, on the other hand, court decisions allowed Quebec to legislate in areas reserved for the federal government in order to preserve a distinct society, Mulroney's assurances would be worthless. How the courts would interpret the distinct society clause was hypothetical, but Meech opponents, both federalist and sovereignist, rejected a clause that appeared to abandon such an important question to the judiciary.

Apart from the distinct society clause, the two aspects of the accord that drew the most fire were cost-sharing provisions and the unanimity required for constitutional amendments. Supporters of particular amendments believed that the unanimity clause would permanently dash hopes of reform. For the aboriginal peoples, who had been one province short of a crucial amendment just months before Meech Lake was announced, the unanimity clause was a particularly bitter pill. Aboriginal self-government appeared to have been sacrificed on the altar of provincial rights. Senate reformers in Western and Atlantic Canada also believed that the accord doomed their hopes, although even the

*Clyde Wells and Brian Mulroney.*
Ron Poling/Canapress

1982 constitution had required unanimity for changes to the Senate.

Outside Quebec, a large majority of Canadians opposed the accord. Women's groups, trade unions, and anti-poverty groups were not pleased with the provision that allowed provinces to exempt themselves from new federal shared-cost programs to set up their own programs. Groups working for new national policies, particularly in the childcare area, suspected that provincial opposition would block the establishment of new programs. After all, medicare had been legislated with

popular support but with limited enthusiasm from provincial governments. Similar opposition to a national childcare program would result in federal abandonment of the notion or a hodgepodge of "opt-out" programs with federal money but no national standards.

National women's groups demanded that women be included in a clause that exempted aboriginal people and multicultural groups from the application of the distinct society clause. Quebec women's groups were divided on the issue. Many feminist nationalists decried the suggestion that a Quebec government might use the distinct society clause to limit women's abortion rights or to bar women from certain occupations. They claimed that anglophone women who feared that Quebec might revert to Catholic conservatism and roll back women's victories were out of touch with modern Quebec, which had the most progressive women's legislation in Canada.

Although northerners had no direct voice in the constitutional amendment process, most were relieved at the growing opposition to the accord. Residents of the Yukon and the Northwest Territories could hardly support an agreement that would virtually preclude them from becoming provinces. Without provincehood, they would have no right to nominate senators or Supreme Court judges and they would have no say at constitutional conferences or regarding constitutional amendments.

Much of the Meech Lake debate might have become academic had three elections between 1987 and 1989 not changed the provincial arithmetic. Newly elected Liberals Frank McKenna in New Brunswick and Clyde Wells in Newfoundland had reservations about the accord. Under Wells, the Newfoundland legislature rescinded its ratification that had been secured under Brian Peckford. A minority Conservative government, led by Gary Filmon, was elected in Manitoba in 1988. Both opposition parties in the province opposed Meech, with the NDP under a new leader reversing the position it had taken when in power. Filmon's party was divided on the issue, uniting against the accord only after Robert Bourassa used the notwithstanding clause to nullify a Supreme Court decision regarding Bill 101, which had prohibited the use of languages other than French on store signs. Filmon appeared to take up the cause of the anglophone minority on the language issue, but Quebec politicians pointed out that he had been part of the Conservative caucus that had bitterly and successfully opposed NDP attempts in the early eighties to legislate greater bilingualism in Manitoba.

At first, the Mulroney government stuck to its hard line that not a word of the accord could be changed. Later, just weeks before the ratification deadline, Mulroney reassembled the premiers and used the threat of Quebec separation to try to force the dissenters to accept the accord with an accompanying statement that granted a degree of Senate reform and acknowledged the views of several constitutional lawyers regarding the scope of the distinct society clause. Frank McKenna, who had come to believe that ordinary Quebeckers would misunderstand Meech's rejection, asked his legislature to ratify the accord with its accompanying statement. In Manitoba, the leaders of the three parties, who had worked together to produce a set of changes to the accord that would preserve a strong federal government and protect the rights of women, aboriginals, and northerners, accepted the agreement under pressure.

Clyde Wells, who opposed Meech because it weakened the federal government and failed to recognize the concept of the equality of the provinces, was displeased with Mulroney's tactics and Bourassa's unwillingness to budge. He wanted Newfoundlanders to decide in a referendum whether the legislature should ratify the accord. When Quebec refused to extend the deadline, Wells resolved instead to have a free vote on the revised accord in the Newfoundland legislature.

Meanwhile, Elijah Harper, the lone Native member in the Manitoba legislature and a former minister in the provincial cabinet under the NDP, used procedural methods to prevent the accord's passage in Manitoba before the deadline. The party leaders could have changed the procedures to force a vote on time, as Ottawa pressured them to do, but they decided to let the agreement lapse. Manitobans had generally disapproved of the

province's capitulation at the constitutional conference, and Harper's last stand for Native peoples seemed a fitting way to let the accord die. When it became clear that Manitoba could not pass the accord in time, Clyde Wells called off the Newfoundland vote. Meech Lake was dead, killed

*Elijah Harper.*
Office of Elijah Harper

off by the misgivings of several have-not provinces and the aboriginal peoples.

Bourassa was furious, arguing that the accord had been designed to meet Quebec's demands, and not to address the discontent of all the other provinces. Quebec francophones also reacted angrily to the defeat of the accord: for several months, polls suggested that a majority of Québécois were prepared to vote in favour of sovereignty. In the fall of 1990, Bourassa established a commission on the future of Quebec. Headed by two businessmen, federalist Michel Bélanger and sovereignist Jean Campeau, it filed a majority report in 1991 that favoured Quebec remaining in Confederation only if Ottawa recognized its sovereignty in most jurisdictions. By then, some nationalist MPs from Quebec, mainly Conservatives, had formed the Bloc québécois, a federal party supporting an independent Quebec and attempting to defend Quebec rights in Ottawa until such time as independence was achieved. The party was headed by Lucien Bouchard, a renegade Conservative cabinet minister. This was the first time since Confederation that a Quebec party dedicated to removing the province from Confederation had a presence in Ottawa.

Although Bourassa continued to support federalism, his party adopted a tough constitutional policy demanding that Quebec have absolute jurisdiction in many areas of economic and social policy where the federal government had total or shared power. To appease sovereignists and put pressure on the rest of the country, the Quebec National Assembly passed legislation calling for a referendum on either sovereignty or an offer of constitutional renewal from the rest of Canada.

## THE CHARLOTTETOWN ACCORD

As the clock ticked toward Bourassa's referendum deadline, Brian Mulroney convened a marathon session of the premiers and some Native leaders, producing the Charlottetown Accord of 28 August 1992. The accord was a complex document that included concessions to each of the players in the room. Quebec was to receive much of what it had been promised during the Meech Lake discussions, but it did not gain important new powers. The federal government agreed to turn over certain areas, such as housing and forestry, to the provinces, but this fell far short of Quebec's demands.

To achieve agreement on special status for Quebec, Bourassa had to make a concession that was galling to most Quebec nationalists: equal provincial representation in the Senate. Quebec nationalists maintained that Canada was a partnership between two founding nations. They did not accept the implicit thrust of the proposed Senate reform, that Canada was a federation of ten equal provinces. Nonetheless, the so-called triple-E Senate—equal, elected, effective—had become the price of support from Alberta and Newfoundland, and Bourassa agreed to accept it after its proponents agreed to whittle down its powers. The other provinces agreed to guarantee Quebec that its representation in the House of Commons would not fall below 25 percent, its approximate percentage of the population of the country in 1992.

The premiers recognized Native rights to self-government, but the perimeters were to be determined in subsequent negotiations. A social charter, the brainchild of Ontario's NDP government, committed governments to maintain existing social programs but made this commitment "non-justiciable": no one could take a government to court for failing to live up to the social commitments in the constitution.

Several provinces, including Quebec, agreed to test support for the constitutional proposals in binding referenda. The Mulroney government, despite its opposition to popular consultation on constitutional changes, therefore decided to hold a national referendum on the Charlottetown Accord. It was only the third national referendum in Canadian history and the results of the first two—on prohibition in 1898 and conscription in 1942—had not been binding.

Initially, a constitution-weary public led pollsters to believe that the Charlottetown Accord would receive a majority in all provinces. Soon, that support began to unravel. The language of the accord, often left deliberately vague, led to rival interpretations of the consequences of various sections. So, while the National Action Committee on the Status of Women saw no value in a "non-justiciable" social charter, Preston Manning, leader of the Reform Party, worried that the charter would discourage governments from cutting social spending. Manning charged that the agreement went too far in conceding group, as opposed to individual, rights; NAC countered that it ignored the rights of women and aboriginal women in particular. If NAC and Reform made strange political bedfellows on the "No" side of the accord, the Canadian

*Cartoonist's view of Brian Mulroney turning his attention from the constitution to the economy.*

*Globe and Mail*, Toronto

Labour Congress and the Canadian Chamber of Commerce were a dubious pairing in the "Yes" camp. What generally united supporters was the belief that the accord represented the best possible compromise in a country of endless divisions. They argued that the constitutional obsession had to end so that governments could concentrate on the country's economic problems.

Ultimately, the "Yes" forces could not withstand the many-pronged "No" campaign. Some Canadians felt left out of the constitutional process; many more did not like certain features of the accord and resented being told that they had to accept the deal as a package. Mulroney alienated others when he opened the referendum campaign in Quebec with a speech in which he threatened that rejection would be the beginning of the end of Canada. Such scaremongering backfired. Weary of continued constitutional impasse, disillusioned by political dishonesty, incompetence, and scandal, and uneasy because of the long recession that

showed no sign of lifting, many Canadians simply wanted to send their politicians a message. On 26 October 1992, three have-not provinces—Newfoundland, Prince Edward Island, and New Brunswick—supported the accord in the hope that constitutional bickering could be put to an end. Ontario voters were split virtually down the middle. In the remaining six provinces, the accord suffered a clear defeat.

Popular disillusionment with the constitutional process and politics in general was directed primarily at Prime Minister Mulroney. When he announced early in 1993 his intention to resign as prime minister, there was widespread rejoicing. Voters virtually obliterated his party in the federal election that year, with only two Conservatives elected across the country, and the new party leader, Kim Campbell, Canada's first woman prime minister, soundly defeated in her own Vancouver riding. The Liberal Party under Jean Chrétien returned to power with a comfortable majority.

## QUEBEC AFTER THE DEFEAT OF THE CHARLOTTETOWN ACCORD

The Bloc québécois, after a fiery campaign by leader Lucien Bouchard, won 49 percent of the Quebec vote in the federal election, enough to give the party fifty-four of Quebec's seventy-five seats and to make it the official opposition in Parliament. The Bloc's promises to defend Quebec interests appealed to many francophones not prepared to support Quebec leaving Confederation, but it was clear that the desire for independence and the exasperation with the rest of the country's apparent inflexibility regarding Quebec were growing.

In the provincial election in 1994, the Parti québécois, led by Jacques Parizeau, won an impressive majority of seats. The PQ enjoyed much greater support among francophones than did the Liberals under their new leader Daniel Johnson. Johnson's political pedigree was impressive—he was the son of former Union nationale premier Daniel Johnson and the brother of former Parti québécois premier Pierre Marc Johnson—but he was a less than dynamic leader. Nonetheless, the Liberals' overwhelming support from anglophones and allophones, as well as support from francophones on the Island of Montreal, meant that they virtually tied the PQ in the popular vote. About 10 percent of the francophone vote went to a new party, the Action démocratique du Québec, formed mainly by breakaway Liberals and led by the youthful former president of the Liberal youth wing, Mario Dumont. It was generally unclear to campaign observers whether Dumont was a sovereignist or a supporter of "special status" for Quebec within Confederation. Dumont's supporters, as well as PQ supporters who hesitated before the party's sovereignty option, were called "soft nationalists" to distinguish them from the hard-liners, such as Parizeau, who wanted Quebec to become an independent nation-state first and worry about its relations with Canada afterwards.

During the 1994 election, Parizeau promised a referendum on sovereignty during the PQ's mandate. There was a great deal of debate among sovereignist leaders about what the referendum question should be. In the end, the question put before Quebec voters was: "Do you agree that Quebec should become sovereign, after having made a formal offer to Canada for a new economic and political partnership, within the scope of the bill respecting the future of Quebec and of the agreement signed on June 12, 1995?" The agreement to which the question made reference was between Parizeau, Bouchard, and Dumont regarding the "formal offer" that would be put to Canada. The leaders studiously avoided the issue of what they would do if Canada refused to negotiate or if it negotiated but could not come to terms with the sovereignists. Federalists charged that the question was a trick to get Québécois to think they could have their cake and eat it too. The sovereignists, they charged, were duping people into believing that they had given the government of Quebec a conditional acceptance of sovereignty.

Voters did appear to be confused. Polls suggested that a third of the voters planning to vote "Yes" believed that a sovereign Quebec would continue to have representatives in the Canadian Parliament and that its citizens would keep Canadian citizenship and social benefits. Even more voters accepted the claim of the sovereignist forces that an independent Quebec could continue to use Canadian currency. The "No" side asserted that the sovereignists were telling lies to attract the support of soft nationalists. They pointed out that the government of Canada, contrary to what the sovereignists said, could not negotiate sovereignty-association with Quebec. Canada's remaining nine provinces would not agree that Quebec, which had enjoyed just one-tenth of the constitutional decision-making power allocated to provinces and one-fourth of the representation in the federal parliament, should suddenly become an equal partner to the federal government of Canada. Quebec could leave Confederation but, if it did, it could not continue to enjoy the benefits that came with Canadian citizenship.

In the early stages of the referendum, such arguments seemed to sway a comfortable majority of the people of Quebec, but the campaign momentum took a swing in the other direction when Lucien Bouchard became its unofficial leader. Premier Parizeau, the official leader of the "*oui*" forces, recognizing that his own unpopularity was a barrier to the success of his dream of an independent Quebec, announced that if the pro-sovereignty forces won the vote, Bouchard would be the one to negotiate for Quebec with Canada. Bouchard was popular in Quebec; for some, he became an almost saintly figure when he survived an attack of a rare and usually deadly disease in 1994. Publicly less strident than Parizeau, he seemed better able to convince the Québécois that Canada was bluffing when it claimed that it would not negotiate with Quebec.

Bouchard was also able to take advantage of the mean-spiritedness taking hold of much of the rest of the country to create pessimism about the advantages for Quebec of staying in Canada. The federal government had announced massive cuts in social spending. As most opinion surveys showed, the Québécois were far more social democratic in their values than Canadians as a whole. Bouchard's attempt to portray a Canada that was no longer caring and sharing struck a responsive chord. With the province's unemployment rate seemingly stuck in permanent double digits well above the Canadian average, there was a great desire for change in Quebec.

Although individuals often had difficulty defining exactly what changes they wanted or why the federal system was necessarily an impediment to achieving those changes, there was a sense that the federalists represented the status quo while the sovereignists, particularly Bouchard and Dumont, had a fresh vision. Prime Minister Chrétien's decision not to offer Quebec any changes, constitutional or otherwise, should its citizens vote no, alienated some soft nationalists and made life difficult for Daniel Johnson, the official leader of the "*non*" forces. Only in the last week of the campaign, with polls suggesting the sovereignty forces were taking the lead, did Chrétien actively step into the campaign. On nationwide television, he made an emotional plea to Quebec not to throw away the benefits of Confederation, promising recognition of the province as a distinct society as well as decentralization of power in Canada. Meanwhile, an estimated one hundred thousand Canadians from outside Quebec joined a last-minute rally in Montreal to plead with Quebec not to break up the country.

Referendum night was a nail-biter for both sides. The ultimate voter distribution was 2 362 355 votes for "*non*," 2 308 504 for "*oui*," and 86 473 spoiled ballots: the margin of victory was actually smaller than the number of spoiled ballots. The complete division within Quebec society was obvious.

Premier Parizeau responded gracelessly to defeat, telling supporters, "It's true we have been defeated, but basically by what? By money and the ethnic vote." While the "ethnic" vote was solidly against leaving Canada, about 40 percent of francophones also voted to reject the vague offer represented in the referendum question. Bouchard made equally ill-advised statements during the campaign, but was able to weather the controversy that followed. Within months after the referendum defeat, Parizeau had resigned the premiership, and Bouchard had moved from Ottawa to Quebec City to become the province's premier and the undisputed leader of the sovereignist forces.

Sovereignists continued to scoff at suggestions that Quebec would pay a heavy economic price for separating from Canada, but the close result of the referendum seemed to contribute to decisions by some corporations to end or reduce their dealings in the province. In the month following the referendum, Canadian Pacific "downsized" and moved its headquarters from Montreal to Calgary, while aircraft engine manufacturer Pratt and Whitney announced that it would recruit the lion's share of its engineers to work in its small Toronto operation, bypassing the firm's larger plant in Longueuil. Union representatives claimed that Pratt and Whitney was using the referendum as a pretext to move jobs from Quebec to Ontario. In the age of the global corporation, smaller concerns than the potential break-up of a nation became reasons for transferring jobs and assets. In 1996, while the employment picture in some parts of Canada brightened, Quebec's economic performance remained mediocre.

Language tensions also heightened in the wake of the referendum. Bitter about the narrow defeat, some nationalists raised concerns again about the threat to the French language posed by the extensive use of English in Montreal. Although most of the population opposed any changes to the province's existing language legislation, well-organized sovereignist groups demanded that the province further restrict the use of English.

Quebec's anglophones and allophones were also in a more combative mood. During the Lévesque period, the non-francophones of Quebec had reacted cautiously to language legislation. The leaders of Alliance Quebec argued that anglophones and allophones could best ensure national unity by avoiding all militancy in defence of their rights so as not to alienate federalist-leaning francophones. The majority francophone vote for sovereignty left such a strategy in tatters. New leaders arose who suggested that federalists must demand the right to linguistic pluralism and militantly oppose separatism to ensure that soft nationalists understood that sovereignty would be costly. Advertising executive Howard Galganov used threats of boycotts to persuade stores in downtown Montreal to post bilingual signs inside their premises. A militant movement within the non-francophone community gained considerable support for its demand that should Quebec separate, federalist regions of the province such as the West Island of Montreal, the Hull region, and northern Quebec be allowed to hold a referendum on remaining in Canada. This "partition movement" made clear the prospects for civil war that could accompany the birth of an independent Quebec.

Meanwhile, Premier Bouchard reacted angrily to a campaign in the courts by former sovereignist Guy Bertrand that sought to establish the illegality of any attempt by Quebec to declare independence unilaterally. Bertrand pointed out that constitutional changes required the support of the federal government and of all the provinces. A referendum in one province could not legally become the basis for that province to leave Confederation. Bouchard insisted that the right of the people of Quebec to self-determination was more important than whatever the constitution of Canada might say, particularly since Quebec had never signed the new constitution.

In the aftermath of the referendum, Canada's future seemed less assured than ever. Nor was it only Quebec that seemed restive and unsure about its political future. In every region of the country, economic slowdown produced social and political instability and the search for scapegoats.

## POST-PROSPERITY ONTARIO

Throughout Canada's history and particularly during the period of postwar prosperity, Canadians outside southern Ontario were fairly united in their dislike of Canada's industrial heartland. Its denizens, accused of reaping all the advantages of the national policies, were believed to have been unfairly subsidized by the sufferings of the rest of the country. For average workers and the poor in Ontario, the notion that Bay Street could be conflated with the whole province was always baffling.

After 1975, it became increasingly clear that the economic crisis had engulfed Ontario as well as other parts of the country. Manufacturing jobs disappeared, particularly during the recessions of 1982–85 and 1990–93. The jobless recovery in the manufacturing sector hit the industrial heartland particularly hard. High-paying jobs in such sectors as steel, automobiles and automobile parts, aerospace, and electrical appliances, which had been the cause of envy by much of the rest of the country, dried up considerably.

The succession of Conservative administrations that had governed Ontario from 1943 to 1985 came slowly around to the business view that the state could no longer afford the full range of services that it was providing. When the newly chosen premier, Frank Miller, put forth this message in 1985, the Conservative dynasty came crashing down. The Liberals formed a minority government with NDP support and then won a big majority in 1987. By then, the Ontario economy was booming again and the Liberals, led by David Peterson, stood squarely against the Mulroney government's program of social spending cuts and free trade with the United States. The government eliminated extra-billing by physicians and extended full funding to separate schools up to grade 13. But the Liberal bubble soon burst. A party fund-raising scandal weakened the Liberals, and voters reacted angrily to an election call in 1990, just three years into the government's mandate. They replaced Peterson with the New Democrats headed by Bob Rae. The right-wing message delivered by Conservative leader Mike Harris received the support of about a quarter of the voters.

The New Democrats proved unable to adopt a consistent policy. In their first budget in 1991, they defied the neo-conservative logic that had gripped most governments in Canada, producing a stimulative budget with a $10 billion deficit. The business community and the media condemned this return to Keynesianism, which would have looked perfectly respectable to all political parties in the late forties or the fifties, as socialist irresponsibility. Social organizations were generally supportive of the thrust of the budget, but concern was expressed that the main beneficiaries were professionals such as university professors, teachers, and senior civil servants, despite the additional funds allocated for public housing and public childcare.

Over the next two years, the NDP largely recanted its first budget and cut social spending. After a frenzied campaign by the insurance industry, it also abandoned the popular election promise of public auto insurance, which had been introduced in the three other provinces where CCF or NDP governments were elected. Rae attempted to maintain the general principles of the postwar social compromise, but he alienated much of the union movement when he imposed an across-the-board wage cut of 5 percent on all public sector workers in provincial or municipal institutions. Those whose salaries were under $30 000 were spared, and the government's "social contract" attempted to compensate for wage cuts with job security guarantees and greater worker involvement in implementing programs. Nevertheless, unionists were appalled by a supposedly pro-labour government violating union-negotiated contracts.

One area where the NDP government had considerable success was in bailouts of large private companies that ran into trouble either because of changing economic circumstances, poor management, or international corporate strategies. Spruce Falls Power and Paper, Algoma Steel, de Havilland Aircraft, Mitel Corp., Provincial Papers, St Mary's Paper, Algoma Central Railway, Urban Transportation Development Corp., and Ontario Bus Industries, among others, rebounded with state aid, saving many jobs. Still, unemployment remained high.

In 1995, as Ontario voters went to the polls after five years of sluggish economic performance during which the hapless Bob Rae had the misfortune to govern, they were in a mood to punish. Liberal leader Lyn McLeod, the first woman to lead a major party in Ontario, focused on the need to cut the deficit without raising taxes. The voters, and particularly middle-age, middle-class white males, wanted an even sharper right turn. Mike Harris's Conservatives received 45 percent of the vote, almost double their previous total, running on a campaign of cutting the civil service, slashing social assistance, privatizing government services, and cancelling employment equity programs. Many liberal Ontarians had once thought that right-wing populist revolts were only possible in rural parts of the country. The Harris victory, which included a near sweep of suburban Toronto seats, demonstrated that the appeal of right-wing ideology could not be explained so simply.

In office, the Harris government cut taxes for the middle and upper classes while slashing health, education, and welfare expenditures to pay for the tax cut. The government cut programs to aid battered women, the disabled, and the mentally ill, closed dozens of hospitals throughout the province, and weakened environmental regulation. It initiated extensive reform at the municipal level, attempting to offload welfare expenditure on to the municipalities and initiating plans to create a "megacity" in Metro Toronto. All of these policies provoked vocal resistance. The megacity plan was decisively rejected in local referenda, and on-going "Days of Action" were organized by a coalition of labour and community groups. The Tories dismissed the opposition as "special interest groups" and continued to pursue their neo-conservative agenda.

## THE POST-PROSPERITY WEST

Battles over control of natural resources in the early seventies marked the return of western alienation as a major factor in national politics for the first time since the Second World War. Throughout the 1970s the question of resource rents caused a considerable falling-out in Ottawa's relations with the three most westerly provinces. In 1980, the National Energy Program (NEP) brought matters to a head. Introduced by Trudeau, the main features of the NEP were a low "made-in-Canada" price for oil, larger federal revenue from energy production, and greater Canadian ownership of the energy industry. The energy-producing provinces wanted Canadians to pay international prices for energy, claiming that the made-in-Canada price simply deprived them of revenues and drove away projects to develop the tar sands of northern Alberta. The costs of removing oil from the tar sands could not be justified if the price of oil was kept artificially low. This debate pitted the three most westerly provinces and the oil-producing "wannabes" in the Atlantic provinces—Newfoundland and Nova Scotia—against energy-poor provinces and the federal government, at least while oil prices were high. When prices began a steep decline in 1982, major oil-sands projects in Alberta came unglued. By the time the prices revived in the 1990s, cheaper processes for extraction of oil had become available.

Although the NEP was modified sufficiently to cause a truce between Trudeau and Alberta premier Peter Lougheed in 1981, it would be blamed by many, perhaps most, westerners, for an economic downturn, beginning in 1982, in which many people lost their homes and their savings. A separatist party, the Western Canada Concept (WCC), held huge rallies in Calgary and Edmonton in the wake of the announcement of the NEP and elected a rural MLA in a provincial by-election in 1982.

Trudeau claimed that the NEP was an instrument of nationalism but, if so, it was more central Canadian than pan-Canadian nationalism. Its goal to provide cheap energy meant that energy-producing provinces, along with the multinationals that dominated the sector, had to sacrifice revenue to fuel the industries of Central Canada. There was nothing in the policy that would help western provinces to use energy revenues to foster secondary industry. Ultimately the policy was a costly one for all Canadians: the grants and tax incentives offered to Canadianize the industry proved expensive for the public purse, particularly at a time when deficits were beginning to soar. Unlike transfer payments to individuals, these incentives had no obvious stimulative impact on the economy.

The NEP was not the only source of western alienation. Grain farmers were angry at the decision of the Trudeau government in the early eighties to phase out the historic Crow rates, which had kept the cost of grain shipment competitive with American farmers' transportation costs. Another common complaint in the region was that the lion's share of federal contracts were awarded to Quebec. Western outrage greeted the announcement that Montreal's Bombardier had received a large contract for maintenance of Canada's CF-18 military aircraft despite the fact that Winnipeg's Bristol Aerospace had submitted a lower and technically superior bid.

Such events joined to a resurgence of right-wing sentiments helped to produce the Reform Party in 1987. Led by Preston Manning, son of Alberta's long-time Social Credit premier Ernest Manning, the Reformers declared that the West did not want out of Confederation: rather it wanted in, and it wished to reconstruct that Confederation to better reflect the regions. While they were anti-separatist, Reformers shared the WCC's right-wing agenda. They wanted the federal deficit slashed, even if it meant sacrificing subsidy programs to farmers and abandoning universality in social programs, and they wanted Canadian immigration policy to favour Europeans as it had before 1962. Manning's iron grip over the party ensured that members of Canada's extreme right were excluded from membership and that the original racist immigration plank was partially modified.

By the 1993 federal election, the Reformers were wooing Ontario voters, appearing more like a Canadian version of the Republican Party in the

United States than a regional protest party. They appealed to many traditional Conservative voters who believed that the Mulroney Tories had been too awash in patronage and shady dealings. Their support in Saskatchewan and Manitoba—both recipients of more in federal grants and transfers than Quebec, on a per capita basis—was significant but not overwhelming. The party's opposition to most programs of wealth redistribution had more appeal for rich provinces. While they carried 20 percent of the vote in Ontario, where they won one seat, it was in Alberta and British Columbia that the Reformers swept all before them, becoming, for the moment, the major federal party in the two wealthy western provinces. The "New Canada" that Preston Manning and his colleagues promoted from the floor of Parliament was one that was largely under the control of the provinces, with the federal government bowing out of social programs such as medicare.

## PROVINCIAL POLITICS

### BRITISH COLUMBIA

Provincial politics in Western Canada underwent considerable change after 1975. The divide between right and left remained fairly rigid in British Columbia before the 1990s. The New Democrats took between 39 and 46 percent of the vote in provincial elections, but repeatedly lost to Social Credit in what was essentially a two-party province. The Socreds demonstrated the shift away from the postwar consensus after the 1983 provincial election, when, despite their marginal victory in the popular vote, they implemented a program of massive cuts in education and social spending, and privatization of a large variety of government services. Civil servants, and state employees such as teachers, nurses, and social workers, joined with client groups to form Operation Solidarity. For a week they shut down most state operations in the province to protest the cuts. Leaders of the private sector unions shunned a request to make the shut-

down a general strike, and in the end Solidarity had to be content with fairly minimal concessions on the part of Bill Bennett's government.

Social Credit became a spent force after Bennett's successor, William Vander Zalm, a charismatic millionaire, resigned over allegations of conflict of interest in his sale of the family firm. Vander Zalm was replaced by Rita Johnson, Canada's first woman premier. In the election that followed, the New Democrats won a large majority without increasing their traditional vote. Much of the Social Credit vote had gone to the Liberals, who formed the official opposition. Mike Harcourt, the New Democrat premier, resigned in late 1995 after a flurry of criticism about his feeble attempts to deal with a party fund-raising scandal. The Harcourt government had also had a difficult time trying to balance the demands of environmentalists and unionized forest workers, both traditional NDP supporters in the province. Clear-cutting at Clayoquot Sound on Vancouver Island became a defining issue for the organized environmental movement not only in British Columbia but across the country. Hundreds of protesters, including NDP MP Svend Robinson, were arrested as they tried to prevent loggers from clear-cutting. Forestry workers protested that the environmentalists were unconcerned about the economic devastation that would affect families and communities if the logging stopped with nothing to replace it.

The triumph of the right wing in the Liberal Party gave Harcourt's replacement, Glen Clark, a chance to revive a government battered by scandal. As voters headed to the polls in May 1996, they were promised a large tax cut by the Liberals. Clark accused the Liberals of having a hidden agenda of cutting health, education, and social services, warning British Columbians that if they rejected the NDP government, they would face the same cuts that other Canadian provinces had experienced. The NDP won a majority of seats, even though the Liberals led in the popular vote. A provincial Reform Party had proved the spoiler for the Liberals, hiving off enough of the right-of-centre vote to allow the NDP to win.

## ALBERTA

In Alberta, the Conservatives remained in office continuously after 1971, but they underwent an ideological sea change as prosperity oozed away in the 1980s and 1990s. The government of Peter Lougheed had been interventionist within the economy and relatively generous in its funding of education, medicare, and social assistance. Lougheed's successor, Don Getty, promised a leaner government and did make some cuts in social programs, but loans and loan guarantees to businesses continued unabated, most of them exploding in the government's face. By the government's own figures, an estimated $1.5 billion was lost as firms went bankrupt without repaying their loans and the government sold their assets for a pittance. A cellular phone company, a magnesium smelter, a meat-packing plant, and a heavy-oil upgrader were the main losers.

This program of "socialism for the rich," as detractors called it, was scaled back with the election of Ralph Klein as premier in 1993. Klein embarked on a program to slash the costs of government, with social programs taking most of the punishment. Nurses, school teachers, welfare recipients, and the elderly suffered the most in a program that attracted national attention. Within the province, the most controversial move was closing down a large number of intensive care units in hospitals and encouraging private medical entrepreneurs to make up for deficiencies in a slimmed-down public health system.

## SASKATCHEWAN AND MANITOBA

In the 1980s, Saskatchewan broke with its socialist traditions, replacing the NDP administration of Allan Blakeney with a free-enterprise Conservative government under Grant Devine. The Tories privatized some Crown corporations and copied Alberta's attempt to lure businesses with subsidies and loans, with much the same dismal results. Floundering in a sea of corruption, the Conservatives lost the 1991 election to the NDP led by Roy Romanow, but much of its populist zeal

was gone. Although the new government used a combination of taxes and cuts to deal with declining revenues, and developed a reputation for prudent fiscal management, it had few ideas about how to diversify the Saskatchewan economy.

Manitoba's political parties were perhaps more sharply divided than Saskatchewan's. Following the NDP government of Ed Schreyer in 1977, Sterling Lyon's Conservatives, unlike other Tory administrations of the prosperity era, were dedicated to cutting programs for the poor, as well as health and education spending. In the 1980s, NDP premier Howard Pawley reversed directions again and, despite the province's relative poverty, ignored the growing neo-conservative campaign of the business classes. Tax increases necessary to maintain public expenditures eventually led to a tax revolt that deposed Pawley's government. The Conservatives under Gary Filmon, initially vague about the direction in which they would take the province, had, by the mid-1990s, clearly joined the neo-conservative camp.

## ATLANTIC CANADA AND THE ECONOMIC CRISIS

Through the era of postwar prosperity, the Atlantic provinces had depended upon federal equalization grants and transfers to offset the poor economic performance of the area. Regional economic development programs had produced few permanent jobs and people continued to leave the region to find work. Federal fisheries management remained ineffective, and there were continuing denunciations of Canada's weak efforts to prevent foreign overfishing within the two-hundred-mile limit that Ottawa claimed to enforce.

The fisheries boom of the 1970s quickly turned into a bust. By the early 1980s, processing companies were in trouble, and two corporate giants, Fishery Products International and National Sea, swallowed up their competitors. With the collapse of the fish stocks in the late 1980s, quotas were cut, fish plants shut down, and many fishing communities faced extinction. People in Canso, Nova Scotia, protested loudly when their fish plant was closed in 1990. Although they won a reprieve, they remained hostages to a corporation whose survival depended on profits, not people, and whose decisions were determined by forces far removed from the Canso town limits.

In July 1992, the federal government announced that there would be a two-year moratorium on northern cod fishing. This meant unemployment for nineteen thousand Newfoundland fishers and plant workers. The future of dozens of communities on Newfoundland's east coast became doubtful. Some compensation was offered the workers, and although the levels of compensation were increased after threats by fishers to ignore the moratorium, a bleak future seemed to await families dependent on the fishery. Even before the moratorium expired, it was clear that the Atlantic cod fishery was over for at least a generation. The industry that had first brought Europeans to Canada's shores was providing testimony to the limited extent to which the world's people were husbanding the earth's scarce resources.

In the late 1970s, the large Hibernia oil field was discovered off Newfoundland. Brian Peckford, Newfoundland's Conservative premier, insisted that the province have equal control with Ottawa over offshore developments. He argued that the province was more sensitive than Ottawa to the need to balance oil developments with protection of the fishery and to use the new economic activity to foster spinoffs throughout the provincial economy. Trudeau disagreed, and the Supreme Court in 1984 upheld his view that the federal government need not share control over oil development with St John's. The election of the Mulroney Conservatives resulted in a victory for Peckford, as Ottawa conceded Newfoundland's claims for co-management of offshore oil developments. But with oil prices down, Hibernia proved not to be the cash cow initially envisaged.

Expectations in Newfoundland and Nova Scotia that they might follow Alberta's lead to become energy-rich provinces had largely evaporated by the early nineties. Instead, the four Atlantic provinces joined the rest of the country in trying to attract manufacturing and service companies with offers of low wages and few government regulations. New Brunswick, with advertisements inviting wealthy investors to get in contact with the premier personally, was particularly aggressive in this respect. Nonetheless, the region remained an area of high unemployment, with average incomes well below the rest of the country.

Governments in Atlantic Canada resorted to desperate measures to accommodate corporate interests in the region. In the late 1970s, Michelin, the French-owned tire manufacturer and the largest manufacturing concern in Nova Scotia, threatened to quit the province if one of its three sites was unionized. The province quickly passed legislation requiring that a majority of the workers from all three sites had to vote for the union before it could be legally recognized. Since two plants were in rural areas, where people tended to be suspicious of unions, the bill effectively killed chances for the union to gain a toehold. The government that was so willing to accommodate corporate concerns seemed deaf to complaints from miners at the Westray coal mine in Pictou County about rock slides, cave-ins, and dangerous levels of methane gas. When an explosion destroyed the mine in 1993, eight months into its operation, twenty-six men were left dead below the earth.

Discontent with the sluggish economy of the region led to a degree of political instability. In New Brunswick, voters unhappy with flamboyant Conservative premier Richard Hatfield gave every seat in the province to Frank McKenna's Liberals in 1987. In the next provincial election, although the Liberals held on to most of the seats, the Confederation of Regions (COR), a party that attacked official bilingualism in a province where 38 percent of residents had French as their first language, managed to become the official opposition. Internal bickering soon made COR an ineffective component of the province's political spectrum.

By the early 1990s, the Liberal Party was also the beneficiary of voter disenchantment in the other three Atlantic provinces, but the differences between the two major parties remained, for the most part, differences of personalities. Both parties, having embraced the welfare state in the postwar era, came to proclaim the need for more individual entrepreneurship and for cuts to state expenditures in an effort to attract global corporations with the promise of low taxes. Although the region's need for federal subsidies to provide a minimal standard of health, education, and social assistance was as great as ever, the willingness of Ottawa to attempt to redistribute wealth was ebbing.

## FEDERAL CUTBACKS

The combination of slow economic growth, increased taxes on ordinary income earners, and the return to the prewar philosophy of business–government relations all worked together to move Canadians away from the social values that had marked the era of prosperity. Increasingly, poverty was seen not as a product of impersonal forces in the competitive marketplace but as the result of shiftlessness. "Welfare bums" who preferred government handouts to hard work, including new immigrants, were blamed for higher taxes and the appearance—though statistics demonstrated it was not a reality—of increasing crime and violence. Such views overlooked the composition of the poor. Single mothers of young children, many of whom lacked job training and most of whom lacked access to affordable quality day care, had become the largest group of poor householders. Also, many of the poor were not social assistance recipients; rather they were the "working poor," who could barely support themselves, let alone their families, on minimum wages that rose less quickly than inflation. Among the social welfare recipients, an increasing proportion were part-time and even full-time minimum-wage workers.

The inadequacy of minimum wages and the Canada Assistance Plan meant that many families ran out of money before their next paycheque was due. Children whose parents were unable to afford even basic groceries regularly went hungry the last week of the month before the welfare cheque arrived. Such families were forced to rely on private initiatives, such as food banks, to survive. Food banks started modestly in the early 1980s in some urban centres. By 1992, 150 000 people were served each month by the Daily Bread Food Bank

in Toronto alone, and an estimated two million Canadians relied on food banks at some point that year.

Public funds had been important throughout the postwar period in placing a floor on poverty and guaranteeing citizens of all social classes improved access to quality education and health services, but in the post-prosperity era, governments became less willing to provide these funds. The Mulroney government, seeking to cut the deficit while also reducing corporate taxes and taxes on wealthy individuals, cut transfer payments to the provinces. Attempts by the federal government to limit growth in grants to the provinces had begun under Trudeau in 1977 when block funding replaced equal federal–provincial sharing of medicare and postsecondary education costs. The new arrangement was called "established programs financing" and gave the provinces a percentage of federal income and corporate taxes plus a cash grant. While cash grants initially were increased by the annual rate of inflation, the Trudeau government set limits to increases in federal spending on postsecondary education for 1982 and 1983.

In 1986, the Mulroney government announced that federal cash grants for medicare and postsecondary education would be reduced by 2 percent annually, and in 1990 it introduced a bill to speed up withdrawal from established programs financing so that by 2004 the federal government's cash transfer for medical and educational spending, which was $9 billion in the 1989–90 fiscal year, would be zero. Campaigning in 1993, the Liberals promised to stop the cuts to the provinces, but once they were in office, they announced they would actually speed up the Conservative timetable for getting rid of established programs financing. The Liberals also cancelled one of the pillars of the Pearson social reforms: the Canada Assistance Plan. Under the plan, there had been some federal control over provinces to ensure that legitimate social welfare recipients were not denied aid. By the 1990s, it was clear that federal governments were unwilling to take a stand against provincial governments that discriminated against certain groups of poor people.

## DEFICITS, GENDER, AND RACE

The public discussion of cutbacks in the welfare state, much like the public discussion of the introduction of social programs, tended to make gender and race invisible. The neo-conservative focus on the deficit made cutbacks appear to be an almost technical matter and across-the-board cuts were presented as fair to the entire population. Yet a study by political science professors at the University of Alberta demonstrated that the cutbacks affected women more than men, as had been the case in British Columbia's cutbacks in the eighties. Women were more likely to be in the jobs gutted or privatized by the government, and they were more likely to be recipients of social assistance. Such a suggestion met an angry response from Conservative MLAs, some of whom even suggested the researchers should be disciplined for coming to such conclusions, but the fact remained that different groups within the population were affected differently by the downgrading of social programs.

The politicians who preached the gospel of a smaller state called for "families" to play a larger role in caring for the sick, the elderly, and the disabled, rather than depending on the state to hire people to do this work. The "family" should play a larger role, they argued, in helping out local schools so that the number of teachers and teachers' aides could be reduced. Similarly "families," not publicly subsidized caregivers, should look after young children. In all cases, "families" was simply a euphemism for "women," and what was being sought was no less than a gradual turning back of the clock. Overall, the neo-conservative vision involved the return to society's dependence on the unwaged caring work of women in the home to look after the young, the old, and the ill.

Women's continued economic dependence on men and their continued responsibility for the welfare of children meant that women figured disproportionately in the ranks of the poor. Cuts in payments to the elderly tended to hurt women more than men because most women had smaller savings and pensions, given their more limited participation in the labour force. Social assistance cuts struck hardest at single mothers and their children. Women of colour, including Native women, were over-represented in the ranks of those on social assistance as well as in the least-skilled public-sector jobs, which were the first to suffer cuts.

## THE TRADE UNION MOVEMENT

Canada's trade union movement was under attack in the age of neo-conservatism, but it fared much better from 1975 to 1995 than its American counterpart. In the United States, southern and western states passed "right to work" legislation that banned the closed shop. As northern firms moved south to take advantage of cheap labour and poor environmental standards, workers in the northeast often abandoned their unions to preserve their jobs, albeit at a high cost in wages and working conditions. The central government, for both constitutional and ideological reasons, did nothing to stop a trend towards rolling back workers' gains. By the mid-1990s, only about 15 percent of American workers were unionized, about half the rate twenty years earlier.

In Canada, by contrast, more than one in three workers was unionized in 1995. Nevertheless, in the era of free trade, Canadians were not immune to trends south of the border. As many Canadians were learning in the age of globalization, local governments had little ability to protect citizens against the often take-it-or-leave-it demands of mobile multinational corporations. In Quebec, governments often neglected to enforce the law against replacement workers, which had been enacted by Lévesque in 1977. Ontario's NDP government passed similar legislation, but it was repealed by Mike Harris in 1995. Both the PQ and the NDP, supposedly friends of organized labour, had at one time or another imposed wage rollbacks on public employees. Things were worse for organized labour in provinces where the social democratic parties were never in power. Alberta, though a rich province, boasted of its American level of unionization to companies looking for a low-wage,

## TRADE UNIONS AND THE CANADIAN—AMERICAN BORDER

Until the 1970s, the Canadian trade union movement was dominated by "international" unions, that is, unions that were headquartered in the United States and had Canadian branches. In some unions, such as the United Steelworkers of America, the Canadian branches had considerable autonomy from American headquarters, while in others, such as the construction trades, locals enjoyed little independence. Beginning in the mid-1970s, "breakaways"—Canadian locals separating from the internationals to form national unions—became common. Those that remained in internationals often found that their grievances were subordinated by the American union leadership to other goals. In the case of the International Ladies' Garment Workers' Union, the New York leadership's desire to appease American employers resulted in suppression of a strike by Montreal workers in 1983. The workers, mainly immigrant women, were protesting the increasing transfer of their jobs to homeworkers, who were outside the union and were paid piece-rates that often made it impossible to earn the equivalent of the legislated minimum wage.

The consequence of having a conservative American-controlled union representing workers was brought home to Fatima Rocchia, an employee of Sample Incorporated in Montreal. She was fired six times between October 1980 and January 1981 for taking too many bathroom breaks. At Sample, an operator was forbidden to leave her machine "even to take a drink, even when it is 108˚ in the shop." No exceptions were made, even for pregnant women. Rocchia's union upheld this rule and gave her little support as she filed grievances against her firings. Rocchia maintained that both the company and the union were violating the collective contract, and she was elected shop chair. While she was able to stop the manager from yelling at workers, arbitrarily speeding them up, and docking their pay when they forgot to punch in, Rocchia and her fellow workers knew the limits. As she observed, "The women have the feeling now that they have some power ... but they also know that I don't have the backing of our union." [4]

no-union environment in which to establish.

The trend towards a greater feminization of the labour movement, apparent since the sixties, continued after 1975, though mainly in the public sector. The huge retail and service sectors proved determined to resist attempts by their largely female workforce to organize. Eaton's workers in Ontario and Manitoba, who unionized in the early eighties, found that their employer did not accept their democratic decision to deal collectively with management. When Manitoba's Labour Relations Board imposed a first contract on a recalcitrant Eaton's in Brandon, the store responded by firing half of its workers and demanding concessions from the union for the workers who remained. By the mid-nineties, Eaton's was again virtually union-free.

## CANADA IN THE WORLD

Pierre Trudeau continued throughout his tenure as prime minister to make cautious steps towards detaching Canada from its Cold War subservience to the United States. He denounced the American invasion of Grenada in 1983 and called for international efforts to improve the global imbalance in wealth between the North and South. The Americans responded coolly to such efforts.

By contrast, under Mulroney, Canada and the United States moved even closer on foreign policy issues. As the Cold War thawed in the late 1980s, neither country seemed to have a clear vision of what diplomatic issues were likely to preoccupy the "new world order." Iraq's invasion of Kuwait, an American ally, in August 1990 marked the first major post–Cold War incident. Canada supported a tough United Nations embargo against Iraq and appeared ready to endorse American plans for an invasion of Iraq should it refuse to withdraw from Kuwait. Iraq proved intransigent, and the United States led massive strikes against the country. The Gulf War was enormously popular in the United

States, but less so in Canada, particularly in Quebec where a majority opposed Canadian participation. Nonetheless, Mulroney lent his full support to President George Bush, extending him a hero's welcome when he visited Ottawa after the war. Mulroney had also refused to criticize the United States for its invasion of Panama in 1989 and seemed incapable of viewing American foreign policy, however bellicose, with anything but uncritical approval.

The morality of Canadian external policies appeared particularly suspect in the area of arms sales, including sales to both Iraq and Iran as the two countries waged a territorial war in the 1980s. Canada sold $1.9 billion in military commodities in 1985, an increase of almost sixfold since 1970. Almost 90 percent of these arms were sold to the Americans. The federal government continued to subsidize defence industries, even though studies suggested that the expenditures would create more jobs in other areas of the economy.

Canada's role in peacekeeping remained the aspect of foreign policy that made Canadians proudest. The nation's long record of service in Cyprus and the Middle East drew praise from many quarters in the world. That record was supplemented by Canada's peacekeeping efforts in the chaotic and dangerous atmosphere of a Yugoslavia that flew apart in the early nineties, leaving a variety of competing ethnic-based groups to vie for territory in a series of bloody civil wars. The image of Canadian peacekeeping was tarnished by racist and murderous behaviour on the part of some of its peacekeepers in Somalia. In any given year, Canada spent far less on peacekeeping than it received in receipts from foreigners for its weapons.

In its public pronouncements, the Chrétien government defended the need for citizens of all countries to have basic human rights such as free speech and the right of assembly, but Ottawa's actions on the trade front belied this rhetoric. In 1994,

Chrétien and nine of the ten provincial premiers (Jacques Parizeau stayed home) conducted a trade mission to the People's Republic of China. Largely willing to ignore Chinese human rights abuses, "Team Canada" came home with a billion dollars in contracts. The government rejected calls to suspend defence orders for such countries as Turkey, Vietnam, and Thailand because of their questionable human rights records, and was slow to respond to concerns over the use of child labour by some of its Asian trading partners.

## THE FEDERAL ELECTION OF 1997

On 2 June 1997, Canadians marked their ballots in a federal election that was held just three and a half years after the Liberal sweep of 1993. Polls suggesting that the Liberals might make major gains in the West and Quebec tempted the Chrétien gov

**Table 17.1**

| 1997 FEDERAL ELECTION RESULTS | | |
|---|---|---|
| Party | Popular Vote % | Seats |
| Liberal | 38.36 | 155 |
| Reform | 19.34 | 60 |
| Bloc québécois | 10.73 | 44 |
| New Democratic | 11.04 | 21 |
| Progressive Conservative | 18.88 | 20 |
| Green | 0.42 | 0 |
| Natural Law | 0.29 | 0 |
| Christian Heritage | 0.23 | 0 |
| Independent | 0.13 | 1 |

*Source:* **Globe and Mail,** *13 June 1997*

**Table 17.2**

| 1997 FEDERAL ELECTION RESULTS BY REGION | | | | | |
|---|---|---|---|---|---|
| Party | West | Ontario | Quebec | Atlantic | North |
| Liberal | 15 | 101 | 26 | 11 | 2 |
| Reform | 60 | 0 | 0 | 0 | 0 |
| Bloc québécois | 0 | 0 | 44 | 0 | 0 |
| New Democratic | 12 | 0 | 0 | 8 | 1 |
| Progressive Conservative | 1 | 1 | 5 | 13 | 0 |
| Independent | | 1 | | | |

*Source:* **Globe and Mail,** *13 June 1997*

ernment to call an early election. By the time the votes were counted, it was clear that regional divisions in Canada were deeper than ever. The Liberals took 101 of the 103 seats in Ontario and picked up enough seats elsewhere throughout the country to give them a slight majority—155 out of 301—but they lost 20 of the 31 seats they had held in Atlantic Canada and failed to make the gains they had anticipated in the West and Quebec.

To some extent, regional differences were exaggerated by the first-past-the-post electoral system. The Liberals were able to take most of the seats in Ontario while receiving less than half of the province's popular vote. Similarly, support for the Reform Party in the West and for the Bloc québécois in Quebec was distorted by a voting system that gave these parties a majority of seats in their respective regions despite the fact that they attracted only about 40 percent of the votes cast in their regional enclaves. Both the New Democratic Party and the Bloc received about 11 percent of the overall popular vote, but the NDP won only 21 seats to the Bloc's 44. Although the Reform and Progressive Conservative parties both earned approximately 19 percent of the overall popular vote, Reform won 60 seats to the PC's 20. Had seats been apportioned, as they are in some democratic countries, according to the percentage of the popular vote received by each party, the House of Commons would have had a much different look and several small parties, including the Green Party, Natural Law Party, and the Christian Heritage Party, would each have won a seat.

Yet, it was clear that each region of the country approached the federal election from a different perspective. Distraught by the cutbacks in federal transfer payments, the collapse of the fisheries, and Depression-level unemployment rates, voters in Atlantic Canada turned to the New Democratic Party led by Alexa McDonough and the Progressive Conservative Party under Jean Charest to express their protest. The badly divided Bloc québécois, under its new leader Gilles Duceppe, managed to retain the allegiance of most nationalists in Quebec, but lost enough seats to the Liberals and Progressive Conservatives to prevent it from forming the official opposition in the House. That role was assumed by the Reform Party, which took a majority of seats in Alberta, Saskatchewan, and British Columbia. Preston Manning had hoped to make breakthroughs for his party in Ontario and the Atlantic region but his tough talk on Quebec alienated most voters east of the Manitoba border. By contrast, Reform's western supporters applauded Manning's rejection of any form of "special status" for Quebec.

Thus, rather than resolving regional differences, the 1997 election only served to highlight them. Ontario clearly called the shots in the second Chrétien administration and Canadians living elsewhere in the country remained wary of a government so beholden to one region.

## DOES CANADA HAVE A FUTURE?

Neo-conservatives maintain that the attack on the deficit has to be the country's first priority even if some people get hurt. The country will have no future if it drowns itself in a sea of debt. Opponents counter that such arguments betray a lack of understanding of the country's economic history and an unwillingness to consider such alternatives as strict controls over financial markets to keep interest rates down, and a more redistributive taxation system.

As Quebec faced its second referendum, industrialist and press magnate Conrad Black made a blunt speech in which he ridiculed attempts made by many liberals to distinguish Canada from the United States on the basis of its social programs. From his viewpoint, it was absurd to try to define Canada in terms of programs that merely made Canadian businesses less competitive than their American counterparts. Indeed, there was a growing view within Canada that it was too expensive to maintain the country. The Free Trade Agreement and NAFTA, agreements that would not even have been considered in the age of prosperity, when public pressure forced governments not only to maintain some trade barriers but also to place some limits on foreign investment, are seen by supporters—and even some opponents—as inevitable. Canada, they say, is too small a market to maintain an independent economic existence in an age of globalization. If it is to be internationally competitive, it cannot afford to continue subsidizing a national railway passenger service or a national airline. It cannot generously fund the national broadcaster, the CBC. It cannot offer its citizens significantly more in the area of social programs or environmental protection than the Americans offer their citizens.

Commentators continue to repeat familiar claims about how Canadians differ from Americans: Canadians are less demonstrative, more humble, less violent, less racist. Much of the Canadian character had been shaped by decisions

to make much greater use of the state as a means to knit the nation together and protect more vulnerable citizens from the fate that the marketplace reserved for its weakest elements. The dispersal of a relatively small population across a vast expanse of geography had always argued against the view that the market alone could be depended upon to solve problems and create a degree of unity. As the twentieth century came to an end, many hoped that the Canadian difference could be preserved, despite the economic pressures that seemed to militate against a distinctly "Canadian dream."

# IF QUEBEC LEAVES

## A Debate

Increasingly, social scientists—if not governments—have been prepared to speculate on the political and economic impact of Quebec sovereignty on both Quebec and the remaining Canadian provinces. Historian David J. Bercuson and political scientist Barry Cooper have marshalled arguments as to why the rest of Canada would be better off without Quebec. They argue that Quebec nationalism is incompatible with the liberal-democratic values that they believe are central to English-Canadian politics. Quebec nationalists, they maintain, place the rights of French Canadians above both majority and individual rights. Bercuson and Cooper suggest that majority rule ought to be—and, without Quebec, would be—the essential principle of governance in Canada. [5]

Some authors point to liberal democracies that accommodate minority communities without losing their liberal character. Political scientist Alain Gagnon cites the examples of Switzerland and Belgium, where regional governments "have the right and the obligation to protect their respective linguistic community against any infringements." Gagnon labels this "a charter of rights and freedoms whose application varies according to specific regions." [6]

Bercuson and Cooper reject such regionalism, and they suggest that a Quebec-free Canada could avoid decentralization by giving each province equal representation in the Senate. Other scholars are sceptical that such a proposal would be acceptable to Ontario. They predict that, if Quebec left Confederation, Canada would begin to fall apart. Economist Tim O'Neill observes that Ontario's dominance in population and economic activity could lead other provinces to "forge separate regional and interregional alliances with other provinces and possibly with contiguous areas of the United States." [7]

Federal bilingual policy is a sore point for many scholars. Bercuson and Cooper scoff at those who claim that "what makes us great is official bilingualism and French on our cereal boxes." [8] While few other anglophone scholars share this rejection of legislated bilingualism, many Quebec nationalists do. They argue that Quebec's government should operate only in French, while governments outside Quebec should offer services in French only in heavily francophone areas. Sociologist Hubert Guindon, a sovereignist who supports unilingualism for Quebec, maintains that "the official bilingualism adopted by the Canadian state was politically irrelevant." [9]

Bercuson and Cooper argue that a

Canada without Quebec would be more prosperous than today's Canada. Adopting the neo-conservative view that the federal government's spending has been out of control for several decades, they suggest that Quebec pressures have played a key role in preventing the government from trimming its programs. Although they provide no figures to corroborate this view, they conclude, "By ending the wasteful transaction costs of official bilingualism and especially the ongoing transfer of wealth from Canada to Quebec, the citizens of Canada would undoubtedly be more wealthy, not less." [10]

Quebec economists of a nationalist bent have rejected the view that Quebec is a net gainer from tax transfers in Canada. Georges Mathew has produced "a balance sheet of federalism for Quebec," which claims that Quebec had a marginally favourable balance from 1973 to 1986 but afterwards was a net loser.[11] Pierre Fortin also argues that Confederation continues to have a negative economic impact on Quebec. He claims that the federal debt, failed federal development policies, and monetary instability as well as duplication in powers between the federal and provincial governments have hurt Quebec's economy. [12] Indeed, such policies hurt every province's economy, and Fortin suggests that radical decentralization might be of benefit to the whole country. If emotional attachments to Canada make residents of other provinces reluctant to support decentralization, then Quebec must either receive special status or become sovereign.

Scholars in have-not provinces, especially Atlantic Canada, have been less sanguine about the economic prospects of their provinces should Quebec leave. Tim O'Neill notes that "neither extensive decentralization nor separation will have a positive impact on Atlantic Canada" because the region depends more on federal transfers than other areas.[13] O'Neill also observes that notions that either Quebec or the rest of Canada will benefit economically from a break-up take as a given that the break-up will

be amicable and cause little short-term economic disruption. Yet, there has already been an indication that the two sides would have difficulty determining how to divide up the national debt.

Political scientist Peter Russell suggests that the aftermath of Quebec sovereignty might well depend on how it is achieved. If it comes through a unilateral declaration of independence rather than through a long process of negotiations, "the climate of uncertainty and tension generated by such a move will reduce international confidence and put severe strain on the Canadian economy."[14] Opponents of independence, particularly anglophones and First Nations, "might insist on federal protection of their rights against a Quebec government operating outside Canadian law. Civil disobedience and violence cannot be ruled out." While such views strike many as alarmist, some Quebec nationalist intellectuals readily concede that the sovereignty-association formula is probably impossible. There is no guarantee that the rest of Canada would negotiate a common market with a seceding province. Hubert Guindon, reflecting on the debate in the 1980 Quebec referendum, observes: "The common myth shared by both those opposed to sovereignty association and those in favour was that should the 'oui' forces have won decisively, it would have led automatically to the creation of a sovereign state with association with Canada.... Such naivete, in a sense, honours us. But it augurs poorly for the kind of sophistication that will be required to inch our way toward sovereignty."[15]

The accuracy of these analyses will only become apparent if Quebec does in fact leave Canada. While the "constitution industry" and most Canadians, including most Quebeckers, still hope that accommodation is possible, Quebec's leaving is no longer unthinkable. It is therefore only natural that scholars continue to paint scenarios of Canada without Quebec and Quebec without Canada.

## NOTES

1  *Edmonton Journal*, 9 Nov. 1995

2  Mel Hurtig, *The Betrayal of Canada*, rev. ed. (Toronto: Stoddart, 1992), 339

3  Gwen Brodsky and Shelagh Day, *Canadian Charter Equality Rights for Women: One Step Forward or Two Steps Back?* (Ottawa: Canadian Advisory Council on the Status of Women, 1989), 3

4  Carla Lipsig-Mummé, "Organizing Women in the Clothing Trades: Homework and the 1983 Garment Strike in Canada," *Studies in Political Economy* 22 (Spring 1987): 61

5  David J. Bercuson and Barry Cooper, *Deconfederation: Canada Without Quebec* (Toronto: Key Porter, 1991), 15–16

6  Alain Gagnon, "Other Federal and Nonfederal Countries: Lessons for Canada" in *Options for a New Canada*, ed. Ronald L. Watts and Douglas M. Brown, (Toronto: University of Toronto Press, 1991), 232

7  Tim O'Neill, "Restructured Federalism and Its Impacts on Atlantic Canada," in *The Constitutional Future of the Prairie and Atlantic Regions of Canada*, ed. James N. McRorie and Martha L. Macdonald, (Regina: Canadian Plains Research Center, 1992), 63

8  Bercuson and Cooper, *Deconfederation*, 134–35

9  Hubert Guindon, *Quebec Society: Tradition, Modernity, and Nationhood* (Toronto: University of Toronto Press, 1988), 143

10  Bercuson and Cooper, *Deconfederation*, 140–41

11  Georges Mathews, *Quiet Resolution: Quebec's Challenges to Canada* (Toronto: Summerhill Press, 1990), 139–40

12  Pierre Fortin, "How Economics Is Shaping the Constitutional Debate in Quebec" in *Confederation in Crisis*, ed. Robert Young (Toronto: Lorimer, 1991), 3–44

13  O'Neill, "Restructured Federalism," 63

14  Peter H. Russell, "Towards a New Constitutional Process" in *Options for a New Canada*, 148

15  Guindon, *Quebec Society*, 166–67

## SELECTED READING

International economic and environmental developments are assessed in M. Patricia Marchak, *The Integrated Circus: The New Right and the Restructuring of Global Markets* (Montreal: McGill-Queen's University Press, 1991); Nigel Harris, *The End of the Third World* (London: Penguin, 1986); and Susan George, *A Fate Worse Than Debt* (New York: Grove Press, 1988).

On the Canadian economy after 1975, directly opposed views are found in Harold Chorney, John Hotson, and Mario Seccarecia, *The Deficit Made Me Do It* (Ottawa: Canadian Centre for Policy Alternatives, 1992) and Linda McQuaig, *Shooting the Hippo: Death by Deficit and Other Canadian Myths* (Toronto: Viking, 1995), on the one hand, and David Laidler and William Robson, *The Great Canadian Disinflation: the Economics and Politics of Monetary Policy in Canada, 1988–1993* (Toronto: C.D. Howe Institute, 1993), and Kenneth Norrie and Douglas Owram, *A History of the Canadian Economy* (Toronto: Harcourt Brace Jovanovich, 1991), on the other. Feminist readings of the changing socio-economic environment include *Through a Feminist Lens: Macroeconomic Restructuring in Canada*, ed., Isabella Bakker (Ottawa: Status of Women Canada, 1994), and *Women's Caring: Feminist Perspectives on Social Welfare*, Carol Baines, Patricia Evans, and Sheila Neysmith (Toronto: McClelland and Stewart, 1991). An attempt to place recent Canadian economic developments within the country's larger economic and intellectual history is Harold Chorney and Philip Hansen, *Toward a Humanist Political Economy* (Montreal: Black Rose, 1992).

On Canadian–American economic relations before the Free Trade Agreement, useful works include Stephen Clarkson, *Canada and the Reagan Challenge*, 2nd ed. (Toronto: Lorimer, 1985), and G. Bruce Doern and Glen Toner,

*The Politics of Energy* (Toronto: Nelson, 1985). The argument for free trade is put forward in the three-volume *Report of the Royal Commission on Economic Union and Development Prospects for Canada* (Macdonald Report) of 1985. Views from the opposite side are found in James Laxer, *Leap of Faith: Free Trade and the Future of Canada* (Edmonton: Hurtig, 1986); and Marjorie Griffin Cohen, *Free Trade and the Future of Women's Work: Manufacturing and Service Industries* (Toronto: Garamond, 1987). On the early impact of the Canadian–American Free Trade Agreement, see Duncan Cameron, Daniel Drache, and Mel Watkins, eds., *Canada Under Free Trade* (Toronto: Lorimer, 1993); Mel Hurtig, *The Betrayal of Canada*, rev. ed. (Toronto: Stoddart, 1992); and Maude Barlow and Bruce Campbell, *Take Back the Nation* (Toronto: Key Porter, 1991). Works on NAFTA include Mario F. Bognanno and Kathryn J. Ready, eds., *The North American Free Trade Agreement: Labor, Industry and Government Perspectives* (Westport, CT: Praeger, 1993), and Ricardo Grinspan and Maxwell A. Cameron, eds., *The Political Economy of North American Free Trade* (New York: St Martin's Press, 1993). Opposing perspectives by Canadians are represented by Ian Robinson, *North American Trade as if Democracy Mattered: What's Wrong with NAFTA and What Are the Alternatives?* (Ottawa: Canadian Centre for Policy Alternatives, 1993), and Stelios Loizides and Gilles Rheaume, *The North American Free Trade Agreement: Implications for Canada* (Ottawa: Conference Board of Canada, 1993).

On Quebec since 1975, see Paul-André Linteau et al., *Quebec Since 1930: A History* (Toronto: Lorimer, 1991); Kenneth McRoberts, *Quebec: Social Change and Political Crisis*, 3rd ed. (Toronto: McClelland and Stewart, 1988); René Lévesque, *Memoirs* (Toronto: McClelland and Stewart, 1986); Pierre Godin, *René Lévesque: un enfant du siècle* (Montreal: Boréal, 1994); and Robert Chodos and Eric Hamovitch, *Quebec and the American Dream* (Toronto: Between the Lines, 1994).

Ontario developments are discussed in Thomas L. Walkom, *Rae Days* (Toronto: Key Porter, 1994); Patrick Monahan, *Storming the Pink Palace: The NDP in Power, a Cautionary Tale* (Toronto: Lester, 1995); and Daniel Drache, ed., *Getting on Track: Social Democratic Strategies for Ontario* (Montreal: McGill-Queen's University Press, 1992).

On Western Canada, see Gerald Friesen, *The Canadian Prairies*, rev. ed. (Toronto: University of Toronto Press, 1987); Trevor Harrison and Gordon Laxer, eds., *The Trojan Horse: Alberta and the Future of Canada* (Montreal: Black Rose, 1995); James M. Pitsula and Ken Rasmussen, *Privatizing a Province: The New Right in Saskatchewan* (Vancouver: New Star, 1990); Patricia Marchak, *Green Gold: The Forest Industry in British Columbia* (Vancouver: UBC Press, 1983); Rennie Warburton and Donald Coburn, eds., *Workers, Capital, and the State of British Columbia: Selected Papers* (Vancouver: UBC Press, 1987); and Jim Silver and Jeremy Hull, eds., *The Political Economy of Manitoba* (Regina: Canadian Plains Research Center, 1990). On the Reform Party, see Trevor Harrison, *Of Passionate Intensity: Right-Wing Populism and the Reform Party of Canada* (Toronto: University of Toronto Press, 1995).

On the Atlantic provinces, see E.R. Forbes, "The Atlantic Provinces, Free Trade, and the Consitution," in *Challenging the Regional Steriotype* (Fredericton: Acadiensis Press, 1989): 200-216; Gary Burrill and Ian McKay, eds., *People, Resources, and Power in Atlantic Canada: Critical Perspectives on Underdevelopment and Primary Industries in the Atlantic Region* (Fredericton: Acadiensis, 1987);Wallace Clement, *The Struggle to Organize: Resistance in Canada's Fisheries* (Toronto: McClelland and Stewart, 1986); and Shaun Cornish, *The Westray Tragedy: A Miner's Story* (Toronto: Fernwood, 1994).

Useful works on the constitutional debates include David Milne, *The New Canadian Constitution* (Toronto: Lorimer, 1982); Keith Banting and Richard Simeon, eds., *And No One Cheered: Federalism, Democracy and the Constitution Act* (Scarborough: Nelson, 1983); Michael D. Behiels, ed., *The Meech Lake Primer: Conflicting Views of the 1987 Constitutional Accord* (Ottawa: University of Ottawa Press, 1989); C.E.S. Franks, *The Myths and Symbols of the Constitutional Debate in Canada* (Kingston: Institute of Intergovernmental Relations, 1993); and Deborah Coyne, *Roll of the Dice: Working with Clyde Wells During the Meech Lake Negotiations* (Toronto: Lorimer, 1992).

On the trade union movement, see Bryan D. Palmer, *Working-Class Experience: Rethinking the History of Canadian Labour, 1800–1991* (Toronto: McClelland and Stewart, 1992), and Leo Panitch, *The Assault on Trade Union Freedoms: From Wage Controls to Social Contract*, rev. ed. (Toronto: Garamond, 1994).

On Canadian foreign policy, see Norman Hillmer and J.L. Granatstein, *Empire to Umpire: Canada and the World to the 1990s* (Toronto: Copp Clark Pitman, 1994), and Ernie Regehr and Simon Rosenblum, eds., *Canada and the Nuclear Arms Race* (Toronto: Lorimer, 1983).

Aberdeen, Lady, 146
Aberhart, William, 243, 276, 288, 289
Aboriginal peoples. See First Nations.
Abortion, 11, 426
Abott, Douglas, 384
Abott, John, 58
Acadians, 9, 31, 52-53, 101, 129
    education, 169
    quiet revolution, 354
    renaissance, 161-63
Acheson, T.W., 95
Act of Union, 29, 30
Action libérale nationale, 244
Actors, 277
Adams, Thomas, 133
Adolescence, 20
Affleck, Minnie, 63
African Americans. See Blacks.
African Canadians. See Blacks.
Africville, 419
Agri-business, 386-87
Agriculture Rehabilitation and Development Act, 350
Aho, Maria, 111
AIDS, 429
Aircraft transportation, 74
Aird, John, 276
Aitken, Max, 77, 89, 216
Alaska purchase (U.S.), 7
Alaska-Yukon boundary dispute, 63, 64
Alberni Canal, 42
Alberta, 59, 482
    Heritage Trust Fund, 351
    ranching, 80
Alderdice, Frederick, 267
Algoma Steel Company, 76, 317
Algonkin, 8
Alien Labour Act (1897), 94
All People's Mission, 131
Allan Steamship Lines, 45
Allan, Hugh, 45
Allard, Edwige, 71
Allen, Judith, 152
Alloway and Champion, 90
Alouette I, 389
Aluminum, 259
Alverstone, Lord, 63
Amalgamated Association of Street Railway Employees, 138
American Revolution, 8, 24, 28
Ames, Herbert, 119, 132
Amulree Commission, 267
Anderson, Doris, 425
Anglicans, 23, 114
Anglo-conformity, 103
Anicinabe Park, 422
Anik, 389

Anishanabe Spiritual Centre, 421
Annapolis Valley, 79
Anti-combines laws, 88
Anti-Semitism, 241
Anti-smoking campaign, 452
Anti-war protests, 319, 366
Aquin, Hubert, 439
Arcand, Adrian, 318
Arcand, Denys, 441
Archambault, Joseph, 219
Archibald, Adams, 41
Architecture, 178-80, 294
Arctic, Canada's claim to, 116-17
Arctic Waters Pollution Prevention Act, 373
Artists, 184, 185, 293-94, 315, 446-47
Arts, 180-88
Asbestos mines, 83
Asbestos strike, 402-403
Asian immigrants, 110, 266, 417-18
    in BC, 60
    in First World War, 213
    racial discrimination against, 20, 82, 107-108
Assembly lines, 87-88
Assembly of First Nations, 420
Athabasca tar sands, 116
Atlantic cable, 26
Atlantic Canada, see Maritimes
Atlantic Provinces Adjustment Grants, 350
Atomic bomb, 305
Atomic Energy of Canada, 368-69
Attlee, Clement, 326
Atwood, Margaret, 443
Auk, 12
Aurora, Ontario, 46
Auto industry, 76
Automobiles, 74, 256, 260, 438
Avery, Donald, 103

Baby bonus, 421
Baby boom, 408
Baby boomers, 411-12
Bacchi, Carol Lee, 151
Baden-Powell, Robert, 172
Baffin Island, 48
Bailey, Donovan, 451
Baldwin, F.W., 74
Balkan Wars (1912-13), 107
Bank of Canada, 248
Banking institutions, 78, 89-90
Banks, Hal, 365
Baptists, 11, 23, 128, 130
Baseball, 174, 450
Batoche, 50
Bay of Pigs, 366-67
Beaverbrook, Lord. See Aitken, Max.

Bell Canada, 89, 136
Bell, Alexander Graham, 74, 75
Belsen Concentration Camp, 315
Bengough, J.W., 45
Bennett, Charles Fox, 44
Bennett, George, 134
Bennett, R.B., 89, 238-39, 240, 246, 248-49, 276
Bennett, W.A.C., 341, 374
Benson, Edgar, 361
Beothuk, 1, 8
Bercuson, David J., 489
Berger, Thomas, 421
Bering Sea, 56
Berlin (Kitchener), Ontario, 11, 211
Bernard, André, 358
BESCO, 262
Beveridge, William, 321
Big Bear, 49, 51
Bilingualism, 54, 353-54, 358
Bird, Florence, 425
Birth control, 11, 147, 279-80, 286, 410.
Birth rate, 11, 103, 410, 411.
Bishop, Billy, 207
Bissoondath, Neil, 455, 456
Black United Front, 419
Black, Conrad, 431, 454, 488
Black, Martha. See Munger, Martha.
Blackfoot, 8
Blacks, 8-9, 108-110, 266, 418-20
    in British North America, 8-9
    Emancipation Day, 177
    in First World War, 213
    racism against, 20, 108-109
    sports, 175
Blair, A.G., 55, 58
Blais, Marie-Claire, 438
Blake, Edward, 46, 57
Blakeney, Allan, 482
*Bleus*, 26, 31
Bloc québécois, 474, 476, 488
Blood Indians, 112
Board of Broadcast Governors, 375
Board of Grain Commissioners, 198, 199
Board of Moral and Social Reform and Evangelism, 141
Board of Pension Commissioners, 217
Boat people, 418
Boer War. See South African War.
Bolshevik Revolution. See Russian Revolution.
Book publishing, 454-55
Bootleggers, 129
Borden, Robert Laird, 64-65, 139, 197-200
Borduas, Paul-Émile, 438
Bouchard, Lucien, 476, 477, 478
Bourassa, Henri, 61, 62, 140, 149, 160, 223
Bourassa, Robert, 355, 472, 473-74
Bowell, MacKenzie, 58
Boy Scout movement, 172
Bracken, John, 320, 339

Branch-plant economy, 72-73, 372
Brand, Dionne, 444, 456, 457
Breynat, Gabriel, 236
Britain. See Great Britain.
British-American Joint High Commission, 56
British Columbia Packers Association, 82
British Columbia, 6, 8, 13
    entry into Confederation, 42-43
    mining industry, 83
    post-1975 politics, 481
    salmon fishery, 81-82
    timber, 82
British Commonwealth Air Training Plan, 312-13
British Empire, 6
British North America, 6, 7, 8-12, 14-15
British North America (BNA) Act, 6, 30, 32, 52, 54, 89, 101
Brittain, Miller, 293
Bronfman family, 262, 386
Brown, George, 26, 29-30, 36 , 44, 134
Bruce, John, 40
Buck, Tim, 239, 246
Bukovyna, 106
Bunkhouse men, 136
Burger King, 390
Burgess, Helen, 407
Burrard Inlet, 42
Bush, George, 487
Business cycles, 71, 73
Butler, Benjamin, 43
Byng, Governor General, 233

C.D. Howe Institute, 393
Caisses populaires, 142
Caledonia Township, 54
Calgary, 117, 118
Callwood, June 456
Campbell, Kim, 475
Campbell, Maria, 444
Canada
    international status, 216-17
    name, choosing, 32
    people and culture, at Confederation, 8-12
    written histories of, 161
Canada Assistance Plan, 345, 347, 484
Canada Carbide Company, 77
Canada Cement Company, 77, 89
Canada Council, 445
Canada Development Corporation, 373
Canada East, 29
Canada First movement, 46-47, 158
Canada Pension Plan, 345, 347
Canada Temperance Act (1878), 128-29
Canada West, 9, 29. See also Upper Canada.
Canadian Airborne Regiment, 420
Canadian Army Nursing Service, 63
Canadian Army Overseas in Britain, 311
Canadian Authors' Association, 292
Canadian Bankers Association, 88

Canadian Broadcasting Corporation (CBC), 276, 375, 431, 453
Canadian Citizenship Act (1947), 343
Canadian Clubs, 159
Canadian Commission of Conservation, 132
Canadian Conference of Catholic Bishops, 431
Canadian Congress of Labour, 270, 402
Canadian content rule, 447
Canadian Corps, 206
Canadian Council of Agriculture, 142, 222
Canadian Council on Children and Youth, 345
Canadian Expeditionary Force, 201
Canadian Girls in Training (CGIT), 172
Canadian International Development Agency, 356
Canadian Labour Party, 232
Canadian Legion, 218
Canadian Manufacturers Association, 47, 65, 88, 464
Canadian Medical Association, 14, 344
Canadian Memorial Association, 62
Canadian Mortgage and Housing Corporation, 341
Canadian National Council of Refugees, 319
Canadian National Railway (CNR), 232
Canadian Northern Railway, 60
Canadian Pacific Railway (CPR), 45, 47, 60, 83, 107, 117, 118
Canadian Party, 39
Canadian Patriotic Fund, 203
Canadian Radio-television Commission (CRTC), 375-76, 447
Canadian Radio League, 276
Canadian Seamen's Union, 365
Canadian Social Science Research Council, 291
Canadian Wheat Board, 249, 316
Canadian Women's Army Corps, 308
Canadian Women's Suffrage Association, 149
Cannizzo, Jeanne, 456
Canol pipeline, 326
Caouette, Réal, 341
Cape Breton, 18, 238, 242, 262, 266, 342
Capitalism, 263
Capitalists, 12-13, 14
Caraquet Riot (1875), 52-53
Card, Charles Ora, 104-105
Caribana, 419
Caribbean Domestic Scheme, 419
Caribbean immigrants, 408, 419
Carleton House, 18
Carr, Emily, 181, 188, 293
Carson, Rachel, 396
Carter, Frederick, 44
Carter, Gerald Emmett, 431
Cartier, George-Étienne, 30, 36, 42, 45
Casgrain, Thérèse, 235, 425, 343
Casgrain, Marie-Elizabeth (Sister Sainte-Justine), 145
Casselman, Cora, 235
Castro, Fidel, 366
Catherwood, Esther, 297
Catholic Byzantine Rite, 106

Catholic Emancipation, 22
Catholics. See Roman Catholics.
CBC. See Canadian Broadcasting Corporation.
Cattle, 79, 80
CCF. See Cooperative Commonwealth Federation.
CEGEPs, 414
Censorship, 278, 454-55
Céntrale de l'enseignement du Québec, 414
Chalk River, 305
Chapais, 37
Charest, Jean, 488
Charlottetown Accord, 474-76
Charlottetown Conference, 30-31
Charter of Rights and Freedoms, 469, 470-71
Chase, Lillian, 170
Cheese industry, 79
Chelsea, Phyllis and Andy, 424
Chemical industry, 386
Child abuse, 281
Child-rearing practices, 282-83
Children's Aid Society, 129
Children, 20
    entertainment for, 453-54
    illegitimate, 11
    as labourers, 91-92, 93, 94
    moral reform of, 129
    poor and neglected, 148
    in suburbs, 415
    training schools for delinquents, 148
China, People's Republic of, 487
Chinese immigrants, 9, 103, 266
    Exclusion Act, 299
    in First World War, 213
    head tax, 107
    labourers, 48
    prostitutes, 112
Chipman, C.O., 84
Cholera, 12
Chorney, Harold, 405, 435
Chown, Reverend S.D., 131
Chrétien, Jean, 467, 477, 487
Christian Socialist League, 140
Church of England. See Anglicans.
Church of Jesus Christ of the Latter-Day Saints, 104-105
Churches, and social gospel, 130, 131
Chysler, 76
Cities. See also Urban growth.
    boards of control, 133
    farmers markets, 176
    garden city planners, 133
    growth of, 117-21
    municipal development laws, 120
    postwar, 414-16
    poverty in, 119-20, 122-23
    unemployment, 121
    urban reform, 132-33
    water systems, 120
City beautiful movement, 132

Civil Code (Quebec), 28
Civil War (U.S.) 7, 15, 28
Clark, C.S., 129
Clark, Esther, 170
Clark, Glen, 481
Clark, Joe, 463
Clark, Paraskeva, 293
Class, 20-21
    and cultural activities, 176
    housing differences, 282
    and sports, 175
Clergue, Frances Hector, 76
Clerical work, 85
Cleverdon, Catherine, 150
Coady, Moses, 289
Coaker, William, 142
Coal mining, 18, 42, 82-83, 238
Cochrane, Matthew, 80
Code of Civil Procedures (Quebec), 28
Cohen, Leonard, 442
Cold War, 338, 341, 362-63, 368, 377, 486
Colombo Plan, 356
Colonies, British in North America. See British North
    America.
Columbia River Treaty and Protocol, 374
Comeau, Anselme and Charlotte, 163
Comfort, Charles, 294
Committee on Reconstruction, 321-22
Committee for an Independent Canada, 376
Common Front, 3, 402
Common law, 20
Common schools, 22
Communication, developments in, 73-74, 388-89
Communications revolution, 276-78
Communism, 239-41, 245
Communist Party of Canada, 221, 237-38, 246, 319
Communists, 377
Computers, 386, 389-90
Confédération de Travailleurs catholiques du Canada,
    270
Confederation, 5, 6, 42-44
    failure of United Canadas, 24
    opposition to, 31
    pro-forces, 31-32
    road to, 28-32
    transportation, effect on, 13
Conscientious objectors, 319
Conscription, 222-23, 306-307
Conservative (Tory) Party, 26
Conservative, defined, 26
Consolidated Mining and Smelting Company of Canada
    (COMINCO), 83, 383
Constitution Act, 1982, 470
Constitution, patriating, 469-70
Consumer durables, 260
Consumerism, 434-35
Cook, Ramsay, 188, 223, 358
Cooper, Barry, 489

Cooperative Commonwealth Federation
    (CCF), 235, 242-43, 252, 286, 320, 321, 340-341
Cooperative movement, 142-43
Copp, Terry, 122
Corbett, E.A., 292
Cosmos, Amor de, 42
Cottages, 172-73
Council of Tribes, 113
Craven, Paul, 73
Credit, 256-57
Cree, 49, 112, 422-23
Creighton, Donald, 378
Crerar, H.D.G., 311
Crerar, Thomas, 222, 230, 231
Crime, in immigrant communities, 112
Crimean War (1854-56), 7
Criminal Code, 221
*Croisade d'adolescents*, 161
Cross, James, 354
Cross, Ronald (Lasagna), 423
Crow rate, 231, 232
Crow's Nest Pass Agreement, 73-74
Crow, John, 463
CTV, 452, 453
Cullen, Maurice, 315
Cult of the folk, 296
Culture of protest, 427
Culture, 176-78
    interwar years, 292-95
    U.S. influence on, 374-75
    who speaks for, 455-57
Currie, Arthur, 206
Custodian of Enemy Property, 318
Customs, 14-15. See also Tariffs.
Cutbacks, federal, 484-85
Cypress Hills, 41

Dadson, Ebenezer William, 163
Dafoe, John W., 223
Dairy farming, 80, 91
Dalhousie University, 25
Dance, 178, 448
Dandurand, Raoul, 306
Danysk, Cecilia, 111, 301-302
Darwin, Charles, 25, 163
Darwinism, 172
Davies, Robertson, 443
Davies, William, 79
Dawson City, 59
Dawson, William, 163
Day care, 348
Defence of Canada Regulations, 318
Defence Production Sharing Agreement, 361, 364
Defence spending, 384-85
Deficits, 485
Dene, 116, 236, 383, 421-22
Denison, George Taylor, 158
Denominational schools, 40

Manitoba, 54, 168
New Brunswick, 52-53
Prince Edward Island, 43
Quebec, 166-67
Dent, John Charles, 161
Department of Indian Affairs, 112, 235, 236
Department of Labour, 139
Department of Munitions and Supply, 316
Department of Soldiers Civil Re-Establishment, 217
Depression, See Great Depression.
Desbiens, Jean-Paul, 413, 414
Desjardins, Alphonse, 142
Deskadeh, Chief, 235-36
Devine, Grant, 482
Dewar, Marion, 345
Dewar, Phyllis, 297
Dewdney, Edgar, 48, 49, 50
Diefenbaker, John, 197, 339, 344, 345, 367-68, 378
Dieppe, 310
Diet, changes in, 452
Diphtheria, 12
Dirty Thirties. See Great Depression.
Disabled, schooling for, 168
Disease, 12, 120-21
Distant Early Warning (DEW) Line, 364
Distinct society clause, Meech Lake Accord, 471
District of Franklin, 48
Divorce, 148, 281, 410, 425
Dofasco, 262
Domestic International Sales Corporation, 373
Dominion Day, 14
Dominion Housing Act, 249
Dominion Iron and Steel Company, 76
Dominion Lands Act (1872), 41, 100
Dominion Securities, 89
Dominion Steel and Coal Corporation, 317
Dominion Wholesale Grocers Guild, 88
Dorion, A.-A., 31
DOSCO, 351
Douglas, C.H., 243
Douglas, Tommy, 242, 320, 321
Doukhobors, 105, 106
Downsizing, 462
Draft dodgers, 366
Drapeau, Jean, 355
Drew, George, 339
Drought, 257
Drury, E.C., 141, 222
Drysdale, Arthur, 216
Dubois, Norbert, 100
Duceppe, Gilles, 488
Duck Lake, 50
Dufferin, Lord, 46
Dumont, Gabriel, 50, 175
Dumont, Mario, 476
Duncan, Andrew Rae, 233
Duncan, Sarah Jeannette, 183
Duncan, William, 114

Duplessis, Maurice, 244, 245, 306, 319, 341, 352
Dupuis Frères, 402
Durbin, Deanna, 277

East Indian immigrants, 103, 108, 418
Eastern Townships, 79
Eaton's, 86, 486
Eaton, Margaret, 308
Eayrs, James, 379
Economic Council of Canada, 399
Economic disparity, 398-99
Economic nationalism, 369-72, 373
Economy
    continental economic integration, 368
    cycles in growth, 71, 73
    fifties growth, 385-87
    jobless recovery, 465-67
    postwar reconstruction, 384-85
    stagnation, 460-63
Edmonton, 117
Education
    bilingual, 168-69
    compulsory attendance, 167, 290
    at Confederation, 21-22
    curricula, 167
    high schools, 167
    in interwar years, 289-92
    kindergartens, 167
    Native peoples, 114-15, 420
    Ontario, 169
    postwar, 412-13
    provincial systems of, 166-67
    universities, 25-26, 169-71, 291-92, 413
Edwards, Henrietta Muir, 234
Electrical appliance industry, 260
Electrical power, 83-84
Empire Day, 159
Energy crisis, 351, 392
Engels, Friederich, 26
English immigrants, 10
Enlightenment, 23-24
Ens, Gerhard, 66
Entertainers, Canadian, 375
Environment, 132-33, 461
    effects of growth on, 396-97
    and western farmers, 258
Environmental movement, 427-28
Equal Rights Association (Ontario), 53-54
Equal rights feminists, 149
Equalization payments, 482
Ethnicity, and housing, 283
Eugenics, 131-32, 280
Eugenics Board, Alberta, 411
European Economic Community, 461
European Union, 461
Evangelicals, 11
Ewart, John S., 160
Ewen, Stuart, 434

Ewing, Juliana Horatia, 16
Exports, 15
External Affairs, Department of, 56

Fabre, Edouard-Charles, 166
Factory system, 13, 21
Fairclough, Ellen, 342
Family Allowances, 322
Family, 17, 19
    blended, 410-11
    gender distinctions in (1867), 19-20
    nuclear, 410
    single-parent, 410, 425, 466
    social changes, 147-48
    work and, 91-93
Famous Players, 277
Farm labourers, 286
Farming, 15-17, 285-86, 393-94
    commercialization of, 79
    in interwar years, 301-302
    scientific and technological innovations in, 80
    supervisory boards, 202
    wealth, 21
Farrer, Edward, 57
Federal election (1997), 487-88
Federal system, 30
Federal-provincial conference, 355
Fédération des Femmes du Québec, 425
Fédération des francophones hors Québec, 353
Feminism, 149, 234
Fenians, 27, 32
Fennario, David, 442
Ferdinand, Archduke Franz, 200
Ferland, Jean-Baptiste-Antoine, 161
Ferron, Jacques, 437
Ferry Command, 313
Fessenden, Reginald, 75
Fielding, W.S., 55, 58
Fillmore, Roscoe, 377
Film industry, Canadian, 277
Filmon, Gary, 472, 473, 482
Films, 178, 256, 275, 277, 375-76, 441-42, 445-46
Financial institutions, 89-90
Findley, Timothy, 443
Finkel, Alvin, 330
Finns, 111, 237
First Canadian Army, 311
First Nations, 8, 40-42, 49-51, 82, 84, 112-115, 213,
        235-37, 300-301, 397-98, 420-24.
          See also Inuit and entries for individual nations.
   artists, 446-47
   authors, 444
   Charter, right under, 470-71
   and European contact, iv-v
   Indian treaties, 40-42, 49, 116, 236
   land claims, 115, 422-23
   life expectancy, 410
   Meech Lake Accord, 472

   political activism, 113, 235-37, 420-24
   racial discrimination against, 20, 420
   recording artists, 447-48
   residential schools, 115, 420
   Red River Rebellion, 38-40
   women, 17, 424
First World War, 197, 200-218
Fischer, Lewis R. 78
Fisheries, 18, 394-95, 482-83
Fishermen's Protective Union, 142
Fishing, 17, 81-82
    Canadian-U.S. disputes, 56
    canning and cold storage, 81
    salmon fishery, 81-82
    Smith butchering machine, 82
Fitzpatrick, Alfred, 292
Flag debate, 343
Flanagan, Thomas, 66
Flappers, 275, 279
Flavelle, Joseph, 202
Fleming, Sandford, 75
Folk culture, 185
Fontaine, Phil, 420
Food banks, 484
Football, 449-50
Forbes, Ernest R., 151, 233
Ford, 76
Ford, Henry, 87
Foreign aid, 356
Foreign Exchange Control Board, 316
Foreign investment, 90
Foreign Investment Review Agency, 373
Foreign ownership, 371
Foreign policy
    post-Cold War, 486-87
    Third Option, 373, 464
Forestry, 17, 82
Forke, Robert, 231
Fort Garry, 40, 41
Fort Resolution, 383
Fortin, Pierre, 404, 490
Foster, W.A., 158
Fowke, Vernon, 301
Fox, Terry, 450-51
France, 7, 18, 311
Francophones. See French Canadians.
Fraser Institute, 393
Fred Victor Mission, 131
Free Schools, 22
Free trade, 15, 58. See also North American Free Trade
      Agreement.
French Canadians, 28, 30. See also Nationalism,
      French-Canadian; sovereigntists, Quebec;
      Sovereignty-association.
   birth rate, 103
   conscription, 208
   cultural alienation, 51, 53
   marriage rates, 11

nationalism, 160-63
racist attitudes towards, 158
settlement patterns, 100-101
writers outside Quebec, 444
French language instruction in public schools, 290
French Regime in North America (1604-1760), 9-10
French Revolution, 24, 28
French Shore, 18
French Wars (1793-1815), 10
Friday, Bill, 173
Friedman, Milton, 462
Friesen, Gerald, 107
Frog Lake, 50
Front de libération du Québec (FLQ), 354-55
Frontier College, 292
Frost, W.A., 157
Frum, Barbara, 453
Fumoleau, René, 421
Fur industry, 84
Fur trade, 12, 17-18

Galbraith, John Kenneth, 462
Galician immigrants, 99, 106
Gallant, Mavis, 443
Garneau, François-Xavier, 161
Gay clergy, 432
Gay rights, 428-30
Gélinas, Gratien, 440
Gender distinction, 19-20
General Agreement on Tariffs and Trade (GATT), 384, 461, 465
General Electric, 89
General Motors, 76, 269
Generation gap, 20
Generation X, 467
George, Henry, 139-40
German immigrants, 11, 104, 105, 166, 241
Getty, Don, 482
Girl Guides, 172
Globalization, 460-61
Gold rush, 9, 18, 42
Godbout, Jacques, 439
Gordon, Arthur, 31-32
Gordon, Margaret, 209
Gordon, Walter, 370, 371-72
Gordon Report, 369-70
Gouin, Paul, 244
Gouzenko, Igor, 362
Graham, Roger, 223
Grain elevators, 179-80
Grain Growers' Grain Company, 142
Granatstein, J.L., 223, 330
Grand Indian Council of Ontario and Quebec, 113
Grand Trunk Railway, 6, 29, 59, 60
Grange Movement, 141
Grant, G.M., 159
Grant, George, 378
Grant-Cummings, Joan, 427

Gray, Herb, 373
Great Britain, 7, 10
cultural ties, 157
and free trade, 15
immigration from, 103, 110
Great Coalition, 30, 36
Great Depression, 227, 238-41, 250, 262-268, 272-73
Great Famine (Ireland), 10-11
Great War. See First World War.
Great War Veterans Association, 218
Green, Howard, 366
Greenpeace, 427-28
Greenway, Thomas, 54
Grenfell Mission, 131
Grenfell, Wilfred, 131
Grey Nuns, 145
Grierson, John, 277
Gross Domestic Product (GDP), 76
Gross National Product (GNP), 71, 75, 76, 256, 264, 391
Grosse Île, 11
Groulx, Lionel, 161, 241
Group of Seven, 188, 294-95
Gruchy, Lydia, 288
Guaranteed Income Supplement, 345, 347
Guèvremont, Germaine, 438
Guibord, Joseph, 165
Guindon, Hubert, 490
Gulf of St. Lawrence, 18
Gulf War, 486-87
Gzowski, Peter, 453

Haliburton, Robert Grant, 158
Halifax, 12, 81, 121, 171,
explosion, 213-16
Halifax Platform, 64, 198
Halifax Relief System, 214-15
Hall, Esther Marjorie, 294
Hall, Maggie, 109
Hamilton, 13
Hanlan, Ned, 174
Hansen, Rick, 451
Harcourt, Mike, 481
Hardy, Laura, 348
Harkness, Douglas, 366
Harlequin romances, 444
Harper, Elijah, 473
Harper, John Joseph, 423
Harrington, Eric, 337
Harris, Arthur, 314
Harris, Mike, 479, 485
Hart House Theatre, 177
Hatfield, Richard, 350, 483
Hayden, Dolores, 434
Heaps, A.A., 238
Hébert, Anne, 440
Heinze, F.A., 83
Hepburn, Mitchell, 245, 269
Heritage conservation, 448-49

Hewitt, Foster, 297
Hexagone Group, 438
Hibernia oil field, 483
Hill, James J., 47
Hind, Cora, 212
Hitler, Adolf, 241, 251, 305
Hitsman, J. M., 223
Hockey, 174, 449, 450
Holt, Herbert, 263
Home Children, 109
Homeopaths, 14
Homestead policy, 110
Homosexuality, 12, 132, 427
Homosexuals, 241, 377, 410
Hong Kong, 309, 417-18
Honorary Advisory Council for Science and Industrial
        Research. See National Research Council.
Hoodless, Adelaide, 145, 167
Horn, Michiel, 262
Horner, Ralph C., 164
Houde, Camillien, 319
House of Commons, 30
Houses of Industry, 25
Housing, 283, 284, 349, 415-16
Howe, C.D., 305, 316, 317, 328, 384, 385, 388
Howe, Joseph, 5, 26, 31, 37-38
Howland, William, 129
Hubbard, William Peyton, 109
Hudson's Bay Company, 6, 17-18, 29, 38, 84
Hughes, Sam, 201-202, 208
Human rights legislation, 417, 419-20
Huntington, Lucius, 45
Hurtig, Mel, 465
Hutchinson, Leonard, 293
Hutterites, 106
Hyde Park Agreement, 324-25
Hydro-electric power, 83-84, 91, 259, 374, 388
Hydro-Québec, 352

Icelandic immigrants, 104
Ilsley, J.L., 322
Immigrants. See also entries for ethnic groups.
        assimilation, 168
        crime, 112
        postwar, 416-17
        solidarity, 111-12
Immigration, 47-48, 72
        open door policy, 103
        policy, post-Confederation, 101-103
        postwar, 408-409
        settling in Canada, 110-12
        turn of the century, 99-100
Imperial Federation League (1884), 57
Imperial Oil, 89, 388
Imperialism, 61-63, 159, 241
Imperial Order of the Daughters of the Empire (IODE),
        62, 203
Income, 361, 466

distribution, 399
Independent Labour Party, 221
Indian Act, 41, 112, 235, 420, 424
Indian Rights for Indian Women, 424
Indian treaties, 40-42, 49, 116, 236
Indians. See First Nations.
Industrial Development Board, 322
Industrial Disputes Investigation Act, 139, 323
Industrial Relations Disputes Act, 401
Industrial Revolution, 12-13, 14, 26
Industrial Woodworkers of America, 377
Industrial workers, 395
Industrial Workers of the World, 136, 139
Industry, secondary, 75-77
Infanticide, 11, 129
Inflation, 384, 392
        vs. unemployment, 467
Information Age, 388
Innis, Harold Adams, 324, 349, 376
Institut canadien, 165
Intercolonial Railway, 31, 32, 38, 78, 232
International Commission for the Northwest Atlantic
        Fisheries, 394
International Commission of Control and Supervision, 376
International Control Commission, 364-65
International Harvester, 87
International Nickel Company (Inco), 83, 361
International relations, 356-57
Internment camps, 210-11, 319-20
Inuit, 8, 117, 236, 393, 421
        art, 446-47
        land settlement, 422
Iraq, 486
Irish immigrants, 10-11, 15, 52
Irish Republican Brotherhood, 27
Iron and steel industry, 262
Iron Ore Company, 387
Iroquois, 8, 112
Irving, K.C., 386
Isolationism, 251
Italian immigrants, 103, 107, 112, 241

James Bay hydro-electric project, 423
James, Cyril, 321
Japanese immigrants, 99, 103, 107, 108, 266, 299-300
        in First World War, 213
        picture brides, 108
        sports, 175
Jehovah's Witnesses, 318-19
Jelf, George, 148
Jesuit Estates Act (1888), 53
Jewett, Pauline, 343
Jews, 241, 244, 418
        immigration, 104
        refugees, 298, 319
Johnson, Ben, 441, 455
Johnson, Daniel, 476, 477
Johnson, Harry, 371

Johnson, Lyndon, 361
Johnson, Pauline, 182
Johnston, Franz, 315
Jost Mission, 131
Joual, 440
Judicial Committee of the Privy Council, 47, 54-55
Juvenile Delinquent Act (1908), 148

Kamouraska, 37
Kennedy, John F., 362, 366-67
Kenny, Edward, 36
Keynes, John Maynard, 249-50
Keynesianism, 384, 404-405, 479
King, George, 52
King, Thomas, 444
Kingsford, William, 161
Kittson, Norman, 47
Kizima, Senefta, 127
Klein, Ralph, 482
Klondike gold rush, 59, 82
Knights of Labor, 134-35, 165, 166
Koeppen, Ebe, 111
Kogawa, Joy, 310
Korean War, 363
Kraft, J.L., 79
Ku Klux Klan, 241, 242
Kwakiutl, 114

L'Association catholique de la jeunesse canadienne-
        française (ACJC), 160-61
La Bolduc (Marie Travers), 295
La Ligue nationaliste canadienne, 160
Labour force, unionized, 94
Labour Party, 237
Labour politics, 139, 237-38
Labour Progressive Party, 239
Labour unions. See Unions.
Labour
        and government, 137-39
        post-First World War unrest, 220
        shortage, First World War, 203-204
Labrador, 6
        fisheries, 18
Lachine Canal, 13
Lacombe, Albert, 116
Lacrosse, 24
LaMarsh, Judy, 343, 425
Land ownership, 15
Landry, Israel-D., 161
Lang, k.d., 447
Lapointe, Ernest, 306, 319
Laporte, Pierre, 354
Laurence, Margaret, 443
Laurier, Wilfrid, 54, 57, 71-72, 108, 142-43
        1911 election, 64-65
        Liberal government of, 58-59
        prohibition referendum, 129
Laval University, 22, 63

Lavallée, Calixa, 188
Leacock, Stephen, 149, 183, 218
League of Indians of Canada, 236
League of Nations, 217, 250
LeBlanc, Édouard, 162
Leclerc, Félix, 440
Leduc, Alberta, 387
Lefebvre, Camille, 162
Lemelin, Roger, 438
Lemieux Act, 139
Leo XIII, Pope, 53, 166
Lesage, Jean, 352, 355
Lesbians, 427
Letelliers, 37
Levant, Victor, 379
Lévesque, René, 352, 353, 441, 468, 469, 470
Liberal (Reform) party, 26
Liberal Party, 228, 306, 338-42, 352, 355, 463, 465, 478-79,
        483, 487-88
Liberal, defined, 26
Liberal-Conservative Party, 26, 36, 37
Liberalism
        post-Second World War, 337-58
        vs. conservative social order, 26, 28
Liberation theology, 421
Libraries, 455
Life expectancy, 12, 298, 410
Linteau, Paul-André, 434
Literacy, growth of, 19, 166
Literature, 181-82, 218, 292-93, 443-45
Lockhard, Grace Annie, 147
Loft, Fred O., 236
Log drivers, 17
Logging disputes in BC, 422
Longley, J.W., 150
Lord's Day Act (1907), 130
Lord's Day Alliance, 130
Loring, Frances, 294
Lougheed, James, 217
Lougheed, Peter, 482
Lower Canada, 10, 29
Lower Canada rebellion, ii
Lowland Presbyterian Scots, 10
Loyalists, 8, 10
Lubicon Cree, 422
Luftwaffe, 314
Lunenburg County, Nova Scotia, 11
Lutherans, 11, 104
Lynch, John Joseph, 165
Lyon, Sterling, 482

Macdonald, Angus L., 269, 349
MacDonald, Hugh, 38
Macdonald, John A., 30, 36, 107
        1891 election, 57-58
        Pacific Scandal, 44-46
MacDonald, Margaret, 201
MacDonald, Robert H., 172

MacDougall, John, 141
Macedonian immigrants, 107
Machar, Agnes, 163, 182
MacInnis, Grace, 337, 343
MacIntosh, William, 321
Mackenzie King, William Lyon, 94, 228-29, 240, 249, 251
    five-cent piece speech, 238, 239
    isolationist policy, 229
    King-Byng Affair, 233
    U.S. relations, 324-26
    conscription, Second World War, 306-307
Mackenzie Valley Pipeline, 421
Mackenzie, Alexander, 44, 45, 46
Mackenzie, Donald, 60
Mackintosh, W.A., 250
MacLennan, Hugh, 443
MacMillan, H.R., 317
MacMillan-Bloedel, 386
Macphail, Agnes, 219, 234-35, 238
Macphail, Andrew, 146
Macpherson, C.B., 301
MacPherson, David, 45
Magazines, 184, 277-78, 454
Mair, Charles, 158
Makaroff, Peter, 105
Management, modern, 87-89, 94
Manhattan Project, 305
Manifest Destiny (U.S.), 7
Manitoba Act (1870), 40, 54
Manitoba Grain Growers' Association, 141-42
Manitoba, 6, 40, 41, 48, 60, 482
    schools question, 54
Mann, Donald, 60
Manning, Ernest, 244, 341, 412-13
Manning, Preston, 474, 480-81, 488
Manufacturing, 72-73, 259-60
Marconi, Guglielmo, 75
Maritime Freight Rates Act (1927), 233
Maritime Rights Movement, 232-34
Maritime union, 30
Maritimes
    anti-Confederation feelings, 31-32, 35
    bilingual education, 169
    deindustrialization, 77-78
    Depression, 266-67
    economic crisis, 482-84
    economic slowdown, 60-61
    farming in, 79
    floundering economy, 350-51
    outmigration, 100
    post-Second World War politics, 342
Marriage
    and property laws, 20
    companionate, 23
    rates (1867), 11
Married Women's Property Acts, 86, 148
Marsh, Leonard, 321
Marshall Plan, 328

Marshall, Donald, 423
Martin, Médéric, 133
Martin, Paul, 329, 368, 379, 467
Martin, Clara Brett, 147
Marx, Karl, 26
Mass production, 87-89
Massey, Harris, 72, 87
Massey, Vincent, 343, 374
Massey-Harris, 466
Maternal feminists, 149, 219
Matthew, Georges, 490
Mavor, James, 105
McCarthy, D'Alton, 54
McCarthy, Joseph, 377
McCarthy, Leighton, 326
McClung, Nellie, 150, 151, 182, 212, 234
McCurdy, J.A.D., 74
McDonald, H.F., 326
McDonough, Alexa, 488
McDougall, William, 39-40
McEwan, C.M., 314
McGee, Thomas D'Arcy, 26, 27, 36, 158
McGill University, 25, 63
McGinnis, David, 301
McKenna, Frank, 472, 473, 483
McKenna-McBride Commission (1912), 112
McKinley Tariff (1890), 57
McKinney, Louise, 234
McLachlan, J.B., 238
McLaren, A.F., 79
McLuhan, Marshall, 388
McNaughton, A.G.L., 307
McPherson, Aimee Semple, 289
McRitchie, Donald, 64
McRoberts, Kenneth, 358
Mechanics Institute, 24
Media concentration, 454-55
Medicare, 344-45, 484
Meech Lake Accord, 471-74
    notwithstanding clause, 471, 473
    opposition, 472
Meighen, Arthur, 223, 230, 233, 320
Men
    farming duties, 16-17
    in industrial workforce, 14
    marrying age (1867), 11
    whipping for wife-beating, 148
Mennonites, 11, 104
Mercantile system, 14-15
Merchant-Heeney Report, 361
Mercier, Honoré, 53, 55, 160
Mercredi, Ovide, 423
Merger movement, 88-89
Methodists, 11, 23, 128, 130, 163, 287
    social gospel, 131, 132
Métis Friendship Centres, 421
Métis, 8, 158, 236, 300-301, 421
    as lost nation, 116

Bill of Rights, 50
migrations, 65-67
National Committee, 39
Northwest French-speaking, 9
rebellion, 49-51
Red River Rebellion, 38-40
Metlakatla, 114
Mi'kmaq Indians, 113, 216, 423, 483
Middle class, 21, 23
reformers, 24-25
Military Service Act, 208
Military-industrial complex, 385
Miller, Frank, 478
Miller, Gray, 264
Milne, David, 315
Minifie, James, 366
Mining, 259,
Mining industry, 82-83
Missionaries
Anglican, 114, 116
Roman Catholic, 116
Mitchell, Margaret, 426
Mohawks, 75, 423
Monk, D.F., 198
Monopoly, 88
Montcalm, Mary Beth, 358
Montgomery, Lucy Maud, 183, 184
Montreal Massacre, 426
Montreal Trust, 89
Montreal, 12, 13, 29, 117, 118, 119-20
City Improvement League, 132
labour unrest, 13, 14
Moores, Frank, 343
Moral and Social Reform Council of Canada, 130-31
Morgan, Henry, 158
Morgentaler, Henry, 426
Mormons, 104-105
Morris, Edward, 142
Morrison, J.J., 141
Mortality
infant, 12, 247, 282, 410
Mother's allowances, 246
Motherhood, 282-83
Movies. See Films.
Mowat, Oliver, 55, 58
Muir, Leilani, 411
Muise, D.A., 122
Mulroney, Brian, 462, 463, 464-65, 471, 486-87
Multiculturalism, 417
Munger, Martha, 61, 212
Munro, Alice, 443
Murphy, Emily, 234, 281
Murray, George, 199
Murray, L.W., 312
Murray, Margaret Polson, 62
Museums, 295-96
Musgrave, Andrew, 42
Music, 184

francophone, 440
in interwar years, 295
popular, 276-77
Musqueam band, 422
Mussolini, Benito, 305

Nagano, Manzo, 99
Naismith, James, 174
Napoleonic Wars (1793-1815), 10
National Action Committee of the Status of Women,
425-26, 474
National Council of Women of Canada, 146-47
National Employment Commission, 268
National Energy Program, 480
National Film Board, 277, 441, 443
National Hockey League (NHL), 449
National Housing Act, 322
National identity, 157-59
National Indian Brotherhood, 420
National Native Women's Association, 424
National Policy, 47-48, 57
importance of, 72-73
and regional development, 95-96
National Progressive Party, 222
National Research Council, 91
National Resources Mobilization Act, 319
National Trades and Labour Congress, 135
National Unity Party, 318
Nationalism, 27, 28, 62-63,
Nationalism, French-Canadian, 160-63
Native peoples. See First Nations.
Natural Products Marketing Act, 249
Natural resources, 12, 60, 78
Nature, 171-72, 182. See also Environment.
Naval Aid Bill, 198-99
Naval policy, 64, 65
Naval Service Bill, 64
Nazis, 241
Neo-conservatism, 462-63
Neo-Nazis, 420
New Brunswick, 5, 6, 8, 31, 32
fisheries, 18
timber trade, 16
New Brunswick Common Schools Act (1871), 52
New Deal, 248-49
New Democratic Party, 242, 321, 340, 341, 465, 478-79,
481, 482, 488
Newell, Dianne, 82
Newfoundland, 6, 8, 31, 142
denominational schools, 22
effects of Depression on, 267
enters Confederation, 342-43
fisheries, 18
immigration, 100
refusal to join Confederation, 43-44
Newfoundland and Labrador Federation of Labour, 270
Newfoundland Federation of Labour, 345
Newspapers, 26, 184-85, 278, 454

Newsprint industry, 259
Newton, Janice, 152
Niagara Falls, 83
Nielsen, Dorise, 235
Nisga, 113
Norman, E.H., 377
Normandy, 311
Norquay, John, 56
Norrie, Ken, 95
North American Commercial Company, 56
North American Free Trade Agreement, 461, 464-66, 488
North Atlantic Air Defence Treaty (NORAD), 364, 366, 368
North Atlantic Treaty Organization (NATO), 363, 364, 366, 368
North Atlantic Triangle, 56-57
North Pole expeditions, 116-17
North-West Mounted Police, 41, 49
Northern Electric, 390
Northern Pacific Railway, 45
Northwest Rebellion (1885), 116
Northwest Territories, 6, 48
Northwest Territories Act (1875), 54
Noseworthy, Joseph, 320
Notre Dame Congregation, 145
Nova Scotia, 5, 8, 31
    better terms for in Confederation, 38
    coal mining, 18
    farming oppurtunities, 16
    fisheries, 18
    secessionist movement, 37-38
Nova Scotia Association for the Advancement of Coloured People, 418
Nova Scotia Steel Company, 76
Nuclear arms, 364
Nunavut, 422

O'Neill, Tim, 489
Oblate Missionaries of Mary Immaculate, 116, 117, 421
October Crisis, 354-55
Official Languages Act, 353
Oil industry, 236, 351, 373, 387-88, 480, 483
Oil and Petroleum Exporting Countries (OPEC), 351, 392
Ojibwa, 112
Oka confrontation, 423
Old age pension, 246
Oliver, Frank, 102, 112
Olmstead, Frederick Law, 171
Olympic sports, 450-451
On-to-Ottawa trek, 240
One Big Union, 220, 270
Ontario, 5
    anti-Catholicism, 53-54
    anti-French, 53-54
    Big Blue Machine, 342
    boundary dispute, 55
    mining industry, 83
    opportunities in, 15-16

post prosperity, 478-79
    religion in, 23
    universities, 169
Ontario Farmer's Association, 141
Ontario Housing Corporation, 349
Ontario Hydro, 91
Operation Solidarity, 481
Oppenheimer, J. Robert, 305
Orange Order, 23, 40, 53
Order of Sleeping Car Porters, 137
Order-in-Council PC 1003, 324
Organization for Economic Co-operation and Development, 346
Orphanages, 11-12, 25, 285
Osborne, Helen Betty, 423
Ottawa, 120-21
Otter, Sir William, 210
Outmigration, 100-101
Owram, Douglas, 95, 404

Pacific Scandal, 36, 44-46
Padlock Act, 245
Pal, Leslie, 330
Paley Commission, 369
Palmer, Howard, 103, 122
Palmer, Phoebe, 164
Parent, Madeleine, 270
Parents' Information Bureau, 280
Paris Peace Conference, 217
Parizeau, Jacques, 476, 477, 487
Parlby, Irene, 231, 234
Parti acadian, 354
Parti national, 53
Parti ouvrier, 139
Parti québecois, 341, 353, 355, 468, 476
Participaction, 452
Partridge Island, 11
Partridge, E.A., 142
Passchendaele, 206
Patriarchal ideal, 20
Patriotic Fund, 62
Patrons of Industry, 144
Paul, Aleck, 113
Pawley, Howard, 482
Payment, Diane, 66
PCBs, 396
Peacekeeping, 487
Pearl Harbour, 306
Pearson, Lester, 197, 340, 361
Peary, Robert, 116
Peckford, Brian, 472, 483
Pellan, Alfred, 293
Penfield, wWlder, 291
Penman, John, 110
Perley, E.E., 241-42
Perley, Sir George, 206
Permanent Joint Board on Defence, 363
Peterson, David, 478

Petro-Canada, 373
Petroleum, 259
Philip, Marlene Nourbese, 456, 457
Pierson, Ruth, 330
Pine Point, 383
Piva, Michael, 122
Poets, 172, 182, 292, 442
Poirier, Pascal, 162
Polish immigrants, 166
Poor, organizations of, 430-31
Pope, James, 43
Population
    Canada at Confederation, 5
    census enumeration, 7
    in interwar years, 298-300
    nineteenth century, 100
    postwar boom, 408-410
Populism, 252
Porter, John, 398
Portland, Maine, 6
Postindustrial Age, 388
Potash, 17
Potatoes, 262
Poundmaker, 49, 51
Poverty, 398-99, 484
    immigrants, 416-17
    regional, 399-400
Prairies
    French-speaking settlers, 101
    rural reform, 141-42
    settlement of, 104, 105
    universities, 169
    wheat boom, 79-80
    wheat production, 257-58
Prairie Farm Rehabilitation Act, 249
Premiers' Conference (1887), 55-56
Presbyterians, 11, 23, 128, 130, 141, 257-58
Prince Edward Island, 6, 13, 16, 30-31
    entry into Confederation, 43
    potato farming, 79
Professional services, 14
Professionals, education, 170-71
*Programmistes*, 51-52, 58
Progressive Conservative Party, 320, 338-42, 463, 465,
    478-79, 482, 488
Progressive Party, 230-32
Progressivism, 130-33
Prohibition, 129, 140, 147, 288
Prostitution, 129, 132, 143, 281
Protectionism, 15, 22, 23, 57, 72, 248. See also Customs;
    Tariffs.
Protestants, 10, 11, 163-64, 188-89, 287-89, 431-32
Provinces
    continentalism and, 374
    opting-out principle, 352, 472
    post-Second World War liberalism, 349-52
Provincial rights, 60-61
Provincial Workmens' Association, 135

Provincial-Dominion conflict, 54-56
Public health, 247
Pulp and paper, 82, 258-59
Puttee, A.W., 139

Quebec, 5, 6, 17, 100, 441-42, 443
    Catholic Program, 51-52
    conquest of (1763), 9
    education, 169-70, 413-14
    effect of leaving Canada, 489-90
    elite, 20
    farming in, 79
    French colonies, 9
    language legislation, 356, 414
    legal reform, 28
    mining industry, 83
    modernization, 352
    nationalism, 352-56, 358, 439-41, 467-69
    opposition to Confederation, 31
    *rattrapage*, 414
    religious orders, 145
    Roman Catholics, 22-23, 166
    seigneurial system, 16
    special status, 355-56
Quebec City, 12, 99
Quebec City Bridge, 75
Quebec Pension Plan, 352
Quebec Resolutions, 31, 32
Quiet Revolution, Quebec, 352-53, 398, 414

Racism, 20, 39, 107-110, 131-32, 241, 418-19, 455-57
Radio, 276
Radio-Canada, 441, 452
Railways, 13, 42, 59, 60, 71, 262
    Board of Railway Commissioners, 90-91
    growth of, 73-74
    nationalizing, 204
    unions, 137
Ralston, J.L., 307
Reagan, Ronald, 462, 463
Rebellion, Upper and Lower Canada (1837-38), 7
Rebick, Judy, 426
Recession, 73, 465
    postwar, 255
    1912, 199-200
    1920-24, 257
Reciprocity, 56-57, 58, 65
Reciprocity Treaty, 15, 18, 32
Reconstruction Party, 249
Recording artists, 447-48
Red Cross, 203
Red River Rebellion, 38-40
Reform
    environmental, 132-33
    labour, 133-39
    progressivism, 130-33
    sexual practices, 131-32
    socialism, 137, 40

temperance movement, 128-29
Reform Party, 465, 474, 480-81, 488
Reform Party (George Brown), 29-30
Regehr, T.D., 96
Regent Park, 415-16
Regina, 118
Regina Manifesto (CCF), 242-43
Reisman, Simon, 464
Relief camps, 239, 240
Relief Camp Workers Union, 240
Religion, 22-23, 287-89, 431-33
Religious art, 181
Religious orders, 145
*Report of the Royal Commission on the Status of Women*, 348
Representation by population, 30, 31
Reproductive technology, 411
*Rerum Novarum*, 166
Reserves, 8, 112, 113
        restrictions on Indians, 20
Residential schools, 115, 420-21
Resource industries, 387-88
Respectability, 278-82
Responsible government, 15, 26
Restructuring, 462
Retail Merchants Association, 88
Retail, Wholesale, and Department Store Union, 402
Retailing, 85-87, 260
Revivalism, 164
Rhinoceros Party, 437
Rhodes, E.N., 233
Richler, Mordecai, 376, 442
Riddell, Walter, 250
Ridley, Ethel, 212
Riel, Louis, 39, 40, 49-51, 53
Rioux, Marcel, 358
Ritchie, Samuel J., 83
Ritchot, Abbé N.J., 40
Roback, Lea, 270
Robertson, James W., 167
Robinson, Svend, 481
Roblin, Duff, 341
Roman Catholics, 14, 22, 23, 26, 116, 166, 289
Romanow, Roy, 482
Roosevelt, Theodore, 63
Rose, John, 38
Rosenfeld, Fanny, 297
Ross, Douglas, 379
Ross, George, 159
*Rouges*, 26, 31
Rowell-Sirois Commission on Dominion-Provincial Relations, 218
Rowley, Kent, 377
Roy, Gabrielle, 438, 439
Royal Canadian Air Force, 308
Royal Canadian Mounted Police, 240, 270
Royal Canadian Navy, 308, 312
Royal Commission on Bilingualism and Biculturalism, 353

Royal Commission on Canada's Economic Prospects, 370
Royal Commission on Canada's Economic Union and Development Prospects, 464
Royal Commission on Dominion-Provincial Relations, 245, 249, 268, 322
Royal Commission on Health Services, 345
Royal Commission on Maritime Claims (1926), 233
Royal Commission on Newspapers, 454
Royal Commission on Taxation, 400
Royal Commission on the Relations of Labour and Capital (1886), 137, 138
Royal Commission on the Relations of Labour and Capital (1889), 94
Royal Commission on the Status of Women, 425
Royal Navy College, 218
Royal Securities, 89
Royal Society of Canada, 170
Rum running, 262
Rumilly, Robert, 223
Rupert's Land, 6, 7, 8, 22. See also Northwest Territories.
Rural areas, 12
Rural life, 285-86
Rural reform, 140-43
Russell, Peter, 490
Russia, 7
Russian Revolution, 211, 220
Russian immigrants, 105
Ryan, Claude, 468, 469

Sager, Eric W., 78
Saint-Jean, Idola, 235
Salvation Army, 143
Sangster, Joan, 123
Saskatchewan, 59, 111, 123, 482
        medicare, 345
        municipal doctor scheme, 247
Saunders, Charles E., 80
Saunders, S.A., 95
Scandinavian immigrants, 103
Schaefer, Carl, 293
School taxes, 21-22
Schools, compulsory attendance, 22
Schools, separate, constitutional guarantee, 32
Schreyer, Ed, 344, 482
Schumacher, E.F., 397
Science, 25
Scott Act (1878), 128-29
Scott, Thomas, 40
Scottish immigrants, 10
Seafarers International Union, 365
Seal hunt, 56-57
Second World War, 305-307, 313-20, 326-28
Segregration, racial, 20
Seigneurial system, 16
Senate, 30, 234, 464
Separatists. See sovereigntists, Quebec.
Service economy, 390-92
Service industries, 88

Service organizations, 297-98
Seton, Ernest Thompson, 172
Sexual assaults, 280
Sexual mores, 12, 278-80
Sexual practices, reforming, 131-32
Sexual revolution, 412
Shawinigan Falls, 83
Shawinigan Water and Power, 77
Shipbuilding, 17, 43, 78, 202-203
Shortt, Adam, 161
Shuswap, 424,
Sifton, Clifford, 58, 59, 65, 102, 132
Signal Hill, 75
Sikh immigrants, 108
Simpson's, 86
Simpson, Sir George, vi
Single-parent families, 285
Sir George Williams University (Concordia), 419
Six Nations, 235-36
Skelton, O.D., 122
Slavery, 8-9
Slavic immigrants, 102
Smallpox, 12
Smallwood, Joey, 343, 388, 402
Smith, A.J., 31
Smith, Adam, 15
Smith, Albert Edward, 163
Smith, Donald, 47, 62
Smith, Goldwin, 159
Smith, Ralph, 139
Snell, James, 148
Snow, John, 39
Social assistance, 265
Social Credit Party, 242, 243-44, 252, 341, 481
Social Democratic Party, 140
Social Gospellers, 163
Social mores, postwar, 410-12
Social programs, 338, 459-60, 484. See also Welfare state.
Social reform, 24-25
Social security programs, 246, 249
Social Service Council of Canada, 130-31
Socialism, 139-43
Socialist Labour Party, 140
Socialist Party of Canada, 139
Société Saint-Jean Baptiste, 160
Society for the Prevention of Cruelty to Animals, 172
Sojourners, 107, 108
Soldiers Land Settlement Scheme, 217
Soldiers' Wives League, 62
Somalia, 420
Somme, 206
Sons of Freedom. See Doukhobors.
Sons of Temperance, 25, 128
South African War, 62-63
Southam, 454
Sovereigntists, Quebec, 353
Sovereignty, 467-69
     and culture, 439-41

Sovereignty-association, 353, 469, 476-78
Soviet Union, 241, 362
Spanish Civil War, 250-51
Spanish flu epidemic (1918-19), 247
Special Senate Committee on Mass Media, 454
Special status debate, 355-56
Speck, Frank, 113
Spiritualism, 164
Sports, 24, 173-76, 296-97, 449-52
Sprague, Douglas, 66
Squamish, 113
Squires, Richard Anderson, 267
St Jacques ward (Montreal), 71
St John, 12, 13, 120
St John's, 44, 120
St John's Ward ( Toronto), 119
St Laurent, Louis, 339
St Lawrence River, 13
St Louis, 298
St Pierre and Miquelon, 18
St Lawrence Seaway, 385
Stagflation, 392
Stairs, John, 89
Stalin, Joseph, 306, 363
Stall, Sylvanus, 148
Standard time, 75
Stanfield, Robert, 341
Stanley Cup, 174
State power, expansion of, 246
Status Indians, 91, 235
Statute of Westminster, 250
Steel companies, 76, 262, 317, 328
Steel Company of Canada, 76, 89, 262
Steel miners, 238
Stefansson, Vilhjalmur, 116-17
Stephen, George, 21, 47
Stevens, H.H., 249
Steveston, 81
Stock trading, 89
Stowe, Emily Howard, 147, 149, 164
Strange, Carolyn, 123, 129
Strikes, 134, 328, 402-403
Strong, Maurice, 397
Strum, Gladys, 235
Struthers, James, 330
Suburbs, 284, 414-15
Suez Crisis, 357
Suffrage movement, 149-50, 151-52, 209, 219
Sun Life, 268
Supreme Court of Canada, 47
Suzuki, David, 310, 397
Swampy Cree, 112
Sweated trades, 14
Swift's, 72
Symons, Thomas H.B., 376
Syndicalism, 139

Taché, A.A., 46

Taft, William Howard, 64
Tariff Commission, 198, 199
Tariffs, 58-59, 60, 72, 142-43, 248, 464
Taschereau, Louis-Alexandre, 244
Task Force on Structure of Canadian Industry, 372
Taxes, 204, 265, 400-401
    sin, 452
Taylor, E.P., 386
Taylor, Frederick W., 87
Taylor, Jeffery, 301
Teaching, 290-91
Technology, 466
    growth of, 255-57
Television, 374-75, 441-42, 452-54
    in Quebec, 41-42
Temagami Indians, 113, 422-23
Temperance, 25, 128-29
Tenant League, 43
Territorial Grain Growers' Association, 141
Thatcher, Margaret, 462, 463, 469
Theatre, 295
Theatres, 177, 445
Thirteen Colonies (U.S.), 7
Thobani, Sunera, 426-27
Thompson, John Herd, 301
Thompson, John, 58
Thompson, Phillips, 139-40
Tilley, Samuel Leonard, 31, 36
Toronto, 12, 15, 29, 117, 119
    manufacturing centre, 13, 72
    Morality Department, 129
    wealth distribution in, 21
Towers, Graham, 248
Trade Union Act (1872), 134
Trade Unions. See Unions.
Trades and Labour Congress (TLC), 135, 269
Trading blocs, 461-62
Trans-Canada Pipelines, 388
Transfer payments, federal-provincial, 351, 468
Transportation, 73-74
    railroads, 6
    stagecoach services, 6
    steam engines, 12-13
Treaty of Paris, 7, 10
Treaty of Utrecht, 10
Treaty of Washington, 38, 56
Treaty One, 41
Tremblay, Michel, 439-40
Trout, Jenna, 147
Truck system, 18
Trudeau, Pierre, 340, 352, 355, 368, 463, 469-70, 471, 483, 486
Truman, Harry, 326
Tuberculosis, 12, 236-37, 283
Tupper, Charles, 31, 32, 36, 37, 38, 58
Turner, John, 463
Turtle Cove, 216
Tynes, Maxine, 444

Ukrainian immigrants, 127, 237, 299, 417
Ultramontanists, 51
Underground Railway, 8-9
Underhill, Frank, 319
Unemployment, 238, 264, 385, 392
    NAIRU, 404, 405
Unemployment Insurance, 246, 321, 347
Unemployment Relief Act, 239
Union government, 209, 219, 229-30, 257
Union nationale, 242, 244-46, 341
Union of Canadian Municipalities, 132
Unions, 14, 127, 237, 323-24, 401-403
    during interwar period, 269-70
    early history, 133-37
    people of colour excluded from, 137
United Auto Workers, 269
United Canadas, 29
United Church of Canada, 287-88, 432
United Farm Workers of Alberta, 231
United Farmers of Alberta, 230, 231, 232
United Farmers of Ontario, 141, 230, 232
United Maritime Fishermen's Co-operative, 289
United Mine Workers, 94, 135
United Nations Conference on the Human Environment, 397
United Nations Emergency Force, 357
United Nations Relief and Rehabilitation Administration, 325
United Nations, 326
United Province of Canada, 5
United States, 309, 312
    cultural influence, 275, 276-77
    early history, 7
    First World War, 216-17
    tight money policies, 263
    Universities, 25-26, 376, 413
Unwed mothers, 279
Upper Canada, 10, 29
Uranium, 305, 368-69
Urban growth, 12, 13-15
Urban reform, 132-33

Valleyfield, Quebec, 82
Vatican Council, Second, 352
VE Day, 327
Venereal disease, 132
Versailles Treaty, 217
Verville, Alphonse, 139
Veterans' Charter, 322, 326
Victoria, Queen of England, 6, 57
Victorian Order of Nurses (VON), 146
Victory Bonds, 316
Vietnam War, 361, 362, 364-65, 379
Vietnamese immigrants, 418
Vimy Ridge, 206
Violence, in Victorian Canada, 23
Visible minorities, 212-13
Voting, in New Dominion, 37

Wage and price controls, 392-93
War brides, 327-28
War labour policy, 204
War Measures Act, 200, 204, 219, 268, 306, 355
War of 1812, 7, 8
War profits tax, 204
Wartime Elections Act, 209, 210
Wartime Prices and Trade Board, 316
Wartime Shipping Limited, 317
Washington, 38
Waterloo County, Ontario, 11
Watkins Report, 372
Watkins, Mel, 372
Wealth, distribution of, 21
Welfare, 246
Welfare family, 346
Welfare state, 320-23, 329-30, 338, 344-49
Welsh immigrants, 10
West Indian immigrants, 419
Western Labour Conference, 220
Westinghouse, 72
Wheat, 79-80, 257-58, 263, 316
Whilton, Charlotte, 322
White Paper on Indian Policy, 420
White Paper on postwar reconstruction, 384
White, Thomas, 198
Whitney, James, 61
Widows, 246, 285
Williams, A.M., 223
Willson, Thomas "Carbide", 77
Wilson, Cairine, 234
Winnipeg Jewish Orphanage, 285
Winnipeg Labour Party, 139
Winnipeg strike, 220, 221
Wolseley, Garnet, 40
"Woman movement", 234
Woman's Christian Temperance Union (WCTU), 128,
    147, 148
Women's College Hospital, 147
Women's International League for Peace and Freedom,
    377
Women's Labour League, 237, 238
Women's Missionary Aid Societies, 143
Women's movement, 143-47, 425-27
Women's Royal Canadian Naval Service (WRENS), 308
Women
    and social assistance, 265
    battered, 148
    domestic responsibilities, 1867, 16
    double day, 425
    dower rights, 148
    farming duties, 17
    in First World War, 212
    flight, from farms, 141
    interwar Canada, 275
    in labour force, 138, 317-18, 391-92, 398, 402,
    labour protests, 136
    low wages, 93, 94

    marrying (1867), 11
    moral reform of, 129
    persons decision, 234
    in Second World War, 308-309
    subordination of (1867), 20
    in suburbs, 415
    unemployment, 264
    in unions, 403
    university education, 147
    university faculty, 292
    voting rights, 209, 219
    wages, 264
    welfare state, 347
    work, and family, 284-85
Wood exports, 15, 17
Wood Gundy, 89
Wood, Henry Wise, 231
Woodsworth, J.S., 131, 221, 237, 238, 242, 243, 287
Woodward, Charles, 87
Woodworkers Industrial Union of Canada, 337
Workers Unity League, 239 240, 269, 270
Working poor, 400
Workman's Compensation Acts, 94
World War I. See First World War.
World War II. See Second World War.
Wreck Commission, 216
Wright, Bertha, 145
Wrigley, G. Weston, 140
Wrong, Hume, 325
Wyle, Florence, 294

Youmans, Letitia, 143
Young Men's Christian Association (YMCA), 25
Young Woman's Christian Association (YWCA), 143, 147
Ypres, 201, 205, 206
Yukon gold rush, 61
Yukon Territories, 59